THE DARTNELL

OFFICE ADMINISTRATION HANDBOOK

J. C. Aspley, *Editor*

THE DARTNELL CORPORATION
CHICAGO and LONDON

Printed by Dartnell Press, Inc., Chicago, Illinois 60640, U.S.A.

FOREWORD

ADMINISTRATION of the business office is, if anything, growing to new stature in the overall scheme of corporate management. The responsibilities that rest on the shoulders of the office manager or administrator are growing as well.

It is significant that the men and women who perform these duties recognize the effect of change on their role. After a four-year effort of reorganizing and reprogramming, the members of the National Office Management Association took a major step forward by changing the name to the Administrative Management Society. The reasoning was sound. More and more the office manager is involved in administrative problems, in administrative services and in administrative management.

At the time of the change, International President J. W. Gawthrop, vice-president and planning director of Pilot Life Insurance Co., Greensboro, N. C., emphasized one important fact: "AMS is professionally interested in all administrative management affairs, from the simplest and most rudimentary clerical operations to the most sophisticated systems of information retrieval and supervisory or management training."

The very ability to change in meeting new situations is a prerequisite to holding the title of manager. Just how important was pointed up recently by Richard Wytmar, partner in Maichle & Wytmar, Inc., Chicago, when he warned: "In this day and age everything seems to become obsolete in a relatively short period of time—machines, methods, materials, even men."

Middle management, Mr. Wytmar emphasized, is a target for oblivion. Substantial chunks of middle management responsibilities have been taken over by the computer—from the actual direction of operational activities to the rapid, accurate gathering of comprehensive data.

Rather than an ominous threat, the alert office executive accepts this as a challenge. In concerted action, NOMA re-established itself as the AMS. Individually, the members have been making the change since the middle 50's. Those who make the transition successfully are well aware that management is still their major function, no matter what their modern title may be.

Handling people in a complex, more automated environment demands a growing amount of skill and knowledge. A recent ad featuring a new business machine reaches the core with the headline: "Yesterday, Marion was a billing clerk. Today, she is a whole department."

Justifying the need for the new machine offers a statistical challenge. Orienting Marion to her new position can prove to be a much bigger job.

To keep in step with these changes, Dartnell editors have produced a new handbook, with a new title and copyright, supplanting the former OFFICE MANAGER'S HANDBOOK. The primary concern of the Dartnell editors is to focus attention on the human relationships involved in office administration. To this end, better than 50 percent of the pages are given to reporting the working experiences—problems and solutions—of companies and executives directly concerned with office management.

Most of the material in this HANDBOOK is drawn from the Dartnell Office Administration Service and from hundreds of personal contacts with people directly concerned with administration in the modern business office. The publishers wish to acknowledge the contribution made to the Dartnell concept by C. M. Weld, editor of the first handbook, and E. M. Ryan, co-editor of the second edition; their insight set a pattern for orderly growth and change which is so necessary. Dartnell editors contributing to this new title include Robert S. Minor and Edward L. Throm.

CONTENTS

APPENDIX

ACKNOWLEDGMENTS

The Dartnell editorial staff has been assisted in the preparation of this handbook by hundreds of business executives who have been generous with their time, advice, and case-history material. Their cooperation is sincerely appreciated by the editors and the publisher. Among companies contributing to the content of this handbook are the following:

ABBOTT LABORATORIES, North Chicago, Ill.
ADMINISTRATIVE MANAGEMENT SOCIETY, Willow Grove, Pa.
ADMIRAL CORPORATION, Chicago, Ill.
AETNA CASUALTY & SURETY CO., Atlanta, Ga.
AETNA INSURANCE CO., Hartford, Conn.
AGRICULTURAL DEVELOPMENT CO., Topeka, Kans.
AGRICULTURAL INSURANCE CO., Watertown, N. Y.
AIRPORT PARKING CO. OF AMERICA, Cleveland, Ohio
THE ALBERTA GENERAL INSURANCE CO., Edmonton, Alta., Canada
ALDENS, INC., Chicago, Ill.
ALEXANDER FILM CO., Colorado Springs, Colo.
ALLEN MANUFACTURING CO., Hartford, Conn.
ALLIED MUTUAL INSURANCE CO., Des Moines, Iowa
ALLIED PAPER CORP., Kalamazoo, Mich.
ALLIED VAN LINES, Broadview, Ill.
ALLIS-CHALMERS MANUFACTURING CO., Milwaukee, Wis.
AMERICAN ABRASIVE METALS CO., Irvington, N. J.
AMERICAN CHICLE CO., Long Island City, N. Y.
AMERICAN ENKA CORP., Enka, N. C.
AMERICAN INSTITUTE OF BANKING, New York, N. Y.
AMERICAN MANAGEMENT ASSOCIATION, New York, N. Y.
AMERICAN NATIONAL BANK AND TRUST CO., Chicago, Ill.
AMERICAN OPTICAL CO., Southbridge, Mass.
AMERICAN SEATING CO., Grand Rapids, Mich.
AMERICAN STANDARDS ASSOCIATION, New York, N. Y.
AMERICAN SURETY CO., New York, N. Y.
AMERICAN TOBACCO CO., New York, N. Y.
ANCHOR CASUALTY CO., St. Paul, Minn.
ARMCO STEEL CORP., Middletown, Ohio
ARMSTRONG CORK CO., Lancaster, Pa.
ASSOCIATED TRANSPORT, INC., New York, N. Y.
ATLANTIC COAST LINE RAILROAD, Jacksonville, Fla.

BALTIMORE AND OHIO RAILROAD CO., Baltimore, Md.
BEAR BRAND HOSIERY CO., Chicago, Ill.
BELL & HOWELL CO., Chicago, Ill.
BELL TELEPHONE LABORATORIES, INC., Murray Hill, N. J.
BILOXI-GULFPORT HERALD, Gulfport, Miss.
BLUE CROSS—BLUE SHIELD, Chicago, Ill.
BOEING AIRPLANE CO., Seattle, Wash.
THE BORDEN CO., New York, N. Y.
BOWMAN DAIRY CO., Chicago, Ill.
BRIDGEPORT BRASS CO. (Div. of National Distillers & Chemical Corp.), Bridgeport, Conn.
BURROUGHS CORP., Detroit, Mich.
BUTLER MANUFACTURING CO., Kansas City, Mo.

15

ACKNOWLEDGMENTS

CALLAWAY MILLS CO., La Grange, Ga.
CARGILL, INC., Minneapolis, Minn.
CARNATION CO., Los Angeles, Calif.
GEORGE B. CARPENTER & CO., Chicago, Ill.
CARRIER CORP., Syracuse, N. Y.
CATERPILLAR TRACTOR CO., Peoria, Ill.
CENTRAL NATIONAL BANK, Chicago, Ill.
CENTRAL SURVEYS, INC., Shenandoah, Iowa
CESSNA AIRCRAFT CO., Wichita, Kans.
CHASE BRASS & COPPER CO., Waterbury, Conn.
CHRYSLER CORP., Detroit, Mich.
CITIZENS FINANCE CO., Grand Junction, Colo.
CITY PUBLIC SERVICE BOARD, San Antonio, Texas
CLARY CORP., San Gabriel, Calif.
CLEVELAND ELECTRIC ILLUMINATING CO., Cleveland, Ohio
THE COLEMAN CO., Wichita, Kans.
COLONEL WILLIAMSBURG, INC., Williamsburg, Va.
COLUMBIA BROADCASTING SYSTEM, New York, N. Y.
COMBINED INSURANCE COMPANIES OF AMERICA, Chicago, Ill.
CONNECTICUT GENERAL LIFE INSURANCE CO., Hartford, Conn.
CONTINENTAL ILLINOIS NATIONAL BANK & TRUST CO., Chicago, Ill.
CROMWELL PAPER CO., Chicago, Ill.
CROWELL-COLLIER & MACMILLAN, INC., New York, N. Y.
CURTISS CANDY CO., Chicago, Ill.

DALE ELECTRONICS, Columbia, Nebr.
DENNISON MANUFACTURING CO., Framingham, Mass.
DETROIT EDISON CO., Detroit, Mich.
A. B. DICK CO., Chicago, Ill.
DICTAPHONE CORP., New York, N. Y.
DOUBLEDAY & CO., INC., New York, N. Y.
E. P. DUTTON & CO., INC., New York, N. Y.

EASTERN MORTGAGE SERVICE CORP., Washington, D.C.
EASTMAN KODAK CO., Rochester, N. Y.
EGRY REGISTER CO., New York, N. Y.
WALTER E. ELLIOTT ASSOCIATES, Cincinnati, Ohio
EMPLOYERS INSURANCE OF WAUSAU (Wis.)
EQUITABLE LIFE ASSURANCE SOCIETY OF THE UNITED STATES, New York,
  N. Y.
ESSO STANDARD (Div. of Humble Oil & Refining Co.), New York, N. Y.
EVATYPE CORP., Eva Tone Div., Deerfield, Ill.
EXECUTONE, INC., Long Island City, New York, N. Y.

THE FAFNIR BEARING CO., New Britain, Conn.
FAULTLESS RUBBER CO., Ashland, Ohio
S. J. FECHT & ASSOCIATES, Ridgewood, N. J.
FEDERAL OUTFITTING CO., San Francisco, Calif.
FEDERAL RESERVE BANK OF PHILADELPHIA
THE FEDERATED BROKERAGE GROUP, INC., New York, N. Y.
FIELD ENTERPRISES, INC., Chicago, Ill.
FIRST FEDERAL SAVINGS AND LOAN ASSOCIATION, New Haven, Conn.
FIRST NATIONAL BANK OF ATLANTA

ACKNOWLEDGMENTS

First National Bank of Miami
First National Bank of Oregon, Portland, Ore.
First Trust Co. of St. Paul (Minn.)
Florida Savings & Loan League, Orlando, Fla.
Ford Motor Co., Dearborn, Mich.
The Foxboro Co., Foxboro, Mass.
Franklin Electric Co., Inc., Bluffton, Ind.
Friden, Inc., San Leandro, Calif.

Gamble-Skogmo, Inc., Minneapolis, Minn.
The Gates Rubber Co., Denver, Colo.
General Dynamics Corp., Liquid Carbonics Div., Chicago, Ill.
General Electric Co., New York, N. Y.
General Fireproofing Co., Youngstown, Ohio
General Mills, Inc., Minneapolis, Minn.
General Motors Corp., Detroit, Mich.
General Telephone Co. of California, Santa Monica, Calif.
General Tire & Rubber Co., Akron, Ohio
Gibson Refrigerator Div., Hupp Corp., Greenville, Mich.
Glens Falls Insurance Co., Glens Falls, N. Y.
Globe-Wernicke Co., Cincinnati, Ohio
Golden State Mutual Life Insurance Co., Los Angeles, Calif.
Goodyear Tire & Rubber Co., Akron, Ohio
Great Lakes Carbon Corp., Los Angeles, Calif.
A. P. Green Fire Brick Co., Mexico, Mo.
Greenville Industries, Inc., Greenville, N. C.
L. Grossman & Sons, Inc., Braintree, Mass.

W. F. Hall Printing Co., Chicago, Ill.
Hammermill Paper Co., Erie, Pa.
John Hancock Mutual Life Insurance Co., Boston, Mass
Hansen Glove Corp., Milwaukee, Wis.
Hardware Mutuals, Newark, N. J.
Edward N. Hay & Associates, Inc., Philadelphia, Pa.
Herbst Shoe Manufacturing Co., Milwaukee, Wis.
The High Standard Manufacturing Corp., Hamden, Conn.
Honeywell, Inc., Minneapolis, Minn.

Illinois Bell Telephone Co., Chicago, Ill.
Illinois Mutual Life & Casualty Co., Peoria, Ill.
Illuminating Engineering Society, New York, N. Y.
Inland Steel Container Co., Chicago, Ill.
International Harvester Co., Chicago, Ill.
International Telephone and Telegraph Corp., New York, N. Y.
International Textbook Co. of Scranton (Pa.)
Interstate Finance Corp., Evansville, Ind.
Interstate Securities Co., Kansas City, Mo.
Intertype Co. (Div. of Harris-Intertype Corp.), Brooklyn, N Y.
Iowa Mutual Insurance Co., DeWitt, Iowa
ITT Cannon Electric Co., Los Angeles, Calif.

Jack & Heintz, Div. of Siegler Corp., Cleveland, Ohio
Jefferson Standard Life Insurance Co., Greensboro, N. C.

ACKNOWLEDGMENTS

Jewel Tea Co., Barrington, Ill.
Johnson & Johnson, New Brunswick, N. J.
Johnson Motors (Div. of Outboard Marine Co.), Waukegan, Ill
Joslyn Manufacturing & Supply Co., Chicago, Ill.

Kaiser Aluminum and Chemical Corp., Oakland, Calif.
A. T. Kearney & Co., Chicago, Ill.
Kelly-Read & Co., Inc., Rochester, N. Y.
Kemper Insurance Group, Chicago, Ill.
Kimberly-Clark Corp., Neenah, Wis.
Frank M. Knox Co., New York, N. Y.
Koppers Co., Pittsburgh, Pa.
Kraft Foods, Chicago, Ill.

Lafayette National Bank, Lafayette, Ind.
Lambert Co. Ltd., Los Angeles, Calif.
Lampson and Sessions Co., Cleveland, Ohio
La Salle Steel Co., Hammond, Ind.
Leading National Advertisers Inc., New York, N. Y.
Leath and Co., Chicago, Ill.
Lennox Industries, Inc., Marshalltown, Iowa
Liberty Life Insurance Co., Greenville, S. C
Lincoln Telephone & Telegraph Co., Lincoln, Nebr.
Thomas J. Lipton, Inc., Englewood Cliffs, N. J.
Litton Industries Inc., Royal Division, Beverly Hills, Calif.
Liquiflame Oils., Ltd., Toronto, Can.
Lord Manufacturing Co., Erie, Pa.
Raymond Loewy William Snaith, Inc., New York, N. Y.
Luria Brothers & Co., New York, N. Y.
Lynch Corp., Anderson, Ind.
Lynn Insurance Group, Kansas City, Mo.

E. F. MacDonald Co., Dayton, Ohio
Marathon Oil Co., Findlay, Ohio
Martin Co., Denver, Colo.
Maryland Casualty Co., Oklahoma City, Okla.
G. A. Mavon & Co., Chicago, Ill.
H. P. Maynard & Co., Pittsburgh, Pa.
Maytag Co., Newton, Iowa
McCarthy Hicks, Inc., Baltimore, Md.
Merck & Co., Rahway, N. J.
Meredith Publishing Co., Des Moines, Iowa
Metropolitan Life Insurance Co., New York, N. Y.
Metropolitan Utilities District of Omaha (Nebr.)
Minneapolis-Honeywell Regulator Co., Minneapolis, Minn.
Minnesota Mining & Manufacturing Co., St. Paul, Minn.
Moncrief Lenoir Manufacturing Co., Houston, Texas
Monsanto Chemical Co., St. Louis, Mo.
Montgomery Ward & Co., Chicago, Ill.
Motorola Inc., Franklin Park, Ill.
Murphy & Rochester, Inc., Odessa, Texas
Mutual Benefit Life Insurance Co., Newark, N. J
Mutual of New York, New York, N. Y.

ACKNOWLEDGMENTS

NATIONAL ASSOCIATION OF FOOD CHAINS, Washington, D.C.
NATIONAL BANK OF COMMERCE, Pine Bluff, Ark.
NATIONAL CANNERS ASSOCIATION, Washington, D.C.
NATIONAL CASH REGISTER CO., Dayton, Ohio
NATIONAL FAMILY OPINION, INC., Toledo, Ohio
NATIONAL GYPSUM CO., Buffalo, N. Y.
NATIONAL INDUSTRIAL RECREATION ASSOCIATION, Chicago, Ill.
NATIONAL RECORDS MANAGEMENT COUNCIL, INC., New York, N. Y.
NATIONAL SAFETY COUNCIL, Chicago, Ill.
NATIONAL SOCIETY FOR THE PREVENTION OF BLINDNESS, New York, N. Y.
NATIONAL STATIONERY AND OFFICE EQUIPMENT ASSOCIATION, Washington,
 D.C.
NATIONWIDE INSURANCE CO., Columbus, Ohio
NEW YORK TELEPHONE CO., New York, N. Y.
NORDBERG MANUFACTURING CO., Milwaukee, Wis.
NORTHRUP, KING & CO., Minneapolis, Minn.
NORTHWESTERN MUTUAL INSURANCE CO., Seattle, Wash.

OAK PARK TRUST & SAVINGS BANK, Oak Park, Ill.
OLIVETTI UNDERWOOD CORP., New York, N. Y.
OLSON TRANSPORTATION CO., Chicago, Ill.
ONEIDA, LTD., Oneida, N. Y.
OPINION RESEARCH CORP., Princeton, N. J.
ORDNANCE RESEARCH LABORATORY, Pennsylvania State University, Univer-
 sity Park, Pa.
OWENS-CORNING FIBERGLAS CORP., Toledo, Ohio
OWENS-ILLINOIS INC., Toledo, Ohio
OXFORD FILING SUPPLY CO., Garden City, N. Y.

PACIFIC TELEPHONE & TELEGRAPH CO., San Francisco, Calif.
PALMETTO STATE LIFE INSURANCE CO., Columbia, S. C.
PARKE, DAVIS & CO., Detroit, Mich.
PEACEDALE MANUFACTURING CO., Peacedale, R. I.
PENNSYLVANIA NATIONAL MUTUAL CASUALTY INSURANCE CO., Harrisburg,
 Pa.
PEPSI-COLA COMPANY, INC., New York, N. Y.
PERSONAL PRODUCTS CORP., Milltown, N. J.
PHILCO CORP., Philadelphia, Pa.
S. S. PIERCE CO., Boston, Mass.
PILLSBURY CO., Minneapolis, Minn.
THE PIONEER RUBBER CO., Willard, Ohio
PITNEY-BOWES, INC., Stamford, Conn.
PORCELAIN STEEL BUILDINGS, Columbus, Ohio
PORTER-CABLE MACHINE CO., Div. of Rockwell Mfg. Co., Syracuse, N. Y.
PROVIDENCE INSTITUTION FOR SAVINGS, Boston, Mass.
PRUDENTIAL INSURANCE CO. OF AMERICA, Newark, N. J.
PUBLIC BUILDINGS SERVICE, Washington, D.C.
PUBLIC SERVICE COMPANY OF NEW MEXICO, Albuquerque, N. M.

RADIO CORPORATION OF AMERICA, New York, N. Y.
RECORDAK CORP., New York, N. Y.
RECORDS MANAGEMENT INSTITUTE, New York, N. Y.
REED INTERNATIONAL, INC., Houston, Texas

ACKNOWLEDGMENTS

REMINGTON RAND DIV. (of Sperry Rand Corp.), New York, N. Y.
REPUBLIC STEEL CORP., Cleveland, Ohio
RESEARCH INSTITUTE OF AMERICA, New York, N. Y.
REVERE COPPER & BRASS, INC., New York, N. Y.
REVLON, INC., New York, N. Y.
REYNOLDS METALS CO., Richmond, Va.
JENS RISOM DESIGN, INC., New York, N. Y.
GEORGE D. ROPER CORP., Newark Div., Newark, Ohio

SKF INDUSTRIES, INC., Philadelphia, Pa.
SACRAMENTO MUNICIPAL UTILITIES DISTRICT, Sacramento, Calif.
SANDUSKY FOUNDRY AND MACHINE CO., Sandusky, Ohio
SAN GABRIEL CORP., San Gabriel, Calif.
THE F. & M. SCHAEFER BREWING CO., Brooklyn, N. Y.
JOS. SCHLITZ BREWING CO., Milwaukee, Wis.
GEO. T. SCHMIDT, INC., Chicago, Ill.
SEARS, ROEBUCK & CO., Chicago, Ill.
SECURITY FIRST NATIONAL BANK, Sheboygan, Wis.
SELECTED RISK INSURANCE CO., Branchville, N. J.
SHAMPAINE INDUSTRIES, INC., St. Louis, Mo.
SHELL OIL CO., New York, N. Y.
SIMPLICITY PATTERN CO., New York, N. Y.
SKELLY OIL CO., Kansas City, Mo.
SLIGO, INC., St. Louis, Mo.
SOCONY-MOBIL OIL CO., New York, N. Y.
SORG PAPER CO., Middletown, Ohio
SOUNDSCRIBER CORP., North Haven, Conn.
SOUTHERN PACIFIC CO., San Francisco, Calif.
SOUTHEASTERN EMPLOYER'S SERVICES CORP., Bristol, Tenn.
SOUTHWESTERN BELL TELEPHONE CO., St. Louis, Mo.
SPECTOR FREIGHT SYSTEM, INC., Chicago, Ill.
SPIEGEL, INC., Chicago, Ill.
SPRAY PRODUCTS CORP., Camden, N. J.
SMITH, KLINE & FRENCH LABORATORIES, Philadelphia, Pa.
A. E. STALEY MANUFACTURING CO., Decatur, Ill.
STANDARD OIL CO. OF CALIFORNIA, San Francisco, Calif.
STERNS & FOSTER CO., Lockland, Ohio
STEELCASE, INC., Grand Rapids, Mich.
STEWART-WARNER CORP., Chicago, Ill.
SUN OIL CO., Philadelphia, Pa.
SUPER MARKET INSTITUTE, Chicago, Ill.
SUPERTEST PETROLEUM CORP., LTD., London, Ont., Can.
SUPREME STEEL EQUIPMENT CORP., New York, N. Y.
SURFACE COMBUSTION CORP., Janitrol Div., Columbus, Ohio
SWIFT & CO., Chicago, Ill.
SYLVANIA ELECTRIC PRODUCTS, INC., Towanda, Pa.

TANDY CORP., Fort Worth, Texas
TENNESSEE VALLEY AUTHORITY, Knoxville, Tenn.
THOMSON-DIGGS CO., Sacramento, Calif.
3M COMPANY, St. Paul, Minn.
TIDEWATER OIL CO., Los Angeles, Calif.
TIMKEN ROLLER BEARING CO., Canton, Ohio

ACKNOWLEDGMENTS

TOKHEIM CORP., Fort Wayne, Ind.
TONI CO., Chicago, Ill.
THE TRANE CO., La Crosse, Wis.

UNION ELECTRIC CO., St. Louis, Mo.
UNION STEEL PRODUCTS CO., Albion, Mich.
U.S. ELECTRICAL MOTORS, INC., Milford, Conn.
U.S. GOVERNMENT PRINTING OFFICE, Washington, D.C.
UNITED STATES STEEL CORP., New York, N. Y.
UNITED VAN LINES, INC., Maplewood, Mo.
THE UPJOHN CO., Kalamazoo, Mich.

VAPOR HEATING CO., Niles, Ill.
VAPOR RECOVERY SYSTEMS CO., Compton, Calif.
VICTOR BUSINESS MACHINES CO., Chicago, Ill.

WANG LABORATORIES, Tewksbury, Mass.
WARNER BROTHERS CO., Bridgeport, Conn.
WARNER-LAMBERT PHARMACEUTICAL CO., Morris Plains, N. J.
WASHINGTON GAS AND LIGHT CO., Washington, D.C.
WELCH GRAPE JUICE CO., INC., Westfield, N. Y.
WESTERN ELECTRIC CO., New York, N. Y.
WESTERN UNION TELEGRAPH CO., New York, N. Y.
WESTINGHOUSE ELECTRIC CORP., Pittsburgh, Pa.
WESTON INSTRUMENTS, INC., Newark, N. J.
WEST PENN POWER CO., Greensburg, Pa.

Chapter 1

THE OFFICE AS THE CONTROL CENTER

A NYONE who has viewed the drama of a manned spacecraft launching knows the heart of the operation is in the control center. The equipment-packed room hums with the activity of scientific and technical personnel who direct the countdown. Attention is focused on the men in the capsule, but decisions are made in the control center.

Nothing could be closer to the drama unfolding every day in the business world. The control center, complete with electronic and electric equipment of varying degrees of sophistication, is the modern business office. Attention is focused on production and sales, but decisions are made in the office.

Ask the office manager what's under control, and he'll tell you: "Documents, records, finances, systems and procedures, work flow, personnel and costs!" Executives are based in this control center and they need information to help them make major decisions.

Today no business head would think of taking an important step without first calling upon his controller or office manager for all the facts available from the records of the business, as well as outside sources. The company budget, so important in modern management, could not be successfully operated without office records. The many reports required by federal, state, and local governments must be made out in the office. Tax records and returns are an office responsibility. And the daily information needed by management to make day-by-day decisions is supplied by the office. The office has, in fact, become the very heart of the business.

The office manager of today, therefore, has a responsibility far beyond being a good keeper of the accounts. He must understand the overall problems which top management is called upon to solve, so that he can maintain the records and systems necessary to provide data helpful in solving those problems. And the office must keep the records efficiently, so that all information needed for the profitable operation of the business will be immediately, or at least quickly, available and up to date. There is nothing so dangerous in management as for the head of a business, or its executive committee, to have to make important decisions with outdated information. Stale facts are usually worse than none at all.

Forecasting Future Growth

One responsibility of top management, and perhaps the most important, is to make long-range plans for the growth of the business. It is all very well, as happened in the case of one steel company, for management to say we will build all the plant capacity we need to make all the steel we can sell. But in order for its management to plan intelligently, buy wisely, and organize most efficiently, a business should know where it is going, how long it will take to get there, and what it intends to do after it gets there. Haphazard expansion, without first determining how the expansion is to be financed or how the increased sales are going to be obtained, can wreck any company. In fact, more businesses fail from overexpansion than from any other cause.

However, a business can lose both money and opportunity by following an overcautious, overconservative policy. There is no such thing as standing still in business. You either go ahead or go stale, and once a business goes stale, it begins to die. Top management's job is to look ahead five years, and with the aid of all the information available from office and other records, project as best it can the growth of the business over that period. It may prove to be a poor guess. But it is better than no guess at all.

The Office Manager and His Job

With the pressure on the office manager to provide top management with many of its managing tools, what is the nature of his job, and what should be his qualifications?

The office manager is the connecting link between the sales and the production ends of the business. He reports to the president, general manager, or chief financial executive and is held responsible for office efficiency and personnel. He works closely with the controller in the development of cost-reducing office methods.

What are his qualifications? He should have a thorough knowledge of accounting, the ability to select and manage people, and an inquiring attitude toward improved office methods. He should be fair and sympathetic in his dealings with employees. Membership in local office managers' groups is desirable. He should maintain avenues of information about the latest developments in business machines and modernized equipment for offices. He should be alert for new ideas at all times and, having become convinced of their desirability, be ready and able to sell them to top management.

It used to be that any good bookkeeper with a flair for working with people could be promoted to office manager and do a fairly good job—or, at least, things went along smoothly enough so that no one questioned the way he managed the office. Then business methods changed, and the salaries of office workers doubled and tripled. The office payroll became a matter of concern to top management.

Perhaps it is because the office and the paper work involved in its management are not "productive" in the eyes of the owners of a business that the question of whether a more experienced and skillful office manager might not bring down administrative costs has been often overlooked. When the office management of a business begins to assume more important functions, we find the office not only the control room of the business, where the facts and figures needed to manage the business successfully are prepared, but also the department where the *control* of all costs is centered. The greatly increased number of transactions, the endless records required by government, and the need of statistical data upon which to base decisions have multiplied the number of people needed in the office. As a result, today's office manager must be a personnel expert as well as an accountant, a systems expert as well as a purchasing agent, an authority on taxes, a forms expert, and a "wizard" with figures.

The Prime Responsibility

The office manager's first responsibility is to get office production out efficiently, economically, and accurately. All other aspects of his job are only contributory to that all-important end. In these days of rising labor costs and higher prices for everything used in the office, the office manager's job has become infinitely more complex than it once was. But his responsibility remains the same, whether in a large company where he must delegate most of the supervision (but not the control), or in a small one where he is able to perform many of the functions himself.

In offices where production lags, causes are usually to be found among these:

1. No record kept of production, and no one knows what production is expected.

2. Inadequate or obsolete equipment.
3. Overcrowding due to poor arrangement.
4. Too little supervision.
5. Help retained through slack periods and not temporarily transferred to busier departments.
6. Failure to require good deportment, prompt attendance, and good office manners.
7. No central authority to assign work and workers.
8. Continuation of old practices, old methods, use of obsolete forms, preparation of reports no longer needed.
9. Friction and failure to cooperate between departments.
10. Poor lighting, too much noise, bad housekeeping.

One of the commonest faults revealed by Dartnell studies is failure to provide overall supervision of offices; in many organizations each department manager runs his own department according to his own ideas, without help or assistance from some central authority. Almost invariably this leads to uneven management, with one department operated strictly and efficiently and an adjoining department operated so loosely that the morale of the entire organization is ruined. A seemingly high-priced office executive can earn his salary many times over in a surprisingly small organization, just by tightening up the operation and getting the different departments synchronized.

Organization Checking Points

1. Does each individual—worker, supervisor, or executive—know to whom he reports?
2. Does each supervisor, department head and executive know what individuals report to him?
3. Is there an organization chart?
4. Can a copy of the organization chart be found quickly?
5. Is the organization chart kept up to date?
6. Are individuals in the organization specifically acquainted with their respective sections of the organization chart and generally acquainted with the rest of it or appropriate divisions of it?
7. Is there an organization write-up describing each position on the organization chart?
8. Are there standard practice instructions covering each operation standardized?
9. Is there a pamphlet for distribution to employees that tells of all office rules?
10. Is there an office manual describing the various routines and procedures and their relation to each other?

THE COMPANY ORGANIZATION CHART

Oxford Filing Supply Company

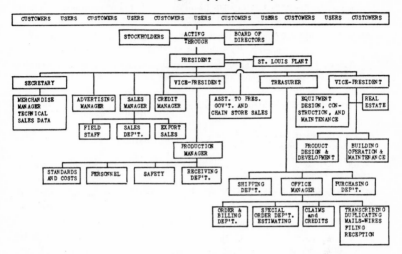

NOTES: (1) This chart shows lines of authority. It does not attempt to show lines of contact. In the transaction of business, there must necessarily be contacts, by each department or division of the company, with practically all other departments. All departments and individuals must work together as a team.

(2) As jobs may be shifted from one individual to another, individuals' names are not shown.

(3) Any differences in levels (distance from top) between departments, as shown on this chart, do not reflect their relative importance. Such differences in levels were necessary for space and printing reasons only. All departments are equally important since no machine can function without all of its parts.

---

11. Is the work functionalized—that is, so far as possible is work of a similar kind assigned to specified workers (as in centralized departments like transcribing, calculating, statistical, and so on); and similarly with individuals where appropriate?

12. Is each individual responsible solely to one person for each function performed?

13. In sections, does one person at a time go to the supervisor's desk?

14. Are technical and functional contacts and sources of information differentiated from lines of operating responsibility?

15. Does each executive have four or fewer subexecutives, department heads, or supervisors reporting directly to him?

16. Is there a periodic inspection and checkup of department heads and supervisors?

17. Do executives and department heads know of the work, ability, special achievement, and special shortcomings of their immediate subordinates' assistants, the men in the second rank below them?

18. Are expense accounts and budget items arranged according to the organization chart and, thus, according to operating responsibilities?

19. Are only those costs charged to divisions, departments, and sections for which the division, department, or section head is responsible and which he can regulate?

20. Are all costs allocated to divisions, departments, and sections that can be thus allocated?

21. Are detailed analysis of their financial results available to division, department, and section heads?

22. Is there a program for training men for supervisory and executive positions?

23. Is it recognized that anyone may appeal to the president or some other top executive?

24. Is decision-making decentralized as far as possible?

25. Are decisions made at the lowest point in the organization at which the decider possesses all the facts necessary for a sound decision?

26. Do men who possess the facts do the deciding?

27. Have there been eliminated nominal approvals that destroy subordinates' confidence in their ability and that encourage "buck passing"?

28. In making executive changes is there too strict an adherence to a fixed organization plan regardless of the qualification of the executive personnel?

29. Are executives, department heads, and supervisors in the same general rank of similar intelligence and taste?

Declaring War on Turnover

The office manager, more than any single person in the organization, is in a position to do something positive about the basic causes of high office costs. While increased material costs have a lot to do with the high price of output, the effect of the present labor situation is even more far-reaching. This is where the office manager's skill at managing people comes in. If he knows what motivates his people and how to use the right motivating forces to get their best efforts, he can make invaluable contributions to the welfare of his company.

Much of the high cost of office production comes from turnover rates that are higher than they need be. The competent office manager knows that unpleasant working conditions contribute heavily to excessive turnover rates and make his job that much more difficult to carry out successfully. Targets of his attack are some of the physical factors that hold no attraction for office employees—especially female employees: office noise; lack of clean, well-lighted rest rooms; and other conveniences now common to better equipped offices. In many offices that are housed in old buildings, for example, it would be profitable to lower ceilings, install acoustic tile, and step up lighting.

Many resignations are simply inarticulate protests against noise, dirt, overcrowding, and poor tools in the office. People object to these things without realizing exactly what it is that makes the work disagreeable. High turnover rates and high absenteeism are often nothing more than unvoiced protests against an unpleasant working atmosphere.

Effective Administration

The office manager's job is to get things done through people and to make his concern a good place in which to work. Here are two dozen practical ideas on successful administration gathered from the experience of many successful business leaders. The ideas, suggested by the Small Business Administration, are worth a good deal of careful thought, for they can help an office manager build the more alert, effective, and responsible staff he needs to do his job better.

1. Emphasize skill, not rules, in your organization. Judge your own actions and those of your subordinates by their effects— effects in terms of increasing both the competitive strength of your business and the satisfaction of the human needs of the people who work in it. Go easy on pat rules for running a business. Doing it "by the book" isn't always the most satisfactory way. If an unorthodox solution works effectively and pleases the people who use it, don't discount it just because it doesn't seem exactly "according to Hoyle."

2. Set a high standard for your organization. If you are irregular in your work habits, late for appointments, fuzzy in expressing yourself, careless about facts, bored in attitude, your supervisors probably will be, too. If, on the other hand, you set a high standard for the organization, in all probability your supervisors will be eager to follow your good example.

3. Know your subordinates and try to determine what is important to each. Continuous study of individuals is a "must" for getting things done through people. Motives and attitudes are important tools for the executive, and they can be determined only by study. Since security is the main drive in many people, giving recognition to the contribution of others and to their roles is a useful starting point in getting the best from people of future executive caliber.

Individuals vary widely in their other characteristics. Well-timed praise may spur one person to new heights of achievement, but it may only inflate another. A better key to the latter's effort might be constructive criticism. A third individual may wilt under any kind of criticism and some other approach is needed. The skillful executive constantly hunts for the appropriate procedure. He also searches beyond the office for background. People's motives and attitudes are heavily conditioned by their personal situations. For this reason, tactful drawing-out of subordinates can often supply invaluable information for understanding them. Remember that people often act on the basis of emotional, nonlogical reasons, even though they try to appear completely logical.

4. Try to listen thoughtfully and objectively. The executive who knows his people—their habits, worries, ambitions, touchy points, and pet prides—comes to appreciate why they behave as they do and what motives stir them. The best and fastest way to know them is to encourage them to talk freely, without fear of ridicule or disapproval. Try to understand how others actually feel on a subject, whether or not you feel the same way. Never dominate a conversation or meeting by doing all the talking yourself if you want to find out where your people stand. If both you and one of your people start to say something at the same time, give him the right of way.

One objection to the idea of being a good listener is that it takes time to draw people out. The answer is that it takes time to plan, too. Both are essential in the executive's job. The time invested will pay big dividends.

5. Be considerate. Few things contribute more to building a hard-working supervisory team than a considerate chief. Try to be calm and courteous toward your lieutenants. Consider the effects on them of any decisions you make. Take into account the problems they have of their own, both business and personal. Try to build up their pride in their work, and their self-respect. Start by treating personal characteristics as assets and being careful not to trample on them.

6. Be consistent. If you "fly off the handle" and "set off fireworks" you are likely to frighten subordinates into their shells; if you vacillate wildly in reaction, mood, and manner you will probably bewilder them. Neither sort of behavior can win you the confidence and cooperation of your lieutenants, which you must have to get things done.

You and your supervisors are in the position of a leader and his followers. One wants to follow only the leader whose course is steady and whose actions are predictable.

7. Give your subordinates objectives and a sense of direction. Subordinates should know where they're going, what they're doing, and why they're doing it, in order to plan their time intelligently and to work effectively. Good supervisors seldom enjoy working just day to day. Therefore, make clear the relation between their day-to-day work and the larger company objectives.

For example, don't merely ask people to analyze the variable costs of a particular department. Tell them also that it's part of a longer-range plan to provide leeway for salary increases, and that the knowledge they provide will strengthen the operating efficiency of their company.

8. Give your directions in terms of suggestions or requests. If your people have initiative and ability, you will get vastly better results in this way than you will by giving orders or commands. Issue the latter only as a last resort. If you find that you *have* to give orders all the time, maybe you'd better look for some new assistants—or reexamine the way you have been handling your own job. Be sure, also, to tell why you want certain things done. Informal, oral explanations are often as good as or better than written ones; let the individual circumstances be your guide here.

9. Delegate responsibility for details to subordinates. This is another "obvious" point that is frequently overlooked. Delegating

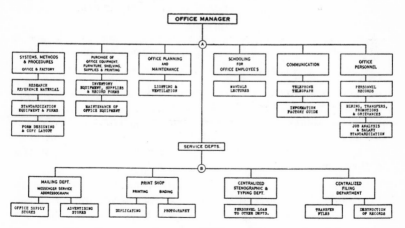

The office manager's responsibilities are many and varied

responsibility is basic to competent administration. You are not doing your real job as an executive if you do not delegate, because, as office manager, if you insist on keeping your hand in details, you discourage your subordinates by competing with them. Moreover, by doing everything yourself, you prevent subordinates from learning to make their own decisions. Sooner or later the capable ones will quit and the others will sit back and let you do all the work. Ultimately, you will have no time for the thinking and the planning that are so important in your job. Think of your supervisors as working *with* you, not *for you.*

10. Show your staff that you have faith in them and that you expect them to do their best. Supervisors—and everyone else, for that matter—tend to perform according to what is expected of them. If they know you have the confidence in them to expect a first-rate job, that's what they will usually try to give you.

11. Keep your subordinates informed. Bring them up to date constantly on new developments and let them know well in advance whenever changes are in the offing. As members of a team, they are entitled to know what's going on. If they do, their thinking will be geared more closely to reality and their attitudes will be more flexible. Give them enough information about conditions and events in your company and industry to let them see themselves and their work in perspective.

12. Let your assistants in on your plans at an early stage. It's true that many plans can't be discussed very far in advance. They should, however, be discussed with subordinates before they are in final form. It will give your assistants that all-important chance to participate. Furthermore, because they will have taken part in shaping the plan, it will be as much theirs as yours, and they will feel a personal responsibility for its success. Hence, they will usually carry out the program with vigor and precision.

13. Ask subordinates for their counsel and help. Bring them actively into the picture. It will help to give them a feeling of "belonging" and to build their self-confidence. It will often make them anxious to work harder than ever. What is just as important, they may well have good ideas which may never be utilized unless you ask for them.

14. Give a courteous hearing to ideas from subordinates. Many ideas may sound fantastic to you, but it's important not to act scornful or impatient. There's no surer way to discourage original thinking by a subordinate than to disparage or ridicule a suggestion he makes. His next idea might well be the very one you want—make it easy for that next idea to come to you.

15. Give your subordinates a chance to take part in decisions. When your people feel they have had a say in a decision, they are much more likely to go along with it cooperatively. If they agree with the decision, they will look at it as their own and back it to the hilt. If they don't agree, they may still back it more strongly than otherwise because of the fact that their point of view was given full and fair consideration.

16. Tell the originator of an idea what action was taken and why. If you do so, he'll study other problems and make suggestions on ways to solve them. If his idea is accepted, he will be encouraged by seeing the results of his thinking put into effect. If his idea is not adopted, he will accept that fact more readily and with fuller understanding if you show him that the reasons for rejection are clear and sound. In addition, knowing exactly why his idea was impractical will help the suggester analyze the next problem more clearly.

17. Try to let people carry out their own ideas. Occasionally it happens that equally good suggestions on a particular problem come from two individuals at the same time; one person directly responsible in the situation, the other person essentially detached from it. In such cases, it's usually desirable to choose the recommendation developed by the person who will ultimately carry it out. He will then have a personal stake in proving that his idea is, in fact, workable. It's good administrative practice, therefore, to keep subordinates constantly aware of your willingness to have them work out their own solutions to problems in their particular operating areas.

18. Build up subordinates' sense of the values of their work. Most people need to think their jobs are important. Many even have to feel that they not only have an important job, but are essential in it, before they start clicking.

19. Let your people know where they stand. The day of "treat 'em rough and tell 'em nothing" has passed. A system providing periodic ratings for employees is the first step. However, the full value of such a system is realized only if ratings are discussed with each person individually so that each can bolster weak points, clear up misunderstandings, and recognize his particular talents.

A formal rating system may be worthwhile, but is not necessarily essential if the office manager talks at least once a year with each supervisor about his performance during the past period.

20. Criticize or reprove in private. This may, perhaps, seem obvious, but administrators forget to do it every day in hundreds of organizations. Reprimands in the presence of others cause humiliation and resentment instead of a desire to do better next time. Criticizing a subordinate when people from his department are present undermines his authority, his morale, and his enthusiasm to do his best for your company.

21. Criticize or reprove constructively. First, get all the facts; review them with those concerned, and reach an agreement on them. Then be ready to suggest a constructive course of action for the future. When you criticize, concentrate on the method or the results, not on personalities. If you can precede the criticism by a bit of honest praise, so much the better. Note, however, that some executives do this so regularly and unimaginatively that the compliments lose their value.

22. Praise in public. Most people thrive on appreciation. Praise before others often has a multiple impact. It tends to raise morale, increase prestige, and strengthen self-confidence—important factors in the development of capable supervisors. But be sure that those you praise are really the ones who deserve it, and that you don't encourage "credit grabbing."

23. Pass the credit on down to the operating people. Taking for yourself credit that really belongs to one of your operating people tends to destroy his initiative and willingness to take responsibility. Giving him fair recognition for what he does has a double benefit; he gets appreciation for doing a good job, and you get the help and support of a loyal staff. If you take all the bows when somebody else played the leading role, you can rapidly lose the respect of your supervisors and other employees.

24. Accept moderate "griping" as healthy. In small doses, griping can serve as a safety valve for your people. If they worked under a perfect administrator they would probably still complain, just because he *was* perfect. Vicious, personal sniping is, of course, another matter; here, you should make every effort to have the cause discovered and rooted out. Remember, too, that without some dissatisfaction there would be little incentive to do or get something better.

A striking example of the trend to modernization in bank lobbies: The terrazzo-floored entrance to the First National City Bank of New York. Above the pool and around the walls of the lobby is display space for telling the story of the bank's services.

Courtesy, First National City Bank of New York

Chapter 2

EQUAL EMPLOYMENT
OPPORTUNITY REQUIREMENTS

THE Equal Opportunity Act of 1966 brought new and unfamiliar responsibilities to the office administration executive. The act put real teeth into the federal government's efforts to achieve a nationwide pattern of fair employment practices. Noncompliance can subject a company to severe penalties. Therefore, an entire chapter of this handbook properly is devoted to this important legislation.

On July 2, 1967, companies engaged in interstate or foreign commerce, with eight or more employees for each working day in each of at least 20 calendar weeks in the current or preceding year, become subject to the Equal Employment Opportunity Act. Prior to July 2, 1967, only those employers with 50 or more employees were subject to the legislation. In counting the number of employees, the whole work force is included from top to bottom.

Most of the material which follows was prepared by Southeastern Employer's Services Corporation, a management consulting firm specializing in equal employment opportunity analysis.

Unlawful Employment Practices

There are a number of actions by employers that are considered unlawful employment practices (UEP) if they are based on race, color, religion, sex, or national origin. A number of these prohibitions are subject to some important exceptions which will be discussed later. Although employers are prohibited from engaging in specified unlawful employment practices, they are not required to take any affirmative action or to apply quotas so as to rectify existing imbalances in employment.

The provisions of fair employment make it unlawful for employers to take the following discriminatory actions where they are based on race, color, religion, sex, or national origin:

1. To discharge, or fail or refuse to hire, or

2. Discriminate with respect to compensation, terms, conditions, and privileges or employment, or

3. Limit, segregate or classify in any way that would tend to deprive any individual of employment opportunties, or

4. Indicate a preference, limitation, specification, or discrimination in printing or publishing any notice or advertisement for employment, or

5. Discriminate against an employee or job applicant because he has opposed any unlawful practice or made a charge, testified, assisted, or participated in any investigation, proceeding, or hearing under the requirements.

In short, employers may not discriminate against individuals because of their race, color, religion, sex, or national origin in hiring or firing, employment conditions, segregation or classification, advertisement, or job notices, training programs, or because a person has brought a complaint of alleged discrimination.

Exceptions to Prohibitions

There are a number of exceptions to the prohibitions just discussed. That is to say, employers are permitted to discriminate for or against individuals or disregard certain prohibitions in the following instances:

1. An employer may disregard the prohibitions of discrimination against religion, sex, or national origin where they are a bona fide job qualification reasonably necessary to the normal operation of the employer's business. This includes hiring and employment by employers and admission to apprenticeship, training, or retraining programs and also includes advertising or employment notices.

2. If an employer is subject to a government security program and the individual involved does not have security clearance, the employer will not be liable if he discharges or refuses to hire a person because of his inability to obtain a security clearance when the position involved requires such clearance.

3. Employment discrimination is permitted against an individual who is a member of the Communist Party of the United States or of any other organization required to register as a Communist-Action or Communist-Front organization by final order of the Subversive Activities Control Board, pursuant to the Subversive Activities Control Act of 1950.

4. The fourth broad exception says that it shall not be an unlawful employment practice for an employer to apply different standards, or compensation, or terms and conditions of employment where they are applied pursuant to a bona fide seniority system, a merit system, or a system that measures earnings by quantity or quality of production.

5. An employer is permitted to apply different pay scales, conditions and facilities of employment according to the location of different plants. An employer having a plant in one state or geographical area need not apply the same terms of compensation, conditions or facilities of employment as it had in plants located in other geographical areas.

6. An educational institution employer which is owned or supported by a religion or a religious corporation may employ members of that religion without such religious discrimination being declared an unlawful employment practice.

7. A business operating on or near an Indian Reservation may give preferential treatment in the employment to Indians without such being an unlawful employment practice.

8. An employer may rely upon the results of a professionally developed ability test that is not designed or intended to be used to discriminate against persons because of their race, color, sex, religion, or national origin.

9. An employer may justify pay differentials based on sex that are authorized under the Equal Pay Act of 1963. Thus, the provisions of the Equal Pay Act are not nullified.

10. An employer may continue to observe veteran re-employment preference rights without such being declared an unlawful employment practice.

The Equal Employment Opportunity Act does not require preferential treatment be given to any individual or group because of imbalance that may exist without respect to the total number or percentage of persons of any race, color, religion, sex or national origin employed in comparison with the total number or percentage of such persons in that or any other area. As a matter of fact, the requirements prohibit hiring members of minority groups on the basis of quotas in order to rectify existing imbalances in employment.

The Equal Employment Opportunity Act is administered and enforced by the Equal Employment Opportunity Commission (EEOC). This five-member commission seeks to obtain voluntary compliance through methods of persuasion, conciliation, and mediation, but it is empowered to conduct hearings and issue cease-and-desist orders if there is noncompliance. The commission has established recordkeeping requirements, including the posting of official notices and the annual reporting requirements.

Recordkeeping and Reporting Requirements

On or before March 31 of each year, every employer subject to the Equal Employment Opportunity Act must file with the commission copies of the information report entitled Employer Information Report Form EEO-1.

The commission reserves the right to require reports other than that designated as the Employer Information Report on Form

EEO-1 about the employment practices of individual employers or groups of employers whenever in the commission's judgment special or supplemental reports are necessary.

The commission has not adopted any requirements, generally applicable to employers, that records be made or kept. It however reserves the right to impose recordkeeping requirements upon individual employers or groups of employers. The EEO-1 Information Report regarding the number of minority group employees in various job classifications may be obtained by a visual head-count of the work force *or* by the maintenance of post employment records as to the identity of employees where such is permitted by state FEP requirements. In the latter case, the commission recommends the maintenance of a permanent record as to the racial or ethnic identity of an individual for purpose of completing the report form *only* where the employer keeps such records separately from the employee's basic personnel file or other records available to those responsible for personnel decisions.

Unless the employer is subject to a state or local fair-employment-practice regulation governing the preservation of records and containing requirements inconsistent with the present policies of the EEOC, any personnel or employment record made or kept by an employer should be preserved by the employer for a period of one year from the date of the making of the record or the personnel action involved, whichever occurs later. Such forms would include, but are not necessarily limited to, application forms submitted by applicants, records having to do with hiring, promotion, transfer, layoff, termination, rates of pay, or other terms of compensation and selection for training or apprenticeship programs.

In the instance of involuntary termination of an employee, the personnel records of the individual terminated shall be kept for a period of one year from the date of termination. Where a charge of discrimination has been filed, or an action brought by the U.S. Attorney General, the employer must preserve all personnel records relevant to the charge or action until the final disposition of the charge or the action. The term "personnel records relevant to the charge," for example, would include personnel or employment records relating to the charging party and to all other employees holding positions similar to that held or sought by the charging party; an application form or test papers completed by an unsuccessful applicant and by all other candidates for the same position as that for which the charging party applied and was rejected.

The date of "final disposition of the charge or the action" means the date of expiration of the statutory period within which the charging party may bring an action in a United States District Court, or where an action is brought against an employer either by a charging party or by the U.S. Attorney General, the date on which such litigation is terminated.

The commission requires every employer covered by the act to post an official "Notice to Employees." Such notices may be obtained directly from the Equal Employment Opportunity Commission, Washington, D.C. Such official posters should be conspicuously displayed in each establishment covered by the act.

Sex Discrimination

The Equal Employment Opportunity Commission has established its guidelines and interpretations as it applies to discrimination because of sex. When Franklin D. Roosevelt, Jr. was chairman of the EEOC, he stated that the commission would proceed with caution in interpreting the scope and application of the prohibition of discrimination in employment on account of sex. The commission is mindful that there is little relevant legislative history to serve as a guide to the intent of Congress in this area. The guidelines issued by the commission are an effort to temper the bare language of the act with common sense and a sympathetic understanding of the position and needs of women workers. Nevertheless, where the plain command of the act is that there be no artificial classification of jobs by sex, the commission feels bound to follow it even where such segregation has worked to the benefit of the female worker.

One of the most difficult areas is the relation of the act to state labor requirements designed originally to protect women workers. The commission has ruled that it cannot assume that Congress intended to strike down such state legislation. The commission goes further to say that its study of some state legislation revealed part of these requirements are irrelevant to present-day needs of women and much present state legislation is capable of denying effective equality of opportunity to women. The commission does not believe that Congress intended to disturb state labor regulations which were intended to and have the effect of protecting women against exploitation and hazard.

Accordingly, the EEOC will consider limitations or prohibitions imposed by such state regulations as a basis for application of the bona fide occupational-qualification exception. However, in cases where the clear effect of a state regulation is not to protect women but to subject them to discrimination, the state labor regulation will not be considered a justification for discrimination. For example, restrictions on lifting weights will not be deemed in conflict with the act except in cases where the limit is set as an unreasonably low level, which would not endanger women.

The commission states that an employer will not be considered to be engaged in an unlawful employment practice when he refuses to employ a woman in a job in which women are prohibited from being employed or which involves duties which women may not be permitted to perform because of hazards reasonably to be apprehended from such employment. On the other hand, an employer will be found to have committed an unlawful employment practice if he refuses to employ or promote a woman in order to avoid providing a benefit for her required by a state regulation—such as a minimum wage or premium overtime pay for women.

As is outlined earlier in this manual, the EEOC permits discrimination because of sex where sex is a "bona fide occupational qualification reasonably necessary to the normal operation of the employer's business." In applying this standard, the commission believes that the bona fide occupational qualification exception as to sex should be interpreted narrowly. Labels—"Men's Jobs" and "Women's Jobs"—tend to deny employment opportunities unnecessarily to one sex or the other.

The EEOC will find that the following situations do not warrant the application of the bona fide occupational qualification exception:

1. The refusal to hire a woman because of her sex, based on assumptions of the comparative employment characteristics of women in general. For example, the assumption that the turnover rate among women is higher than among men.

2. The refusal to hire an individual based on stereotype characteristics of the sexes. Such stereotypes include, for example, that men are less capable of assembling intricate equipment. The principle of nondiscrimination requires that individuals be considered on the basis of individual capacities and not on the basis of any characteristics generally attributed to the group.

3. The refusal to hire an individual because of the preference of co-workers, the employer, clients or customers, except where it is necessary for the purpose of authenticity or genuineness where sex might be a bona fide occupational qualification in the case of an actor or actress.

4. The fact that the employer may have to provide separate facilities for a person of the opposite sex will not justify discrimination under the bona fide occupational qualifications exception unless the expense involved would be clearly unreasonable.

It is an unlawful employment practice to classify a job as "male" or "female" or to maintain separate lines of progression or separate seniority lists based on sex where this would adversely affect any employee unless sex is a bona fide occupational qualification for that particular job. Accordingly, employment practices of employers are not permitted which arbitrarily classify jobs so that:

1. A female is prohibited from applying for a job labeled "male" or for a job in a "male" line of progression and vice versa.

2. A male scheduled for layoff is prohibited from displacing a less senior female on a "female" seniority list and vice versa.

A seniority system or line of progression which distinguishes between "light" and "heavy" jobs constitutes an unlawful employment practice if it operates as a disguised form of classification by sex, or creates unreasonable obstacles to the advancement by member of either sex, or creates unreasonable obstacles to the advancement by member of either sex into jobs which members of that sex would reasonably be expected to perform.

The commission has determined that an employer's rule which forbids or restricts the employment of married women and which is not applicable to married men is a prohibited discrimination based on sex. The commission states that it does not seem relevant that the rule is not directed against all females, but only against married females, because so long as sex is a factor in the application of the rule, such application involves a discrimination based on sex. The commission says that a bona fide occupational qualification must be justified in terms of the peculiar requirements of the particular job and not on the basis of a general principle.

Advertising Requirements

Help-wanted advertising may not indicate a preference based on sex unless a bona fide occupational qualification makes it permissible to specify "male" or "female." When a newspaper or other publication classifies such advertising in separate "male," "female," and "male and female" columns, advertising will most clearly avoid an indication of preference by using the "male and female" column. However, ads for help may be placed in either column—"male" or "female"—and the advertiser is not required to specify that both sexes may apply. However, if an employer specifically asks for a male or a female, he must be prepared to justify his preference as a bona fide occupational classification.

The EEOC will consider only the actual advertisement of the covered employee, exclusive of the classification headings used by the advertising media.

Employment Agencies

The Equal Employment Opportunity Act specifically states that it shall be an unlawful employment practice for an employment agency to discriminate against any individual because of sex. The EEOC has determined that private employment agencies which deal exclusively with one sex are engaged in an unlawful employment practice, except to the extent that such agencies limit their services to furnishing employees for particular jobs for which sex is a bona fide occupational qualification.

An employment agency that receives a job order containing a prohibited sex specification will share responsibility with the employer placing the job order if the agency fills the order knowing that the sex specification is not based upon a bona fide occupational qualification. However, an employment agency will not be deemed to have committed an unlawful employment practice if the agency does not have reason to believe that the employer's claim of bona fide occupational qualification is without substance and the agency makes and maintains a written record of each order. This written record should include the name of the employer, the description of the job, and the basis for the employer's claim of a bona fide occupational qualification. Furthermore, it is the responsibility of employment agencies to keep informed of opinions and decisions of the commission on sex discrimination.

Pre-Employment Inquiries

A pre-employment inquiry may ask "male (yes or no), female (yes or no)," or "Mr., Mrs., Miss," provided that the inquiry is made in good faith for a nondiscriminatory purpose. A pre-employment inquiry in connection with prospective employment which expresses directly or indirectly any limitation, specification, or discrimination as to sex will not be permitted unless based upon a bona fide occupational qualification.

The Equal Pay Act of 1963

The Equal Employment Opportunity Act requires that its provisions be harmonized with the Equal Pay Act of the Federal Wage-Hour Requirements in order to avoid conflicting interpretations. Therefore, the EEOC states that the standards of "Equal Pay for Equal Work" set forth in the Equal Pay Act for determining what is unfair discrimination in compensation are applicable under the EEO Act. Accordingly, the commission will make applicable to equal pay complaints the relevant interpretations of the Wage-Hour Administrator of the U.S. Department of Labor. Relevant opinions of the Wage-Hour Administrator in interpreting "the equal pay for equal work standard" will also be adopted by the commission. The commission also states that it will consult with the administrator before issuing an opinion on any matter covered by both acts.

Preparation for Equal Employment Demands

Since the beginning of the civil-rights movement, the various civil-rights organizations, their representatives, and other interested parties have contacted many employers for the purpose of achieving their goals of equal rights—equal housing, equal education, and equal employment. Knowing that the future will bring forth additional contacts by these organizations and their members, it is recommended that certain steps be taken by your organization so that you may be better prepared to discuss and negotiate with any civil-rights organization regarding demands and goals as they apply to your particular business.

RECOMMENDATIONS

1. Find out the percentage of the population of each minority group in your city and state.

2. Attempt to find out the percentage of the population of each minority group in your particular industry.

3. Compute the percentage ratio of each minority group on your payroll compared with other employees of your company.

4. Compare the number of minority-group employees with other employees by hourly and salaried classifications. List the types of positions minority-group members hold in your company, their educational backgrounds, and compare these minority-group members with the number of other employees holding a similar position and having a similar educational background.

5. Find out the ratio between minority groups and those of the Caucasian race who are on unemployment and relief rolls in your city and county.

6. Attempt to recall and list in writing how many members of minority groups applied for jobs in your company during the past 180 days. List the jobs they applied for, the results of their pre-employment interview, the results of any aptitude and achievement tests, and any other pertinent data available on minority-group members that was obtained through the screening process.

7. Locate any written communication you may have sent to private and state employment agencies indicating that you are an equal opportunity employer and that you do not discriminate on the basis of race, religion, sex, color, or national origin.

8. Locate copies of any newspaper or magazine "Help Wanted" ads you have used in the past which further document your company as providing equal employment opportunities and fair employment practices.

9. If your company has had to undergo any layoffs or recalls during the past 180 days, describe how members of your minority groups were affected by such personnel action.

10. If possible, locate copies of newspaper and magazine clippings providing statements that civil-rights leaders advocate nonviolence and self-preparation for employment.

11. Carefully study and review your present labor contract or employee handbook to determine if you have any clauses in the agreement or handbook which discriminate against minority groups for any reason involving race, color, sex, religion, or national origin.

Principal Rights Organizations

The following six "minority group" organizations are primarily concerned with the civil-rights movement, and, in particular, with the administration of the Equal Employment Opportunity Act. A brief background of these organizations should be known by the principal corporate officers and key management personnel in your organization because they should know the people they may have to deal with in the future concerning the broad field of equal employment opportunity. Many employers have been and will be contacted in the future by representatives of these organizations. By preparing for any such meeting, it's always desirable to begin your preparation by knowing as much as you can about the background of the particular organization being represented. You can be certain that minority group representatives will be well informed about the employment background of *your* particular organization. They will know their immediate and long-range objectives, and they will be armed with as many facts as possible to reinforce their demands.

NATIONAL ASSOCIATION FOR THE ADVANCEMENT OF COLORED PEOPLE (NAACP)

The National Association for the Advancement of Colored People was established in 1909 by approximately 60 white and Negro citizens. Their goal has been to work toward future equality for the American Negro. At present, the NAACP is the nation's largest civil-rights organization with approximately 400,000 members.

The NAACP has four primary objectives in its day-to-day activities:

1. Enforcement of constitutional rights of Negroes in both state and federal courts.

2. Enactment of state and federal laws to protect civil rights and prohibit racial discrimination.

3. Conduct educational and training programs designed to create an atmosphere of opinions favorable to equal rights and human brotherhood.

4. Conduct direct-action campaigns involving selective buying, sit-ins, picketing, and demonstrations.

NATIONAL URBAN LEAGUE, INC.

The NUL was established in 1910. It is a professional community-service agency whose goal is to secure for Negro citizens equal employment opportunity, education and youth centers, improvement in health and social welfare, and better housing in order that they may share equally in the rights and responsibilities of American citizenship.

The NUL is interracial in both its staff and voluntary leadership. The present staff consists of more than 500 members. The volunteer members of the NUL number in the thousands. The NUL conducts its activities throughout the nation. Offices of the NUL are located in at least 65 key American cities which serve 77 percent of the urban Negro population. The NUL is a nonprofit and nonpartisan organization. To achieve its objectives it uses the methods of fact-finding, negotiation, persuasion, and public education.

NATIONAL COUNCIL OF NEGRO WOMEN

The National Council of Negro Women was established in 1935 by Mary McLeod Bethune with the assistance of approximately 35 prominent women leaders. Their goal was to plan for united, concerted action by various women's organizations.

At present the National Council of Negro Women acts as a clearing house in uniting over 1,000,000 women in 25 national organizations. This unity of women exists in church, business, professional, sorority, city, fraternal, and social groups in communities and college campuses across the nation.

The National Council of Negro Women is an active affiliate of the National Conference of Women of the U.S. and the International Council of Women. It is also affiliated with the Pan-Pacific Southeast Asia Women's Association of the United States. At the United Nations, the National Council of Negro Women has an observer status which is accredited but nongovernmental. The council also has members on the U.S. Commission to UNESCO. The council's national headquarters are in Washington, D.C., and New York City. The activities of this organization are directed toward strengthening the family, with particular emphasis on behavior of American youth, problems in housing, education, employment, citizenship, and international affairs.

CONGRESS OF RACIAL EQUALITY (CORE)

CORE was founded in 1942. It is a national interracial civil-rights organization which utilizes the methods of nonviolent, direct action. It pioneered these methods for the purpose of ending discrimination in employment, housing, education, and public accommodations.

CORE has been responsible for training many of the Southern student sit-in leaders in its nonviolent, direct-action program. CORE is also responsible for the national organization and direction of the Freedom Riders, which resulted in desegregated transportation of vehicles and terminals in many areas of the South. In the northern section of the United States, CORE has been developing direct action programs for the purpose of combating discrimination in housing. The CORE membership now exceeds 61,000 members located in approximately 75 chapters across the nation.

SOUTHERN CHRISTIAN LEADERSHIP CONFERENCE

This civil-rights organization was founded in 1957 by approximately 100 Southern clergymen who were interested in nonviolent-protest action programs. Today, the SCLC consists of over 85 local affiliates. Each affiliate has its own organization name and determines its own policies within the framework of nonviolent action. The SCLC also directs its attention and assistance to local civil-rights activity such as voter registration, direct-action, and leadership-training programs. The goal of the SCLC is to secure the right to vote for every American citizen, regardless of race, as well as working toward the integration of the American Negro into all aspects of American life.

Methods of Approach From Civil-Rights Groups

The history of the civil-rights movement reveals that certain patterns of communications have been used by various organizations and their representatives. Usually, one of the following three approaches, or a combination of them, have been utilized:

1. A personal phone call to the employer.

2. A visit to the employer's place of business.

3. A letter to the employer.

The primary purpose of these "contacts" is to obtain a verbal or, preferably, a signed statement that you will not discriminate in hiring, promotion, payroll procedures, or any other employment matter because of race.

In order to achieve a stated purpose or demand, the representative making the initial contact will usually suggest a meeting to discuss his group's primary objectives.

How to Conduct Yourself During These Initial Approaches

1. Immediately contact all top-management personnel and corporate officers. In addition, keep the personnel director and your company equal employment compliance officer, if such a man is on the company staff, informed of all developments without delay.

2. Set up a meeting of all company officials and supervisors. Present this group with all information you have received to date concerning the proposed meeting. Describe the demands and objectives presented to you thus far in these initial contacts by representatives of minority groups.

This management meeting should be held with the objective of orienting everyone as to the possible future action that can be taken by the minority groups or the representatives. The meeting should also be held for the purpose of everyone reviewing the information you have already prepared concerning the percentages of minority-group members in your community, your company's equal employment opportunity policy in the past, and the other pertinent information you collected earlier as recommended.

At this meeting you should also review with your other management personnel the background of the particular minority-group organization you are to meet with.

During your management meeting, inform your group that the company must show good faith in the future meeting requested. Above all, representatives of the company who will attend are to be polite, patient, tolerant, noncommittal, *but interested in the discussions which will take place.*

3. Come to an agreement as to which company representatives will attend.

4. Explain to your management group possible demands which may be made at the future meeting which have been used elsewhere at other companies.

The following are some of the demands presented to companies by minority groups:

A. Your company should hire a specific number of minority-group applicants and these applicants should be placed in jobs suggested by the "committee" by a date established by the committee.

B. The company should turn over its personnel records to the committee for their study. The committee will want to keep these records for several weeks so that it may analyze them for the purpose of reviewing your past employment policies as they may pertain to minority-group members.

C. Your company should hire *only* members of minority groups until it reaches either a certain percentage of your employment or a specific number of jobs.

D. Your company should upgrade a specific number of minority-group employees into supervisory and managerial positions. If training is needed to accomplish this request, then the company should train them on the job and at the company's expense.

E. The company should cease the seniority and length-of-service rights of present employees in order to begin upgrading employees of minority groups.

F. If an apprenticeship program presently exists in your company, the requirements to enter such a program should be temporarily waived and employees of minority groups should be put directly into the skilled jobs without having experienced apprenticeship training.

G. The company should finance training programs which should be initiated as soon as possible.

H. If layoffs become necessary in the future, the company should revise its layoff policy so that employees who are not minority-group members are to be laid off first.

I. The company should *actively* recruit qualified minority-group applicants to apply for positions in the company.

J. The company should no longer hire minority-group employees to be exclusively used in "behind-the-scenes jobs" such as janitors or maids, but should also hire them for jobs such as receptionists, cashiers, salesmen, and so forth.

K. The company should agree to hire a specific number of minority-group applicants according to a time schedule. This request may also include a stipulation describing specific jobs to be filled by minority-group applicants.

Before meeting with the representatives of the minority group or groups, try to find out whether other employers in your area or industry have also been contacted. Try to find out what their plans will be in regard to the demands of the minority groups. Compare the objectives and demands given to other employers with those presented to you thus far. Also, if you know of other companies who have already participated in such meetings, find out what demands the civil-rights organizations made and the final outcome of these negotiations.

Compose a letter to the representative who initially contacted you and propose that the meeting he requested be held at a neutral location at a definite time and that the chairmanship of future meetings be rotated between the minority group and the company representatives.

You should suggest in your letter that the meeting be held at a neutral spot such as a hotel or motel meeting room. If the representative in his initial contact proposal suggested a meeting at *their* headquarters, it is recommended that you not counter by suggesting a meeting be held at *your* office. It would be undiplomatic to oppose their suggestion. Furthermore, the committee's appearance at your office might cause rumors to circulate throughout the company which could be detrimental to your overall company objectives. Having a meeting at either party's headquarters could possibly fail to achieve the desirable objective atmosphere which both parties should be seeking.

Your letter should also request that you think more could be accomplished at the proposed meeting if no publicity is given to the meeting and that no reporters be present. Based upon past history and experience, there is every likelihood that your suggestions as to the meeting place and the absence of publicity will be acceptable to the minority group if you are firm in making these a condition of your acceptance.

The closing part of your letter should request that the minority-group representative let you know who will be representing the minority group at the meeting. Your letter should also state the names of company representatives who will be at the meeting with you.

Lastly, ask the representative you are corresponding with to confirm agreement with your suggestions by written reply.

What You May Encounter

You may expect the initiative to be taken seriously and offensively by the minority-group committee. Some minority-group committees present their demands in a point-by-point manner and try to insist on each point being answered and disposed of before going on to the next demand.

However, it is certainly reasonable and desirable for you to insist on knowing the whole proposed package before agreeing to any part of it. You should state that your company feels that good-faith discussions involve being informed concerning all aspects of the demand before reaching a decision on any one point. Such a request will normally be granted by the minority-group committee.

You can expect the minority-group demands to be backed up by rather impressive documentation of statistics concerning the working status of minority-group members in your company, in your community, your state, your industry, and the nation. You can also expect these statistics to be supported by written statements from governmental agencies, industrial, business, and educational associations with which you are affiliated, by unions, and by religious organizations.

You should become familiar with the pertinent statistics being given to you by the committee and take careful notes. Above all, take good minutes of this meeting and any future meetings, and carefully note verbal statements by the minority-group committee which indicate any desire to avoid violence and the necessity of minority-group applicants to *prepare* for higher skilled jobs.

We recommend you have your labor agreements, employee handbooks, and personnel policy manuals available at this meeting. You will need these for reference.

There is a possibility that you will be asked by the committee to place your signature on an agreement stipulating that your company will hire a specific number of minority-group applicants and place them on particular jobs. Also, the agreement may stipulate that you will educate and train minority-group applicants to hold specific jobs and that you will promote minority-group employees wherever possible.

Avoid signing any such agreements. Certainly, you should not commit your company to anything before discussing the agreement with management after this meeting. It is recommended that you also check your present union contract, if your workers are organized, to be sure that the contract has no clause which bars any verbal or written agreement with other outside organizations. Furthermore, a union agreement may contain specific clauses which prohibit specific requests made by the minority-group committee concerning hiring, promotions, and seniority rights.

In discussing the suggested agreement presented by the minority-group committee, you should persuasively convince the representatives that signed documents and agreements are not worth anything unless they are based upon good faith. If good faith is present, signed agreements are not necessary. You should further communicate to the minority-group committee that the subject of civil rights and equal employment opportunities involves a complex and changing social situation which does not lend itself to simply drawing up a written agreement with signatures of both interested parties. Certainly, it will be timely for you to state that any amount of time and effort spent in persuading your company to execute the signed contract or agreement could be better used in implementing a constructive program of fair employment practices. You could also say that continuing demands for signatures can cause a negative reaction by possibly encouraging additional resentment and frustration. Above all, avoid committing yourself and the company to any requests before you take it up with your management representatives at the conclusion of the meeting.

Your Objectives and Strategy

OBJECTIVES

1. You should convince everyone that your company will approach the problem in good faith, objectively, with a sincere effort to assist in using the available manpower resources effectively within the framework and philosophy of the Civil Rights Act of 1964 and the Equal Employment Opportunity Act of 1966.

2. You should avoid making any promises or commitments that have not been approved by the company or that cannot be kept.

3. You should avoid surrendering any of management's rights to manage and operate your work force.

4. You should bring home the point very clearly to the committee that your company has a continuing obligation to its present employees. For example, your company should not and cannot discharge present employees for the purpose of creating a job for an applicant of a minority group. Another example of a point that you should bring home very clearly to the committee is that you are morally and perhaps legally required by the present union agreement to honor seniority rights of your present employees which they have earned by their past employment record involving preparation, application of talent, and hard work.

5. You should communicate to the committee that your company is willing in good faith to recognize the employment desires of minority-group applicants in an orderly, businesslike manner but without lowering your reasonable personnel job specifications and hiring standards.

6. You should communicate the fact that your company's personnel policy is to promote from within whenever possible and that you cannot undertake any action inconsistent of this policy.

STRATEGY

1. Listen and listen closely.

2. Question the committee as often as necessary so that you can be absolutely certain you clearly understand the demands and their significance. Be absolutely certain you and your representatives know what the committee expects of you and the company.

3. Don't argue. Avoid arguments and hot discussions about any point or position taken by any member of the minority-group committee. However, you should try to get a verbal observation from every member of the minority-group committee.

4. Take good minutes of all observations and verbal comments made from the minority-group committee as well as your company representatives.

5. Avoid giving the minority-group committee any information concerning your company until after they have presented you their whole package of demands and described their specific goals for your company. Pin down the committee to specifics before you really get into the negotiations.

Remember that this committee knows what it wants to talk about and has definite opinions. Let them speak and listen to everything they have to say even though you may be anxious to speak up.

When you are certain that each member of the minority group committee has expressed himself fully, and that their specific goals are clearly defined as they apply to your company, request a brief adjournment of the meeting so that you and your representatives may discuss their demands in private. Although it is desirable to go forward with the meeting, after your caucus you may desire to schedule another meeting after you and your representatives have had time to go back to the company and discuss the minority-group's demands and present them to management in detail. If the committee agrees to do this, set a definite time, date and place for your next meeting before leaving the conference.

6. If you and your company representatives decide to continue the meeting after your caucus, return to the conference room and make the following points clear to the minority-group committee:

a. Express your concern and sympathy of your company to the needs of the minority-group the committee is representing.

b. Pledge your company's sincere desire to be constructive in your efforts to provide equal employment policies in good faith.

c. State that your company will not dodge the problem presented.

d. Emphasize strongly that the presence of you and your company representatives is an open indication that your company wishes to search for practical, workable solutions to the minority-group's desires.

e. After reviewing your company's record and personnel policies toward equal employment opportunity in the past, if you can present written policies for examples of your past efforts to solve such civil rights areas of concern, you should state what these are in both general and specific terms. For example, the minority-group committee may have stated that one of its objectives is that your company should have the same percentage of minority-group employees that exists in other companies in your community or industry. If your statistics reveal that your company equals or exceeds this percentage, you should certainly state this fact.

7. Suggest to the minority-group committee that you would like to call the meeting to a close so that you may take their objectives and demands to your company officials for good-faith discussions as soon as possible. At this stage, avoid any requests to sign their prepared statement or agreement. In all probability, the minority-group committee will agree to postpone their request.

8. At this stage of your first meeting, be persuasive in your concluding remarks that the problems presented by the minority-group committee do not involve easy solutions or simple answers because the situations they have described are problems that have been created over many years. Suggest that the complexities of their demands warrant further meetings and discussions.

9. If you are working under a union agreement, advise the committee that binding commitments in your union contract may prohibit some solutions or agreements to their demands.

10. Attempt to adjourn this first meeting with a harmonious atmosphere remaining between you, your company representatives, and the minority-group committee.

11. Return to your company, set up a meeting of the corporate officers and company officials and advise them of the outcome of your first meeting. Describe in detail the objectives and demands of the minority-group committee in terms of what they expect your company to do. Allow plenty of time for comments, criticism, and recommendations from other members of management not present at your meeting. Review again your past employment policies and personnel practices as they apply to minority-groups and attempt to prepare yourself for the next meeting with concrete suggestions and recommendations which will tend to prove your good faith in coming to a workable program of equal employment opportunity for everyone regardless of race, color, religion, sex or national origin.

The Second Meeting

At the second meeting you should present to the committee the feeling, attitudes, and desires of your company as reflected by the corporate officers and key management representatives. You should definitely communicate to this minority-group committee that your company will actively meet all requirements of civil-rights legislation.

If your corporate officers have given you the authority to commit the company to personnel policies which exceed the requirements of the Equal Employment Opportunity Act, you can make these known to the committee at this time. If you are unionized, and your present labor agreement prohibits taking any action toward the demands of the minority group because of specific contract language, it is suggested that your union business agent be present at this meeting to discuss such contract bars and be prepared to answer any questions in good faith that may be raised by members of the minority group committee.

At this stage of your second meeting, you must remain patient and flexible. The longer you can talk with the committee, the better chance you will have to come up with constructive solutions.

What to Do If Negotiations Fail

There is always a possibility that your counterproposals will not meet the ultimate demands and requests of the minority-group committee. However, you should continue to be persuasive enough in your meetings to show your fairness, consideration, objectivity, and good faith. The committee should be sold on the fact that your company is trying its best to meet these challenges of the civil-rights movement and to work out the problems of employment in a harmonious, good-faith manner. Certainly, it is hoped that your patience, diplomacy, tolerance, and good-faith negotiations will prevent any threats of picketing, demonstrations, or violence. Nevertheless, it is the responsibility of your company's management to plan for every possibility and to take reasonable precautions to avoid threats to company employees and undercutting of your company's reputation.

If your company's counterproposals are not satisfactory to the committee, and you are threatened by picketing, sit-ins, stand-ins, or demonstrations, it is recommended you take the following steps:

1. Contact your state fair employment practice committee if you have one and inform them of the developments to date.

2. Contact the Equal Employment Opportunity Commission in Washington. If an investigator is requested, bring him up to date on all developments which took place in all previous meetings with the minority-group committee.

3. Contact your local law-enforcement agency and inform them of your present situation. Keep them informed.

4. Contact the heads of local government offices in your community and inform them of your present situation.

5. Keep your corporate officers and officials, including all ranks of supervision, completely informed of every development.

6. Inform all employees, including minority-group employees, of the present status of your situation by letters to the homes. Request that your employees avoid violence. Suggest that the employees not cross picket lines if it appears that this may result in harm to them. Suggest that employees not congregate where pickets or demonstrators are in action and to avoid arguments with pickets or demonstrators.

Instruct your plant guards, if any, not to attempt to move or arrest pickets or demonstrators. This is the responsibility of your local law-enforcement officers.

7. Contact your company's legal counsel and request that he undertake any legal action which may be available to avoid violence or picketing which will be harmful to your employees, the company's reputation, or destructive to your property.

8. Be certain that your local news media (newspapers, radio and TV) have all the facts concerning your good faith effort to meet the demands of the minority group which is behind the present picketing, sit-ins, stand-ins, or demonstrations.

When Federal Men Come

Here are recommended guidelines to follow when the EEOC investigator arrives to investigate a charge:

1. Provide the investigator with a suitable and comfortable place to work. You can expect many borderline questions to arise during his investigation. Therefore, there is no point in creating any animosity or antagonistic feelings because of discourtesies. Certainly, it is to your advantage to have all your personnel records in such an orderly manner that it will not be necessary for the investigator to become engaged in a hunting expedition.

2. Select a competent office employee to assist him. The person you select should reflect a pleasant attitude, patience, and a willingness to help. This person should do the leg work for the investigator in obtaining the records and other personnel data he may request.

3. Don't be overfriendly. Most investigators are alerted to expressions of honest courtesy as well as to false and meaningless expressions of generosity. Therefore, do not offer to buy his meal, or offer him your cigars. You should expect the investigator to be an honest and a decent man, just as you would want him to feel that you are above cheap chicanery.

4. Don't try to tell your employees what to say to the investigator. It won't work. In the first place, it isn't fair to put your employees in this type of embarrassing position. If your employees are not in the habit of making false or misleading statements, they certainly wouldn't want to do so when questioned by an EEOC investigator. Remember also, that if perjury or falsification of information is detected by the investigator, it can be really embarrassing for you in the long run.

5. Don't hold back confidential or personal information or records. If you are concerned about your present employment practices and personnel procedures, check in advance with your consultant or attorney. Above all, don't wait until the EEOC investigator gets into your office to begin any changes.

6. Before the EEOC investigator finishes his inspection, and is ready to leave your premises, find out how you stand if at all possible. It is recommended that you ask the investigator very frankly upon what points he may feel you might be on the borderline of a violation. Request his recommendations on what you should do to put your house in order. Obtain all the information you can. Find out where your personnel policy procedures and practices have failed to meet the requirements of the Equal Employment Opportunity Commission.

7. Don't agree to commit yourself to anything. You should not commit yourself to taking any personnel action on any present employees or job applicants involving race, color, religion, sex, or national origin. However, you should write down all requests and recommendations made by the EEOC investigator before he leaves your premises. Thank him for his assistance and his recommendations. Above all, tell the investigator that you will give his recommendations and suggestions careful consideration and that you pledge future compliance in all aspects of the requirements.

8. Contact your consultant and attorney as soon as possible. Tell them of the investigator's findings and recommendations. You will then be given practical steps on what to do next.

Company and Personnel Records

It is recommended that the following company and personnel records be made available for review by an EEOC investigator:

1. Organizational chart of your company.

2. All company policy statements from top management to supervision and employees covering equal employment opportunity at your company.

3. Copies of letters or notices to recruitment sources and employment agencies concerning your policy on equal employment opportunity.

4. Copy of your personnel policy manual if it contains a policy statement on equal employment opportunity.

5. Copy of an employee handbook which you have distributed which contains a statement of your company's position on equal employment opportunity.

6. Copy of your collective bargaining agreement if workers are unionized.

7. Sample copies of any newspaper or magazine advertisements for employment (want ads).

8. Copies of all reports filed with the EEOC or with the President's Commission on Equal Employment Opportunity (annual compliance reports).

9. Copy of your company's present apprenticeship program, if such a program exists.

10. If available, copy of your company's recruiting program.

11. If available, sample copies of all job specifications and job descriptions used for hiring and promotions.

12. Sample copies of all psychological tests used for hiring or for promotion purposes.

13. Copy of pay scales or pay rate ranges.

14. Copy of your seniority list by name, seniority date, and job classification.

15. A list of all minority-group employees presently employed. Compile this list by name, job classification, rate of pay, and date of hire.

16. List of new employees hired during the past six months by name, job, rate of pay, and date of hire. Also identify each minority-group employee who was hired during this six-month period.

17. Copies of all applications received by the personnel office for the past 12 months.

18. Copies of all forms used in screening all job applicants during the past 12 months. For example, you should have available in your personnel files written results of your telephone reference check, pre-employment interview, results of reference checks by letter, psychological test results, credit bureau reports, and physical examinations, if any.

19. Have available in your personnel files documentation on reasons for employee raises, promotions, transfers, disciplinary action, and terminations.

In order for an employer to fully understand what types of discrimination are being filed with the Equal Employment Opportunities Commission, we list below a number of complaints filed with the EEOC alleging various types of discrimination.

THE NEW YORK TIMES/PRENTICE-HALL INTERNATIONAL CASE

The NAACP field a charge against an employer in connection with newspaper advertising. The complaint was lodged against the New York *Times* and Prentice-Hall International, Inc. It was filed under Title VII forbidding publication of "any notice indicating any preference, limitation, specification, or discrimination based on race." The NAACP alleges that the New York *Times* "carried a Prentice-Hall advertisement for which a Negro was not accepted." The position was that of a sales representative in South Africa. In rejecting the Negro applicant on whose behalf the complaint was filed, Prentice-Hall explained that the policies of the South African Government precluded the employment of a Negro in the position. In effect, the NAACP is urging the EEOC to rule that newspapers must find out whether their help-wanted advertisers intend to discriminate in employment even if the advertisements themselves state no discriminatory exclusions.

The NAACP has been a leader among minority-group organizations in filing complaints on behalf of its members and members of minority groups. For example, seven employees of the Republic Steel Corporation, Canton, Ohio, allege that their company established a pattern of discrimination against Negroes.

Eight employees of the P. Lorillard Company alleged that Negro employees were limited to menial jobs and filed charges against the company and Local 317 of the Tobacco Workers International Union, Greensboro, North Carolina.

Complaints have been filed against federally aided state employment services in South Carolina, Arkansas, North Carolina, Georgia, Alabama, Mississippi, and Louisiana, alleging job discrimination because of race and color. In addition, a complaint was lodged against a vocational training school operating a training program under the Manpower Development and Training Act. Two students at the unnamed school charged discriminatory operation of the vocational program.

A Negro employee filed a charge through the NAACP against the Hayes International Corporation, Birmingham, Alabama. The Negro employee was allegedly threatened with discharge because of his voter-registration activities.

CROWN-ZELLERBACH'S "PROMOTION LADDER"

An EEOC announcement was recently made that it has worked out integrated lines of progression for certain departments in the Crown-Zellerbach plant at Bogalusa, Louisiana. The past practice of the company has been that one group of jobs led up to a foreman designed for white employees and another group led up to a wood unloader which was reserved for Negroes. The commission's plan, agreed to by the company and union, merged the two groups into a single promotion ladder without regard to race or color.

The EEOC indicated that this settlement was reached through "technical assistance" by the EEOC. The parties also agreed to change promotion lines in other departments on the basis of principles incorporated into the agreement. The commission indicated that it will attempt similar technical assistance in other plants that have a history of segregated lines of progression.

Questions and Answers About the Act

Some of the most common questions and answers about the Equal Employment Opportunity Act can be a helpful guide to management. Included in this section are questions and answers about the most troublesome problems that concerned participants in a Dartnell seminar for executives on this legislation.

Question: Is a single employer who operates more than one establishment considered a single employer for purposes of coverage?

Answer: A single employer who operates more than one store or establishment is a covered employer and the relevant figure in determining coverage is the total number of employees in the multistore chain. Both fulltime and parttime employees are included, with the exception of seasonal employees who might not be employed for more than 20 calendar weeks in the current or preceding year.

Question: What is the definition of a single employer for purposes of determining number of employees?

Answer: The definition of a single employer for purposes of determining the number of employees presents problems in situations such as vertically integrated enterprises, chains of retail outlets, concessions or other similar establishments, and independent contractors, and must be decided on a case by case basis. Criteria to be considered are: Interrelations of operations, common management, centralized control of labor relations, common ownership and power of control over employees.

Question: Is an employer with a home office in Canada and branches in the United States subject to the act?

Answer: A company with its home office in Canada and branches in the United States and Canada is covered with respect to its operations in the United States if there are eight or more employees in the United States after July 2, 1967.

Question: Is a private club such as a country club covered?

Answer: The Equal Employment Opportunity Act does not apply to membership applications of private men's clubs and country clubs.

Question: Is an employer required to fill vacancies without giving present employees preference to bid on such jobs?

Answer: Hiring new employees to fill vacancies without giving present employees an opportunity to bid on such jobs is not, without more, a prohibition.

Question: Is age discrimination prohibited?

Answer: The commission has no authority over discriminatory employment practices based on age. It is highly probable that such discrimination will be added to the list of prohibitions whenever the Civil Rights Act is amended in succeeding Congresses.

Question: Is a company permitted to refuse to hire an employee because of weight limitations?

Answer: A company refusal to hire employees who weigh more than a stated number of pounds is not a prohibition.

Question: May a company discriminate for or against applicants based on educational qualifications?

Answer: Discrimination based on educational qualifications is not prohibited.

Question: Is it permissible for an employer to maintain separate male-female seniority lists?

Answer: No. Segregation by race, sex, or national origin in collective bargaining units or lines of promotion in seniority lists is not permissible under the EEOC rules.

Question: What is meant by "segregated facilities"?

Answer: Any physical segregation of employees by race, whether with respect to working area, toilet or locker facilities, recreational activities, etc., is not permitted. No general answer can be given with regard to permitting employees "freedom of choice" to choose lockers when this may result in racial segregation. Experience has shown in somewhat analogous situations that where a pattern of compulsory segregation is replaced by "freedom of choice" the freedom to make a choice which would disturb that pattern is often effectively denied in subtle ways. An employer who has participated in maintaining segregated facilities prior to July 2, 1965, therefore, should take positive steps to prevent the pattern of segregation from perpetuating itself.

Question: Is it permissible to have a provision in a collective bargaining agreement obligating the employer not to "employ female help in specific departments coming under the jurisdiction of the union as long as adequate manpower is available"?

Answer: A provision in a collective bargaining contract obligating the employer not to employ female help in those departments coming under the present jurisdiction of a union as long as adequate manpower is available is not permissible unless sex is a bonafide occupational qualification for the jobs involved.

Question: Does the Equal Employment Opportunity Act of 1966 supersede any labor-management agreement in conflict with the act?

Answer: The federal EEO requirements supersede any labor-management agreement in conflict with the act.

Question: May an employer adopt an employment policy of not hiring relatives of company employees?

Answer: Company policy prohibiting the hiring of relatives of company employees, including, or limited to, spouses, is not discrimination based on sex and is therefore not prohibited.

Question: May an employer discharge a female employee because she marries?

Answer: An employer's rule which forbids or restricts the employment of married women and which is not applicable to married men is a prohibited discrimination based on sex. It is irrelevant that the rule is not directed against all females, but only married ones, for so long as sex is a factor in the application of the rule, it is prohibited discrimination.

Question: Is it permissible for an employer to adopt a policy of not employing females with preschool-aged children unless the female is divorced?

Answer: A policy of not employing females with preschool-aged children unless the female is divorced or putting her husband through college constitutes an unlawful employment practice.

Question: May an employer pay part of the cost of "family plan" medical coverage for male employees while requiring female employees to pay the entire cost of such coverage?

Answer: A company practice of paying part of the cost of "family plan" medical coverage for male employees while requiring female employees to pay the entire cost of such coverage is prohibited.

Question: May a company refuse to grant time off from work for an employee to attend religious services?

Answer: A company may refuse an employee the right to be absent from work to attend religious services, provided other employees are not allowed equivalent time for such purposes.

Question: How long must I keep personnel and employment records?

Answer: The commission requires all relevant records be kept for six months following the date a personnel action was taken such as a failure or refusal to hire.

Question: Are employers required to keep minority employees when their services are unsatisfactory or no longer needed?

Answer: No. The employer has complete freedom to hire and to fire so long as the decision is not based on race, religion, sex, or national origin.

Question: Do fair employment practices subject employers to continuous time-consuming investigations?

Answer: No. The EEOC can only make an investigation when a complaint has been filed. Our experience has shown that the commission members and employees are intelligent in handling expeditiously civil-rights complaints. Only those employers who refuse to cooperate with the commission find that such investigations are time consuming.

Question: How can an employer best defend his employment practices?

Answer: In short, an employer's best assurance that he will not be unfairly accused of discrimination is to establish sound, objective job analysis, and to keep all records pertaining to employment or separation, including application forms of rejected applicants.

Question: Can members of minority groups be assigned by an employer to one department only?

Answer: Generally, no. Segregation of workers or facilities because of race, religion, color, sex, or national origin is discrimination in conditions or privileges of employment.

Question: Is an employer permitted or required to maintain a certain percentage of minority-group workers?

Answer: Emphatically no. Every complaint must be judged on its own merits. The presence or absence of other minority group members does not affect the merit of a complaint. Every employer has complete freedom of decision in job qualifications, job specifications, and the number of employees he wishes to employ. Hiring on the basis of racial quotas in order to rectify existing imbalances is specifically prohibited.

Question: May job qualifications include personality and appearance factors?

Answer: Yes, depending upon the job. Appearance and personality factors cannot include color or racial characteristics, religious affiliation or national origin.

Question: What if two applicants for employment possess equal qualifications?

Answer: The choice of the applicant is entirely at the discretion of the employer, but he must not make his decision on the basis of race, color, religion, sex, or national origin.

Question: If two applicants apply for one opening, one a Negro and one a white, and both have the minimum qualifications for the job but the one is hired because the employer feels that happier employee relations will prevail, will such a case constitute an unlawful employment practice?

Answer: Yes, if the reason that the employer believes that happier employee relations will prevail is based on the color of one of the applicants. The employer would be committing an unfair employment practice by denying employment to the white or the Negro simply because he believes that employee relations will be benefited by employing that applicant.

Question: Who may file a charge of unfair employment practices?

Answer: The aggrieved individual or a member of the Equal Employment Opportunity Commission.

Question: May the EEOC make public the filing of a charge or the results of its investigation or conciliatory efforts?

Answer: No.

Question: What happens if the commission's efforts to gain voluntary compliance are not successful?

Answer: If the Commission's efforts at mediation to gain voluntary compliance are not successful within 30 days after the filing of the charge—which time may be extended to 60 days by the commission, a complaint and notice of hearing will be issued.

Question: Do we have to refer to previous application forms when a job opening occurs or merely hire a current walk-in applicant?

Answer: We feel that it is always best to refer to previous application forms for a specific job wherein other applicants have expressed a desire in that job. If an employer does not do this, he is in fact not providing other applicants with "equal opportunities" for the job. It is entirely possible that an employer may overlook a qualified minority-group candidate if he simply hires a walk-in applicant without checking his applicant file.

Question: If a company provides a scholarship program which is open only to sons of employees (employees are male and female) would this be discriminatory?

Answer: No. So long as an employer's scholarship program is open to male dependents of men and women employees, this is not a sex discrimination prohibited by the Act.

Question: If application forms must be kept for six months, is this an indication that an applicant has a six-month period to file a complaint against an employer?

Answer: No. In a state without an FEP law, an aggrieved party must file his complaint within 90 days after the date of the alleged discriminatory act.

EQUAL EMPLOYMENT OPPORTUNITY REQUIREMENTS

Question: Our company has an executive stock option plan. Levels below the executives are not permitted to participate in this stock option plan. Is this discriminatory?

Answer: Even though your stock option plan is not open to nonexecutives, the plan is not a prohibited discrimination.

Question: Must application forms be held six months if there is a written notice on all applications which states, "Void after 60 days"?

Answer: An employer subject to the EEO requirements must keep all application forms at least six months regardless of any such language which may appear on the application form.

Question: We have two company-sponsored golf tournaments and two company-sponsored bowling leagues. One is for men and the other is for women. The company gives some financial assistance to these activities. Is there any violation here?

Answer: No, unless either of these company sponsored activities are not open to minority-group men and women. Otherwise, an employer is permitted to have separate recreational activities for male and female employees provided the activities are equal and the *company sponsorship or financial contribution is equal.*

Question: We have a pension plan which requires men to wait two years to become participants, but it requires women to wait five years. Is this permitted?

Answer: In our view, such eligibility requirements based on sex are discriminatory.

Question: Could our company hire applicants referred only through one private employment agency, using no other source?

Answer: Generally, yes. Such an employer would have to be very careful that the private employment agency referred all candidates without regard to race, color, religion, sex, or national origin.

Question: Can a position that is clerical in nature be called "Office Girl" or should its title be changed to "Clerical Worker"? Another example would be "Maintenance Man," "Stock Boy," etc. In other words, must the job title be free of any indication of a sex preference?

Answer: Unless sex is a bona fide occupational qualification for the specific job in question, we recommend a sex designation be deleted from any jobs. In the above examples, the employer might use, "Office Clerk," "Maintenance Mechanic," "Stock Clerk."

Question: Is any change necessary on personnel records of older employees where they have been with the company 10 or 15 or even 20 years? On these we have color, race, church affiliation, clubs and lodges—are we in trouble?

Answer: An employer may place racial or ethnic information on post-employment records *provided* such designations do not appear on permanent personnel records which are used regularly in the process of making decisions regarding transfer, promotion, termination, etc. We feel it is best to remove such designations from old permanent employment records.

Question: In our warehouse the clerical staff is primarily female and works a consistent 35-hour week. The production staff is primarily male and consistently works a 40-hour week. Is this discrimination based on sex?

Answer: No.

Question: A corporation has a subsidiary that is independently operated. The parent corporation is nonunion, the subsidiary is unionized. Must both companies have the same benefits?

Answer: Differences in rates of pay, fringe benefits, and other terms and privileges of employment may be made between plants so long as they are not based on race, religion, color, sex, or national origin.

Question: I understand that the federal act does not allow a company to make a special effort to hire or select minorities in order to correct a racial imbalance in employment. Please explain on what basis the government does require special efforts to correct racial imbalances in employment.

Answer: Employers subject to the Equal Employment Opportunity Act are not required to apply quotas in their hiring practices so as to bring in more members of minority groups. On the other hand, government contractors or subcontractors who are subject to Executive Order 11246 are required to take "affirmative action" which means that in these cases such employers must actively seek and recruit qualified minority-group applicants.

Question: Can majority groups (whites) file discrimination charges under the act?

Answer: Yes. Whites as well as nonwhites are protected against discrimination.

Question: We use professionally prepared psychological tests as a screening device. We have established local norms. However, from time to time, these norms have been lowered due to the need for employees in a tight labor market. We therefore vary our test norms depending upon the need at a specific time. Can this practice be construed as discriminatory?

Answer: An employer is permitted to rely upon the results of a professionally developed psychological or ability test provided the results of such testing do not discriminate because of any of the five prohibited factors. Ideally, an employer should not change norms because of the inconsistencies which might result and the difficulties which might be encountered in properly documenting the reasons why norms were changed. On the other hand, of necessity an employer must change norms from time to time in order to assure himself of an adequate work force. At such times, we therefore suggest that deviations from standards be carefully documented as to the specific reasons why and the results of such deviations. For example, if the lowering of norms causes an employer to hire more minority-group members, let your records indicate such and similarly, above all, do not continuously change norms from one day to the next but set periods of deviation for a week, two weeks, etc., before returning to standard norms.

Question: If you accept an application for employment, does the applicant have any recourse for not being considered for comparable openings during the 90-day period following the date of application?

Answer: Ideally, the employer should consider the applicant only for the specific job which is being applied for. If an applicant expressly applies for a specific job and cannot meet those job requirements, then the employer would have a bona fide reason for refusal to hire. On the other hand, if an applicant simply states on the application form that he wants "any job available" then it might be difficult to defend an employer's position if he does not consider the applicant for any job which he might qualify for.

EQUAL EMPLOYMENT OPPORTUNITY REQUIREMENTS

Question: If you have a union contract and this contract has a nondiscrimination clause and a grievance procedure clause, must the employee use the grievance procedure before filing a charge with the Equal Employment Opportunity Commission?

Answer: The EEOC, we think, would prefer the individual to first use the grievance procedure in adjusting a complaint under the nondiscrimination clause in the contract. If these efforts prove fruitless, then the aggrieved union member should file a charge with the EEOC.

Question: The employee-requisition form which we use to indicate job openings to our personnel department has space to indicate male or female. Is this permitted?

Answer: Generally, no. Unless the job in question is such that sex is a bona fide occupational qualification, sex designation should be left off of the requisition form.

Question: Our union contract specifies that no married women may be hired and if a female employee becomes married she must then terminate her employment. If the union refuses to eliminate this from the contract, is the company in violation, or is the union in violation?

Answer: First of all, the company should make a good-faith effort to eliminate this language from the contract because it is, per se, discrimination based on sex. If the union absolutely refuses to remove such language from the contract, and the employer has made a good-faith effort to correct the situation, then the union would be in violation.

Chapter 3

SELECTING OFFICE WORKERS

E VERY employee on a payroll represents thousands of investment dollars. Executives, for example, according to a member of the faculty of the University of Michigan, are worth from $250,000 to $500,000 to a business like General Motors. This is equally true whether the employee has been selected, trained, and placed in accordance with modern management techniques, or tossed into a job and left to sink or swim.

In either case, the company's investment is an extremely important one. In the first case, however, the employer has a good chance to realize on his investment; in the second—the hit-or-miss method—the employer too often loses his investment in a short time by reason of high turnover.

One of the most important factors in labor turnover has been, experience shows, the proper screening and placement of workers. Such techniques carefully set up *and as carefully administered* give the company better workers. And, because they enjoy their work more when properly placed, they are better satisfied.

Several years ago a research organization conducted a survey for a company to find out what employees really thought about their jobs and what they wanted to be contented. Much to management's astonishment, it learned that the first desire of employees was not higher pay, new washrooms, or shorter hours, but a sense of being important to the business. These particular needs can best be met by:

1. Getting the right employee for the right job.
2. Following through on the placement to see that it is correct.
3. Evaluating jobs so that salaries are *equitably* set up.
4. Providing for adequate communication between worker and management, so that the employee becomes an integral part of the whole.
5. Giving supervisory groups adequate training to eliminate areas of friction between worker and "boss."
6. Giving employees a sense of participation in the company's progress.

Reducing Turnover Through Careful Selection

Labor cost is constantly taking a bigger bite out of the business dollar. The dollar cost of poor selection and placement is, in fact, becoming startling. The man who started out at $2,400 to $3,600 a few years back is now starting at $6,000 to $8,000.

It is not unusual to find the following situation prevailing in many sound companies. Management in this case found that its turnover cost, all factors included, was $400 per man. This applies to semiskilled, not management personnel. The company was hiring at the rate of 10 people per week, more than 40 a month. Out of every three people employed, only two reached minimum standards of production—one man out of every three was a "dud." By improving the selection process in this particular company, a saving of $3,000 every month would result.

What are the advantages of good selection? The first is, of course, decreased turnover, for improved selection will, it has been proved many times, decrease turnover. No company should be without some turnover; otherwise the "deadwood" would accumulate to the detriment of the company. Some management engineers believe that turnover should not go below 25 percent. That is, of course, an arbitrary figure, and much would depend upon the industry, management policies, future growth possibilities, age of the company, as well as other factors.

While there is no selection system which will not make mistakes, better selection and placement means higher standards of quality from employees from the start of their employment. Also, by better selection and placement, management can do a better job of planning for future needs and a company will not be in the quandary of being "caught short" and having to take anybody at all just because a job must be done.

In addition, by picking people of high potential in the beginning, management can train and develop them to the point where a vacancy in a high-level position is not likely to become an expensive catastrophe. Too frequently, new men are brought in by management looking at the possibilities for an open job. Men such as these are difficult to get rid of. On the other hand, good recruiting and selection techniques can bring in personnel of high promise and such individuals can move up rapidly to fill vacancies.

One management engineer explains the technique of hiring and selection as follows. First, determine the philosophy of the business. Will it expand or contract? An expanding business requires different personnel in low-level jobs than if the *status quo* is to be maintained or if the business is to be contracted. The expanding business must select people who can move up rapidly. On the other hand, the business that is cutting down will require personnel which will be content to stay on a lower-level job for, perhaps, years.

Second, employment interviewing must be so set up that it will adequately check the information that cannot be had from any other source. Third, there should be a good psychological testing program, handled by well-trained personnel. These three factors will enable management to secure the right type of person for the right type of job insofar as is humanly possible. It does not, however, end there. All selection programs should be subjected to continual checks. Conditions change, people change, labor supply changes, the business alters—all these things should be considered so that as changes occur over the years, the program, too, can be changed. A continuous follow up is an essential of any program, no matter how well it has been set up.

A recently revised Dartnell evaluation summary which follows lists the important factors that should be considered in appraising job applicants or candidates for promotion. The trick here is to plot the particular requirements for the job *before* rating the applicant. For example, a show-off type with no regard for consequences would be a good candidate for a job of diving off a 100-foot platform into a pail of water; a man with destructive tendencies should work out very well on a wrecking crew.

It is important not to add or average the listed factors in making a rating. Match the qualifications of the applicant against the special requirements of the job.

Good Recruiting Simplifies Selection

Some turnover is necessary to prevent a business from going stale and to keep the line of promotion moving. Building your company's reputation as a good place to work will attract employees of high caliber. Spadework in neighboring schools and colleges— sending company men to address commercial classes, distributing company literature, or conducting plant tours for students—will pave the way.

Schools and colleges; YMCA's; manufacturers of typewriters, dictating machines, and other office appliances; trade organizations and businesswomen's clubs maintain employment bureaus which are dependable sources of help. Reliable private employment agencies which specialize in supplying office personnel are also helpful.

SELECTION AND EVALUATION SUMMARY

Applicant's Name_____ Date_____ 19____

Position Applied for _____ Job Class_____

		Rating on Each Factor	Out-standing	Good	Mar-ginal	Poor
"CAN DO" FACTORS	Appearance, manner.........					
	Availability for this work................................. .					
	Education, as required by this job........................ ...					
	Intelligence, ability to learn, solve problems............ ...					
	Experience in this field..					
	Knowledge of the product......					
	Physical condition, health, energy........................					

"WILL DO" FACTORS

CHARACTER TRAITS (Basic Habits)

STABILITY; maintaining same jobs and interests..........				
INDUSTRY; willingness to work.				
PERSEVERANCE; finishing what he starts........				
ABILITY to get along with people........................				
LOYALTY; identifying with employer......................				
SELF-RELIANCE; standing on own feet, making own decisions				
LEADERSHIP....................................				

MOTIVATION

BASIC ENERGY LEVEL (Vigor, Initiative, Drive)............				
NEED FOR INCOME......................................				
NEED FOR SECURITY..				
NEED FOR STATUS...................................				
NEED FOR POWER.......................................				
NEED TO INVESTIGATE...............................				
NEED TO EXCEL.......................................				
NEED FOR PERFECTION...............................				
NEED TO SERVE......				

DEGREE OF EMOTIONAL MATURITY

Freedom from dependence.............................				
Regard for consequences................................				
Capacity for self-discipline.............................				
Freedom from selfishness...............................				
Freedom from show-off tendencies........................				
Freedom from pleasure-mindedness.......................				
Freedom from destructive tendencies.....................				
Freedom from wishful thinking............................				

Important: Do not add or average these factors in making the Over-all Rating. Match the qualifications of the applicant against the requirements of the *particular position* for which he is being considered.

Strong Points for This Position_____

Weak Points for This Position_____

Over-all Rating: [1] [2] [3] [4]   Recommendation to Employ: [ ] Yes [ ] No   Rating by_____

Form No. EB-404R

This form makes it easy to consider important factors in appraising job applicants

Classified ads pull well for many companies, especially in large cities like New York. A carefully worded ad that gives the basic requirements will screen unsuitable job seekers at the outset. Tricky ads may gain attention, but they do not attract good prospects. A Chicago oil company ran a misspelled and poorly typed message to dramatize how badly stenographers were needed, for three days. The ad pulled five replies—and only one was from a likely candidate.

When Dartnell recently surveyed the situation, it found the shortage of stenographers and good secretaries to be more acute than in any other line of work. Incompetent help is fairly easy to find; but capable, efficient personnel is short in most areas. James W. Horan, of the Sandusky Foundry and Machine Company, Sandusky, Ohio, suggested that, "Too many young people are going to college who would be better off to obtain office jobs locally." E. G. Sherman, of General Mills, analyzed the situation this way: "There are now more girls attending college and marrying at a younger age. More demand for office workers is prevalent because of business expansion in the past decade."

Most comments about the "tight" market pertain to female employees. An advertising executive in the East put it this way, "Competition is very keen, resulting in a high rate of turnover. Unemployment among competent office workers is rare." The personnel manager of a utility complains, "Some applicants have delusions of grandeur and some are only going through the motions of job seeking." Other comments from executives faced with the problems of finding and keeping good office employees follow a similar vein.

It is apparent from Dartnell's probing of the subject of getting clerical and office employees that policies established for continuous recruiting are more effective than "one shot" recruiting efforts to get a particular employee. As part of the continuous plan many companies are using the talents of former employees, or housebound women who cannot come to the office. They can do home typing and take pressure off present employees engaged in routine work, such as addressing and other simple typing jobs.

Employee Referrals Prove Choice Applicants

Ninety percent of the employees of the Tokheim Corporation in Fort Wayne, Indiana, came there through friends. The choicest job applicants, claims Tokheim, are referrals. Experts agree that this is true, but also concede that most companies can get few applicants by this method. How did Tokheim manage this achievement? Its method is so good that 95 percent of the supervisory personnel is "promoted from within."

In a spot check, when 25 Tokheim employees were asked how they happened to come to work there, 24 immediately told stories of being recommended by relatives or friends. And even the twenty-fifth, who said he got the job "on his own," admitted that his first contact with the company occurred when he visited the plant with a friend.

In the past 20 years there have been only a few cases at Tokheim of a referred job applicant being rejected as undesirable, and even fewer instances where an employee hired in this way later proved undesirable. And in most of the cases where a referred employee proved unsatisfactory and was released, the sponsoring employee later offered an apology and expressed amazement that he could have been deceived by the individual. No doubt part of this sense of responsibility is due to the liberal profit-sharing plan which creates in Tokheim employees a profound concern about the efficient operation of the plant.

Although the selection and indoctrination program at Tokheim developed out of years of experience and observation, the company keeps fully abreast of all new developments in recruiting and hiring and, unlike some firms, is glad to have would-be employees fill out application forms at any time. This is a policy which, Tokheim management says, has produced many valuable employees through the years.

Employment of Relatives

Views of large and small companies show the problem of employing relatives is not the property of companies of any given size. If the company is large enough and has divisions or plants that are physically separated, problems seem to be lessened. The small compact concern, with few employees, is more worried about the personalities of its employees and their ability to integrate within.

Preselection procedures should apply to all, regardless of whether they are relatives of present employees or not, is the predominant opinion among employers today. If the applicant is recommended by an employee and he fails to meet hiring standards, he should not be hired. It is the prevailing opinion that this basic principle should be thoroughly explained to workers who recommend relatives, thus eliminating any chance of hard feelings or resentments when their relative is not hired.

Blood is thicker than water, and most companies find the dissatisfaction of one employee is usually shared by his relatives. Those who make it a practice to hire related persons indicate the need to keep personalities out of work problems. It can usually be done if relatives are assigned to unrelated sections, or if they are the kind who can get along without friction with others. Again, preselection standards do much to determine this characteristic.

While few companies indicate that employment of related persons is a major problem within the organization, it has been one of those little irritating things that sometimes affects other areas of personnel administration. It is quite clear that the concern which has a set policy, whether it is for or against employment of relatives, has better control of the situation than one who merely goes along with no policy at all.

Recently, Dartnell asked a number of companies how they felt about hiring relatives. These are some of the replies. A rubber manufacturing firm with 325 employees commented:

"Being in a rural area we have many relatives working—some do a good job— others work in groups and cause trouble with other groups—we would operate better, since we have a union, with no relatives in the plant."

From a large insurance company:

"Whenever relatives are employed in same office, we recommend they be placed in jobs where one does not supervise the other. No relatives of the general manager or personnel director may be employed in the same section where they are employed."

Metropolitan Utilities District of Omaha, Nebraska, reported through its assistant industrial relations director:

"Although both sides have considerable merit, we feel our policy avoids discrimination, either for or against another relative. Morale of nonrelated employees is higher. We have fewer interdepartmental labor problems."

(Metropolitan Utilities does not employ husbands and wives, but will allow them to remain, if married while working for the company, provided they work in different departments. It employs no immediate relatives, including in-laws.)

Douglas Catling, personnel director of The Cromwell Paper Company, states the policy with his firm is to employ either husband or wife, but not both. Other relatives are employable. If problems occur between relatives, both resign.

The vice-president of a small chemical company in the Midwest says:

"I have never been in favor of relatives working for the same company. Personnel problems, promotions, demotions are always aggravated by having to consider what a relative will do because of company action, either good or bad."

Lauren R. Cooper, director of methods research, The Alexander Film Company of Colorado Springs, Colorado, says his company allows employment of relatives, but not in the same department:

"This makes for good, loyal, family-type employees—though we insist relatives meet the same standards as strangers. In contrast, this also offers a problem when one or other of the relatives must be laid off or discharged, or hours changed, etc."

Abbott Laboratories' director of employee relations reports that its policy does not allow relatives to work in the same department. A grandfather clause in the policy provided assurance that departmental situations existing at the time the policy was made effective would not be disturbed. The policy applies to employees hired or transferred after the effective date of the policy.

The industrial relations manager of a Pennsylvania sheet-metal firm says:

"We feel that in most cases, if a good employee on the payroll suggests a relative when we are looking for help we usually will hire on his or her recommendation. This has worked out very well. This, naturally, assumes the applicant meets the company hiring standards."

A small manufacturing firm in Los Angeles with 60 employees commented through its vice-president:

"If it can be avoided, relatives should not be hired, as it breeds politics and 'rumor grapevines,' particularly if relatives are working in different departments of a smaller business."

The personnel director of a building materials firm in the East gave the following report:

"A real reason we discontinued employing relatives was that when it became necessary to discharge an employee who was related to another employee, there was bitter feeling on the part of the one who remained. In fact, because of this resentment which was built up on a few such occasions, we have kept a few employees who would otherwise have been automatically discharged.

"Then there is the matter of resentment when one of the relatives is advanced, which leads to flaunting of take-home pay. On one occasion, a father and daughter were working for the company, and because the daughter was going to college, the father always picked up her check to bank it for her.

"The daughter became resentful toward both the company and her father. Although the father meant well, the girl did not have the opportunity to watch her savings grow. There have been other occasions where relatives worked in close harmony, but because of the few times when they could not get along with each other we have had to make it a rule that no relatives may work within the same company."

An official of an Iowa life insurance company, employing 66 people in the office, said:

"Our philosophy is that you solve one problem and create another by hiring relatives. I believe a sister combination is the exception, provided they work in different departments."

Raymond Bauer, employment manager of The Stearns & Foster Company of Lockland, Ohio, reports his firm will hire husband-and-wife combinations and other relatives if they do not work in the same department. This concern has over 60 percent of its employees related to others in the firm. Mr. Bauer writes:

"We conduct 95 percent or more of our hiring by this process. It has proved to be efficient and the workers are very cooperative. We are well satisfied with the results."

This comment from M. C. Campbell, vice-president of personnel of The First National Bank of Atlanta, is interesting:

"One of the factors against which banks particularly have to guard is the reputation of being 'closed family affairs.' Rightfully or wrongfully, some banks have such a reputation which militates against capable young men of real potential seeking employment unless they are 'related.' Our policy in this regard has worked well in our bank. Of course, the employment of close relatives does mean that when one is absent for one reason or another, someone else may be absent for the same reason. The nonemployment of relatives means that very desirable potential employees might be passed up. In banks, a security measure also is present which might be an argument against employment of relatives. There are definite advantages and disadvantages to such a policy."

Mr. Campbell reports the policy of the bank is not to allow the husband-and-wife combinations. If they should marry while with the bank, both may be retained, but not in the same department. No one of closer kin than third cousins is employed.

How Ford Avoids "Burying" Workers' Skills

Workers' skills need not become "buried," even in a large company like the Ford Motor Company. A system of keeping employee qualifications and work preference cards on hand, and reviewing them quarterly, helps to fill openings by the upgrading process.

Some 32,000 salaried employees fill approximately 1,700 different job classifications in Ford offices and plants. Thousands of others have applications on file. No one person or even a group of people could possibly be familiar with the abilities of all these people. The usual result in such cases is one big organization consists of many small organizations, and the abilities of individual employees are known only to their immediate associates. Upgrading is likely to be limited to departments.

Capable employees get "buried" in their departments because there is no opening for promotion, while other departments hire new employees to fill positions which in all likelihood could be filled more competently by these "buried" employees.

This was true of Ford until the salaried personnel record system was introduced a few years ago. Prior to that time the salaried personnel record consisted of a 4- by 6-inch employment envelope into which were stuffed forms and papers pertaining to employment, transfer, reclassification, promotion, and salary changes. The only method of discovering employees' skills was by personal recommendation of those who were acquainted with them.

To correct this condition and to establish every employee as an individual whose combined talents could be brought under constant surveillance, the salaried personnel department was reorganized and the present personnel record system installed.

There are 81 salaried personnel offices in the Ford organization. These include a central salaried personnel office, a central personnel records department, and, perhaps most important of all, a planning and records section of central salaried personnel.

When an application for employment in a salaried position is received and there is no immediate opening, the application is coded. Then it is filed by code so that it is immediately accessible when an opening does occur.

Suppose a woman applies for a position as a comptometer operator and she is considered desirable, but there is no immediate opening for her. Her application will be coded 1-8AF- and followed by a number. The "1" denotes that the applicant is desirable, "8" means clerical, "A" means comptometer operator, and "F" means female. The number following the code denotes the folder in which the application is filed.

Applicants for clerical positions are tested for accuracy and speed and are given an aptitude test. Results are entered on the front of an interview rating form, together with comments. On the back of the same form, the applicant is given an overall evaluation. This form is stapled to the application.

As needed, supervisors requisition personnel. Interviewers then search the application files for the most desirable applicants and call them in for another interview.

When a person is hired he or she fills out a salaried employee history card, similar to the application form, but more detailed. It provides for a list of four positions for which the applicant considers himself best qualified, in order of preference; for languages which he reads, writes, or speaks fluently; and for his military service, if any.

This history card goes to the planning and records section of central salaried personnel, where it is checked. Then it goes to an IBM room, and much of the information on it is coded and punched in a set of seven cards. These include a master card, four "qualifications" cards, a salaried personnel status card, and a military status card.

The history record card then is photographed and returned to the records agency. The photograph, meanwhile, is inserted in a pocket in a Kardex file, together with a status posting card (not the punched card referred to above). The posting card bears a running record of the employee's classification, salary, location, organization, etc. Personnel status changes average about 350 a day and these are posted as fast as received.

Once each month a roster of all salaried employees, grouped by areas and by classifications, is run from the punched salary status cards and distributed to the personnel offices, which in turn distribute copies to the supervisors in their areas. At this time the status posting cards are posted on a transfer posting machine from the revised IBM status cards.

Every three months a qualifications roster of all salaried employees is made up from the IBM qualifications cards and distributed to the various organizations for their use in searching for people with qualifications for position openings. The personnel offices keep these rosters on file and refer to them constantly for personnel to fill positions for which they receive requisitions.

When they are unable to find suitable personnel through such searches, they request an IBM qualification run, and the information is furnished on a companywide basis.

Special Hiring Problems

Not too long ago at a local chapter seminar of the Administrative Management Society, a panel discussion dealt with recruiting problems as seen through the eyes of several executives. From the personnel director and training director of Time, Inc., responsible for hiring and training a large clerical group, came some interesting comments on a phase of employment much in the limelight today—that of hiring older people. He had this to say:

" 'Middle age' is a flexible term at best. To the teen-ager it is probably from 25 years up. From the viewpoint of the 25-year-old it may begin at 40. Those at that age have other ideas.

"Unfortunately many firms set clerical hiring age limits at 30 or 35 years of age, some lower, giving the following as some of the reasons:

   1. Loss of adaptability or decline in learning ability.

   2. Not as active physically.

   3. Suspicion as to why the individual is on the market.

   4. Adverse effect on pension plan.

"Actually, many of the reasons given are simply not so, and others may be offset by planning. More important, there are compensating and, in today's society, compelling reasons for the employment of this so-called 'middle-aged' group, at least in a balanced relationship to total staff.

"Among the advantages are:

1. Greater stability of performance.

2. Less turnover for marriage and maternity.

3. More incentive, more compelling reasons for working.

4. Previous experience.

"In any event, ours is a population of advancing age. The younger group is being siphoned off by college, early marriage, and maternity. Further, anyone who is unemployed at any age must be supported in one way or another. Our economy needs the productive efforts of all. It ill behooves us to set up arbitrary barriers to employment or to refuse to alter our ways even slightly to make use of a great productive potential."

Discussing another aspect of securing workers, an official of one of Chicago's largest hotels commented on the matter of hiring handicapped individuals:

"Defining the word 'Handicapped' presents some interesting problems when we couple our definitions with the prospect of employing someone. Obviously we will not hire anyone who, for one reason or another, is incapable of doing the work. The incapability may be a result of physical limitations or mental limitations. The first bugaboo to remove from our minds is one that implies we are seriously considering employing someone who cannot do the work.

"At one time a person who wore eyeglasses—or perhaps a better word for our purposes, corrective lenses—was considered a liability. A person who wore a hearing aid to assist him to overcome his physical limitation was also considered a liability. Today, corrective lenses and hearing aids are commonplace in our offices. Perhaps, too, the time will come when a crutch or an artificial limb will be equally acceptable. If a crutch or artificial limb is all that separates an otherwise capable worker from securing a job, and he is willing to buy it himself, he is worth our consideration.

"Sometimes the corrective measures are as simple as a cushion on a chair or a raised platform to help some physically limited person reach the work area. If such people are otherwise capable, are we willing to extend ourselves to the point where we will make such adjustments?

"It is axiomatic that in order to intelligently interview an applicant for a job, we should know the content of that job. Frequently we are inclined to associate the job content with the person who formerly held the job. If he or she kept bouncing around the office, we might be inclined to believe that such activity was necessary. Actually, however (and perhaps a little more frequently than we realize), much more production work would have been accomplished if the person had stayed put for eight hours. A person who had an artificial leg, for example, and who is otherwise capable, could certainly fill that job requisition.

"Experience of employers who hire so-called handicapped workers is, generally speaking, excellent. There's less turnover, less absenteeism, less tardiness, and more loyalty. As in any group of human beings, there are exceptions; but if we do an intelligent screening of all applicants, we should not be too concerned about acquiring misfits—physically limited or otherwise."

Chapter 4

TESTING THE QUALIFICATIONS
OF APPLICANTS

W HILE a testing program is essential to organized training, the misuse or too complete reliance upon tests is both dangerous and common. One of the mistakes being made by a large section of business and industry is buying tests from catalogs rather than investigating to see if particular company needs are served by their use.

Dr. Robert N. McMurry, an industrial psychologist, defined another danger in using tests as follows:

> Aptitude testing, intelligence testing, all testing except actual job-sample or proficiency testing should only be conducted by trained personnel. The ready availability of tests from catalogs and elsewhere should not lead to their use; it would be indiscriminate. It would not differ from a man getting into a druggist's laboratory and dousing himself with the basic drugs used to fill prescriptions. They could do him a lot of harm; any good they did him would be accidental. They have to be administered by someone trained to know what they can and cannot do.

> Testing, however scientifically conducted, is just one tool. It is dangerous and ineffective unless accompanied by a sound selection and placement program. The "can-do" of the applicant has been determined; his "will-do" must next be discovered. It is useless to place a person with an I. Q. of higher than 85 in a job sorting papers all day; intelligent people cannot successfully do monotonous jobs. The personality, aptitudes, and proficiencies of the person must be discovered and used as a basis of placement.

Simple proficiency tests are, of course, another matter. For example, a number of companies have developed job-sample tests to be given prospective employees which consist of typical assignments the applicant would have received if hired. A dictating cylinder to transcribe, bills to post, or a column of figures to add usually constitute the tests. Because there is less uniformity in the time limits which are established for these tests, standards which may serve as yardsticks for those who want to get more out of their proficiency tests are discussed later in this chapter.

When a Midwest manufacturing plant found its turnover rate going higher and higher, labor shortages developing, and heavier production schedules piling up, something drastic had to be done. No longer could the company, which had grown under the impetus of emergency conditions, get along with its old methods of selection and placement.

The reorganization of this 500-worker plant's personnel procedures started with the hiring of a management consultant. A new testing program was the first step he took, and responsibility centered in the personnel placement supervisor's hands.

Under the new set-up, all applicants get a preliminary screening test to weed out the obviously unfit. Following the passing of the screening test, the actual selection procedure includes four things: A patterned interview, an application blank, a physical examination, and checkup of references. Under this procedure, nearly one out of three was rejected.

The company is hiring three distinct groups of people from day to day: (1) Clerical jobs; (2) shop jobs; (3) engineering jobs. For clerical jobs, the Wonderlic Personnel Test (mental alertness) and the Minnesota Clerical Test are used. Clerical jobs fall into four classes: Stenographer, general office clerk, timekeeper, and expediter and expediting clerk.

On shop jobs, only one test is used. This is the MacQuarrie Test for Mechanical Ability. There are several things in favor of this test—it is short, it is simple, and it is easy to administer. Yet it covers a number of types of shop jobs—punch press, coil winding, calibrator, riveting machine jobs, inspecting, and so on.

A battery of six tests is used in the selection of applicants for engineering jobs. These are: Wonderlic Personnel Test; Minnesota Clerical Test; Minnesota Paper Form Board; Bennett Test of Mechanical Comprehension; a test of supervisory ability; and the Kuder Preference Record. The last is a vocational interest test.

By the use of this series of tests (in the case of newly hired) the rate of turnover was cut 74 percent in five months. Furthermore, the company secured enough information in this period of time to set up a test pattern or "profile," as the management engineers call it, to aid in the hiring of future employees.

Thus, not only did management secure an immediate result in decreased turnover, but a long-range program could be worked out that meant better planning of future selection procedures.

No Perfect Tests—Many Good

Take the best of the tests published for employee selection or up-grading, and there's something wrong with them. There isn't a perfect test on the market, no matter who gives it or who interprets it. That's one thing you'll get out of reading between the lines of the answers received in a Dartnell survey of employee testing techniques. But there are many good tests and there are many people qualified to interpret results among the companies using them at some stage of their personnel programs.

If you check any large sample of companies, you're going to find opinions ranging from, "Tests stink," to, "They're the best tool in my bag." You will also find some who think they compare with the Delphic oracle—just a few, and usually these will be people with short experience or a new acquaintance with testing. At first, the tests seem almost miraculous to some, especially if they test in the genius scale themselves, or if a few predictions hit on the nose. Those who think tests are for the birds usually fall in the category of executives who find from the preference tests that they should have been choir leaders, artists, or clerks (and some of these have occupational ulcers) ; or those who have hired outstanding men and been dissatisfied with results (for which there could be any number of reasons).

Herbert P. Bearak, the personnel manager of L. Grossman Sons, Inc., says:

"At Grossman's, until three years ago, no use was made of psychological testing in evaluating the potential of applicants and selecting employees for promotion. Our first step was the use of various pencil and paper tests which were purchased from reputable publishing firms. After using these tests for about a month and a half, we realized that we were wasting our money and time on something which could not be an effective measure in determining the potential of an individual taking these tests.

"The next step was to send our applicants to a local university for personnel appraisal; and after about a month, we realized that this method, too, was inadequate. The reports we received were not sufficiently comprehensive to cover the needs of the company.

"We then considered another means—that of 'Mail Testing.' This is the type of testing program whereby we would administer a battery of tests to an applicant, and then mail the package away to be evaluated so that we could receive a written report by return mail. After extensive investigation, we realized that this type of testing program could not properly serve our needs; and, therefore, looked elsewhere.

"I have always felt that each company had its own specific problems to cope with—that no one testing program could be good for all. In other words—this was one case where 'What is good for one is NOT good for all.' We, therefore,

TESTING PROGRAMS IN SELECTED COMPANIES

S. S. Pierce Company, Boston, Mass.

We are currently using the following tests and analyses in selection and placement including, as applicable, for upgrading:

SRA Verbal
Thurston Mental Alertness
Thurston Temperament,
Remington Rand, 5 Minute Typing Test
Short Employment Test—Verbal, Numbers Clerical Aptitude

Associated Transport, Inc., New York, N. Y.

Following tests are for selection of operations and sales personnel:
Thurston Mental Alertness
Cardall Practical Judgment
Thurston Temperament

Timken Roller Bearing Company, Canton, Ohio

At present, we are using the following testing material and equipment:

Wonderlic Personnel Test
Seashore's Recordings

Lamson and Sessions Company, Cleveland, Ohio

At present, we are using the following tests and analyses in the selection and placement of personnel:

Wonderlic Personnel Test
E. J. Benge Basic Employment Tests
E. J. Benge Tests for:
  Occupational Interests
  Self-Analysis Scale
  Personnel Audit

Oneida Ltd., Oneida, N. Y.

We use tests for all applicants (Activity Vector Analysis), transfers, upgrading, and counseling. Other tests used are:

Wonderlic Personnel Tests, Forms A and B
Wesman Personnel Classification Test
Differential Aptitude Tests for:
  Clerical Speed and Accuracy
  Space Relations
  Abstract Reasoning
  Numerical Ability
  Verbal Reasoning
Kuder Preference Record
General Clerical Test (Psychological Corporation)
Blackstone Stenographic Proficiency Test

employed a clinical psychologist to do a thorough research study into the requirements of a successful man in our various sales departments, as well as those of administrative capacities.

"After running a validation study over a period of four weeks, and administering tests to both successful and unsuccessful personnel, the psychologist was able to determine the qualifications necessary for an effective man in each position. Our experience with testing of this nature over 12 years has indicated 86 percent accuracy; we have reduced turnover in executive and sales positions, decreased voluntary terminations substantially, and kept involuntary terminations to a minimum.

"Testing is used to determine the applicant's capabilities and potential for advancement. Upon receipt of a written report from the clinical psychologist, we are then able to establish a training program for newly hired employees, who are thoroughly trained in the necessary departments. At the same time, we are also able to minimize and direct the individual away from those areas in which he will have difficulty, or where he will not enjoy job satisfaction. Job satisfaction is stressed, because we believe there is a definite correlation between the ability of a man to produce effectively, and his liking for the job. This also eliminates our having to recheck the employee's work, because we can almost assume, or even insure, that what he does will be done properly. For example, if a man is interested in and has aptitude for sales, rather than administrative work, it would be ridiculous to assume that he could do an effective job and be happy in work which required paying attention to clerical details and little association with people.

"The tests which are employed by these consulting psychologists measure intelligence, interests, aptitudes, and personality. In preparing the individual for testing, we explain to the applicant that these tests are for his benefit, as well as the company's—that it will enable the company to determine in advance where to properly place him with the company, and will insure him that he has potential for advancement within a given field. We explain to the applicant that both he and the company will benefit, that the tests are designed solely for our particular company, and that if he is employed he may be assured of job success and continued advancement. At the same time, we point out to him that it is better to know before he is employed that he is able to perform a certain job; otherwise, in a few months he might be dissatisfied and would start looking for a new position—or the company would recognize his inability to perform the work, which would make it necessary to transfer him or let him go.

"Since using the psychological testing program, we have been able to employ a better qualified applicant, build up a reserve of potential for advancement, and receive full cooperation from our entire staff of employees, because they realize that the testing program is of benefit not only to the company, but to themselves—because it insures advancement in an area which will allow the greatest job satisfaction, as well as financial success.

"The consulting firm states, and I agree, that psychological testing has its place; that it should never replace the judgment of a personnel manager, but should be complementary to it. We also realize that a testing program is not something which can be pulled out of a file, administered to an applicant, and selection made solely on the basis of the score that the individual receives. Rather, a psychological testing program consisting of scientifically validated testing batteries, combined with an individual consultant's services, will insure most effective utilization of all available techniques."

CLERICAL STANDARDS FOR NEW EMPLOYEES

Definite standards are used in many companies to evaluate accurately and fairly the performance of new employees. While these standards should be high enough to encourage proficiency, caution should be exercised lest they be so high as to discourage the less experienced.

Larger companies usually make their own job studies and arrive at their own performance standards, but companies employing only a few people in their offices must depend on standards developed by a national research agency such as the Administrative Management Society (AMS). This organization has worked out a series of tests covering certain office operations, and high-school and commercial-school students who satisfactorily pass the tests are awarded certificates of proficiency. The certificates are accepted by many employers as proof of the applicant's vocational qualifications for certain types of office work.

A nationwide study of vocational requirements made jointly by AMS and the United Business Education Association established the speed rate of typing from straight copy between 45 and 60 words a minute. The majority of companies reported a minimum requirement of 45 words a minute. This might be a satisfactory speed for most offices that are able to use high-school graduates for typing positions, but it is too low as a national standard.

In the same way, shorthand speeds of 80 words a minute and transcription speeds of 30 words may be all very well in times of extreme shortages when the quality of applicants is relatively low, but such standards are below those set by commercial schools under normal conditions. Most offices consider a shorthand speed of 100 words a minute as the very minimum for a stenographer. Anything less than that means too great a loss of both the dictator's and the stenographer's time.

Clerical Standards at Merck & Company

All testing is handled by the Employment Department. An official explains company policies this way:

Since we find it necessary to "trim our sails to suit the winds," it is rather meaningless to set arbitrary standards. This in spite of the fact that the company attracts the best applicants on the labor market for typists and stenographers.

While Merck & Company sets no minimum standards for the typists and stenographers it selects, it recognizes that the median international speed score on the S.R.A. Typing Skills Test is 45 words a minute and the 75th percentile

CLERICAL STANDARDS

Stenography

Dictation..100 words a minute

Transcription... 20 words a minute

Transcribe six letters (150 words) in an hour

Maximum of one error per 100 words

Business Machines

Burroughs Adding Machine—Minimum: 100 key strokes per minute (average)

Billing Machine   —Minimum: 35 correct lines of typing per minute in a 10-minute test

Bookkeeping Machine   —Minimum: 150 postings per hour on a combination typewriter and bookkeeper
200 postings per hour on a straight listing machine

Key Punch (Electric)   —Minimum: 200 cards per hour

Calculating

Number of Problems Correctly Solved in One Hour

Addition 160 *Key Strokes*	*Multiplication* 3 & 4 *Digits*	*Subtraction* 4 *Digits*	*Division* 4 *Digits*
60	340	280	140

Accounting

Ability to handle partnership and corporate accounting records and books. The same authority has drawn up a curriculum which, with proper instruction, should prepare commercial high-school students to pass the tests above. This curriculum could be compared with that of local high schools.

Clock Hours Spent on Each Major Course

Accounting Major ....533-1/3 hours

Calculating Major ....333-1/3 hours Calculating Machine
66-2/3 hours Accounting Machine

Business Machine Major ....133-1/3 hours Calculating Machine
266-2/3 hours Accounting Machine

Stenography Major ....266-2/3 hours Theory
466-2/3 hours Transcription Practice

Clerical standards should be high enough to develop proficiency but not so high as to discourage the less experienced. Most companies publish performance standards.

score is only 50. After sufficient guidance and practice newcomers are expected to reach the following rates of speed:

Typist-Clerk Trainee ....50 words a minute

Typist-Clerk ....60 words a minute

Steno-Typist Trainee ....50 words a minute

Steno-Typist ....60 words a minute

Training of employees who will take dictation is based upon a maximum speed of 120 words a minute. Anyone having this rate upon employment needs no further training, but the others are assisted to improve their speed as follows:

From:	To:
80- 85 words a minute	85- 90 words a minute
85- 95 words a minute	90-100 words a minute
95-100 words a minute	100-110 words a minute
100-115 words a minute	110-120 words a minute

The Values of Psychological Tests

In discussing the use of psychological tests for selecting and up-grading clerical workers, a consulting psychologist, Charles M. Morris, Ph.D., of Easton, Pennsylvania, reports as follows:

Psychological tests have been designed to screen individuals on the basis of what the tests are intended to measure, be it intelligence, personality, aptitude, or achievement. Too often, the users of tests have in their enthusiasm placed more finality on the test results than the designer ever intended. The bulk of the criticism leveled at employment tests have been of this nature. Since, with the possible exception of group intelligence tests, clerical tests are more widely used than any other employment tests, a word of caution is in order.

In this situation where no tests are used in the selection of clerical workers, be they clerk or executive secretary, both the employee and the employer suffer. When the employee resigns or is separated, there is little or no objective evidence as to the causes. Neither the employer nor the employee has learned anything from the experience. The clerical test thus can serve even minimally as a cumulative personnel research tool in future initial interview screening.

In instances where the personnel department utilizes employment tests, the shortcomings of clerical tests should be evaluated in terms of the complexity of the placement situation. For example, the applicant may show a low tolerance for repetitive work when the position calls for just that. This could be determined in the initial interview or through an interest or personality test. A screening test would not be likely to indicate this low tolerance, and yet it might spell success or failure on the job. Again, there is the person who has the prerequisite clerical aptitude or achievement but has more intelligence than is required. He is thus overqualified for this particular position. An intelligence test would screen him as not qualified. This person might be employed, however, if there are sufficient opportunities for promotion.

Many personnel departments as well as management consultants are attempting to remedy these so-called shortcomings by having the prospective employer draw up a list of specifications for the position that would include statements such as "large amount of repetitive work required" or "average intelligence adequate—small clerical staff with little opportunity for advancement." Depending on the specifications, a clerical test may be sufficient or more testing may be required, such as personality and intellectual measures, to mention only two possibilities.

Clerical employment tests were designed to measure clerical aptitude or achievement, and were never intended to sample more than that. The test user is thus cautioned to evaluate the work situation before he makes the hasty conclusion that the clerical test has failed him.

Speaking on the same subject, another industrial psychologist, R. D. MacNitt, Ph.D., of Walter E. Elliott Associates, Cincinnati, has found such tests useful in the following situations:

For present employees they:

1. Determine fitness for the job held.

2. Indicate potentialities for greater efficiency.

3. Measure promotion on a fair, impartial, and successful basis.

4. Indicate in what fields an employee is worth training.

5. Improve employer-employee relationships.

6. Suggest advisability of replacement.

For new employees they help:

1. Determine the approximate potential worth of the new employee.

2. Replace costly trial-and-error processes

3. Safeguard against being misled by an attractive exterior.

4. Remove the possibility of getting the slow-to-catch-on worker into work he cannot do.

Employment tests, when combined with the interviews, can help in:

1. Placing the right man in the right job.

2. Getting the most out of the payroll dollar.

3. Promoting better employee-employer relationships because selection and promotion are more objective and impartial.

4. Improving employee morale through a feeling of greater security.

5. Eliminating fear and other negative emotions caused by discontent that results from improper placement.

6. Providing an intelligent basis for training.

7. Insuring the selection of responsible types for distant and unsupervised jobs.

8. Eliminating waste through unnecessary turnover.

9. Discouraging "hit or miss" selection.

10. Predicting success or failure on a job.

TESTING THE QUALIFICATIONS OF APPLICANTS

Dr. MacNitt reports:

Unused aptitudes, interests, and personality traits can create dissatisfaction and restlessness. When employees do not have the necessary abilities and other characteristics, nervousness and tension may result.

Therefore, employment tests are a yardstick for intelligent initial placement. They also reveal promotional possibilities. However, employment tests were never meant to be a substitute for the personal interview. When combined with the best judgment of the interviewer they make for more effective placement.

Test results cannot always be taken at their apparent face value. A good personnel man soon learns to take the raw scores from the tests and to interpret them with increasing accuracy. Some employees underrate themselves, and others tend to oversell themselves. There are good employees who have difficulty accurately revealing themselves in tests, while some will try to "kid" the tests just as they try to "kid" the interviewer.

Reliable and valid tests reduce such error to a minimum, but a margin for error must still be allowed. However, this does not seriously alter the value of employment tests. You must learn to use these tools skillfully. They do not automatically give you the answers.

Sources of Tests

As there is a tendency in the field of psychological testing for the practitioners to move about, from one group of associates, and from one educational institution, to another, printed lists of such sources tend to go rather rapidly out of date. Office executives interested can secure a recent list of qualified psychological testing concerns by writing to the Purdue Research Foundation, Lafayette, Indiana, or to the American Psychological Association, 1333 Sixteenth St., N.W., Washington 20006, D.C.

Chapter 5

HIRING PROCEDURES

I N addition to proficiency and dexterity tests, picking applicants most likely to stay "put"—that is to say, with a high stability rating—requires skillful interviewing and careful checking of references. In the selection procedures recommended by Dr. Robert N. McMurry, a leading consultant on personnel problems, the use of a patterned interview blank is required. This is to overcome the inability of most interviewers to establish both what an applicant *can* do and what he or she *will* do. The interview blank is fitted to each classification of jobs for which applicants are to be selected, and is based upon characteristics which experience has shown are essential for specific types of work. These tests enable the interviewer to measure with some degree of accuracy such basic qualifications as:

Stability	Self-reliance
Industry	Ability to get along
Perseverance	with others
Loyalty	Leadership

A good application form is of inestimable value in weeding out applicants who could not possibly fill the bill and who therefore would not be retained on the payroll. It is important today that these application forms conform to laws respecting race or religious discrimination—laws which are now on the books of some states and several major cities.

The application blank shown on the following page has been carefully prepared by The Dartnell Corporation for the purpose not only of securing the best possible employees, but also to conform with fair employment practices laws.

Equally as important as the patterned interview is the telephone check recommended by Dr. McMurry. It is the quickest way of getting information about a job applicant. It saves money, even in cases where long-distance calls are necessary. The principal objectives of the telephone check are:

1. To verify statements made by applicant in his application.

2. To obtain previous employers' *estimates* of the applicant's strong and weak points.

3. To obtain a general appraisal of the applicant from people with whom he has actually worked.

4. To help the interviewer prepare in advance to get complete information *during* the interview.

In brief, the McMurry system involves three fundamental processes of scientific selection: (1) The application, (2) the investigation, and (3) the examination. The latter is the most important of the three.

While some personnel departments prefer to make use of an individually typed letter of inquiry in checking the references of an applicant, the trend has been toward the use of a printed or

Name (last name first)	Mr. Mrs. Miss		Date of Application
Permanent Address		Phone Number	Age____Born; Month____Day____Year
City and State			Temporary Address
			Whom do you know personally in this company?

References (*Not* Former Employer or Relative)	Position They Hold	Address	Phone Number

Is your mother living?____Occupation?____Father living?____Occupation?____
Do you live with parents?____; with relatives____; board____; or____
Did you serve in World War II?____Date of entering service____; Date discharged____; Kind of discharge____
Are you a member of an armed forces reserve?____What is your rank or rate?____Draft Classification____
Are you single?____Married____; Separated____; Divorced____; Widowed____; How many children?____Age____
Why do you want a position?____Do you desire a steady position?____How long?____Salary expected____
What kind of work do you think you can do best?____

EDUCATION

Schooling	Name of School	Kind of Course	Check Last Year Completed	Did You Graduate?	What Year?
Grammar School			5 6 7 8		
High or Preparatory School			1 2 3 4		
College or Technical School			1 2 3 4		
Night High School			1 2 3 4		
Correspondence Course			Number of Months		
Business College or Trade School			Number of Months		

In which two subjects did you excel in high school?____In college?____
What are you doing now to improve yourself mentally?____

What magazines do you read regularly?____Newspapers?____
Give names of a few of the books you have read recently (not in school)____

In what activities did you participate in high school or college? (Do not include sports; and exclude organizations which would indicate race, religion, or nationality)____

Check special training in: Dramatics ☐; Singing ☐; Speaking ☐; or____ What musical instrument can you play?____
What honors did you win in high school and college?____

A comprehensive application form reduces the risk of hiring the wrong candidate

---

TELEPHONE CHECK

Name of Applicant_____

Former
Supervisor_____Title_____

Company Where   Telephone
Applicant Worked_____   Number_____

1. Mr. (name) has applied for employment
   with us. I would like to *verify* some of
   the information given us. When did he
   work for your company?   From_____19____To_____19____

2. What was his job when he started to
   work for you?   _____

                   When he left?   _____

3. He says his earnings were $_____
   per_____Is that correct?   ☐ Yes,   ☐ No, $_____

4. What did you think of him? (Quality
   and quantity of work, attendance, how
   he got along with others, etc.)   _____

                                        _____

                                        _____

4a. What accidents has he had?   _____

5. Why did he leave your company?   _____

                                        _____

6. Would you re-employ him?   ☐ Yes,   ☐ No, (If not, why not?)_____

                                        _____

                                        _____

Additional comments_____

_____

_____

                Date of Check_____19____Made by_____

Form No. OT-261

The telephone check, rather than written information, uncovers pertinent facts about an applicant. It enables an employer to screen out applicants unlikely to stay "put."

Courtesy, Dr. Robert N. McMurry

mimeographed form. Unfortunately, when such a form is printed or mimeographed the job is not always well handled, with the result that it looks so much like a cheap circular that it may reach the wastebasket instead of the intended recipient. Some companies even use a post card form which in itself prevents a prospective employer from securing definite information on an applicant because such a form prevents securing confidential information. Where hiring is done in large numbers and the card is simply a more or less routine checkup of dates, occupation filled, etc., the post card is about the cheapest and simplest means of securing information. The check of fingerprints and other data also helps to establish the employee's background. There are several reporting services that investigate applicants for a small fee.

The form used to make a checkup by telephone, which has been developed for office and plant use by Dr. Robert N. McMurry, makes it easy to check information provided by job applicants. Previous employers will often divulge information in a telephone conversation which they might hesitate to put in writing.

The Physical Examination Form

Another highly important factor in keeping down turnover rates is the use of a good physical examination form. For both office and plant jobs, or for jobs in the shipping and maintenance divisions of an organization, such examinations should be based on a standard form which covers all possible variations in health or physical condition which would later necessitate separation of the employee from the payroll.

A form which is in use today by a well-known equipment firm is shown below:

PHYSICAL EXAMINATION Form IR-309. PRINTED IN UNITED STATES OF AMERICA

..............................Works

Name.............................. Birth Date.......... Sex....... Marital Status..........

Occupation.............................. Years Service..........

Present Complaints or Interval History..............................

Pre-placement ☐ Periodic: First ☐ Subsequent ☐ Transfer: Domestic ☐ Foreign ☐ S.D.A. ☐ Other ☐

Present Weight____ Usual Weight____ Height____ Temp.____ Pulse____ BP(1)____ (2)____ Vaccination____ Vaccinated By Examiner____

(If 1st is elevated, take 2nd at end of exam)

Vision (Distant) Without Glasses R 20/ L 20/ (Near) R WD/ L WD/

With Glasses R 20/ L 20/ R WD/ L WD/

Color vision____ Depth Perception____ Hearing: Right Satis. ☐ Unsat. ☐ Left Satis. ☐ Unsat. ☐

Mark (+) if Findings are Abnormal, and (-) if Findings are Normal, Explain in Detail Abnormal findings. (List by Number)

1 Scalp ☐	8 Teeth ☐	15 Lungs ☐	22 Varicose Veins ☐	29 Reflexes ☐
2 Skin ☐	9 Throat ☐	16 Heart ☐	23 Peripheral Circulation ☐	30 Neurologic, other ☐
3 Cranial Nerves ☐	10 Tonsils ☐	17 Abdomen ☐	24 Feet ☐	31 Deformities (old injury) ☐
4 Eyes ☐	11 Neck Glands ☐	18 Hernia ☐	25 Spine ☐	32 Deformities (Congenital) ☐
5 Ears ☐	12 Neck Vessels ☐	19 Genitalia ☐	26 Rectum ☐	33 Scars, Disfiguring Marks ☐
6 Nose ☐	13 Thyroid ☐	20 Muscle Atrophy ☐	27 Hemorrhoids ☐	34 Mental Reaction, Attitude ☐
7 Mouth ☐	14 Breasts ☐	21 Ankle Edema ☐	28 Prostate ☐	35 Personal Hygiene ☐

Explanation of Abnormal Findings: (List by Number)..............................

Laboratory Findings: Chest X-Ray____ Urine sp. gr.____ Alb.____ Sugar____ Micro____ Blood Serology____ Rbc.____ Hgb.____ Wbc.____ Blood (other)____ EKG____

Recommendations..............................

Recall to Medical Dept. on____19__for Physical Examination ☐ X-Ray ☐ Special Examination ☐ Laboratory ☐ Follow-up Injury ☐ Other, Specify ☐

Do (Do not) approve individual for: Placement ☐ S.D.A. ☐ Transfer ☐ Other ☐ (Disability permanent as of____19__: Approved Supvr. of Medical Service____)

If not approved, state why briefly____

Date____ Occupational Disability Group 1 2 3 4 5 6 (Circle one) Physical Classification A B C D (Circle one) Examined by____M.D.

Better than two-thirds of the companies responding to a Dartnell inquiry require health examinations before hiring office employees. A small number reported a policy whereby men actually took an examination but female employees merely filled in a form before hiring.

In most instances, 85 percent, the examination is conducted by the company doctor. It is also given without charge to the employee in all of these cases. About 15 percent of the examinations are made by the employee's own physician; in very few companies does the employee pay the bill. One respondent reported a policy whereby the company will pay part of the fee for the employee's examination by his own doctor. Another firm, which does not always require a physical examination, pays the employee's physician for the examination when requesting such a checkup. The executive reporting for this firm, a bank, said, "We maintain a flexible policy on physical examinations. We only require one of a prospective employee if we have serious doubts about his physical ability and stamina."

Physical examinations for office employees are, as a rule, not as stringent as examinations for work calling for physical strain and effort. Few companies require office employees to take periodical physical checkups. Some have a yearly check required of all office workers, but others are "optional."

THE PERSONNEL FILE

Having complete data on every employee readily available is extremely important. While setting up accurate personnel records with all the detail needed to make them yield the utmost in value involves a great of time and effort, such an effort pays handsome dividends in the long run. There are probably as many ways of setting up personnel files as there are companies. Virtually all types of records, to be really satisfactory, must be adapted to the individual situation. Even so, helpful ideas and suggestions are to be had from learning how a few companies handle this phase of record keeping.

Signal System on Personnel Records

By a series of tabs or signals, attached to each employee card, the Washington Gas Light Company's employee history system can show:

1. Green signal at extreme left indicates "new" employee.
2. Green over a figure (1 to 12) indicates month in which rate increase is due.

3. Orange signal placed over figure flashes the expiration of 5 months of employment—send first rating sheet.

4. Yellow signal over a figure shows which month of year employee is to return to doctor for medical examination.

5. Purple signal placed over figure reveals expiration of 9 months of employment—time to send second rating sheet.

6. Blue signal over figure shows number of reprimands.

7. Orange progressive signal traveling over the present rating chart flashes general employee efficiency.

8. Yellow signal over sick benefits column indicates prolonged illness.

9. Blue signal over department code section indicates "utility" employee.

10. Purple signal over department code means "confidential" payroll.

11. Green signal over employee number indicates exemption from the Fair Labor Standards Act.

Approximately 2,000 present employee cards are housed in three tiers of visible index drawers, occupying less space than a small desk.

Locating Personnel by Punched Cards

In all personnel systems, two features are mandatory: (1) Ability to locate rapidly the complete record of an individual; (2) the ability to locate the cards of all individuals with common qualifications. To save cross indexing, many personnel departments use a punched-card system which enables a clerk to do both with only one record.

One such system is the "Keysort" by Royal McBee. Its distinguishing characteristics are small holes punched in the card adjacent to the margin. These holes are given sorting classifications either by assigning a number to each hole, or by printing the actual names of the classifications under the corresponding holes. For example, under Education, on the card illustrated, the holes are labeled "Some H. S." (high school), "Grad. H. S.," etc. If the individual represented on the card had graduated from high school (but had no further education) this hole, "Grad. H. S.," would be slotted or notched. Then, if from several hundred cards it was desired to obtain all individuals whose academic education ended after graduation from high school, all that would be necessary under this method would be to run a steel tumbler through that hole (Grad. H. S.) in all cards involved, and lift up the tumbler. All cards having that hole slotted would drop out of the pack—and the sort would be accomplished.

This particular "Keysort" personnel card, when completely filled out and slotted, permits 25 characteristics of the individual to be coded into the margins. Thus, there are 25 cross references eliminated.

Another advantage of this system is that an individual's primary as well as secondary skill can be coded into the margin in such a manner as to permit a direct sort for either skill. Today there is continued shifting of skill or job qualification requirements. In filling such openings it is deemed best to choose from existing personnel, especially where an increase in salary is involved.

For instance, when military orders became important, manufacturers of certain materials changed their catalog drawings from plan views to a full pictorial method, showing three-dimensional views of the part or machine, in relation to the whole assembly. This change was brought about by the need, on the part of the Army, for easier identification of repair parts as well as more comprehensible installation instructions.

This requirement placed a load on personnel managers to find men qualified and capable of such illustrative design. In the industry using the card illustrated, a sort for pictorial draftsmen was made of the secondary skills of all employees after ascertaining that they had none with this type of experience as a primary skill. This sort, necessitating a sort on four holes at one time, was done with a multiple needle tumbler.

As a result of this sort, the card of one man was found who had made a hobby of this particular branch of drafting. He was immediately transferred to this pictorial work, and, thanks to the foresight of the personnel manager, became chief of the division.

Forms Used in Employing Office Workers

In a busy office where many persons are constantly being interviewed, having their references checked, and finally being employed, there is need for an assortment of timesaving forms. Use of some forms depends upon the disposition made of the applicant when hired. In a large office, when the applicant is hired and notified to report to work he reports to the personnel department, not to the employment manager or office manager. Here most of the forms—such as notification of employment, notification to payroll department, preparation of clock cards, assignment to work, assignment to locker space, application for insurance, application for membership in company clubs, preparation of personnel records, and similar records—are taken care of by the personnel department. Who does the work is immaterial. Here is a list of some of the forms which are in current use:

Application blanks	Employee's change of address cards
Interview or rating blanks	Requisition for employee
Telephone check forms	Application for Social Security Account
Termination forms	Number
Physical examination record	Employee history cards
Reference investigation blanks	Credit union membership cards
Return envelopes	Identification cards or badges
Notification of employment	Shop passes
Application for group insurance	Period rating cards
Payroll deduction for insurance	Change of rate cards
Employee's address cards	Transfer cards
Payroll deduction cards	Change of status blanks
Insurance	Locker room tickets
Benefits	Lunchroom credit cards
Hospital	Rule books, or employee handbooks

There is a tendency, however—and this is common with most administrative departments of a business—to keep too many records that are really not necessary, and to keep records too long. Periodical checks should be made to be sure profitable use is being made of all employment records.

Keeping adequate records of those who apply for work has sometimes solved a serious help problem. Many skilled workers have been located through almost antiquated but complete personnel records. One manufacturer located a toolmaker who came to him more than 25 years earlier in search of work.

Some companies are checking over the records of college alumni to locate long-lost engineers who have drifted into other fields. A once-famous engineer was found writing juvenile fiction stories. Another engineer was about to be drafted into the Army, because having found engineering tough sledding, he had drifted into the millinery business.

Terminating the Office Worker

Since the complex pattern of employment today does not make it possible for employers to fire a worker without cause or without thought of future consequences, personnel records must be kept which will show that the proper procedure has been followed—a procedure which will satisfy Government regulations as well as union agreements. As the unionization of offices and retail stores continues, such records may well be as important in the firing of office workers as they now are in firing plant employees.

<table>
<tr><td colspan="2" align="center">EXIT INTERVIEW</td></tr>
</table>

EXIT INTERVIEW

Clock No. .... S. S. No. .... Employee ....

Male .... Female.................. Dept. ....

Present Position or Duties ....

....

Date Started .... Date Ended .... Length of Service ....

Initial Rate .... Present Rate .... Hired by ....

Would Rehire .... Reinstated by .... Date ....

Reason for not Rehiring ....

....

Supervisor .... Interviewer .... Date Paid Off ....

Reason for Resigning	Reason for Dismissal
☐ Gave Notice Yes .... No	☐ Inefficient ☐ Insubordination ☐ Lazy
☐ Not satisfied with Rate ☐ Return to School	☐ Inattentive ☐ Does not work consistently
☐ Temporary Lay Off.................. ☐ Eyestrain	☐ Poor Attendance ☐ Poor Health ☐ Tardiness
☐ Does not like Nightwork ☐ Illness in Family	☐ Will not work overtime ☐ Will not take transfer
☐ Does not like Hours ☐ Does not like Work	☐ No Work ☐ Under Age ☐ Lack of effort
☐ To take another Job ☐ Family moved out of town	☐ Agitator ☐ Loafing ☐ Character
☐ To get married ☐ Reason Unknown	☐ Not fitted for work ☐ Low production
☐ Other	☐ Other ....

F52 7-48 1M

This exit interview form can usually be used without further change or adaptation

In addition, it is now generally agreed that carefully planned procedures for terminating employment of workers are necessary to insure absolute fairness to the worker as well as protection for the employer.

The exit interview is particularly important in this procedure for it not only helps to get the real story of the employee's desire to terminate his employment with the company, but enables an alert management to locate the trouble spots which may have been conducive to a high turnover rate.

Furthermore, it is advisable that the responsibility for firing an employee not be left to the discretion of a department head, but be handled by the personnel department according to a standard procedure or plan. It is also important that in the case of a discharge, the company have accurate and complete data in the employee's personnel record or employee history files to show the cause of discharge and that the employee had been given a fair hearing. Such records are essential for unemployment insurance as well as the retention of seniority rating where such ratings are guarded in the union contract.

An important reason for not permitting department heads to take the responsibility for discharging employees is that only the personnel department can be fully cognizant of and responsible for compliance with the Wages and Hours Act, the Equal Employment Opportunities Act, other Federal and State laws, as well as any regulations dealing with labor union practices.

All termination orders, instructions, and reports should be *in writing,* and copies kept on file for at least four years. The Wages and Hours Act requires that the records must show the following 12 items of information about each employee who is terminated:

1. Name and identification number, if used.
2. Home address.
3. Date of birth, if under 19.
4. Occupation in which employed.
5. Time of day and the name of the day on which employee began work.
6. Regular hourly rate of pay when overtime is worked.
7. Basis on which regular wages are paid.
8. Hours worked each day and total hours of each week.
9. Total daily or weekly straight time earnings.
10. Total weekly overtime excess compensation.
11. Total wages paid each period.
12. Date of payment and pay period covered by payment.

SUMMARY OF EXIT INTERVIEWS
Supplement to Labor Turnover Report

Reasons for Desiring Separations	Separations			Retentions		
	Male	Female	Total	Male	Female	Total
1. Wages unsatisfactory						
2. Job level unsatisfactory						
3. Working conditions unsatisfactory (Hot—cold—dusty—wet—noisy—fumes—etc.)						
4. Not adaptable to the work						
5. Returning to home duties, joining husband in military service, married, etc.						
6. Inadequate transportation or housing, moving from district, etc.						
7. Hours of work unsatisfactory						
8. Health reasons (employee's health)						
9. Differences with co-workers or supervision						
10. Reasons not known—Quit without notice Failed to report after absence Failed to return following furlough or leave of absence						
Grand Totals						

Reasons for separations, when entered on a form like this, offer revealing clues to the problem of excessive turnover.

EXIT INTERVIEW FORM

Employee's Name..Interview Date...........................

Department...Separation Date...........................

Job Title..Employment Date.......................

Reason for separation (be specific) : ....

1. What were the things you liked most about your job?..

2. What were the things you disliked most about your job?....................................

3. What were the things you liked most about the company?...................................

4. What were the things you disliked most about the company?..............................

5. Were you satisfied with the training you received?..................If no, why not?

6. What do you consider to be your greatest asset for contributing to the success of a business?...

7. Do you feel the company fully capitalized on this quality or experience?...............

8. Do you feel you received sufficient orientation as a new employee and were made to feel at home quickly?....................Did your supervisor devote ample time to explaining things, and did he answer all your questions or get the answers for you?...

9. Is there any point of disagreement or uncertainty that you have not been able to settle satisfactorily?....................If so, would you like to discuss it now?.............

10. What specific suggestions can you make that you feel would lead to improvements in company procedures?..

11. What comments would you care to make regarding general working conditions? ....

....

....

....
(Interviewer's Signature)   (Department Head)   (Personnel Director)

Use the reverse side for any additional comments or suggestions.

In order to maintain an accurate record of the causes of all voluntary terminations, it is necessary to provide a form which will be easy to maintain in the personnel department, yet which will give complete information.

Such a form enables the personnel department to maintain a record on "quits" for either office or plant personnel which gives the picture of "causes" at a glance.

Each company will, of course, want to prepare its own form, depending upon how it will eventually be used for the record. However, the standard form shown can generally be used in most cases "as is."

It is suggested that the interviewer use the form only as a guide in asking questions and to prepare a record for the files. Actually, best results are secured by letting the employee talk. In this way, the interviewer will be more likely to find out the *real* reason the worker wants to quit. The more often the employee goes over his story, the more likely the truth will come out. To be a good listener should be the interviewer's aim.

Aldon Rug Mills, Incorporated, is currently using the exit interview sheet at left for all employees leaving the company. The interview is a personal one between the employee and the personnel manager. The interview is private and informal with the personnel manager asking employee specific questions and expanding on those of importance to the employee and the company.

The form is used as a general outline and the personnel manager moves into any area the employee wishes in regard to constructive (and sometimes destructive) criticism or comments regarding company policy, procedures, pay, conditions, etc. The employee is asked to review the form and sign it at the termination of the interview.

Fill-in notes are made on the sheet during the interview. If the employee quits without notice, the form is mailed with his last check and a self-addressed envelope is included. In most cases these are returned with added comments.

Chapter 6

ORIENTING OFFICE EMPLOYEES

FIRST impressions are the lasting ones. What happens the first few days a new employee is on the job often determines how he will like the job and how long he will stick.

Without proper preparation for the first few days, the new worker can become discouraged enough by the end of the week to be ready to quit when the first misunderstanding occurs over a minor infringement of the rules.

In its need to get an employee into production, a company may speed up the induction procedure too fast, with the result that the worker starts on the job insufficiently prepared.

While the time devoted to the induction procedure varies considerably from company to company, it is not a good idea to allot less than a full day to it. The process of induction rightly begins with the initial employment interview. If this interview is handled with sincerity and dignity—if the interviewer himself is sold on the company—the new employee will get off to a good start.

Second, if the supervisor has been trained in the process of handling new employees, the induction job won't be muffed when the new worker is turned over to the department where he will work.

Third, if a well-planned program for inducting new employees has been set up, every employee hired will get the benefit of a good start. Another advantage of having a well-planned program in writing is that, as it is tested over a period of time through use, it can be added to or steps may be eliminated as usage determines.

The start of the induction program is an excellent time to bring the supervisor into the picture. One company in the communications field handles this phase of the program by including a page in its employee-induction booklet which serves to install confidence in the worker toward his supervisor.

YOUR SUPERVISOR IS READY TO HELP YOU

Right now, when starting a new job, you're undoubtedly full of questions. There are a hundred and one things you'd like to know . . . and dozens of new situations to meet.

Your supervisor is always ready to help you. As leader of the group in which you work, he or she has a real interest in your welfare and progress and wants you, as a member of the team, to contribute to the overall accomplishments of the group.

So, when you have a question or problem, talk things over with your supervisor. With such friendly guidance, you'll soon feel right at home on your new job.

You will be given all the instruction and help you need. Your supervisor and your fellow workers want you to succeed.

The important thing to remember is to keep an open mind toward your job. Learn all you can about your work and the telephone industry by observation and by asking questions. Knowledge and sureness in your work will come gradually with experience.

Excerpt from employee-induction booklet

The Induction Manual

The largest group of manuals in use by business and industry are the induction or "welcome" manuals prepared to simplify the orientation of new employees. These manuals received great impetus during World War II as a means of helping to orient thousands of new employees suddenly thrown into war production—many of whom had never worked in an office or a plant before.

Strictly speaking, this type of manual is not an office manual. However, the induction manual must be considered such to some extent since, in a number of companies, it substitutes for the more comprehensive office manual. Also, the employee or induction manual, embodying rules and policies, can well be a step toward the more essential office or job manual.

Many of these early induction manuals were, unfortunately, pretty extravagant in pointing out the benefits of employment. Too often the prose consisted of plenty of "sweetness and light," but little understanding of human relations. Today's induction manuals are, as a rule, far superior to these early efforts, although there still exists in many cases a strange lack of understanding of what should go into such a manual. For example, too much space is given to the "greeting" from the president of the company. This message should be brief and factual; it should not go overboard to the extent that the new employee will think everyone has just been awaiting his arrival!

Letter From the President

A combination greeting and policy statement from the chairman and president of Cessna Aircraft Company, Wichita, Kansas, is presented in the form of a short letter. It appears in the company's employees' guide, opposite a statement of company objectives.

To all of us:

KNOW THE ROPES is intended to help you understand our policies and procedures. As you become thoroughly familiar with them and know why we do things, you can have the fullest opportunity to develop yourself on the job and to contribute to our collective prosperity.

"You'll like working at Cessna - ask any Cessna employee" is a reflection of our real interest in newcomers and old timers alike. And it establishes a standard of excellence that you can help to maintain.

We have been fortunate in the many busy years of progress we have enjoyed. Working together in a friendly, informal way, we have built a reputation for "on time" production. We have improved old products and developed new ones. Some are built for our country's defense; others anticipate the needs of our commercial customers. Still others help diversify our production and increase job security. The cooperative efforts of people with every kind of skill and talent have carried Cessna to the top of a progressive, highly competitive industry.

From the achievements of the past, we face the future with confidence. The years ahead will challenge the best we have in creative imagination, technical know-how, and operating efficiency. We know that the sum of our individual contributions will mean continuing success for our company with greater opportunities for each one of us.

Del Roskam
Del Roskam
President

Dwane Wallace
Dwane L. Wallace
Chairman

The booklets have a variety of names. *Within the Selected Circle* is the title of the guidance booklet prepared for new employees of Selected Risks Insurance Co. in Branchville, N. J. *This Is Your Company* is the Coca-Cola handbook. *Your Job With CW* describes working rules and policies for new employees at the restored Colonial Williamsburg community in Williamsburg, Va. A simple *Welcome* has been selected by several firms as the handbook title.

Cartoons Are Used

Many of the employee guidebooks use clever cartoons to illustrate major points. If the company has a cartoon character as a mascot, he may deliver the message. Some of the more elaborate booklets are printed in three or four colors, but the majority are printed in two colors.

Keep History Brief

Anyone preparing a new employee's guide or induction manual will benefit from the modern trend to keep company history short and to the point. This means that pictures of the plant or plants in all stages of development for the past 50 years or so can well be omitted. What the new employee wants to know about the organization is simply what it makes, where its offices and plants are located, the names of the products and possibly an indication of its future development or potential.

Most important is that all of the essentials are given to the new employee. Pay Day, Holidays, Payroll Deductions, Vacations, Absences and Overtime are some key titles in Cessna's "Know the Ropes." Jury duty, service in the armed forces, garnishments, solicitations, personal business and security are other subjects of importance.

Personnel Policy Information Is Essential

An attractive personnel induction manual is produced by the Continental Illinois National Bank and Trust Co., of Chicago. As in all well prepared induction manuals, emphasis is placed in this 12-page booklet on personnel policies. Drawings and a minimum of copy explain such matters as hours of work, paydays, merit increases, vacations, holidays, sick leave, jury duty, military service, fringe benefits, and retirement.

Personnel policies are essential in an induction manual. The important point concerning this part of the manual is that the policies be made understandable. Material should be clear and concise and, at the same time, written so that the employee immediately understands that all policies, rules, and regulations are an integral part of the proper functioning of the whole organization. To accept company procedures from the very beginning of his employment makes a man a better worker and guarantees more certain teamwork later.

No orientation program is complete unless the department head or the supervisor under whom the employee is to work contributes his or her full measure to the program. The important role of the supervisor is shown in this report from the Newark Division, Geo. D. Roper Corp., Newark, Ohio.

A new person is, of course, interviewed thoroughly in the personnel department. When he is assigned to a department, he is taken to that section and introduced to the department head. The department head also interviews the individual, explains all the ramifications of what will be of interest to him on his job, shows him how to ring his card, and where the rest rooms are located. He then introduces him to the other employees in the department and gives him further information essential for his complete indoctrination.

We carry through practically the same procedure with the executive force. The new executive's immediate superior is the guiding light as far as introductory work is concerned, except that we also have multiple management. In this case, whenever a new executive is hired the personnel manager notifies the chairman of the junior board of directors, he introduces him to the man, and the chairman of the board in turn selects some specific person on the executive force to show the man through the plant, explain things thoroughly, take him to lunch the first day, preferably in the plant cafeteria, etc.

We believe the new employee's immediate superior is the person who should acquaint him with the company and its products, policy, rules and regulations, and any other pertinent information at the time of his first employment.

This is in line with our thinking that the department head, being the manager and supervisor in the various departments, is management's representative.

The Indoctrination Schedule

In most larger companies the employee orientation program takes at least one day or, more often, an entire week. During this time when the new employees are required to attend meetings or lectures, they are paid at their regular rates of pay.

Such a program may include talks by the personnel director, the safety director, and the president of the company, or some other officer representing top management.

A change of pace is highly desirable, otherwise induction meetings can become rather dull. One way to prevent monotony is to interspace the talks with sound-slidefilms and demonstrations. The demonstrations may include right and wrong procedures on the job and safe methods of working. The sound-slidefilm may show the whole process of induction or just a history of the company and it products.

A good sound-slidefilm showing the various departments is particularly helpful when the organization is so large that it is spread over acres of ground. For the smaller company, while the sound-slidefilm is useful in presenting a picture of the company's activities, an actual trip through the office and plant is even more effective in giving the new worker a picture of the company's activities.

If an auditorium or special room in the office can be set aside for regular use as a meeting room, large charts and posters of the company's products can be displayed to give employees an idea of the ramifications of the company's business.

If only one day can be allowed for the induction program, it must be scheduled carefully in order to include all the necessary steps. Such a program might be time scheduled as follows:

	Time
COMPANY HISTORY:	
A talk on the company's history	15 minutes
Sound-slidefilm showing departments and operations in making products	45 minutes
Talk on the company's markets	15 minutes
TOUR OF THE PLANT:	
Conducted trip through the plant	2 hours
LUNCH	30 minutes
COMPANY RULES AND POLICIES:	
Employee rules and regulations, company policies, wage rates, merit rating, promotions	1 hr. 30 min.
TRAINING PROGRAM:	
Details of the training program	20 minutes
INTERMISSION	10 minutes
EMPLOYEE WELFARE:	
Talk on group insurance, life insurance, retirement plan, etc.	25 minutes
EMPLOYEE HEALTH:	
Talk on hospital facilities, first aid, hospitalization insurance	20 minutes
Sound-slidefilm	30 minutes
ACCIDENT PREVENTION:	
Talk on safety on the job	20 minutes
Sound-slidefilm on handling tools	20 minutes
Sound-slidefilm on safe work methods	20 minutes

Individual induction programs will, of course, vary in companies according to size of office and number of new employees being hired. However, few of the items scheduled above can be omitted without seriously limiting the program.

International Textbook Company's Program

The International Textbook Company of Scranton, Pennsylvania, has a record for low employee turnover. Perhaps one of the greatest contributing factors to this low turnover in personnel is the company's comparatively simple, but effective, indoctrination program. The procedure is as follows:

At the time the new employee is "signed up" a member of the personnel department staff goes over a specific check list with the idea of telling the employee certain fundamental things about the job such as: Hours of work, rate of pay, timecard use, vacation policy, absence from work, tardiness, etc. An employee handbook covering all of these items is given to the employee to take with him for later review of the items that have been discussed.

When the employee reports to the department head, the department head carries along the same line covering another specific check list of items such as: Duties of the job, change of address, method of wage payment, safety rules, first-aid room, rest room, recreation room, smoking regulations.

Within 10 days after the employee starts to work, he is sent an appointment slip through his supervisor requesting his attendance in one of our conference rooms on a specific date and at a specific time. When the employees gather in the conference room, they have already been at work for approximately 10 days and have some general idea of their job and the work procedures involved. At this meeting, a member of the personnel department staff discusses briefly the company history and company organization including a functional description

---

Mr. John J. Doe
Street Address
City, State

The first several days on a new job, Mr. Doe,

. . . are difficult ones indeed . . . new environment, new faces, different office procedures . . . new everything. Your Supervisor and your Personnel Department are aware of the anxiety that exists with being "brand new" in an organization. We know how uncertain those initial days can be.

At this early stage of your association with us, you no doubt are aware of our efforts to make you feel "at home."

People, working together toward a common business objective, inevitably have mechanical as well as human problems. Your Personnel Department is geared to actively assist you, Mr. Doe, in any problem you may have. It stands to reason we cannot have all the answers, but, working together, we can concentrate on making your career with us a satisfying experience.

. . . Anyway, Welcome! We feel sure you'll enjoy your association with us.

Sincerely,

Personnel Manager

Welcoming the new employee

of the companies comprising the corporate structure. Some fundamental company policies are further explained. Questions are asked by the employees and answers given by the personnel department representative.

After discussion has ended, one of the company guides takes the new employees on a tour of the home office operations. All departments are visited and the guide explains the basic work being done in each department. After the tour, employees are encouraged to present questions they might subsequently have about the company or its operations to their supervisor. Supervisors have been instructed to answer such questions and to contact the personnel department whenever a question might be raised that they cannot answer.

Part of a good new employee orientation program is the checkup given each worker at a specific date following his employment. A checkup or interview should take place somewhere between three weeks and three months after the employee has been added to the payroll. Such an interview not only succeeds in determining whether the employee has been properly placed in his job and is satisfied, but it can also help to assure the worker of the company's interest in his welfare and future security.

In order to cover the ground thoroughly, a standard outline may be of some help to the interviewer. An employee interview form shown nearby should serve only as a *guide* to the interviewer—questions for the purpose of getting the worker to talk about his job, his department, and his foreman. The more he talks the better the interviewer may determine whether the new employee is well integrated.

EMPLOYEE INTERVIEW FORM

NAME...

DATE...

ADDRESS...

PHONE..

SOCIAL SECURITY NO...

CLOCK NUMBER...

SINGLE...................MARRIED.....................DIVORCED...................

DATE STARTED WITH COMPANY...

1. Do you think you are working at the job for which you are best fitted?...............

2. Is there any other type of work in the company for which you think your background and experience are better suited? ....

3. Is there anything about your present job you don't like? ....

4. Are you taking any courses of education or special training at this time? ....

5. Would you like to take a series of tests to determine your aptitude for some other type of work in the company? ....

6. Have you submitted any suggestions for improving methods of doing the work in your department?...............

7. Have you any suggestions for improving working conditions in your department?..... In the company?...............

8. Do you have any suggestions or comments regarding the food or the service in the cafeteria?...............

9. Do you participate in any of the recreational activities offered by our company such as bowling.........., golf ...., dancing ...., horseshoe pitching ...., baseball? ....

10. Is there anything about our merit-rating system you do not understand? ....

11. Do you understand the salary rate ranges? ....

12. Do you thoroughly understand how the retirement trust program benefits you? .... Did you know that the company pays entire cost? ....

An interview form designed to uncover evidence of dissatisfaction before an employee decides to look for another job

EMPLOYEE SPONSORSHIP AT KEMPER INSURANCE

Recognizing that informal contact with veteran employees is invaluable in helping new employees adjust themselves to unfamiliar faces and surroundings and to unaccustomed routines, we feel that it will help to reduce our employee turnover if we assign to each new employee a sponsor.

There are several reasons why a sponsor system will help you retain a higher percentage of the new employees. Through the sponsor system the employees feel that someone is taking a special interest in them. Sponsors "know the ropes"; as workers themselves they are in a position to know what kind of information incoming employees want; routine information regarding location of washrooms, time clocks, elevators, exits, etc., can be furnished by sponsors—thus saving valuable supervisory time. Introductions to other employees tend to be less formal when handled by another employee not in a supervisory capacity. New employees are often backward about asking supervisors certain questions that they would not hesitate asking another employee. In addition, sponsorship has been found a valuable means of developing leadership and responsibility in the sponsors themselves.

Here are some of the things about which a sponsor could give information to an employee:

1. Working hours.
2. Method and time of pay.
3. Washrooms and time clocks.
4. History of the company.
5. Type of business, particular job of new employee and its place in the department and in the organization.
6. Lunch periods and cafeterias.
7. Hospital and insurance plans.
8. Holidays and vacations.
9. Personal phone calls.
10. Absences and tardiness.
11. Half days.
12. Suggestion system.

The sponsor should also see that a new employee has someone to go to lunch with, either an old employee or the sponsor for at least the first week of work. Also, through questions asked by the new employee and opinions expressed, the sponsor could be a great help in baring ideas that would help to improve our orientation of new employees.

It must be borne in mind that the many benefits possible under the sponsor system may be nullified if the sponsors are selected indiscriminately. An employee who is dissatisfied with his own job, who cannot get along with his supervisors or his associates, or whose concept of company operations is confined to his own particular duties, unconsciously dampens the enthusiasm of the new employee.

We feel that sponsors should be selected on their ability to get along with other people, their tact and poise, initiative, production record, length of service, and progress they themselves have made.

LINCOLN TELEPHONE AND TELEGRAPH COMPANY

INDUCTION CHECK LIST FOR USE BY SUPERVISORS
AS A GUIDE IN INDUCTING NEW EMPLOYEES

Supervisor..Date................................

Employee..Dept................................

Check when
completed   FIRST DAY

................1. Review the job.
   a. Importance of his work.
   b. Relation of his job to others in the department.
   c. Give assurance that he will learn quickly.
   d. Let him know that you are depending on him.

................2. Explain hours of work.
   a. Starting and quitting time, and hours per week.
   b. Relief periods.

................3. Review compensation.
   a. Amount.
   b. When paid.
   c. Deductions—Income Tax—Social Security.
   d. Payment for absent time.
   e. Overtime pay.

................4. Introduce to immediate associates and sponsor.
   a. To supervisors.
   b. To workmates close to workplace.
   c. Sponsor.

................5. Discuss and explain employee benefits.
   a. Group insurance.
   b. Mutual Benefit Association.
   c. Company pension and benefits.
   d. Employees Cooperative Credit Association.

................6. Company literature.
   a. Discuss and give copy of Working Agreement and Wage Schedule.
   b. Give copy of booklet, "Your Company and Your Job."

................7. Give job instruction.
   a. Have a trainer well prepared and suited to teach.
   b. Show him examples of the work he will do.
   c. Practice.
   d. Encourage him to ask questions.
   e. Show where to store work overnight.

................8. Explain quality and quantity of work.
   a. Importance of accuracy.
   b. Quality before quantity.
   c. Speed will come with experience.
   d. Accident prevention and safety.

Check when
completed

SECOND DAY

........................1. Give instruction on how to answer the telephone.
    a. Speak clearly.
    b. Give your name when answering.
    c. Take messages in writing for those not present.
    d. Keep personal calls to a minimum.
........................2. Give employee opportunity to say how he is getting along.

THIRD DAY

........................1. Explain policy on donations.
    a. Community Chest, Red Cross, etc.
    b. Start no lists for gifts without approval of supervisor.
........................2. Discuss suggestion plan.
    a. How to submit.
    b. How awards are made.
    c. Should be well-thought-out ideas.
    d. All suggestions are thoroughly considered.
    e. Don't be discouraged if first suggestion is not accepted.

FOURTH DAY

........................1. Discuss vacation plan.
    a. How length of vacation is determined.
    b. The part seniority plays.
    c. Time selected must be approved by supervisor.

FIFTH DAY

........................1. General review.
    a. Answer any questions employee may ask.
    b. Encourage him to discuss problems with his supervisor.
    c. Let him know how he is getting along.

FIRST PAY CHECK

........................1. Pay check will be transmitted to immediate supervisor for delivery to the new employee.
........................2. Discuss compensation and deductions.
    a. Explain deduction slip.
........................3. Discuss wage progression.
    a. Explain.

PROGRESS INTERVIEW

........................1. Conduct at the time of the first wage progression step and each subsequent step.
    a. Review with employee his work and progress.
    b. Assure the employee that he is not being overlooked and that the supervisor is interested in his welfare.
    c. Discuss with employee his strong points and weaknesses. This enables the supervisor to learn about employee problems and grievances, before they become acute. The supervisor, of course, has kept in close contact with employee, during entire period, and has lost no opportunity to make him feel at ease and to direct his work constructively.

Chapter 7

PREPARING A JOB EVALUATION PROGRAM

JOB evaluation today is recognized as the first step in securing the right employee for any particular position. Without a clearly defined description of the function of the job, it is very difficult to determine who should perform, what results should be expected, and what pay should be given.

In truth, many companies, especially smaller office operations, do not have clearly defined job descriptions. This often proves as costly for them as it does for a larger corporation, where chaos would be the result.

Procedural changes made to eliminate duplicate or unnecessary work in offices will result in a greater productivity on the part of clerical employees. Increased office productivity is the only way to reduce total office costs and will provide other benefits such as better office discipline, better customer service, a better basis for evaluating methods, procedures, and policy changes, and a basis for changing personnel policies and staff to meet changing volumes and conditions.

Job analysis can increase productivity in instances where mechanization is not feasible, and where work activities are definable. Typical activities include calculating, filing, posting, typing, and billing.

What Is Job Evaluation?

Job evaluation means exactly what it says. It means setting a value on each and every job in the organization. This includes office jobs as well as those in the plant or shop. It presupposes that some jobs are worth more than others because they require more than others. Some jobs require more skill from the worker; some more experience; some more physical effort; and some more mental effort. Many jobs require considerable responsibility; others require but little. Boiled down to its simplest explanation, job evaluation means *defin-*

ing job requirements. If it is possible to define the requirements of the individual jobs in any given office or plant, it is possible to work out a plan of job evaluation.

In every case, emphasis is put on the job, not the worker. Job evaluation does not rate employees—it does rate jobs. A good maxim to keep in mind is one that management engineers emphasize in every approach of job evaluation: *Rate the job—not the man.*

Every company has some sort of job evaluation. Even if no formal plan has been set up, a job must be evaluated every time a person is hired and put to work. First of all, the employer must determine what the person is worth or what the job is worth. Thus the job is evaluated (after a fashion) in order to determine the rate of pay.

An evaluation made this way may be a good guess—it may be a poor one. Frequently what happens is that the person who does the best job of selling himself gets the best pay, regardless of the job itself. By the hit-or-miss method of evaluation, one employee may be getting a good salary whereas another, doing much more skilled work or whose job requires more ability and intelligence, will be underpaid by comparison. Much of the dissatisfaction in offices and plants is due to such inequities.

Some time ago, the works manager of an industrial machinery firm expressed the part job evaluation plays: "Job evaluation is a reasonably scientific means of distributing *x* dollars of payroll to any specific group of workers so that each one gets his fair share." Any other concept of job evaluation's contribution is likely to be wrong and may lead to faulty operation of the plan as well as to future salary trouble.

What Will Job Evaluation Accomplish?

It is not, of course, the answer to all problems of employee relations. But since it is tied in with the worker's take-home pay, job evaluation is an important factor in solving some of the problems. Without a fair and equitable salary structure, the chances of maintaining favorable employee relations are likely to be extremely poor. Furthermore, a well-planned and carefully executed job evaluation program which provides for continuous operation can help reduce labor turnover, help fit the right person to the right job, reduce employee grievances over salaries, and enable management to gauge labor costs more accurately. It can also, of course, help to set up a salary structure which more nearly conforms to going rates for the community and the industry.

The majority of companies using job evaluation feel that the program has results in better industrial relations. Many also feel that it has brought lowered unit costs.

Preparing the Organization for Job Evaluation

Because no new program affecting employee relations should be installed without consideration of the company's policies and requirements, it is a good idea to undergo a "period of contemplation" before the first steps are taken toward installing a job evaluation program.

First of all, management must have a clear picture of what the program can accomplish. One way to get such a picture is to analyze the results secured by other companies. Another is to make a list of all the things that are wrong with the company's present wage administration plan. If a clue to such faults is needed it may be found in the salary grievances which have come from employees over a period of time.

Together, these two processes should make it possible to arrive at a list of objectives which a company may reasonably expect to realize through a job evaluation program—provided it is properly set up and maintained.

Another point to consider is determination of company policies. What, for instance, is management going to do about the problem of overpaid jobs? That there will be such a problem is a certainty, for when *employees* are rated instead of *jobs* (as is generally true when there is no job evaluation program) some jobs are bound to be out of line. The general policy followed is to try to upgrade the employee —get him into a higher-rated job which can make better use of his skill. This is preferable to decreasing his salary in line with reclassification of his job.

Another question of policy—one which is exceedingly important— revolves around the matter of union participation. This is a problem which *cannot* be side-stepped. The experience of many companies indicates that it is far better to settle on a definite policy at the very beginning than to muddle along, hoping the matter will work out somehow during the process of getting the evaluation program under way.

It is never easy to shift from the laissez-faire method of handling salaries to a more scientific procedure. Because it goes counter to previous policies, "rating the job and not the worker" will make for changes not only in salary administration, but also in the executive group's attitudes toward the entire salary structure.

THIRTY RESULTS SECURED BY
JOB EVALUATION

As Reported by Companies With Job Evaluation Plans

JOB EVALUATION HAS:

1. Eliminated odd or personalized rates.
2. Smoothed out rate ranges which were out of line.
3. Established definite requirements of skill and responsibility for each operation or job.
4. Allowed for preparation of logical promotional steps.
5. Provided for departmental manuals of value to managers and to those they supervised.
6. Allowed for better job specifications for personnel department which were helpful in considering employee qualifications.
7. Provided a basis for incentive rates.
8. Insured better union relations.
9. Made for a more realistic alignment of job rates.
10. Made possible a uniform schedule of increases.
11. Pointed up overpaid jobs.
12. Provided uniform program for upgrading and testing employees.
13. Eliminated an outmoded bonus system.
14. Insured "equal pay for equal work."
15. Provided for closer control of classifications and rates.
16. Established basis for rates in labor contract wage negotiations.
17. Secured more and better production.
18. Stabilized the employment force.
19. Aided in settling wage disputes and eliminated many wage rate grievances.
20. Decreased per unit cost.
21. Provided for flexibility under wage stabilization program.
22. Provided adequate hiring and merit adjustments.
23. Facilitated setting up new plants or departments.
24. Made better budgetary control possible.
25. Provided better supervisory understanding.
26. Provided sound basis for making area wage surveys.
27. Reduced turnover.
28. Lowered clerical costs.
29. Improved selection, placement, and transfer of employees.
30. Eliminated feeling of favoritism in departments.

Consequently, the executive and supervisory groups should be thoroughly prepared in advance for the new program. This educational process is more important than it would seem to be at first glance, for without cooperation and understanding of department heads and supervisors, the whole evaluation program can well bog down.

Selling the Employee on Job Evaluation

Nor should management fail to prepare rank-and-file employees for the coming of the job evaluation program. Companies with the most success in employee relations consider it poor policy to spring any new plan or activity "cold" on the worker. They always arrange for an adequate selling job to precede important changes in policies that affect employees.

It is virtually impossible to keep secret the first steps of any major change such as introduction of a job evaluation program. Efforts to do so will only result in employees becoming suspicious when the actual process of analysis and rating gets under way. In the case of job evaluation it is particularly poor policy to ignore the natural interest of employees in procedures affecting their income. Further, management is going to need their cooperation if the program is to be a success—and cooperation is difficult to secure if employee and management get off on the wrong foot at the start.

Much suspicion and resentment can be built up by the sudden appearance of someone in the office who goes from one worker to another making notations on the various jobs. Let a group of time-study men or job analysts suddenly appear where the workers are unprepared for their arrival and rumors immediately start going the rounds. The grapevine practically sizzles with misinformation! Management would be considerably startled if it could know how "off the beam" most of these rumors are.

When it is realized how little the average employee actually knows about basic company policies, this reaction can readily be understood. What the worker does not expect and does not fully understand is bound to be resented because he is confused by any sudden change or any deviation from routine practices. When he is prepared for the new procedure and given adequate reasons why the project is undertaken, his reaction is much more favorable—and cooperative. Such efforts make him feel that he is part of the enterprise—that his cooperation and understanding are important and that he, too, is important.

The *modern* procedure is to offer employees a chance to participate in the development of a new program. This makes the new program *their* program as well as the company's.

Announcing the Program

Giving the employee information about new plans and programs can be done by means of bulletins, letters, meetings, use of space in the employee magazine, visual aids (movies or sound-slidefilms), and the public address system. From a check of materials used over the last decade, one of the best vehicles is the employee magazine. The bulletin board seems to be too abrupt—that is, at first. After the program gets under way, attention can be called to its progress by means of posters. It is in the employee magazine, however, that the employee can be told in an informal way about the new program. Such articles can easily answer many of his questions before he even gets around to asking them.

While the majority of companies include some reference to the job evaluation program in the employee manual, only a few have prepared special booklets on the subject for employees. Among these few are the York Corporation and the American Seating Company.

Your Salary is the title of the booklet prepared by the York Corporation to explain the evaluation of its salaried jobs. It is printed in black on white paper stock and makes use of pert cartoons throughout its 12 pages to insure reader interest. The story of job evaluation is told in simple terms easily understood by the average employee. Why and how jobs are evaluated is explained; how committees are set up; and details of the mechanics of job evaluation included. The employee is also told why the following 12 job evaluation factors were chosen: Education, experience, judgment, analysis, originality, responsibility, accuracy, supervision, contacts, independence of action, working conditions, and physical demand. Emphasis is placed on the fact that when all salaries from the lowest to the highest in the corporation have been established through job evaluation, they will conform to the average paid in the community and in the industry for the same types of work.

JOB EVALUATION PROCEDURES

There are three main operations involved in setting job rates. They are: (1) job description, (2) job analysis, and (3) classification. These are the three basic steps, but the whole procedure is much more comprehensive. The overall picture of the entire program, step

WHAT IS JOB EVALUATION?

As the company is about to undertake a program of JOB EVALUATION and as the success of such a program depends to a great extent upon your cooperation, there will be a series of discussion meetings for the purpose of getting better acquainted with the whole subject. The schedule for these meetings appears below. In the meantime, the following is a brief outline of the purposes and scope of job evaluation:

WHAT IS JOB EVALUATION?

There is no mystery in job evaluation. This is simply the process whereby the relative values of jobs are determined.

DOES JOB EVALUATION RATE THE WORKER?

Job evaluation rates the job, not the man.

DOES JOB EVALUATION DETERMINE RATES OF PAY?

Job evaluation does not determine rates of pay, but does establish proportional comparisons which allow for the determination of rates of pay.

DOES JOB EVALUATION DECREASE THE AMOUNT IN THE PAY ENVELOPE?

The purpose of job evaluation is not to increase or decrease the amount in the pay envelope. Rather, it makes for a more equitable basis of wage rates.

HOW ARE THE DUTIES AND REQUIREMENTS OF A JOB DETERMINED?

The duties and requirements of a job are determined by a job analyst who will secure this information from employees on the job. From this information, job descriptions will be prepared which will be approved by the employee concerned and by his department head.

WHO MAKES THE JOB EVALUATION?

A special committee makes the job evaluation. This committee will consist of two representatives of management, two employees, and an impartial member.

WHAT FACTORS WILL BE CONSIDERED?

The following factors will be considered in the analysis:

Skill Requirements	Physical Requirements
Mental Requirements	Working Conditions

SCHEDULE OF MEETINGS:

A bulletin sent to supervisors to announce a series of meetings to launch a job evaluation program.

by step, conforms pretty much to the following pattern:

1. Determine company policies on wage rates.
2. Select committee members, including subcommittees.
3. Set time limits on the program.
4. Determine job factors.
5. Select job analysts.
6. Establish educational and training procedures.
7. Prepare job descriptions.
    a. Get necessary information regarding jobs from:
        (1) Interviews with workers.
        (2) Interviews with supervisors.
    b. Prepare rough draft of job on a regular job description form.
    c. Submit rough draft of job for approval by employee on the job and his immediate superior. (Another step may take place here if approval is not secured.)
    d. Submit all job descriptions (when approved) in a department to the department head for his approval.
8. Classify jobs according to their relative difficulty expressed in terms of job evaluation points.
9. Set salaries in accordance with findings.
10. Check results by crafts and the labor market.
11. Review job titles and job descriptions.
12. Prepare the job manual.
13. Arrange for maintenance of plan.
14. Set up re-evaluation program.

While these steps will vary somewhat from company to company in the order of procedure, they are not likely to vary much as to content. In other words, they are the steps that will be required if the program is to be complete and if it is to continue functioning once it has been installed.

A company contemplating a job evaluation program may find it helpful to set up such a check list in order to determine in advance just what the procedure must include. It may even be more helpful if a time limit is assigned to each of the steps since this will give impetus to the plan and prevent it from becoming stalled on dead center.

Job Evaluation Committees

Before the job evaluation program can get under way, committees must be appointed to handle the policies and details of the plan. The main committee, usually called the steering committee, is made up of representatives of management and labor (where unions are involved)—generally two representatives of management, two of labor, and one or two impartial members.

The number of subcommittees to be set up will be determined chiefly by the size of the company and whether the organization is centralized or decentralized. The small company with a well-knit centralized organization may be able to operate with just one committee—the steering committee. However, the company which has branches and plants through the country will require many subcommittees to carry out the program.

One comparatively large company in the Midwest set up seven job analysis committees consisting of four salary committees, one wage committee, one field salary committee (nonselling), and one sales salary committee.

The Job Analysis Committee

The plan of procedure generally provides for an evaluation or job analysis committee which must define the requirements of each job or occupation and evaluate the relative importance of those requirements.

Management representatives should always include those who are most intimate with the jobs being evaluated; i.e., foremen, supervisors, superintendents. The inclusion of these people on the committee helps to speed up the procedure considerably inasmuch as they are more familiar than others with all the aspects of individual jobs in office or plant. The impartial member of the steering committee frequently acts as the chairman of the job analysis committee and is responsible for the selection of the job analysts.

The job analysts, who are generally selected from the rank-and-file employees, must be chosen with great care. They are often selected by merit rating, but when a company has no merit-rating information, they may be asked to volunteer for the job. The group of volunteers can then be screened by simple tests which will determine analytical ability, ability to handle details, and ability to get along with others. Selectees should also have a good reputation for accuracy and general "know-how."

It is not difficult to train carefully selected employees to do a good job of analysis. They must, of course, learn the correct terminology of the job analysis process and understand and be able to differentiate between physical effort and working conditions; between mental effort and skilled effort; between the requirements of a job and the responsibilities of that job.

How a Textile Firm Set Up Its Committee

A company in the textile field in the East set up a job evaluation committee consisting of seven permanent members. The chairman was the assistant general manager of the company and other members included the personnel manager, the controller, a job analyst, and three plant superintendents. Provision was made for additional members to be added temporarily at the discretion of the permanent committee.

The position of job analyst on this committee was described and his work defined as follows:

The position of job analyst has been established and is under the direct supervision of the personnel manager. The analyst will act as a technical co-ordinating head for the company-wide evaluation program. The responsibility of the job analyst will include the following:

1. Instructing and directing in the correct procedure all representatives of management who are called upon to prepare job descriptions.
2. Supervising the development of job descriptions by department superintendents.
3. Reviewing all job descriptions.
4. Evaluating the description of each applicable occupation within the company in accordance with accepted company policy and procedures.
5. Reviewing and securing approval of all evaluations from the department superintendent of jobs within his line of authority.
6. Contacting each department superintendent at regular intervals for the purpose of reviewing each job under his jurisdiction to determine and record any and all changes in job content that may have occurred since the preceding review. Any corresponding changes in evaluation which are required are to be made concurrently.

The part the department superintendent played in helping the job analyst carry out his assignment was defined by this company as follows:

Each department superintendent shall assume the following responsibilities in respect to occupations falling under his line supervision:

1. Reviewing and approving each job description as prepared by those designated by the department superintendent.

2. Reviewing and approving, in conjunction with those selected by the department superintendent, each job evaluation prepared by the job analyst.

3. Conferring with job analyst at regular intervals for the purpose of outlining any changes in job content of occupations within his jurisdiction which may have occurred since the preceding review.

4. As any changes in job descriptions occur, the job analyst shall be notified immediately of such changes, so that a re-evaluation of the revised job description can be promptly made.

Getting the Committees to Work

Everyone who has had any experience with committees knows how easy it is for them to get stalled. Part of this is due to buck-passing and part to the fact that no one person has any *real authority* to push the job through from start to finish. In order to get a committee down to work and to keep it working, management must back up the person who is to be responsible for the job with sufficient authority to keep things in motion.

One of the most effective ways to get the job evaluation committee going is to set up a "deadline" or time limit for the job. The committee should estimate the number of jobs to be evaluated and then specify the time when they should be written up and ready for review. One management engineering firm suggests building a schedule chart which would list the various departments to be covered and the individual jobs in each.

At the minimum, the chart should indicate the time allotted for finishing each department. However, the committee may go even further than this and indicate the time allotted for each individual job. As each employee is interviewed, the date and the initials of the interviewer are entered on the chart.

Securing Union Cooperation

Some companies seem to have had unusual success in getting union cooperation in the job evaluation program; some have gone ahead with the program in spite of failure of the union to cooperate; while still others have given up the idea completely because of union opposition.

Generally speaking, the first reaction of a union to the suggestion of job evaluation is one of suspicion. There is an underlying fear that management is out to reduce wages or to straitjacket them. It is readily understandable that inasmuch as one of the prerogatives of the union is wage negotiation, any attempt to put such matters on another footing will arouse resentment. In companies where good labor relations have prevailed over a period of time, there is less likelihood of active opposition.

Most companies have found that a well-planned educational program will do a great deal toward smoothing the path and make it easier for management and labor to get together on an evaluation program. This educational program may take a little time, but in the long run it will pay for itself many times over.

While most companies take the initiative in securing union cooperation, the union sometimes makes overtures to management. In at least one case, the union itself has asked for a job classification. In another, the union suggested that the principle of job evaluation be applied instead of a general increase. In still another case, both the union and the company felt that a job evaluation program was necessary. Unknown to each other, each went to a well-known management engineer to check on such a program. While the union was still talking it over, the company hired the management engineer to do the job, telling him at the time that the union was violently opposed to job evaluation. When negotiations got under way, the engineer (unknown to the company) was better informed than management was as to what labor wanted.

Even though representatives of labor may not be included in the committee membership, it is a good idea to arrange for their attendance at meetings when jobs are evaluated and points set up. At this time, many difficulties may be ironed out which could cause trouble later on. As one industrial relations director explains: "Getting approval on each job description at the time it is written up, prevents stalling of the program when it is ready to go into operation. It certainly throws a monkey wrench into the proceedings if some job descriptions are found to be unacceptable just when the evaluations are about to be approved!"

One organization, the H. B. Maynard and Co., Inc., management engineers, has found in its experience with job evaluation work that getting labor representatives to participate in the work is the best way to sell the program to the union. H. B. Maynard, chairman, states:

> Where a union is involved we always make it a point to take them in on the study from the very outset. Working with them and with members of management, we develop step by step the job descriptions and job evaluations. By the time this part of the job is done, it is sold to all concerned because they have all had a part in developing it. There remains then only the task of making wage surveys and determining a reasonable wage scale which is subjected to collective bargaining for approval.

Those companies which seem to have the least difficulty selling the union on a job evaluation program are those in which an evaluation plan was in operation before the office was organized. The union, in such cases, seems to accept the program as a matter of course. One company which had a job evaluation program set up under such conditions, reported that the union not only accepted the entire program but also asked to have specific jobs (previously omitted from the program) evaluated in order to get the proper rates set up.

There are actually two schools of thought regarding union participation. One favors participation of the union from the very beginning when the job evaluation committee is set up. The idea is to secure cooperation all along the line so that when the job analysis is completed and salary rates are determined, the union will be in complete agreement. A hitch in the proceedings when the program is about to be put into operation may well delay installation of the plan for many months.

The other school of thought favors leaving the union out of the picture until job analysis is completed. At this point, union representatives may be consulted on the contents of various jobs in order to make sure that every factor has been given proper credit. The union will still have the opportunity to review the program and to negotiate with management on items with which it disagrees. This presupposes that there is no clause in the union contract which provides for union participation in the work of the committees.

It should be remembered, however, that even though the labor union may recognize the value of job evaluation, it may hesitate to enter into any joint sponsorship for fear of being party to a commitment which would set up a pattern too rigid for future salary negotiations. Management must be prepared to meet this argument when it gets ready to sell the union on participation.

Job evaluation is sometimes sold to the union during the period of negotiation and is then made a part of the labor contract. Following is the type of clause usually set up in such an agreement on job evaluation:

When a new job is created which has not been evaluated or any major change occurs in a job that has been evaluated, the company will, within 30 days, assign it to an appropriate labor grade by the regular job evaluation procedure then in effect and immediately will notify the union in writing of its action. A major change shall be one which is sufficient to place the job in either a higher or a lower labor grade. Any dispute shall be subject to the grievance and arbitration procedure.

Another important point in the matter of union cooperation is that is can help to clear up a number of job-class differences which

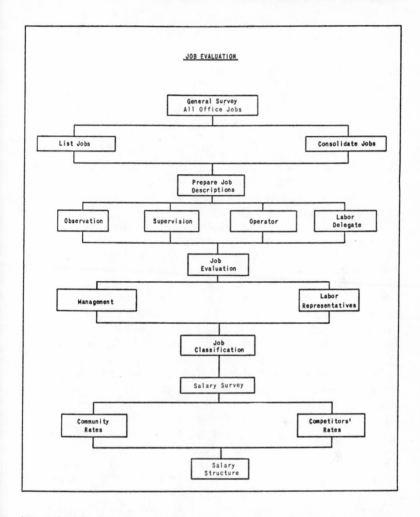

have already been responsible for grievances. Through such participation, management may be able to get the union to agree not to turn job-class questions into grievances. Such questions can then be brought up for committee analysis before they assume the importance of a grievance.

If cooperation is secured, management may also be able to set up an informal agreement which will make it possible to settle, by re-analysis, a number of questions on job classification. Such questions may not properly be considered as grievances but they still cause a great deal of friction, distrust, and irritation between union and management.

Job Evaluation and the Supervisor

The supervisor must be shown just what job analysis can contribute in the way of better supervision. When he realizes that the results will be of as much benefit to him as to the company, then he will be assured that the program is something to get behind and push. Job analysis alone makes for better supervision because it gives the supervisor an opportunity to evaluate all the jobs under his control and thereby improve the routines.

It should be explained to the supervisor that many jobs are likely to contain a mixture of high- and low-grade work in one job. This often happens in a department when, in changing workers, additional work is given to a newcomer because he knows how to do it— not because the extra work goes with the job. Thus, after a time, many workers are doing a number of tasks involving a higher or lower type of work than that for which they are being paid. Job analysis leads to an improvement in such job classifications by means of specialization. It also happens that by narrowing jobs so that they take in less territory, the training period can be reduced for new workers and additional help can be added to a department in less time than it might ordinarily take.

The supervisor should also be made to understand that job descriptions reveal overlapping where it exists. This is particularly true of jobs involving responsibility and authority. Removal of overlapping prepares the way for a smoother organization.

All this makes for easier and better supervision, and it is this phase of job evaluation that appeals the most to the supervisory group. In handling a meeting for supervisors on job evaluation, therefore, it is best to cover *results in terms of supervision* in order to sell the group on the whole program.

Careful job evaluation also makes it possible to select, transfer, and promote employees with much greater skill and accuracy. Knowing the exact requirements of a given job makes it easier to set up the proper training program for such a job. It makes it possible to arrange for training that will cover not only the job the applicant is to fill, but to bridge the gap between that job and the next higher one so the employee is better prepared for the next step up. This, too, is an angle of job evaluation which should be interesting to the supervisory group. Promotions and upgrading are not easy to handle if there is a lack of definite policy to follow.

Most management engineers are emphatic on the desirability of securing the cooperation of supervisory groups. So important do they consider this phase of job evaluation, they have been known to decline to take on a job whenever opportunity to inform and educate the supervisory group is denied them by the company. Usually, this part of their service is an integral part of the job evaluation plan and is explained as such at the time the ramifications of the plan are discussed with the company. Therefore, if an outside organization has been retained to handle the installation of job evaluation, the task of selling supervisors on the program will generally be theirs.

In addition to giving supervisors information and making them feel that they are an important part of the program, meetings between the outside consultant and the supervisory group have another purpose—to get the program off on the right foot. These meetings usually follow the procedure already described, wherein supervisors are given information regarding (1) the importance of the job evaluation program, (2) the need for such a program, and (3) the overall results of job evaluation.

Improving Employee Morale

The job evaluation project offers an excellent opportunity to improve employee morale, provided the supervisory group has been sold on the program and takes a real part in its installation. When the supervisor participates actively in preparing job descriptions and in helping to make job analyses, he will have considerable contact with each worker in his department. The talks between supervisor and worker on job evaluation help to make the worker's job seem more important to the organization. This is particularly true if the supervisor has been properly prepared for this contact work.

The fact that job evaluation leads to more intelligent selection and promotion of employees and that it eliminates favoritism and bias, tends to improve employee morale. If a real effort is made through the supervisor to present such a picture to all his employees, management will be able to realize this important by-product of the job evaluation program.

Chapter 8

JOB EVALUATION IN ACTION

THERE are four generally accepted systems of job analysis. They are: Job Ranking Method, Classification Method, Point Evaluation Method, Factor Comparison Method.

Some management engineers favor one method, some another. Before the job evaluation committee decides which system should be used, it may be well for the managing engineer or some other qualified person to study the four methods to learn which would be the most suitable. Sometimes a better program can result from a combination of the best features of two or three systems.

The first method—Job Ranking—takes into account the entire job and compares it with all other jobs in the department, the division, or the company. The system is set up by having department managers, supervisors, and executives rank various jobs under their jurisdiction in the order of their importance. The opinions of those participating in the job ranking are then averaged and salary and wage ranges are established in accordance with the averages.

One of the objections to this method is the difficulty of ranking jobs. Few persons are really familiar enough with the intricacies of all jobs under their control to rank them intelligently. The larger and more complex the organization, the more obvious this objection becomes. Thus the method is usually confined to companies having relatively few jobs to be rated.

Another disadvantage is that ranking may be done without the use of job descriptions and as a result existing rates for these jobs may sway judgment. Furthermore, the lack of records may make it difficult to defend the relative rank of jobs. When it comes to revising rates, the job analyst may find it almost impossible to back up his reasons.

The second, or Classification, method (sometimes called Predetermined Grading) is based on a process of establishing uniform salary ranges and general job classifications. This method is not only logical, but it is, necessarily, a part of the average salary administration plan. It has met with small success, however, because classifying jobs by job levels is usually done by department heads who, having already set up approximate values for each job, tend to distribute jobs in accordance with the salaries of those already in them. It is obvious that this tendency is likely to continue any inequalities already existing. Because it is the way in which the system is applied rather than the system itself that causes the difficulty, devising a better way to classify jobs makes the classification method more practical.

The Point Evaluation Method and the Factor Comparison System are actually variations of the same process since they both break down jobs into component factors or job elements. The chief difference between the two methods is that the Point Evaluation Plan compares the job against a point scale, whereas the Factor Comparison Method compares job against job. Actually, the Factor Comparison Method is a refinement of the Point Evaluation Process. It is, however, a little more difficult to explain to employees and requires a more intensive selling job on the part of management. Some of the failures management has experienced with this method are due not so much to the method itself as to its own failure to sell the employee (and supervision) on the process. Because both methods provide for a better analysis of the individual job, they are to be preferred generally to either the Job Ranking or Classification Methods.

The two systems take advantage of the fact that all jobs possess certain attributes or elements in common and thus make it possible to compare unrelated jobs or job classifications. Without a factor breakdown, it would be quite impossible, for instance, to compare such jobs as porter and stenographer. Comparative factors must be set up as a basis of comparison.

The Point Rating System

In applying the Point System of job evaluation, the attributes or characteristics common to all jobs are considered separately; points are assigned to show the relative amounts of each characteristic found in each job, and the total number of points is then converted to a salary rate. The Point Plan is the one most widely used, principally because it is not difficult to apply and is easily understood by the average person.

Generally speaking, point rating involves the following steps:

1. Establish and define a series of basic factors, usually around five or 10

in number, which are common to most jobs and which reflect the principal elements of value inherent in all jobs.

2. Define the degrees of each factor.
3. Establish the maximum points to be accredited to each factor.
4. Establish the maximum points to be accredited to each degree of each factor.
5. Prepare a job description of each job, arranged to show the extent to which each factor is applicable.
6. Convert the job points into dollars.

Here is how one company, using the Point Rating System, has set up its point ranges:

Job Grade	Point Range	Job Grade	Point Range
1	140-159	7	260-279
2	160-179	8	280-299
3	180-199	9	300-319
4	200-219	10	320-339
5	220-239	11	340-359
6	240-259	12	360-379

The attributes and point values used in determining the value of a job are as follows:

The relative value of a job is considered to depend on the following attributes which are present in varying degrees in the various jobs. These attributes are not of equal importance, and to give recognition to these differences in importance, weights or points are assigned to each degree of each attribute in accordance with the following table. Any job under consideration will properly fall into some one of the several degrees of each attribute.

JOB ATTRIBUTE	1st Degree	2nd Degree	3rd Degree	4th Degree	5th Degree
Skill					
1. Education	14	28	42	56	70
2. Experience	22	44	66	88	110
3. Initiative and Ingenuity	14	28	42	56	70
Effort					
4. Physical Demand	10	20	30	40	50
5. Mental or Visual Demand	5	10	15	20	25
Responsibility					
6. Equipment or Process	5	10	15	20	25
7. Material or Product	5	10	15	20	25
8. Safety of Others	5	10	15	20	25
9. Work of Others	5	10	15	20	25
Job Conditions					
10. Working Conditions	10	20	30	40	50
11. Unavoidable Hazards	5	10	15	20	25

The Cessna Aircraft Company, Wichita, Kansas, uses a combination of factor-comparison and point-rating systems as a method of establishing job relationship.

The personnel department is responsible for describing, analyzing, and evaluating all jobs. Personnel executives are further responsible for establishing wage structures and for administering a wage and salary program.

The shop job-rating plan considers skill, effort, responsibility, and job conditions. The office and technical plan considers skill, monetary responsibility, contacts, and supervisory responsibility.

A variety of techniques is used to gather facts concerning the assignment of job duties. The analyst may use a questionnaire to be completed by the job incumbent. He may observe the employee at work or he may interview the employee at his work station. In all cases he will interview the employee's immediate supervisor to determine what has been assigned to the job.

The final job description is approved by management.

Determining the Factors

As the job analyst cannot begin his work until the job factors have been decided upon, the first step in job analysis procedure is to determine what job characteristics or job factors should be included.

There are usually four main characteristics to be considered in analyzing a job. These are Skill, Responsibility, Effort, and Working Conditions. Each of these elements may be broken down further so that there may be 20 or more factors altogether.

In choosing factors, it is important to make sure that all the fundamental elements reflecting the full value and relative importance of all jobs be included. There is no set number of factors to be considered in job evaluation, however. Some management engineers use as few as eight while others favor the use of 20 or more. One expert in the field believes that upward of 30 factors are necessary to do a thorough job of evaluation. The usual tendency today is to keep the number as low as possible for simplicity's sake.

When the factors have been selected it becomes necessary to define them and determine their degrees in terms that can be readily understood. It is extremely important to have these definitions set up clearly and concisely for they will be used later as a basis for classifying all jobs and assigning points. The aim should be to make the definitions brief without sacrificing clarity.

Each factor, then, is assigned a certain point value range. The reason for this is obvious—various factors are not of equal value, although they do have a definite relationship to each other.

How are these point values determined? When companies first pioneered in the field of job evaluation, they had to use the trial-and-error method to establish point allotments. Today, the management engineer has the benefit of many plans previously devised and, consequently, there is an established uniformity in the point weighing in most evaluation plans. Certain standards are set up which make it possible to rate the same job in any given organization by any individual reasonably familiar with the substance of the various factors.

For example, the maximum point values for each factor may be indicated as follows:

Job Factor	Maximum Evaluation Points
Mental requirements	150
Skill	
Experience and training	200
Dexterity	100
Responsibility	
Materials and equipment	150
Safety of others	25
Working conditions	
Personal hazard	50
Surroundings	50
Physical effort or fatigue	75
Total	800

These are the maximum point values and indicate, of course, the highest evaluation possible in rating an occupation. On Mental Requirements, for instance, an occupation may be rated as low as 25; on Skill, as low as 5 points; on Personal Hazard, the assigned points may run as low as 10 points.

There is no mathematical formula that can be relied upon to compute the exact percentage of a total point allotment which should be accredited to any one of the factors; decisions as to the actual allotment must be the result of judgment and past experience.

This method of rating jobs may be compared somewhat with the method of grading examination papers in school. Proper wording and grammar, for instance, would count more (get more points) in an English course than accuracy and neatness. However, accuracy would count more in arithmetic than neatness, wording, and grammar. Thus the number of points will naturally vary with the nature of the job. Some jobs require more experience than others, some more education, and others more mental effort. The individual factors must be weighed in order to take into consideration these differences.

Job Classification Procedure

When determining salary rates, it is usually a good idea to group jobs of approximately the same rating in classes, each class to cover a certain rating range. This results in fewer rates and greater rate differentials from one class to another.

In actual practice, this works out about as follows. A fairly large-sized manufacturer has, say, 220 different kinds of jobs. Let us assume that the 220 different kinds of jobs fall into 10 main groups. Assuming that all employees in each job group are "equal" in performance, the salary-point relationship would, in chart form, be something like that shown in the job values chart which follows. This shows the step-up in pay in proportion to the number of points required for each job group.

Each job group, however, has variations depending upon the amount of knowledge, skill, and experience required to perform the jobs within the various groups. Assuming there are four degrees of such knowledge, skill, and experience required, then each salary group would be broken into four sections and each section evaluated accordingly. When allowances are made for the four sections within each job group, the salary-point relationship would be like that shown in the chart.

When setting up job classifications and specifications, it is important to look ahead to a national emergency. We might expect a heavy drain on manpower for the Armed Services. An employer should know how many workers of draft age would be called to the colors, how many replacements would be needed to maintain the working force, and the minimum skill that can be accepted for each classification. Since salaries and wages will be frozen without warning in the event of another emergency, the farsighted employer will establish minimum and maximum pay ranges for each classification, breaking down each main classification into as many subclassifications as feasible. This is to provide an employer with as much turning room as possible in case of another pay freeze, so that employees can be moved up from one job classification to another without the ne-

JOB VALUES SHOWN IN POINTS BY JOB GROUPS AND BY VARIATIONS WITHIN JOB GROUPS

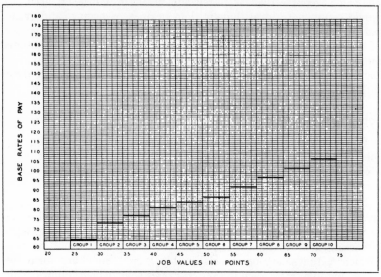

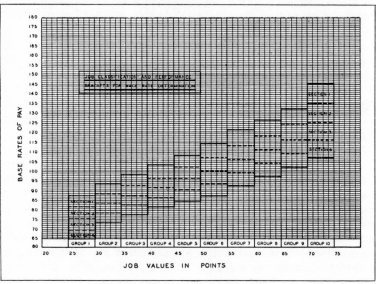

The top chart shows a salary-point relationship where all employees are "equal." Below, allowances are made for different degrees of skill and knowledge required of workers.

cessity of applying to a wage control board for authority to grant an increase in salaries. Such foresightedness will put the company in a favorable position when it comes to competing for office help.

Automation Brings Change

Another good reason for an active job evaluation program is the changing face of the office. New equipment and new techniques call for a new classification in some cases. As fast as new jobs are created, it is a wise move to provide for them within the basic structure. If old employees are going to do the work, they will be very interested in their new prospects. If new personnel is needed, both the new jobs and their relationship to the regular jobs will have to be evaluated.

JOB DESCRIPTIONS

Before jobs can be analyzed, they must be described, so an important step in job evaluation is preparing or setting up the descriptions of various occupations. It is important that descriptions be accurate and foolproof because they will become part of the employment and advancement routine.

Descriptions should be exact, simple, and clear statements of what the worker is expected to do on his particular job. Much of the verbiage can be eliminated from descriptions if such phrases as these are omitted: "Must know something about," "must be able to," "should be interested," etc. Not only do these phrases make the job description sheets unduly long, but they are subject to numerous interpretations by those who are concerned with what each employee must be capable of doing in a particular job.

There are several ways of securing job descriptions. They may be prepared by an analyst; they may be written up by the individual employee; or they may be worked out by the supervisor for all those jobs under his jurisdiction.

To obtain uniformity, however, employees and supervisors need help in writing up descriptions. While the employee may know more about his job than anyone else and the supervisor may know more about the jobs in his particular department, still it is not always possible for these people to be able to view the jobs with which they are so familiar as an integral part of the whole organization. Therefore, when preparing descriptions, the worker or supervisor may overemphasize the responsibilities and functions of their jobs. In addition, while they may be able to *think* in terms of their jobs, *written* descriptions are another matter. Few individuals can write clear, concise, and comprehensive job descriptions, even when they know them thoroughly.

Some companies have been unusually successful in securing job descriptions by means of questionnaires. However, the usual way of securing the information is through interviews with workers and supervisors. The main objection to the questionnaire method is that, as a rule, no one questionnaire can be set up which will cover all jobs. Thus, a company may find it necessary to set up dozens of questionnaires—no small undertaking. Another point in favor of gathering information by the interview method is that greater accuracy will be realized, resulting in descriptions which are more likely to stand the test of classification criticism that may be brought up later.

The proper person to secure interviews with employees is the job analyst. In a small company, one person may be able to do this work, but in a medium-sized or large company, it will require several. This part of the job is generally coordinated under the chairman of the job analysis committee which is responsible for training analysts in the technique of preparing necessary information for setting up the descriptions.

The job description should indicate: (1) What the employee does, (2) how he does it, and (3) the conditions under which he does it. Furthermore, the summary or description must be broad enough to include all those who do a particular kind of work, yet it must exclude, beyond any question or doubt, all those working on other jobs.

It is also important that the analyst make certain that descriptions indicate, for each job described, the relative values of all the job evaluation factors—skill, effort, responsibilities, and working conditions.

How Jobs Are Analyzed

The job analyst secures the necessary information regarding individual jobs by interviews with workers on their jobs. Next, he reviews this information with the worker's immediate supervisor for the purpose of verifying the information received from the worker. The job description is then written up and presented to both the worker and his supervisor for their approval. If there is disagreement regarding the job description, the department head is called into conference with the worker and the supervisor.

After descriptions are written up for each job in a department, they are submitted to the head of that department for his approval. It is a good idea to make up a departmental summary sheet to cover each department. Such a summary makes it possible to tell at a glance how many job titles or occupations there are in each department and how they are correlated with the main job factors. The summary may also indicate the maximum number of points required for each occupation. An example of a departmental summary form is shown in this chapter.

Department heads concerned with the classifications should be consulted before the forms are filled out, and their approval secured once they are completed.

Administering the Job Evaluation Program

Before final classifications are approved and put into operation, all salary groupings or classifications should be checked against the prevailing salary structure for the community. This is important because it would be poor policy for a company to set up evaluated rates so low as to enable other companies in the locality to get the cream of available workers. It would also be poor policy to set rates so high as to imperil the surrounding labor market. While this situation may never present any trouble, it is a good idea to make certain that it cannot do so. Furthermore, since workers today are well informed regarding going rates in their communities they resent any effort to pay less than those rates.

JOB EVALUATION SUMMARY

A departmental summary form used by the analyst in job evaluation

At one time, securing comparative rates was a difficult if not impossible task because of the great secrecy surrounding them. Today, however, the picture is different. Most companies now—even competitors—are willing to aid in a community check.

When making comparisons, it is important to make certain that the other employers' job classifications are similar to yours. It is useless to compare salaries for jobs which have similar titles but are dissimilar in content. And titles can be exceedingly misleading. Therefore, clear and accurate descriptions are essential for proper comparison. This means that salary studies should be made of *actual jobs,* not job titles. Too often companies are satisfied with passing rate sheets back and forth in order to set up comparative rates.

A short cut in setting up comparative salary-rate sheets is to compare job titles at the time the job descriptions are being set up. The usual procedure is to secure job description forms from other companies in the same locality and then to check each form against the job titles you have set up. No attempt should be made to follow these forms to the point where your own form will be exactly identical. The idea is simply to use the other forms as a guide in setting up your own description titles. Once the job titles have met the comparison test, it is an easy matter to compare rates later, and there will be no danger of camparing like titles for jobs unlike in content.

THE JOB EVALUATION MANUAL

By the time the job evaluation study is finished, the job manual is, in fact, completed. Job titles have been determined, job descriptions set up, and the rate groups specified. The information has been gathered and all that remains to be done is to put it together in logical form in writing.

If an outside organization is handling the job evaluation study, it will prepare the job manual as the work progresses. If, however, the study is being made by the company itself, then the job manual is prepared by the job analyst or by the salary committee.

If job evaluation is being installed in both office and plant, it is well to set up two separate manuals—one for the office and one for the plant. The characteristics or factors for both kinds of jobs are dissimilar, and the classifications will be used by supervisors of two different groups of employees.

The job manual is complete only after all factors have been determined, definitions of degree written, and the points assigned to each degree. In addition to job descriptions and rates, job manuals may also cover company policies in respect to salaries and wages and include an outline of the merit-rating plan and/or seniority rate increase procedure, if one has been established. Thus, the department head or any member of the supervisory group has all the general rules and regulations at hand regarding salary increases as well as the rates for each job.

Most of the job manuals in use today range in size from 4 by 6 inches to 9 by 11 inches, but the majority are around 8½ by 11 inches, in loose-leaf binders. The loose-leaf type of manual is a good choice since it permits the addition of reclassifications at a later date.

A common mistake made in preparing the job manual is to set it up on a poor grade of paper which soon becomes yellowed and dog-eared with handling. The expense of a better grade of paper is so slight it is well warranted, since it not only will stand up better under constant use, but it will have a psychological effect on the supervisory group using it. Management engineers have found that a good-looking, sturdy manual lends importance to the job evaluation program and helps to sell supervision on the plan.

By-Products of Job Evaluation

Jobs are not static and it therefore follows that job evaluation cannot be static, either. Allowances must be made for reclassification of old jobs as their content changes and for the addition of new jobs as operations change or are modified by technological improvements. To fail to take into consideration the necessity for such changes is the same thing as admitting that the job evaluation is complete at any one time and that it may be filed away and considered finished.

Nothing is further from the truth. Not only must job evaluation be considered a continuing process, but preliminary preparations for a job evaluation study should be based on this concept. From the very beginning of the program, provision should be made for restudy and reclassification of jobs.

Furthermore, if the program is not administered from the start as a *permanent* feature, the company will fail to receive the full value of the job evaluation installation since its purpose goes well beyond analyzing, describing, and rating jobs. These are only the initial processes; there is a broader meaning to the whole program if it is properly planned. The real value of a well-organized and properly installed job evaluation program lies in the resulting by-products. What are some of these? They will vary in individual cases, but over a period of time such by-products should include the following:

1. Control of turnover by reduction of discontent over salary rates.
2. Improved hiring practices by fitting the right person to the right job.
3. More amicable relations with the labor union if there is one.
4. Reduction of employee grievances.
5. Provide a basis for the incentive plan.
6. Gauge of labor costs each year.
7. Reduction of labor costs by providing a balanced salary structure.
8. More intelligent basis for promotion and transfers.
9. Improvement of routines and procedures in departments.
10. Provision for proper instruction of new workers.

It is in the maintenance of the program that most of these by-products will be realized. By achieving them the job evaluation program pays for itself over and over again. Failure to realize results like these simply increases the total cost of any job evaluation installation.

RE-EVALUATION

It has already been pointed out that the job evaluation committee usually includes one member who is responsible for the job analysis procedure. When the study is completed it is usually this individual who becomes chairman of the reclassification committee and takes charge of maintaining the program.

Because of his experience in making the analyses of the various jobs in the plant, the job analyst is the ideal person to handle re-evaluations of old jobs or evaluation of new ones as they are added. His work is so important to the success of maintaining the program that he should be selected for the job with very great care.

Before he begins to analyze jobs, someone in authority should decide whether the job analyst will concern himself with job evaluation only, or if he will go further afield and look for better methods of work performance. If time is a factor—that is, if the company must put through the job evaluation program in a hurry—then the job analyst will probably have to confine himself simply to the process of analyzing the jobs in each department. Even under those circumstances, he can make supplementary notes of situations which seem to require correction and put them aside for a special committee to consider after the job evaluation installation is completed. He would not, of course, discuss such things with supervisors or workers on the spot. They can await the later attention of the committee. In this way the analyst can pick up numerous worthwhile ideas which will eventually be helpful to management. In fact, such ideas may more than offset the whole cost of the evaluation program.

The need for job re-evaluation may exist because:

1. The job has changed in content.

2. The department has expanded.

3. Personnel factors.

The first two reasons are self-explanatory. The third may be a result of any one of several factors. A good example is the job which has been held by an unusually efficient person who has initiative and originality. He quits, and a replacement of the same caliber is not available. Consequently, the job will have to be broken down further, making re-evaluation necessary. This circumstance is particularly true when jobs have been filled in a hit-or-miss fashion and some individuals have gradually assumed additional duties or functions not inherent in their particular jobs simply because they are capable of handling more varied and more difficult types of work.

Part of maintaining the job evaluation plan is the review of jobs at regular intervals. In order to insure that job content has not changed for any of the jobs in the office, it is well to have each supervisor review all job descriptions covering positions in his department or group at least once a year.

Another precaution to take which will insure correct job descriptions is to provide for a definite system of rotation so that all job descriptions are rewritten once every five years. This procedure eliminates any possibility that a job may gradually change in content over a period of time until the original job description no longer fits it.

WHO SHOULD RUN THE PROGRAM?

When it comes to installing a job evaluation program, one of the first, sometimes troublesome, questions is: "Who should do the job?" This is a question that can be answered only by management itself since there is no cut-and-dried approach. An outside organization and the company's own employees can both do the job well; each approach has its advantages.

In support of an outside organization, one company official said recently: "I am strongly of the opinion that a well-qualified management engineering firm is necessary to job evaluation since job evaluation itself requires an analytical and detached approach to each job. It is difficult, if not entirely impossible, for one person within an industrial organization to have this viewpoint. There are many other reasons to be considered, too, such as the saving of time that results from having an outside organization undertake such studies, the assurance of a broad experience in arriving at evaluation, and the ability to rate jobs from knowledge of many similar jobs in comparable companies."

Because job evaluation requires the kind of technical training and background of experience not usually to be found in the average company, it is often advisable to call in a management engineer to handle the job.

If time is a critical factor and the evaluations must be prepared quickly, it will be hard to give members of the company's regular staff the thorough training and preparation essential to the undertaking. Under such circumstances, an outside organization will provide the answer to the problem.

If job descriptions and classifications are to be used in negotiations with the union later on, they must be set up with the utmost technical skill. A poorly prepared job evaluation by company employees with little experience and technical knowledge may do untold damage to good labor relations and leave many a loophole to cause serious complications later.

The outside organization is not involved in the company's minor politics—and politics are bound to appear in the best of companies. The company employee may find it difficult to make recommendations or to get management to make changes without treading on someone's toes. The outsider, of course, is not afraid of becoming "unpopular" and, therefore, is not afraid of the effects his decisions will have on various groups.

Another point to consider is that the outside organization will usually tailor the job evaluation plan to fit the company. Too often, when the company installs the program itself, it makes the mistake of trying to use a standard plan "as is." The best results in job evaluation can be achieved only when the plan is tailored to the company's needs.

When the Company Handles the Job Evaluation Program

Because job evaluation is a technical project rather than a scientific one, it is possible for any company to set up its own program, *provided* it has an engineering staff which can handle such technical matters as wage incentive plans, merit rating, time studies, and job evaluation. Without the necessary technical knowledge, however, there is little chance of doing a really good job with the program. Furthermore, if the staff has had no experience in working out a job evaluation program it must necessarily do a bit of experimenting before getting fully launched on the project. This takes extra time which adds to the cost.

When the program is handled by the company it is usually set up by the company's industrial engineering department. In some cases— usually in the retail or banking fields—the controller's department may handle the program. The office manager and personnel department will also be concerned with the job since they will supply some of the staff for the project and be responsible for maintaining the records.

An obvious advantage when the company handles the job itself is the uncovering of intimate details of each job which are valuable in the selection and placement of new employees. This one factor alone, however, will not offset the damage which may be done to employee morale or to labor relations as a result of a poor job.

Nor will the use of "home talent" serve to cut the hidden costs which will eventually show up, even though unaccounted for at the time the evaluation is made. Furthermore, when an outside organization takes over the job evaluation program, the company knows in advance what the total cost will be. In handling the program itself, the company will not be sure until the job is entirely finished. And the biggest cost might turn out to be a plan which is not usable at all and which can only be shelved until the job may be properly done later.

Another way to handle the job evaluation program is to arrange for a combination company-consultant method of installation. The actual evaluation job is done by the company's engineering department and a consultant is retained to give such technical advice as may be needed along the way. The person with responsibility for the project should be an employee who is familiar with the work of the various departments and with the company's production methods in general. He will take charge of the job analysis procedure, the education of the supervisory group, and the installation of the program. When the job is completed he will be in a position to administer the program or train an assistant to handle it.

When the job evaluation procedure is handled by the company in this way, it is less likely to run into blind alleys or to bog down along the line. Constant checking of the technical processes by an outside consultant—a management engineer—will tend to rule out any such difficulties and prevent failure of the project.

FIGURING COSTS OF JOB EVALUATION

Job evaluation costs are dependent on such factors as size of company, type of organization (centralized or decentralized), as well as on the type of job evaluation study to be undertaken. This last factor does not refer to the system to be used, but rather to the extent of the project. If, for instance, the study is to include only job analysis, classifications, and the setting of salary rates, then it will be less expensive than a program which includes not only those essentials, but also provides for better methods of work performance and, possibly, a merit-rating program or a wage incentive plan.

There is, of course, a lot to be said for combining with job analysis a study which will lead to simplification of work routines or better methods. But it should be understood that it will take longer to accomplish such a program, which will increase costs. It is possible to get these results without seriously slowing up the program by deciding beforehand that job analysts are to make notes of recommended changes at the time they are preparing job analyses. After the program has been completed, the analysts' notes can be consulted for information on matters that need correcting.

It is obvious that the more that is expected of job evaluation—and the more time it takes to install it—the more it will cost. However, it is also true that such immediate costs may well be offset over a period of years by such results as smoother production methods and a more closely knit organization.

There are different ways to make cost estimates. Some management engineers determine costs according to payroll; others according to man-hours worked. In figuring costs against the payroll, some of the larger companies have found that the cost of installing job evaluation ran around .5 percent of the yearly payroll, with maintenance costs about .1 percent of payroll. Because most of this expense is usually charged to getting job facts, setting up definitions, and so forth, the overall cost will not vary to any great extent regardless of the type of plan used to evaluate jobs. Obviously, the percentage costs of installation will be slightly larger for the small company.

Here is how one management consultant sees the situation:

Costs vary widely in accordance with the degree of thoroughness used by the analyst in preparing an accurate job description, and the detail and care used in rating each job factor. There are other variables such as the total number of jobs involved in one installation, the amount of assistance provided the consultant by the client's staff, and the fees charged by the consultant. Another and most important variable is the amount of time taken by the consultant in training the client's staff to continue and maintain a job evaluation and merit-rating installation.

A CHECKLIST ON JOB EVALUATION
Fifteen Reasons Why the Program May Not Work

1. Failure to provide for adequate administration after the plan has been installed.

2. Undue pressure to speed up the installation of the plan.

3. Lack of support for the plan by top management.

4. Failure to get the full cooperation of supervision.

5. Failure to sell employees on the value of the program *to them.*

6. Bypassing the union.

7. Inadequate training of personnel to maintain the program.

8. Failure to set up job evaluation as part of a *long-range* program.

9. Choosing the wrong type of plan for the company's needs.

10. Lack of "selling program" for new group when key personnel changes.

11. Lack of provision for the regular job of re-evaluation.

12. Failure to allow for the elimination of inequities in allocating costs of the plan.

13. Lack of centralized control of wage and salary rates.

14. Failure to give recognition to factors other than job content in determining rates, such as merit rating and the seniority factor.

15. Lack of simplicity. Unnecessary technical procedures, leading to a multiplicity of staff training problems and difficulty in selling the plan.

This is a point very frequently overlooked with unfortunate results in job evaluation installations. It is probable that job evaluation installations properly and soundly done will run in cost around $50 per job covered. You cannot calculate the cost per worker for it costs no more to establish job evaluation for a job on which 100 workers are employed than it does for a job on which but a single worker is engaged. The measure of time and cost required in job evaluation is therefore the total number of jobs covered by the evaluation and not the total number of workers employed.

Another management consultant emphasizes one factor that has a direct bearing upon costs, *the time required,* "which will be entirely dependent," he says, "upon the cooperation and speed with which management furnishes assistance to the consultant."

Costs are estimated at somewhat higher figures by a number of management engineers. For instance, one management consultant in the East puts the figure at from $65 to over $100 a job, depending upon its complexity and the extent to which all jobs in the plant have been standardized and written up. "The extent of employee participation is another factor that helps determine the cost of an installation," he said. "We always include in our figures ample time for acquainting the workers with full details of the plan so that they can take active part in its development."

If a company wants to hold down the costs of job evaluation, it is suggested that a time schedule be set up before the program gets under way. The schedule need not be followed so closely as to impair the value of the project. Given some idea of the time required, however, it is possible to check on the program's progress from time to time and to keep costs within reasonable bounds.

SUMMARY OF JOB EVALUATION

The salary administrator of one company made this statement regarding his company's experience with job evaluation:

We have found that when properly applied, job evaluation can help to improve employee relations, stabilize the monthly labor budget, assist in future budget estimates and, in general, offer a concrete salary and employment placement and classification program based upon logic rather than guesswork. Along with time and motion study, it enables a company to offer a sound wage incentive system, for job evaluation serves as the proper basis for computing wage incentives. Furthermore, job evaluation plus time and motion study permit lower unit labor costs to be accomplished.

Job evaluation procedures have become so standardized today that there need be little question about costs, time required, or any such details. This is especially true when an outside organization installs the program.

The end result of the average job evaluation program is, of course, to arrive at equitable job evaluations. However, in achieving that goal, numerous by-products are also realized and these may be almost, if not entirely, as important as the evaluations themselves. Such by-products will undoubtedly include better production methods, the simplification of work routines, the reduction of wage-rate grievances, and better employee morale. A properly engineered system should, by accomplishing such results, pay for itself within a reasonably short time.

Job evaluation is not a cure-all for everything that may be wrong with employee relations. Instead, it is an aid to better employee relations—and an important aid—for there is nothing quite so essential to good employee morale as an effort by management to put the problem of pay on a fair and equitable basis.

Chapter 9

SALARY ADMINISTRATION
IN THE OFFICE

WHILE nearly all large employers have salary and wage administration divisions, smaller companies often shy away from the idea as being too expensive. On the contrary, *not* to have such an operation can be far more expensive than the cost of maintaining it. Much of the work has to be done by someone in the office anyway, and it would ordinarily be better to have it done by someone trained to do it.

The establishment of wage levels for office positions is only a part of the job. Just as important today is the establishment of wage policies. The workweek, overtime, holidays and benefits are areas where policy is a must. Thanks to the annual effort of the Administrative Management Society, it is possible to get measurements over the country for a large variety of office jobs. But, there is no such animal as a broad salary policy.

Employees have a deep concern about their wages. Alert management is aware of this and can do much to promote understanding. Here is "The Story of Your Salary," prepared by the Federal Reserve Bank of Philadelphia and submitted by William A. James, personnel officer:

This story is important because it deals with your job and your salary. Read it carefully and feel free to discuss it with your supervisor, department head, officer or the Personnel Department. There is nothing mysterious about the way your salary is determined and the method should be known to you.

Jobs

There are some 1,000 people employed in the bank. In all, we occupy nearly 500 different positions. In the Department of Collections, for example, there are about 65 different jobs; in the U.S. Savings Bond, 35; in Cash, 40, and so on throughout the bank. It is evident that there are numerous jobs which have more than one occupant. Each position is necessary and therefore important; but they are not, of course, equally complex or difficult.

Jobs differ in many ways. Some are quickly learned, others require long training or experience. Most of them call for high school education while some require years of specialized preparation. Some positions consist largely of making important decisions while others require ability to follow instructions accurately. There are wide differences, also, in the physical effort called for. In these and many other ways, jobs differ from each other.

Just as jobs differ from each other in responsibility, complexity and difficulty, so they differ in salary rates. How are these rates determined? They cannot be pulled out of thin air. They ought not to be made subject to anybody's guess. Above all, rates of pay should be regarded as fair. A salary may be said to be fair when it is soundly related to the salaries paid for other jobs in the bank and to rates paid in the community for similar work. In determining salaries we start by carefully studying the content of each job and comparing the jobs with each other and then measuring the differences. Let us look at this process, called Job Evaluation, more carefully.

Job Evaluation

A series of steps are taken in determining the relative difficulty and importance of jobs:

1. Each job in every section of the bank is carefully observed and studied. This is done by one or more job analysts (fellow workers specially trained for this duty). All the duties and responsibilities of the job are set down in a "job description." Your supervisor and your department head, as well as many of you, participated in this work.

2. All of the jobs, thus analyzed and described in writing, are measured or evaluated by the analysts sitting in a group, as a sort of "board of judges." There is no one "yardstick" that can be used to measure them. Think, for example, of the difficulty of comparing the job of a paying teller with that of an electrician. We can, however, measure jobs quite accurately by separating them into five essential parts and measuring each part with an appropriate yardstick. These parts or factors are:

   1. Mental and educational requirements
   2. Skill requirements
   3. Responsibility for one's own work
   4. Responsibility for supervision
   5. Physical effort and working conditions

Each part is assigned a weight or score and the sum of the scores of the parts is the total score for the job. Since a great deal is left to human judgment the method is not *scientific*. But since the same method is used to analyze and weigh all jobs and since decisions are made not by one person but by a group of competent fellow workers, the results may be said to be accurate and fair.

3. Jobs of similar difficulty and importance, as measured by the scores, are placed together in a group. There are sixteen of these groups or job grades, as they are technically called. Group One is at the lower end of the scale and Group Sixteen is at the upper end.

4. A range of pay is set for each job grade. There is a minimum rate and a maximum rate. The spread or pay range between the two exists because individuals doing the same work do not always do it equally well. Some

are more efficient, or work harder, or possess more experience, or have a greater natural flair for the job. Whatever the cause, those who excel merit higher pay. An individual in the lower range of a grade can expect to move up in the grade by improving quality, quantity, etc. To the extent that length of service enables one to gain the experience which results in better work, it is an important factor in advancement. It is to be emphasized that performance is judged by those who continuously observe your work—your supervisor, department head, and officer.

5. We have not yet mentioned how our general level of salary rates is determined. We believe the best way of setting our salaries is to relate them to those paid by other Philadelphia firms for similar work. We believe our rates should compare favorably with rates for comparable work in banks, insurance companies, utilities, manufacturing concerns, and other applicable groups in this area. Although we take into account levels of salaries paid by other Federal Reserve Banks we principally compare ourselves to employers in the Philadelphia area because this is where we live. We pay Philadelphia prices for things we buy and receive Philadelphia salaries for services we render. The salary rates being paid in the Philadelphia area are checked several times each year. This is done by careful, accurate surveys in which many leading companies take part.

PROMOTION

It is the policy of the bank to promote from within wherever possible. In general there are two ways of moving up. One can move upward in his grade, and he can move into a job in a higher grade.

Sometimes an employee starts with a fairly elementary assignment. The beginner becomes more valuable in his job as he learns to do it better. Practice may not make perfect, but it helps one to improve. Some individuals have a stronger will to improve than others and, sooner or later, advance beyond those who show less initiative. It is one of the important duties of a supervisor to observe changes in the way you work. It is also his job to help you improve. You will find, however, that it is human for supervisors to help most those who seek to improve themselves in doing their immediate job and in preparing for the jobs ahead. Performance is important and so is progress. We consider both in setting salaries.

Individuals may be moved into a job in a higher grade. A change, however, may not result in an immediate change in salary. As an example, when one is placed in a higher-graded job he is given opportunity to demonstrate his ability to fill it before a salary adjustment is made. It is important to remember that it is not always possible to promote a person to a higher-graded job when he is ready for it and deserves it. There may not be a vacancy. There are, obviously, not as many jobs "up the line" as there are in the lower and middle grades. There is, for example, only one head of each of our twenty-three departments and, usually, but one assistant head. Only the larger departments have division supervisors. We make every effort to find higher-graded positions for those who have attained the maximum salary for their present jobs but the problem of vacancies is always with us. Because this is true we always stand ready to assist talented and able employees in obtaining advancement with other concerns.

To summarize: it is the intention of this bank to see that you are paid fairly. Salaries vary. This is because there are differences between jobs and differences in the way people do their work. Jobs are restudied periodically and the performance of employees is observed constantly. The salary of each employee is reviewed once a year; new employees and those in lower-numbered grades, more frequently. A review may be made at any time for the employee who has made an unusual contribution to his job, or who has been transferred from one job to another. A review may or may not result in a salary increase.

Every employee may feel free to ask questions about his job, his status and his pay. He may ask to have his job restudied. Supervisors, department heads, officers, and the Personnel Department may be consulted at any time.

Determining Type of Salary and Wage Ranges

If a company correctly classifies individual positions with standard job classifications, and has uniform salary ranges, all its employees then have the same opportunity, and a fair and equitable distribution of the total payroll is possible. The problem of administering salaries is, therefore, primarily one of determining the type of salary range schedule and job classifications to be established.

In most companies, in order to handle all salary adjustment problems, it is desirable to have salary ranges with a 50 percent spread from minimums to maximums. This 50 percent spread should, in turn, be broken down into three parts as follows: (1) A probationary or training period for beginners; (2) a merit range for average employees; and (3) a special merit range for outstanding employees. Generally, the probationary, the merit, and the special merit ranges should be approximately the same, although this is not necessary. There are, in fact, two schools of thought on this point. One school maintains the ranges have to be uniform at all levels; and the other, the merit ranges above a certain level should always be the same fixed amount.

Under one company's salary program:

(a) Employees starting at the special training period minimum for their classification are granted probationary adjustments at certain intervals during the training period. Normally, the training period varies from 30 to 180 days, depending on the job.

(b) Employees starting at the merit minimum, or above, are eligible for merit adjustment consideration every three months, subject to the following limitations: (1) The total merit adjustments to individual employees shall not exceed in any one year more than two-thirds of the difference between the "Merit Range Minimum" and the "Special Merit Maximum"; (2) average employees shall be entitled to merit adjustment consideration between the "Merit Range Minimum" and the "Merit Range Maximum" only; (3) below-average employees shall not be eligible for merit adjustment consideration.

The administration of (b), above, entails maintaining up-to-date merit ratings on all employees falling under this plan. This is accomplished by asking department managers to grade all employees once each six months in accordance with the following formula: A— Above company average (maximum each department, 20 percent) ; B—company average (minimum each department, 60 percent) ; and C—below company average (maximum each department, 20 percent).

The form used for requesting this information is simple, and department managers are asked only whether the employees under their jurisdiction are A, or B, or C employees. This company believes the merit-rating form used for salary administration purposes should be the simplest form possible and entirely separate from merit-rating forms used for other purposes.

Descriptive Organizational Titles

In large organizations today, the duties of individuals are so complex and varied, a great number of descriptive organizational titles are in constant use. This is sound practice, because otherwise, there would be utter confusion. That the number of individual job titles runs high is brought out by a survey an industrial engineer made of three firms. This survey showed: Company A had 3,500 office employees, and 950 job titles; Company B had 2,800 office employees, and 650 job titles; Company C had 2,000 office employees, and 490 job titles; or, approximately, one individual job title for every four employees. While that may be all right from an organization viewpoint, it is a monstrosity from a salary administration angle.

For this reason, after establishing a salary range schedule, the next step in solving salary administration problems is setting up of standard, general job classifications. To control salaries and to have flexibility under stabilization regulations, it is almost mandatory to have general job classifications. And yet, surprisingly enough, few companies have job classifications for office employees except for a comparatively few clerical and stenographic classifications. Most executives and most department managers do not realize there is a distinction between: A descriptive "job title" used for organizational purposes, and a general "job classification" used for job evaluation and salary administration purposes.

In fact, if 10 employees in managerial positions in almost any company were asked how the words, "job," "position," and "job classification" differed, eight of the 10 would say there is no difference. Yet there is a tremendous difference. The words, "job" and "position," refer to individual jobs or positions; the words "job classification" refer to a group of individual jobs or positions similar in nature and content requiring a given amount of knowledge, skill, responsibility, education, experience.

To establish general job classifications in any company is not difficult. After all, in most companies there are really only five types of salaried employees to be classified: Clerks; stenographers; professional and administrative specialists and supervisors; supervisors of hourly workers; miscellaneous employees such as messengers, porters, and so forth.

Under this setup, any position (the duties of which are primarily clerical) classified to job level No. 4 automatically carries a job title of Senior Clerk, Class B. The position might also carry an organizational title, such as Accounts Payable Clerk, but that is unimportant from a salary administration viewpoint. Likewise, a stenographic position classified to job level No. 5 would carry the job classification title of Junior Secretary, etc. A company doesn't even need a formal job evaluation plan to set up a program like this, although job evaluation might help to eliminate internal inconsistencies.

Employees who earn more than $350 a month may be staff specialists or supervisors, and can be classified under such general titles as senior and junior specialists, supervisors, etc.

With such general and special clerical and stenographic classifications as the basic pattern, it should be easy to set up standard job classifications for 90 to 95 percent of employees. One company, which has had a program similar to this in effect for many years has found it took only a few hours to classify all accounting positions.

Such an arrangement as this does not mean organizational titles or descriptive job titles can no longer be used. It means job titles can no longer be used alone. A general job classification is a tool which management uses to designate a particular salary range. To illustrate, the title, Payroll Clerk, by itself, means nothing from a salary administrative angle, but the title, Junior Accountant (Payroll Clerk), means a salary range of $350 to $500 a month.

From a salary-administration and a salary-control viewpoint, individual jobs which are similar in nature and in required amounts of knowledge, skill, experience, and responsibility should be combined under general job classifications if at all possible. This simplifies internal salary administration tremendously. Strangely enough, many companies have overlooked this possibility of simplifying their operations. Apparently, they have not yet realized they have the right to arrange and rearrange the work assigned to individuals so that a number of individual positions will have approximately the same value to the company. Consequently, they make no attempt to combine positions under general job classifications, but treat each position as though it were a separate entity. This not only results in untold confusion, but makes difficult the administration of a salary or wage program on any intelligent basis. Most companies were guilty of this prior to the stabilization of wages during World War II, which partly explains why stabilization regulations were such a burden.

In job evaluation, reclassification is a routine everyday occurrence. The value of one job increases, the value of another decreases, so the job analyst rerates the jobs and reclassifies them to different general job classifications. This is most confusing to those individuals who do not know the difference between a "job title" for organizational purposes and a "job classification" for job evaluation purposes. They are afraid the job analyst is doing something illegal, and they are inclined to believe he is breaking stabilization regulations. Yet these individuals will take a File Clerk who does nothing but filing, give her a couple of reports to prepare each month in addition to her filing, reclassify her as a Junior Accounting Clerk, and think nothing of it. Why? Because in the lower classifications the standards have been set, and this has been routine practice for years. In most companies, management has been lax in establishing general job classifications beyond the lower levels. This mistake has been costly, because in order to administer salaries intelligently, job classifications must be established wherever possible, even up to the officers of the company.

If a company has general job classifications and a salary range schedule, it has almost complete freedom of action. To illustrate, a man can be called a Chief Accountant from an organizational viewpoint and still be classified to three different job classifications merely by changing the responsibilities of the position.

Whether the Chief Accountant should head two, three, or four subdepartments depends entirely on the qualifications of the individual available. Unfortunately, in business, the type of employee management would like to have is not always the kind management has. For this reason, management frequently has to rearrange the work within the organization in order to utilize best the employees on hand.

Ordinarily, job analysts should be employed to rate jobs and to determine whether proposed reclassifications are in order. A company can, however, establish a sound program without them. Job evaluation is not an exact science; it is an approximation.

Salary Review Procedures

Unfortunately, many companies do not place enough emphasis on internal consistency (i.e., a uniform relationship between jobs within a company), but try to maintain external consistency by paying individual market averages for each position. This is a mistake because, in most companies, employees tend generally to compare their salaries with salaries paid to other employees within the organization rather than with salaries paid to employees in similar capacities in other firms. When establishing a salary administration program, it is more important to provide for a uniform internal relationship than to attempt to meet the salaries paid by competitors for individual jobs.

In one large Midwestern company, the management tried to establish an internally consistent salary program at a time when individual department managers were complaining employees under their jurisdiction were being paid less than employees in similar capacities in other firms. While the newly created job evaluation unit was trying to establish a fair internal relationship between the Accounts Payable Supervisor and the Power Plant Engineer, and other jobs in the organization, individual department managers were swamping this unit with requests to find out the market averages for positions and classifications on which the company had but one or two employees. The trouble was, the various department managers were confused as to the ultimate goal of salary administration. The primary purpose of salary administration is to achieve internal consistency, and all other aims are secondary.

A company should never ask another company what the salary or rate range is for a classification unless both companies have at least 10 employees in the classification to be compared. Due to internal differences in organizations, it would be a miracle if an individual position in one company carried the same duties and responsibilities as an individual position in another company. For this reason, unless two companies have enough employees in a classification so that the duties are standardized in both, the company requesting a comparison is merely wasting its time and the time of the company from which the comparison is requested. Many companies do not realize the truth of this statement and the daily mail of almost any firm in recent years includes requests from other companies for comparisons involving a wide variety of job titles in which the company receiving the request has but one or two individuals. These requests became such a burden on one company, it finally adopted a policy of returning all such requests with the notation, "No comparable classification," unless there were at least 10 employees in its organization who had that same classification.

For the reasons just outlined, the management of all companies should strive for internal consistency and pay no attention whatsoever to what other companies are paying for individual jobs. Once a company establishes rates for hourly workers and clerical classifications, and sets up a relationship between these rates and the rates for the supervisors of these employers, it automatically establishes rates for all other jobs.

As the first step toward achieving internal consistency, each company should establish: (1) A uniform salary schedule; (2) general job classifications for individual jobs similar in nature and content; (3) an orderly upward arrangement of job classifications within each department; (4) a "normal" salary for each job classification; and (5) a job evaluation plan for rating jobs.

As the final step in achieving internal consistency, management should divide salary administration into two parts, namely: The control over the total amount of adjustments, which is a function of management, and the control over individual adjustments, which is a function of departmental supervisors.

To handle individual adjustments, a job evaluation unit should prepare monthly salary control reports for management's consideration, and, whenever the percentage of "actual" salaries to "normal" salaries drops to an undesirable figure, management should authorize a general review of salaries. At that time, each department manager should be told the approximate amount of monthly adjustments he should grant to his employees. Under this method of control, as long as the department manager stays within the amount that is authorized by management, and within the general policies prescribed by management, he should have complete freedom of action, and his decision should be final.

The salary committee, which has handled proposed merit adjustments heretofore in most companies, should be abolished, because no group can intelligently pass on proposed adjustments when they know but very few of the individuals concerned.

In place of a salary committee, management should appoint a

salary and wage administrator to administer the salary and wage policies established by management. The primary functions of this individual should be:

1. To review all proposed adjustments (or lack of proposed adjustments) in order to maintain internal consistency between departments. This function is primarily a policing function designed to prevent deviations from established salary policies.

2. To supervise the job evaluation unit.

3. To analyze the various reports prepared by the job evaluation unit, and to recommend to management corrective steps which are necessary.

4. To supervise periodic salary reviews.

As soon as a salary and wage administrator is appointed, all merit adjustments should be granted at salary review periods only. Such a policy simplifies salary administration and leads to better internal consistency. On salary reviews, a department manager looks over the records of all employees at the same time, instead of just one or two at a time as is the case when adjustments are processed individually.

By controlling the total amount a department manager can give, and making him grant it all at the same time, management forces department managers to analyze their individual problems and to distribute their adjustments where they will do the most good.

The salary review form should be designed for the convenience of department managers and should contain space for the following information:

1. Job classifications.

2. Employees' names (and organizational titles).

3. Employees' merit ratings (i.e., A or B or C).

4. Salary range—minimum, normal, maximum.

5. Present salaries.

6. Date of last adjustment.

7. Salary adjustment recommended.

8. Effective date of salary adjustment.

Under this method of operation, columns (1) through (6) should be filled in by the job evaluation unit, and department managers should merely insert their recommendations in (7) and (8).

It is possible to maintain constantly a desired relationship between "actual" salaries and "normal" salaries with this method. This is very important because, unless a company maintains a desired relationship between "normal" salaries to be paid to all employees and "actual" salaries paid (exclusive of overtime and bonuses), it cannot have a true control over salaries and wages. This method has another advantage during a time when the working force is being reduced, and when it might even be desirable to uproot employees who are not too well satisfied with their jobs, or employees who are uninterested in their work. It is sometimes necessary to move out restless employees without arbitrarily discharging them. Most employers dislike discharging an employee, unless for cause, merely because he is not an especially capable worker. It sometimes shatters his self-confidence and makes it more difficult to secure another position.

A sound salary review program is one way of "easing out" the less desirable employees but at the same time giving them an opportunity to "save face." This is especially true when layoffs are on a seniority basis and there is a tendency for the organization to become top heavy with people who feel their jobs are secure, so there is no need to try to do better. A business which has stopped expanding needs some turnover in its employees to avoid hardening of the arteries, as its working force grows older and less progressive.

Salary Determination

While methods used in determining wage rates for employees doing repetitive operations, such as in the factory, can be based on job evaluation without too much chance for error, when it comes to determining salaries for white-collar employees many intangible factors enter into the picture. Good practice generally recognizes, along with length of service, certain fairly well-defined merit considerations for advancing employees within the salary range, such as the following: (1) The minimum or starting rate for the position; (2) the rate for improved production; (3) the rate for skill reflected in production at or above standard; (4) the rate for versatility or ability to do several kinds of work, or even to accept a higher degree of responsibility upon occasion; and (5) the maximum rate, reserved to compensate an employee for all-around ability and future value to the company.

Adjusting Clerical Salaries to a Pattern Wage Increase

In order to maintain a balance between wages in the shop and salaries in the office when production workers are increased according to a national pattern, the pattern should be translated into terms of weekly or monthly increase and applied directly to existing salaries and, in most cases, to existing range minimums, maximums, and

EMPLOYEE APPRAISAL

NAME _____ PLANT _____ DEPT. _____ SHIFT _____

CLOCK NO. _____ PRESENT JOB CLASSIFICATION _____

Date Employed
Last Increase _____ Date _____ Amount _____

Check   **ACTION**

☐ Recommend change RATE from _____ to _____ per hour _____

☐ Recommend change JOB classification from _____ to _____

☐ Recommend change SHIFT from _____ to _____ starting _____ 19 _____
                                                                    Date

☐ Recommend transfer in DEPARTMENT from _____
                                         Department Name   Department No.

to _____ starting _____ 19 _____
    Department Name   Department No.   Date

☐ Recommend that NO ACTION be taken at this time.

REASON FOR ACTION
_____
_____
_____
_____
_____
_____

APPRAISAL

CHARACTERISTICS	Check	EXCELLENT	Check	GOOD	Check	FAIR	Check	POOR
ABILITY Skill, Knowledge, Judgment, Versatility, Follow Instructions and Accept Responsibility.								
EFFICIENCY Production, Saving of Time, Energy and Materials, Care and Maintenance of Equipment.								
PERSONAL HABITS Cooperativeness, Conduct, Temperament, Cleanliness, Honesty, Tact, etc.								
PHYSICAL CONDITION General Health, Strength, Physical Defects.								

APPRAISAL BY _____

Date _____ 19 _____
      Foreman or Supervisor

ACTION EFFECTIVE _____ 19 _____
         Personnel Division

Date	APPROVED BY
	Personnel Director
	Plant Superintendent

A simple form for use by supervisors in recommending pay increases, upgrades, shift changes, and transfers. An interesting feature of the form is that it requires the person recommending the action to rate the employee on essential characteristics which must support the recommendation. The form thus provides a simplified merit-rating plan, which could serve as a basis for layoffs and rehires along with seniority.

intermediates. For example, if the pattern increase is 12½ cents, the indicated weekly increase for clericals will be, in most cases, 40 times 12½ cents, or $5 weekly. In the case of a monthly payroll, the proper increase would seem to be 173⅓ hours times the pattern amount. Assuming a pattern increase of 12½ cents, the monthly increase would be $21.66, which in practice would be leveled off either to $21.50 or $22.00.

The real problem arises in the treatment of related rates in the ascending scale, chiefly the rates of supervisors, administrators, and professional employees. As the salary goes up, the significance to the individual of an increase of $22 a month diminishes and altogether disappears at about the level of $500 a month. To the production workers in many firms such an increase would have been approximately a 10 percent increase and there has been some suggestion that the higher rates should be increased by that percentage. This latter treatment of the problem, however, is extremely expensive and tends to interfere with the concept of merit which is much more rigidly applied at the higher levels. Therefore, it would seem that some compromise between the uniform flat rate increase and the uniform percentage increase is desirable. The compromise, however, should manage to preserve, insofar as possible, the existing rate structure. Some companies have made this compromise in the past by taking the percentage and applying it over a selected range of salaries in juxtaposition to the earnings of production workers and applying a selected flat increase to all salaries over that amount up to the point where it is felt that further increases are unnecessary, which, in the case of one company, was at the level of $10,000 a year.

This latter method, however, has certain disadvantages in that it tends to disrupt the relationship of the rates at or near the various breaking points and may, to some degree, distort evaluated rates.

"Selling" the Wage Schedule to Supervisors

Whatever wage policy is decided upon, it should be explained carefully to employees and especially to supervisors. The policy should be supported by ample facts and these facts should be the result of an impartial survey. In recent years, more companies are following the policy of "taking employees into the confidence of management," and are issuing annual reports to their *job holders* as well as to their stockholders, showing how the wage structure in their plants compares with others in the industry and area of operation.

In summary, factors to be considered in setting wage and salary

PAYROLL CHANGE (TYPE IN DUPLICATE)
FORM O-848C

☐ REMOVE ☐ CHANGE

_____ COMPANY

TO PAYROLL DEPARTMENT: _____ DATE

EFFECTIVE_____ DATE _____ A.M. _____ TIME P.M. PLEASE CHANGE THE PERSONNEL RECORD OF

NAME_____ EMPLOYEE NO_____

FROM	TO
DEPARTMENT_____	DEPARTMENT_____
GANG OR SECTION_____	GANG OR SECTION_____
OCCUPATION_____	OCCUPATION_____
OCCUPATIONAL STATUS—	OCCUPATIONAL STATUS—

TEMPORARY ☐ PROBATIONARY ☐ NORMAL ☐   TEMPORARY ☐ PROBATIONARY ☐ NORMAL ☐
UTILITY ☐ CONFIDENTIAL ☐   UTILITY ☐ CONFIDENTIAL ☐
RATE OF PAY $_____ ☐ HOUR ☐ MONTH   RATE OF PAY $_____ ☐ HOUR ☐ MONTH

GIVE REASON FOR CHANGE IN STATUS (IF REMOVAL, COMPLETE UNDER REASON FOR TERMINATION)_____

IF CHANGE OF DUTIES:—DOES EMPLOYEE USE PERSONAL AUTOMOBILE FOR COMPANY BUSINESS NOW? YES ☐ NO ☐
WILL NEW DUTIES REQUIRE USE OF PERSONAL AUTOMOBILE FOR COMPANY BUSINESS? YES ☐ NO ☐
DOES CHANGE INVOLVE HANDLING OF CASH OR SECURITIES? YES ☐ NO ☐
PRESENT ADDRESS_____ PHONE NO_____ MARRIED ☐ SINGLE ☐

REASON FOR TERMINATION

VOLUNTARY	INVOLUNTARY	GIVE DETAILED STATEMENT OF EXACT REASON FOR TERMINATION___
☐ SICKNESS	☐ MISCONDUCT	
☐ HOME DUTIES	☐ PERSONNEL REDUCTION	
☐ ANOTHER POSITION	☐ WORK UNSATISFACTORY	
☐ DISSATISFIED	☐ VIOLATION OF RULES	
☐ LEAVING CITY*	☐ LATE OR ABSENT	
☐ _____	☐ _____	

* FORWARDING ADDRESS_____

DATE EMPLOYED_____ DATE OF LAST DAY WORKED_____
PAY THROUGH_____ FOR_____ DAYS EARNED VACATION FOR_____ DAYS SEPARATION PAY
☐ RECOMMENDED FOR REEMPLOYMENT
☐ NOT RECOMMENDED FOR REEMPLOYMENT IN THIS DEPT   ☐ NOT RECOMMENDED FOR REEMPLOYMENT IN COMPANY
IF NOT, GIVE REASON_____

THE FOLLOWING ITEMS ENTRUSTED TO THE ABOVE EMPLOYEE FOR USE IN THE PERFORMANCE OF HIS DUTIES HAVE BEEN RETURNED AND ACCOUNTED FOR
☐ MONEY ☐ TOOLS ☐ KEYS ☐ AUTO · ☐ DOCUMENTS ☐ BADGE ☐ IDENTIFICATION CARD_____
ADDITIONAL REMARKS_____

PREPARED BY_____
APPROVED—(IN CASE OF INTERDEPARTMENTAL TRANSFER, HEADS OF BOTH DEPTS. MUST SIGN)

_____ DEPT. HEAD   _____ DEPT HEAD   _____ DEPT HEAD

_____ PERSONNEL DEPT   _____ VICE PRES   _____ VICE PRES

FOR USE OF THE PERSONNEL DEPARTMENT DATE	FOR USE OF THE PAYROLL DEPARTMENT DATE
IDENTIFICATION CARD RECEIVED_____	GROUP INSURANCE CANCELLED_____
PERSONNEL RECORD POSTED_____	ALL DEDUCTIONS CHECKED_____
NOTIFIED UNION_____	PERSONNEL DATA CARD POSTED_____
TO TAX AND INS.—BOND APPLICATION_____	ADDRESSOGRAPH DEPT NOTIFIED_____
NOTICE RE AUTO INS._____	ALL TABULATING CARDS CHECKED_____
	NO OUTSTANDING INDEBTEDNESS EXCEPT AS NOTED—
EXEMPT F. L. S. A. BEFORE THIS CHANGE? YES ☐ NO ☐	ACCT REC_____
EXEMPT F. L. S. A. AFTER THIS CHANGE? YES ☐ NO ☐	MDSE. CONSIGNMENTS_____
REMARKS:_____	

Form used by aircraft corporation for payroll changes. In the case of an employee's services being terminated, the supervisor filling out the blank is required to state specifically the reasons for the termination. These reasons are later broken down into ten classifications for analysis purposes.

rates, all of which involve research work if they are to be effectively used in wage administration, are:

1. Cost of living—generally and locally.
2. Wages in the industry of which your company is a part.
3. Wages in the community, and comparison among companies and regions.
4. Job differentials; job evaluation.
5. Individual differences among employees; personnel ratings.
6. Collective bargaining and union differentials.
7. Management differentials; the adequate management of personnel and industrial relations.
8. Governmental regulations; legal minimums and other wage considerations.
9. Seniority and special wage problems.

Natural Lap

The Labor Relations Bureau of the Commerce and Industry Association of New York developed formulas for lapping-in the increase so as to preserve existing rate relationships with very little distortion.

This formula will taper off a pattern increase to a limit of twice the amount of the increase at the lowest level; i.e., if at $300 an employee receives $33 a month, no employee will receive more than $66 a month, however great his salary. Practically then, the formula will result in a flat sum increase in the upper brackets.

$$RH \left(1 + \frac{P-L}{P}\right) = I$$

Where R = Pattern increase in cents per hour.

H = Hours in month (173⅓).

P = Present monthly salary of employee, or class rate, range minimum, maximum, or intermediate.

L = Level of salaries above which it is desired to taper off the increase ($300 monthly minimum).

I = Increase in dollars per month.

NOTE: If H, P, and L are expressed in weekly terms, I will be the weekly increase.

Company Payment Policies

Because salary scales vary so greatly in different geographical sections of the country, any table of earnings can only be taken as a general guide. The most accurate information on comparative salaries in clerical jobs can be had from the following reliable sources:

Administrative Management Society
Willow Grove, Pennsylvania 19090
(or through your local AMS chapter)

Wage & Salary Reporter
Research and Editorial Office
Farm Credit Building
2180 Milva Street
Berkeley, California 94704

U.S. Department of Labor
Bureau of Employment Security
Washington, D.C. 20025

In surveys made of company payment policies, Dartnell has found that most offices pay employees twice a month—over 50 percent of them do. Companies paying employees every week total 38 percent. Some companies gave employees a choice of whether they want their check each week or twice a month. In 7 percent of responding companies employees are paid once a month.

In cases where men and women are doing the same type of work (and not too many respondents say they are) pay is equal 85 percent of the time. But 15 percent of the companies that have men and women doing the same jobs give men a better pay scale. Here's the reason one company official gives for doing this. "Men need more money than women. It is an economic fact that men carry greater financial burdens what with the responsibility of rent or mortgage, car payments, and the thousand and one other obligations the average husband faces." While this may not be taken with favor by many capable career women, some employers still feel it's a man's world. But, apparently, they are in the minority.

How 155 Companies Handle the Office Payroll

Dartnell had the cooperation of 155 office administrators in preparing this report on management policy and experience. Large and small groups are represented from a diverse group of businesses. Nearly 730,000 clerical employees work in the surveyed organizations which represent 23 states and parts of Canada.

In slightly more than 41 percent of these organizations, the basis of clerical employee compensation is a fixed salary. Fifteen percent of the companies pay an hourly rate and 28 percent have a combination of the two methods. For instance, the office manager for Lennox Industries, Inc., Marshalltown, Iowa, represents a number of firms making up the latter group when he explains: "People in professional and administrative jobs are on 'exempt' payroll, not subject to overtime."

Another typical combination is explained by the area manager, Agricultural Development Company, division of Bartlett and Company, Topeka, Kansas: "Supervisory personnel are on a monthly basis, regular personnel on an hourly basis."

Union-organized office personnel are usually on an hourly rate; however, only a small fraction of office workers are unionized.

Reporting the length of the pay period, respondents indicated as follows:

Monthly	2 percent
Semimonthly	36 percent
Weekly	27 percent
Biweekly	23 percent
Combination	11 percent

Some office administrators report a policy whereby employees have a choice between being paid weekly or semimonthly. The sex factor enters into the picture at Fiddes Moore & Company, Fort Wayne, Indiana, where men are paid semimonthly and women weekly.

Supervisors are frequently paid in a different pay period than rank-and-file employees. Following are statements by contributors attesting to this:

Biweekly for regular employees; monthly for department heads and higher bracket executives.

Biweekly for employees on time cards; monthly for all other employees.

Hourly, biweekly; executives and department heads, semimonthly.

Payroll checks are by far the most common means of paying employees, 95 percent of the firms using them. Only 2 percent say they now pay with cash, and 1 percent pay with cash or checks. A Chicago publishing company gives department heads and executives a choice of cash or check and selection of pay period, "providing they stay with it and don't go changing about frequently."

Lafayette National Bank of Lafayette, Indiana, has still another procedure, whereby a deposit in the amount of his or her pay is deposited to the individual's account. Glens Falls Insurance Company of New York has a similar policy; Salary is deposited to employees' checking accounts, which are maintained in either of two local banks of the person's choosing.

Most companies (69 percent) do not provide a check-cashing service for employees. However, 25 percent do have such an accommodation, 9 percent use an outside check-cashing service, and 12 percent have a carrying account at a nearby bank.

Spray Products Corporation, Camden, New Jersey, schedules a payroll clerk to cash checks for employees at noontime on payday. This is common with firms providing a check-cashing service—having a set time when it will be done, rather than allowing employees to cash them at any time.

Tabulation on computation of payrolls indicates the following:

Payroll sheets	32 percent
Time Cards	31 percent
Combination	17 percent
Punch cards	10 percent
Other methods	10 percent

A spokesman for Lynch Corporation, Anderson, Indiana, explaining "other methods" used by his company, says: "The permanent rate card has a section showing earnings and deductions for each pay period. These remain fairly constant, eliminating the need of computation each pay period. If a change is required, a paper reproduction is attached to the front of the rate card, showing changes and pay period. This is removed after the check is written. Each payday we compute the exceptions."

The following tabulation shows replies of executives joining in this exchange of experience when asked, "How are names imprinted on checks and/or payroll reports?"

Typewriter	28 percent
Addressograph	18 percent
Punch-card machine	17 percent
Payroll machine	14 percent
By hand	10 percent
Combination	2 percent

Lynn Insurance Group, Kansas City, Missouri, computes payroll records on a pegboard. Others report the use of Elliott addressers, Ditto payroll systems, Royal McBee systems, NCR accounting machines, IBM machines, and Burroughs Todd-Hadley Pegboard systems. A few respondents point to the fact that "confidential payroll" in their firms is manual.

Eighty-two percent of the firms show deductions for Social Security and withholding tax separately on the paychecks; 9 percent do not. These deductions are usually shown on the check itself or on a perforated checkstub. Those firms paying by cash usually have pay slips, showing deductions, stuffed in the pay envelopes.

There is considerable variance between the actual end of the pay period and payday among responding companies. One rather interesting fact—nearly 34 percent say there is no time lapse between the end of the pay period and payday: It is the same day. These are by no means all small firms, either. One West Coast utility employing some 600 office employees is in the group. However, even among these firms, quite a few mention "delays" due to overtime computations. In such instances, it is a common practice to pick up overtime incurred the following week.

Following is a breakdown of time lapses between the end of the period and payday among many of the other concerns, excluding the 34 percent which pay the same day:

Five days	5 percent
One day	7 percent
Two days	7 percent
Three days	11 percent
Four days	5 percent
Seven days	9 percent
Six days	2 percent

Others include: one and a half weeks, four and a half days, three to five days (it varies), 10 days, and two weeks.

The use of payroll messages for employees apparently hasn't caught on as a major communications device. Only 22 percent of the firms use them and 66 percent say they do not. Some use them "rarely" when they have a special message to deliver, such as holiday closing announcements, vacation policy statements, or other statements of concern to employees.

Of course, since many companies using checks do not have pay envelopes, the need for payroll stuffers is limited.

Preparing a Basic Salary Structure

In preparing a basic salary structure for the various levels of sales management, some attempts have been made to use point systems similar to those used in job evaluation of production workers, clerical workers, and supervisors. Such elements as complexity of work, degree of responsibility, educational requirements, and conditions under which the work is performed have been considered.

Many executives believe that this approach does not lend itself as readily to a study for top and middle sales management groups as does the method outlined below. The data shown should not be considered applicable to any individual company; they have been selected merely to illustrate the method.

1. Each department head is asked to grade the positions under his jurisdiction into their relative rank. Emphasis is placed on the *position* being rated, and *not* on the *man* holding the position.

   Positions between departments are interrelated by a salary committee made up of major executives; their positions are excluded. The president rates all top positions. Promotional and traditional relationships of positions are discussed and considered before final ranking decisions are made.

2. The positions are then inserted on a salary schedule chart (illustrated). (Not all positions found in a company are shown here, nor are the rankings to be assumed as typical; they should be different for individual companies.)

3. The salaries currently being paid to the incumbents of the positions are then plotted, as shown by dots on the Salary Graph (illustrated).

4. A curve is then sketched on the chart (dotted line) to represent approximately the salary pattern being paid. In this example, the president was a heavy stockholder and received much of his income from dividends; he therefore had held his salary very low ($25,000). This reflected in a low salary for the executive vice-president ($30,000). Since the company had always been production-minded, the vice-president for manufacturing received a relatively high salary ($29,000), almost equaling that of the executive vice-president. The vice-president-finance was related to the president, and although his responsibilities were not large, he received a comparatively good salary ($23,000). Marketing was rated rather low, the vice-president-marketing receiving $17,000 and the sales manager, $14,000. The managers of "A" and "B" branches received the same salaries, although there was considerable difference in the size and responsibilities of the two branches. There were a number of prima donna salesmen who received greater incomes than the branch managers and there were other salesmen who were underpaid.

		Current Salary	Proposed Salary		
			Min.	Mid-Point	Max.
Ranking	Position				
16	President	$25,000	$42,500	$50,000	$57,500
15			36,800	43,300	50,000
14	Executive Vice President	30,000	32,000	37,600	43,300
13			27,800	32,700	37,600
12	Vice President-Marketing	17,000	24,100	28,400	32,700
11	Vice President-Manufacturing	29,000	21,000	24,700	28,400
10	Vice President-Finance	23,000	18,300	21,500	24,700
9	Sales Manager	14,000	15,700	18,500	21,500
	General Factory Manager	19,000			
8			13,700	16,100	18,500
7	Advertising Manager	9,000	11,900	14,000	16,100
	Merchandising Manager	8,000			
6	District Manager	11,000	10,400	12,200	14,000
	Research Manager	11,000			
5	Manager Branch A	8,500	9,000	10,600	12,200
	Customer Service Manager	11,000			
4	Manager Branch B	8,500	7,800	9,200	10,600
3	Senior Salesman	12,000	6,800	8,000	9,200
2	Salesman	5,000–9,500	5,900	6,900	8,000
1	Junior Salesman	4,000–5,000	5,100	6,000	6,900

Salary Schedule Chart

SALARY GRAPH BASED ON SALARY CHART

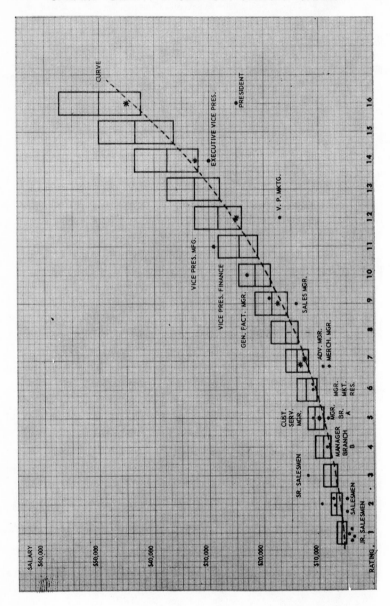

Chapter 10

PROBLEMS IN SALARY DETERMINATION

WHILE seniority has nothing to do with the technique of job
evaluation, it is often taken into consideration in determining
salary rates because many employees—and employers, as well—believe that a person's length of service with his company should be
compensated for to some degree. There is plenty of loose thinking
about the subject, and many an employee is thoroughly convinced
that because he has been with a company a long time he is worth
considerably more money than the man who has only a year or two
of seniority. Naturally, this does not follow, but the problem is to
convince the employee of the fact and make him accept it.

Because it has always been easier to measure length of time than
an employee's increasing (or decreasing) ability on the job, management has found it simpler to compensate an employee by length
of service rather than by performance. Thus, length of service,
rather than ability, becomes the criterion of a person's value to his
company. Actually, it is a measure of loyalty and stability, not necessarily skill at the job.

When a job evaluation study is made, it will often reveal that
employees who have been on the job many years are getting higher
pay for the same type of work than those who have been on the job
a shorter period of time. In order to conform to the classifications
set up, the rates would ordinarily be decreased in such cases. Management's problem is what to do with such a situation. Shall the
employee's rate be decreased? Shall he be upgraded to a higher-rated job? How can an adjustment be made without disturbing the
employee's morale too severely?

The best thing to do, of course, is to find higher-rated jobs for
such employees which will justify their present rates. To reduce
the employee's earnings would be to penalize him for management's
faulty judgment in the past and would not only be basically unfair,
but would tend to lower morale. If it is impossible to justify a

169

higher-priced job for the employee, then the usual procedure is to keep him at the present rate in his old job. Every employee, however, should know what the minimum, maximum, and intermediate rates are for all jobs so that he may not be under the impression that the high rate for the old employee with long seniority is the standard one.

Companies feeling strongly about the seniority factor sometimes set up rate schedules that apply to all employees according to length of service. Here is how one company does it:

Those employees who have completed five years of continuous service get 5 percent over their evaluated rates;

Those who have completed 10 years of continuous service, get 10 percent over their evaluated rates;

Those who have completed 15 years of continuous service get 15 percent over their evaluated rates;

Those who have completed 20 years or more get 20 percent over their evaluated rates.

In periods of depression, a company's payroll costs may be larger because of seniority increases. This is because older employees do not look around for other jobs when work is scarce. Thus, turnover is cut and seniority accumulates. On the other hand, during a period of prosperity when the company is in a good position to pay higher labor rates, seniority payments are likely to decrease. During such a period, turnover among older employees tends to go up.

As a rule, seniority increases are not as desirable as merit increases, yet on some jobs it is obvious that if increases are to be given they must be for seniority. These are the routine, repetitive jobs which allow little leeway for the individual to show superiority over other workers doing the same kind of work.

Undoubtedly, seniority is one of the toughest nuts to crack in salary administration. If allowances for seniority must be made, it is well to align them carefully within the range of rates for each job. This prevents an employee's rate of pay from exceeding the maximum rate for his job classification. Care must also be taken that increases are not given so frequently or in such large amounts as to overload the payroll. Seniority increases should be limited to every six months at least. It is still better not to grant them more often than once a year.

INCENTIVES IN THE OFFICE

Wally E. George, a Grand Rapids (Michigan) management consultant, points out that the basic requirement of a good incentive plan is *incentives for everyone*. He emphasizes that ineptly conceived, poorly run incentives are worthless, while installations limited to a chosen few are not much better. Seldom does a sizable organization find a single plan suited to all its employees, he points out. And, all too often, after partial incentive coverage is attained, human lethargy forestalls any additional planning or applications.

"Incentives must be pointed to a purpose," says Mr. George. "The plan that works well for one segment of personnel is not necessarily appropriate to the others. Accurate measure of performance is the key to success of an incentive plan."

He indicates that "responsibility patterns" dictate the basis for gauging performance, as the following five premises declares:

1. *Those who formulate the policy* should share in the profits.

2. *Those who sell* should earn more as their volume increases.

3. *Those who supervise* should be compensated for their control and reduction of costs.

4. *Those who produce* should be rewarded for their production.

5. *Those who serve* should be paid in relation to their services.

The broad incentive programs of an enterprise may embrace various plans, each designed to offer tangible premiums for superior work. The several plans should fit into an integrated policy which, among other things, will provide an upgrading ladder that the individual can scale.

An Incentive System for Typists

An insurance firm's incentive system enable it to measure a girl's output and determine her rate of pay. The system also shows when a typist is ready to be trained as a transcriber.

Each typewriter in the pool has a cyclometer which registers one stroke for every 100 keys hit. The typist keeps a record of her daily strokes by reading the cyclometer in the morning and at closing time. The girls are allowed credit for "idle" hours—proofreading, attending meetings, using special typewriters (long carriage and the Executive Model) which do not have cyclometers, and time lost through illness or visiting the doctor or dentist.

The transcribers record "abnormal time credit," as well. Usually, it takes 45 minutes to an hour to transcribe a belt. If transcription takes longer, due to poor dictation (the dictator may not have given proper instructions or may not have marked the ends of memos and letters), the operator records the extra time. The company allows 2,137 strokes for every hour of such abnormal work. This figure represents the hourly strokes the average operator types on normal work. Although this figure was calculated some time ago, periodic checks have revealed that it stays about the same.

Allowance is also made when a new typewriter or other piece of equipment is installed, because it takes time to master a different machine.

At the end of the month, the supervisor collects the stroke sheets. She figures the girls' averages every three months. This quarterly average determines each girl's rate of pay for the next three months. In other words, a girl can change her salary four times a year. However, the pay rate does not always increase; sometimes it decreases, if a girl's production dips.

Eventually, each typist hits a leveling-off place, the top speed of which she is capable. A good, fast typist can type 90,000 strokes a day, according to company records, so the maximum salary is based on that figure. Most girls will not reach that speed; some consistently type between 80,000 and 85,000 strokes daily. But the incentive is there to try to hit the maximum production and salary.

When a typist is hired, she is given a starting salary, which she receives until she has established a stroke record, usually within three months. The incentive schedule starts at 30,000 strokes, but most new girls type between 35,000 and 45,000 strokes a day the first quarter. Generally, a girl's speed increases every three-month period.

After a girl can average 60,000 strokes a day on copy work, which is the maximum, she is ready for training as a transcriber. Because the company sometimes finds it necessary to train a typist for transcription before she has hit this peak, the transcriber's schedule starts at 50,000 strokes a day.

Allen Manufacturing Company's Plan

Survey after survey has proved that employees want recognition from management more than any other one thing. While management in hundreds of companies is cognizant of this fact, little or nothing is done to capitalize on this one little gesture of good will toward the employee.

An exception to this is the Allen Manufacturing Co., which a few years ago found a merit award system the answer to the problem of how to recognize those employees who were outstanding during the year. The factors used in determining the winners—small gold lapel pins—were: Job performance, production average, attendance, safety, off-the-job activities, and suggestions.

The awards were divided among five groups: Supervisors, office employees, production operators, toolsetters, and nonproduction employees. Details of the basis for the awards are given as follows:

Employee Rating Report—Unless the last two rating reports are "good" or "better," an employee will not be considered for an award. Ratings will be graded according to the point total.

Production Average—If the production average of an operator equals the department average or is between 1 and 4 points above, he receives 5 credits on the Production Factor. If between 5 and 9 points above the department average, he gets 10 credits; if between 10 and 14 points above, 15 credits; if 15 points or higher, the maximum number of credits or 20. Production foremen and toolsetters receive credit in proportion to the 12-month average bonus earned by their departments. If it is between 20 percent and 24 percent, they get 5 points; if between 25 percent and 29 percent, 10 points; if 30 percent or higher, the maximum number of points or 15.

Suggestions—For a "Class A" suggestion accepted by the Suggestion Committee during the year, an employee receives 10 points; for a "Class B" suggestion, 5 points; for a "Class C" suggestion, 2 points; for each rejected suggestion up to five, 1 point or a maximum of 5 points.

Attendance Record—For Groups 1, 3, 4, and 5, credit for attendance will be given on the following basis:

Days Lost	None	1	2	3	4	5	6	7	8	9	10
Points	15	14	13	12	11	10	8	6	4	2	0

Since office employees (Group 2) are on salary, the attendance factor is weighted more heavily for them:

Days Lost	None	1	2	3	4	5	6	7	8	9	10
Points	25	23	21	19	17	15	12	9	6	3	0

Safety Record—For a perfect safety record, the maximum number of points shall be given. If an employee has one accident without losing any time, he receives 5 points. For a lost-time accident or more than one accident without losing time, no credit.

Off-the-Job Activities—The chairman of any committee in the plant, the head of any activity, or the initiator of any worthwhile endeavor receives 5 points. To an officer, or leading member of any activity, 2 points; to a member of any activity, 1 point.

Recommendations—Recommendations of candidates for a Merit Pin Award must be made to the General Committee as follows:

1. The superintendents shall recommend production and nonproduction foremen; the office manager shall recommend office supervisors.

2. The office supervisors with the approval of the office manager shall recommend office employees.

3. Production operators, toolsetters, and nonproduction employees shall be recommended by foremen with the approval of their superintendent; stewards with the approval of the shift chief steward.

D. J. Ridings, former Porter-Cable Machine Co. head, said recently: "Profit sharing is not a generous handout of excess profits, but an enlightened business principle for increasing benefits to the company, its employees, and its customers alike. We have just as many financial burdens as any other manufacturer, but we believe that people who share in the company's success take a proprietary interest in its welfare. They produce more units per day, work more intelligently, suggest more efficient methods, and take more pains with their work."

While profit sharing works fairly well for hourly rated employees, it runs into complications when used to provide incentive pay for salaried employees in the higher tax brackets. Uncle Sam takes most of their pay away, with the result that the incentive value of the bonus is nullified.

The experience of most employers who have profit participation plans for key employees is not too satisfactory. After a few good years with big bonus checks, employees gear their living standards to their expected bonus, which they take for granted. The bonus, they feel, is something they are entitled to, regardless of whether business is good or bad. They are well aware the company has a substantial surplus which they assume it will tap for the bonus if profits do not permit paying it out of the year's earnings. They seldom stop to figure that this surplus is probably in the form of bricks and machinery which cannot very well be used for bonus checks. At any rate, when the bonus which they have come to anticipate is not forthcoming or is reduced materially, they feel they have been bilked and react as you might expect a person who has just had a cut in salary to react.

To get around this objection to profit sharing in the form of a cash bonus at the end of the company's fiscal year, management often sets up an irrevocable trust into which it pays each year the maximum profits permitted by law, or nothing at all if there are no profits. Such a trust must conform to the current federal tax code. Payments into the fund will then be tax-free to the company and not taxable to the employee until the time funds are paid to him by the administrator or trustees.

Life Insurance for Profit Plans

There is considerable difference of opinion whether a profit-sharing trust for salaried employees should be self-administered, administered by an impartial trust company, or possibly invested in ordinary life insurance contracts under a recent ruling affecting

Section 165(a) of the Internal Revenue Code. The ruling permits investment in ordinary life policies provided that aggregate premiums on the life of an employee are less than 50 percent of the aggregate of contributions allocated to him at any one time and the life insurance is converted to a retirement income contract upon the employee's retirement. Under the plan, retirement income is not predetermined but depends on the allocations of profits to the participant's account; a portion of the annual allocation to the account of an uninsurable participant is invested in an annual premium deferred annuity contract.

Setting Up an Executive Incentive Pay Plan

There are, of course, many factors bearing on incentives for a salaried employee, not the least of which is a person's natural interest in his work. He gets a great satisfaction from doing his job well. He wants to be important to the management. To him it is not just a matter of pay, but also a matter of pride and the sheer joy of winning.

It would therefore be a grave mistake to approach the problem of providing key men with greater incentives with the assumption that they only are interested in their pay checks. But pay is a part of job satisfaction. It therefore should be approached in an intelligent and realistic way.

The best plan is one which blends company and executive objectives. The executive seeks maximum take-home pay, capital build-up, family and personal security. He wants tax protection and inflation protection. The company wants the maximum incentive arrangement. It wants to control the net cost of meeting the executives' requirements and still stimulate the build-up of capital values for its stockholders. Here, then, are three key questions to be answered in approaching the problem:

1. What can be done to put the executive in a position comparable to that which he would occupy if he were running his own business? This means direct incentives and the opportunity to participate in the enhancement of capital values.

2. What can be done to accumulate financial security for the executive within a corporation; i.e., in the form of annuity values, future payments on disability or retirement, and family security payments subsequent to death?

3. What can be done to carry expenses which the executive finds it difficult to meet in the face of the current level of taxes and the deterioration of the dollar; i.e., group life insurance, health and medical protection, physical examinations, training opportunities, etc.?

The answers to these key questions give an approach to establishing a plan which will provide the maximum incentive. At the same time, they offer the salaried employee more assurance that he is better off working for an established company at a salary plus contingent pay than he would be in business for himself, or taking a job with a new company even though the management of that company might dangle a nice block of stock before him to get him to make the change. There are five steps to take in setting up a fair plan:

1. Make up a list of the individuals in your executive group, their ages, compensation, and length of service with the company. Full data should be gathered on their stakes in any existing pension plan, profit-sharing arrangements, or other programs now in force.

2. Conduct a study of your present compensation practices, including their history. The study will indicate how and why a particular plan was adopted and its appropriateness at the present time.

3. Appraise the personal and family needs of the executive group, so that the program selected will be best adapted to meet those needs. Depending upon the needs of the executive group, the program may emphasize present earnings rather than security or vice versa. Projections should be made to show how each of the individuals in the executive group would stand to come out in take-home working income, retirement income, and capital over his working life if some of his present compensation and foreseeable increases were applied to installing or expanding one or more of the available methods of compensation.

4. Examine your relations in the past with Government agencies, with stockholders, and with labor. The program eventually adopted must take into consideration any positions you may have adopted in a tax case, with the SEC, at a stockholders' meeting. or in collective bargaining.

5. Evaluate alternative plans in terms of what they cost you and your stockholders in out-of-pocket dollars and in dilution of equity. This must then be weighed against what the hoped-for results in executive performance promise to do for you and your stockholders. Of course, final adoption of any plan will require reasonable assurances that it will meet approval from stockholders and other employees, and that it will comply with rules laid down by SEC and tax authorities.

The Contingent Bonus

It goes without saying that when tax considerations are not important, as in the case of middle management employees in the middle tax brackets, a bonus paid quarterly or semiannually, or annually with a quarterly draw, contingent upon departmental or division profits, is the most effective. Indeed, it is important in any incentive plan to tie the size of the bonus to a specific objective. The objective might be unit production, sales, savings, or departmental or branch profits. But it should be visible.

If profits are to be used as a base, it is most important that it be clearly understood how the profits are to be determined. There is nothing worse for the morale of a business than to have a dispute arise as to whether the management has changed the rules for computing profits in the "middle of the game." This is especially important during a period of high corporation taxes when management is inclined to make decisions which are advantageous to the business from a tax standpoint, but which adversely affect the immediate profits available for distribution under a profit-sharing plan. One common objection to contingent bonuses is that they tend to overemphasize near-term profits at the expense of the long-range good of a business.

Many companies are following the lead of General Motors in providing for the payment of bonus awards in annual installments over a period of up to five years. This method of delivery recognizes that one basic purpose of a bonus plan is to furnish incentive for the executives to remain in the employ of the corporation. In addition, installment delivery should make a plan more effective in that deliveries over a period of years will tend to reduce fluctuations in the recipient's taxable income, compared with a lump-sum payment, and thereby may be beneficial to him from a tax standpoint.

DISMISSAL PAY

When the time comes that a person is willing to work but is unsuited to the job and dismissal is necessary, the Monsanto Chemical Company has established a definite scale for dismissal wages. The scale follows:

Length of Service With the Company	Dismissal Pay
1 to 3 months	1 day
3 to 5 months	2 days
5 to 8 months	3 days
8 to 10 months	4 days
10 to 12 months	1 week
1 to 2 years	2 weeks
2 to 3 years	3 weeks
3 to 5 years	4 weeks
5 to 7 years	5 weeks
7 to 10 years	6 weeks
More than 10 years	8 weeks

Those rates are for people with dependents. If the dismissed employee has no dependents, two-thirds of the above rates apply. The company grants general managers permission to suspend dismissal wages when in their opinion a man will have no difficulty finding prompt re-employment in his usual trade.

Employees leaving the company from choice, layoff, or because they have been discharged for dishonesty or insubordination, are not eligible for dismissal wages.

Schedule for Dismissal Payments

Another large, well-known company, famous for its fair policies toward employees, uses the following schedule of payments in cases of dismissal:

Length of Service	Workers on Weekly Basis	Workers on Hourly Basis
Up to 12 weeks	1 week's pay	None
12 weeks up to 24 weeks	1 week's pay	8 hours' pay
24 weeks up to 52 weeks	1½ weeks' pay	12 hours' pay
52 weeks up to 3 years	2 weeks' pay	24 hours' pay
3 years or more	3 weeks' pay	40 hours' pay

Some companies would like to set aside reserves for future dismissal wage payments, but the present tax situation does not encourage such reserves. However, there may be a strong demand for dismissal wages in the future. This is a problem which every company should bear in mind in setting up any policies on dismissal wage payments at this time.

HOW 85 FIRMS HANDLE WAGE GARNISHMENTS

Of 85 concerns joining in an exchange of management experience, 33 percent have a set policy governing wage garnishments of employees. There are 34,018 office employees in these companies and 13 states are represented in the tabulation.

Many concerns report that while their policy is not actually put in writing, it does exist. Typical of these is Superior Coach Corporation, southern division, Kosciusko, Mississippi, whose assistant treasurer reports: "Our policy is not set down in writing for the reason that it has been used so seldom. Our division has not averaged more than two garnishments a year, and those have been with plant personnel—not office."

The office manager, Robertson Company, Louisville, Kentucky, says "Sorry, or rather fortunately, we are unable to comment on this subject. We have never had any credit complaints against our office employees. Undoubtedly, we—as much as the majority of people—are living 'over our heads,' but, somehow or other, have been able to scrape by."

Of the companies replying "No" to the question about having a set policy, 21 percent have a thorough discussion about the problem with the employee when a garnishment writ appears. Ten percent say it "never happened," 7 percent say the "garnishment is honored," and 14 percent deduct from the payroll. Five percent feel they would dismiss the employee, but 6 percent would loan him the money to pay the debt. So it would appear that even many of those concerns who don't have a formal policy do know what they would do in the event the situation arose.

The First Garnishment

What happens among participating companies when the first garnishment on an employee arises? Thirty-four percent of respondents say the individual is "talked to"—that disciplinary action isn't taken and that the company tries to help the employee through counseling. Four percent issue a warning to the employee, 7 percent set up payroll deduction plan to cover the debt, 3 percent dismiss the employee on the spot, and 2 percent "don't do anything." One concern has a plan whereby the credit union steps in and assists the employee "if he is a valued and dependable worker."

One firm, a farm-equipment manufacturer, says the "employee is invited to fully discuss the matter with an aim toward satisfying the garnishment and preventing future difficulties. Often the employee is referred to a reliable lending agency (bank, credit union, etc.) for assistance."

Summing up, on the first offense few employees lose their jobs. Rather, the company tries to help out and salvage the employee.

The Second Garnishment

When an employee has a second garnishment offense, chances of his dismissal from the company increase. Of those replying:

—11 percent fire the employee
— 6 percent counsel and advise
— 8 percent issue a warning
— 3 percent consider each case separately

Many respondents do not indicate exactly what happens on the second offense but imply that it is "very seriously considered."

The Third Garnishment

By the time an employee has a third offense it is generally concluded that he is a chronic offender and disciplinary action gets more severe. Again, many respondents do not specify exactly what happens in cases like this (usually because many have never faced them), but 14 percent say the employee is dismissed at once. Two percent "have no policy," and 3 percent feel "it depends upon circumstances."

The finance director, City of Wichita, says, "In a 12-month period, the City Treasurer sends a memo to the employee's departmental director with a copy to the personnel office." He reports that three garnishments in any 12-month period are grounds for written notice of dismissal. The treasurer, Hunter Bed Mfg. Corporation, Des Moines, Iowa (a nonunion organization), says, "We separate the employee, although the third offense has never occurred, yet, to test the rigidity of our policy. Evidently, employees do not wish to test it." And the office manager, Cities Service Oil Co., South Bend, Indiana, adds, "Although it has never gotten this far, it certainly would necessitate release of the employee for repeated offenses. If the employee cannot manage his money any better, I'm sure he could not manage the company's money, either."

Aid for Debt-Ridden Employees

Most concerns—60 percent—do not, as a matter of policy, provide legal aid to employees who are swamped by creditors. Only 7 percent actually offer such assistance as a matter of standard policy. However, other concerns would "assist" the employee, and that help might include legal aid. Another small group would help "if necessary and the employee was deserving." Seven percent of respondents would help through the credit union in accordance with its provisions. Typical replies follow:

"Not in any formal way. However, our assistance is offered any employee, and, occasionally, legal service would be provided by the company attorney."—Farm-equipment manufacturing company.

"If it seems to be a pretty hopeless debt situation, we urge the individual to use the services of a credit management firm."—Furniture manufacturer.

"Credit union stands ready to provide this type of aid."—Radio manufacturing firm.

"It may sound like locking the door after the horse is gone," says one office executive, "but we've salvaged more than one worthy employee from the clutches of financial ruin by good, old-fashioned counseling on the importance of living within one's means. They will accept it, too—if you will really help them."

Despite this rather eloquent plea for counseling debt-ridden employees, well over 50 percent of the responding companies offer no such aid. Nine percent have a formal program to help, and another 7 percent call their program "informal." Again, the credit union helps in 7 percent of the cases.

The director of personnel of a large railroad says his organization "avoids such counseling wherever possible. But we do counsel and have gone to bat for some employees at local banks to get them out of the clutches of high-interest loan sharks."

The secretary-treasurer, Zimmer-McClaskey, Inc., Louisville advertising agency, says, "We have very few problems of this nature. However, the firm's business manager is always available and willing to discuss personal problems with employees." And the supervisor of systems and procedures, The Steckler Company, Inc., New Orleans insurance group, says that while theirs is not a "fixed program," the head of the particular department concerned would speak to the employee and try to counsel him on his problem.

Asked whether they feel there has been an increase or decrease in garnishments over the past three years, executives joining in this exchange of management views and experience replied as follows:

No change—39 percent	Decrease—8 percent
10 percent increase—2 percent	Slight decrease—8 percent
20 percent increase—3 percent	Very few—3 percent
Slightly higher—9 percent	Can't say—7 percent

The following personal observations of office executives about employee indebtedness, garnishments, or trends toward living over one's head in these days of creeping inflation reflect the problem as it now exists:

"Most of our troubles stem from easy credit terms on the part of retail furniture and jewelry stores . . . We refuse to verify employment by telephone and advise written requests if the person has a previous history of debt troubles."

"In examining the cases of these employees receiving garnishments, it does not seem to appear that inflation, etc., affects the cases as much as might be anticipated. The same employee might well experience the same problems under different economic circumstances."

"The lack of early education in budgeting and managing money and credit coupled with small downpayments and easily acquired credit are a cause of these 'poor managers' becoming debt-ridden. Also, as most transactions are turned over to some financial institution, the local businesses don't seem to be concerned about a customer's financial status as long as the sale can be completed."

"This is a personal view: Anything less than garnishment is the individual's sole responsibility. However, for the benefit of public relations and employee morale in general, management should encourage its people to handle finances properly."

"We do not recognize wage garnishments. Since we stopped accepting them, suits have dropped off until now they are a rarity. Business houses know we do not accept garnishments, so they are a bit more careful in extending credit. Nearly all actions were against factory hourly rated help—probably 99 percent."

"It is less costly to adjust an occasional garnish than to try to replace an otherwise satisfactory employee."

"I feel that the use of the credit union has been a very good thing for our employees. We encourage them to use it. It can be used for saving and borrowing."

Establishing a Garnishment Policy

A number of companies include the subject of garnishment handling in their policy manuals. The following offered through the courtesy of the Burroughs Corporation, is typical.

SUBJECT: GARNISHMENTS

Policy: Garnishments are an inconvenience and a burden to the Corporation and to employees who receive them. In order to minimize this inconvenience, the Corporation will provide the employee with suggestions and information to help keep himself free from debt. However, if the employee continues to receive garnishments, he will be subject to disciplinary action as herein stated.

Definition: A garnishment is an order received from a duly constituted court requesting the Corporation to withhold certain monies from wages due an employee. Failure to act promptly may render Burroughs subject to a default judgment from which no appeal can be taken. A wage assignment, letter of inquiry or request by an outside concern stating that an employee will not pay monies owed to them, will be considered for the purposes of this policy the same as a garnishment.

Outside Aids: Employees receiving garnishments should be counseled regarding the aids that are available to them to avoid further action.

Disciplinary Procedure: It is not the Corporate policy to discharge seniority employees solely because of garnishments unless the offense becomes habitual, and the employee refuses to take steps to relieve himself of financial difficulties. Therefore, the severity of the disciplinary action to be applied should be based on a complete review of his record, so as to give consideration to the employee's history and past performance.

Probationary employees who are garnished will be subject to immediate dismissal unless the employee has established a satisfactory work record, and the garnishment is the result of some misfortune or other extenuating circumstances.

STANDARD WEEKLY SALARY TABLE

40 Hours a Week Basis—5 Days to a Week, 52 Weeks to a Year

Rate Per Week	Rate Per Year	Rate Per Month	Rate Per Day	Rate Per Hour	Rate Per Week	Rate Per Year	Rate Per Month	Rate Per Day	Rate Per Hour
$ 56.00	$ 2912.00	$242.67	$ 11.20	$1.40	$142.00	$ 7384.00	$615.33	$ 28.40	$3.55
58.00	3016.00	251.33	11.60	1.45	144.00	7488.00	624.00	28.80	3.60
60.00	3120.00	260.00	12.00	1.50	145.00	7540.00	628.33	29.00	3.62½
62.00	3224.00	268.67	12.40	1.55	146.00	7592.00	632.67	29.20	3.65
64.00	3328.00	277.33	12.80	1.60	148.00	7696.00	641.33	29.60	3.70
65.00	3380.00	281.67	13.00	1.62½	150.00	7800.00	650.00	30.00	3.75
66.00	3432.00	286.00	13.20	1.65	152.00	7904.00	658.67	30.40	3.80
68.00	3536.00	294.67	13.60	1.70	154.00	8008.00	667.33	30.80	3.85
70.00	3640.00	303.33	14.00	1.75	155.00	8060.00	671.67	31.00	3.87½
72.00	3744.00	312.00	14.40	1.80	156.00	8112.00	676.00	31.20	3.90
74.00	3848.00	320.67	14.80	1.85	158.00	8216.00	684.67	31.60	3.95
75.00	3900.00	325.00	15.00	1.87½	160.00	8320.00	693.33	32.00	4.00
76.00	3952.00	329.33	15.20	1.90	162.00	8424.00	702.00	32.40	4.05
78.00	4056.00	338.00	15.60	1.95	164.00	8528.00	710.67	32.80	4.10
80.00	4160.00	346.67	16.00	2.00	165.00	8580.00	715.00	33.00	4.12½
82.00	4264.00	355.33	16.40	2.05	166.00	8632.00	719.33	33.20	4.15
84.00	4368.00	364.00	16.80	2.10	168.00	8736.00	728.00	33.60	4.20
85.00	4420.00	368.33	17.00	2.12½	170.00	8840.00	736.67	34.00	4.25
86.00	4472.00	372.67	17.20	2.15	172.00	8944.00	745.33	34.40	4.30
88.00	4576.00	381.33	17.60	2.20	174.00	9048.00	754.00	34.80	4.35
90.00	4680.00	390.00	18.00	2.25	175.00	9100.00	758.33	35.00	4.37½
92.00	4784.00	398.67	18.40	2.30	176.00	9152.00	762.67	35.20	4.40
94.00	4888.00	407.33	18.80	2.35	178.00	9256.00	771.33	35.60	4.45
95.00	4940.00	411.67	19.00	2.37½	180.00	9360.00	780.00	36.00	4.50
96.00	4992.00	416.00	19.20	2.40	182.00	9464.00	788.67	36.40	4.55
98.00	5096.00	424.67	19.60	2.45	184.00	9568.00	797.33	36.80	4.60
100.00	5200.00	433.33	20.00	2.50	185.00	9620.00	801.67	37.00	4.62½
101.00	5252.00	437.67	20.20	2.52½	186.00	9672.00	806.00	37.20	4.65
102.00	5304.00	442.00	20.40	2.55	188.00	9776.00	814.67	37.60	4.70
104.00	5408.00	450.67	20.80	2.60	190.00	9880.00	823.33	38.00	4.75
105.00	5460.00	455.00	21.00	2.62½	192.00	9984.00	832.00	38.40	4.80
106.00	5512.00	459.33	21.20	2.65	194.00	10088.00	840.67	38.80	4.85
108.00	5616.00	468.00	21.60	2.70	195.00	10140.00	845.00	39.00	4.87½
110.00	5720.00	476.67	22.00	2.75	196.00	10192.00	849.33	39.20	4.90
112.00	5824.00	485.33	22.40	2.80	198.00	10296.00	858.00	39.60	4.95
114.00	5928.00	494.00	22.80	2.85	200.00	10400.00	866.67	40.00	5.00
115.00	5980.00	498.33	23.00	2.87½	205.00	10660.00	888.33	41.00	5.12½
116.00	6032.00	502.67	23.20	2.90	210.00	10920.00	910.00	42.00	5.25
118.00	6136.00	511.33	23.60	2.95	215.00	11180.00	931.67	43.00	5.37½
120.00	6240.00	520.00	24.00	3.00	220.00	11440.00	953.33	44.00	5.50
122.00	6344.00	528.67	24.40	3.05	225.00	11700.00	975.00	45.00	5.62½
124.00	6448.00	537.33	24.80	3.10	230.00	11960.00	996.67	46.00	5.75
125.00	6500.00	541.67	25.00	3.12½	235.00	12220.00	1018.33	47.00	5.87½
126.00	6552.00	546.00	25.20	3.15	240.00	12480.00	1040.00	48.00	6.00
128.00	6656.00	554.67	25.60	3.20	245.00	12740.00	1061.67	49.00	6.12½
130.00	6760.00	563.33	26.00	3.25	250.00	13000.00	1083.33	50.00	6.25
132.00	6864.00	572.00	26.40	3.30	255.00	13260.00	1105.00	51.00	6.37½
134.00	6968.00	580.67	26.80	3.35	260.00	13520.00	1126.67	52.00	6.50
135.00	7020.00	585.00	27.00	3.37½	265.00	13780.00	1148.33	53.00	6.62½
136.00	7072.00	589.33	27.20	3.40	270.00	14040.00	1170.00	54.00	6.75
138.00	7176.00	598.00	27.60	3.45	275.00	14300.00	1191.67	55.00	6.87½
140.00	7280.00	606.67	28.00	3.50	280.00	14560.00	1213.33	56.00	7.00

STANDARD ANNUAL SALARY TABLE

40 Hours a Week—5 Days of 8 Hours

Annual Rate	Quarterly	Monthly	Weekly	Daily	Hourly	¼ Hour
$ 3,000	$ 750.00	$250.00	$ 57.69	$ 11.54	$ 1.44	$ .36
3,500	875.00	291.67	67.31	13.46	1.68	.42
4,000	1,000.00	333.33	76.92	15.38	1.92	.48
4,500	1,125.00	375.00	86.54	17.30	2.16	.54
5,000	1,250.00	416.67	96.15	19.23	2.40	.60
5,500	1,375.00	458.33	105.77	21.15	2.64	.66
6,000	1,500.00	500.00	115.38	23.08	2.88	.72
6,500	1,625.00	541.67	125.00	25.00	3.13	.78
7,000	1,750.00	583.33	134.62	26.92	3.37	.84
7,500	1,875.00	625.00	144.23	28.85	3.60	.90
8,000	2,000.00	666.67	153.85	30.76	3.84	.96
8,500	2,125.00	708.33	163.59	32.72	4.09	1.02
9,000	2,250.00	750.00	173.08	34.62	4.33	1.08
9,500	2,375.00	791.67	182.70	36.54	4.57	1.14
10,000	2,500.00	833.33	192.31	38.46	4.81	1.20
11,000	2,750.00	916.67	211.54	42.31	5.29	1.32
12,000	3,000.00	1,000.00	230.77	46.15	5.77	1.44
13,000	3,250.00	1,083.33	250.00	50.00	6.25	1.56
14,000	3,500.00	1,166.67	269.23	53.85	6.73	1.68
15,000	3,750.00	1,250.00	288.46	57.69	7.21	1.80
16,000	4,000.00	1,333.33	307.69	61.54	7.69	1.92

STANDARD MONTHLY SALARY TABLE

Monthly Rate	Annual	Quarterly	Weekly	Daily	Hourly	¼ Hour
$ 250	$ 3,000	$ 750	$ 57.69	$11.54	$1.44	$0.36
260	3,120	780	60.00	12.00	1.50	.38
265	3,180	795	61.15	12.23	1.53	.38
275	3,300	825	63.46	12.69	1.59	.40
285	3,420	855	65.77	13.15	1.64	.41
300	3,600	900	69.23	13.85	1.73	.43
325	3,900	975	75.00	15.00	1.87	.47
350	4,200	1,050	80.77	16.15	2.02	.51
375	4,500	1,125	86.54	17.31	2.16	.54
400	4,800	1,200	92.31	18.46	2.31	.58
425	5,100	1,275	98.08	19.62	2.45	.61
450	5,400	1,350	103.84	20.77	2.60	.65
475	5,700	1,425	109.61	21.92	2.74	.69
500	6,000	1,500	115.38	23.08	2.88	.72
550	6,600	1,650	126.92	25.38	3.17	.79
600	7,200	1,800	138.46	27.69	3.46	.87
800	9,600	2,400	184.61	36.92	4.62	1.16
900	10,800	2,700	207.69	41.54	5.19	1.30
950	11,400	2,850	219.23	43.85	5.48	1.37
1,000	12,000	3,000	230.77	46.15	5.77	1.44
1,050	12,600	3,150	242.31	48.46	6.06	1.52
1,100	13,200	3,300	253.85	50.77	6.35	1.59
1,150	13,800	3,450	265.38	53.08	6.63	1.66
1,200	14,400	3,600	276.92	55.38	6.92	1.73
1,250	15,000	3,750	288.46	57.69	7.21	1.80
1,300	15,600	3,900	300.00	60.00	7.50	1.88
1,350	16,200	4,050	311.54	62.31	7.79	1.95
1,400	16,800	4,200	323.08	64.62	8.08	2.02

WEEKLY EQUIVALENTS OF HOURLY RATES

Overtime Included in 44- and 48-Hour Week

Hourly Rate	Hours Per Week		
	35	37½	40
$1.25	$43.75	$46.88	$50.00
1.26	44.10	47.25	50.40
1.27	44.45	47.63	50.80
1.28	44.80	48.00	51.20
1.29	45.15	48.38	51.60
1.30	45.50	48.75	52.00
1.31	45.85	49.13	52.40
1.32	46.20	49.50	52.80
1.33	46.55	49.88	53.20
1.34	46.90	50.25	53.60
1.35	47.25	50.63	54.00
1.36	47.60	51.00	54.40
1.37	47.95	51.38	54.80
1.38	48.30	51.75	55.20
1.39	48.65	52.13	55.60
1.40	49.00	52.50	56.00
1.41	49.35	52.88	56.40
1.42	49.70	53.25	56.80
1.43	50.05	53.63	57.20
1.44	50.40	54.00	57.60
1.45	50.75	54.38	58.00
1.46	51.10	54.75	58.40
1.47	51.45	55.13	58.80
1.48	51.80	55.50	59.20
1.49	52.15	55.88	59.60
1.50	52.50	56.25	60.00
1.51	52.85	56.63	60.40
1.52	53.20	57.00	60.80
1.53	53.55	57.38	61.20
1.54	53.90	57.75	61.60
1.55	54.25	58.13	62.00
1.56	54.60	58.50	62.40
1.57	54.95	58.88	62.80
1.58	55.30	59.25	63.20
1.59	55.65	59.63	63.60
1.60	56.00	60.00	64.00
1.61	56.35	60.38	64.40
1.62	56.70	60.75	64.80
1.63	57.05	61.13	65.20
1.64	57.40	61.50	65.60
1.65	57.75	61.88	66.00
1.66	58.10	62.25	66.40
1.67	58.45	62.63	66.80
1.68	58.80	63.00	67.20
1.69	59.15	63.38	67.60
1.70	59.50	63.75	68.00
1.71	59.85	64.13	68.40
1.72	60.20	64.50	68.80
1.73	60.55	64.88	69.20
1.74	60.90	65.25	69.60
1.75	61.25	65.63	70.00
1.76	61.60	66.00	70.40
1.77	61.95	66.38	70.80
1.78	62.30	66.75	71.20
1.79	62.65	67.13	71.60
1.80	63.00	67.50	72.00
1.81	63.35	67.88	72.40
1.82	63.70	68.25	72.80
1.83	64.05	68.63	73.20
1.84	64.40	69.00	73.60
1.85	64.75	69.38	74.00
1.86	65.10	69.75	74.40
1.87	65.45	70.13	74.80
1.88	65.80	70.50	75.20
1.89	66.15	70.88	75.60
1.90	66.50	71.25	76.00
1.91	66.85	71.63	76.40

Hourly Rate	Hours Per Week		
	35	37½	40
$1.92	$67.20	$72.00	$76.80
1.93	67.55	72.38	77.20
1.94	67.90	72.75	77.60
1.95	68.25	73.13	78.00
1.96	68.60	73.50	78.40
1.97	68.95	73.88	78.80
1.98	69.30	74.25	79.20
1.99	69.65	74.63	79.60
2.00	70.00	75.00	80.00
2.01	70.35	75.38	80.40
2.02	70.70	75.75	80.80
2.03	71.05	76.13	81.20
2.04	71.40	76.50	81.60
2.05	71.75	76.88	82.00
2.06	72.10	77.25	82.40
2.07	72.45	77.63	82.80
2.08	72.80	78.00	83.20
2.09	73.15	78.38	83.60
2.10	73.50	78.75	84.00
2.11	73.85	79.13	84.40
2.12	74.20	79.50	84.80
2.13	74.55	79.88	85.20
2.14	74.90	80.25	85.60
2.15	75.25	80.63	86.00
2.16	75.60	81.00	86.40
2.17	75.95	81.38	86.80
2.18	76.30	81.75	87.20
2.19	76.65	82.13	87.60
2.20	77.00	82.50	88.00
2.21	77.35	82.88	88.40
2.22	77.70	83.25	88.80
2.23	78.05	83.63	89.20
2.24	78.40	84.00	89.60
2.25	78.75	84.38	90.00
2.26	79.10	84.75	90.40
2.27	79.45	85.13	90.80
2.28	79.80	85.50	91.20
2.29	80.15	85.88	91.60
2.30	80.50	86.25	92.00
2.31	80.85	86.63	92.40
2.32	81.20	87.00	92.80
2.33	81.55	87.38	93.20
2.34	81.90	87.75	93.60
2.35	82.25	88.13	94.00
2.36	82.60	88.50	94.40
2.37	82.95	88.88	94.80
2.38	83.30	89.25	95.20
2.39	83.65	89.63	95.60
2.40	84.00	90.00	96.00
2.41	84.35	90.38	96.40
2.42	84.70	90.75	96.80
2.43	85.05	91.13	97.20
2.44	85.40	91.50	97.60
2.45	85.75	91.88	98.00
2.46	86.10	92.25	98.40
2.47	86.45	92.63	98.80
2.48	86.80	93.00	99.20
2.49	87.15	93.38	99.60
2.50	87.50	93.75	100.00
2.51	87.85	94.13	100.40
2.52	88.20	94.50	100.80
2.53	88.55	94.88	101.20
2.54	88.90	95.25	101.60
2.55	89.25	95.63	102.00
2.56	89.60	96.00	102.40
2.57	89.95	96.38	102.80
2.58	90.30	96.75	103.20
2.59	90.65	97.13	103.60

Hourly Rate	Hours Per Week		
	35	37½	40
$2.60	$91.00	$97.50	$104.00
2.61	91.35	97.88	104.40
2.62	91.70	98.25	104.80
2.63	92.05	98.63	105.20
2.64	92.40	99.00	105.60
2.65	92.75	99.38	106.00
2.66	93.10	99.75	106.40
2.67	93.45	100.13	106.80
2.68	93.80	100.50	107.20
2.69	94.15	100.88	107.60
2.70	94.50	101.25	108.00
2.71	94.85	101.63	108.40
2.72	95.20	102.00	108.80
2.73	95.55	102.38	109.20
2.74	95.90	102.75	109.60
2.75	96.25	103.13	110.00
2.76	96.60	103.50	110.40
2.77	96.95	103.88	110.80
2.78	97.30	104.25	111.20
2.79	97.65	104.63	111.60
2.80	98.00	105.00	112.00
2.81	98.35	105.38	112.40
2.82	98.70	105.75	112.80
2.83	99.05	106.13	113.20
2.84	99.40	106.50	113.60
2.85	99.75	106.88	114.00
2.86	100.10	107.25	114.40
2.87	100.45	107.63	114.80
2.88	100.80	108.00	115.20
2.89	101.15	108.38	115.60
2.90	101.50	108.75	116.00
2.91	101.85	109.13	116.40
2.92	102.20	109.50	116.80
2.93	102.55	109.88	117.20
2.94	102.90	110.25	117.60
2.95	103.25	110.63	118.00
2.96	103.60	111.00	118.40
2.97	103.95	111.38	118.80
2.98	104.30	111.75	119.20
2.99	104.65	112.13	119.60
3.00	105.00	112.50	120.00
3.01	105.35	112.88	120.40
3.02	105.70	113.25	120.80
3.03	106.05	113.63	121.20
3.04	106.40	114.00	121.60
3.05	106.75	114.38	122.00
3.06	107.10	114.75	122.40
3.07	107.45	115.13	122.80
3.08	107.80	115.50	123.20
3.09	108.15	115.88	123.60
3.10	108.50	116.25	124.00
3.11	108.85	116.63	124.40
3.12	109.20	117.00	124.80
3.13	109.55	117.38	125.20
3.14	109.90	117.75	125.60
3.15	110.25	118.13	126.00
3.16	110.60	118.50	126.40
3.17	110.95	118.88	126.80
3.18	111.30	119.25	127.20
3.19	111.65	119.63	127.60
3.20	112.00	120.00	128.00
3.21	112.35	120.38	128.40
3.22	112.70	120.75	128.80
3.23	113.05	121.13	129.20
3.24	113.40	121.50	129.60
3.25	113.75	121.88	130.00

Overtime Included in 44- and 48-Hour Week

Hourly Rate	Hours Per Week 35	37½	40	Hourly Rate	Hours Per Week 35	37½	40	Hourly Rate	Hours Per Week 35	37½	40
$3.26	$114.10	$122.25	$130.40	$3.92	$137.20	$147.00	$156.80	$4.59	$160.65	$172.13	$183.60
3.27	114.45	122.63	130.80	3.93	137.55	147.38	157.20	4.60	161.00	172.50	184.00
3.28	114.80	123.00	131.20	3.94	137.90	147.75	157.60				
3.29	115.15	123.38	131.60	3.95	138.25	148.13	158.00	4.61	161.35	172.88	184.40
3.30	115.50	123.75	132.00	3.96	138.60	148.50	158.40	4.62	161.70	173.25	184.80
				3.97	138.95	148.88	158.80	4.63	162.05	173.63	185.20
3.31	115.85	124.13	132.40	3.98	139.30	149.25	159.20	4.64	162.40	174.00	185.60
3.32	116.20	124.50	132.80	3.99	139.65	149.63	159.60	4.65	162.75	174.38	186.00
3.33	116.55	124.88	133.20	4.00	140.00	150.00	160.00	4.66	163.10	174.75	186.40
3.34	116.90	125.25	133.60					4.67	163.45	175.13	186.80
3.35	117.25	125.63	134.00	4.01	140.35	150.38	160.40	4.68	163.80	175.50	187.20
3.36	117.60	126.00	134.40	4.02	140.70	150.75	160.80	4.69	164.15	175.88	187.60
3.37	117.95	126.38	134.80	4.03	141.05	151.13	161.20	4.70	164.50	176.25	188.00
3.38	118.30	126.75	135.20	4.04	141.40	151.50	161.60				
3.39	118.65	127.13	135.60	4.05	141.75	151.88	162.00	4.71	164.85	176.63	188.40
3.40	119.00	127.50	136.00	4.06	142.10	152.25	162.40	4.72	165.20	177.00	188.80
				4.07	142.45	152.63	162.80	4.73	165.55	177.38	189.20
3.41	119.35	127.88	136.40	4.08	142.80	153.00	163.20	4.74	165.90	177.75	189.60
3.42	119.70	128.25	136.80	4.09	143.15	153.38	163.60	4.75	166.25	178.13	190.00
3.43	120.05	128.63	137.20	4.10	143.50	153.75	164.00	4.76	166.60	178.50	190.40
3.44	120.40	129.00	137.60					4.77	166.95	178.88	190.80
3.45	120.75	129.38	138.00	4.11	143.85	154.13	164.40	4.78	167.30	179.25	191.20
3.46	121.10	129.75	138.40	4.12	144.20	154.50	164.80	4.79	167.65	179.63	191.60
3.47	121.45	130.13	138.80	4.13	144.55	154.88	165.20	4.80	168.00	180.00	192.00
3.48	121.80	130.50	139.20	4.14	144.90	155.25	165.60				
3.49	122.15	130.88	139.60	4.15	145.25	155.63	166.00	4.81	168.35	180.38	192.40
3.50	122.50	131.25	140.00	4.16	145.60	156.00	166.40	4.82	168.70	180.75	192.80
				4.17	145.95	156.38	166.80	4.83	169.05	181.13	193.20
3.51	122.85	131.62	140.40	4.18	146.30	156.75	167.20	4.84	169.40	181.50	193.60
3.52	123.20	132.00	140.80	4.19	146.65	157.13	167.60	4.85	169.75	181.88	194.00
3.53	123.55	132.37	141.20	4.20	147.00	157.50	168.00	4.86	170.10	182.25	194.40
3.54	123.90	132.75	141.60					4.87	170.45	182.63	194.80
3.55	124.25	133.13	142.00	4.21	147.35	157.88	168.40	4.88	170.80	183.00	195.20
3.56	124.60	133.50	142.40	4.22	147.70	158.25	168.80	4.89	171.15	183.38	195.60
3.57	124.95	133.88	142.80	4.23	148.05	158.63	169.20	4.90	171.50	183.75	196.00
3.58	125.30	134.25	143.20	4.24	148.40	159.00	169.60				
3.59	125.65	134.63	143.60	4.25	148.75	159.38	170.00	4.91	171.85	184.13	196.40
3.60	126.00	135.00	144.00	4.26	149.10	159.75	170.40	4.92	172.20	184.50	196.80
				4.27	149.45	160.13	170.80	4.93	172.55	184.88	197.20
3.61	126.35	135.38	144.40	4.28	149.80	160.50	171.20	4.94	172.90	185.25	197.60
3.62	126.70	135.75	144.80	4.29	150.15	160.88	171.60	4.95	173.25	185.63	198.00
3.63	127.05	136.13	145.20	4.30	150.50	161.25	172.00	4.96	173.60	186.00	198.40
3.64	127.40	136.50	145.60					4.97	173.95	186.38	198.80
3.65	127.75	136.88	146.00	4.31	150.85	161.63	172.40	4.98	174.30	186.75	199.20
3.66	128.10	137.25	146.40	4.32	151.20	162.00	172.80	4.99	174.65	187.13	199.60
3.67	128.45	137.63	146.80	4.33	151.55	162.38	173.20	5.00	175.00	187.50	200.00
3.68	128.80	138.00	147.20	4.34	151.90	162.75	173.60				
3.69	129.15	138.38	147.60	4.35	152.25	163.13	174.00	5.01	175.35	187.88	200.40
3.70	129.50	138.75	148.00	4.36	152.60	163.50	174.40	5.02	175.70	188.25	200.80
				4.37	152.95	163.88	174.80	5.03	176.05	188.63	201.20
3.71	129.85	139.13	148.40	4.38	153.30	164.25	175.20	5.04	176.40	189.00	201.60
3.72	130.20	139.50	148.80	4.39	153.65	164.63	175.60	5.05	176.75	189.38	202.00
3.73	130.55	139.88	149.20	4.40	154.00	165.00	176.00	5.06	177.10	189.75	202.40
3.74	130.90	140.25	149.60					5.07	177.45	190.13	202.80
3.75	131.25	140.63	150.00	4.41	154.35	165.38	176.40	5.08	177.80	190.50	203.20
3.76	131.60	141.00	150.40	4.42	154.70	165.75	176.80	5.09	178.15	190.88	203.60
3.77	131.95	141.38	150.80	4.43	155.05	166.13	177.20	5.10	178.50	191.25	204.00
3.78	132.30	141.75	151.20	4.44	155.40	166.50	177.60				
3.79	132.65	142.13	151.60	4.45	155.75	166.88	178.00	5.11	178.85	191.63	204.40
3.80	133.00	142.50	152.00	4.46	156.10	167.25	178.40	5.12	179.20	192.00	204.80
				4.47	156.45	167.63	178.80	5.13	179.55	192.38	205.20
3.81	133.35	142.88	152.40	4.48	156.80	168.00	179.20	5.14	179.90	192.75	205.60
3.82	133.70	143.25	152.80	4.49	157.15	168.38	179.60	5.15	180.25	193.13	206.00
3.83	134.05	143.63	153.20	4.50	157.50	168.75	180.00	5.16	180.60	193.50	206.40
3.84	134.40	144.00	153.60					5.17	180.95	193.88	206.80
3.85	134.75	144.38	154.00	4.51	157.85	169.13	180.40	5.18	181.30	194.25	207.20
3.86	135.10	144.75	154.40	4.52	158.20	169.50	180.80	5.19	181.65	194.63	207.60
3.87	135.45	145.13	154.80	4.53	158.55	169.88	181.20	5.20	182.00	195.00	208.00
3.88	135.80	145.50	155.20	4.54	158.90	170.25	181.60				
3.89	136.15	145.88	155.60	4.55	159.25	170.63	182.00	5.21	182.35	195.38	208.40
3.90	136.50	146.25	156.00	4.56	159.60	171.00	182.40	5.22	182.70	195.75	208.80
				4.57	159.95	171.38	182.80	5.23	183.05	196.13	209.20
3.91	136.85	146.63	156.40	4.58	160.30	171.75	183.20	5.24	183.40	196.50	209.60
								5.25	183.75	196.88	210.00

ADJUSTMENT FACTORS FOR ELIMINATING PREMIUM OVERTIME PAYMENTS FROM GROSS AVERAGE HOURLY EARNINGS

Average Weekly Hours*	Adjustment Factor	Average Weekly Hours*	Adjustment Factor	Average Weekly Hours*	Adjustment Factor	Average Weekly Hours*	Adjustment Factor
36.0	0.990	42.0	0.957	48.0	0.913	54.0	0.878
.1	.989	.1	.956	.1	.913	.1	.878
.2	.989	.2	.955	.2	.912	.2	.877
.3	.989	.3	.954	.3	.912	.3	.877
.4	.988	.4	.953	.4	.911	.4	.876
.5	.988	.5	.952	.5	.910	.5	.876
.6	.988	.6	.952	.6	.910	.6	.875
.7	.988	.7	.951	.7	.909	.7	.875
.8	.987	.8	.950	.8	.909	.8	.874
.9	.987	.9	.949	.9	.908	.9	.874
37.0	.987	43.0	.948	49.0	.907	55.0	.873
.1	.987	.1	.947	.1	.906	.1	.873
.2	.986	.2	.946	.2	.905	.2	.872
.3	.986	.3	.945	.3	.904	.3	.872
.4	.986	.4	.945	.4	.904	.4	.871
.5	.985	.5	.944	.5	.903	.5	.871
.6	.985	.6	.944	.6	.902	.6	.870
.7	.985	.7	.943	.7	.902	.7	.870
.8	.984	.8	.942	.8	.901	.8	.869
.9	.984	.9	.941	.9	.901	.9	.869
38.0	.984	44.0	.941	50.0	.900	56.0	.868
.1	.984	.1	.940	.1	.900	.1	.868
.2	.983	.2	.940	.2	.899	.2	.867
.3	.983	.3	.939	.3	.899	.3	.867
.4	.982	.4	.938	.4	.898	.4	.866
.5	.982	.5	.937	.5	.898	.5	.866
.6	.981	.6	.936	.6	.897	.6	.865
.7	.981	.7	.935	.7	.896	.7	.865
.8	.981	.8	.934	.8	.896	.8	.864
.9	.980	.9	.933	.9	.895	.9	.864
39.0	.980	45.0	.933	51.0	.895	57.0	.864
.1	.979	.1	.932	.1	.894	.1	.863
.2	.979	.2	.932	.2	.894	.2	.863
.3	.978	.3	.931	.3	.893	.3	.862
.4	.978	.4	.930	.4	.892	.4	.862
.5	.977	.5	.930	.5	.892	.5	.861
.6	.977	.6	.929	.6	.891	.6	.861
.7	.976	.7	.929	.7	.891	.7	.860
.8	.975	.8	.928	.8	.890	.8	.860
.9	.974	.9	.927	.9	.889	.9	.859
40.0	.973	46.0	.926	52.0	.889	58.0	.859
.1	.972	.1	.926	.1	.888	.1	.859
.2	.971	.2	.925	.2	.888	.2	.858
.3	.970	.3	.925	.3	.887	.3	.858
.4	.969	.4	.924	.4	.887	.4	.857
.5	.969	.5	.923	.5	.886	.5	.857
.6	.968	.6	.923	.6	.886	.6	.857
.7	.968	.7	.922	.7	.885	.7	.856
.8	.967	.8	.921	.8	.885	.8	.856
.9	.966	.9	.921	*.9	.884	.9	.856
41.0	.965	47.0	.920	53.0	.883	59.0	.855
.1	.964	.1	.919	.1	.883	.1	.855
.2	.963	.2	.919	.2	.882	.2	.854
.3	.962	.3	.918	.3	.882	.3	.854
.4	.961	.4	.917	.4	.881	.4	.853
.5	.961	.5	.917	.5	.881	.5	.853
.6	.960	.6	.916	.6	.880	.6	.853
.7	.959	.7	.916	.7	.880	.7	.852
.8	.958	.8	.915	.8	.879	.8	.852
.9	.957	.9	.914	.9	.879	.9	.851
						60.0	.851

*For practical purposes, premium overtime payments in industries averaging less than 36 hours a week may usually be ignored.

Use of the table assumes that the average weekly hours of work during the period represented by the average hourly earnings is known. The steps to be taken in making the adjustment are as follows: (1) In the column headed "Average Weekly Hours" find the average hours for the period being studied, and (2) multiply the gross average hourly earnings figure by the adjustment factor opposite this average of weekly hours. Example: In one period the aircraft industry had average weekly hours of work of 47.7 and average hourly earnings of 94.8 cents. Inspection of the table reveals that the adjustment factor for 47.7 hours is 0.916. This ratio multiplied by 94.8 cents yields 86.8 cents, the estimated hourly earnings corrected to eliminate premium overtime pay.

U. S. Department of Labor

Chapter 11

COMPENSATING OFFICE EXECUTIVES

WHAT, specifically, is an office manager supposed to do for his pay check? To find out, Dartnell's editors put this and other questions to managers of 197 companies, including those with employees numbering less than one hundred all the way up to many thousands.

The answers prove, in the aggregate, that today's office manager is a versatile, several-sided person. It turns out that 41 times out of 100, much of his time and attention are tied up with major financial responsibilities; running the office is a side line, although an important one. Forty percent of the office managers canvassed have other important outside duties that cannot be classified as financial, and only 35 percent of them are allowed to devote full time to keeping office production humming. (The figures given here add to more than 100 percent because a number of office managers have extra responsibilities in both financial and nonfinancial areas.)

There are differences, of course, as offices change size. For present purposes we are assuming that an office is large if the administrative staff (the employees who are under the direction of the office

OFFICE MANAGERS' TITLES

TITLE	Percentage of Office Managers Surveyed		
	Office Service Staff of		All Offices
	Less Than 50	50 or More	
None (office manager only).........................	30	55	35
Treasurer or controller...........................	18	13	17
Assistant treasurer or assistant controller...........	12	11	11
Assistant secretary...............................	9	5	8
Personnel manager...............................	7	8	7
Chief accountant.................................	8	3	6
Credit manager..................................	9	....	6
Secretary.......................................	8	....	6
General manager.................................	6	5	6
Purchasing agent................................	4	3	4
Traffic manager.................................	2	3	2
Auditor..	2	....	1
All others......................................	7	8	7

FUNCTIONS AND RESPONSIBILITIES OF OFFICE MANAGER

Oxford Filing Supply Company, Inc.

The Office Manager is responsible to the Treasurer.

Assists the Treasurer in the control function of the business, in the preparation of forecasts, budgets, and financial reports.

Responsible for and coordinates all administrative and office activities, cooperating with department heads.

PERSONNEL

    Hiring, transfers, promotions, grievances
    Personnel records
    Introduction of new employees
    Office manual
    Training (new and old employees)
    Vacations, holidays, and office hours
    Employee attitudes (guidance)
    Employee welfare, rest rooms
    Job analysis, job evaluation, salary standardization, merit rating
    Payroll policy and salary changes

OFFICE EQUIPMENT AND SUPPLIES

    Standardization   Inventory   Purchase
    Maintenance—storage, distribution   Forms design

OFFICE PLANNING

    Layout   Lighting, heating, ventilation, noise reduction

OFFICE METHODS AND PROCEDURES

    Organization setup   Flow of work   Research   Systems
    Measurement of clerical production and establishment of standards
    Inspection and departmental audit

SERVICE UNITS

    COMMUNICATION

        Telephone, teletype, telegraph, interoffice
        Messenger service   Reception

    MAILING

        Distribution of incoming   Dispatch of outgoing
        House mail   House mail

    STENOGRAPHY AND TYPING

        Centralization   Transcribing   Duplicating

    FILING

        Centralization   Storage   Destruction

manager and whose only purpose is to serve the rest of the office) consists of 50 or more persons. It is to be expected that managers of offices that size would be more apt to find the demands of running the office occupying all their time, and such is the case. In 55 percent of the instances reported to us, the office manager in a large situation has no other title, whereas in small offices the percentage drops off to 30. As the office decreases in size, the manager is better able to assimilate some of the other important duties connected with the business.

Other Responsibilities

Even though he may not carry additional titles suggestive of further duties, there are sometimes certain "fringe" responsibilities in the life of an office manager that are not listed in the textbooks. Yet, they show up often enough to be considered part of the office manager's assignment. One of these is employment, or some phase of it.

When office managers told us they had no other titles, we asked them if they held responsibility for the employment function. More than three-quarters of them (76 percent) said "yes." Responsibility usually extends to the office force only, leaving the plant side to the personnel department. In practice, the office employment responsibility is usually shared in some measure by the personnel executive and the office manager.

Over half of those same office managers bear the responsibility for working up and administering the office payroll. A third of them have specific accounting department functions to worry about. Beyond these, a wide variety of activities have been reported. Those mentioned several times are accounts payable and receivable, billing, fleet supervision, budgets, financial statements and reports, employee and corporate insurance, cost accounting, community and public relations, corporate taxes, salary administration, statistical analysis, and inventory control.

Salaries of Office Managers

For the last 20 years at least, the office manager has been among the poorly compensated administrative officials. A recent Dartnell survey shows this still to be the case, with the office manager near the bottom of the compensation ladder once again.

The duties and responsibilities ascribed to office managers are many and exacting. If he were the personnel and payroll expert he is supposed to be, if he were competent in tax matters and electronic data processing, if he were an accomplished systems and procedures man, he would deserve a much higher salary than he is presently drawing. The fact of the matter is that few office managers have all the responsibilities and obligations that are included in many job descriptions. It is almost too much to expect one man to be proficient in all.

General office administration, either in a company or a large department of a company, is the one common denominator for all office managers. Beyond that, duties vary. Of the companies participating in this survey, for example, 26 percent ask their office managers to be responsible for clerical employment; 19 percent place them in charge of data-processing activities.

Relatively small numbers combine management of the office with other functions. Only 8 percent make a part-time credit manager out of the office administrator, while 7 percent have him in charge of purchasing. These figures, incidentally, are lower than similar figures turned up in surveys of other years, suggesting that many companies are finding it necessary to place specialists in charge of such activities as employment and data processing.

While the median salary of the office manager is $9,200, it is well over $10,000 in 90 percent of those companies where he has charge of clerical employment and data processing. Very rare, however, are salaries of more than $15,000.

The office manager's total compensation, as measured by this recent survey, runs to just $10,000. He has come off fairly well in the past 5 years, increasing his base pay by 11 percent, the all-executives-all-companies average, and bringing his total compensation up 14 percent.

The office manager's salary and full pay are 21.3 percent and 20.0 percent, respectively, of the chief executive's. He stands third from the bottom in the ranking of 37 executives making up the compensation ladder.

What happens when the office manager is given more responsibility? Responsibilities may come in two ways: through an enlarged office staff or by assumption of more outside duties. In either case, the effect is the same: Compensation increases. When he is given a second-level financial job to handle, in addition to managing the office, his salary goes up by from $500 to $1000 per annum. Such a job might be assistant treasurer, assistant controller, chief accountant, credit manager, or auditor. If his additional duties are outside the financial field—such as personnel director, secretary, administrative assistant, purchasing agent, traffic manager, or the like—his salary is similarly affected.

The Office Manager's Bonus

Bonuses, gifts, and extra incentive pay account for the difference between base salary and total compensation in all of the tables. In this department, the survey shows, office managers are overlooked more often than most of their brother executives; only 47 percent of the companies surveyed give them cash bonuses.

The amount of the office manager's bonus ranges, in the majority of instances, from 4 percent to 18 percent of base salary. The median amount is exactly 10 percent of salary. Sources of bonus awards are just as varied as for other executive groups. Most popular, however, is profit sharing, which accounts for almost four out of every 10 bonuses paid to office managers.

Seventeen percent of the office managers polled describe their bonuses as gifts, given at Christmas or at the end of the fiscal year. Fourteen percent say bonuses are discretionary, varying from year to year according to executive committee decision. About the same number of bonuses, 13 percent, are subject to stated formulas which are almost always based on the office manager's salary and/or years of service. One company, for example, has a plan called "Additional Living Compensation." Under it, salaried employees receive 5 percent of their salaries as a bonus. They get another 5 percent if they have been with the company for more than three years.

Eleven percent of the office managers surveyed work under special incentive arrangements by which bonus amounts are dependent upon office production, savings, or some other measure of the office manager's effectiveness. Bonuses paid to the remaining 6 percent of those under survey must be classified as miscelleaneous or not otherwise identified.

COMPENSATING OFFICE SUPERVISORS

In the companies that took part in Dartnell's survey, it appears that the representative office manager who has supervisors under his direction has an average of 3.7 of them, and that each of the supervisors controls exactly 10 employees. In small companies (fewer than 50 office service employees), there are 2.5 supervisors on the average, each with 7.3 employees; in large companies (50 or more employees), there are 7.4 supervisors directing 11.9 employees each. What are these people getting for their supervisory efforts?

The range of salaries and total compensation paid to office administrators is shown on the tables following.

How do supervisory salaries stack up against the office manager's and against each other's? Ascribing an index value of 100 to the office manager's base salary, we find that the supervisors' indexes look like this:

	INDEX
Office manager	100
Supervisor, statistical tabulating	78
Supervisor, billing	73
Assistant office manager	70
Supervisor, general accounting	68
Supervisor, order department	65
Supervisor, payroll	64
Supervisor, office communications	58
Supervisor, mailroom	55
Supervisor, stenographic pool	53
Supervisor, files	47

Bonuses in the supervisory group are spotty and irregular. It often happens that when the office manager gets a bonus, those down the line have it too. But it does not happen often enough to bring the bonus incidence among supervisors up to the office manager's frequency.

Bonuses are most common in the order department where 46 percent of supervisors are on the bonus list. Next come supervisors of general accounting, 37 percent of whom rate bonuses. After that, there are the stenographic pool supervisors at 31 percent, the files heads at 18 percent, and mail department supervisors at 15 percent.

The amount of the supervisory bonus is proportionately less than the office manager gets. The majority fall between 4 and 10 percent of base salaries, with the median at just 5 percent of salary.

COMPENSATION OF THE OFFICE MANAGER

All Industries

Gross Sales	Number of Employees		Median		Percentage Increase 1959–1964	Range of the Middle Half		Percentage Receiving Bonus	
			1964	1959		1964	1959	1964	1959
Under $5 million	all sizes	base	$ 8,000	$ 7,500	7	$ 7,000–$10,000	$ 6,000–$ 8,800	32	31
		total	8,900	7,800	14	7,700– 11,000	6,300– 9,200		
$5 million–$25 million	all sizes	base	9,200	8,400	10	8,100– 11,000	7,500– 10,000	45	45
		total	9,900	8,900	11	8,500– 11,800	7,800– 10,500		
Over $25 million	under 1,000	base	10,100	8,000	26	8,800– 13,800	7,400– 10,400	33	44
		total	10,500	8,500	23	8,800– 14,400	7,500– 10,400		
Over $25 million	over 1,000	base	11,000	9,800	12	9,300– 13,900	8,300– 12,000	42	32
		total	12,100	10,600	14	9,800– 15,100	8,600– 13,500		

Chemicals, Petroleum and Rubber Products

All companies	all sizes	base	$ 8,500	$ 7,500	13	$ 7,500–$10,500	$ 7,300–$ 8,400	39	32
		total	9,200	7,800	18	8,300– 10,800	7,400– 9,400		

Fabricated Metal Products

All companies	all sizes	base	$ 9,700	$ 8,500	14	$ 8,300–$11,100	$ 7,200–$ 9,600	33	21
		total	10,000	8,500	18	8,400– 11,700	7,200– 10,100		

COMPENSATION OF THE OFFICE MANAGER (continued)

Finance, Insurance and Real Estate

Gross Sales	Number of Employees	Median		Percentage Increase 1959-1964	Range of the Middle Half		Percentage Receiving Bonus	
		1964	1959		1964	1959	1964	1959
All companies	all sizes	base $11,400 total 12,000	$10,000 10,300	7 16	$ 9,000-$14,500 9,500- 15,800	$ 7,900-$15,100 7,900- 16,100	30	39

Food and Tobacco Products

All companies	all sizes	base $ 9,000 total 9,900	$ 8,200 8,800	10 12	$ 7,800-$11,000 7,900- 11,400	$ 6,300-$ 9,900 6,600- 10,200	47	67

Transportation, Communications, Public Utilities

All companies	all sizes	base $ 9,300 total 9,400	$ 8,400 8,400	11 12	$ 7,300-$11,600 7,800- 12,000	$ 7,500-$13,600 7,500- 14,100	20	13

Wholesale and Retail Trades, Services

$5 million-$25 million	all sizes	base $ 8,100 total 9,000	$ 7,500 8,500	8 6	$ 7,300-$10,000 7,800- 10,200	$ 6,300-$ 9,000 6,400- 9,900	40	38
All companies	all sizes	base 8,100 total 8,900	8,000 8,800	1 1	7,200- 9,900 7,500- 10,000	7,000- 9,500 7,500- 10,100	38	37

Chapter 12

SUPERVISING OFFICE EMPLOYEES

A NALYSIS of the "quit" records of selected companies shows the highest percentage of quits is due to failure of the employer to make the worker feel he is important to the company, and that good work and loyalty will be rewarded. This is especially true of white-collar employees. While a high percentage of quits is due to dissatisfaction with an employee's compensation or his inability to get along with the supervisor or for other personal reasons, the most important reason employees who have been with a company two or more years quit is the belief they have no future with the company.

There are, of course, many angles to the turnover problem. To begin with, it is important that proper care be used in selecting persons qualified for the type of work they are to do. Employees who like their work and are doing the things they are best qualified to do are more likely to stay with the company than those who do not like their work because they are not proficient at it.

But after the selection has been made and before the new employee goes to work (or at least soon after), it is important that he be thoroughly indoctrinated. That is to say, he must be "sold" on the company, the economic importance of what he is doing, and the opportunity he has to advance with the company.

How well the indoctrination job is done has a great deal to do with how long the employee will remain with the company and how happy he will be in the new environment.

And, finally, there is the problem of supervision and all that it involves. The solution of this problem is most difficult. It embraces not only having as supervisors persons who understand the importance of human relations in modern business organization and management, but also a system for periodically rating both employees and supervisors on the work they are doing, their attitude toward their jobs and the company, and their capacity for advancement with the company.

A University of Illinois Survey

A survey taken a few years ago by the University of Illinois attempted to find the real reasons for job dissatisfactions. The findings are based on some 2,000 questionnaires covering the fields of retailing, clerical, and manufacturing occupations.

The survey revealed that more than three-quarters of the employees questioned quit for reasons *within the control of the employer and because of ineffective management.* Thirty-nine percent (the greatest percentage) of employees quit their jobs because of *supervisory* problems. Here are a few of the reasons former employees gave for leaving previous jobs:

1. Company training program poor.
2. Supervisor discouraged suggestions.
3. Supervisor treated employees unfairly.
4. Too many bosses.
5. Not placed in right job.

Since supervision seems to be mainly at fault in many of those quits, one of management's first steps in securing lower turnover should be a better program of supervisory training.

According to a booklet published by a well-known management engineer, labor turnover costs average from $170 to $700 per worker, depending upon the type of job. This is exclusive of any training expense. "Today," states the booklet, "21 percent of all newly hired employees leave before completing one week on the job. Trained foremen can reduce turnover materially. On the average, a 10 percent reduction in turnover will more than pay for the training of five foremen." Thus, foreman and supervisory training is an investment, not an expense.

Improving Morale Through Good Supervision

One of the hardest jobs in training the supervisory group is to give those people an understanding of the manner in which employee morale can be improved and especially the manner in which they, the supervisors, can help to improve it.

One of the best statements of how such a goal can be achieved appeared in a bulletin Johnson & Johnson prepared for its supervisory force. The bulletin follows:

1. Give a great deal of attention to discovering emotions, feelings, and highly colored personal attitudes which block highest efficiency. Study your men—use their personalities to work for the

program, not against it. Discuss undesirable attitudes as they begin to develop. Anticipate them; prevent them.

2. Work on yourself first. Get yourself straightened out.

3. Consider causes for dissatisfaction fairly and promptly, and try to do something about them. Point out at once what is being done.

4. Always give credit when credit is due.

5. When you have to criticize a man, follow the procedures and principles given in this course.

6. Tell your workers WHY. Give them the reasons.

7. Take a conscientious interest in improving each worker's working conditions.

8. Do your utmost to make jobs safe and healthful.

9. Don't make promises you cannot keep, and keep the promises you do make.

10. Whenever possible, avoid too frequent change. Let your men get set. If you must change, prepare your workers in advance. Tell them about it.

11. Place your men where their training and experience can be used best.

12. Take the worker into your confidence. Tell him about things. Make him a part of the organization. Develop that "we" attitude.

13. Remember that the reasons first given by workers for their complaints or dissatisfaction are usually not the real reasons for their low morale or disinterest.

14. Build up the job. Show its importance. Show where the product goes, what it is used for.

Motivating Employees Through Good Supervision

There have been a lot of scientific studies made on the subject of motivation. Today, it is generally agreed, the problem of employee motivation rests on the shoulders of supervisors—where so many other responsibilities rest. According to studies made in many different kinds of companies, high production and job satisfaction result from supervision that tends to delegate some authority and responsibility to members of the work group and give the members of the group greater freedom of action. Naturally, this doesn't mean that discipline is relaxed. It does mean willingness on the supervisor's part to let employees shoulder some of the responsibility and thus feel more important to the group. It means that workers must feel free to make suggestions, recommend better ways of doing things, talk freely and exchange ideas with the supervisor.

The supervisor must set the climate for motivation. The studies that have been made show clearly that low production goes along with supervision which is inclined "to put the pressure on" for greater production, that wields the whip.

Supervisors who practice good human relations techniques in dealing with employees generally have groups that outproduce those of supervisors who see their people just as workers paid to turn out so many units of work per day. An understanding of people and their problems and a sincere interest in them are vital to good supervision. Treat them like people, fellow workers, not as if they are merely parts of the machine.

Supervisors who establish the climate that all employees are part of the work group see their job as leading, not dictating or ruling. This holds true for office as well as for shop, and for every level of supervision. The same supervisors have less poor work in their groups. They don't snoop around hunting for employee errors and mistakes. They don't hover over employees like an old mother hen expecting the worst. Instead they spend their time in training people for their present jobs and for advancement to better jobs.

While a lot of supervisors don't realize it, they are supervising individuals rather than a work group. This has the effect of preventing the group from feeling the team spirit, from working together as a unit. It prevents the good feeling that can exist when a group of people work together in a common cause to reach common goals. True, there are individual problems that must be handled with certain employees. But successful supervisors keep the climate as a group effort rather than individuals. A good example of team effort is a well-organized basketball team. True, some teams have high individual scorers, but the really great teams have five men all working together in a single effort. High scorers are fine to have—providing they are working together for the common good of the team.

Supervisory Duties

A clear-cut statement of the duties and responsibilities of a supervisor can do a great deal to clear up many of the ambiguities that all too often handicap the supervisory group.

The following list of 30 duties and responsibilities covers the area of supervision quite thoroughly. However, the individual company may find upon analysis of the general supervisory duties, that still others can be added—depending, of course, upon the extent to which the supervisor "supervises."

1. Getting the right man on the right job.
2. Economical use and placement of materials.
3. Attendance control—absence and tardiness.
4. Accident prevention, providing first aid, making reports.
5. Morale—keeping the worker satisfied.
6. Adjusting grievances and complaints.
7. Maintaining discipline.
8. Keeping records and making reports.
9. Handling workmen's compensation matters.
10. Maintaining quantity of production.
11. Maintaining quality of production.
12. Improving work or production methods.
13. Keeping costs down.
14. Planning and scheduling production in the department.
15. Training workers on the job.
16. Requisitioning equipment, materials, and tools.
17. Inspection and care of equipment.
18. Cooperating with other supervisors and departments.
19. Checking and inspecting work.
20. Settling differences among workers.
21. Promoting teamwork and cooperation.
22. Checking workers' time.
23. Keeping workers informed.
24. Eliminating false rumors.
25. Reporting conditions requiring attention to operating officials.
26. Maintaining good housekeeping on the job.
27. Maintaining an adequate work force.
28. Making best use of the work force.
29. Carrying out instructions.
30. Taking an interest in the employees.

CHECKLIST FOR KEEPING TURNOVER LOW

HIRING: Are we hiring the right applicants?

1. When we interview, are we enthusiastic and aggressive in telling our story—the many advantages of working with our company?
2. Do we thoroughly describe the job—its rewards and its demands?
3. Are we making full use of available tests?
4. Do we do most of the talking or do we encourage the applicant to talk—to tell his or her story, training, experience, and *job desires?*
5. Is each applicant sufficiently informed to be sure he or she wants the job; are we sufficiently informed to be sure we want this person as an employee?

INDUCTION: Are we adequately introducing each newcomer to the job, the office, and the company?

1. Do we use an introduction check list to be sure all items are covered thoroughly over a reasonable period of time?
2. Do we encourage questions and answer them fully?
3. Do we continue induction long enough? Do we *review* and *repeat?*
4. What do those we hired two months ago think of the adequacy of our induction program and procedures?

TRAINING: Are we meeting our responsibilities to employees in job training?

1. Is the trainer qualified? Does he know the job? *Does he know how to teach it?*
2. Have we given the trainer time to train?
3. Does the trainer tell *and* show *and* watch *and* check back?
4. Is the pace of training geared to the ability of the learner?
5. *Do we continue training long enough?*

SUPERVISION:

1. Is supervision aggressive, steady, and understanding, or soft, erratic, and demanding?
2. Is our supervision that of leadership and working together or "bossism" and work assignment?
3. Do we inspect enough and assure proper control of quality or do we inspect too much and create tension and frustration?
4. Is there adequate communication up and down the line?

SALARY ADMINISTRATION: Are we getting full value for our wage dollar?

1. Are our starting rates right; i.e., are they such as to assure employment of qualified applicants?
2. Do we get value out of the increases we give? When they are for merit, does the employee understand how merit has been shown? Is a raise an incentive for continued production and progress or merely an acknowledgment of the passing of time?
3. Do those who do not get expected increases understand why . . . do they know their deficiencies?

Check list for use in reviewing office with high turnover rate, prepared by Robert Teel, was printed in NYPMA Bulletin. Suggestive rather than all-inclusive, the list spotlights areas where improvements can be made.

How ITT Cannon Electric Picks Supervisors

Selection of supervisors to fill vacancies, always a major problem in industrial organizations, is now being put on a more practical and scientific basis at ITT Cannon Electric Company, Los Angeles. The plan, which became effective only a short time ago, centers around a supervisory selection committee, charged with the objective of "assuring the selection of best qualified personnel for all levels of supervision."

Not only does the new plan make for a better selection system for the company, but it also opens the path of promotion for many ITT Cannon Electric employees who might otherwise never be given consideration. With a committee in charge of selection, due consideration can be given to a number of individuals both in and out of supervision. The selection committee has two permanent members, one of whom is a company general manager, and the other is the industrial relations manager. Other members are the department head in whose department the appointment is to be made, and the supervisory head directly concerned with the proposed promotion. Should the proposed appointment involve transfer from one department to another, both department heads serve on the committee.

The committee does not make the final selection of the individual to fill the supervisory job—its function is to appraise the qualifications of all candidates for the job and to make recommendations to the department head concerned who will make the selection. To insure a large field of candidates for any job opening, the head of the department in which the opening occurs is required to notify the committee at that time and to select candidates for the job. The committee has power not only to appraise the candidates' qualifications, but also to select candidates from other divisions. Except in cases of emergency (death, for example), the opening must be announced 30 days in advance.

Among the procedures set up to handle this selection program are: (1) Employee folders and other records will be carefully reviewed to determine qualifications; (2) industrial relations manager will contact other departments to seek possible qualified employees for promotion; (3) qualifications of each candidate will be listed on a special appraisal form to be reviewed by each committeeman; (4) not less than two nor more than five of the highest rated candidates will be asked to participate in a psychological evaluation; (5) after reviewing qualifications of all candidates, the committee will make its recommendations to the department head. He will designate the

WHY A WORKER LACKS PERSONAL PRIDE IN HIS JOB

CAUSES

1. Lack of job understanding.

2. Failure to understand his contribution to company's overall result.

3. Inability to get social satisfaction as a member of the work group.

4. Inability to satisfy creative ideas.

5. Poor supervision.

6. Poor selection and training of workers.

7. Lack of recognition of individual skills in the same job.

8. Does not know company goals.

9. Does not know how he benefits by doing a good job—financially, personally, economically.

10. Does not feel personally responsible for his work.

11. Loses his identity in production line.

12. He is ashamed of his job title.

13. Thinks company has poor public relations status.

SOLUTIONS

1. Encouragement for a good job. Explain the importance of the job. Job rotation to give workers entire picture. Train supervisors to set up goals. Hold an open house.

2. Explain "why" of job. Better understanding through better communications.

3. Train management in human relations. Group incentives to help develop teamwork.

4. Install suggestion system. Attention of foreman when approached by an employee with an idea. Incentive program for future supervisory positions. Do not hire, but upgrade.

5. Better selection and training of supervisors.

6. Set up progressive selection and training procedures.

7. Merit rating and periodic discussion with direct supervisor to find out where worker stands.

8. Departmental meetings to explain objectives. Employee committees to help establish company goals.

9. Financially: Explanation by foreman of pay procedures. Personally: Establishment of definite promotional procedures. Economically: Training in basic economics.

10. Hold worker directly responsible for his work.

11. Merit rating. More personal contact with the individual worker. Job-relations training for foremen.

12. Glamorize the job. He is still a clerk, but make him proud of his job by having a good job title. Systematic job evaluation. Give thought and careful analysis to job titles.

13. Employees should be kept up to date about company.

SALARIED EMPLOYEE'S PROBATIONARY REVIEW

A. IDENTIFICATION DATA

(1) Plant.............

(2) Name...................   (3) Dept.................   (4) Occupation...........

(5) Date Started   (6) Date Started on   (7) Scheduled Com-
     With Company...........   Present Position........   pletion Date...........

Instructions: To be filled out in duplicate by employee's immediate supervisor and reviewed by the department head. Immediate supervisor will place a check in the appropriate response column depending upon his experience with the employee.

B. EMPLOYEE'S QUALIFICATIONS REGARDING:

	Very Good	Satisfactory	Questionable
1. Previous Experience...................	☐	☐	☐
2. Apparent Physical Condition............	☐	☐	☐
3. Educational Background and Training.....	☐	☐	☐

C. EMPLOYEE'S ABILITY TO:

1. Follow Through on Assignments..........	☐	☐	☐
2. Produce Quality Workmanship...........	☐	☐	☐
3. Produce Quantity of Work...............	☐	☐	☐
4. Function Without Close Supervision......	☐	☐	☐
5. Understand and Follow Instructions......	☐	☐	☐

D. EMPLOYEE'S ATTITUDE TOWARD:

1. Cooperating With Supervision...........	☐	☐	☐
2. Cooperating With Associates............	☐	☐	☐
3. Accepting Instructions.................	☐	☐	☐

(8) Submitted by...................   (9) Date.........   (10) Submitted to...........

E. DEPARTMENT HEAD'S COMMENTS:

Note: Following discussion with employee's immediate supervisor, clearly indicate your personal opinion of this employee's present value to your department and his potential value to the company

....
....
....
....

F. REMARKS   (If Insufficient Space Use Reverse Side of Form)

....
....
....

(11) Dept. Head Approval............................

(12) Date Approved.................................

(13) Discussion Date...............................

After a new employee has been on the job for a short time, it is desirable to review his performance and potential value to the business. This form may be used for that purpose.

successful candidate for the position in question, after obtaining approval on the promotion from the general manager.

Managing Women

Elisha Canning, district traffic superintendent for the New York Telephone Company, has had over 30 years' experience in telephone central office administration and in meeting and solving problems of training, turnover, absenteeism, recruitment, and promotion as they exist in a predominantly female employee group. These are some of Mr. Canning's thoughts on special problems related to supervision of women:

A book of working conditions is an important factor in hanging on to a capable force once it is secured and trained. We have found there's no point in talking about our pension plan to 16-year-old girls who have the firm idea that they'll be with us a month or two and then Prince Charming will come along and take them off our hands. We do supply comfortable, spacious rest rooms, quiet rooms, relief periods in each session, and we operate a dining room in the building that handles $200,000 of volume a year at cost prices.

We have an induction program which may be of interest. All employees are interviewed from time to time on significant features of the job. The bulk of the interviews are by the employee's immediate supervisor or group chief operator. The Chief Operator herself, however, handles some selected subjects, and my assistants on the district staff and I get in on at least one discussion with every girl who is added to the payroll. The aim of this induction program is really to cater to the principal basic desires of the girls who take up operating as a living. Number one is the matter of making money. Paying the grocery bill, buying clothes—survival, in other words. Number two, I suppose, is the desire for recognition as an individual, as a valued member of the crew. The girl wants to feel she is an important part of the organization (as she certainly is), that she belongs.

In the early days in our department, girls formed in line as they prepared to enter the operating room to take their places at the switchboard and the requirement—unwritten but fully recognized—was that the girls speak only when spoken to. Bosses were largely stuffed shirts and it was a case of production, production, production. We even were insistent on the type of dress worn by the girls. Our ideals, I can assure you, of dress were on the conservative side.

As time went on, a great deal of that, of course, went by the board. You just couldn't expect people to work for you any longer under such stiff conditions. I feel many companies developed something of a pseudo buddy-buddy style which is well intentioned, but certainly not genuine enough for our present day standards. It is all right to be cozy and say, "How's the family and the kids?" but do you know the family and the kids and does your employee know your family and your kids?

Should women be treated differently from men? Well, I certainly don't think so, except that it's the *little important things* that loom awfully big. There should be a difference here. I have in mind particularly good manners, courtesy, interest, greeting people by name, knowing them as individuals, asking their opinions, holding doors for them, helping with their coats, noticing and remarking on new hairdos, new outfits, and so forth.

A HUMAN RELATIONS TEST FOR SUPERVISORS

Through the courtesy of Kelly-Read & Co., Inc., Rochester, N. Y., we list the following "Human Relations Check List for Supervision." The instructions given with the check list are: Think each question through carefully, then check "yes" or "no" in the space provided. Your honest "yes" measured on the yardstick (at the end of the check list) will help you figure your human relations effectiveness:

	YES	NO
1. Do you know the first names of your employees?	☐	☐
2. Do you feel your employees confide in you?	☐	☐
3. Do you have a below-average absentee rate in your group?	☐	☐
4. Have you had employees promoted from your group?	☐	☐
5. Do you try quickly to solve causes of potential grievances?	☐	☐
6. Do you ever visit a sick employee at his home?	☐	☐
7. Do you try to handle your employees as individuals?	☐	☐
8. Do you consider it more important to save an employee than to "scrap" him?	☐	☐
9. Do you try to sell your people new methods instead of just "shoving them down their throats?"	☐	☐
10. Do you call employees in for face-to-face private discussion of problems?	☐	☐
11. Do you try to understand the employee's point of view when problems arise?	☐	☐
12. Do you get quick, straight answers for employees' questions?	☐	☐
13. Do you try to get both sides of an argument before attempting to reach any decision?	☐	☐
14. Can you discipline an employee and still hold his sincere respect?	☐	☐
15. Do you treat all your people fairly—without playing favorites?	☐	☐
16. Are your employees loyal to you—and do they speak well of you?	☐	☐
17. Do you make yourself clearly understood to your employees at all times?	☐	☐
18. Do your employees put in a full day's work—no loafing, no long coffee breaks, and so forth?	☐	☐
19. Do you have a good safety record in your group?	☐	☐
20. Do you believe people work for more than money alone?	☐	☐

"Yes" to all 20 questions............Tops   "Yes" to 13 questions...............Acceptable

"Yes" to 18 questions.............Excellent   "Yes" to 11 questions.............Fair

"Yes" to 15 questions............Good   "Yes" to 9 questions.............N.G.

Chapter 13

SUPERVISORY TRAINING

THE development of training programs for office supervisors has generally lagged behind similar programs for plant personnel. But there are many companies that are becoming convinced that training programs for office supervisors can be just as productive and as easily organized as those for factory foremen. The experience reported by an official of the Caterpillar Tractor Company is typical:

When we first started supervisory training it was largely for production people, but we later discovered that there were many advantages in having production and office people in the same conference.

It has been our experience that the problems were the same whether the supervisor be in the shop or in the office, but that the illustrations need to be changed in the conference material. Another question was whether or not we were helping our supervisors to do a better job of training. Our supervisory training program has always emphasized that phase of supervision, and whether it be "Job Instruction Training" or any other discussion of "how people learn," we emphasize it.

Many companies agree with Caterpillar that their office supervisory training programs were first organized around materials developed for plant supervisors and eventually developed into more specialized training efforts. This is particularly true in those cases where factory employees are members of unions and office employees are not; such problems as the formalized handling of grievances and union-company relationships could be omitted from office supervisory courses of study. Many other elements, though, can be left intact.

Common to most training programs is the fact that they are not aimed at improving specific job-skills, but rather at improving supervisors as leaders, administrators, and instructors. As one training director has explained:

There are lots of people who know their jobs and technical operations very well, but are amateurs in the more valuable skills of dealing with people, leadership, organization, planning, staffing, control, and communications. Our emphasis in the training is strongly educational and developmental rather than on the mastering of prescribed subject matter. It is a drawing-out of the mind rather than a filling of it. For this purpose, discussion periods, where actual supervisory cases are reviewed and each supervisor attempts to arrive at his best solution to the problem with guidance from the leader and the group, will bring the best results.

Of course, the emphasis is not solely on increasing supervisors' skills in human relations: the supervisor who decides that he can earn executive success by winning a perpetual popularity contest is not likely to have a much more productive department than the Simon Legree who snaps a long and formidable whip periodically during the day to keep his people on their toes. Hence, most programs attempt to improve the supervisory skill of seeing to it that departmental assignments are carried out efficiently and promptly. This means that the supervisor must be able to analyze his responsibilities and authorities, and be able to know what duties to pass along to subordinates and what to retain. A good supervisor does not follow the example of the farmer who bought a dog but barked at intruders himself.

Supervisory Training at Sentry Insurance

Much of the average supervisor's time each day is spent, consciously or unconsciously, in training subordinates. Moreover, most training directors agree that training can best be done by "line" supervisors—when they have been taught how to do it correctly. The attitude of the training department at Sentry Insurance is typical:

It is a proven fact that results will be better if job training is done by the line supervisor or someone in his unit whom he designates. The supervisor knows the ins and outs of the particular job better than any outsider from the personnel department or training division ever will. He also is responsible for the results which his unit achieves, and if he does the training himself he cannot blame anyone else for the shortcomings of his people.

Second, it is a proven fact that most supervisors are not good teachers and will not be effective in training unless they themselves are trained in training methods and techniques. Nowhere is there such a glaring difference between right and wrong, good and bad training methods as in job instruction. Until supervisors know this and what to do about it, their training effort is liable to be a boring misdirected chore, and the training return and reduction of cost negligible.

In the training of supervisors to train others, it is necessary to apply the same sound educational principles which they are being asked to adopt and use.

Some companies have used books on educational theory which they expected the supervisors to absorb and apply. Unfortunately, very few of the supervisors held PhD. degrees in education and the programs missed the bus entirely. Other companies have tried manual systems which give detailed and technical directions for every operation including training. Again, unfortunately, a manual system by its very nature is a reference system which is useful to people who already know the job. If the manual is complete and serves its reference purpose, it cannot adequately serve as a source of initial learning on the part of supervisor or trainee. It is the difference between a dictionary devised for the use of a skilled linguist and a speller that says c-a-t spells cat for a beginner.

We find a better method is to take the supervisors from their daily work for five sessions on "How to Teach." During this time, we not only present the latest training methods and techniques, but we do it in such a way that just watching the instructor is an object lesson in itself.

The first session shows the supervisor the need for effective training and lets him know that management not only thinks training is essential, but is making it one of the greatest responsibilities that the supervisor has to perform. The customary cry of the supervisor at this time is that he does not have time to train. It is forcefully brought home in the session that he cannot afford not to train and that very likely the reason he has no time is that a training job has not been done in the first place. Because his people do not know their jobs, he must do production work, must be continually answering questions, correcting errors, and providing close and time-consuming detailed supervision.

The second and third sessions present and apply sound modern educational theory to various training jobs. Filmstrips, motion pictures, visualcast slides, case studies, discussions, and demonstrations are all utilized. Many of the supervisor's conceptions of what constitutes effective training are torn down and rebuilt. He learns first that we can build things into a trainee's mind just as you build blocks into a house. Each unit and part of the subject matter has a place and order, and it does not do much good to build the roof without the foundation and walls to hold it up.

He is usually chagrined to learn that the average individual can learn only about four to six new ideas at a time. When he presented more than that, as was his custom, without a tying-in and clinching of each unit as he went along, the trainee left him after the saturation point and learning ceased. The supervisor finds that in arranging the units in such a way that learning takes place, he must build logically from the simple to the complex, from the basic and fundamental to the involved and technical. He sees that if you are going to do the job right, it will take careful planning and a blueprint of operations.

Several types of training plans are presented. First, he sees the simple outline which he can make up himself in a few moments' time. It lists the operations making up a job along one side of the sheet of paper, in the center the key points that make or break the job are listed, and in a third column he places hints to aid him in putting over the material. He learns that the way he does it is more important than the subject matter which he knows so well.

From here, he progresses to more complex training guides prepared for his use by the training department. These guides are used by supervisors for:

—Job Training

—Product Training

—Introduction of Changes Affecting Employees and the Business

—Management Training

The supervisor will find these training guides incorporate sound educational principles and techniques. Learnable units, methods of presentation, suggested time schedules, checks and examinations to test the trainee's progress are all included. He learns how supervisors who use the guides as they are written are, in most cases, able to reduce the time and effort they previously expended in training.

Next, methods of presentation and putting over the units are discussed and illustrated. The supervisor reviews the wartime training within industry methods and picks out the best in that program for his own use. He learns how to gain rapport and how to erase worries and fears from the mind of the trainee so that learning can take place. He learns to find out what the trainee already knows and then builds from the known to the unknown.

Once started with the actual instruction, he applies our own four-step method to each small, learnable unit. We call it the "Tell-show-do-check" presentation. It continues to amaze us that such a simple little device can make such large savings in training time.

He learns that telling is not teaching. Actual statistics show an average retention from telling alone of about 10 percent. "In one ear and out the other" is more than an idle theory. But telling is important in letting the trainee know what he is being taught. In telling, the supervisor must keep it simple. It is anybody's guess as to how many fine training programs or methods-improvements programs or professors' lectures for that matter have missed completely, simply because they did not get it on the level of the learner. We avoid technical terms and business vocabulary. The supervisor also learns how to stress the key and vital points of the material. The instructor knows what is important but the trainee does not unless shown.

In applying the "show" step, the supervisor learns that the more senses applied in the training process, the more rapid will be the learning and the longer the retention of the material. It is estimated that about 85 percent of the knowledge which we have at the present time came to us through our eyes rather than our ears.

We like to use the "grapefruit" technique here. When training navigators in the Air Force, one thing they just couldn't seem to remember was that they were not to measure along the edges of their maps, but rather in the center of the map. Any map has distortion at the edges because something has to "give" when you place a part of a sphere on a flat plane. The instructors would tell the cadets that it was vital, that we were losing ships every day because of it, but some way the next day there they would be merrily measuring along on the edges of the map and missing their targets by miles.

Finally, in desperation, a plan was devised. Each instructor having that particular lesson would bring to the field with him the half of a grapefruit peel, the juicier the better. He would hold it up in front of the class and say: "See this?" Immediately every man in the class was up on the edge of his seat. This was something out of the ordinary—something that they could see. Then the instructor would say: "This peel is just like part of the earth; it is a sphere. I am now going to place it on a flat surface just as we do when we take part of the earth and place it on a map."

He would then haul off as hard as he could and smash the half grapefruit flat against the blackboard. Then he would hold the peel up in front of the class again and ask the men if they could measure from one place to another along the edge and be accurate. It was obvious that they could not for the peel had been broken and there were quarter-inch splits all along the edge. In the center it was still sound and measurements could be made accurately.

Not letting it go at this, the instructor would take the old juicy peel and pass it to the first man in the class and say: "Here, mister, pass this around the class." The man would gingerly take it, look at it, smell the juice, pass it on, and reach into his pocket for a handkerchief to clean his hands. There was not a man in that room who would forget the lesson he had learned as long as he lived. He couldn't forget it. He had heard about it, he had felt it, he had seen it, he had smelled it, and it had grooved itself into his mind in such a way that he couldn't forget it if he wished to.

That is teaching by the showing method. Instructors probably will not be able to use grapefruit. They can, however, use charts and blackboards and graphs and actual machines, to bring about the same effect in their teaching. Often, it may be no more than a word picture, a parable, or an illustration which clarifies the point to be made.

The supervisor learns that the "doing" step with each small unit is vital to the clinching of that unit in the mind of the trainee. It is only coincidental if observation alone results in learning. Subject matter must become a part of the trainee through action of his senses, not through action of the instructor. Too often, we see new employees sitting at the desk of an experienced operator as that operator performs operational duties. After three or four days of 'his, they finally put the trainee at the machine and ask him to do the operation. It is a truly outstanding trainee who can perform the operation any better than he could have had they placed him at the machine after his first 10 minutes of instruction.

Since the supervisor is responsible for learning, he finds that he cannot take it for granted that material presented has been learned. He must apply a "check" to each small unit. There is little good in going on to the next until he knows that the trainee has accomplished what has gone on before. This final step also helps him in timing his training. If the check shows that the trainee is learning well, he moves on more rapidly. If the trainee is not learning, he goes back and moves more slowly, since adding unknown to unknown will lead to nothing but complete confusion.

The last two sessions of the "how to teach" are used for doing and checking of the supervisors themselves. Each supervisor prepares a plan for the teaching of an operational unit under close supervision of the instructor. Then, before the group each of the supervisors actually presents his unit to one of the other supervisors. The rest of the group watch each presentation carefully and then make constructive criticism as to how it might be bettered and how the educational principles might be more completely applied.

The course is followed up by the personnel manager in each office. We believe that training is more than a "one-shot" deal. No matter how well you did the original training, there will always be more thaining to do. Operations that are not done regularly will be forgotten by the trainee, and will require retraining. Changes in ways of doing things, new equipment, increased speed and efficiency, all will take additional training. Periodic checks and records are made to be sure that effective teaching methods are being used, and that the instructors are not falling back upon the old trial-and-error approach. Emphasis is placed upon spotting training needs in advance and the objective keeping of records and time-tables which will do the training job before it is needed. We don't wait to train until we need a trained employee.

Cargill's "Teacher-Pupil" Methods

The "teacher-pupil" method of training supervisors, in which the students rotate as discussion leaders, is popular among many companies. Cargill, Incorporated, is one of these, and a Cargill official reports:

"We have recently instituted a rather extensive supervisory training program for the 135 supervisors in our Minneapolis offices. The evaluation of such a program is obviously somewhat difficult, but we have considerable evidence from upper management that supervisors are now doing a more creditable job.

"In brief, we offer four supervisory courses, and each is repeated three times yearly in fall, winter, and spring quarters. Attendance at these conferences is voluntary, but we have been quite successful in selling supervisors on the idea of attending at least one conference series each year. I do the arranging and always lead the first conference in each series. Thereafter, the members of the conference rotate as conference leader. However, I furnish them all of the materials they need; such as suggested discussion questions, case studies, appropriate references, magazine articles, clippings, etc. Usually, we have one appropriate visual aid for each topic. After each conference is completed, I summarize the general findings which are mimeographed and distributed at the next session."

The Human Element

A 10-day course called "Principles of Supervision" is a vital step in the Bear Brand Hosiery Company's goal to provide its supervisory personnel with the ability to meet and solve the problems of employees.

The Chicago-based firm has manufacturing plants in various locations in Illinois, Arkansas, and Kentucky. E. R. Middleton, director of industrial relations, travels to each plant to conduct and direct the course and other training programs.

By using audiovisual aids such as films and filmstrips, textbooks with outside reading assignments and other teaching tools, Middleton has established a program which helps train supervisors to deal with the human element in their jobs as well as the technical aspects. This supervisory program supplements concentrated training activities for production workers and enables them to earn higher wages in less training time.

Leadership Training at Personal Products Corporation

Considerable emphasis is being placed on improving conference leadership techniques of office supervisors. The feeling is that departmental conferences, when controlled and disciplined, can be productive and do much to increase employee morale and knowledge of the department's function. Personal Products Corporation uses this approach:

So far we have conducted four courses with our office supervisors. The first course, titled "Principles of Supervision," was a 16-session course devoted to such subjects as organization principles and controls, handling women workers, handling grievances, etc.

The next course was an eight-session one in which we reviewed our salary evaluation and merit-rating structure for clarification and proposed revisions.

At the present time we are conducting conference leadership for this group for the purpose of teaching proper procedures and techniques in conducting conferences, with a by-product of improved participation in conferences. This course was originally scheduled for 10 sessions but has since evolved into 18 additional sessions as a combined conference leadership session for the participants and staff meetings.

In order to develop a greater appreciation of the problem and services of other departments connected with our office work we are presently scheduling each supervisor for a visit to each of the other departments. These visits will last somewhere from two to six or eight hours, depending upon the complexity of the work in the various departments.

Teaching Supervisors the Analytical Approach

The First Trust Company of St. Paul, Minnesota, is one of the few companies with a definite program for teaching supervisors to use an analytical approach in getting solutions to their problems:

It is the practice of our company to devote a portion of every monthly department head meeting to the study of methods designed to improve these office supervisor's abilities to handle subordinates and to plan and control.

At these meetings informal discussions are held of problems which are currently confronting the various supervisors. Timely books and articles are sometimes read aloud and discussed and criticized. "Let's Be Human" by John L. Beckley and "The Supervisor's Management Guide" of the American Management Association have been so used. An interchange of ideas and possible solutions takes place between the men. Plans are accepted or rejected only after considerable discussion and consideration. Throughout all of these periods the basic principle which we try to implant in the minds of our supervisors is the need for a constructive, analytical approach to everyday problems. This is the one underlying thought behind our entire program.

In recent years all of our supervisory employees have taken two formal courses. The first was the Job Instructor's Course under the auspices of the War Manpower Commission given by one of our officers. The second was sponsored by the American Institute of Banking and was adapted from the Job Relations Program material developed by the War Manpower Commission. It was designed to provide supervisors with an organized plan for gaining the loyalty and cooperation of their fellow workers.

The need for planning in our operational departments has been stressed for many years. Overloads and peak periods are anticipated and the importance of advance preparations and interdepartmental cooperation is definitely recognized. The result of this is a minimum of confusion and unnecessary expense in busy seasons.

We are aware of the lack of those qualities which are requisite to teaching ability in most of our supervisors. To overcome this we have prepared procedure manuals covering, in detail, the work performed by each of our workers. These manuals when used effectively by the supervisor compensate quite appreciably for the shortcomings of the supervisor as an instructor. For the same purpose our department heads maintain organizational charts which are also useful in explaining the flow of work and interrelationship of jobs to the employees.

From time to time pamphlets and literature of general interest on the subject are distributed to all supervisory employees. They are encouraged to read and discuss this material with their supervisors.

CARGILL'S SUPERVISORY TRAINING COURSES

DEVELOPING LEADERSHIP (Presupervisory training course)

Inclusive Dates................Weeks of October 10 to December 12.

Duration and Time........10 weeks, one 1½-hour session each week. Day of the week and time of day to be arranged for the convenience of the majority.

Recommended for............Any individual in the Minneapolis area who has already demonstrated leadership ability and who gives promise of being able to accept greater responsibility in a supervisory capacity at a later date.

Method...............................Lecture and conference. The material is designed to be informative for those whose background of experience is limited. Lectures will be given on each topic by members of our own upper management. Enrollees will rotate in leading the discussion periods which will follow.

Content............................Our Role in Free Enterprise
Selecting Subordinates
Handling New Personnel
Training New Personnel
Work Planning
Cost Control
Building Employee Morale
Causes of Supervisory Problems
Basic Desires of Employees
The Supervisor's Role in Fulfilling Management's Responsibilities

THE JOB OF SUPERVISION (First half of supervisory training course)

Inclusive Dates................Weeks of October 10 to December 12.

Duration and Time........10 weeks, one 1½-hour session each week. Day of the week and time of day to be arranged for the convenience of the majority.

Recommended for..............Any supervisor of any rank in the Minneapolis area. Staff or nonsupervisory personnel may be scheduled to attend if deemed advisable by respective supervisors.

Method...................................Conference. Case studies, questions, and films will be used to bring out the experience and opinions of those enrolled. Members will take turns as conference leaders on topics of this choice.

Content...................................Supervisory Skills and Responsibilities
Recruiting and Selecting Employees
Induction Procedures for New Personnel
Placement and Transfer
Motivation and Incentives
Discipline and Discharge
Principles of Job Evaluation and Job Instruction
Gripes and Grievances
Commendation and Reprimands
Selling the Free Enterprise System

PROBLEMS OF MIDDLE MANAGEMENT (Second half of supervisory training course)

Inclusive Dates................Weeks of October 10 to December 12.

Duration and Time........10 weeks, one 1½-hour session each week. Day of the week and time of day to be arranged for the convenience of the majority.

Recommended for..............Any supervisor of any rank in the Minneapolis area. Staff or nonsupervisory personnel may be scheduled to attend if their respective supervisor so desires.

Method...................................Conference. Case studies, questions, and films will be used to develop the collective opinions of the group on the basis of their past experience. Members will rotate as conference leaders on topics of their choice.

Content...................................Leadership in Management
Delegation of Authority
Employee Appraisal
Coordination of Company Policies
Work Planning and Waste Control
Public Relations
Promotion Policies and Problems
Communication, a Two-Way Proposition
Maintaining and Building Morale
Employee Problems and Problem Employees

"Supervisory Development Seminars"

The Public Service Company of Colorado in Denver relies on an initial 54-hour classroom course on the "Basics of Supervision" for new supervisors and a continuous program for supervisor training after that.

The extended program, called "Supervisor Development Seminars," is made up of eight monthly two-hour discussion sessions each year, beginning in October and ending in May. The supervisor remains in the program until he is removed from it by the vice-president of his department, usually because of promotion to a higher echelon of management.

Each group is limited to about eighteen supervisors for reasons of promotion discussion. This group is a carefully balanced cross section of the total company, with the number of supervisors from any major department limited to the same percentage ratio as the total number of supervisors in the department bears to all the supervisors in the company.

Meeting dates of the various groups are spread across the month. Meeting time runs from 9 to 11 a.m. and from 1 to 3 p.m. This permits a supervisor to start his work force out in the morning and to be with them at the close of the day.

An important key to the success of the program is the careful selection and training of the group leaders who must also be supervisors. The responsibility of leadership is a two-year assignment given each man by top management. The first year is spent as assistant conference leader. Natural speaking ability, tenure with the company and group acceptance are among the qualifications sought. The conference leader, in preparation for his responsibility, should have some formal conference leadership training. Valuable preparation is also afforded during his first year in this assignment as an assistant conference leader.

The assistant conference leader is an observer and recorder. He does not participate in the conference discussion. He watches for things which either help or hinder progress of discussion. There are many factors that may be involved; such as participation of conferees, ability of conference leader to keep discussion on the track, good use of questions on the part of conference leader, domination by one or more conferees, good use of summaries, etc.

As a recorder, the assistant leader fills out a report form that covers attendance, general subject discussed, objectives, questions, conclusions, suggestions, etc. The knowledge gained from using the form helps the assistant to prepare for his job as leader and guides the program in general. Each form is returned to the Education Department of the company which is responsible for the training program.

Subjects covered in seminars are the result of suggestions by the supervisors themselves and requests made by executive management. Such topics as economics, the study of a company public relations survey and subjects covering local conditions affecting the whole company are the choice of management.

Each discussion group is required to cover the same subject of the month to coordinate the program. Two training sessions are held the last week of each month in order to prepare leaders for the subject to be discussed the following month. The conference leaders meet with a member of the Education

Department who acts as the conference leader for these sessions. Different subjects require different planning patterns which are worked out in advance.

Advance planning for each supervisor seminar contributes to a meaningful session. The conference leader is under injunction to see that the conference ends with some conclusions agreed upon by the group, and a good summary is necessary.

Management has an opportunity to review the results of all the monthly conferences, and the supervisors themselves also receive additional information through a special monthly publication, *The Messenger,* beamed only to them. The lead article of each *Messenger* is a summary of the previous month's conferences.

An excellent book for use in supervisory training programs is *A Short Course in Skilled Supervision,* written by Grace Paul and published by The Dartnell Corporation of Chicago.

Chapter 14

MAINTAINING OFFICE DISCIPLINE

O NE of the biggest stumbling blocks to good supervision is the lack of know-how in giving reprimands to employees. There are more lost tempers, more misunderstandings, and waste of time in this area than in almost any other in human relations. No company should neglect the careful and thorough training of the supervisory group in the technique of discipline. It is the very core of getting things done in the office or the plant.

A few years ago, Homer Smith, an expert in supervisory training, discussed the principles involved in taking proper corrective measures. Reprimanding, said Mr. Smith, should be considered an integrated and vital part of disciplinary control. Supervisors should be made to realize that their own skill in reprimanding is evidenced or determined by the manner in which the supervisor conducts himself and influences the conduct of the employee being reprimanded; and that the future conduct, attitude, and reactions of the employee will, to a large degree, be affected by the manner in which the reprimand is administered.

The reprimand has on occasion proved an opportunity for the supervisor to strengthen the loyalty of his employee. By handling the difficult situation in a tactful and positive manner, he has won the respect of an otherwise resentful employee.

Because of the wide differences in personality and conditions under which regulations are violated, each case must be considered as one demanding individual attention. This means that the supervisor must study temperament, background, environment, social attitudes, and physical condition of each employee. He must know thoroughly the rules and regulations which control the conduct of employees, the penalties for violation, the extent of his authority as a supervisor, and the manner in which each case is to be investigated to determine responsibility.

No reprimand should be given unless preceded by:

1. Explanation of the regulations, the advantages to be gained by observing them, and helpful suggestions relative to observing them.

2. Explanation of the penalties.

3. Cautions on avoiding infractions.

Supervisors should be on the alert to remove any factor which encourages employees to violate regulations. It should be remembered that it is difficult for a supervisor to reprimand when he conscientiously knows that he is partially to blame for the violation.

Under normal conditions reprimanding should take the form of private counseling. If an employee, through the medium of effective counseling, can be brought to realize the folly of his infraction of regulations and make the necessary correction himself, better results are obtained.

The primary objective in reprimanding is that of securing better performance from the employee, without creating dissatisfaction or resentment during the process. Therefore we must make a careful distinction between the "Bawl-Out" technique and the Reprimand.

THE REPRIMAND	THE BAWL-OUT
1. Is done when calm	1. Is done when angry
2. When sure it is deserved	2. Without checking facts
3. With worker and boss alone	3. In front of others
4. Is straightforward without cussing	4. Uses strong language
5. Includes encouragement to do better	5. Makes the man angry or discouraged
6. Leaves man anxious to improve	6. Leaves him beaten or resentful

Justice in reprimanding means the prompt, fair, and open application of impartial rules. It includes a desire to forgo self-interest in order to promote the welfare of all. Despite the efforts of management to establish the most desirable working conditions, infractions of regulations will occur. Reprimanding is an essential function of management and thought must be given as to how it shall be done.

Planning the reprimand interview is as necessary as planning any other management function. The supervisor who is able to follow a previously thought out plan of action will never be sorry for things that happened in the heat of a reprimand or for things that were left undone until it was too late to be effective. Following is an outline that can be used in preparing for any reprimand interviews:

BEFORE THE INTERVIEW:
1. Get all the facts.
2. Evaluate the facts.
3. Organize the facts into a plan of action.
4. Arrange for the interview.

DURING THE INTERVIEW:

1. Give the reasons for reprimand.
2. Give employee opportunity to explain.
3. Keep cool.
4. Focus attention on situation rather than on person at fault.
5. Do not make threats, use sarcasm, nor display authority.
6. Talk straight.
7. Be constructive—point out ways to improve.
8. Encourage employee and express confidence in his ability and desire to improve.

AFTER THE INTERVIEW:

1. Follow up and give praise for improvement.
2. Indicate by casual contacts that friendly relationship is not impaired.

One large midwestern company has laid down its own instructions in this form:

"There are many situations in which supervisors, foremen, and department heads must correct workers who have made mistakes, who have done their work carelessly, who have disregarded instructions and regulations, who have spoiled material and abused equipment, who have developed unsafe work habits, whose general attitude has developed in an unhealthy direction, and who, for one reason or another, are 'off-side' and need to be brought back into line.

"In correcting workers there are certain principles which should be followed:

"1. Always start the correcting process with the attitude that you sincerely want to be helpful. Don't think primarily of punishment. Think in terms of helping. Be sure to do more than point out the error—*show how to correct it.*

"2. Size up the situation carefully before becoming critical, and then base your tactful handling of the situation on the *actual facts.*

"3. Make sure you, yourself, have not contributed in any way to the worker's need for correction, and if you have contributed to his mistakes be sure to share the responsibility.

"4. Remember that a man will accept suggestions much more open-mindedly if you do nothing to belittle him, to anger him, or to make him feel 'dumb' and inferior.

"5. Proceed to correct a man calmly, without anger, patiently, and with the tactful attitude of one who has confidence that the man corrected has the interest, the intelligence, the ambition, and initiative, and the ability to do the right thing."

Reprimand Check List

Here is a "Reprimand Check List" which has been used with excellent results in training supervisors in the art of disciplining employees. Such a check list has value, too, in giving old-timers on the supervisory force a new slant on the problem. The supervisor who has been on the job for any length of time is likely to develop bad habits in handling discipline—habits which if allowed to continue can account for a steady rise in employee turnover.

1. Did not know WHAT was expected... ....
   Full details of job not explained.. ....
   Details explained but forgotten.. ....
   Sufficient explanation not given of policies and conduct expected ....
   Policies explained but forgotten... ....

2. Did not know HOW to do what was expected............................ ....
   Improper instruction ....
   Insufficient practice ....
   Too complicated to remember.. ....
   Did not pay attention to instructions.. ....
   Other (record).. ....

3. COULD NOT DO what was expected....................................... ....
   Too much skill and training required... ....
   Lacks background of education... ....
   Lacks background of experience... ....
   Illness ....
   Fatigue ....
   Nervousness ....
   Worry ....
   Insufficient intelligence ....
   Did not have time.. ....
   Not permitted to perform duties required.................................. ....

4. WOULD NOT DO what was expected...................................... ....
   Duties too unpleasant.. ....
   Angry with supervisor.. ....
   Just didn't feel like it.. ....
   Against personal principles... ....
   Not in line with company policies... ....
   Wants to be transferred... ....
   Wants to be discharged... ....
   Not part of the job.. ....
   Nobody else follows rule... ....
   Wanted to have some fun.. ....
   Job was too monotonous... ....
   Preferred to do another job first... ....
   Didn't see any sense in it... ....
   Preferred to do things the old way.. ....

Sell It Out

Putting the rules in writing and explaining the discipline procedure gives the employee every opportunity to cooperate. No one can argue that rules are unnecessary. Most of them are designed to protect the employee himself, his fellow employees, and the company.

Here is an adaptable Dartnell compilation of rules and discipline procedure which will fit most situations:

ONE COMPANY'S RULES AND DISCIPLINE PROCEDURE

Employees will be subject to disciplinary action for any of the following offenses:	1st Offense	2nd Offense	3rd Offense	4th Offense	5th Offense
1. Engaging in horseplay, running, scuffling, or throwing things.	Verbal warning	Written warning	3 Days off	1 Week off	Discharge
2. Failure to observe parking and traffic regulations on premises.	Verbal warning	Written warning	3 Days off	1 Week off	Discharge
3. Eating at working area except during rest periods and lunch periods.	Verbal warning	Written warning	3 Days off	1 Week off	Discharge
4. Being habitually tardy, absent, or unauthorized absence.	Written warning	3 Days off	1 Week off	Discharge	
5. Contributing to unsanitary conditions or poor housekeeping.	Verbal warning	Written warning	1 Week off	Discharge	
6. Operating, using, or possessing machines, tools, or equipment to which the employee has not been assigned; or performing other than assigned work.	Verbal warning	Written warning	3 Days off	Discharge	

ONE COMPANY'S RULES AND DISCIPLINE PROCEDURE (Cont.)

Employees will be subject to disciplinary action for any of the following offenses:	1st Offense	2nd Offense	3rd Offense	4th Offense	5th Offense
7. Causing scrap of material or parts due to carelessness.	Verbal warning	Written warning	3 Days off	Discharge	
8. Wasting time, loitering, or leaving place of work during working hours.	Verbal warning	Written warning	1 Week off	Discharge	
9. Posting, altering, or removing any matter on bulletin boards or company property unless authorized.	Written warning	3 Days off	1 Week off	Discharge	
10. Gambling on company premises.	Verbal warning	Written warning	1 Week off	Discharge	
11. Violating a safety rule or safety practice.	Verbal warning	Written warning	1 Week off	Discharge	
12. Using elevator, fire-escapes, or lunchroom during working hours without specific permission.	Verbal warning	Written warning	3 Days off	Discharge	
13. Using or having possession of another employee's tools without the employee's consent.	Written warning	1 Week off	Discharge		
14. Carelessness affecting personal safety.	Written warning	1 Week off	Discharge		
15. Threatening, intimidating, coercing, or interfering with fellow employees on the premises.	Written warning	3 Days off	Discharge		
16. Misusing, destroying, or damaging any company property or property of any employee.	Written warning	Discharge			

ONE COMPANY'S RULES AND DISCIPLINE PROCEDURE (Cont.)

Employees will be subject to disciplinary action for any of the following offenses:	1st Offense	2nd Offense	3rd Offense	4th Offense	5th Offense
17. Distributing written or printed matter of any description on company premises unless it is approved.	Written warning	1 Week off	Discharge		
18. Making false, vicious, or malicious statements about any employee, the company or its products.	Written warning	3 Days off	Discharge		
19. Leaving plant during work shift without permission.	3 Days off	1 Week off	Discharge		
20. Failure to punch out clock card when employee leaves the plant during the working day for personal reasons.	Written warning	1 Week off	Discharge		
21. Failure to follow company job instructions, verbal or written.	Written warning	3 Days off	Discharge		
22. Vending, soliciting, or collecting contributions for any purpose whatsoever at any time on the premises, except for contributions for flowers for sick employees, or unless authorized by the management.	Written warning	1 Week off	Discharge		
23. Deliberately restricting output.	Written warning	Discharge			

ONE COMPANY'S RULES AND DISCIPLINE PROCEDURE (Cont.)

Employees will be subject to disciplinary action for any of the following offenses:	1st Offense	2nd Offense	3rd Offense	4th Offense	5th Offense
24. Provoking or instigating a fight, or fighting during working hours or on company premises.	2 Weeks off	Discharge			
25. Reporting for work obviously under the influence of alcohol or drugs.	1 Week off	Discharge			
26. Sleeping on job during working hours.	1 Week off	Discharge			
27. Insubordination.	1 Week off	Discharge			
28. Receipt by the company of a wage assignment or garnishment against employee's wages.	Written warning	Discharge			
29. Falsifying company records.	Discharge				
30. Knowingly punching another employee's timecard; having one's timecard punched by another; altering timecard, for any reason whatsoever.	Discharge				
31. Unauthorized possession of firearms or explosives on premises.	Discharge				
32. Smoking, except in specified areas at specified times.	Discharge				

NOTE: The accumulation by an employee of any five (5) such written notices for breaking of the above company rules during any 12-month period is cause for discharge. Warnings are cumulative for 12 months.

CORRECTIVE INTERVIEW*

The Corporation Trust Company

PURPOSE—To discuss and correct an employee's weaknesses and thus improve his performance. This discussion should be done by the supervisor.

It is good planning to fill in I a, b and c before talking to the employee. In doing so give serious consideration to actual facts and *avoid generalities.* Telling an employee he's a good man isn't enough—let him know why he's a good man and what he's good at. A pat on the back isn't the answer—your employee wants a straightforward explanation of his good and bad points. He wants to know where he stands and why. You won't fool him by being general—remember, *he knows the facts about himself but hasn't recognized them or hasn't admitted them.* Don't try to fool him—you have to live with him.

The need for such an interview can be determined by checking the following points:

1. Has the employee's performance been really substandard?
2. Is it typical or unusual for him?
3. Is it worse than your other employees?
4. Has the employee been told of his weaknesses and given a chance to improve?

If a valid need for improvement is shown, remember:

Always be prepared. Get all the facts and use the work sheet to have them at hand.

Respect his membership in the human race—the same human race you belong to. Always discuss the problem in private. Listen to the employee; he may have something to say that you don't know about.

NEVER ARGUE—Do not get annoyed or exhibit sentiments or feelings. Don't expect your employees to be like you—we're all individuals.

Do not treat everything that is said as fact or error. You're dealing with feelings, attitudes, and opinions which may be true or false but express the employee's point of view *as he sees it.*

Get below the surface—At times the obvious trouble is not the real trouble at all. Try to look for contributing causes. Listen in a friendly way—do not give personal or moral advice. Let the employee tell you what's wrong and he'll recognize and accept the fault a lot easier.

FOLLOW THROUGH—Don't let the problem die on the vine. You might find it easy to forget about it, but the employee won't. Check to see what the results are. Give praise for improvement—the employee deserves it.

The keynote to a successful discussion is real sincerity—not paternalism. Jocular remarks tend to reduce the desired effectiveness of the discussion. It is more important that the supervisor provide an atmosphere of appropriate relaxation and mutual respect by indicating real pleasure in having an opportunity to discuss with the employee those things which can ultimately make the employee more valuable to himself, as well as the company. The supervisor must be *sure that he is prepared* to do a good constructive job of discussing the employee before he talks with the employee.

Developed by John J. Grela, director, Edward N. Hay & Associates, Inc., Philadelphia.

WORK SHEET

I. THE PROBLEM

    a. State the purpose of the discussion. (I'd like to talk to you about—your job, something you are doing) or (I have a problem on which I could use your help—cooperation) etc. NOTE THE PROBLEM.............................

    b. Tell him good points. (There are some things you are doing well) or (You're valuable to—me, the company, because) etc. NOTE GOOD POINTS employee has, things he does or has done well...........................

    c. Tell him weak points—(I think you can do a better job than you are doing if—) or (I would like to talk to you concerning what we can do about—). NOTE THE FACTS AND CLEARLY STATE to employee

    ....

II. GET THE EMPLOYEE'S REACTIONS

    d. Are the facts so? (Do you agree that this is true?) or (Is that the way things are?) NOTE EMPLOYEE'S ANSWER.

    EMPLOYEE AGREES...........................

                 (go to step III)

    EMPLOYEE OFFERS ACCEPTABLE REASONS OR NEW FACTS

    ....

        (Terminate discussion for present and investigate)

    EMPLOYEE DISAGREES AND HAS NO GOOD REASON...........

                 (go to step III)

III. CONSIDER APPROPRIATE ACTION

    e. Get employee's suggestions to eliminate problem. (What do you think we can do?) or (What suggestions do you have?). If suggestion required study or new facts are presented, terminate discussion and investigate. NOTE SUGGESTIONS...........

    If no suggestion go to Step IV-f. If suggestion no good (I'm sorry but I don't think that would do it. However—go to Step IV-f).

IV. THE PLAN OF ACTION

    f. No suggestion or not acceptable suggestion (Suppose we try this—state plan of action).

    g. Employee argues but has no valid objection (I'm sorry but this is a valid problem and I'll have to ask you to do this - - - - - - - - - - - -). NOTE PLAN ....

V. CLOSE WITH FRIENDLINESS—*Be sure* he understands *exactly* what you have suggested or that he understands what's expected of him.

VI. FOLLOW UP—and tell employee if he has improved within reasonable length of time.

Chapter 15

TRAINING AND DEVELOPING OFFICE WORKERS

T HE glamour associated with the modern, automated office is wearing off. Glowing forecasts of upgraded skills and interesting new jobs have been replaced by complaints that EDP jobs are less varied, less interesting, and not as well paying as they were supposed to be.

The fact is the jobs are more demanding in terms of speed, accuracy, and alertness. People-to-people relationships are replaced by people-to-machine relationships. The idea of "doing something" has a new concept. A computer-console operator, as an example, mounts tapes containing programs and data on a tape drive. A button is pressed and the computer does the calculations. The contact is purely between the operator and the machine he operates. The operator is getting a calculation, but he is not calculating.

A stenographer or even a secretary may, in some cases, never receive dictation except from a machine. To a degree, this is a stronger person-to-machine relationship than a person-to-person relationship, at least in this particular area of her job. In turn, she may transcribe the dictation on a machine that cuts a tape which is transmitted to another machine miles away and this typed automatically on still another machine.

A clerk may sit at a large filing unit on an automatic chair that moves her from point to point to reach records which are retrieved at the push of a button. She may also sit at an automatic unit that locates a film record atnd displays it on a screen or automatically prepares a copy.

Challenge in Training

Varying degrees of automation and a change in office concepts calls for new thinking in training and new goals. An early question that arises is whether to train employees in groups or singly.

One company's experience is that group training is best for the initial stages which cover policy, wages, rules, and general skills. The next step is individual training for the specific job. This job is normally the one that the new employee applied for, and he must be made aware of how it is performed here.

During this early orientation the supervising personnel must note how well the new employee is absorbing the training. Does he really understand what he is doing? Does he know how to do this job already? Is he better at this job than the standard set for the operation? Does it appear that he will never be able to reach the standard?

Flexibility is a major advantage to a company at this point. If a person undergoing job training shows more than a natural amount of ability at this point, he should be exposed to other areas of employment that might be open. Marked aptitude or a proficiency in some skill should be duly recorded.

Topsy Turnover

Hard, cold statistical facts gathered by the U.S. Department of Labor point to increasing turnover in office employment. Why? Because the available work force during the next 10 years will be made up of very young people and women over 35 years of age.

Within five years some 26 million young people will move into the ranks of the employed, and by 1975 that number will have increased another 16 million. Very young people, both men and women, have a high rate of turnover as they try out various jobs, moving about to find something better. Young girls, well trained in office tasks, normally leave the work force between the ages of 20 and 30 to marry and raise a family.

Adequate training and a sound program of job progression can cut back the costly turnover. Planned, organized orientation of a new employee goes a long way toward keeping him on the job.

Supervisor's Responsibility

The supervisor must help a new employee develop his knowledge and skills for the best productivity on his job. It is also up to the supervisor to help the new worker develop favorable attitudes toward management, the supervisory staff, his associates and the job itself.

The supervisor is also charged with the responsibility of seeing to it that the new employee has the necessary training—on-the-job or classroom—to adequately do his job. It is the supervisor's job to continue to counsel and guide an employee while he progresses in his first job, and finally it is up to the supervisor to evaluate work performance at regular intervals, preparatory to recommending wage or job improvement.

Promotion-From-Within Programs

Many promotion-from-within programs fail, not because of any lack of sincerity on the part of the company, but because the necessary mechanics of the program are not complete or the program is not adequately promoted or understood by supervisors and employees.

No matter what the job, a new employee's performance should be reviewed frequently in the beginning. This will taper down until he moves into a different job. A review at the end of 30-60-90 days is not uncommon. During the review period, the employee certainly should have the freedom to make mistakes and deal with them as part of the learning program.

The advantage of a promotion-from-within policy is that it means there is a continuous program of education, of job posting, of testing, and finally, of promoting. The desire to improve is kept alive, and the employees know there is a chance to advance.

Of the problems and risks involved in such a policy, one training director says:

"Naturally, any program of this type involves certain risks and in the administration of it one encounters problems. We feel, however, that the problems we have experienced are less serious than the ones we were living with prior to the establishment of the program. For example, we feel that it is better to have some individuals feel disappointed at not receiving a particular job opportunity than to have many people feel that there are no effective means for recognizing ability and for providing opportunity within the company itself.

"Another problem which we have experienced is that some people have felt favoritism existed in some of the appointments. This, however, is to be expected among a certain percentage of people, particularly if they make several applications for different jobs and do not measure up to any of them. We have tried in these cases to alleviate this as much as possible by talking directly to employee groups made up of those people who have indicated a desire for promotion plus a personal interview with each of the individuals. We still feel that despite a certain amount of this criticism which is perhaps to be expected to some extent in any new project, we have provided a very definite and effective mechanism for recognizing abilities and making promotions possible.

"Another problem which we have encountered was the increase in required training time due to a succession of promotions. We have attempted to remedy this by the following plan. Each job posting is now restricted to 48 hours. Second, we have made it mandatory for supervisors whose people have been selected for advancement to release them at least on a part-time basis initially. This serves to provide a certain amount of leverage on the supervisor who now needs a replacement, to come to a decision more quickly. Since neither supervisor is wholly happy with a part-time individual there is a strong desire on everyone's part to get the situation corrected as rapidly as possible.

"To make such a program successful over a period of time requires a strong belief in its essential soundness and a willingness to accept some of the inevitable problems in the belief that long-run experience will prove the final value of the procedure."

The Right Choice

In line with promotion-from-within policy, the Administrative Management Society has compiled 15 selection techniques which are most used to determine an employee's fitness for promotion:

1. Performance appraisal reports or merit ratings—Formal evaluation of the performance of the employees by the manager or supervisor.

2. Skills inventory—Formal record of skills, prior experience, hobbies, etc.

3. Management judgment—Best judgment of the individual manager, based on the supervisor's recommendations.

4. Observation—Total observation of the employee on and off the job site.

5. Tests—Personality and aptitude tests, professionally administered and interpreted.

6. Posting job openings—Announcements on all bulletin boards indicating the type of job openings and the requirements, so that interested employees might apply.

7. Seniority—Selection of most senior qualified employee.

8. Understudy system—Assignment of individual to training and a specific job leading toward promotion.

9. Three-position plan—Organization chart showing the best three qualified employees for each position, including code indicating readiness.

10. Selection by management—A formal promotion committee.

11. Promotion lists—Formal listing of best qualified employees for promotion.

12. Training—Training for a specific job opening, together with on-the-job coaching or formal training.

13. Personal characteristics—Personality, appearance, social maturity, education, etc., of candidates.

14. Family factors—Does position require, say, social maturity and special abilities in the employee's family.

15. Other—Techniques not already mentioned.

Some 200 members of the New York chapter participated in a survey to see which of these techniques were followed. Management judgment was the first choice for all reporting. This was followed by formal performance appraisal, personal characteristics and training. In a closer breakdown by type of company, those involved in manufacturing and sales rated management judgment and appraisal reports as equal in value and they also selected training and the understudy system as equal in value, ranking these immediately above personal characteristics.

To round out the selection techniques used, the understudy system closely followed training for all companies. Next in line were observation, skills inventories, tests, seniority, family factors, posting job openings, management committee, promotion lists, three-position plan and other methods.

One interesting finding of the survey was the relatively frequent use of the newer selection technique, the skills inventory. It carried more strength than tests or seniority.

Only 79 of the 200 companies interviewed use formal tests administered and interpreted by trained psychologists. The majority of these companies were manufacturing, sales and insurance companies which have qualified personnel available. The understudy system, used by 133 companies, correlates closely with training in the promotion picture.

The Intangibles

One factor that shapes the future of an employee is his loyalty or his ability to be loyal. This can be developed by him or he can be "sold on his company" in a planned way by his supervisors.

When a man is pleased with and proud of the company for which he works, he is likely to be pleased with himself. His position may not be great so far as jobs go, but his sense of importance is identified with the importance of the company. He will merge his ambition with the achievements of the company. To bring a man to this point will usually take conscious effort on the part of executives. They must plan to win the confidence, the goodwill and the loyalty of employees.

In order to develop a keen sense of loyalty to a company, an employee must believe that the company is worthy of his loyalty, that it is as loyal to him as it is practically possible to be for a company.

To develop loyal employees a company must be accurate and completely honest in all its dealings. Supervisors must show that they are trustworthy in their dealings both with the company and with the employees. Promises that cannot be backed up should not be made at all. Everyone under the supervisor should be known as a person, not just as a number.

Working with a group of loyal and contented employees makes it much easier for a supervisor to supply candidates for a better position within the company.

A Bank Trains Programmers

A classic example of developing employees for a specialized job is that reported by the Security First National Bank of Sheboygan, Wisconsin. When management realized it must computerize its operations, it turned to a woman assistant cashier, Mrs. Beatrice Radke. No one in the bank, including Mrs. Radke, had had previous electronic data processing or programming experience when she began her study of computer systems.

However, the bank's board of directors elected to go "all the way." Based on Mrs. Radke's recommendations, the board ordered a National Cash Register 315 computer system. Following placement of its computer order, Security First National searched both within and outside its organization for programming talent. The bank placed advertisements in local and regional newspapers and in Milwaukee and Chicago dailies.

It failed, however, to receive a single response from an experienced bank programmer. Of those programmers who did respond, most had only a year or less of experience in programming and none in banking. In addition, they generally made demands which the bank considered unrealistic.

"In retrospect, we were very fortunate in finding young people within our organization who could be trained to do programming," Mrs. Radke comments. "This eliminated the personnel problems which invariably occur when you bring somebody in from the outside. In addition, lacking banking knowledge, even experienced programmers could not have produced any more satisfactory results than we have achieved with our staff."

The staff's personnel was selected by means of a programmer's aptitude test which bank officials invited all of Security First National's employees to take. Of the approximately 40 bank employees who took the test, seven passed. Three were executives who had taken part simply to learn more about programming. The remaining four were invited to become computer programmers. Two refused.

But Bonnie Hoppe, age 21, and Jill Meyer, 18, indicated that they would like to try. Bonnie, who is married, had come to the bank directly from high school. Her high school studies had included college "prep" and commercial courses and two years of math (algebra and plane geometry). At the bank, Bonnie had worked in the bookkeeping department and had been a teller in both the savings and commercial departments. She had also handled teller operations at a "drive-in" window.

Jill had likewise started working for the bank immediately after her graduation from high school. She took the programming test after 6 months' experience in the proof department. Her high school secretarial course had included both algebra and math.

Bonnie, Jill and Mrs. Radke attended a three-week programming course at the NCR training center in Chicago. The course provided a basic background in NCR computer programming. Meanwhile, the bank gave the programmer's aptitude test to a number of its part-time employees. Barbara Behnke, 18, a senior in high school who was working afternoons at the bank as an electronic bookkeeping machine operator, was enlisted as a result of her test performance.

NCR then assigned a site representative, Russell J. Puuri, to the bank. His job is to provide continuing assistance in programming training and to maintain close liaison between the manufacturer and the customer. Puuri was to work from a desk at the bank for the next year and a half until Security First National's computer conversion was completed.

The tempo of the work picked up. Mrs. Radke began developing extensive procedure books defining bank systems in detail. She determined the informational needs of bank officers in terms of computer reporting requirements.

Puuri continued the programming instruction begun by Bonnie, Jill, and Barbara at the training center. He assigned them simple "nonsense" problems which became increasingly complex and sophisticated. As the girls programmed solutions, they gained growing experience in working with the computer.

After several months, production programming of demand-deposit accounting was initiated. The girls proceeded to develop three conversion programs and 14 daily and monthly processing programs. Testing of these programs was done at the NCR Chicago data center.

In 1965, the girls wrote programs for both the bank and outside customers. These included:

- Six programs for handling bank transit operations.

- Five programs for Christmas Club applications.

- Thirteen programs providing sales analysis for a manufacturing concern.

- Other sales analysis programs for a local furniture and appliance store chain.

- Five programs providing statistical analyses of hospital revenue and services.

- A department store sales analysis program involving 300,000 to 400,000 transactions per month.

- Three programs for preparing a quarterly state report on behalf of a public welfare agency.

- Payroll programs for the Sheboygan board of education.

- Payroll programs for the bank.

Programs for bank operations such as mortgage loans, consumer credit, time certificates and dividends were also begun. In addition, a "package program" for handling 10,000 savings accounts was adapted to the bank's computer system.

Except for this use of a "package program" for savings, Security First National's young women programmers wrote and are continuing to write all of their own programs. The girls even do some of their own systems work in developing programs for outside customers. They remain under the general supervision of Mrs. Radke on these advanced jobs, but write actual programs with little or no supervision.

Preparing Employees for Advancement

American business owes much to its managers, much to its salesmen, much to those who work behind the desks of its offices. And the greatest asset of any business is its people—all people. Emphasis upon good teaching, both on and off the job, together with the progressive promotion of those who take the training and show capacity for advancement, should be cardinal planks in every management platform. Helping employees to improve their position in life is a social as well as a management responsibility.

Then, too, helping employees improve their educational background is an excellent method of stabilizing employment for it brings about two much-to-be-desired results: (1) aid in upgrading employees, and (2) gives the employee reason to believe that the company is interested in his advancement and in his future security.

One of the earliest plans set up to augment the educational background of employees appeared in banks. Through the American Institute of Banking—the educational division of the American Bankers Association—a program of courses especially adapted for bank employees was inaugurated many years ago. The charge made for these courses has always been a nominal one and the entire amount is refunded when the student completes his course and receives credit for it.

While the courses given by the A.I.B. are many and varied, employees have an even wider choice since they are permitted to take educational courses in other schools and colleges. Naturally, such courses must be taken at accredited schools and enrollment must be approved by the personnel department if the employee is to receive a refund on his tuition.

"Outside" courses similar to those permitted under the American Institute of Banking's educational program are also set up by a great many companies individually. While the regulations governing such programs must, necessarily, vary considerably, there are usually just four rules set up by management:

1. The course of study must be in line with the employee's work or have some bearing on it.

2. The course must be studied at an approved school.

3. The employee's enrollment must be approved by an executive of the company.

4. The employee must make a passing grade to receive a refund of the tuition.

Refunds made to employees, after these four rules have been met, vary from 50 percent of the cost of tuition to payment of the entire bill. Some companies pay one-half, some 60 percent, some two-thirds, and others the full amount, plus registration and laboratory fees.

In order to stimulate the employee's interest in his course, some companies increase the amount of refund as the employee's grade goes up. Among the companies following this plan of procedure is the Bowman Dairy Company of Chicago which inaugurated an educational program for employees some years ago. The rule covering tuition refunds is as follows:

> Upon completion of each semester's work, the company will reimburse you for tuition, matriculation and laboratory fees in keeping with the following schedule: For a grade of A, 100 percent; for a grade of B, 85 percent; for a grade of C, 75 percent. For marks or grades below C, no payment will be made.

Good grades mean free studies when the employees of the Clary Corporation go to school with "PEP."

PEP, as explained by Jack Harper, the personnel director of the San Gabriel, California, corporation, stands for "Personnel Education Program." It means that after the employee has submitted his proposed studies to a screening committee and they have been approved, he registers at the selected school and begins his studies on his own hours.

The employee pays the tuition and textbook fees, but if he completes the studies with a grade of "A" (100 percent) or "B," (80 percent) Clary pays back the entire amount of these fees. If he obtains a grade of "C," the company rebates 50 percent.

"Our aim," Mr. Harper says, "is to encourage specialized training that will, or can, be used to improve an employee's abilities on his present job or a logical better job such as a tool and die maker taking drafting and machine design courses."

Dartnell Institute Clinics

The Dartnell Institute has from time to time held special training clinics for secretarial personnel. These have often been attended by newly appointed office supervisors as well as by secretaries and correspondents, the new supervisors coming to learn how to conduct their own training meetings along Institute lines.

Some companies have found Dartnell's secretarial-training publications of considerable value in training new stenographers. The Dartnell "Correspondence Manual," now in its fifth printing, is in use in several hundred companies which adapt it to their own use for secretarial training.

Training Typists and Stenographers

During a shortage of typists, a number of companies may hire employees who do not quite meet the standards in job skills usually required and give them refresher training. The Chase Manhattan Bank hires typists even though they cannot pass the bank's test for immediate placement. These employees are paid while they are at-

TRAINING AND EDUCATION SURVEY

(When completed, please return this form to the Personnel Department)

....   Payroll No.................
(Last Name)   (First Name)

Date of Birth.................Married or Single.................Height.............Weight.............

Present Position.................................Social Security No.....................

EDUCATION OR TRAINING ACQUIRED SINCE YOU BECAME EMPLOYED WITH THE COMPANY

Education	*Special Training*	*Special Interests and Abilities*
Years Attended	(List Courses)	(Please Check)
Grade School	....	*Business*
High School	....	☐ Read Blueprints
		☐ Use Micrometer
College	....	☐ Operate Comptometer
		☐ Typing
Other	....	☐ Shorthand
		☐ Accounting
....	....	☐ ....
		☐ ....

List Choice of Positions in the Order of Preference:

(1)................................   (2)..............................   (3)................................

Remarks, if any...

....
(Date)   (Employee's Signature)

In large organizations it is important to determine periodically what skills or education an employee has acquired during employment. Employees should be made to feel they are in the "line of promotion" and not in a "dead-end" job. Some companies make it a practice to inventory the newly acquired talents of their employees every two years, or even more often. A simple form like this one helps bring to light much information of value to both the company and the employee.

tending a refresher course. If they qualify within two weeks, they are given typing positions. Otherwise, they are assigned as general clerks.

When necessary, newly hired stenographers get individualized training in the bank's secretarial-skills training center to help them develop speed and accuracy and to improve their spelling and punctuation.

If an employee who has been working at the bank as a typist expresses an interest to use a stenographic skill that was learned but never used, the accuracy of that skill is determined through testing. If the employee passes a pretest, she comes to training for one hour per day until she has qualified as a stenographer according to the bank's standards.

At a Chicago bank, beginning stenographers receive 22 training lessons, including spelling drills. These sessions last from 8:30 a.m. to 11:45 a.m. After lunch, the young women work at assigned tasks. Besides training employees in methods, helping them do their work better makes them loyal to the company.

One of the most effective methods, used by Merck & Co., Inc., Rahway, New Jersey, and numerous other employers including Government agencies, is the central pool for training clerical, stenographic, and secretarial help. The employee is not hired for any specific job, but may eventually do one of several jobs and is sent directly into the pool unassigned. She is then "farmed out" on various temporary jobs, always returning to the pool for further training until a position she can handle opens up. A synopsis of the curriculum at Merck shows the thoroughness of the training:

1. ORIENTATION
   General indoctrination, including rules of Typing Service Department where newcomer reports.

2. TYPING
   Guidance and practice to attain required speeds of 40 to 60 words a minute.

3. DICTATION
   Improvement of shorthand speed.

4. BUSINESS ENGLISH
   Grammar, punctuation, and completion of "A Work Book Course in Business English" at employee's own speed.

5. SPELLING AND VOCABULARY
   Increasing vocabulary.

6. OFFICE MACHINES
   Working knowledge of duplicating, adding, calculating machines.

7. OFFICE SERVICES FACILITIES

   Routines and facilities of Office Services Department.

8. FILING

   Filing manual and actual practice (modified Remington Rand system).

9. TELEPHONE TECHNIQUES

   Newcomer makes and answers calls in Typing Service Section for at least a week.

10. MATHEMATICS

   Employee who scores low in arithmetic comprehension test is encouraged to study on her own time.

11. GENERAL SECRETARIAL PRACTICES

   Guidance from supervisor on duties, office etiquette, and getting along with superiors and co-workers.

12. COMPANY ORGANIZATION

   Organizational Manual and other material; explanation of her future department, its work and personnel.

13. OFFICE PROCEDURES

   Instruction and tests based on Office Practices Manual.

14. MISCELLANEOUS

   Arranged where need arises; possibly collating, chart work, or checking lists.

Improving Typing Skills

Another area where training has proved beneficial is in typing jobs. For several years, Employers Mutuals only hired typists who could type 50 words a minute or more. When it became impossible to hire enough fast typists, the company discovered that if it hired a girl who typed 25 or 30 words a minute *accurately,* she could increase her speed considerably with a little special training. It is easier to increase an accurate typist's speed than to train a fast typist to become more accurate.

The company tried the plan with one girl before changing its employment policy. A girl whose speed was 37 words a minute was chosen for the experiment. The company hired her and tried to increase her speed before giving her any actual work to do. The typist practiced the following drills: Speed building, finger strengthening, alternating finger, high speed, location of keys, balanced movement, rhythm, concentration, and alphabetic words and sentences.

Besides the drills, the girl spent considerable time on straight typing. She practiced about 30 hours that first week. This period is equal to about six weeks of typing practice in the average high-school class of an hour a day. The supervisor tested the typist daily after the first day. Here are the results:

Employment Test, Monday ....37 Words a Minute
Tuesday ....38 Words a Minute
Wednesday ....46 Words a Minute
Thursday ....48 Words a Minute
Friday ....53 Words a Minute

With her typing speed increased by 16 words a minute, the typist began practical work the following Monday. She concentrated on learning the kind of work she would be doing, and her speed took care of itself.

This experiment worked so well that the company decided to increase the speed of every new typist before putting her on production. Going a step further, Employers Mutuals trained girls qualified for other jobs requiring some typing. Usually, this practice entailed a two- or three-day brushup. In four cases picked at random, speeds were increased five, 10, 15, and 26 words a minute. To allow more space for this training, the room adjoining the stenographic pool was converted into a typist training room with all the necessary equipment.

How Doubleday Trains Secretaries

Now several years old, the annual training program at Doubleday & Company, Inc., has proven to be double-barreled. Not only does the training prepare young women to fill secretarial spots and other positions, but it also has brought more qualified applicants than the publisher can hire. All the 30 to 40 trainees are still at Doubleday, except several women who have married and moved away and three others who were dismissed because they did not measure up to the high standards of the group. Most of the training-squad graduates hold key secretarial posts; one is a copywriter, another is an assistant in the export department.

When the program was launched, Doubleday solicited most of the major eastern colleges for applicants and interviewed 150 candidates before selecting nine trainees. Since then, the need to campaign has lessened because word-of-mouth has swelled the number of applicants.

Doubleday selects college girls with "good academic records and social adaptability," plus training in typing and shorthand (50 and 100 words a minute, respectively). Its program involves assignments in the various major departments, wherever there is work to be done. The object is to give each girl a broad view of publishing, in an effort to place her eventually in the department she will enjoy the most. The training period may last from three to six months, until openings for regular positions occur.

Another by-product of the basic training is revealed by Miss Carola Diehl, employment manager, who points out that most of the present women members of management have worked there as secretaries. "We are convinced that secretarial training offers the best possible background for executive and junior executive work."

Armstrong Cork's Program

Just as good secretarial training has enabled women at Doubleday to step into executive positions, thorough training of stenographers at Armstrong Cork Company in Lancaster, Pennsylvania, has smoothed the transition from senior stenographer to secretary.

Armstrong employs 80 secretaries, who have qualified for top jobs by specialized training and years of company experience. At the general office, the stenographic section serves as the training ground for future secretaries. Girls are hired on the basis of interest, aptitudes, and school records, and are given on-the-job instruction. "They all have a background in typing and shorthand," says Charles Rees, Jr., section supervisor, "but there's a lot for them to learn about Armstrong and its office methods. It usually takes at least two years to get an all-round training, and some of the top secretaries in the company have worked in 'stenographic' twice that long."

Thorough training includes refresher classes in grammar and stenography; demonstrations and practice on office machines; and seeing films on office etiquette, telephone courtesy, use of the Dictaphone, and typing shortcuts. In addition, the trainees hear talks by members of the various divisions and tour the Floor and Closure plants to understand the company's work.

Assignments within the section vary. Some girls handle all the correspondence of one person or one department. Others work for from three to six people, depending upon the volume of work and their own speed. As the girls gain experience, they are given more and more responsibility. Finally, as senior stenographers, they handle almost any type of assignment with very little supervision. From this group secretaries are chosen on the basis of efficiency, poise, personality, and real interest in their work.

Once again, the successful candidate finds herself a beginner, for she still has much to learn in taking over an office of her own. She has new contacts to make outside and inside the company. Moreover, each boss has his favorite methods for doing his work, and the new assistant must learn them as quickly as possible. With a good stenographic background and knowing the company procedures, the new secretary can concentrate on adapting herself to her employer.

Montgomery Ward & Company has set up a unique secretarial training plan to help the type of secretary the firm wants. Ward-Ette trainees go to school half days and work half days, get paid for a 40-hour week. Girls who have had commercial training take an eight-week course, while those with little or no business training attend classes for 16 weeks. In some cases, the trainees increase their shorthand and typing speed as much as 50 percent.

The course stresses typing, shorthand, grooming, business etiquette—"everything a secretary ought to know." Students use letters written at Ward's for practice, have their own copies of "Ward's Stenographer's Handbook," hear a company organization lecture, see slides on telephone manners, and learn phraseology peculiar to the mail-order company. Although no trainee is obliged to work at Ward's when she finishes the course, virtually all the girls stay.

Helping the Secretary Cope With a New Situation

It is natural enough that secretaries, particularly the new ones, should have trouble spelling words like "adiabatic," or "alidade," or even "dibutyl para-cresol." Putting words like those into shorthand and getting them out again is no small matter. A booklet produced by Socony Mobil Oil Company tells how.

The "Petroleum Shorthand Glossary" is provided for all secretaries, stenographers, and typists of the Socony Mobil Oil Company. Standard shorthand outlines in both Gregg and Pitman are set up for the more difficult words used in the business. Helpful, too, is the section defining some of the unusual terms.

This is a good idea for any business that has unusual or technical terms. Such a glossary need not be elaborate. A mimeographed page or two may be adequate and more than pay for the time and effort by cutting down on errors and retyping time. (We know an executive who dictated the title "Illuminating Engineer" and it came back "Eliminating Engineer.")

GLOSSARY

PITMAN		GREGG
	absolute vapor pressure	
	absorber	
	absorption	
	acceleration	
	acetate	
	acetylene	
	acid heat test	
	acidity	
	acid sludge	
	acidizer	
	additives	
	adiabatic *	
	adsorption	
	aerial photographs	
	air compressor	
	air drive	
	air lift	
	alcohol	
	alidade *	
	alkali	
	alkylate	
	alkylation *	
	aluminum chloride	

Defined in dictionary.

DEFINITIONS OF UNUSUAL TERMS

The following definitions are not to be considered as complete but are merely intended to give a little information concerning the meaning of specific words.

ADIABATIC: *A change occurring without loss or gain of heat although temperature may change.*

ADSORPTION: *Taking up of a subject by a solid surface. Not to be confused with absorption.*

ALIDADE: *A rule equipped with sights used in surveying to determine direction.*

ALIPHATIC: *Pertaining to an open chain carbon compound.*

ALKYLATION: *A substitution of an aliphatic hydrocarbon radical for hydrogen in a compound.*

AMORTIZATION: *Creation of a sinking fund.*

ANEROID: *Containing no liquid.*

ANHYDROUS: *A compound which has lost all its water.*

AQUIFER: *A water-bearing bed or stratum of earth, gravel or porous stone.*

ARGILLACEOUS: *Clayey; applied to rocks containing clay.*

AROMATIC: *Derivative of benzene or carbon compound whose molecule contains one or more benzene rings.*

ATTRITION: *Wearing by friction; abrasion.*

BAUME GRAVITY: *Gravity according to hydrometer scale devised by Baume.*

BENZAL-XYLIDINE: *A compound of benzal and xylidine.*

BLEEDER: *A connection which allows only a small amount of fluid to flow.*

BUTADIENE: *A colorless gas of bivinyl group.*

BUTANE: *One of paraffin hydrocarbon series.*

glossary for secretaries

TAKE-HOME BOOKLETS

The man or woman in the plant or office thinks about many things, but one thing of never-ceasing interest is how to make some extra money to buy a better home or a new car or take a nice, long vacation. They think a lot about having fun off the job, of course. They think about their hobbies—photography, touring, gardening, home crafts, sports, and stamp collections. The women think about raising their families, home furnishings, sewing, cooking, clothes, and entertaining friends. Both men and women, fathers and mothers alike, think about taxes and government, about the cold war and what can be done to prevent another world war, about getting along with people. When an election comes along, they both get excited about who will get their vote.

Since what people think about determines largely what they do off the job, as well as the kind of work they do on the job, employers are giving more consideration to activities or projects to guide the thinking of their workers into constructive channels and, at the same time, clear up any fuzzy ideas they may have about our economic system. Just as modern safety planning concerns itself with off-the-job accidents, so modern employee education concerns itself with what the employee does between the time he leaves the plant or office in the evening and the time when he reports for work the next morning. Obviously, if the employee spends his time raising hell, drinking, and keeping bad company, he is not as valuable to himself, to the community, or to his employer as if he employed his time to purposeful advantage.

General Motors Corporation, Pacific Telephone & Telegraph Company, and numerous other employers want their employees to lead fuller, happier lives. So does any employer who has a sincere interest in the welfare of those who work in his plant and office. These employers have found an especially effective way of doing this by making available to employees easy-to-read pamphlets designed to sharpen their interest in better living and better government. For years, employers have been distributing reprints of magazine articles, syndicated publications put out by employers' associations, reprints of important speeches, copies of the company's annual statement, etc., to guide employee thinking. But some workers took exception to what they termed "company" propaganda being mailed to them at home and objected to being required to attend meetings, even on company time, to listen to lectures on economic problems.

The solution to the problem was found in placing "take home" booklet racks throughout the plant and office, and in sales and branch offices, very much like the racks used in hotels for distributing advertising literature of railroads, airlines, other hotels, and resorts to travelers. In each rack, according to the nature of its location and the problems of the employees, there is an assorted supply of pamphlets on all kinds of subjects, which are slanted to build character, increase morale, improve health, and help employees to make better use of their time when they are off the job. Employees are invited to select from the rack one or more of the pamphlets that interest them, and take them home. There is, of course, no charge for the pamphlets and no obligation to return them. It is just one more thing the company does to help its people grow and get more happiness out of life. Because reading the booklets is voluntary, with no pressure from the "boss," these booklet racks have proved to be very popular. In the opinion of most users, the booklets are a definite contribution to better employer-employee relations.

PLAN FOR BUILDING SHORTHAND SPEED

Objectives

1. To build shorthand speed to 120 words a minute.

2. To build a correct shorthand vocabulary.

3. To acquaint students with technical terms used in the various departments of the company.

4. To help prepare employees for stenographic promotion.

Philosophy

A stenographer's worth to a department depends in large part upon the ability to take correct shorthand at the speed of the dictator. Thus, in the increasing of stenographic skill, the efficiency of the department will be increased proportionately, and, as individual efficiency goes up, so does employee morale.

Such a course should make a student aware of shorthand weaknesses and should provide a basis for review in both class and on the outside. In this way, the student is initiated into the correct habits for shorthand improvement which will be of benefit long after the actual course is completed. The writing of correct shorthand makes possible the interchange of notes throughout the department for transcription.

This training program is in line with the company's policy of promotion from within since it makes available to management a better qualified group from which to select applicants for higher stenographic positions.

Scope

Letter dictation, technical dictation, word drill, and graded 5-minute tests at speeds of 90 to 120 words a minute.

OFFICE ADMINISTRATION HANDBOOK

Location and Schedule

The three-month course will be held in Room................, from 9:30 to 10:00 on Wednesdays and Fridays.

Eligibility

Selection of candidates for this training group will be made by each department head. Such selection should be made first from those employees whose improvement will be of most value to the department and then from those expressing a desire to attend these classes.

Quotas

The class will be restricted to 20 because of limited facilities. Departmental quotas will be based on departmental need. Requests for quotas should be directed to the personnel division.

Course Administration

The Training Division will furnish the instructor who will have complete charge of administering this course.

Method of Presentation

As much dictation material as possible will be taken from company files, both correspondence and technical material. Short periods of dictation, such as two-minute and three-minute letters, will serve to prepare students for the graded five-minute tests which will be used as the criterion for determining speed.

Since the ability to *write* correct shorthand is largely dependent upon the ability to *think* correct shorthand outlines, emphasis will be placed upon a systematic review of shorthand theory, with an opportunity being given to the student to apply the shorthand principles to an increased vocabulary.

This training should enable those who have the required minimum speed of 90 words a minute to increase that speed to 120 words by the conclusion of the course. In class, students will be asked to read their shorthand notes, and these notes will be collected periodically for correction by the instructor.

Texts and References

Mimeographed lists of shorthand forms and other such material will be distributed for reference material. At the end of the course, this reference material will include a comprehensive glossary of terms peculiar to the oil industry. Shorthand dictionaries will be available for use of the students.

Student Activity

In addition to the students' reading shorthand notes in class for determining accuracy, they will be given short dictation assignments several times a month to be transcribed during office hours at the convenience of the supervisor.

Special Information

Each student at the completion of the course will be awarded a certificate for the maximum speed reached.

PLAN FOR IMPROVING LETTER WRITING

Objectives

1. To improve the quality of letters written in a designated department of the company.

2. To make everyday business more efficient by a saving of the dictator's time and the stenographer's time.

3. To stimulate an interest in a desire for the improvement of letters from a departmental viewpoint and from a company one.

Philosophy

Letters many times are the only contacts a company or department has with another; therefore, it is most important that they reflect credit on the organization. Much can be accomplished in a directed discussion course covering proper letter-writing techniques. It is highly desirable in letter writing that a cooperative spirit be fostered between the dictator and the person taking dictation. This cooperation is obtained most effectively by the formation of a training class including both groups. With the benefit of the same training at the same time, one group can be a check on the other. This training is most helpful if offered on a departmental basis, because those in attendance will have a common knowledge of the subject matter in the sample letters.

Scope

Course content will cover all phases of letter writing. Some typical subjects are as follows: The Letter Setup, Beginning the Letter, Closing the Letter, The Letter as a Whole, Word Usage, Use of Hackneyed Expressions, Types of Letters, and Salient Points of Composition.

Location and Schedule

Classes will be held in a conference room or office convenient to the department. The time and frequency of meetings will be decided by the department head and the Training Division, but one-hour weekly meetings are suggested. The program is planned for 14 hours, but this length factor is quite flexible.

Eligibility

Persons connected in any way with the subject of letter writing are eligible for this training program. This group embraces dictators, stenographers and secretaries, ediphone operators, and those who write their own letters.

Size of Group

The ideal group should consist of approximately 25 employees.

Course Administration

The course will be established at the request of department heads, who will in turn select and notify personnel scheduled to attend sessions. The Training Division will furnish an instructor who will have charge of administering the course.

Method of Presentation

The laboratory method will be used as the most practical approach to this type of subject. A presentation of the day's topic with appropriate expansion will be given first, then mimeographed sample letters from departmental files illustrating this topic and their revisions will be distributed to the class for complete analysis. Members of the class will receive also mimeographed lists of punctuation rules, capitalization rules, hackneyed expressions, and other such items. Student participation is urgently requested, so that an informal atmosphere will always prevail. The sound-slide film, "Frailey's Letter Clinic," may be used to supplement this instruction.

Texts and References

A number of selected books on the subjects of business English, English composition, secretarial practice, and business letter writing will be recommended to the students. It is suggested that all mimeographed material distributed be placed in a loose-leaf binder with any notes taken, in order that each trainee will have prepared his own text and reference book by the end of the training program. Departments may wish to develop from such material a "Correspondence Style Book" for their groups.

Student Activity

Periodically, students will be given letters to revise for discussion at the subsequent meeting; however, the principal activity is that each group member make a conscientious effort to put into practice the good-letter qualities evolved in the training classes.

TRAINING PLAN FOR THE RECEPTIONIST

Objectives

1. To insure the courteous and efficient handling of all outside and employee visitors to the building.
2. To develop a set of standards for the ideal receptionist.
3. To evolve a uniform procedure for receptionists to follow in normal situations.

Philosophy

The receptionist, usually the first personal contact made with the company, is the most important public relations agent in the office. The first impression in many cases is a lasting one and as such should be the most favorable. Much emphasis has been placed recently on the public relations aspect of every job, so it is important that the same stress be given the job with which public relations starts. The receptionist is the vital link between the company and the outside; consequently, her assignment requires much thought and consideration.

Scope

This training program will include the history and organization of the company, the location and functions of affiliates, and the floor plans of the building. Detailed discussions on receptionist responsibilities, good telephone procedure, and general business decorum will be given.

Location and Schedule

The first two days of this three-day course will be spent in Room............, from 9 a.m. to 4:45 p.m. The group will be divided into two sections and each section will be with a scheduled orientation group.

Eligibility

All receptionists in the company and their substitutes are eligible for this training course. This first group will consist of those employees actually having the classification of receptionist.

Course Administration

The Training Division will furnish instructors who will administer the program.

Method of Presentation

A very informal conference method will be used with this training group. Some of the orientation material, including films, charts, and company pamphlets, will be shown and discussed. Charts on representative floor plans of the building, data on the company and its affiliates, receptionist responsibilities, and general business decorum will be used extensively.

Round-table discussion of case problems will serve as the best medium for an analysis of a receptionist's duties. An expression from each person about her experiences will help the group to develop a set of standards for the ideal receptionist and to establish a uniform procedure for the handling of certain problems. Group participation with respect to their own jobs will greatly stimulate their interest. The leader should guide the discussion so that the maximum benefit may result. Some lecturing will be necessary for a coverage of certain subject matter and for the adherence to a time schedule.

Follow-up Procedure

Every six months this group should meet to present new problems encountered; to check up on their duties; to compare notes on their experiences; and to gather new, and bring up to date old, information. If new receptionists enter the picture, then they will have the opportunity of getting additional training to that given them by their predecessors. The Training Division will call these meetings and coordinate this follow-up training.

How 101 Companies Train Clerical Workers for Maximum Productivity

The Dartnell Office Administration Service made a survey of 101 companies, coast to coast, to study this question. One thing seems quite clear from this sampling of clerical training policies—most offices (80 percent) do not appear to have a planned, established, and standard way of going about it. However, the one out of five companies that does formalize the procedure goes about it in an efficient and generally scientific manner.

As a spokesman for one of these concerns says, "We have a planned policy to meet this important area of employee development. But, quite frankly, though we've been doing it for some six years now, we've barely scratched the surface of possibilities in training clerical employees." He adds, "We'll continue to work on it, and in several years maybe we can say we do a first-class job. In the meantime, all we can say is we're doing the best we can and we strongly urge others to start."

Obviously, the above-quoted office administrator is a bit modest in his convictions. But he really hit the nail on the head when he concluded, "I believe the professionalization of the clerical work force is one of our great needs of the day."

When Training Starts

Of those offices having clerical training programs, over 50 percent start the action when an employee is hired. Twenty-three percent say do it "periodically," and the rest range from "prior to advancement" to "when it's needed." W. J. Tait, supervisor of training, Standard Oil Company (California), explains that clerical training in his company "varies with departments and locations." But Standard does have planned programs.

Quite a few of the organizations joining in this exchange of experience have on-the-job apprentice training. Typical of these is Oak Park (Illinois) Trust & Savings Bank, where an executive, W. W. Allen, explains, "We have organized training periods in some areas of work for apprentices. We also supplement with evening courses at the American Institute of Banking facilities."

Carl F. Distelhorst, executive vice-president, Florida Savings & Loan League, Orlando, explains: "While we do not call it a 'formal' program, once it appears an employee is permanent, he attends courses offered by the local chapter of the American Savings and Loan Institute, which will familiarize him with various aspects of this kind of a business operation. This doesn't, however, include clerical secretarial training."

Who Trains Clerical Workers?

In most instances, the immediate supervisor or department head is charged with the responsibility of training the clerical staff under his direction. Typical replies follow:

"Training is the responsibility of line management with assistance from staff trainers."

"We encourage them to train themselves at night school."

"Office manager, via assignment of coworkers to help new employees."

"The personnel manager helps the department head in training—sees that certain basic procedures standard within the company are used."

"Instructors designated for each unit or department."

"Supervisors under direction of the personnel training department."

Use of Tests and Other Evaluation Instruments

Dartnell researchers asked, specifically, "Are tests, merit-rating techniques, or other personal evaluation instruments used as part of the training program?" Fifty-four percent of the participating office administrators say yes and 46 percent, no.

C. O. Bower, treasurer, Brink's Incorporated, Chicago, says his firm uses an aptitude test, and section heads review for merit rating "periodically." J. H. Turner, hospital personnel officer, Patton State Hospital, Patton, California, explains: "The new employee begins on a six-month probationary period, with written evaluations each 60 days. If probation is successful, he or she becomes a permanent employee and annual performance reports are made."

Other explanations follow:

"Merit rating is used only as a source of evaluation—twice yearly."

"We use tests before hiring. In fact, those prospects making the best scores on tests usually get the jobs."

"I'm afraid ours is strictly a trial-and-error method."

"Test results are used as indicators of employee's ability to grasp and retain instruction. A performance review program is also used as a tool to point up training malfunction in either the system or the trainer."

"We use tests in hiring and in considering employees for promotion (along with performance, of course). We also believe strongly in professional counseling with each employee after he is tested. We've seen such personal counseling actually change negative attitudes to positive ones."

Subjects and Phases of Training Programs

A personnel department spokesman for General Mills, Inc., lists the following two-step process:

Step 1. Indoctrination includes all phases of the company, benefits, and potential job areas.

Step 2. On-the-job training includes learning all phases of each department, so as to be experienced in a general way with all functions.

A spokesman for the First National Bank of Miami, Florida, lists the following:

Orientation—3 hours

Introduction to banking—12 hours

Machine operation for certain departments—varies

Procedures training is part of on-the-job training

Wayne L. Doty, sales-promotion supervisor, The Vapor Recovery Systems Company, says, "Our people are given a thorough job description, are familiarized with office forms and acquainted with the job routine." Other comments:

Troy E. Wade, secretary-treasurer, Valley Federal Savings and Loan Association, Grand Junction, Colorado: New employees are given a complete tour of the office and make the acquaintance of the other employees. The various phases of the work are explained to them, on the basis of who does what and how they do it. Weekly staff meetings are very helpful, not only to the new employees, but also to keep the old employees up to date on new regulations and plans. We feel that it takes at least six months for a new employee to be really on his own because of the complicated and confidential nature of our business.

W. M. Fletcher, office manager, The Navigators, Inc., Colorado Springs, Colorado: "(1) Overall organizational policies and objectives; (2) Skills related to the particular job; (3) Cross-training in the related jobs; (4) Human relations, attitudes, etc.; (5) Health; (6) Spiritual life (in line with the fact we are a Christian education house)."

Training Vs. Turnover

Although few respondents hazard a guess as to the percentage, most agree training helps reduce the turnover rate. Over 75 percent of those replying felt there is definitely some kind of relationship between such orientation, training, and the ability to keep employees on the job. On the subject of reducing turnover by training, one respondent observes: "Most of our turnover is attributable to marriage, pregnancy, or moving out of town. What training programs can reduce these?"

Using Training As a Recruiting Aid

Thirty-six percent of the responding companies emphasize training possibilities within the organization in their recruiting efforts; 57 percent do not. A few others do "sometimes." There are, of course, varying circumstances involved. For instance, the finance manager of a state mental hospital in California explains, "Because of civil service requirements, the employee *must* be trained before hiring." Robert T. Dickson, industrial relations and educational director of The Gates Rubber Company, Denver, says: "Yes, to the extent that we say to applicants, 'You are entitled to receive careful and skilled training and supervision—and you will get it.' "

Organizing the Training Program

One office manager explains, "Our training program just grew up." He means, of course, it started originally in a small way and, by process of company growth and increase in job demands and skills, became more complex and thorough. A bank spokesman says, "Ours started through departmental needs to train new employees during a period of rapid expansion." This is a typical reply—those firms having such training started their efforts at a time when it was needed because of growth and a shortage of qualified personnel on the labor market.

The concept of clerical training is closely related to that of promotion from within the organization. Many promotion-from-within programs fail, not because of any lack of sincerity on the part of the company, but because the necessary mechanics of the program are not complete or the program is not adequately promoted, planned, or understood by employees and supervisors alike. Those firms having a policy of upgrading within the organization find it means they must have a continuing program of education, of job posting, of testing, and, finally, of promoting. This means employees have to be told about it, too.

Training Clerical Employees Outside the Organization

By far the majority of the 101 companies joining in this exchange of experience do not send clerical employees outside the company (evening schools, association courses, etc.) for training. The Gates Rubber spokesman replies: "Send them? No! But we do make evening school classes available to them—if they wish to go."

The American Institute of Banking—used by many banks for employee education and training—has a wide experience with regulations governing tuition and refund programs. Here are four criteria which this organization finds to be generally applied by its participating banks:

1. The course of study must be in line with the employee's work or have some relation to it.
2. The course must be studied at an approved school.
3. The employee's enrollment must be approved by an authorized executive of the bank.
4. The employee must achieve a passing grade to receive any refund of the tuition paid.

These rules generally apply with most concerns that are willing to pick up the tab for outside training of employees who are willing to prepare themselves for self-improvement. Refunds made to employees, after these four rules have been met, vary from 50 percent of the cost of the tuition to payment of the entire bill. Some of the companies pay one-half, some two-thirds, and the others the full amount, plus registration and laboratory fees.

Other aids used in clerical training are take-home booklets, selected by the company to improve efficiency, and the use of outside training specialists to come in and work with present employees in class sessions.

Using Outside Consultants for Clerical Training

While most of the responding companies do not, there is an appreciable number (about 30 percent) that have used outside consultants for training. In this regard, the State Beverage Department of Florida, enforcement and collection-of-taxes agency for the state, reports it has often called upon personnel from Florida State University for training purposes, "and we have been most pleased with the results."

Standard Oil of California, typical of organizations using outside services, reports, "We have used outside instructors for courses in rapid reading, letter writing, and so forth. Results have been good." William H. Cole, training director, Johnson Motors, Waukegan, Illinois, tells Dartnell his concern has had good results with a shorthand course offered personnel by an outside consultant. A Cincinnati oleomargarine manufacturer brought in a human relations consultant to work with clerical employees in reducing some of the tensions and personal negative attitudes that had developed in the office. Results here were good, too.

As one office manager comments: "While we like to think we have a specialized and well-rounded staff, it is foolish to think we can do it all ourselves when it comes to employee training and development. So, like many others, we use consultants who can bring us the benefit of their skills and abilities to supplement our own training efforts in specialized areas."

What Clerical Training Programs Need

Summing up replies to the question, "What, in your opinion, is the most needed part of a clerical training program?" Dartnell researchers found a general feeling among the executives that, after orientation to departmental procedure, the striving professionalization of the clerical work force is the most needed portion. A spokesman for the Oak Park (Illinois) Trust & Savings Bank points out, "There is a need for the provision of sufficient time during working hours for regularly scheduled training sessions with the assurance that all personnel will be available." Others concur—feel it is a management responsibility to train, but do it in such a manner that productive output is not hindered.

Among the important observations on what training needs are the following, selected from respondents' varying views:

"A sincere belief by management that clerical training is of real importance, benefit, and necessity, for the organization and its employees."

"A better understanding of the nature of the business helps personnel to exercise better judgment in the operation of a business."

"We need a realistic approach to the problem of hiring the proper person for the proper job. More turnover is caused by the 'misfit' of the individual than any other reason—adequate training notwithstanding."

"Company familiarization. Theoretically, they are already technically proficient, so learning the company, its procedures, its 'personality,' its policies, are most important in training."

"Clerical training should emphasize the basics—spelling, grammar, punctuation, accuracy."

"We need more programs—with employee participation—to minimize duplication of work and, above all, reduce paperwork."

"Teach people how to make better use of their time."

"If I were to set up a training course for clerical personnel, it would be based on company procedures with primary emphasis on where to find answers and whom to ask for assistance. This course, however, would be designed to try to teach employees how to solve their own problems when they are on the job."

"Greater emphasis should be placed on the quality of instructors who do the actual training. Some supervisors are excellent in running their departments and getting the work out, but fail miserably in teaching others how to do it."

"Employees should be taught a thorough understanding of their jobs and WHY they are doing them."

"Taking pride in one's work is certainly a thing of the past and it is doubtful a training program could overcome the laxity existing in today's office."

"The ideal program stresses consistency and uniformity. Performance standards must be decided on and agreed to. They should be enforced all across the board."

Whether they have a formal program for training clerical workers or not, respondents agree such programs can be worthwhile. Consensus puts stress on the importance of helping employees improve their educational backgrounds as an excellent method of stabilizing employment. Two much-to-be-desired results of such activities are pointed out: (1) They aid in upgrading employees;

and (2) they give the employee reason to believe that the company is interested in his advancement and his future security.

Purposes of training vary. This is to be expected because of the diversity of business and industry involved in this survey. However, as one office administrator concludes, "Training should be a 'tailored' sort of activity. What works for General Electric may not be exactly right for the Joe Blow Company. Therefore, whether yours is a small, medium, or large organization, time would be well spent in listing the objectives of such a course and what it can best do for your organization, its management, and its employees." He adds, "Once you've reached that goal, you are ready to develop a training program. But training for training's sake is unprofitable, time-consuming and unproductive." And, one might add, demoralizing to employees.

How General Telephone of California Trains Secretaries

The General Telephone Company of California, Santa Monica, has given several secretarial-development training programs aimed "to broaden the level of interest and techniques" among its 120 secretaries. In groups of 12, the women have attended four-day programs conducted by the general personnel training instructor. As a result, some secretaries have qualified as certified public accountants, and others are preparing for similar job advancement.

The company's director of personnel reports, "The program has been received with a great deal of interest and enthusiasm on the part of the secretaries. Bosses tell us they have noticed a marked improvement in the performance and self-confidence of their secretaries as a result of attending the program."

Given once a month, the General Telephone program mentions technical skills briefly, concentrates on the less tangible abilities, as shown by the agenda that follows:

Monday

Welcome

Introductions and Conference Arrangements

The Secretary as a Management Representative

    1. What does the secretary owe to her boss and to other management people?

    2. What are her responsibilities to other employees?

Job Planning and Organizing

Tuesday

Making the Job Easier and More Pleasant for the Boss

    1. What are some of the things you can do for your boss before he asks you to do them?

2. How can a secretary learn to anticipate her boss's needs?

3. Why is a secretary's attitude toward her job important in making the job easier and more pleasant for her boss?

The Secretary as a Leader—A Secretary's Authority

Office Etiquette and Reception of Callers

Wednesday

Effective Use of Telephones

1. Techniques in handling calls

Understanding the Boss

A Secretary Deals With People

Thursday

Effective Use of Telephones

1. Developing telephone personality

Opportunities for Advancement

Self-Development

Summary

Each secretary attending the program receives a secretarial handbook and booklets such as "Poise for the Successful Business Girl" and "The Successful Secretary." Case studies of situations a secretary may encounter are read and discussed. To improve telephone techniques, a tape recorder and teletrainer are used for practice calls, which are played back for discussion. Films shown include "A Manner of Speaking" and "Office Courtesy."

Group luncheons are scheduled each day with a company executive as guest speaker. He speaks "off the cuff" on qualities he looks for in a secretary and answers questions the girls may have. In addition, the conferences pave the way for better understanding between departments.

Programmed Instruction

Growing interest has developed in the techniques offered by programmed training. Enough time and effort has gone into this comparatively new form of education to indicate that it is highly effective. Over 1,000 P.I. training books have already been published. Some are excellent, many are adequate and some are bad, but all indicate a growing reliance on the technique.

Advantages of programmed instruction include a uniformity in training and a basic consistency of learning. The quality of training is proving to be high. Training time is reduced to a very important degree. Individuals can be trained for a job without waiting for a formal class to be formed. The time of the instructor is cut to a minimum, and, in most cases, the trainees seem to enjoy learning with the new method.

Chapter 16

RECOGNITION AND REWARD

PEOPLE live better than they used to live. They have better homes, more conveniences, more home entertainment. It is, therefore, natural that in choosing a place to work, they apply first to the establishment where the working environment is at least as good as they have at home. After all, we spend one-third of our day at work.

By the same token, people work more effectively, are happier and less inclined to change their jobs when working conditions are good. Clean washrooms and rest rooms, ample lighting, cool water, adequate parking facilities, soundproofing, orderly arrangement of equipment and tools—these are just a few of the factors which attract and hold employees. That is why American business is spending millions of dollars to modernize its offices and plants. It is not just that businessmen want their establishments to be known as good places to work, but they have found that modernization is good business.

New and improved offices not only, as a rule, lead to greater and better production without increasing the number of employees, but more pleasant surroundings have proved their worth in decreasing labor turnover. This is particularly true of offices in which the majority of employees are girls. Girls like pleasant, clean, and modern offices; desks and chairs that are comfortable and do not snag their nylons; efficient lighting and air conditioning. With the emphasis today on bright, cheerful, modern offices, there is no reason why an employee—especially a woman employee—should continue to work in a dirty, old-fashioned office. Even if the salary is slightly better, the constant irritation of old-fashioned files, desks, and chairs, plus the dirt, makes the small difference in salary unimportant.

The National Canners Association moved to its new headquarters office building in Washington, D.C., a few years ago—headquarters in which the layout and facilities were the result of suggestions solicited from and offered by 1,000 of the association's member companies.

Good office and laboratory facilities have not only enhanced the service of the association to its members, but also have resulted in low employee turnover. The office employs 80 persons, and their reactions to their new working quarters could be summarized like this:

"We appreciate our present working conditions. In the old building, the roof leaked; the plumbing and lighting were poor; dust was prevalent despite daily removal; wooden files and other old office equipment were difficult to handle; the noise distracted us, we could

---

THE AIMS OF A COMPANY AND ITS PEOPLE ARE THE SAME

The Employee Wants:	The Company Wants:
A steady job	Steady, increasing employment— This indicates a growing demand for its products
High wages	High wages—Only by paying high wages can management secure top-skilled workmen.
Opportunity for a better job	Opportunity for its workmen to progress—Top management's greatest problem is to find men willing and able to assume increased responsibilities.
Comfortable, safe working conditions	Comfortable, safe working conditions—Intelligent management knows that without such conditions its workmen cannot remain steadily on the job.
Lower prices for what he buys	Lower prices, quality considered— Only by providing better products at lower prices can it hope to stay in the competitive market, expand its business, and continue to grow.

ACTUALLY, YOU AND YOUR COMPANY ARE TRAVELING THE SAME HIGHWAY TOWARD THE SAME GOAL.

Statement of employee-employer aims used by one company

overhear most of the telephone conversations; we ate our lunches at crowded desks; and on hot, humid days, we wondered if we could last the full day or how soon arrangements would be made to let us go home early."

Now the office staff works comfortably in air-conditioned rooms, with soundproofed ceilings, cheerful surroundings, and the latest in office furnishings.

As surveys have shown, employees are not so often discontented because of wage rates or salaries today as they are because they lack a feeling of being needed or of being important to the success of a business. Sometimes the simplest little change in policy will supply this need.

The South Wind Division of the Stewart-Warner Corporation, Indianapolis, does not believe it is always necessary to inaugurate new personnel programs in order to improve or maintain employee morale. Opportunities already exist to create in the employee a favorable attitude toward the company and his job. A good example of how a little thought can go a long way is shown in the way South Wind handled its industrial plant-painting program. Instead of proceeding along the usual lines, South Wind management decided to let employees review the color plans for painting factory and office areas before the work was begun. After some deliberation, two color schemes were chosen and scale-size mock-ups of a typical office or factory area were painted. These were then placed in the company cafeteria with slips of paper available to all employees to indicate their choice. This seems like a "little" thing, but good employee relations is made up of just such little things.

LIBERALIZING OFFICE RULES

During World War II when many offices and plants had to be completely manned by women and the pressure of work was unusually heavy, old hidebound policies had to be cast overboard. After that war ended, the majority of offices found the labor supply still short and instead of going back to prewar policies regarding office rules and regulations, some of the wartime policies were even further broadened. In many instances, when attempts were made to return to prewar strictness of rules, turnover took a sudden jump.

What are some of these broadened policies? Just to name a few: Permitting women workers to smoke at their desks; coffee periods; handy soft drink, milk, and ice cream dispensers; better-arranged and more pleasant rest rooms; production bonuses; definite policies relating to promotions and raises; liberalized policies relating to sick leaves and vacations.

A typical company is Allied Mutual Insurance Company of Des Moines. Allied has no established rest periods for workers, but sees no necessity for them with its arrangement. There are Coke machines and milk and ice cream dispensers in strategic spots in the building, and any employee can get up from a desk whenever there is a desire for a refreshing pause. In reality, people in the office can "rest" when they wish, and there are no bells ringing to warn them when it is time to return to work.

Before moving into its new office building a few years ago, Allied Mutual rented space in downtown Des Moines, and a great deal of time was lost during the workday when girls went down to the drugstore for a Coke and cigarette. The new policies have not only reduced turnover, but have increased working time as well.

While the company has developed some ideas for increasing office efficiency, some of the credit must be given to the new building. Before moving into its new structure, the company was so cramped some of the files were even placed in corridors. The arrangement was not too convenient, because the offices had to be split up—some on one full floor and some on a part of another. It does not take a great deal of time—with salaries where they are—to add up to a lot of money.

Time-study experts estimated that working efficiency could be increased as much as 25 to 30 percent under a new one-roof arrangement, as compared to the divided departments in the old building. The estimates proved accurate, for officials say that efficiency figures have risen throughout the various departments in the company. In the filing section, for example, it is believed that the new setup is 25 percent more efficient than the old.

RECOGNIZING FAITHFUL SERVICE

As every employer knows, an employee's years of service with a company or in a job mean a great deal to him. It is his job security and assurance that he will not be among the first to be laid off, if business goes sour. If the company has a retirement plan, his pension is partly determined by the number of years he has been on the job. That is why the unions attach so much importance to seniority. Many strikes have been called because of infractions of union seniority rules as applied to a craft or an industry.

Employees who have been in the service of a company for a number of years value highly the privileges that go with that service.

They hesitate to quit or change jobs, since by doing that they would lose their seniority. So employers strive to make seniority as meaningful as possible, and, in addition to the benefits accruing to an employee, they make him feel important to the company because of his seniority status. Here are ways to accomplish it:

The service award as a morale builder cannot be overestimated. In the first place, the awarding of a service pin and the inclusion of a man or woman in a group such as a Twenty-Five-Year Club, lifts the individual out of the big impersonal mass of workers, and he becomes an entity, not just a member. If, in addition, the award carries some special privilege such as extra vacation time with pay, management has succeeded in filling the strong need most employees have for recognition.

Furthermore, the service award recognizes the fact that man does not work for pay alone. He wants—and needs—something in addition to pay; something that adds a little importance to his stature among other men. An outstanding authority in the field of employee relations has this to say about it:

Management has fallen far short in two ways in dealing with individual and mass frustration. First, we have failed for the most part to understand the basic needs and aspirations of people. We have been preoccupied by the unrealistic belief that men work for wages alone.

The implication of the fact that men and women almost automatically tend to rate their company as a better place to work, as engaged in finer research, as making better products, as giving the public more for its money—these implications have not yet been understood or capitalized by American management.

The man with a job wants to believe that where he spends his working hours is the best place for him to be.

Recognizing Seniority

"You can't buy an employee's loyalty and good will with a $10 pin or a $50 watch," said one company official recently. "If you think you are giving something away when you give service awards, you had better quit. It's the spirit and sincerity with which such an award is given that counts. I have seen older workers, their eyes filled with tears, receiving a service award. I have seen others who actually resented the 'paltry' offering." What's the difference between these two reactions?

There seems little question but that the recognition of an employee's years of loyal service with a company is of importance to management, to the employee himself, and to the company as a whole. For this reason, over 95 percent of the companies participating in a Dartnell survey on the subject have a policy for recognizing length of service. Firms not using service awards have, generally, some other form of recognition such as longer vacation periods for senior workers, pension funds, bonus increases, and other extras. It is a rare company that allows an employee to stay 25 years without some sort of recognition.

Certainly you don't start giving service awards when a man has only been with your company six months. But policies covering the proper time to recognize years of service vary in different companies. The popular time to start recognizing service is at five years with 10 years and 25 years next in order.

Many companies report award systems that include pins with added diamonds or other valuable stones as the employee acquires greater seniority. The Todd Division of the Burroughs Corp. gives a pin for each five years of service, a certificate at 25 years, a $75 bond at 30 years, and a $100 bond at 40 years.

Swift & Co., Chicago, gives pins after each five years of service with stars to show length of service. At 40, 45, and 50 years, a congratulatory letter signed by the president is sent to the employee's home. A. H. Robins Company, Richmond, Virginia, gives a pin for five years of service. Men receive a ring for 10 years of service and women a bracelet. Union Switch & Signal Division of Westinghouse Air Brake Co. has no service award policy, allows a vacation bonus in addition to regular vacation pay: One dollar for each year of service, beginning with 25 years.

In many offices, employees are given an extra day of vacation for each year with the company after the first five years. In some instances, this additional vacation is allowed after three years' service. Banks and other financial institutions frequently give all employees a vacation of three weeks with pay (when the usual vacation period is two weeks) after they have been with the bank 15 years.

In some offices an employee also finds a bouquet from the company on his desk on his service "birthday." This usually begins with the employee's fifteenth anniversary.

Service pins, gold watches, service certificates—all have become useful and important evidences of long service for employees with 25, 30, 40, or more years with a company. However, few companies have looked at the situation like the Armco Steel Corporation, which believes "that behind every good man there is the helping hand of a good woman." Armco has especially created for Armco veterans' wives, gold charm bracelets which are presented to them in appreciation of their helpfulness to the company. Said an Armco executive:

"We believe that behind every good man there is the helping hand of a good woman. She is the balance wheel that keeps her husband on the right road. If it were not for their wives, many Armco men would never have become 25-year veterans. An Armco pin is our way of saying 'thank you sincerely for all your interest and help in the past.' "

The brooches were sent to 2,317 women, including the widows of men who had worked at least 25 years with Armco.

When giving pins, companies sometimes begin the awards with a bronze pin, next a silver pin, then a gold; and for the twenty-fifth year, a gold pin with a diamond. Another common method, however, is to begin the award with a plain gold pin, adding jewels to the pin to indicate the succeeding years. If the plan begins with the tenth year, the plain gold pin is used to commemorate the occasion; a diamond is added for the twenty-fifth year.

Employees of The Coleman Company may select their choice of a lapel pin, tie bar, tie chain, bracelet with charm, or brooch on each five-year service anniversary.

Jewelry is in yellow gold with a red-enameled emblem for the fifth year, blue enamel for 10 years, and black enamel for 15 years. For 20 years a ruby is added to the emblem, and at 25 years a blue sapphire appears. For the intervals of 30, 35, 40 and 45 years, the base metal changes to white gold, with a diamond of increasing size for each five years.

A drug firm in the East has set up a rather unusual system of monetary awards for salaried workers. Length of service and annual salaries are computed at the end of each May and November and the Service Award payment is made twice a year, normally in June and in December. The schedule of payments under this plan is explained to employees in the following table. The percentages refer to the employee's annual salary.

Length of Service of Employee	First Half-Yearly Payment	Second Half-Yearly Payment	Total Yearly Payment
Less than 1 year but over 3 months	$5.00	$5.00	$10.00
1-4 years inclusive	1%	1%	2%
5 years	1⅛%	1⅛%	2¼%
6 years	1¼%	1¼%	2½%
7 years	1⅜%	1⅜%	2¾%

And so on, to retirement. In other words, for each additional year of service beyond 4 years, the annual amount of the Service Award will be increased by ¼ of 1 percent of the annual salary.

This plan was set up at a time when the labor market had tightened up and the problem of retaining experienced workers on the payroll had become acute. The plan was instrumental in cutting down the high turnover rate as well as strengthening employee morale.

In addition to giving employees special pins on their service anniversaries with the company, many organizations present their employees with gold watches on the occasion of the twenty-fifth anniversary. These are usually wrist watches for the men and wrist or lapel watches for the women. It is advisable to permit the employee to indicate his choice before the presentation. If the watch is to be engraved, it is a good idea to check with the employee on this point, too, for the individual has ideas of his own about so personal a matter.

Among "unusual" service awards given by some companies are television sets, desk name plates, a company-sponsored trip to Florida, and other extras. But the most popular is still the wrist watch, with pins, monetary gifts, scrolls, and emblems also well received.

Completion of five years of service has been recognized at Mattel, Inc., by this certificate of award.

Service clubs are growing in acceptance. Of those having such clubs, well over 50 percent are sponsored by the company. The clubs not only act as a means of recognizing length of service, but act as a social center for older employees and retired workers. For instance, The Fafnir Bearing Company of New Britain, Connecticut, has a recently formed group known as the "Fafnir Seniors." The group meets every Wednesday and includes recently retired employees who still want to keep in touch with the company and their friends. Through the "Seniors," recently retired Fafnirites can enjoy a regular social outlet with others of similar age. It's a fine idea and helps to decrease some of the problems of loneliness that befall retired employees.

Presenting the Award

The award is usually presented to the employee at a banquet. One executive explains it this way: "We believe the banquet itself, which is pretty lavish, does more good for morale than the award. Everyone looks forward to it and the award turns out to be a souvenir of a happy and memorable occasion." Other means of presenting the emblem, pin, watch, or scroll include luncheon meetings, at the Christmas party, during the company picnic, or right at the workplace by a company executive.

Most companies agree that the value of service awards is watered down if the event is not given good publicity. For this reason, the company publications, suburban and metropolitan papers, bulletin boards, and other media are used to tell the story of the company's old-timers to employees and the community.

There is another side to this matter of giving awards—a side which must be taken into consideration when a company sets up a system of awards. "Management must not attempt to gain employee loyalty or good will by the recognition of years of service alone," said the president of a Kansas City firm. He added, "The service award is just something extra. It cannot take the place of good labor relations. It cannot undo the damage done to employee morale by years of poor internal relations."

As an example of what happens when a company leans too heavily on service awards, take a well-known firm in the East which was conspicuous for its low pay and its hard-handed dealing with employees. No company ever made a greater event of its "gold watch ceremonies" than this company. Press releases showing the "friendly" president of the concern presenting a watch to a tottering old man or woman went far and wide. This saccharine attempt to undo all the bad labor relations which had existed in this company for years would be laughable if it were not so tragic.

When a new, modern management took over eventually, the gold watch ceremony was not discarded, but it was relegated to its proper place in the employee relations program and the publicity was soft-pedaled. Before the change could be made, however, the dissatisfaction of the majority of employees with management's policies made the workers a pushover for union organizers. Today, the employees are well unionized and, consequently, they regard all the improvements which have been made in the company policies as stemming from the union's demands.

Before setting up a service award system, a company should ask itself these six questions:

1. Can the union poke fun at the plan because of poor labor relations?

2. Does the company have a well-developed program of employee relations?

3. Is this the only time the company attempts to get in touch with the individual employee?

4. Is the wage and salary rate in line with that of other companies in the same industry or with other firms in the community?

5. Does the company have (or plan to have) a program of employee security—group insurance, retirement plan, hospitalization, etc.?

6. Does management handle employee grievances promptly and adequately so that no backlog of employee resentment has been built up?

If management cannot honestly answer these questions with some degree of confidence, then it should defer the service award plan until its "fences are mended." Such a program serves a fine purpose and is effective if it is an adjunct to a well-balanced employee relations program.

Performance Awards

Not so widely recognized is the necessity for rewarding good performance. As an example, a supermarket checkout cashier is extremely important to the success or failure of her store in two ways: (1) in the accuracy of her checkout operations and (2) in the courtesy and consideration with which she handles the customers. For instance, the net profit of a supermarket is somewhere under 2 percent annually. This means, literally, that a 20-cent error by the cashier in favor of the customer would require $20 in sales to recoup! Also, the average steady customer patronizing a supermarket is estimated to spend about $1,500 a year. This is the volume of business lost when a checker-cashier annoys a steady customer with discourteous treatment to the point where she refuses to patronize the store any longer.

Well aware of this, the supermarket industry has taken steps to reward competency at the checkstand with prestige recognition. Many companies conduct an annual "Checker of the Year" Award. Winners are scored for accuracy and courtesy. The first requirement is established by monthly cash-register-balance checks, while "mystery shoppers" visit the store to check on courtesy. Other stores conduct an "Orchid Girl of the Month" campaign, and reward high scorers with a fresh orchid and a small orchid-ornamented lapel pin. These awards are highly prized, and result in improving over-all store performance.

Members of the National Association of Food Chains participate in a somewhat similar competition among store managers, with an annual selection of a "Manager of the Year" who is given an expense-paid tour.

Such award competitions could be adaptable to any business or industry where the work performance can be easily and fairly measured.

Chapter 17

OVERCOMING BARRIERS TO COMMUNICATION

M ANY companies are actively seeking the understanding, loyalty, and cooperation of employees. Yet few of them have set down in black and white the "picture" of themselves, their statement of purpose. In the United States we have our Constitution. This precious printed piece *is* the United States, and millions of people expect the elected officials to live up to the picture of the country that is drawn in the Constitution. They depend upon it, believe in it.

Among all the employee handbooks, the hundreds of "You and Blank Company" publications, there are only a few which attempt to set forth any creed, any basic statement of purpose. Certainly, there is a value to having a published basic policy for employees and customers alike. There is a greater value in living up to such a published policy.

One company's creed, insofar as the employees are concerned is illustrated through the courtesy of the A. P. Green Fire Brick Company. It is a statement of policy whereby employee relations are handled according to the five basic principles given.

In replying to a Dartnell questionnaire on the subject recently, one respondent said, "If our employees were really sold on the merit of all company rules, we wouldn't have any problems." That is a questionable conclusion, however, in the minds of other office and personnel executives who feel the human element is too complex for any one formula to completely solve the problem of personal likes and dislikes.

When it comes to attempting to solve communication problems, most businessmen believe all they need to do is to install a training program, refurbish their house organ, or take some other specific and simple action. They believe this in part because it is human nature to look for easy solutions. But they have also been encouraged

STATEMENT OF POLICY

IT IS THE POLICY of this company to govern relations with employees in accordance with the following principles:

1. Wages will be at rates equal to or better than those prevailing in the area for the tasks performed. Wage surveys to verify the fairness of rates will be made at reasonable intervals.

2. Any employee will be welcomed by the management to discuss improvements in working conditions, hours, policies, or problems of any nature.

3. Any grievance will be fairly and promptly handled through steps provided by the grievance procedure posted in all departments.

4. General conditions, such as vacations, safety, cleanliness, and employee accommodations, will equal or exceed prevailing community practice, and we expect to continue the improvement of working conditions.

5. We will devote our best efforts and thinking to the building of a growing business within which will prevail an atmosphere of friendliness and harmony, with steady jobs and opportunities for all.

A. P. GREEN FIRE BRICK COMPANY,

President

The "creed" of A. P. Green Fire Brick Company has five basic principles.

in their belief by many so-called "experts" in the field of industrial communication.

Here are the ways 185 companies are trying to sell company policy, rules, and regulations to office employees.

Employee handbooks outlining policy..60 percent

Thorough indoctrination upon hiring..80 percent

Orientation programs for new employees..................................45 percent

Posters and bulletin board notices..30 percent

Use of employee opinion polls..25 percent

Through supervisors..85 percent

Public address system announcements......................................15 percent

Emphasizing the "honor" system.. 5 percent

Individual counseling sessions..30 percent

Group meetings to "air" problems..50 percent

Company magazine features..40 percent

Personal letters from the president..20 percent

Much as we would like to have it otherwise, communication is by no means a simple matter. The best minds in the field have barely begun to understand something of its nature, its processes, and its problems. And the more research is done, the more it becomes obvious that there are no "pat answers"—no simple, yet effective, panaceas for the communication difficulties.

For example, many "experts" in the field have espoused the idea of the "open-door" policy as a means of improving communication. The idea is to have the major executives of the company announce that their doors are open to anyone wishing to ask a question, offer a suggestion, or make a complaint.

By carefully questioning the executives of companies which have instituted the open-door policy, we have discovered one very interesting fact. Virtually nobody actually comes through the "open door." Indeed, the idea of going over their superiors' heads to talk with the top men is so fraught with real or imaginary dangers for most employees that they wouldn't dare to do it. And so one more pious platitude in industrial relations is wrecked on the rocks of reality. It sounds sensible and wonderful—but it doesn't work.

At first blush, communication seems like a very simple matter: You want to tell someone something, so you tell him. Or you want to find out something, so you ask someone.

But it isn't that simple. Suppose, for example, that top management issues the following communique to employees: "Starting

Monday morning all employees will use the south entrance to the plant." The employees, individually or as a group, may give that simple communique an entirely different interpretation from the one management intended. The office employees, for example, may decide that it surely doesn't apply to them, since they have always used a separate entrance from the plant employees and the notice speaks only of the entrance to the plant.

Or the office employees may decide that it applies to them and regard it as a "slap in the face" because they are now expected to go in the same door as the plant employees—and an inconvenient one at that. And so on with all the other employees. Each will interpret the bulletin in the light of his own circumstances, emotional attitudes, experience, and background.

Actually, management may have issued the bulletin for a wide variety of reasons, such as: (1) To cut down on jaywalking in front of the plant, (2) to permit repairs or repainting of another entrance, (3) to cut down on the number of plant guards needed, (4) as a spiteful show of authority because of some previous incident, and so forth.

The point is this. It is impossible to communicate a fact or a simple instruction on procedure by itself. It is always sent in a particular context of meaning, and it is always received in a particular context of meaning. In each case, certain goals and attitudes go along with the central message.

To some extent, the "sender" can control the real meaning of his message to the "receiver" by explicitly stating his goals and attitudes in the message. But this is only partially possible. For one thing, the sender inadvertently communicates goals and attitudes in other ways—by gestures, facial expressions, actions in other situations, the method of communication chosen, and so forth. If his explicitly stated goals and attitudes are his real goals and attitudes, this inadvertent communication will reinforce them. But if they are not, then the inadvertent communication is, at least, confusing and, more probably, overriding.

Similarly, the "receiver" already has his own ideas about the goals and attitudes of the "sender," and these have a powerful influence on how he interprets the message—or whether he bothers to listen at all.

Thus, even without considering the added complexities introduced by the fact that we are concerned with communication in a particular environment—namely a business organization—it is clear that the surface simplicity of communication is misleading. We are dealing with a very complex process.

In recent years, there has been so much emphasis upon "getting management's story across to employees," that it is easy to overlook the fact that communication within a business organization is actually a tridirectional process. There is, to be sure, communication downward. But no organization can function effectively unless there is also communication upward (from employees to management) and crosswise (between departments or similar major segments of the business).

Actually, each of these communication directions poses its own unique and special problems. There are strong psychological and sociological barriers inherent in large business organizations (many of which are huge bureaucracies) which tend to block or to distort communication in each of these directions. And no real and lasting improvement in communication can be expected unless these barriers are recognized and either removed or circumvented.

To arrive at a realistic and effective approach to communication problems, then, a business leader needs to:

1. Put aside all thoughts that there are any simple short cuts or "easy answers." There are no workable packaged techniques which he can buy, install, and forget on the assumption that they will function automatically. The basic responsibility for effective communication is so inextricably bound up with other management functions that he cannot even delegate it safely. To attempt to do so is merely to engage in wishful thinking and, in the end, to fail by default in a management responsibility.

2. Realize that communication necessarily includes the indication of (a) goals and (b) attitudes, as well as (c) information and (d) instructions on procedures. If the goals and attitudes are not specifically and truly expressed, they will be inferred, correctly or incorrectly, by the receivers.

3. Be aware of the tridirectional nature of communication and the fact that upward, downward, and horizontal communication each poses different problems because of the specific communication barriers involved.

Information Meetings

While the employee magazine is the "first line" of communication between employee and management, sometimes a situation calls for a more intensive campaign of sharing information with the worker. A leading company in the watch industry found it necessary to spotlight a new communications program a short time ago and for this purpose set up a new employee-management relations program. The backbone of this program is a series of monthly meetings (on company time) designed to provide information for employees concerning their company's operations.

A different employee group attends each meeting to hear and exchange information with management about the company and the watch industry. These meetings were originally scheduled for one year but are being continued as long as there are subjects for discussion. Speakers are questioned in detail at these meetings—no holds are barred. After each session, the minutes of the meeting are printed in a brochure which is mailed to all employees on the payroll and to the board of directors. The program is organized as follows:

The conferences are set up for the particular subject to be discussed. The first—which has been termed an "Advisory" meeting—consists of five members from the foremen group, four employees from the Jobmasters' Association, seven officers of the executive board of the Watch Workers' Union, four members from the International Association of Machinists' Shop Committee, and four employees representing the office supervisory personnel.

After a speaker has been selected to talk before a monthly meeting, the function of this committee is to advise him as to what the employees would like to know within the scope of his subject and where emphasis should be placed for the participants of the second conference. Basically, this committee acts as a critical liaison between the employee and management by telling management exactly what the employee wants to know.

In practice, this first advisory meeting becomes a sort of dress rehearsal in which the speaker presents his entire talk for the benefit of the advisory group. They recommend, ask questions, or request additional information in which their fellow employees are interested. Members of the advisory group are urged to discuss the assigned topic with their fellow employees before attending the meeting.

The second conference, which lasts about an hour and one-half, is attended by employee personnel selected from the two unions previously mentioned and from members with no labor agreements or affiliations. The latter employees are appointed by the personnel director with supervisory assistance. The members of the two unions are chosen by their shop stewards. Different employees are selected to attend each conference in order that as many employees as possible will have an opportunity to attend the meetings.

The minutes of the second conference are taken by five volunteers from the group. After the meeting, these volunteers meet with the personnel director and compare notes and prepare the final draft for their fellow employees. This draft is mailed to their homes, bearing the names of all employees in attendance. When a new employee joins the company, he is given a portfolio containing copies of all the previous talks.

During the question-and-answer period, questions may be asked, the answers to which might reveal confidential information. Such questions are answered as fully as possible during the meeting, but the answers are "off the record" and do not, of course, appear in the written transcript.

Field trips are also considered a part of the program. Groups have been taken to some of the finest jewelers in the community in order to observe retail business operations. Other groups have been taken through parts of the plant entirely foreign to them so that they may become acquainted with all the functions of the business.

Other Ways to Reach Employees

Most large, well-appointed offices have public-address systems. They can be made useful for keeping employees informed about the business and their part in its success. But the talks must be slanted directly to the employees' interests, rather than general lectures which are boring and tiresome to most people. Johnson & Johnson's former chairman, Robert Wood Johnson, once rang the bell with a series of forty-four 15-minute broadcasts about his company. He took up one department after another and in a brief message, often packed with personal references to people in the organization, he told why a certain department is important, how it functions, and its relationship to the business as a whole. These spot broadcasts were subsequently used in other Johnson & Johnson plants and in subsidiary companies all over the world. Interest was so keen, that the management had the talks printed in book form under the title, *Robert Johnson Talks It Over*. Thousands of copies were distributed.

Plastic recordings which can be played on an office phonograph or in employees homes offer a relatively inexpensive means of transmitting important messages. These will be discussed in the following chapter.

The rapid development of television has opened up a new avenue of employee communication, permitting an employee actually to see his employer talking to him, as well as hearing what he has to say. In-plant television is certain to become an increasingly popular way to keep employees informed, as it permits the use of charts, skits, and other interest-building devices. Employees' cafeterias are being equipped with daylight screens and telecasting equipment and companies are finding that such employee relations features are paying off.

If telecasts or spot broadcasts are to be used over the office PA system, it is a good idea to consider calling in a professional script writer to help present the facts in an interesting and dramatic way. Remember that employees do not have to listen, and will not listen to a dry, colorless talk. Using lots of names and personal references helps keep the talk "chatty." Attempts should be made to talk with the employees rather than at them.

Checking Rumors

Nothing is so upsetting to employee morale as rumors—and even the best regulated companies seem to have them. Since employees are bound to receive information—sometimes misinformation—from some source or other, it is better for it to come direct from management. Rumors by co-workers, stories which start from simple unguarded remarks of supervisors, activities of the labor union, disturbing economic or war news—all these have a way of snowballing until the final story has been so embroidered, one cannot tell how it originated.

There are times when it is very hard to stop a rumor or to explain an action. Recently one manager was forced to discharge two employees who had been with the company for some time. The reasons for their discharge were valid, but certainly not for publication.

The company was undergoing an intensive and well-publicized cost-cutting program. It didn't take long for a rumor to spread that the ax was falling because of cost cutting. Other employees became nervous.

Normally, any discharge that doesn't have an obvious base is going to be suspect by the person's fellow employees. A cost-cutting program is a convenient and plausible explanation that could be put to work. It might require an announcement that (assuming it is true) there will be no more separations in the near future. Nothing can be gained by attempting to explain the two dismissals, but much can be gained by giving the remaining group some kind of assurance.

Needless to say, the announcement will not satisfy 100 percent of the group. A certain number will remain fearful because it is their nature. The point is that the majority of the staff will be assured.

An effective anti-rumor weapon is the bulletin board. This could be a top-priority function for the board. It is possible to put more emphasis on this function by using an area adjacent to the board itself. In one company a spike has been driven into the wall next to the bulletin board. On the spike are bulletins quoting rumors, followed by management replies giving the facts. Spiking the rumor is good drama.

Another company has "It's a Fact" sheets posted on the board. These sheets give the facts about rumors reported—but they do not repeat the rumor. The point is that some employees would remember the rumor but forget the fact.

Keep It From Starting

The best defense is a good offense in the case of controlling rumor damage. Offices and companies which recognize that employees are individuals also recognize that they have individual points of view. Cutting through the communication barriers is the responsibility of management.

Let it be known that management wants to know if there are questions concerning a policy change or any action that appears to affect the employees. Keeping the "door open" in the sense of setting up a path of communication between employees and management will kill the vast majority of rumor problems.

Bulletin boards have high readership in offices and plants.

ELEVEN HINTS FOR LETTERS TO EMPLOYEES

1. Write letters only when there's something to talk about; don't make them periodical, or they may become routine.

2. Make the letters friendly but not too familiar or patronizing.

3. Be specific and be brief.

4. Letters sent to the employee's home are more effective than those distributed at the plant or office.

5. Letters should be personalized at least to the extent of being signed by an officer; company names as signatures are cold and impersonal.

6. Letters should be sent by first-class mail, so as not to be confused with advertising matter.

7. Every letter should say something of importance and of interest to the employee and his family; otherwise it is better not to write at all.

8. Check now and then with supervisors or other selected employees to find out how the workers react to the letters.

9. Tailor the letters so that they will be easily understood, but without obvious talking down.

10. Don't let the letters fall into a pattern; make each as distinctive as possible.

11. Subjects that may be used as "pegs" on which to hang such letters include:

   a. Special occasions (holidays, anniversary of company founding, etc.)

   b. The business outlook

   c. Wage and hour matters

   d. Labor-management relations

   e. Job security

   f. Company benefits

   g. Product information

   h. Competition

   i. Future plans

From the Dartnell *"Business-Letter Deskbook"*

Chapter 18

GETTING EMPLOYEES TO LISTEN

NEXT best to hearing the voice of the company president talking about matters of mutual interest, is to get a personal letter from him at home. General letters and printed bulletins are, of course, commonplace among the many ways used to keep employees informed about the company, but they lack the warmth and human touch of a friendly letter. International Harvester Company, for example, uses letters as one of three media in its communications program. These letters go to employees in their homes, and they may be written by the president of the company or by works managers. Subjects covered include the company's side of a labor dispute, reasons behind increased prices or lowered prices, or the letters may tell about a layoff that is anticipated.

In addition to these letters, a weekly newsletter goes to the management organization at each one of the company's manufacturing operations, and the information is passed on to employees. There is also a news bulletin that goes to management people at manufacturing operations. These bulletins are designed to get important news into the hands of the management organization before it is heard from some other source.

International Harvester's program is effective, and there is plenty of evidence it is accomplishing its purpose. Because of the thousands of employees to be reached, though, it is difficult to achieve the desired personal touch.

It may seem like a small matter, but the secret of effective letters to employees is to have them individually typed on automatic typewriters, and, if possible, signed personally and not rubber-stamped. When an employee gets a letter at home, written personally by the president of his company, he feels a sense of importance that he wants his family and neighbors to share with him. It makes him feel he belongs, and is not just a number on the time clock.

A weakness of most employee communications, and especially

letters to employees, is that there is no real reason (in the eyes of the employees) for the letter except to "pep them up." It is possible to double and triple the readership of a letter by a good peg on which to hang it. For example, if a company has a profit-sharing plan, it may help to issue quarterly progress reports. If the reports take the form of personal letters, rather than duplicated bulletins, they have a high interest value and are carefully read because they discuss a matter of mutual interest—the company's profits.

Do's and Don'ts

One way to alienate employees is to write letters to workers which are pompous and stuffy. Equally bad is the letter which is "all sweetness and light"; the letter which tells the employee how lucky he is to live in this country, as if a favor were being conferred on him (remember, he *is* this country!); the letter which makes cracks—either outright or implied—at his intelligence or integrity; or the letter which is patronizing—the "from me way up here to you way down there" type of letter. Such letters are by no means rare—in fact, it is the exception, rather than the rule, for letters to employees to be interesting and in good taste.

One fault in the preparation of such letters is that they are not carefully planned in advance. The writer has to write a letter so he gropes about for a subject of interest and is likely to come up with something on free enterprise, loyalty, or teamwork which is full of platitudes but doesn't have much meat.

Such letters not only fail to hold any interest for employees, but are likely to widen the cleavage between labor and management just at the time when it is essential that they be brought closer together.

When an office or a plant is being organized by a union, and a National Labor Relations Board election is in the offing, it is important that any letter regarding the advantages or disadvantages of union membership be carefully, as well as tactfully, handled. The Labor-Management Relations Act gives an employer more latitude in writing to his employees than the old Wagner Act. But the law is quite specific that employers' letters must not threaten or coerce an employee nor promise him any benefits for not joining the union.

Because the possibility of being charged with unfair labor practices by the union is so great, most employers have letters to be mailed out prior to a union certification election checked by an attorney. It has been found effective to address such letters to the employee's home address. Such letters should be individually typed to be effective.

On the following pages is a list of 16 points to keep in mind when writing a letter to employees:

1. It is better not to attempt to get out a letter at regular intervals. Letters to employees are better when the writer really has something to say.

2. Sentences and words should be short so that the message will be clear and understandable. Many words in common use in the front office are unknown to an unskilled worker in the plant who may be of foreign origin.

3. Never distribute these letters at the gate. Distribute them within the office and plant, or, better still, mail them to the employee's home, thus establishing contact with his family.

4. If you cannot do a good job of writing to employees, use a "ghost" writer. Get the best writer you can find and see that the letters are signed with a company official's name. Beware of the syndicated type of letter which your more alert employees will be likely to detect as phony.

5. Never take anything for granted. You may know all about the business, but the average worker does not have this knowledge. In fact, his ignorance of the business (unless you have done a better job of informing him than most companies are doing) is prodigious.

6. Be specific. Don't beat around the bush and confuse the employee. If you really have something to say, say it.

7. Even though you may now talk frankly and openly with your employees, do not make your letters a means of taking cracks at the union. Not only will you develop bad labor relations, but you will fail to establish good faith between yourself and your workers. It is well to keep in mind that the establishment of good faith between employer and employee is the only way of gaining reader acceptance!

8. Do not write too many letters. Letters gain in importance by their infrequency.

9. Your letters are but one contact with your employees—don't try to make them carry the full burden of employee relations.

10. Send a copy of your letter to the union business agent—he will see it in any event, but it is better policy to have it come from the company.

11. Try to confine your letter to one subject—if you jump from one subject to another you confuse the reader.

12. Keep technical jargon out of your letters. The average employee does not think in such terms. This is particularly important if you are writing him about the company's financial position or the annual report. Much of the language used in annual reports is unintelligible to workers.

13. Soft-pedal the subject of free enterprise, the American way of life, etc. The thousands of words run off on this subject matter (much of it syndicated) have become monotonous and thus have lost all meaning for the average employee. Any worker with common sense—and a surprising lot of them do have common sense—does not want to live under a foreign system of government and therefore does not have to be sold on the

American system. Business is likely to put itself on the defensive—a bad position—by reiterating phrases about free enterprise over and over again. There are other ways of selling democracy to Americans.

14. Much of the information the worker receives from other sources is misinformation. It is management's job to see that he gets his information "straight from the feed box." It is management's job to try to make the average worker a well-informed person so that when others start talking in terms of wages and profits, he will know the score.

15. Vary the tone and the format of your letters to avoid monotony.

16. Check and double check on the way readers react to your letters. A check can be established through representative employees (beware of checking with "yes" men) which will show whether your letters are doing the job they are expected to do.

The Employee Newsletter

Even in a relatively small office, it pays to get out some sort of newsletter for white-collar employees every fortnight or oftener. Such a letter disseminates all kinds of information which might interest employees, such as news about important sales that were closed during the period, new products that are being developed, items about new employees—who they are and where they came from—and, most important of all, news about staff promotions.

When employees of the Illinois Central System get together, they can talk intelligently and interestingly about their work because of a monthly letter.

Without making it too evident, the aim of the newsletter should be to take the employee into the confidence of the management, make him feel that he is a member of a champion team, and demonstrate by concrete cases that the company does reward good work and that its policy is to promote from within the organization rather than to go outside when there is a good job to be filled. Such a newsletter need not be elaborate, in fact, the more personal it is, the better. A few pages of informal notes, run off on the office duplicator, will do very well. But it should be informative and not an office gossip sheet —which may interest those whose names appear in it, but which does not do the job that so badly needs to be done—if the turnover of employees is to be held down and the highest morale maintained.

Employee Counseling

Keeping office employees happy and contented is obviously highly important to the successful operation of any business. But despite great increases in income, better working conditions, and many added benefits in the past decade, the office employee is still often dissatisfied. Add to this condition a wide-open job opportunity market with a great choice of jobs, and it is not difficult to see why turnover is a serious problem to the office manager.

Most of the 165 companies that contributed to a Dartnell report, covering office working conditions, have company-sponsored programs designed to aid employees with personal problems as well as problems that arise from the job situation. They also have programs aimed at making the place of employment a pleasant center of social life. Elsewhere in this book such programs are described, as well as the efforts made by management to keep office employees informed.

Employee counseling services, aimed at helping employees with personal and on-the-job problems, are provided by 65 percent of the companies responding to Dartnell's survey. Large firms, like Boeing Company, consider counseling an important part of the program.

Individual counselors are usually management executives who are qualified by education and experience to assist employees with their problems. Many small firms use outside consultants to help employees through the use of psychological measurements and personal counseling. This type of counseling will many times salvage an employee who is not working out because of attitude or personality difficulties. Walter E. Elliott, director of an industrial consulting concern in Cincinnati, Ohio, has described such counseling as follows:

The elementary purpose of counseling is to help people solve the many complex problems in which the greatest feeling of satisfaction will be achieved. The primary purpose is to help the individual see and do something about the personality factors or attitudes which may limit his success despite the knowledge, intelligence, interests, and aptitudes that are brought to light by tests. For the executive, it pinpoints the problem areas and the best ways of working with his key people in helping them to reduce emotional pressures caused by ever-increasing job responsibilities.

One of the most neglected areas in many school and guidance centers is the failure to stress the attitude factors that will limit the person's advancement to higher levels in the given fields. Hand in hand with this neglect goes the failure to help the individual see the causes behind his wrong attitudes and do what is necessary to overcome them. Closed-mindedness, evasiveness, temper, inferior feelings, indecisiveness, too low or too high self-sufficiency are just a few of the attitudes or personality traits that may short-circuit the individual's success despite his choosing the field that will use his capabilities most effectively.

Surveys disclose continually that about three-fourths of the labor problems, personal failures in management level of positions, lack of promotion from the ranks to supervision, have their foundations in wrong attitudes and personality weaknesses . . . things which could be corrected if a person could only be made aware of the negative effects he has on others.

Group counseling and discussions are provided by 35 percent of companies. These sessions are designed to explain policies, air gripes, and answer questions that bother employees. In the opinion of a General Motors official, counseling is an important job for either the supervisor or the medical department, especially if the medical department includes a psychiatrist or psychologist, depending upon the types of problems that arise.

Group sessions are usually informative and simple. An office manager with an insurance company says, "We have had group counseling for three years. Each department head is schooled in the latest techniques of group meeting administration and we have regularly scheduled meetings with our departments once a month, or, in some cases, twice a month. Employees know they can talk frankly and openly in these meetings and we feel we are getting the gripes out in the open rather than waiting till they build up into major problems of resentment. Whether an employee's complaint is real or imagined, he still likes to have it heard."

A personnel followup in two parts is urged by the Business Management Service of the University of Illinois. First, supervisors should interview new employees at intervals—usually after three months, six months, and one year. The supervisor talks privately with the newcomer about his work and may tell him how it can be improved. At the same time, the employee has a chance to discuss any questions or problems with the supervisor.

Second, the employment office should send a followup form to the supervisor for reporting his satisfaction or dissatisfaction with the employee. This information permits the personnel man to evaluate the placement and, if necessary, shift the employee elsewhere or take steps to change conditions which may be causing difficulties.

The Plastic Recording

Breakthroughs on the part of manufacturers have made it possible to record a message on a flimsy piece of plastic. This plastic, when placed on a phonograph, provides a medium with startling fidelity.

The communicator, faced with larger audiences whose attention is diverted by all manners of outside influence, is hard put to come up with methods for gaining and holding employee attention. A growing number are turning to the phonograph record. This is not the newest idea on the market, but it is proving to be an effective, not-too-expensive way of reaching and holding a group's attention. Since the records can be—and are—used in the home, they provide an excellent medium of reaching a family audience.

Take Dale Electronics, Inc., a Lionel Corporation subsidiary in Columbus, Nebraska. Carl Rafferty, employment manager, reports his company experience: "Our annual report to employees has always been pretty much of a conventional thing, and we simply wanted to *do something different.*"

This desire resulted in the pressing of 1,200 seven-inch, flexible vinyl high-fidelity records, each containing the voice of President William R. Simpson. He spoke to each employee and his family individually. The records were mailed to the employee's home enclosed in a folder. The printed folder highlighted the year's results as well as the record.

Rafferty expresses the results: "The *biggest* thing the record idea has to offer is its sheer novelty—people just naturally play the record to see what's on it. When they do, they hear a *personal* word from the president."

Rafferty also mentions the value of sound and emotion: "There is better emphasis through enunciation rather than italicized or underscored type."

President Simpson's message was recorded on tape and edited at a Columbus radio station. The tape was then sent to a record manufacturer who cut the discs and prepared the folders. The cost, exclusive of postage and making the tape, was about $155.

Last year Motorola, Inc., experienced the greatest growth in the 17-year history of its profit-sharing fund and established a first in communicating the results of the record year to fund members. Speaking as a trustee in the company's own studio, Robert Galvin recorded a talk that was placed in every copy of the company publication, *Voice of Motorola.*

The idea was a good one. Reporting on the favorable reaction, R. A. Orth, assistant to the human relations vice-president, said reception was particularly good in locations that were distant from the Franklin Park, Illinois, headquarters. Employees who have less opportunity to see and hear Board Chairman Galvin were very pleased.

At SKF Industries, Inc., a Zero Defects program called COMPETE was presented as a *complete* industrial communications program. So, it is not surprising that the sound dimension has been utilized in COMPETE, with a record bound into an issue of *The Sphere,* the SKF employee publication. Via this record, E. R. Broden, president and chairman, visited the homes of SKF'ers to link the company's success to the future of employees and their families. He reminded them that COMPETE stands for Customer Orders Mean Protection of Earnings Through Efficiency. "Simply stated," Mr. Broden said, "satisfied SKF customers mean continued roller-bearing orders and the job security and future employee opportunities that go with them." The chief executive was thus able to emphasize to employees, in their homes, the competitive need to keep roller-bearing users satisfied."

What Does It Take?

From Eva-Tone division of Evatype Corporation, Deerfield, Illinois, we get the following information:

A company interested in producing a recorded message must supply two things to a processing company: (1) a tape recording of the message to be pressed into record form and (2) the copy or artwork for the center imprint on the record and the copy/artwork for the folder (if desired).

The tape recording is best if professionally produced in a recording studio. In many cases a community radio station can do the job. The cost of a sound studio effort is in the vicinity of $25 an hour. The recording should be made at a reasonably high level with careful editing. It is normally recorded at 7½ or 15 IPS on a ¼-inch single or double track magnetic tape.

This tape is first reproduced as a master acetate, and in turn this is mounted into machines which produce the required number of flexible records at high speeds.

Eva-Tone tells its customers that its product is made on a "highly resilient, pure vinyl." The speeds for playing are normally 33⅓ rpm (a normal speed on the majority of phonographs) or 16⅔ rpm (on many phonographs today).

EFFECTIVE BULLETIN BOARDS

The bulletin board is one communications device that has not fallen by the wayside in this age of advanced communication techniques. In fact, 98 percent of industry still leans upon it as the best method of keeping employees informed. This was discovered in a Dartnell survey of 223 companies.

Commenting on boards in general, one respondent said, "The only thing that has changed about the use of bulletin boards is the fact that they are getting fancier and sharper in appearance." That this is true is evidenced by the number of companies in business today whose sole service deals with posters, photographs, and other board materials for industry. It is a most unusual company that does not have some type of employee notice device on which to post announcements, statistics, safety slogans, and the dozens of other notices directed to employees.

If you post a vital notice that should reach all workers, what is your percentage of readership? Estimates ranged from as low as 30 percent to "almost 95 percent." Median average of the estimates was almost 75 percent. This does not take into consideration the word-of-mouth reaction that sets in once a vital notice is posted.

A southern food supply house ran an experimental series of notices. It found the well-received notice gets high readership in a hurry. But it also found that notices that don't make employees too happy have a peculiar way of going unnoticed by a large segment of the group. It found, for instance, that 90 percent of the employees were familiar with the fact that Monday before Christmas was a paid holiday three hours after the announcement was posted. But only 35 percent knew that Monday before New Year's was to be "work as usual," though it was posted at the same time. Seems like employees read the things they like to read, but are not keen on retaining information that isn't pleasing to the eye.

Quite a few companies believe that the most effective announcements are those with pictures or cartoons. "They are easy to understand," said one executive, "and employees catch the meaning quickly when the idea is visualized."

Who Maintains the Board

Poor maintenance is listed as one of the chief causes of poor readership among employees. If the board is sloppy and unattractive, if notices remain posted long after they are obsolete, and if anything anyone wants to put up is exhibited it will lower employee interest. The answer to keeping the board up-to-date and attractive lies in having one person, or group of persons, responsible for its upkeep, according to 85 percent of the companies which contributed to the Dartnell survey. In 65 percent of the cases, the personnel department is responsible for servicing the notices. In larger companies, the industrial relations department, which is usually over the personnel function, services the boards. Department heads do the posting in 10 percent of the companies, and various other departments are responsible in 8 percent of the cases.

How 200 Companies Control Office and Plant Bulletin Boards

Most firms—almost 95 percent—have a system for keeping the board up-to-date. Whoever is responsible for maintenance of the notices follows a prescribed system. Here are the methods of companies responding to a Dartnell survey:

Weekly inspection ....40 percent

Biweekly inspection..22 percent

Monthly inspection..10 percent

Outside service .... 5 percent

Announcements dated for posting and withdrawal............................15 percent

No set system.. 8 percent

Besides the methods listed above, a number of concerns reported other controls used to supplement the program. Included are the use of color codes to identify announcements by subject and date, short cycle checks, and the use of an appointed committee to police the boards.

Suggesting ways to make the board more effective, the personnel director of the large Chicago offices of Field Enterprises, Inc., says: "Careful consideration should be given to the location, placement of materials, frequent changing of materials; furthermore some light matter, such as cartoons, should be interspersed with regular announcements, to attract readers."

Another office executive reports, "Some boards are like some people: They talk too much and say nothing." He adds, "A little personality in your office bulletin board will make it individual and interesting—there is a definite art to administering a bulletin board effectively."

As one executive commented, "Bulletin boards are now accepted as the very backbone of effective office and plant communication by

A BULLETIN BOARD CHECKLIST

YES   NO

1. Do you have enough boards to attract the attention of all employees?

2. Is one person or group of persons solely responsible for the upkeep of company boards?

3. Do you have a system for checking boards and keeping them free from obsolete or outdated notices?

4. Are the boards attractive, well lighted, and eye-catching?

5. Have y o u checked employee interest and readership lately as it applies to bulletin boards?

6. Are board notices supplemented by other forms of communication such as public address s y s t e m announcements, supervisor-employee group meetings, company house organ articles, letters to employees, or other methods?

7. Do you have separate bulletin boards for personal employee notices and for official company notices?

8. Are the boards strategically located so that everyone sees them who should see them?

9. Do those who submit official material for posting have it approved by their superiors when required?

10. Is your bulletin board treated as a vital link in the communication system?

If you have answered "NO" to any one of the questions on the list, better look into it. Remember, a poor bulletin board system means a poor communication system.

most companies, and, as such, they should be handled seriously and methodically, not as catch-alls for scraps of paper."

Some respondents commented on the importance of having boards for personal notices from employees separate from those used for official bulletins.

How Schlitz Controls Bulletin Boards

An office executive of the Jos. Schlitz Brewing Company, Milwaukee, Wisconsin, has kindly permitted reproduction of the rules of that company with regard to control of its bulletin boards. As this is one of the subjects on which "everybody agrees something should be done, but few actually do anything about," the following excerpts from the Schlitz personnel manual may prove useful.

I. Types of Boards.

    A. Plant News Boards (Family News Type).

        To Contain:

          1. Announcements of company-wide or plant-wide interest, i.e., new rules, holiday announcements, etc.

          2. Union notices emanating from union headquarters.

          3. Safety posters.

          4. News material, i.e., Family Newsette, sports announcements, advertising pieces, reporters' pictures, TV announcements, etc.

          5. Permanent notices—company and those required by law.

    B. Plant Department Boards (these are the small boards now liberally sprinkled around the plant).

        To Contain:

          1. Notices of department interest only. Such notices may require immediate attention. If notices become permanent, they should be transferred after a reasonable time to the news-type boards in the department concerned.

          2. Special notices for salaried personnel. Such notices would be placed on the department boards accessible to salaried personnel, i.e., scheduling offices, supervisors' lunch rooms, etc.

          3. Thank you cards, etc. (Note—this type of notice should be put up only with approval of department head. He should initial them and list a take-down date. Usually a posting of a week or two is sufficient.)

    C. Timeclock Boards.

        To Contain:

          1. Flash notices—i.e., change in working hours, etc. Notices posted on timeclocks should be few since regular department boards should suffice.

D. Office News Boards (Family News Type). In general offices, Payroll, Tech. Building City Sales.

To Contain:

1. Announcements of company-wide or plant-wide interest, i.e., new rules, holiday notices, etc.
2. News material, i.e., Family Newsette, sports announcements, advertising pieces, reporters' pictures, etc. Men's and girls' club announcements.

E. Office Department Boards (now located at various places in general offices).

To Contain:

1. Permanent notices.
2. Menus for cafeteria.
3. Departmental announcements—both permanent and those requiring immediate attention.
4. Personal thank you notes. (Note—this type of notice should be put up only with approval of department head. He should initial them and list a take-down date. Usually a week or two of posting is sufficient.)

NOTE: A glassed-in board will continue to be mounted in the basement hallway of the General Office Building. This board will contain permanent notices.

II. Posting Regulation.

A. All bulletin boards shall be under the jurisdiction of the Industrial Relations Department.

B. Posting of news boards in plant and offices will be done only by Industrial Relations Department Personnel.

C. Posting on news boards will be done so far as possible on Wednesday afternoons and on weekends. Notices to be posted should be in the family news office by *Wednesday* or *Friday* mornings.

D. Notices for all news and office department boards should be marked with a removal date. For most notices, a week or two of posting is sufficient. Removal dates should *coincide* with posting dates.

E. It is suggested that all notices follow this form:

— — — — — — —

Subject and Date
and Department

Message

Removal Date

— — — — — — —

After notice has been posted a reasonable time, center portion of the notice can be clipped out, transferred to news boards and posted with permanent notices if the notice is of permanent nature. To make efficient use of space in bulletin boards, permanent notices should be single spaced and take full advantage of the width of an 8½" x 11" sheet. Surplus paper can be trimmed off when notice is relocated with other permanent notices.

F. All official notices should include "Jos. Schlitz Brewing Company" in signature.

G. Department boards will be posted by persons designated by department head. Thank you cards and other noncompany material to be posted should have initialed O.K. of department head or designated authority and a removal date noted.

H. It is the responsibility of department heads to see that department boards are kept in neat condition.

Advantages and Disadvantages

Since 98 percent of American companies use the bulletin board to keep employees informed, we asked respondents to list some of the advantages found in posting notices. The greatest advantage listed was the fact that bulletin boards are inexpensive to maintain. Ease of administration, rapid attention, centralized information, quick communication, and authoritative, factual information were also given as reasons for use of bulletin boards.

Poor upkeep and maintenance were the main disadvantages seen by management executives. J. N. Campbell, industrial relations head, Spector Freight System, Inc., observed, "The bulletin board lacks the personal touch—it may not be read." Walter Kante, editor of the company publication of Joseph Schlitz Brewing Company, feels a definite disadvantage lies in the fact that boards "take lots of time to prepare and post."

Here are some typical comments from employees who are on the receiving end of bulletin board announcements and notices. The comments were picked up at random in a spot check of several firms.

Foreman, Chicago tool company: "My biggest gripe with the bulletin arrangement in our company is the fact that notices are posted and seen by employees before supervision even knows about it. For instance, the personnel department recently put up an announcement on job postings which affected my department. I didn't even know it was posted until several employees came to see me about it."

Typist, Indiana insurance office: "We have a fine system here and most of us look at the bulletin board as the best source of information on company plans, letters of praise or criticism from customers, and general news about our people."

Shipping clerk, Chicago publishing house: "Employees get tired of seeing the same notices on the board for weeks and months. We have one on the board right now that has been there since March. It tells about one of our employees who 'is in the hospital.' The fellow has been back to work three months and has had another operation since the original announcement."

Secretary, Midwest bakery: "If you want my opinion, I think companies can do a much better job than they are now doing in posting announcements for employees. First of all, the board should be attractive and easy to see. Second, it should be centrally placed, or several boards should be used so all employees have a chance to see them. Third, it should be kept in neat condition. No one wants to read a dirty, ancient notice."

Requisites of the Perfect Board

While the measurement of perfection is always a rather ambiguous thing, there are certain procedures that make a company notice board about as perfect as things can be. First, the board must be placed where it has the best chance of readership. At entrances and exits, in the department itself, by the time clocks, or any areas where employees gather are good sources of high readership. Second, maintaining the board should become the responsibility of one person or group of persons. Third, a system for posting and withdrawing notices should be devised. Regular checks on the board material should be made by this responsible group. Fourth, spot checks on employee readership will give clues to the strengths and weaknesses of the current system. Several companies have had success with questionnaires given to each employee for his impressions and suggestions about the bulletin board system. Fifth, boards should supplement other means of communication.

Bulletin boards are the very backbone of effective plant communications and, as such, should be handled seriously and methodically. Companies which spend thousands of dollars building employee good will through recreation programs, extra benefits, and other activities, can lose the battle right at the bulletin board. If employees feel slighted by a dirty, slovenly, poorly maintained attempt at board administration, they will show it in morale and—where it hurts the most—in lower productive output. When a bulletin board has not been inspected in some time, it should be looked at critically and put back in shape as quickly as possible.

THE EMPLOYEE HANDBOOK

There is no doubt that high-level office production depends largely upon the morale of an organization and the employees' willingness to give the jobs their best efforts. While this factor in production costs also depends on having supervisors who have the knack of getting people to work with them, or in the human relations aspect of management, it also involves job understanding. To make sure that every employee understands what his job is all about and how he fits into the overall picture, it is now standard practice to prepare and issue to new and old employees a company handbook.

What an Employee Wants to Know

There are many questions on the mind of a new employee. Many of these can best be answered by the employee's immediate supervisor. Similarly, there are things a person considering a job wants to know about the company, but usually he hesitates to ask questions while he is being interviewed. Yet the right answers to these questions may have a decisive bearing on whether or not the applicant takes the job. By the same token, older employees are frequently asked questions about the company and its policies by new employees, which they do not know how to answer.

Then there are situations which come up in managing men, whether they are office workers, retail clerks, or unionized production employees, which call for the "blueprint" treatment. For example, an employee gets into a fist fight on company property. The company has an "unwritten" rule that whoever starts a fight will be discharged for the good of the organization. When the men are called on the carpet for fighting and there is no printed rule about fighting, their natural "excuse" would be they didn't know fighting was against the rules; nobody had ever told them about any rule. The culprits have no alibi if their supervisor or the department manager can open the employee manual to page 23 where it says "in black and white" that fighting on company property is one of those things nice people don't do, but if they do, whoever starts the fight will be discharged.

If the company has a contract with a union and the union has agreed to the rules in the manual, no one can question management's right to take appropriate action if rules are broken.

Generally speaking, there are five things that every employee, new or veteran, wants to know about his job. They are:

> When and how did the company get its start?
> How is the company organized and what does it do?
> What are the important advantages that employees enjoy?
> What is expected of me?
> What is my opportunity for advancement?

The answers to these and similar questions should be clearly set forth in the fewest words possible. There will be other questions to be covered, other rules, other stipulations relating to the employee and his job, but as an approach to planning or revising an employee manual, these five questions should be kept in mind.

Chapter 19

MAKING THE MOST OF
EMPLOYEE PUBLICATIONS

COMPANY publications mean many things to many people today. The familiar mimeographed "house organ" has grown, in some cases, to a slick magazine with external (outside) distribution. The presentation and quality of content rivals the best that general interest can produce.

Such publications as *Kaiser Aluminum News* and *Think* by IBM are not considered employee publications, although employees can read them with pride. On the other hand Western Electric's *WE* and Southwestern Bell's *Scene* are produced for and about employees with the same amount of care.

The normal role of a company publication is to inform employees. This job is well handled by United States Steel Corporation which produces an 11 a.m. and 4 p.m. *News Bulletin*, prepared daily by its public relations department for selective distribution at New York headquarters. This is generally a one-page mimeographed sheet, employee-written for employees, which quotes AP, UPI, and Dow Jones news highlights in paragraph form.

The majority of company publications are prepared in either magazine or newspaper format and distributed monthly or more frequently. Some are still poorly put together, giving little or no real news to the reader. Others are vital links in the corporate communications chain, providing employees with the important news first and in accurate detail.

What Employees Want to Read

To be most effective an employee publication, regardless of format, must be editorially well balanced. It should give the reader information of interest and value to him. In an effort to find the proper balance between news and educational material in an employee publication, a reader survey among workers in several industrial plants of The National Cash Register Company was conducted by L. E. Finley. This survey showed employees were more interested in news about the company than they were in news about other employees.

An exception to this rule would be the small organization having less than 300 employees, most of whom know one another. Another exception would be a publication for members of a specific department, such as a paper for the salesmen or the office employees. But in nearly every poll of employees in organizations with 300 or more persons on the payroll, the "know your company" type of articles ranked at the top. A poll at Socony Mobil Oil Company, Inc., for example, gave this type of article 96 mentions compared with 16 mentions for news about employees, new babies, brides, and so on. The same poll gave jokes, which some editors consider a "must," only 33 mentions. A poll at American Optical Company, to determine what type of articles employees wanted, placed more company stories first, more humor second, and more pictures third.

When a publication for employees is soundly edited and is not a mirror of some executive's pet ideas, it can be a most useful link in the chain of employer-employee communications. Over 6,000 American business and industrial establishments spend more than $100 million annually for employee publications, which is rather convincing evidence of their cash-register value. One large steel company credits its employee publication with its 18-year no-strike record. This company found when employees are given the facts in a publication which presents their side as well as the company side of employment issues, there is no need for paying dues to a union.

The Chamber of Commerce of the United States has issued, as a part of its continuing American Opportunity program, a book which is entitled *How to Tell Your Business Story in Employee Publications.*

The chamber lists the following 10 objectives for employee publications dedicated to the task of improving employee attitudes toward business. They are:

1. Interpret company policies to employees.

2. Keep employees informed about new company plans and developments.

3. Promote employee cooperation and loyalty through better understanding of company problems.

4. Explain financial structure and operation of the company.

5. Expose rumors that breed misunderstanding.

6. Nullify harmful propaganda from antibusiness sources.

7. Promote an employee-company family concept of mutual aims and interests.

8. Build a favorable attitude toward the company on the part of wives and children of employees.

9. Foster friendly press relations.

10. Build community good will for the company.

In short, to do its job, an employee publication should improve employee relations, help to maintain industrial peace, encourage productive labor, stimulate ambition, build morale, express recognition of work well done, give employees the economic facts of life, and speak up for America.

Presenting the Company's Story

There is a story behind every business and it is the job of any publication sponsored by a company for its employees, or its customers for that matter, to tell that story well. That does not mean filling the publication with "puffs" or articles that sound like a page from the company's catalog. But there is a philosophy that motivates a business which an editor should understand and interpret in an interesting and readable way.

William G. Caples, former president of Inland Steel Container Company, in an address to a meeting of industrial editors in Chicago, said: "Anyone charged with the responsibility of a business has sat down and figured out the place of that business in the economy and society; what he wants the business to be, now and in the future; and how he intends to accomplish those objectives. Whether you agree or disagree with that philosophy, it is the philosophy of the management that employs you. It is your obligation to present that philosophy as effectively as you know how. If you cannot do that, you must make one of those decisions that each person makes many times in his life. To do otherwise would be dishonest.

"If the philosophy has not been formalized or put in writing, one of an editor's first duties is to go to the men who run the business and find out from them, by talking to them, what their philosophy is. For instance, I have seen many employee publications issued by companies in which I knew there was considerable controversy with a union. And yet, to read the company publication you would not know that any such thing existed.

"There is a company side to any union controversy and one of the places in which that side can be most clearly stated is in the company publication. Certainly, the workers who read that publication know that it is written with bias from the standpoint of management, but the company is entitled to that view, just as they are entitled to the union view. From these adverse views, they can reach their own conclusions. In this regard, let me quote the *Labor Relations Advisory Letter:*

" 'If management does not undertake to tell its story to employees, no one else will. The employees will, in all probability, be told a story by someone or some organization, but . . . it will *not* be management's story and it will not be designed to do management any good. The effectiveness of management's story will, however, depend on: (a) How sound the story actually is; (b) how well it is told; and (c) whether it is told over the course of the year or saved for an "emergency." You can't blame employees for being a litttle suspicious of management communications that appear only in times of tension or friction.'

"To my mind, a company publication should meet company problems, deal with them and report accurately and fairly the management's viewpoint toward these problems and their probable solutions. An employee publication must be specific and straight forward. Following a 'head-in-the-sand' policy is unrealistic."

Types of Employee Publications

In the smaller office or plant it is customary to issue one employee publication which goes to all employees—the workers in the plant, the office employees, the sales staff, and even to the stockholders. In this way, the whole organization is knit together. The workers can learn about the activities and problems of the office force and the salesmen, and the salesmen and office people become acquainted with the workers and their contribution to the success of the enterprise.

As an industrial enterprise grows, however, the practice is to issue not just one "family" paper but several publications, each dealing with the particular interests of the group that receives it. A common division of publications is as follows:

1. Weekly newspaper for plant workers.
2. Monthly news bulletin for supervisors.
3. Monthly news bulletin for office personnel.
4. Weekly news bulletin for salesmen.
5. Monthly magazine for customers.
6. Quarterly news folder for stockholders.

Each of the major classifications may be, and indeed usually is, broken down according to the needs of the business. Where a company has several plants, it is customary to publish a paper for the workers of each plant with general articles carried over from one plant paper to the other. In the case of news bulletins to the distributing organization, one publication may be edited for the salesmen who represent the company in the field; another for distributors; another for distributors' salesmen; still another for dealers and their clerks. This follows the trend in business journalism toward highly specialized papers dealing with the problems of a clearly defined reader group.

How to Get "Live" News

The value of news as a means of building good will among employees and loyalty and enthusiasm among those who carry your message to the buyer can hardly be overestimated. No plant is too large, no business too small, to utilize it. It will work effectively for the employer or the merchant whose problem consists of spreading the news about the new things he has on sale among a selected group of townspeople. Everybody is news-minded. Even the hard-boiled salesman, who thinks he is too busy to read most of the matter sent to him by the office, stops to read the news.

The trick in getting "live" news for publication in your business bulletins is to develop "a nose for news." While it is possible to create a certain amount of news, the best news comes out of the daily activities of a business. The alert employer keeps a weather eye open for any unusual development that can be passed along. It may be a story about a person; a closeup of someone who is in the news. It may be news about a shipment of merchandise received from abroad; or the experience of a man in "the shop." But always it is interesting; otherwise it is not worth printing. This is the first and great commandment in using news to build employee relations.

Format of Employee Publication

Because employees are vitally interested in other workers and employees and what they are doing, the most effective type of employee publication is the small-sized newspaper, printed inexpensively on newspaper stock. It has been found that by using stock of a little better quality than ordinary newsprint, and using a coarser screen of halftone engravings, results are even better than when a highly coated paper stock is used. Even though the coated paper reproduces halftones better than newsprint, the more expensive coated stock gives the publication an atmosphere of extravagance which is not always desirable. Employees quite rightfully think economy, like charity, should "begin at home."

If the number of copies to be printed is relatively small, the publication is usually produced on the office duplicating machine, either from a stencil or by the offset process. Any one of the methods produces a very acceptable publication, and there is something about the intimacy of the processed news-bulletin that readers like. The same reader reaction is found to newsletters as compared to more expensively printed business papers.

If the size of the company warrants, a magazine format is certainly acceptable for an employee publication. The magazine allows a certain amount of editorial makeup and freedom which can attract the reader's eye. It is also very adaptable for picture stories—those which tell more than 1,000 words.

It is also a fact that the magazine format normally will cost much more money, and that the publication will probably be edited by a professional.

There are many reasons why a company should or should not have a magazine. Often the decision will be made by the public relations man or team working with top management. In many cases, more frequently distributed bulletins supplement the monthly or bimonthly magazine issued by the company. These bulletins are used for news while the magazine tells the company's long-range story in words and pictures.

Changing the Pace

The cardinal sin of industrial journalism is letting a publication go stale. It should be remembered that an employees' magazine is like a show on Broadway. It attracts theatergoers for a few months, and then a new show is needed or the box office will have to close. Even the best employee paper needs stirring up and changes of editorial treatment and format once in a while. The editor who is on his toes and wants to keep his job, will think of new features to keep his readers excited. Good journalism involves not only writing and editing the news, but also creating news to get the publication talked about. One of the reasons for the influence of the Chicago *Tribune*, for example, is that it is always doing something to get readers excited—they may not like the *Tribune's* editorial policies or the way its rewrite men treat the news, but it is never dull. To maintain that kind of reader interest is the real test of industrial journalism.

For some years, the Jewel Tea Company, Barrington, Illinois, used a one-page form carrying the caption, "Fill it out! Send it in!" to secure news for its employee magazine. After some years of use, this form was discontinued in favor of personal letters, which employees are encouraged to write to the editor of the magazine.

The company discontinued the use of printed forms because (1) familiarity with the form led to its being neglected and (2) the standardized forms led to a stereotyped format in reporting. The letter method has been found to give greater variety to the material submitted.

Daily Office Bulletins

Every morning employees of the Skelly Oil Company, Kansas City, Missouri, find on their desks a copy of a bulletin called, *The Office Bugle*. The *Bugle* is only a single-sheet affair, simple and unpretentious, but it reports latest office activities, news, and announcements. Each copy is dated and numbered consecutively.

This is a plan which could be adopted advantageously by many companies. There is much that takes place in every medium-sized or large office that could well be made the subject of definite announcement. There are a thousand and one things which happen daily to fill the columns of a regular office bulletin.

Perhaps of first importance are announcements concerning working time, opening and closing hours, compensation, holidays, time off, etc. Announcements of personnel changes are important, too. Often new employees have a difficult time adjusting themselves, and old employees waste time by sending work to wrong persons and departments because they are not aware of the new workers and their duties. A daily bulletin should announce the names, positions, and duties of each new employee—temporary or permanent. By following this plan everyone in the office is made aware of each new employee and knows whose work he has taken over or what new work he is expected to do. With this definite knowledge the entire staff is usually glad to help newcomers, and their own work often is facilitated.

One of the most insidious causes of unrest and dissatisfaction in any office is gossip. And most gossip is based on uncertainty. When do vacations begin? Will we have vacations with pay? Will vacations be shorter this year, or longer? Will we close the day before Christmas? Will we have a half or full holiday on Washington's Birthday? With the daily bulletin to give the answers to these and a thousand similar questions, much gossip and rumor are stopped before they begin. But when an office staff begins to gossip about overtime, half holidays, and time off, there is an inevitable letdown in production and morale. Office employees are human and want to make their plans as far in advance as possible. Let them become accustomed to getting their news and facts from a daily office bulletin and they learn to await official news rather than rely on the office grapevine.

Other sources of news items for the daily bulletin are promotions, changes, transfers, and addition of new departments or new equipment, and similar developments. Tell who is promoted, why, whose work the fortunate person is to take over, and who will replace the person promoted.

Announce vacations in the daily bulletin; tell who is scheduled to leave each week, how long they will be away, and who will look after their work while they are on vacation. It may be a good plan to announce each week who has returned from vacations, too. When executives plan extended trips, announce this in the daily bulletins so that persons who have business to take up with these executives may do so before they depart.

The knack of maintaining morale, or keeping up employee interest, is often no more than letting them know what is going on and how they fit into the general scheme of things in an office. This calls for an occasional pat on the back for some employee who has done extra good work. Has the accounting department done herculean labor in getting out the annual statement on time? Then comment on it. Has the advertising department performed some splendid feat in preparing for a sales convention, or mailing out a huge campaign? Then tell about it. Has the credit department been unusually successful in keeping down losses this month? Then let others know it.

How far the daily bulletin should deviate from strict business news depends wholly upon the organization and the viewpoint of the men at its head. Should personal news, such as births, deaths, and marriages be included? Where there is an employee house organ such news should be saved for it. But if there is no employee house organ it may be advisable to include at least the most important items of this kind.

Uses of Contests in Employee Publications

A good employee publication, like a good newspaper, must be exciting. People will not read it unless it is exciting. This kind of interest can be attained by doing a human interest reporting job, and also by creating editorial features which interest and excite readers. One such feature is the contest, which has reached a high state of effectiveness in publications going to sales employees. The same idea can be used in publications going to plant and office workers. Suggestion contests are a good example.

A Chicago mail-order company prepared a series of bulletins on its employee relations policies. To make sure employees are familiar with the policies outlined in the bulletins, a series of contests, to be held every six months, was inaugurated. Fifty prizes were awarded for each contest, amounts running from $15 for the first prize down to $1 for the last 47 prizes. All timeclock employees were eligible.

The first contest consisted of 40 questions of the fill-in-the-blanks type, with considerable weight being carried by the answer to the last question. It was "Tell us which personnel policy you like best in from 25 to 50 words." Each question was illustrated by a small pen-and-ink sketch.

Daily House Organ for Store Personnel

For many years the Federal Outfitting Company, with headquarters in San Francisco, operating 21 stores in California and one in Nevada, has issued a daily mimeographed house organ. This veritable "sparkplug" leaves the head office during the final hour of every business day in the year and by noon the next day is in the hands of all employees of all stores, although some of them are more than 400 miles away. This company uses a sales-stimulation program of monthly promotion. This persistent publication solves the obvious problem of maintaining the *full-month* interest of an organization.

Called *The Federal Trumpeter,* this house organ is produced in 4-page form, page size 8½ by 11 inches, entirely on a mimeograph machine. Sometimes two colors of ink are used, and the color of the paper is never the same for two consecutive months. It is edited by the sales promotion manager, who also directs the advertising program. Little or no space is devoted to news of purely social events, and personalities enter into the picture mostly in connection with selling activities. Every issue is profusely illustrated in comic cartoon style, and the writing technique is light and breezy. Stimulation of interstore rivalry is the basic aim. By reason of its daily appearance, the bulletin keeps all concerned posted on the relative standings of all stores. The day-by-day story is told in rivalry-provoking texts and in pictures which show, for example, contestants rolling hoops, rowing in boat races, fishing, riding in horse races, or climbing mountains—always giving, of course, the name of a store to each character and placing them in the relative positions they actually occupy. The copy goes to the duplicating department soon after noon each day—after the sales reports for the previous day have been received and tabulated.

Revere Copper Employee Bulletins

From a series of single-page, illustrated, letter-size folders, Revere Copper & Brass, Inc., employees learn many essential, dramatic, and interesting facts about their company. Notable for the "brass tacks" quality of the messages, the absence of preaching, the factual information, and well-selected pictures, this series of folders sets a new standard in employees' educational and good-will-building material.

In one of the folders there is a message from the vice-president and general sales manager. It begins: "There is a true saying that salesmen get the first order—but factory men get the second. Suppose, for instance, that one of our salesmen persuades a new customer to buy a quantity of Revere brass. The order goes through the mill and is shipped out. If quality and delivery of the shipment are satisfactory to the customer, he will be inclined to give us another order when he needs more brass. But, if he is not satisfied with either quality or delivery, it will be pretty difficult for our salesmen to get any more business from that customer."

Is the Publication Read?

When business is booming and no one is bothered too much about cutting expenses, few question whether the employee paper is worth what it costs. But just as soon as business slackens off and the black ink shows signs of turning pink, then someone in top management is sure to raise this question. The accepted method of proving that the money spent for a company publication or house organ is a good investment is to distribute a questionnaire and find out if it is being read and who in the family reads it, what they think of it, and what features they like best. However, the number of readers who will return such questionnaires will usually be small. Ten percent would be considered a good response. The important thing is the number who say they read it in relation to the number of questionnaires returned.

One of the outstanding papers in the field of employee relations is *Wright at the Moment* (Wright Engineering). As a guide for the information of associates who contribute to the publication, the editor prepared an interesting list of "don'ts." These were widely reprinted and have helped a number of editors to make their publications more effective. They follow:

Don't "salute" anyone. The mere fact that a story or picture appears is in itself a bow and repeated salutes make the expression meaningless.

Don't "Mr." unless you "Mr." everybody from floor sweeper up.

Don't recommend. It's only the editor (one more baldish guy on the payroll) who says it.

Don't reveal the mechanics of news reporting, unless it's part of the story. Only cub reporters and pretenders to Broadway-columnizing say, "Your reporter called on Mr. Frud . . ."

Don't poke fun. A fellow's hobby of collecting old trolley car transfers is probably more important to historians than your collection of orchids.

Don't fill a page, even a back page, with dry copy and no pictures. Try to treat each page as a show window for its own wares.

Don't misquote—not even if it makes it sound smarter. On the other hand, don't quote if you know it may make the quoter look foolish. Just leave it out.

Don't play up an executive's favorite subject because he's your favorite brass hat and might give you a promotion someday. If it's not a story, be polite but firm. Leave it out.

Don't call everybody "genial," "amiable," "lovable" . . . And don't call every buck-toothed, shiny-nosed, bulgy-eyed girl on the assembly line "pretty." Skillfully handled, the pictures and the facts will prove it—if it's so.

Don't print general copy about events or anything else, if you can fight your way out of it. Keep it local. Find an angle. The home-town newspaper, reporting a train wreck on the other side of the county, will always headline "Local Man Killed in Train Wreck," then will tell about the senator who also died.

Don't shake hands with yourself. Even if you did have to stalk somebody for three weeks to get a story, the company paper is supposed to be ubiquitous and omniscient and to get the story if it's to be gotten. Unlike the city papers, company papers have no scoops.

Don't generalize if you can particularize. On the other hand . . .

Don't give all the gruesome details. Unless it's the Holy Grail, a baseball trophy is a baseball trophy, not "an 18-inch-high brass figure of a ball player standing ready to strike, with inscription underneath." The audience knows the company buys these things ready-made, by the dozen.

Don't begin all score-reporting stories with the same corny lead, even if it is the same corny stuff each time.

Don't let a dull subject stay dull if you can help it. Lighten a spread on safety, for example, with a shot of some safety proponent hanging a "For Rent" sign on the first-aid room of a no-accident department.

Don't print irrelevant fillers such as "Iceland is 400 miles from Scotland" and "The sun is 93,000,000 miles from the earth." Make your fillers plugs for products or workers: "Iceland last year consumed four shiploads of Weet-ees," or "The Weet-ees produced in the last five years supplied enough energy to march an army from the earth to the sun."

Don't subordinate people to things. Maybe a lot of them never saw the inside of your plant before Tuesday, but to the company paper, the plant would fold up without them.

Don't "Don't" if you can help it. Company papers must report rules and restrictions, but they can be put in terms of Do just as easily as terms of Don't.

Don't make a Santa Claus out of the company. It's more fitting to let workers feel sports, prizes, and conveniences are their just due, than it is to try to make them think the company is a warmhearted prince who lives on the hill. They all know that the total spent for sports and such is a tiny fraction of net income anyway!

Don't follow a practice of not letting your external public relations hand know what your internal public relations hand is doing. What you tell the outside world should not be contradicted by what's in the company paper. Remember, local newspaper editors read your company paper. And employees read about the company in local papers.

Don't "slop over" in calling affairs "successful" when they were actually short of success. Nothing undermines an editor so much as being overlavish with praise. Strive to win a reputation for accurate reporting, even if it hurts at times. Nothing succeeds like accuracy in journalism.

Don't reject a good story because of one single reason for not using it. The reasons why it should be may be better.

Finally, don't have too many don'ts. Let policies be the slave, not the master.

Getting Publications Into the Home

An analysis of more than 100 bulletins, house organs, and publications shows that five out of 10 completely overlook the importance of the employees' home folks.

About half are edited only for the worker himself. They carry articles about other people in the plant, about the progress of various departments, about employee athletic activities, but little to make the publication interesting to the folks at home.

Yet it has been the experience of sales managers and others who have successfully used contests that the salesman's family has more to do with getting increased interest and sales production than any other one factor.

Labor organizers likewise have found that the point of attack in getting men to join a union is the man's wife. The first step in getting a man to "join up" is to go to his home, sit down with his wife and home folks, and "sell" them the union. If they can be sold, getting the man to join is relatively simple. American men usually do what their families want them to do.

Since it is impossible for management executives to visit personally the families of all employees and talk over the problems which the company and its workers have in common, the next best thing is to use the printed word. A well-edited, well-directed house organ or other employee publication, is a must for any business employing substantial numbers of workers.

While a shop paper is essentially a device for spreading the news of the organization and building worker morale, its most important objective is making the whole family of every worker—the wife, old folks, and teen-age youngsters—feel that they are all a part of an American industrial family, and that they all stand or fall together.

But in order for any publication or literature to do that kind of employee relations job, it must be interesting to the whole family. It must contain articles which the worker's wife will want to read, since she usually calls the signals in an American home. Here is a "rule of thumb" that can be used in checking a publication for feminine readability:

WHAT INTERESTS WOMEN

1. Women are interested in people—especially the families of other men and women like themselves who work in the plant.

2. Women are interested in children—that is why smart employee publication editors always include some news of children's activities.

3. Women are interested in home protection—they are receptive to suggestions which point to a better standard of living for the family.

4. Women are interested in education—they want to see their children go to college and become important men and women in the community.

5. Women are interested in money—not for the dollars alone, as is often the case with men, but for the comforts and opportunities that money will buy.

WHAT DOES NOT INTEREST WOMEN

1. Women are not interested in economics, as such. But they are interested in the security of the family income.

2. Women are not interested in production records. But they want to be able to boast to their friends about what their "man" is doing.

3. Women are not interested in athletics. But they are interested in what the other workers' wives are doing while their men are at the ball game or fishing.

When an employee publication has that kind of family reader interest you may be sure that it not only will be taken home, but also that it will be read and passed along to the neighbors. That is where a strong employee relations program begins—over the back fence.

Educational Articles Must Have Human Interest

Those employee publications which have the greatest home acceptance devote considerable space to articles about the people who work for the company. These are positive articles. They tell of progress in science and industry and the contributions of the employees. Very often they are human interest stories about men and women who have spent years on the job, helping to make a product or a service better for more people. Such articles show principles of Americanism in action.

Another type of item that should go into employee bulletins and house organs is a chart of company expenditures to illustrate the difference between gross profit and net profit. Most workers know what a company charges for a product, they know about how much labor it took to make it, and they know what the labor cost. The difference between these costs and the selling price, to most men in a shop, is the company's "rake-off."

What it costs to provide a worker with the tools he needs to produce the products, what the company spends per worker in taxes and in interest on its investment, what it spends per worker for getting the orders so the workers can work, what it spends for legal and accounting fees—these are all things the average man in the shop knows little or nothing about but is tremendously interested in.

Chapter 20

THE EMPLOYEE OPINION SURVEY

SINCE employee relations are conceded to be the foundation of good public relations, it is highly important to determine as accurately as possible the effectiveness of management and supervision, the training program, and other matters affecting labor-management relations. To do this, most companies survey employee attitudes regularly, so that trends can be established and results measured from one year to another.

Purposes of Employee Opinion Surveys

Surveys should be planned to get the most benefit from them. To do this, it is necessary for the employer to decide just what he wants to get out of the survey—to define his purposes in making it, as well as secondary aims and purposes that he considers important. Surveys usually cost enough money so it is worth a lot of careful planning and thinking about their widely varied uses in order to avoid overlooking points that may later be desired.

The planning should be done so as to develop understanding of the uses and purposes of the survey among all the different executives and employees who may have occasion to work with this tool. The following outline of purposes may be of assistance in this initial planning stage.

A. To measure in *general* the level of employee morale.

B. To measure *specifically* in what ways and to what degree employees are satisfied or dissatisfied with the following:

    1. Such physical working conditions as temperature, ventilation, noise, restrooms, equipment, etc.;

    2. Job security;

    3. Qualifications of their supervisors in matters of technical competence and human relations;

4. Opportunities for advancement, specific reasons for dissatisfaction with promotion policies;

5. Compensation both direct and through fringe benefits, fairness of wage or salary scales between jobs in the employer organization, and compared with other employers in the community;

6. Relations with fellow employees, working with them as a team, ways in which they are most satisfied or dissatisfied;

7. Other specific policies, practices, and factors that affect employee attitudes.

C. To evaluate more exactly both general morale and specific job satisfactions or dissatisfactions by comparisons in each respect with averages or "norms" established in other employee surveys.

D. To find out where specific job dissatisfactions of each type are most concentrated—in which divisions, departments, plants, or smaller work groups in the organization.

Regarding each type of dissatisfaction, this analysis helps to determine what the need is for corrective action, training, or information—whether to apply it uniformly throughout the organization or only in certain employee groups.

E. To test how well employees are informed and their interest in becoming better informed. This refers to subjects of two general types:

1. Matters relating to their jobs, particularly those in which accurate information will contribute to job satisfaction;

2. Company or industry problems in which it is desirable to build greater public support—an aim to which employees can contribute if they are well informed.

F. To provide employees with an organized opportunity for full expression of their job satisfactions and dissatisfactions, and to do so through a form of upward communication which they are assured will get through to the top. This in itself may be expected to have a healthy effect on morale.

G. An ultimate purpose is *improved performance*. The survey is a first step that should lead to action which will improve attitudes and relationships. This in turn should lead to better performance.

H. Looking beyond the first survey and the benefits to be derived from it, another purpose is to establish a benchmark, for the measurement of future progress in improving employee relations.

Which Employees to Survey

In some types of surveys it is adequate to "sample" the opinions of employees instead of getting the opinions of all of them. This is done by limiting the survey to a cross section of the employees. Proportional representation is given to each division, department, plant, and to other classifications by work groups, employee levels, length of service, and so forth.

Such surveys of a "sample" of the employees are most suitable when there is every reason to expect rather uniform replies throughout the organization. Examples are surveys of employee opinion about a company magazine or regarding a company life insurance program.

Such "sampling" is seldom adequate, however, when the survey calls for opinions that may differ widely between one work group and another. Examples are opinions about supervision and, in some cases, working conditions.

In a survey that covers employee opinion thoroughly over a wide range of subjects, it is usually desirable to include all of the employees or substantially all of them. Some 5 or 10 percent will always be missed because of illnesses, off-season vacations, or other reasons.

There may also be good reasons why employees in certain types of work should be excluded. Most often there are employees who are doing temporary work such as construction. Differences in working conditions, however, in union labor relations, or in other respects, may suggest that certain other types of employees should not be included.

The decision may be for every level of employee to take part in the survey. More often top management—department or division heads—will not be included.

All other management personnel will usually take part in the survey, including foremen. In addition to the same questions given to nonsupervisors (so a comparison can be made) they are asked a few other questions that pertain to supervisory functions.

Best Time for a Survey

A survey aims to get the truest possible measurement of employee opinion, without distortion that may result from any temporary situation that is either more favorable or less favorable than "normal" conditions in a business organization.

A survey immediately following a general wage increase probably would not reflect the attitudes about wages that customarily prevail. On the other hand a survey during a strike, or even in a period of wage negotiation, might indicate less-favorable attitudes than actually exist under more usual conditions.

In a strictly literal sense, conditions may never be entirely "normal" at any given time throughout a business organization. But it is desirable at least to select a time for the survey when things are reasonably normal.

Another factor of primary importance in timing surveys is to conduct them when they will interfere least with necessary work that has to be done. Rush seasons in getting out work also rarely provide the near-normal situation that is desirable for a survey.

Vacation seasons should usually be avoided, when many employees are away and would not be included in the survey.

How Surveys Are Conducted

Most surveys—in 55 companies Dartnell polled—were conducted with printed questionnaires which employees filled in themselves. Only a few involved personal questioning of employees by interviewers, a more expensive method.

The surveys were quite comprehensive as to subject matter. All but three of them included at least 20 questions, and about half covered more than 50 points. Subject matter in most surveys included the following, as a minimum:

General attitude toward job	Wages or salaries
Attitude toward management	Employee benefits
Supervisors	Promotions
Working conditions	Job security

Most of the surveys included 100 percent of all employees (subject to a few absences, of course), rather than only a cross-section sampling. The surveys usually covered supervisory personnel, as well as rank-and-file employees—in some cases the questionnaires were also filled out by all top-level executives.

A big majority of these surveys were conducted on company time and on company premises. Very few companies mailed the questionnaires or let employees take them home to complete.

Forty-five of the 55 firms had some help from outside consultants —especially in planning the survey and questionnaire, and in analyzing or interpreting results.

The main advantages cited, in the use of outside consultants, are objectiveness, impartial approach, greater confidence among employees that they would not be singled out or identified, and general skill and experience in the conduct of such surveys. Only three mentioned any disadvantages of using consultants—the cost and the consultants' lack of specific knowledge about the company's operation.

Results Obtained

In most cases, answers were analyzed by departments, divisions, or other work groups, to pinpoint the information from the survey.

Several of them mentioned that these analyses by separate work groups were the most valuable information obtained.

Practically all companies said they obtained new information about employee attitudes, and that results were helpful in giving a more exact measurement of attitudes that were known or expected prior to the survey of employees.

All of the replying companies stated that their employees answered frankly and honestly in most respects, and took the survey seriously.

About half of the companies received a surprise, however, as to the level of their employees' morale. While only two found morale consistently worse than expected, 10 found it better than anticipated, and 17 found it better in some areas, worse in others. Not quite half (26) said morale was just about as expected.

Benefits from the surveys, as reported by these companies, covered a very wide range. Most typical results reported were these:

Improved morale

Located poor morale areas

Disclosed strong and weak points in company policies or administration

Constructive criticism

Attitude toward supervisors revealed

Learned things employees needed to know but did not know

Showed management weakness in communication

Better understanding of supervisors' attitudes

Provided facts instead of guesswork as a basis for planning and appraisal

Improved communications

Material for supervisory development

Cleaned up general misunderstandings

Showed need for emphasis on human relations in supervisory conferences.

Fewer than one-third of the reporting companies had any dissatisfaction with their surveys or the use made of results. And most of these referred to weaknesses or delay in executive follow-through, rather than to any flaws in the conduct of the surveys themselves. Other complaints, voiced by a very few, included these:

"Too small a return—too few employees" (these answers were by firms who mailed questionnaires to employees rather than following the usual practice of distributing questionnaires for completion on company time at the place of work).

"Difficulty in ascertaining general source of complaints."

"Not enough learned about the 'why' behind certain complaints."

"Inconclusive nature of some of analysis."

Reporting Results to Employees

This is one specific use of results that was employed by all but 10 of the reporting companies; almost half reported the complete general results (not detailed breakdowns, of course) to all employees. Most of the others did this in a more limited way—only to supervisors, or only selected results rather than a complete summary.

The experience that many companies have now had with employee surveys has almost eliminated any idea that surveys increase griping and get employees "stirred up" or "upset."

In a recent study it was found, among companies with experience in employee surveys, that nine in each 10 reported no undesirable results whatsoever. And most of the others either said "nothing serious" or referred only to some fear by employees that their answers might be identified.

Employee surveys *do not cause complaints.* They do bring complaints into the open, determine causes, measure how serious they are and how widespread, so it is possible to apply corrective action or information most effectively.

Twenty of the reporting firms have unions representing their employees, and answered four additional questions about union acceptance of their employee surveys.

Twelve of the 20 discussed the survey in advance with union representatives. None of them reported opposition to the surveys by unions, although some of the unions were neutral or noncommittal on the subject. However, it is desirable to work with the union when possible. If this is not done, trouble might follow. Walter Reuther, for instance, complained bitterly that a survey made among union members in the auto industry prior to negotiating for guaranteed annual wage was purposely slanted to prove that they were against provisions of GAW. He charged the questions were loaded. The matter came up before the American Association for Public Opinion Research, but no action was taken.

But there are those who feel that the small samples pollsters often use to determine attitudes of groups (groups sometimes as large as the whole consumer population of the United States) are inadequate.

However, on this point, Opinion Research Corporation, Princeton, New Jersey, one of the largest poll-taking firms, now believes that most people accept the validity of the small-sample technique. The Federal Reserve Board places a lot of confidence in it. For several years, it has used the University of Michigan's Survey Research Center to determine buying attitudes—using a sample of 3,000 from which to draw nationwide conclusions.

ADDING QUESTIONS ABOUT SUPERVISION

The Basic Questionnaire is quite comprehensive in the questions about supervisors. Besides the list of supervisor qualifications in Question 19, Questions 20 through 23 refer to supervision, as do parts of Questions 25 and 32. But one or more of the following four questions about supervision may also be of interest.

B-1. When a new supervisor is named in my department I think it's better to select him:

- ☐ from my department
- ☐ from another department
- ☐ from another division
- ☐ from outside the company

B-2. In carrying out the safety policies of the company, I think my supervisor:

- ☐ does about right
- ☐ is too easy on us
- ☐ rides us too hard about following the safety policies
- ☐ often disregards the safety policies
- ☐ I think my supervisor does all right with the present safety rules, but we need some new rules

B-3. How much attention does your immediate supervisor give to any suggestions about the business that you or other employees make, or to your ideas about how the work should be done?

- ☐ He considers them carefully and tries to use good suggestions
- ☐ He pays some attention but doesn't use many of our suggestions
- ☐ He doesn't pay enough attention to our suggestions
- ☐ He pays almost no attention to our suggestions

B-4. My immediate supervisor:

- ☐ takes a real personal interest in employees as people, not just in regard to the work they do
- ☐ I don't think that he takes enough interest in employees except for the work they do

---

A page from the Dartnell questionnaire.

Using the Results

To make the most of employee opinion surveys is no difficult or costly problem. Charles N. Parker, former chairman of Central Surveys, Inc., a firm with wide experience in public and employee opinion surveys, says, "Not all employee complaints call for correction. Most of them call for information. The action called for by employee surveys leads to action of three general types:

    a. Taking corrective action when complaints are justified and when something can be done about them without delay.

Companies report many such types of action as the result of surveys. These range from minor changes to revisions of company policy in different respects.

b. Recognizing the need for corrective action and explaining fully why it cannot be taken immediately.

This may occur most frequently in regard to complaints about physical working conditions. When a major rebuilding or remodeling program is planned, for example, it is not feasible to undertake some minor repair jobs that would more quickly stop complaints about working conditions.

It may have to be explained why corrective action in other respects is necessarily planned as a long- rather than a short-range activity. For example, certain complaints about supervision may call for a training program that cannot be started immediately.

c. When the answer to complaints is information rather than corrective action.

Complaints often result from lack of information or from misinformation. An example would be the mistaken idea that wages in a certain plant are below average for the community.

"When corrective action is taken or is planned, as the result of a survey, it is usually best to let the employees know it was their survey answers that stimulated this action. It will be most satisfying to employees to know that management has shown this regard for their opinions."

Packaged Opinion Polls

Two packaged employee opinion polls are available to companies and consultants for use in analyzing the attitudes of employees. One of these has been handled for several years by Science Research Associates and is known as an employee inventory. It was originally developed by University of Chicago. The other was released by The Dartnell Corporation in cooperation with Central Surveys, Inc.

The Dartnell-Central Surveys Unit can be self-administered by the company or consultant making the survey, although it is recommended that the tabulations be done by an outside firm. Before release, the questions which make up the survey form were validated in some 50,000 employee opinion interviews.

The questions used in packaged polls are those which have been found to provide the answers which will be most valuable to administrators in improving the attitudes and conditions existing in a company. They spotlight the areas where training is most needed and indicate the type of training needed. They show the communication breakdowns in the company and which communication methods are weak or strong.

The Dartnell Employee Survey is planned so it can be used by an employer with no outside help, if he prefers this method. Detailed directions are provided so this will be possible.

Professional assistance is available at reasonable cost, however, to help as desired with any part of the work—planning the survey, conducting it, analyzing results, or recommending specific action based on the survey.

Such assistance will aid materially in getting the best results in the survey. This is not essential, however; and if desired the survey can be planned, conducted, and results tabulated entirely by the employer organization.

What Questions Are Asked?

Dartnell's Employee Survey and the SRA survey both use a basic questionnaire, to which additions may be made that best fit the needs of each employer. Before considering additional questions, it will be best for each employer to review some of the considerations that have gone into formulating the basic questionnaire. The considerations may help him decide whether the basic questionnaire alone will be sufficient or whether additions are needed.

The Dartnell questionnaire is quite comprehensive. Although it includes only 33 opinion questions, it covers 86 points of employee opinion and information. These are all subjects, however, that are of interest to practically every organization planning or considering an employee survey. These are the subjects the basic questionnaire is intended to cover. Subjects of less universal interest to employers are covered in the supplementary questions, mentioned in an accompanying manual.

The questions relate to subjects that are generally recognized as most important in their influence on employee morale or job satisfaction. Although a few of the questions test general morale, most of them relate to specific things that the employer can do something about, rather than to generalities.

The questions recommended have been used in many employee surveys. They are thoroughly tested both as to design and phrasing. The questions are usually worded to measure shadings of opinion, rather than to force answers into arbitrary extremes of good or bad, agree or disagree. It is these shadings that are frequently of maximum value in measuring differences between organizations as a whole, or differences between work groups.

The questions are adequate for measuring such differences by work groups within the organization. And it is these variations which frequently suggest the most effective approach in efforts to improve employee morale.

Questions are generally excluded if it has been found through experience that the replies are characteristically quite uniform, or one-sided, providing less basis for such comparisons.

As a matter of standard practice, the different status of supervisors is recognized by asking them 11 questions in addition to those asked of nonsupervisors.

Although Dartnell's basic questionnaire is quite comprehensive, it will need to be supplemented by additional questions in some surveys. This is necessary because the basic questionnaire has been limited to subject matter suitable for practically every organization that is planning or considering a survey. For example, questions about a company magazine would almost certainly be desirable if the organization has such a publication, but such questions cannot be included in a basic questionnaire.

Several lists of supplementary questions have therefore been prepared and are available. These may be ordered separately and attached to the basic questionnaire. These supplementary lists include the following:

> Economic education
>
> Employee (fringe) benefits
>
> Desire for information
>
> Testing present information
>
> Employee magazine
>
> Concerning supervisors
>
> Employee cafeteria

Salesmen are important cogs in the public relations program because of the numerous contacts they make in the course of a day's work. For that reason, and in the interest of the highest possible level of morale in the sales organization (in which might be included salesmen of distributors as well as those employed directly by the company), public relations men find it desirable to extend attitude surveys to members of the sales organization. The resulting replies, when tabulated and released in booklet form, help to keep salesmen sold on the company. its products, and its policies.

The Carnation Company's Opinion Poll

When the Carnation Company wanted to evaluate its sales organization public relations-wise, it retained the California Institute of Technology to make the survey, and as a result participation was almost 100 percent.

The Carnation sales organization is scattered across the United States and Canada with no large number of people at any one location. Group meetings could not be held. Carnation decided to go ahead with a mail survey based on confidential returns going directly to Cal Tech.

Prior to conducting the opinion poll, all top sales management people were advised as to how the poll would be handled. This group included division sales managers. They were not only told that Cal Tech was going to conduct the poll, but were also given advance copies of the questionnaire draft for their suggestions or criticisms.

Cal Tech personnel, under the supervision of Professor Robert D. Gray, director of the institute's industrial relation section, also contributed to the construction of the questionnaire from their experience with similar polls made for Carnation and other companies.

Questions about certain items, such as pay, were stated in such a way as to draw written comments that would be more meaningful and valuable than a simple "Yes" or "No" answer.

The survey sheets mailed to each member of the sales force were, of course, blank in the spaces provided for answers. Instructions on the survey sheets included the statement: "Please do not sign your name," at the beginning and end. The request for general information was prefaced with the explanation:

At the beginning of this questionnaire, we are asking some information about you. Answers to the following questions will assist in the study of whether or not opinions are affected by age, length of service, or department. (Note: The numbers preceding the answers will be used in tabulating the replies.)

Over 50 percent of the questionnaires came back almost immediately. A followup postcard from Cal Tech brought the total up to 72.9 percent. The followup was sent to the full list and it said, in effect:

"If you haven't sent in your questionnaire, please do so."

The fact that some salesmen were not without doubts was indicated by the note that Cal Tech received from one man after the postcard followup. It read:

"If you aren't identifying the replies, how did you know I hadn't sent mine in?"

Notice the particular care that was taken in the letter beginning below, to make it clear to all concerned that the followup did go to the full list; and there was no intent to identify replies of the opinion sampling at any stage or for any purpose.

The results of the opinion poll of the Carnation Company sales organization given in this pamphlet are the exact figures which we compiled and submitted to your company.

The summary includes 557 questionnaires which we received on or before April 20. This represents 72.9 percent of the questionnaires which we mailed to you, a phenomenally high rate on any survey by mail. We are very much indebted to the 50 percent who returned their questionnaires immediately and to the others who mailed their questionnaires after we sent a reminder to everybody.

The quality and quantity of your write-in comments exceeded those we have received from other parts of the Carnation Company. Actually 481 of you (86.4 percent) took the time to tell us some of the things you liked best and least about working for your company and to make many constructive suggestions. Since most of you gave more than one idea, we received well over 2,600 separate comments.

To facilitate the tabulation of the questionnaires, we transferred the information you supplied us to punched cards. The original questionnaires have now been destroyed. No tabulation has been, or will be, made that will reveal the identity of any employee or indicate how a specific person answered any question or what comments he made.

On behalf of Cal Tech's industrial relations section, I wish to thank everyone who participated for the co-operation which was given to us in completing the poll.

Over 85 percent of the respondents added written comments. Some of these comments extended over several pages. Broken down by subjects, there were over 2,600 separately written comments in addition to the answers to specific questions asked.

The Cal Tech staff was surprised by the volume of written comments. Compared with other surveys they had run on nonsales groups, it was obvious that salesmen, as a group, are inclined to express themselves in writing.

The Results

Cal Tech coded each returned questionnaire on an IBM card. Analysis and summaries of those cards have made possible studies by areas, by employee groups, by types of supervision, and so forth. For instance, the company wondered how supervision and morale in areas where it operates through brokers compared with that in areas where it maintains its own district offices. Such studies were easy to make.

Reviewing the steps taken to achieve management benefits from the results, the company reported:

Immediately after the overall results were available, a mimeographed copy went to the entire top sales group, including this time the district sales managers, who are the next level of supervision below the division sales managers.

This was followed by a special meeting of our top company management people, at which Robert Gray, from Cal Tech, presented a summary of the results, including some comparative data. The booklet summarizing the results was then prepared and distributed to all participating sales personnel.

We then had a meeting of the original top sales management group that had first been informed of the opinion poll to present detailed results to them. We made many comparisons and discussed in some detail both the problems and good points as highlighted by the opinion poll. Each division sales manager was supplied at this meeting with additional material giving detailed percentage results for his division and, where possible, districts within his division. He was also supplied with the written comments made by people within his division, broken down into various subject matter classifications. All of this material was made available to him for his confidential use within his own organization.

Showing Good Faith

The booklet showing the overall results (*The Company You Keep*) showed all answers, question by question. It also included a cross section of the written comments. Every effort was made to

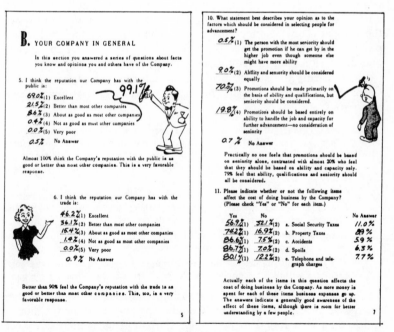

Type of quiz booklet used in the Carnation poll showing how results were publicized to those participating in the poll.

make these comments a representative selection including what might be termed both the "good" and the "bad."

The booklet was prepared as quickly as possible following completion of the poll and sent to all those who had participated. It was felt that this willingness to share the results, promptly and completely, was an important morale factor in itself—and very important to the success of any future opinion polls. It also served as a useful public relations tool since copies were widely distributed throughout the marketing organization.

Interpreting the Results

In general, Carnation was pleased with the results that were shown. Analysis of the figures indicated that the company had good reason to feel this way. Carnation sales employees said they were proud of their company and their jobs. Favorable returns ran up to 99 percent on some questions; only 2 percent said they would pick another company if they had it to do again. The voluntary written comments were favorable at a ratio of 3 to 1. The 3 to 1 ratio on written comments, however, means that over 600 (out of a total of 2,600 separate comments) were critical of something about the company or the individual's job. There was enough criticism, constructive and otherwise, to provide plenty of material for review and discussion and, in some cases, action.

Summarizing the survey project, the sales personnel manager for Carnation commented upon the major values of this opinion poll as follows:

1. The very fact that we made the survey was evidence of our interest in our people and their opinions. This brought an immediate improvement in morale. Turnover in our sales organization was down 18 percent for the three months following the poll, compared with the three months before the poll.

2. The poll gave us facts and figures to use in talking with top management. It was no longer a case of what we "thought" our people liked and disliked—we had proof, the "voice of the people."

3. Some local situations were pointed up, and it was possible to take corrective action before serious trouble developed.

4. The favorable nature of the results improved the stature of the sales operation within the company and the public relations outside the company.

The survey disclosed that Carnation salesmen showed a higher degree of loyalty to the company, and a comparatively better morale index than was found in any other Carnation operation. Cal Tech observed that these factors appeared to be higher than it found similar factors to be in any other industrial survey.

A majority of the opinion surveys that are made to evaluate public opinion are sharp-angled to a particular problem or situation. They usually are confined to questioning—either through trained interviewers or by mail—a single public, such as employees, stockholders, suppliers, or customers. There are occasions, however, when it is necessary for good public relations planning to get the facts on a broad subject, for instance, to determine public opinion regarding a labor dispute, a political situation which might affect the company's operations, or to predetermine the public's reaction to a proposed public relations project.

To make a poll of general opinion, it is best to engage the services of an organization specializing in this type of field work. According to the extent and urgency of the poll and the funds available, the size and composition of the sample are determined.

How big a sample you need depends on your purpose. If you wish to test a campaign theme or sound out the main ideas on an issue, then 100 or 200 cases may suffice. But if you must measure trends, or differences between groups, or publish the findings as an accurate measure of public opinion, then a sample in the thousands may be necessary.

A common idea is that a large sample guarantees reliability. It is not that simple. Though a large sample may well contribute to reliability, other factors taken together can be even more important.

Opinion Research Corporation, one of the leading authorities on opinion polls, offers these guidelines:

1. Determine how much accuracy is required. A 750 probability sample of the general public will produce findings fairly certainly within 4 percentage points, plus or minus. You can cut the range of error to 2 points by taking 3,000 interviews, if the added cost is justified.

2. Set up a sampling plan that assures a representative cross section of the populational group you are studying.

3. Shoot for a high completion rate on the interviews assigned. The hard-to-reach are busy people; they may differ in their views from the stay-at-homes.

4. Validate the field work to make sure each interviewer's work is honest and thorough.

5. Errors can occur in processing. Check each person's work for accuracy, from coding through report typing.

In short, the smart research buyer does not put all his chips on sample size but insists on quality performance in each step of the project.

How to Make Your Own Poll

The first step in making an informal poll without professional help is to decide what you want to find out, then boil it down so that the really necessary facts can be obtained with as few questions as possible. One of the greatest faults of "do it yourself" opinion polls is that they try to cover too much ground. An experienced interviewer who is skilled in "drawing people out" in conversation can take a multisheet questionnaire and get answers to most of the questions from an interviewee. But a novice will soon encounter resistance which may result in the frustrated interviewer supplying his or her own answers to most questions. So you have a poll which simply tells you what the interviewers think or favor.

In preparing a questionnaire for use by either personal interviewers or by mail it is important to decide at the outset what type of reaction you want. Do you want offhand reactions to evaluate the existing state of the public mind concerning a given proposition or situation? Or do you want deliberate reactions; i.e., what the person being polled thinks about a situation or proposition after being given both sides of the question? The former aims to give a picture of public opinion as it exists; the latter concerns itself not so much with existing attitudes or opinions as with what the public opinion will be at the completion of an educational undertaking.

Above all, make sure that the survey is honest. Otherwise it will be a liability rather than an asset. "Loaded" questions designed to support someone's pet theory always give a picture which can lead to costly mistakes and bad strategy. This is a common objection to "do it yourself" polls. The poll-taker is more interested in proving his own theories than in finding out what those he is polling really think. This sort of poll-taking is common in making marketing surveys which are used to gauge the reader response to advertising media. There have been instances where the results of front-door interviews—to determine the influence of a newspaper in creating a demand for a food specialty—have shown as much as a 50 percent error when a pantry check was made of the same homes.

Making the Survey Objective

In connection with making a dependable survey—one that is safe to use in planning a public relations or, for that matter, any program that must be based upon facts rather than fancy—the following suggestions may be helpful:

1. START OFF WITH A "KNOW-NOTHING" ATTITUDE. This will give you a clear, fresh approach, and such an approach is necessary in order to avoid perverted results.

2. CONDUCT SURVEY TO LEARN—NOT PROVE. If the basic idea behind your survey is to produce sales material, it is best that you forget the whole thing. You will get plenty of good sales material as a by-product, and it will be pure and untainted by obsessions of selfishness.

3. AVOID PRECONCEIVED IDEAS OF RESULTS. If you already know the answers, why make the survey? No honest survey will perfectly follow the pattern you *think* it will take, so don't warp the results by striving to have them parallel your unwarranted conclusions.

4. STRIVE FOR ABSOLUTE ACCURACY. You won't achieve it—no one ever did, but the only way to approach perfection is to make perfection your aim. Errors come too easy for us to court such disaster by carelessly inviting them.

5. APPLY STIFF ACCURACY TESTS TO BOTH DESIRABLE AND UNDESIRABLE RE-SULTS. It is just as easy to go wrong in one direction as another, so either test everything from all angles or let the chips fall where they may. The law of averages is a great leveler, but not if you strangle it on one side.

6. DON'T HIDE UNPLEASANT RESULTS—TELL THE WHOLE TRUTH. It is sur-prising how much will be added to the believability of your report if you include those few embarrassing results. There will probably be some answers that will embarrass the recipient, so include yours so you may blush together.

7. USE A SCIENTIFICALLY ACCURATE SAMPLE—THERE'S NO SAFETY IN NUM-BERS. Certainly, get an ample number of reports, but most important, the people interviewed must be typically representative of the whole.

8. INCLUDE QUESTIONS TO CHECK AGAINST KNOWN FACTS. This is the best method of testing the accuracy of your sample.

9. AVOID COMPLICATED, UNEXPLAINABLE METHODS. If the basic problem be-hind your survey is so complex that a complicated method is necessary, call in an outside organization to do the job. This is just as important as calling in a doctor to look after your physical complications.

10. EXPLAIN METHOD FULLY IN ALL PUBLISHED REPORTS. Make certain that you cover the five "W's"—who, what, when, where, and why. Who made the survey, what it's about, when it was made, where it was made, and why it was made. These five things are just as important as your general statements of *how* it was made.

11. POINT OUT ANY WEAKNESS OR LIMITATIONS IN YOUR METHOD. There is no perfect method, so be sure you enumerate those imperfections. The recipient is just as likely to jump to conclusions as you, so prevent such suicidal leaps by plainly stating all limitations.

12. STATE SOURCES CLEARLY FOR ALL OUTSIDE INFORMATION USED. Some an-swers can be better qualified if correlated with outside statistical ma-terial. Label every item of this type so it won't be confused with survey results.

13. DON'T EXTEND RESULTS UNLESS YOU DEFINITELY STATE THE SIZE OF YOUR SAMPLE. Preferably, don't extend results at all, but if you do, make certain that everyone understands how the projection was made.

Finally, after all the reports of interviewers, mail questionnaires, letters of comment from public leaders, and so on, are on hand and tabulated, keep the report of the poll *short*. Give end results and avoid burdening the report with a lot of statistics just to impress the executives who will read it with the exhaustive effort that was made to arrive at the result. Detailed data may be available to anyone who is interested, but it is best to highspot the results when possible, citing conclusions and totals rather than confusing details. It is almost impossible for an executive, especially an executive responsible for policy, to "digest" a mass of statistics. He wants to get a quick picture of what the public thinks about certain matters involved in company policy or operations, with a minimum of reading and study.

From the standpoint of top management, the best polls are so well planned that the required information is quickly obtained. (A mail questionnaire should not exceed a single page, and if the questions can be put on a reply card, so much the better.) Questions should be framed to get honest opinions and reactions; answers should be analyzed intelligently and not just "totted up." Moreover, the report should be conclusive. A survey that is not conclusive in its findings is of little value and executives should not be required to take valuable time to read it.

Chapter 21

INSTALLING A GOOD
SUGGESTION SYSTEM

BEFORE the era of mass production in factory and shop, the boss *was* the boss; he did all the thinking and gave all the orders. The worker was not supposed to have ideas—he was hired to work, not to think. However, with the coming of assembly-line production and sharper competition the boss began to turn to the rank-and-file worker for ideas. One of the first companies to set up a suggestion plan in those early years of mass output was the Yale & Towne Manufacturing Company. Little by little, others began to follow suit.

It is fairly obvious that plans which have survived for 40 years or more have had two things in common: (1) They were properly set up in the beginning, and (2) management played an active part in selling the program to the supervisory group and to the rank-and-file worker.

It was during World War II, when every man and woman had to have a vital interest in high-production levels, that the suggestion plan really came into its own. To encourage the installation of suggestion systems, a special department called the National Suggestion Program went into action. It was conservatively estimated that production suggestions during the war period saved more than 200 million man-hours of work per year. This is equivalent to the full-time labor for a year of about 800,000 workers.

For those who are interested, there is in existence today a National Association of Suggestion Systems. This organization, headquartered in Chicago, has an imposing membership list, an organized program of idea exchange (including publications) and an annual meeting.

To drop names, you'll find among the members, Ford, Du Pont, Eastman Kodak, General Motors, General Foods and General Mills. You will also find much smaller companies on the roster. NASS membership could provide you with enough information to set up a successful program, and it will help you to determine what awards are prevalent today.

As an example you can learn that the highest known award paid out recently was $19,000 to one individual by International Business Machines Corporation. The average award is about $41 for a suggestion.

Why Do Suggestion Programs Fail?

A tremendous number of suggestion programs have failed. Some estimates put the figure as high as 90 percent of all plans inaugurated in the last 25 years.

What was the reason for so many failures? In many instances these failures were due to poor planning and still poorer execution. Lack of publicity in the employee magazine and on the bulletin boards was also a factor. In addition, many a company set up its plan without sufficient funds to carry on and some of the monetary awards for intangible benefits were so small that the employee felt he was being short-changed. Management has long since changed all this by setting up minimum awards of reasonable amounts. In early years the minimum was $2; today it is up to $5 or $10 or more.

Another reason for the failure of suggestion programs was the letdown after the first burst of enthusiasm. Too often those who set the plan in operation leaned back and considered the job completed. Like all other employee campaigns, drives, or contests, enthusiasm must be maintained for the entire duration of the program if it is to succeed. These are the main reasons for failure:

1. Insufficient time spent training the supervisory group to handle employee suggestions.
2. Lack of supervisory enthusiasm for the program.
3. Indifference on the part of employees.
4. Insufficient number of suggestion boxes or poorly placed boxes.
5. Lack of posters to stimulate employee thinking.
6. Too long a time lag between the date the employee sends in his suggestion and the committee's acknowledgment.
7. Unsatisfactory explanations for rejections.
8. Awards too small to interest employees.

If a company's suggestion plan does not come up to par, it is a good idea to make a list of the things needing change before management scraps the whole program. Once the weak spots are uncovered and corrected, the plan is likely to start paying off at once. Most programs which do not click are weak at the supervisory level, and it is here that management should look first.

Elements of a Good Suggestion Program

While a suggestion program should not be expected to cure all employee problems, it will tend to improve employee morale. A good suggestion plan can result in one of the closest contacts there is between workers and the company.

Suggestion plans not only keep management alert, but they also provide a creative outlet for the average employee. If, for example, the employee is working on a routine job which follows a regular pattern each day, any effort he may put into a suggestion identifies him more closely with the company. Other benefits of a good suggestion program will include, to some degree, the following:

1. A SAFETY VALVE—Constructive suggestions may take the place of gripes.

2. SELF-IMPROVEMENT—The employee is encouraged to develop himself beyond and above the requirements of his job.

3. TEAMWORK—A suggestion to management helps build esprit de corps.

4. RECOGNITION—The development of pride in an accomplishment.

5. CASH AWARD—Last, but not least, the award the worker receives for his suggestion.

Management has three types of programs to choose from: (1) A company-planned and administered program, (2) a plan organized and operated by an outside organization, (3) use of a management engineer to study conditions and to suggest a plan best suited to the requirements of the company.

Regardless of which decision is made, the program must be tailor-made. Even if a ready-made plan is selected, it should be studied and so reorganized that it will really fit the company's special needs.

Basic policies regarding the suggestion program should be determined by management and put in writing before any steps are taken to install the plan. Without this preparation, contradictory statements are bound to be made to workers and their supervisors with the result that the program gets off to a limping start. Such a start is sure to kill an enthusiasm for the program just at the time management is trying to stir up an extra measure of interest.

The main policies which must be put in writing cover: (1) Organization, (2) general routine, (3) eligibility, and (4) awards. These policies should be so carefully and clearly set up, the workers will have no trouble understanding them.

In addition to these policies, management should be sure to sell every supervisor on the suggestion program before it is launched. Unless this group is consulted, considered, and sold, the program will break down through lack of constructive interest in each department.

What Is a Suggestion?

This is one of the important questions to decide before the plan goes into operation. Unless employees understand what constitutes a legitimate suggestion, there will be so much confusion that the program never will get off the ground. One way to overcome the problem is for the suggestion committee to circulate a bulletin or poster indicating the types of suggestions that are acceptable. A statement such as this will be helpful:

A suggestion is a constructive idea to improve methods, equipment, and procedures, which will make working conditions better or safer or which will reduce time or cost of such methods.

When defined this way, suggestions concerning repairs, maintenance work, or other matters of a routine nature will be eliminated.

Even though a proper suggestion has been clearly defined, many an employee will still use the suggestion blanks to air gripes or grouches—especially when the program is new. What is more, he may expect to get an award for entering his gripes! The fact that the suggestion blanks are not being used for suggestions should not deter management from continuing with the program. Every employee has some kind of gripe against the company, the work, or his supervisor. He is just getting it off his chest—and that is a good thing for management. Eventually the employee will settle down to the real business of thinking about his job, and when that happens his gripes will become suggestions. Of course, management must continually impress him with the idea that it is his suggestions that count in determining awards—not his gripes.

It is a good idea to examine any and all gripes which make their way to the suggestion box. Often the worker not only voices a gripe which should be considered, but he may include with his gripe the necessary constructive suggestion for its elimination. When handled in this manner, the employee should certainly figure in the awards. If, however, the gripe is just listed without any suggestions which would improve the situation to which it applies, then the suggestion committee is correct in considering it unsuitable for an award.

At the start of the program, management may be impressed with the number of suggestions which land in the suggestion box. After a couple of weeks, however, the number may drop off considerably.

Management should not be concerned with this decrease in number because, as just pointed out, a great many of the early entries will be gripes instead of suggestions. Naturally, too, there must be a letdown after the first rush of enthusiasm on the part of the employees. The questions that are lost as time goes on are usually the ones a company can best get along without.

The thing to strive for in any suggestion program is QUALITY. It is better to have only a half-dozen suggestions, each of which is of real value, than to have hundreds of half-baked ideas or gripes.

Eligibility of Suggestions

The basic principles governing the eligibility of suggestions for an award are generally listed as follows:

1. The suggestion must be adopted or scheduled for adoption.
2. The suggestion must not be under active consideration by management.
3. The suggestion must not be based on an idea in which another employee has priority.
4. The suggestion must not be developed as an assignment from management; such suggestions are within the line of duty.

A company in the Midwest which has set up definite policies regarding the eligibility of suggestions tells the employee that to be eligible for an award the suggestion must accomplish at least one of the following:

1. Conserve material, energy, or time over and above that ordinarily expected in his work.
2. Eliminate or improve an existing operation or method.
3. Eliminate or improve a tool, die, jig, fixture, or other equipment.
4. Eliminate an existing safety hazard, improve working conditions or improve housekeeping.
5. Increase the present output of a machine over and above his responsibility to do so.
6. Improve the quality of the company's products.

The same company considers the following suggestions ineligible for awards:

1. A suggestion pertaining to an integral part of the regular or assigned work.
2. Any suggestion that duplicates one previously submitted or pertaining to a project already under consideration.
3. A routine function, or job still in the development stage.
4. Any suggestion not submitted on a standard employee suggestion blank.
5. When the savings realized will not justify the expenditure involved to carry out the suggestion.
6. When the suggestion covers an obvious error that should be the subject of routine report and correction.

Training the Supervisors

Since the cooperation of supervisors is needed to make the suggestion system operate, management has found that the supervisory group should have special training in the rules, policies, and procedures essential to the smooth operation of the program.

The training is generally informal and takes but a small amount of time from the supervisor's work. In addition to informal meetings, a number of companies either add a section to the supervisor's policy manual which provides the basic information, or they issue a special booklet to cover the operation of the program. The subjects included in these booklets or additions to the manual may be broken down into two parts: (1) purpose of the program and (2) procedures or operation of the plan. Usually the main subjects are listed in the following manner:

Purpose of the plan	Investigations
Organization of the plan	Awards
Procedure	Method of payment
Routine maintenance	Description of forms used
Eligibility of employees	Rejections

One of the supervisor's major concerns is the matter of rejections. The supervisor must be carefully coached or trained on handling rejections for it is especially important that in his personal contact with the suggester he prevent discouragement and keep the employee in the mood to participate again.

Management should not expect the supervisor to do any amount of detail work. This should be handled by the suggestion committee so that the supervisor can concentrate on the more important work of encouraging and inspiring the employees in his section.

When there is some question as to which employee is entitled to an award in those cases where two have made the same suggestion, it is a good idea to include the supervisor in a meeting with the systems manager and the two interested employees.

Because many a supervisor gripes about the additional work the suggestion system makes, management should see to it that he is fully aware of the importance of the work. His part in the program can be emphasized by means of bulletins, letters, and employee magazine articles. He should also understand that his efforts to cooperate in the program will be made a matter of record so that when he comes up for promotion, the record will help him to qualify for the better job or rating. In addition, when the supervisor's promotion is given space in the employee magazine—as it should be—

his achievements with regard to the suggestion system should receive publicity at the same time. Other supervisors who may not have taken the suggestion system seriously, will be made to see what such cooperation actually means.

Acknowledging Suggestions Promptly

It is highly important that suggestions be acknowledged promptly. The worker is in a state of "white heat" when he sends in his suggestion and, since it is HIS suggestion, he expects to get an immediate answer from the suggestion committee. If time drags, his interest has waned and his disappointment may be so great as to affect the cooperation of other employees in his department.

On the following page is a reproduction of a type of blank used by the Allis-Chalmers Manufacturing Company—a form which can be used to acknowledge the suggestions easily and without delay.

In large offices where hundreds of suggestions may be received, suggestion committees have also found it helps to post a daily notice on the bulletin board, listing by numbers the suggestions received by the committee during the preceding 24 hours. Quick action such as this helps encourage more employees to take part in the program.

No specific time can be set up to determine the value of a suggestion an employee has entered. However, if the investigation of the committee must continue for more than two weeks, it is well to contact the employee again and let him know that the committee is still deliberating.

The suggestion committee should operate on the premise that every suggestion should be investigated promptly, completely, and impartially. There should be no deviation from this rule.

Compensation for Suggestions

Because there are many ideas submitted to the suggestion committee which cannot be measured in terms of savings to the company, such suggestions must be rewarded on a flat basis such as $5 or $10 for any accepted idea. It is impossible, for instance, to place a financial valuation on an idea to synchronize the clocks in an organization, or an idea which keeps a department looking shipshape, or a suggestion for paying employees at a more convenient hour.

These are all important suggestions though, and the committee must see to it that promising ideas keep coming from employees. One means of stimulating intangible suggestions is to set up a special award—say $50—for the best one received during each quarter and, at the year's end, an additional $100 for the year's star suggestion.

While it is generally conceded that there should be a minimum award, there seems to be a difference of opinion as to whether a maximum should be set up in the suggestion plan. There are strong opinions on both sides. Those who favor a minimum and a maximum believe that by putting a ceiling on awards the suggestion plan can be kept within certain bounds. On the other hand, executives who approve of having no maximum, believe that the employees become more enthusiastic about a plan by which they can achieve awards amounting to thousands of dollars.

ALLIS-CHALMERS MANUFACTURING COMPANY

SUGGESTION ACKNOWLEDGMENT

Sugg. No.............................

Date:.............................

To...Clock No............................Dept.:.............

Address...City...............................Zone.................

We acknowledge with thanks your suggestion covering.............................

....

....

....

....

Your suggestion will be investigated and a report given to the Suggestion Committee as soon as possible. We will try to keep you informed if any unusual delay occurs, and will notify you promptly of any final decision of the Committee.

Please use the Suggestion number above for reference if further inquiry is necessary.

Sincerely,

HOWARD GABLE
Coordinator, Suggestion Committee

Allis-Chalmers' acknowledgment form illustrates a way of handling one of the important aspects of the suggestion system.

A number of companies started their suggestion programs with a ceiling on awards to employees, but have since discontinued this policy. The main reason is the belief that making the sky the limit is a never-ending source of stimulation to employees. When one worker gets a $500 or $1,000 award, all his coworkers feel that they, too, can hit the jackpot.

A few companies have made use of merchandise awards or prizes in the past, but this practice is now comparatively rare. One of the problems which must be considered is the bookkeeping involved in such an arrangement. For instance, there must be some method of handling "open" accounts over what may be a long period of time while the worker is collecting sufficient points to secure one of the higher value items or prizes. Today, with values fluctuating rapidly, there is also the problem of keeping merchandise in line. If the quality of the award or its value fluctuates too greatly between the time the employee starts to work for it and the time the award is made, the worker may become disgruntled or feel that he has lost out.

In some cases, management has found that prizes awarded to first-time suggesters serve to stimulate interest in the plan. These awards may be of small monetary value, consisting of mechanical pencils, key cases, wallets, cigarette lighters and the like.

Handling Rejections

One of the most difficult problems connected with a suggestion contest is encouraging those whose suggestions have been rejected to try again.

Some companies use a printed notice to inform the employee that his suggestion has been rejected. A better way to do it is to write a letter signed by the manager of the suggestion program. Such a letter should be brief, but it must give the reason for the rejection. It should also be written in such a way that the suggester will not lose interest in the program and will not give up trying for an award.

It is important to tell the disappointed employee that most suggesters do not hit the jackpot on the first try. As a rule, only one out of five suggestions may win an award—this gives the worker a one-to-five chance to succeed the next time.

While most large companies keep the suggestion program in action the entire year, some have found that special suggestion programs at various times during the year are more successful. On top of stimulating employee interest, special contests serve to give the employee a goal toward which he can work.

Best results with special contests are secured by timing the program or contest to coincide with the average employee's need for money. The three best times are: (1) Just before Christmas to provide for extra spending money; (2) just after Christmas when the bills must be paid and extra money is scarce; (3) just before vacation months begin when employees need to put aside money for vacation spending.

If the regular suggestion program has not been too successful, management may find it a good idea to drop it for a few weeks or months and then start a carefully timed special program to create more contest enthusiasm.

Organizing the Suggestion System

When the program has the active support of the president or chief operating officer, the rank-and-file employee is assured that his suggestions are important to top management. Furthermore, an important byproduct of this support is the stimulation of interest and the cooperation of all department heads, supervisors, and other line executives in the success of the program.

The amount of time spent by a top official on the program may actually be very little. It is important to emphasize this point for he may be reluctant to take on the job unless the actual amount of time required for him to sponsor the program is set at a minimum. This may be only the time required for an initial meeting with his operating executives who will come in contact with the operation of the program. It may include a brief—and it really should be brief—talk to the group, and the introduction of the executive secretary. Another brief talk is necessary when some outstanding award has been given to an employee—when the award warrants a special ceremony.

In addition, the president's approval of several other features of the program is essential to indicate his interest. For example, his name signed to letters or bulletins announcing the program is a way to do it; a special suggestion leaflet or booklet with a foreword signed by him, another. In a small company, the chief executive may find that he can participate more closely in the program by reviewing some of the top suggestions and meeting the suggesters.

The Executive Secretary

The executive secretary who will do the actual work of running the suggestion program should be very carefully chosen. Not only must this person be "research minded," he must be receptive to new ideas—have imagination. Furthermore, he must be tactful and be able to secure the confidence of the workers whose ideas are rejected. He must also have the confidence of supervisors who may be—and often are—reluctant to consider new methods and procedures. He must be an enthusiastic salesman for the system.

The executive secretary must not only be able to pledge complete protection of all technical ideas received, but he must be above suspicion of receiving any personal profit from the ideas or suggestions entrusted to him.

In large companies, the secretary or the chairman of the suggestion committee is generally on a full-time basis; in smaller companies, he may be a regular staff member with other duties and only a fraction of his time will be devoted to the suggestion program. In either case, his qualifications should be the same.

The Committee's Job

Because suggestions should be considered promptly, the suggestion committee should normally meet once a week on a specified day. Generally, the order of business follows this pattern:

1. A report on the suggestions received since the previous meeting.

2. A report on the suggestions reported on at the previous meeting which required further investigation.

3. A report on pending suggestions for the consideration of their acceptability.

4. The committee's discussion and consideration of pending awards.

If the committee is to function smoothly and without waste of time, adequate preparations for the meeting must be made in advance. This is particularly true when the number of suggestions being handled is usually large.

One manufacturing company supplies its investigators and suggestion committee with these instructions:

The suggestions are collected from locked suggestion boxes each Monday morning. In the office, the date of collection is written on the face, an acknowledgment form is sent to the suggester, and date of acknowledgment noted on the face. The suggestion is then recorded on the suggester's individual file card and on a card which shows suggestions received, rejected, and awarded each month. An investigation form is attached to the file card and identified by number.

The investigator studies the suggestion, then seeks out the suggester and through discussion gains full understanding of the meaning of the suggestion. The supervisor is then asked his opinion of the suggestion without, if possible, revealing the identity of the suggester. Since the supervisor usually knows who it is (many workers talk over their suggestions with their supervisors) this is not of the utmost importance. If further information is necessary, the investigator turns to whichever other departments are likely to be helpful.

When the story is ready to be told, the suggestion is presented verbally to the consultation committee. This committee considers the acceptability, eligibility, and practicability of the idea. It may reject the suggestion, approve it for trial, ask for further information of a specific nature, or various members may decide they want to look at the operation themselves and report back to the committee.

The committee meets every Tuesday afternoon. Results of each meeting are reported by form to the general manager and employee relations manager.

Upon acceptance, the suggestion is turned over to the award committee. This group authorizes awards for all suggestions. It may also reject a suggestion despite the recommendation of the consulting committee or it may ask for further specific information.

Anonymity of the Suggester

There are two schools of thought on whether the suggester's name should appear on the suggestion form or not. For this reason, there are two main types of forms in use—the coupon form and the open form. The coupon form has a detachable perforated coupon which may have either one or two stubs. Both the form and the stubs bear the same serial number and the employee may write his name on each stub, one of which he keeps, the other being sent to the suggestion secretary. His name does not appear on the form itself, and he can be identified only by means of the stub which is sent to the secretary of the suggestion program. In some cases, only one stub is provided and the worker's identity is not even revealed to the suggestion secretary. This makes it certain that those who pass on the suggestions submitted are not influenced by seeing the name of a suggester.

Companies using the coupon type of form are of the opinion that such confidential handling encourages many worthwhile suggestions which might otherwise never reach the suggestion department.

The open form is designed on the theory that not only should there be no concealment of the identity of the suggester, but there should be no implication that concealment is necessary. Those in favor of this type of form believe that if there is any suspicion on the part of the employee that his supervisor or the suggestion committee cannot be trusted to play fair with him, it is obvious that he cannot depend on getting a square deal in anything else. Proper training of the supervisory group, it is felt, makes the anonymous suggestion unnecessary. Such training emphasizes the importance of getting supervisors to understand that an essential part of their jobs is to develop good ideas from the employees in their department. In addition, they must have the assurance of management that good ideas developed through cooperation with employees are a credit to the supervisor and are taken into consideration at the time candidates are considered for promotion.

Investigating the Suggestion

As a rule, the supervisor of the department to which a new suggestion or idea may apply is assigned to the investigation of that suggestion. What should the investigation uncover? The following

Z 3500		
Z 3500 DATE_____ 19____		DEPARTMENT_____

WATCH FOR THIS NUMBER

On The Suggestion System News Board

UNTIL IT APPEARS

★

This Number Corresponds With The One On Your Suggestion And Identifies You As The One Who Submitted It

KEEP THIS STUB

My Suggestion _____

What Will It Accomplish? _____

How Can It Be Accomplished? _____

DO NOT ATTACH SEPARATE DRAWINGS TO THIS BLANK Simple pencil sketches may be made on back of this blank. If you have other drawings or samples to submit, so state and an appointment will be arranged.

Do you wish help in preparing your suggestion? Yes ☐ No ☐

Date Received_____ Date Posted_____

Date Interviewed_____ Answer_____

Use the Back of This Blank if More Space is Needed. Use a Separate Blank for Each Suggestion.

YOU DON'T NEED TO SIGN THIS SUGGESTION although you may sign all suggestions if you prefer. In either case **TEAR OFF AND KEEP THE STUB**

Name_____

Some companies prefer to let the suggester remain anonymous in the belief that more suggestions will be received that way. A form like this one will keep the employee's identity from the suggestion committee.

is a list prepared by one company to help the investigator to give a complete and detailed reply to the secretary of the suggestion program:

INSTRUCTIONS TO INVESTIGATORS

Your reply should be courteous and complete, giving detailed reasons for your recommendations. If previous consideration has been given to this idea, include reference to specific correspondence, drawings, shop orders, etc.

1. Is the idea new in our practice?
2. Is it already under consideration from another source?
3. If so, who has the matter in hand?
4. Adoption? (Answer "Yes," "In part," or "No.")
5. Improvement in quality of product? Estimated value?
6. Reduction of material? Yearly saving?
7. Saving of labor? Yearly saving?
8. Other savings?
9. Total yearly saving?
10. Show in moderate detail how savings are figured.
11. If suggestion is adopted, when will it be put into effect?
12. Who will be responsible for putting it into effect?
13. Have instructions been issued to put it into effect?
14. Estimated cost of putting it into effect?
15. Other information of interest.

When the Program Bogs Down

When the flow of suggestions from employees shows signs of slowing down perceptibly, the suggestion committee should look for the answers to these 10 questions:

1. Is it possible to reduce the length of time between the receipt of a suggestion and its acknowledgment?
2. Is the length of time between the receipt of a suggestion and its acceptance or rejection over a month? (This does not always apply to technical ideas which may take longer to process.)
3. Is the employee notified promptly if his suggestion is held up because of the time required for investigation of the idea?
4. Is the acceptance letter or memo friendly or just a cut-and-dried proposition? Does it sell the worker on submitting other suggestions in the future?
5. Is the rejection of an employee's suggestion handled tactfully? Is he given adequate and logical reasons for its rejection? Is an effort made to sell him on another try?
6. Are workers given sufficient help by their supervisors in the preparation of their ideas?
7. Has the supervisor been sold on the idea that getting his workers to turn in suggestions is part of his job?
8. Has the style of the suggestion posters become monotonous? Should they be completely changed?

SUGGESTION BLANK

● HAMMERMILL PAPER COMPANY

NO. _____

DATE RECD. _____

BOX NO. _____

DATE _____

I suggest _____

I BELIEVE THE ADOPTION OF THIS SUGGESTION WILL ACCOMPLISH OR RESULT IN _____

BACK SIDE OF THIS FORM MAY BE USED FOR SKETCHES OR FLOW DIAGRAMS.
IF YOU WANT HELP, CONTACT YOUR SUPERVISOR. WHEN COMPLETED, DROP IN SUGGESTION BOX.

Signature _____ Dept. _____ Clock No. _____

A good suggestion form, like this one in use at Hammermill Paper Company, is simple in design. The reverse of this form is gridded to facilitate the making of illustrative sketches.

9. How long has the suggestion form been in use? Should a new style be substituted?

10. Have short suggestion programs been tried for a change of pace?

Unless thought is given to such questions as these from time to time, a suggestion program can easily become static. If it is to be a continuous active means of encouraging employee thinking, it needs to be checked at regular intervals and necessary changes made to keep it fresh and stimulating.

Chapter 22

FRINGE BENEFITS: RETIREMENT PLANS

FRINGE benefits, once the icing on the employee cake, have now taken on the role of a layer. The payment of all benefits has risen above the $75 billion mark, and there is no reason to suppose that the figure will decline.

Between 1955 and 1965, the great spurt years, benefit costs rose some 83 percent as compared to wage increases of 51 percent. In the not-too-distant future, fringe benefit payments will probably top $50 a week for each employee in the United States. In some industries, the figure is already over $40 a week, and in special areas the cost is over $60.

The list of fringe benefits paid to employees today is headed by the paid vacation. Figures taken from a recent United States Chamber of Commerce survey reveal that on a national average each employee receives $4.85 a week in vacation pay. Another $4.35 goes into the national pension payment. The insurance bill (hospital, life, accident, etc.) runs another $3.54 a week, and the Government claims another $3.13 for its insurance programs. Paid holidays cost the employer $3.10, and the rest period (the good old coffee break, lunch period and washup time) costs $2.88 a week on the national average.

What Are the Benefits?

Today, in discussing employment with a candidate, the interviewer makes certain that the "fringe benefits" are spelled out. In most cases these are included in company policy. Most of them are defined and explained in the company manual or policy manual.

The benefits are varied and many. Paid vacations (as indicated) top the list. Next come paid holiday, pension plans, certain paid leaves of absence (illness, jury duty), group life insurance, group hospitalization, group accident and sickness insurance, profit sharing, coffee breaks, rest periods, meal periods, bonuses and last (but not least important) recognition for such things as years of service.

There are also other "fringe" benefits to consider: aid to education programs, employee discounts, employee loans at low rates, relocation payments, recreation programs, and food service at no or low cost.

Do You Get Your Money's Worth?

The important thing to keep in mind is the return for these invested expenses. Do employees *know and understand* what they are getting? These "extras" have added about 25 percent to their paycheck. They are expected benefits, but they are also competitive. If employees are not made aware of the full value, the company is losing a very excellent selling point. This *"invisible paycheck"* will remain invisible unless pains are taken to make it a very real thing on an annual basis.

Most companies today must have at least a minimum benefit program in order to compete in the existing labor market. But aside from this, many employers have provided benefits, or increased them as business conditions allow, from a sense of responsibility to long-service employees—a responsibility to help employees avoid medical catastrophe or indigent old age, for example.

There is also a theory that security is good for employee morale, and high morale means high productivity in the work group. Related to this "high morale, high productivity" theory is the generally accepted doctrine that rest periods and vacations contribute to high productivity during periods of work, that employees can and will work harder if they have an opportunity to relax at periodic intervals.

Another important factor in the record growth of benefits is the realization that group purchases of life insurance, pensions, etc., can provide more benefits per dollar than the employee can purchase individually. This, combined with the fact that employees pay no taxes on money spent on their behalf in company benefit programs, has led many employees to understand that a nickel an hour used to purchase benefits is more valuable than the nickel an hour put into the pay envelope.

Probably the most important factor in management's determination to provide a good benefits program for employees is the desire to attract better employees in the labor market, and to avoid costly turnover in the skilled, experienced labor force which has been built up and trained at a great expense over a number of years. But, as

BILL OF EMPLOYEE BENEFITS

Dear ....:

Last year you cashed an "Invisible Pay Check" although you never saw it. It was just as real as the one you did see, with one exception—you didn't have to pay taxes on much of it.

During the year our average employee received $............................ which is ....c per hour above the straight-time wages you received. This is the amount of money your company spends for benefits which you enjoy as an employee of (*company name*).

The "Invisible Pay Check" paid the following benefits in 1965:

☐ Group Insurance, including:
Life Insurance, Accidental Death and
Dismemberment Insurance, Hospitaliza-
tion, Surgical and Maternity Insurance $......................................

☐ Paid Vacations   ....

☐ Paid Holidays   ....

☐ Paid Rest Breaks   ....

☐ Physical Examinations   ....

☐ Jury Duty Pay   ....

☐ Social Security   ....

☐ Workmen's Compensation   ....

☐ Unemployment Compensation   ....

☐ Overtime Pay   ....

☐ First Aid   ....

☐ Paid Sick Leave   ....

☐ Paid Wash-up Time   ....

☐ Election Day Pay   ....

☐ Pension Plan   ....

☐ Profit-Sharing Plan   ....

☐ Year-end Bonus   ....

☐ Safety Clothing and Shoes   ....

☐ Personal Counselling   ....

☐ Discounts on Company Products   ....

☐ Employee Parking Lot   ....

☐ Company-sponsored Recreation Programs   ....

☐ Christmas Party, or Picnic   ....

☐ Call-in Pay   ....

☐ Reporting Pay   ....

☐ Average Cost Per Employee   ....

Think of it! For the year, your company paid you
more than you realized $......................................

Your company is happy and proud to give you benefits because we believe they help to strengthen your efforts to make our company stronger—and a stronger (*company name*) gives you another benefit—GREATER JOB SECURITY.

Sincerely yours,

(Usual signature)

This is an example of letter which could be sent yearly to homes of all employees.

benefit programs spread and grow, employees tend to forget the value of their benefits, and assume that benefit programs are approximately equal between companies. Thus, an employee may leave Company A and take a job with Company B, where the benefit program is substantially inferior, if he is offered higher *money* wages.

Further, if benefits are to make their proper contribution to higher morale, employees' understanding of their benefits must constantly be reinforced. It's not enough to hand an employee a booklet when he comes to work, and expect him, five years later, to understand and appreciate his benefits. It's only human nature to take for granted that which is received without effort, and received in "hidden" form which only occasionally hits the employee "where he lives"—in his pocketbook.

More important, not everyone accepts the principle that a nickel an hour in benefits is worth more than a nickel an hour in wages. If an employee is hard-pressed, he might rather have a nickel now and the benefit later. And, since the nickels in benefits have accumulated over the years, the average employee has lost track of just how valuable his benefits are in terms of cents per hour or dollars per week.

"Bill of Employee Benefits"

It is therefore extremely important to take time and prepare a "Bill of Employee Benefits" as a means of reminding your employees of the dollar cost of your benefit program. Many employees, supervisors, and no doubt you yourself will be surprised at the amount of money spent on benefits. You can figure the exact payroll cost and hidden cost of benefits paid by your company by using the following formula:

Step 1: Add up the total of what you pay in a year for all the benefits you provide for your employees.

Step 2: To determine what percent of your payroll is paid out for benefits, divide the total arrived at in Step 1 by your total yearly payroll.

Step 3: To determine the cents-per-payroll-hour cost of your benefits, divide the total arrived at in Step 1 by the total number of hours your employees worked during the year.

Step 4: To determine the dollar value per year to each employee of the fringe benefits in your company, divide the total arrived at in Step 1 by the number of your "full-time equivalent" employees.

EXPLAINING YOUR FRINGE BENEFIT PROGRAM

The best designed benefit programs will be unsuccessful unless your employees know what the benefits are, or how they as individuals stand to gain by them. Every benefit must be explained fully and "sold" continually to your employees. Here lies a golden opportunity for direct employee communications from the company. Employees and their families are very much concerned with the subject of employee benefits.

Benefit plans should always be dramatized to show their actual cost—something employees are often unaware of in many companies. Please bear in mind that your employees want to know what the benefits are, and how they may derive most advantage from them. Generally speaking, the amount of employee morale and employee relations advantages your benefit plans will give you *is not* in direct proportion to their generosity, but other things being equal, *to the degree in which your employees understand them.* We recommend you compute your benefit costs and prepare an "Invisible Pay Check" on your letterhead and mail to each employee.

Selling Fringe Benefits

One might think that the very existence of good extra benefits speaks for itself, but most firms still find it necessary to "sell" them to employees. Much of this is caused by the unions' taking credit for all things given by the company; thus, the employee feels the union got it all for him. A midwestern chemical company has a policy that tries to offset this condition. When a new benefit is added, it is always posted on the bulletin board in such a way that the employees "realize the company is responsible for the 'plus' feature, not the union."

Tidewater Oil Company handled the extra benefit story well in the company magazine, *Tidewater News.* Entitled "The Hidden Payroll," the feature explained a survey of oil industry employees which showed how much was gained by each company employee in additional benefits. Actual costs to the company of the contributory pension plan, the accident and sickness disability plan, vacations, holidays, military leaves of absence, excused absences, hospital-surgical-medical insurance, and the group insurance plan were explained to employees.

Negotiators, too, must keep in mind the actual costs of such benefits so that they will know, when sitting at the bargaining table, just how much leeway there is in granting additional employee benefits. Extra services for employees, like credit buying, have a way of becoming very costly over a long period of time, though they seem insignificant at first.

Too often negotiators come to the bargaining table fully prepared with wage rates and labor cost figures, but unprepared with figures on employee benefits. When negotiators on the other side of the table begin to talk in broad terms about pensions, group insurance, longer vacation periods, paid rest periods, and other fringe issues, the prepared negotiator is able to discuss such welfare features in dollars and cents values, since he has studied the actual costs.

Even such benefits as cafeteria service, vending machines, music at work, employee counseling, and recreation programs are extras. True, they are not considered such in many cases, now that they are established, but they started out that way.

Here are some comments on the subject that were made by executives who contributed to the report:

President of a Cincinnati tool company: "With automation upon us, with predictions of a 32-hour workweek within 10 years, and with each round of contracts adding more and more extra benefits—we had better determine if there is such a thing as a saturation point in welfare features. We may reach the day when the employee takes one-third in salary and two-thirds in fringe gifts."

Vice-president, eastern metal products manufacturing firm: "Now that we have the guaranteed annual wage, plus all the other extra benefits above the highest salaries in the history of the world, one begins to wonder when the saturation point will be reached. Apparently it is years away."

What does the future hold? It is certain that new suggestions will be aimed at giving workers greater security. As necessity is considered the mother of invention, economic strains give birth to new employee welfare benefits. By the same token, good times, high production, and climbing sales lead to new employee demands.

It takes no Delphic oracle to predict that more and more extra benefits will be demanded, and in many cases granted. It is also obvious that management will continue to seek ways and means to sell employees on the costs of such benefits to the company.

Not only every worker, but every supervisor and department head should know what these extra provisions cost and it is top management's job to provide this information to the middle-management group.

Pay checks of The Republic Supply Company of California were once used to show each employee exactly how much it had paid him in each of various fringe benefits for the previous year. This is a case where the benefit story struck home in a personal way. Employees rarely realize the high cost of these extras, and here is a dramatic way to get the information across. General reaction among employees at Republic has been surprise at the large total of each individual's benefits. W. Irvin Brennan, company public relations counsel, tells about the plan:

> The checks were made up differently for each individual and were sent to his or her home by mail, instead of being distributed in the office. This move was obvious, so that the wife or husband could also see the figures thereon.

> The smallest check written was for $619.00 and the largest *excluding* executives and administrative personnel was for $2,843.00.

Enclosed with the checks was a letter from H. M. Giller, director of personnel.

Do Pension Plans Pay?

This is a question many businessmen are asking these days. There is no pat answer. While they seem to have little effect upon the turnover among younger employees, pension programs tend to stabilize employment among employees with 10 or more years of service.

The prevailing practice is to regard the cost of a pension plan as a part of the labor cost. The company obligates itself to make regular payments into an irrevocable trust or to pay certain insurance premiums, in accordance with the set requirements of the United States Treasury Department.

Pension plans may be contributory or noncontributory, but unless they are actuarially sound, they are likely to prove more of a liability than an asset so far as employee relations are concerned.

The older, more pension-minded employee is seriously interested in the progress of his company's pension fund. So is the Federal Government. Corporate management is fully aware that pensions are already the second most costly fringe benefit. Cost ranges from approximately 1½ percent to nearly 12 percent of the wage bill. The high cost prevails despite the fact that the actuarial base presupposes that a substantial portion of a company's annual contribution will be reduced through employee termination.

The employee, his union and the Government want assurances that the company is protecting the pension investment. Management is just as interested in its contribution. There are nearly 35,000 pension plans on file with the United States Department of Labor. Some 25 million American employees are covered by such plans, and the number is growing.

The Chamber of Commerce of the United States looks at pension plans in this light:

> Retirement programs are highly desired by many career employees. They are a major item in the fringe benefit package in labor negotiations. They can provide

a measure of financial security to older and disabled employees, the cost of which can be spread over the working life of an employee in a manner that is considered a sound accounting practice.

Most large and medium-size employers have programs in existence. Thousands of small employers have established and are funding deferred benefit plans. However, there are many small employers (those with employee groups of under 100 to 200) that have, for various reasons postponed or not even explored the establishment of a plan. Some of these may feel, incorrectly, that the installation costs of hiring an actuary or other consultant and a lawyer are "too high." A reasonable examination of the facts will soon convince an employer of the fallacy of such views.

There is growing public interest in broadening the coverage of private employee retirement programs. Several million American workers, still not covered by plans, are in types of employment that lend themselves to such coverage. It is a fact that among this number are many who, through individual choice or through collective bargaining processes, have elected not to participate in proferred or suggested programs and, in lieu, have accepted other or more direct forms of remuneration.

Nevertheless, it would seem an eventuality for the great majority of the work force to be covered under private programs within the next decade.

In exploring its particular circumstances, each company which does not now have a plan will be helping to discourage federal and state intervention in what has been and should continue to be a matter to be decided upon by employers for the best interests of their business and their employees.

Basic Types of Deferred Benefit Programs

The two main methods of providing cash payments to employees at or after retirement are through pension plans and deferred profit sharing plans. Each has certain basic characteristics.

Pension Plans

A pension plan can be described as one which provides an orderly flow of payments, usually monthly, to a retired person. The benefit payments are determinable in advance by a formula contained in the plan itself and usually are payable for the life of the pensioner. Frequently, such plans also provide for further payments to the spouse or other dependent of the pensioner.

The above definition is an oversimplification, since there are many variations, but the main characteristic of a pension plan is that of definiteness—either the ultimate benefits or the pattern of contribution to the plan are determinable in advance in accord with its terms.

Pension plan formulas are usually based on an employee's compensation and/or service with an employer. Credit may be given only for service in the future, that is after the date of installation of the plan (called current or future service benefits), but frequently credit is also given for service rendered prior to that date (called past service benefits). Thus a pension plan can, and often does, provide benefits measured by the total service of an employee.

The compensation base for such plans, if one is used, may be the average annual earnings of each covered employee. This would be called a "career earnings" plan. Or the base for the application of the benefit formula might be some form of "final average earnings," such as the average of the five years immediately prior to retirement.

The benefit formula applied to a compensation base is usually expressed in percentages, such as:

a) 1 percent of the final average earnings base, multiplied by years of credit service (both past and future service) or;

b) 1½ percent of annual future service earnings, plus 1 percent of the compensation base in effect at the date of the plan installation, multiplied by credited past service.

Inasmuch as pension plans are often designed to supplement Social Security benefits, the benefit formulas can also integrate with, or take into consideration, expected Social Security payments in whole or in part. This is done by reducing the pension plan benefits by direct offset or by lowering the plan formula in its application to that portion of an employee's earnings subject to Social Security taxes.

Another form of pension benefit formula is called the "flat benefit" type and is frequently found in plans covering hourly or production employees. A typical example might be:

$2.00 (or $3.00 or $4.00 etc.) per month per year of credited service; i.e., $60.00 (or $90.00 or $120.00 etc.) per month for 30 years of credited service.

Under the flat benefit type of plan, there is usually no offset for Social Security payments.

In most pension plans, the "normal retirement age" is usually age 65 at which time the plan benefit becomes payable. However, additional provisions may be included to provide similar or reduced benefits at earlier retirement or upon disability. Many plans also provide for the accrual of a benefit—to be payable at age 65—for employees who terminate their services prior to normal retirement, but after having completed a designated period of service (such as 10, 15 or 20 years) and perhaps a specified age (such as 40, 45 or 50). This is called a "vested benefit."

Deferred Profit-Sharing Plans

A deferred profit-sharing plan is a formal arrangement under which an employer agrees to contribute a portion of his annual business profits to a fund created as part of the plan. The amount of this employer contribution may be in accordance with the application of a specified formula such as:

a) 10 percent of net earnings (before taxes);

b) 10 percent of net earnings (before taxes) in excess of $100,000;

c) 10 percent of net earnings (before taxes) in excess of $100,000 provided that there shall remain after taxes net earnings at least equal to X dollars per share of common stock.

Under certain circumstances it is even possible to leave the amount to be contributed solely to the discretion of the employer; in other words, no specific formula is required under present Federal laws and Internal Revenue Service regulations. However, the application of such discretion must be made with care and free of what the Internal Revenue Service might consider discriminatory practices.

Under a profit-sharing plan, the amounts contributed by the employer are allocated among the covered employees to bookkeeping accounts maintained in their names under the plan. This is usually done on a basis that is pro rata to their respective compensations during each year. However, under certain circumstances it is possible to provide some other form of allocation such as an additional weighting for years of service.

The funds contributed are placed in the selected funding medium, usually a trust fund, and these are invested and administered as a unit. The scope of the permissible investment program is usually spelled out in the trust agreement accompanying the plan. The investment income and gains or losses from the sale of securities or other investments in the fund are allocated to the accounts of the employee participants.

Employer contributions are tax deductible by the employer, but the amounts set aside for the employees (together with any income and investment profits) are not taxable to the employees (or their beneficiaries) until actually distributable to them under the terms of the plan.

Distributions are made upon an employee's retirement (normal or early) and also in the event of death, disability or other termination of employment. To take care of the latter event, a vesting schedule is set forth in the plan which specifies the portion of an employee's account which is payable to him upon termination of employment—usually based on the length of his service or plan participation.

Distribution can take the form of (1) lump sum payments (under appropriate conditions these may be subject to Federal tax as capital gains); (2) installments over a period of years and (3) purchase of an annuity contract from a life insurance company.

There are many variations of both types of plans available in designing a deferred benefit program to suit the needs of an employer and his employees as well as his capabilities to provide the funds.

A New Profit Center

Not too long age, Robert H. Kenmore, director of financial planning for International Telephone and Telegraph Corporation, looked at some interesting statistics concerning his company's pension funds:

1. The funded portion of our pension funds that was trusteed with banks amounted to one-fifth of the company's total net worth.

2. Our charge to the profit and loss income statement in one year for identifiable pension fund costs represented some 8 percent of the company's pretax income.

3. On an actuarial assumption that these funds would earn 4 percent a year, approximately 40 percent of the principal sum required to be paid out in pension benefits would have to be contributed by the company, with 60 percent coming from the compounded earnings of the fund itself. If, however, this sum were to earn 7 percent instead of 4 percent, only 20 cents or roughly half as much of the eventual dollar to be paid out in benefits would have to be contributed by the company and 80 cents would be self-generated by the earnings of the fund. Only a 1 percent improvement in the annual return earned by these funds would be equivalent to roughly $1 million.

The first step was a program of study and contacts with other companies, bank trustees and investment people. Following this a questionnaire was sent to the Fortune 500 group, and the returns were studied and analyzed. The next step was the initiation of a new program:

"The first thing we did was to hire an investment man, whose initial task was to analyze the job that our trustees had been doing and to give recommendations on how a better job could be done if this seemed indicated.

"On the basis of his report, we split off two small pieces—5 to 10 percent of our pension-fund assets—from the total existing pool. One went to a leading mutual fund management organization for their direction. The other was given to our internal staff man to see what kind of management job could be achieved in this manner.

"So now three types of management are being applied to our pension fund assets: bank trustees, professional money-management group, and our internal staff. Over the next year or two, we will be watching closely the results of these different methods of management and will be in a good position to determine which method is the most effective and is likely to produce the best results."

Pension-fund assets have certain attributes built into them which are highly advantageous:

1. Both income and capital gains are completely free of taxes;
2. Flow of money in and out of the fund can be programmed ahead very accurately;
3. Investment judgment is unaffected by external factors such as sales appeal of a published portfolio, legal restrictions on types of investments made, etc.

Management of pension-fund assets represents an opportunity for exercising investment judgment in its most undiluted form to an extent not possible in most forms of money management.

A long-term successful program of pension-fund administration must take full advantage of these factors and be flexible enough to follow investment policies that are in keeping with the long-term corporate objectives.

If management takes an active interest in the growth and development of the pension fund, the employee is going to be interested. Just setting up a program of benefits will not have the effect on turnover it might if it were properly sold to the worker. The presentation to the employee can be as important as the program itself.

Cost of Pension Plans

There is no sound reason why any well-managed company, operating at a profit, should be without some pension plan.

However, shareholders may sometimes prove shortsighted in voting pension plans. Even though the chief executive is thoroughly sold on the need of a pension plan to enable management to attract and hold the better types of workers, and as an investment in human relations, he does not always have the backing of his board of directors. Of course, the standard objection is, "We can't afford it."

If the entire cost of a pension plan must come out of the profit upon which a business operates, this argument of not being able to afford it might be justified. But actually the cost of pensions, since the Federal Government allows payment to pension funds to be taken as a business expense (taxable only to the employee when he receives his retirement pay), is in large measure financed by tax savings. The remainder is treated as a part of the cost of production, which it is if we admit the employer's responsibility to look after his

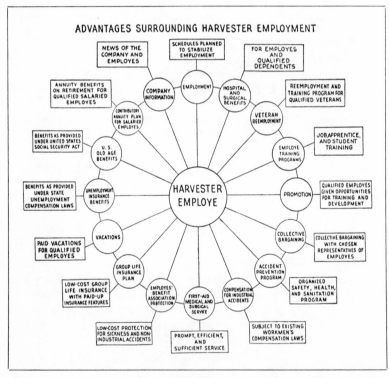

When a company has numerous benefits, these can be dramatized by a chart like this one used by International Harvester Company or by some other device which gets all the employee's benefits before him at one time.

older employees. As a production cost it goes into the selling price. Only when a considerable part of the fund comes out of accumulated surplus, earned before the plan went into effect, does it come out of the stockholders' pockets.

A frequent objection to setting up a pension plan is that having to pay this extra money into an irrevocable fund, or to an insurance company, would place the company at a competitive disadvantage. There was some basis for this argument 10 years ago. But today pension plans are so common, especially in unionized industries, that the company which has no plan is at a disadvantage. It will cost more to get and hold employees.

It is significant that the most successful companies in their industries—Swift & Company, for example, in the packing industry—have pension plans which cost approximately 10 percent of their payrolls to maintain. These companies do not seem to be at a competitive disadvantage for that reason. The Swift pension plan was established in 1916. But a pension plan need not cost 10 percent of payroll. The cost can be controlled in the following ways:

1. By making the normal retirement age 70 instead of 65.

2. By putting a ceiling on benefits to executives.

3. By raising the conditions of eligibility.

4. By excluding new employees over 45 years of age.

5. By requiring employees to contribute to the plan in order to participate.

6. By improving the yield on securities or investments in the trust.

7. By eliminating or restricting the life insurance benefits.

8. By having a committee of employees administer the plan instead of a trust company.

9. By eliminating or restricting the survivor's interest in the plan.

10. By extending the average pay period used in determining retirement pay.

11. By eliminating the disability provision or permitting optional retirement.

12. By not making retirement mandatory and limiting the number of service years in computing pensions.

While there is always the danger of cutting benefits to a point where employees will feel the plan is of little value, so that its value, employee-relations-wise, will be negligible, it is better to start with a plan which the business can finance without damaging its competitive position. Once the plan is established, and the machinery is set up for administering it (if it is to be self-administered), benefits can be increased as experience and earnings warrant.

Shall the Plan Be Contributory or Noncontributory?

This question has bothered employers ever since pension plans came into existence. There are arguments both ways. The contributory plan is favored by insurance companies, and some trust companies, as it costs the company less. It is, therefore, easier to "sell" the plan to an employer. Requiring the employees to contribute gives them a sense of participation and encourages them to save, so that when the time to retire comes, they will receive larger retirement checks. This is a good point, of course. However, there are disinterested bankers who frown on the idea of an employee putting all his savings into any plan that will return just so many dollars. They think employees should be encouraged to invest in homes and in common shares of the company for which they work.

The argument in favor of a noncontributory plan is that it makes administration much simpler. Nor is it necessary for an employee who might be having difficulty in meeting his present expenses to contribute to a plan in order to be eligible for a pension.

Still another objection (which does not exist to the same extent in insurance plans as in self-administered plans) some employers have to the contributory type of plan is that the employee looks upon the money he pays into a pension plan as his savings, because that was the way the plan was "sold" to him. He feels he should be entitled to withdraw his "savings," if he elects to do so. His share of the fund stands there burning a hole in his pocket. If it is necessary for him to quit in order to get the money out, should he want it to start in business or to buy a new car or a boat, he will quit. This, of course, defeats one purpose of a pension plan.

Types of Pension Plans in Use

Generally speaking, pension plans fall into five broad classifications as follows:

1. Group insurance plans (annuities).
2. Self-administered pension trusts.
3. Profit-sharing pension plans.
4. Union-management pension plans.
5. "Pay as you go" plans.

All of these plans can be set up to meet the requirements of the Treasury Department. In preparing a plan, the first step is to retain an actuary who will determine the cost. When the cost and back service liability are determined, what a company can afford as a starter becomes clear. Then an attorney should draft the plan to meet the requirements of the law and obtain the necessary approval from the Treasury Department. The law requires that when the plan has been adopted by the stockholders, it must be made available to all employees concerned in the form approved by the Treasury Department.

All the large insurance companies offer attractive group deals which assure employees of a fixed benefit payable in dollars as provided by an agreement between the insurance company and the employer. An advantage of the group plan is that it relieves the employer from the work and responsibility involved in most other plans. The employee feels more secure when the plan is entrusted to a well-known insurance organization.

The Prudential Insurance Company's Own Plan

On the theory that a big insurance company which has millions of dollars' worth of pension policies in force must know how to set up a practical and economical plan, Dartnell checked the Prudential Insurance Company's plan. Prudential favors the contributory type of plan, and its own plan has that feature. Prudential did not always have a contributory plan. It changed over in 1941. The reason given by the company at the time was that "The steadily increasing number of persons qualifying for retirement, the longer expectation of life of annuitants, and the low interest earnings have caused the cost of a noncontributory plan to become constantly more burdensome. In order to provide an adequate scale of retirement allowance, it has been found necessary to change over to a contributory plan."

Enrollment under the Prudential plan is not necessary to obtain past service benefits at retirement age—65 for men, 60 for women. Participants in the plan who leave the company are given their choice between obtaining a deferred annuity or having all their contributions to the plan returned together with interest at the rate of $2\frac{1}{2}$ percent a year. If certain terms and conditions are met, the deferred annuity will include a substantial amount purchased by company contributions.

If an employee dies before retirement, the beneficiary is paid the amount of the contributions, plus annual interest at $2\frac{1}{2}$ percent. The plan also provides for a benefit payable in the event of death after retirement. In addition, provision is made for an annuity in case of retirement for total and permanent disability, after certain age and service requirements have been fulfilled.

Leath's Half-Pay Retirement Plan

A cooperative retirement plan, supplementing social security benefits and providing a liberal thrift program, has been worked out for the employees of Leath and Company of Lincolnwood, Illinois.

Each employee participating contributes 2 percent of his earnings plus an additional 3 percent on that part of his income in excess of $3,000 a year. The maximum salary in the plan will be $6,000 a year. The company will contribute an equal amount and the total payment is transferred to an insurance company for annuities to mature at retirement age, which may occur at any time during the 10 years between the employee's 55th and 65th birthdays.

For those who are near retirement age, the company purchases annuities based on years of service after age 35, with a maximum annuity credit to any one employee of $7\frac{1}{2}$ percent of his earnings. If an employee leaves the company after he is 45 and has been a contributor to the plan for 10 years, a paid-up annuity contract is given to him, representing his own savings and the company's contributions on his account. If an employee dies or leaves at any time before retirement, his own contributions plus $2\frac{1}{2}$ percent interest compounded annually are returned to him or to his beneficiary.

Retirement Benefit for Staley Employees

It was formerly the policy of A. E. Staley Manufacturing Company, Decatur, Illinois, to transfer older employees to easier jobs, but management knew that, eventually, there would be too many older employees for the jobs available, so a pension plan was adopted in 1941.

Under the plan, each retiring employee receives a fully paid annuity providing for a monthly payment which, when added to the primary insurance benefit received from Social Security, will make his monthly income equal to 40 percent of his average monthly wage or salary since January 1, 1937, the effective date of the Social Security Act. All portions of salary above $250 are excluded from the company's calculations; therefore, the maximum total monthly income of a retired employee does not exceed $100. If 40 percent of the average monthly wages is less than $45, the payment amounts to enough to make the sum from both sources $45.

SELF-ADMINISTERED PENSION PLANS

An alternative to providing retirement pay through group insurance is setting up an irrevocable pension trust which meets the requirements of the Treasury Department, thus making payments into the fund deductible as business expense. In general, the trust cannot be used to evade the taxation of profits, but must be applied uniformly to all, or a particular group, of employees. Plans with a "recapture clause" whereby trust funds may be withdrawn and used by the companies are ineligible. Plans which discriminate in favor of officers, shareholders, supervisors, or other highly paid employees will not be approved. The plan must meet the tests governing trust funds in the state in which it operates. The usual practice is to have a well-known bank or trust company serve as depository, with three or more company officials serving as trustees under a trust agreement.

It is claimed that this type of pension plan is less expensive than the insurance plan, and tax savings are about the same. It is in effect a profit-sharing plan, under which a portion of an employee's compensation is deferred until his retirement when it is paid to him in monthly installments. It may or may not include direct payments into the fund by employees. However, most trust plans carry the provision that the company may, if such is desirable, amend the plan to permit voluntary payments by employees in order to increase the retirement pay or to lighten the burden on the company during a recession.

The form and provisions of any profit-sharing program must depend upon a consideration of the results sought by the particular employer as well as a consideration of the industry.

Requirements

The plan may embrace some or all of the employees. It is customary to establish a minimum period of employment before the employee may participate in the benefits of the trust fund.

Except for that portion of the fund contributed by the employees which must be invested in securities approved by the state for investment of trust funds, it is customary to give the trustees broad general powers as to the investment of the trust funds. Pension funds of less than $100,000 are usually invested in securities of the U.S. Government. Only after that point has been reached is it safe to invest in equities, and then not more than 40 percent of the fund should be so invested.

If an employee resigns or is discharged from service, it is customary to provide that he shall be paid the amount he has contributed and only a part of the corporation contribution plus the trust income credited to his account. The remainder of the corporation credit is a forfeit representing the penalty for withdrawal or dismissal, and reverts to the fund for the benefit of the remaining members. It is advisable to reserve to the employee the right to appeal to an advisory board as a protection against easy or arbitrary dismissal.

In the event of an employee's death prior to retirement, provision is generally made for full and undiminished settlement with his estate or beneficiaries. In this respect proper drafting of the clause may avoid an estate tax on such payments.

Tax Status of Plan

If the pension plan is properly drafted to meet the requirements of the tax law, the trust will be exempt from income taxation. Thus, the plan may provide for investment of the trust funds by the trustees or other persons in control of the trust, but any income or profit realized on such investment will not be subject to tax. Usually, if the established trust is an irrevocable fund in the sense it is impossible for any part of the funds to be diverted for the use of the employer before all liability to the employees has been satisfied, the trust will meet the requirements of the tax law and be exempt.

There are also important tax advantages for the employee participating in a pension trust. Contributions made by the employer to such a trust constitute additional compensation to the employee. If taxable as compensation during the year in which contributed by the employer, they might well raise the employee's income to a higher rate of tax. However, employer contributions are not so taxable to the employee until distributed to him under the terms of the trust plan. Thus, the income tax liability of the employee with respect to this additional compensation is postponed until a time when his income has diminished and his tax is lower.

Pension Trusts for Executives

The law exempting pension trusts from taxation extends the exemption to trusts created by an employer for the benefit of "some or all of his employees." Officers of a corporation, if they perform services for which they receive compensation and are subject to the control usually recognized as existing between employer and employee, clearly come within the meaning of the term "employee." Therefore, a pension trust established for the benefit of executive officers would appear to come within the provisions of the law granting such an exemption. However, the Treasury Department has sought to limit the scope of employees' trusts by providing that the plan must be for the benefit of a large percentage of the total number of employees as distinguished from persons in positions of authority. In fact, the Department has sought to deny the exemption of pension trusts designed to benefit only a small group of selected officials or department heads.

Even if it be conceded the trust itself is not tax-exempt merely because it favors a small or selected group of employees, the tax advantages to the corporation and the employees previously discussed are not thereby lost. In a Treasury Department ruling:

Three pension trusts were created in favor of but 60 out of a total of some 25,000 employees. Trust No. 1 was established for the benefit of a single beneficiary, the president of the corporation. Trust No. 2 covered nine employees, some of whom were officers of the company. Trust No. 3 was designed to benefit some 50 selected employees.

Under Trust No. 1, the corporation contributed a specific amount to the fund each year; the president-beneficiary contributed nothing. Under the provisions of the other trusts, the corporation and the employee-beneficiaries made equal contributions to the fund measured by a certain percentage of the employees' respective annual salaries. All contributions made to the trusts were to be invested in annuity contracts issued on the life of each employee.

Upon these facts the Treasury Department ruled that these trusts were not entitled to exemption upon the ground that they were too restricted in their application, their benefits being limited to a mere 60 out of a total of 25,000 employees. However, the Department clearly indicated that the mere fact that the trusts were subject to income tax did not deprive the corporation and the participating employees of the other tax economies generally associated with a valid pension trust. In this connection, the following portion of the ruling is important:

1. Neither the contributions made by the company nor by the employees constitute taxable income to the trust.

2. The corporation may deduct, as an ordinary and necessary expense, the amount of contributions which it had to pay as long as these contributions, when added to the salaries of the employees, constituted reasonable compensation in comparison to the services rendered.

3. That portion of the corporation's share of the contribution, which was used to purchase retirement annuity contracts for the employees, is not to be considered taxable income to the employees in the year in which contributions were made.

4. Upon retirement, each annuity payment received by the employee will be taxable income to him as received. Since the employee paid part of the cost of these annuities, the entire amount of the payments will not be taxable until he has recovered his cost in accordance with the tax provisions governing ordinary annuity payments.

5. All amounts received by employees upon resignation or discharge are to be included in their tax return for the year in which they are received. If, upon the termination of employment, an annuity contract with a cash surrender value is assigned to the employee, he does not realize taxable income at that time unless he exercises the privilege of receiving the cash. In this event he realizes income to the extent that the cash received exceeds the amount paid into the trust by him.

Thus, while these trusts were not exempt from income tax, the Department ruled that the corporation nevertheless was entitled to a reasonable deduction for the amount which it paid into the trusts, and that the corporation's contributions were not taxable to the participating employees until received by them under the retirement annuity contracts, or in the distribution under the trusts.

PROFIT-SHARING RETIREMENT PLAN

This type of pension plan is similar to the self-administered pension trust, except that no fixed benefits are provided for in the plan. For that reason, it is not commonly considered a pension plan, yet it has the same effect. Rulings of the Commissioner of Internal Revenue restricting profit-sharing trusts from purchasing life insurance contracts on the lives of participants in the plan have been altered. However, the Commissioner warns that insurance may be considered "incidental" only where: "(1) The aggregate premiums for life insurance in the case of each participant are less than one-half of the aggregate of the contributions allocated to him at any particular time; and (2) the plan shall require the trustee to convert the entire value of the life insurance contract at or before retirement to provide periodic income so that no portion of such value may be used to continue life insurance protection beyond retirement of a participant."

The above ruling pertains only to those life insurance contracts where the participant has the right to designate the beneficiary; otherwise the Commissioner imposes no restrictions on life insurance as an investment of the trust when the trust owns the contract and all rights thereunder.

Under a profit-sharing plan, the company is permitted to contribute as much or as little into the fund as it wants to, regardless of the payroll restrictions of the approved pension plan. The amount thus set aside in the fund is not subject to tax, but since it is a form of deferred compensation it is taxable to the participating employee when his share is paid to him. Usually funds are held in the trust and the earnings are permitted to accumulate until the participant reaches retirement age, when his accumulated share is paid to him monthly, or in one lump, as he elects. Under the monthly payment plan, any funds remaining to his credit at the time of his death are paid to his estate.

General Motors' Management Retirement Plan

This plan, effective since 1918, covers salaried employees receiving $250 or more a month, consisting of the General Motors Employees Retirement Plan and the General Motors Service Pension Plan.

Each participant contributes 5 percent of his monthly base salary in excess of $250, and the corporation contributes the balance of the funds necessary to provide such benefits. The maximum period for which an employee may make contributions is 30 years. The annual future service benefit beginning at age 65 or after is equal to 30 percent of the employee's total contributions. The maximum retirement benefits are limited to $25,000 a year, including benefits for past service and benefits under the Service Pension Plan.

The Service Pension Plan provides retirement benefits of $1.50 a month for each year of service up to a maximum of 20 years. An employee is eligible to receive a service pension upon retirement at age 65 or after, provided that at his retirement date he has accrued benefits under the retirement plan, is receiving a base salary of $250 or more a month, and has received such a base salary for at least five years.

All employees eligible to participate in the retirement plan are retired at age 65 unless continued in service upon invitation of the corporation. The corporation may retire an employee under the plan at any time between ages 60 and 65, or an employee may retire under the plan between ages 60 and 65 under conditions mutually satisfactory to the corporation and the employee. In either of these events, any retirement benefits payable on retirement at age 65 to which the employee may be entitled on account of service rendered to the actual date of such retirement shall be payable immediately without reduction because of such earlier retirement. If an employee retires voluntarily between ages 60 and 65, he may elect to have his retirement income begin prior to age 65 on an actuarially reduced basis.

The Joslyn Plan

One much-publicized plan was developed by the Joslyn Manufacturing and Supply Company, Chicago. It has had a far-reaching effect on the employee relations of that business. The plan has been in operation for 45 years and provides for a retirement fund in the case of employees with the company 23 years or more. The plan works in the following manner:

Employees who have been with the company for three years must sign a profit-sharing contract with the company or leave its employ. Under the contract the employee agrees to pay into a trust fund 5 percent of his wages and the company agrees to pay into the same fund not less than 12½ percent of its earnings, but not more than four times the total employee contributions.

The fund is administered by a trustee who acts with the approval of an advisory committee of five, two of whom are officers of the company and three, including the trustee, are elected by the employees.

The funds contributed by employees and interest accumulated on these must be invested, under the terms of the contract, in investments approved by the State of Illinois for trust funds. The funds contributed by the company are invested at the discretion of the trustee and the advisory committee.

M. L. Joslyn, when head of the company, said that in practice the company paid into the fund the maximum amount permitted. This was equal to 20 percent of the payroll, so that the credit to each worker in the fund was 25 percent of his earnings, plus the earnings on the funds previously accumulated. For each $100 contributed by an employee the company paid into the fund to his credit $400.

When the plan was originally drawn, it was hoped that the earnings of the fund would approximate 6 percent a year. In practice they have averaged 9 percent.

The high rate of earnings was the result in part of the transfer of credits from workers leaving the employ of the company to the employees remaining. Under the terms of the plan a member of the fund is entitled to his full credit when he is 60 years old or disabled.

If he leaves the employ of the company or is discharged he gets all he put into the fund, with compound interest and half of the money contributed by the company to his credit. The other half of the money contributed by the company is credited to the accounts of remaining employees. Under no circumstances does the company get a return on any money contributed to the fund.

Sears Roebuck's Retirement Plan

Somewhat similar to the Joslyn plan is that of Sears Roebuck & Company, Chicago. There is, however, no important difference. The

Sears plan is tied up with the success of the business in that it depends upon adequate earnings over a period of years in order to make it work. It also affords a "hedge" against inflation, since it is based upon pooled ownership of Sears Roebuck common shares. The plan was inaugurated in 1916 by the late Julius Rosenwald. It retires men from active duty when they reach the slowdown age. If, for example, an employee participates in the plan 20 or more years, and has earned from $400 to $600 a month, he will leave an estate of $60,000 to $80,000. The plan works like this:

Participation on the part of employees is voluntary, but less than 5 percent refuse it. A worker is eligible to join the fund after being with the company three years. Five percent of his salary is deducted for the fund, and at the end of each year the company contributes 5 percent of the profits. The money thus accumulated is invested at the market price in Sears Roebuck stock, which proportionately is credited to the various employee accounts. This stock, being the same as that held by the regular stockholders, earns dividends which are in turn used to buy more stock, and so the snowball continues to grow larger as it rolls downhill. Those employees who resist the temptation to make withdrawals can build up comfortable estates.

Withdrawals are permitted with full participation in the benefits of the funds after 10 years of service, with one concession made to Cupid. The woman depositor with five years of continuous service who leaves to get married receives full benefits. The same is true of any employee, irrespective of the time served, who is discharged in good standing.

Others—those who wish to withdraw from the fund before the 10 years are up, or those dismissed for inefficiency or misdemeanor —are given the money which they have deposited, plus 5 percent interest compounded semiannually.

Jewel Tea Company's Retirement Plan

Jewel Tea Company employees with two years of service are eligible to participate in a plan whereby the employee contributes from $1 to $5 weekly (or 6 percent of salary if greater) to a retirement fund, to which the company will contribute 15 percent of its net yearly profits in excess of a sum based on common and preferred stock earnings.

A member may change his deposits (but not oftener than once each quarter) or discontinue them. His credits include all that he has paid in plus a percentage of other credits based on his length of service and of plan participation. Funds are held in trust until he retires or otherwise leaves the company. Upon retirement, which may come at the company's option any time after he reaches 50, or at his option after 57, he receives all his credits either at once or in installments over a period up to his average life expectancy at age insured. Full benefits are paid also in case of permanent disability or death.

A Bank's Pension Plan

The American National Bank and Trust Company, Chicago, has a pension plan to give pensions over and above social security benefits and assure satisfactory retirement incomes for employees.

All present employees between the ages of 21 and 65 are included, and new employees between 21 and 50.

While retirement age is 65, men may retire at 60 and women at 55, with proportionate pensions being paid.

Each employee pays into the pension trust 3 percent of his salary and, in addition, the bank contributes from its profits the amount calculated each year to meet the actuarial requirement under the pension trust. It is not obligated to pay more than 10 percent of its net earnings a year.

The pension payments will be figured so that the employee may receive at 65 (the retirement age) an income amounting to 2 percent of his salary for every year in which he participated in the plan, less the amount he will receive from his Federal social security benefits. A maximum total pension has been set amounting to 60 percent of the employee's average annual salary for his last 10 years of service.

If an employee leaves or is discharged, his contribution, plus interest, is returned to him. The rate of interest for the first three years is set at 3 percent. This feature makes the pension trust virtually an investment yielding 3 percent. In case of the death of an employee, his estate receives the total of his contributions, plus interest up to the current month.

In case of an employee's retirement because of ill health after 15 or more years of service, he may draw a pension (not to be over 60 percent of his average salary for the preceding 10 years) based on his and the bank's contributions.

Pay as You Go Plan

This type of plan—if you can dignify it by the name—is just slightly better than no plan at all. It usually calls for the company to set up a reserve on the books, made up from spasmodic entries when profits justify them. Usually such reserves are wholly inadequate to take care of the older employees in a company when they reach retirement age. But to the extent that some of a company's earnings are earmarked for pension purposes, the plan is that much better than nothing at all.

A plan where management "decides how to handle each case when it comes up" gives employees no assurance that they can look forward to more than their bare social security benefits when they retire. If that problem is on their minds, and they have skills or knowledge which competitors who do have pension plans need, it is reasonable to suppose that it will not be long before these valued employees leave for greener pastures.

The statement in an employees' manual that it is the policy of the company to take care of employees when they reach retirement age is not too convincing. The employees want to know: How? They feel they cannot live on the pension they will get from the government and will have to keep on working as long as they are physically able. That attitude hardly makes for harmonious employee relations. While it is true no pension plan can assure an employee of real security in his old age, as German workers well know, they do help to keep employees contented, and the better the plan the more contented the employee.

A Profit-Sharing Retirement Plan

An unusual combination profit-sharing and retirement plan used successfully by a manufacturing company on the West Coast has been found valuable in keeping employees on the payroll. The basic principles of the plan follow:

ELIGIBILITY

All employees who have been in the employ of the company for twelve (12) consecutive full calendar months shall automatically participate in the plan.

EMPLOYEE CONTRIBUTION

Each eligible employee shall contribute three percent (3%) of his salary or wage, such contribution to be made by payroll deduction.

COMPANY CONTRIBUTION

The company agrees to contribute for each fiscal year ending July 31st, a portion of the net operating earnings of the company in accordance with the following graduated scale after provision is made for all operating expenses and commissions, taxes, losses, reserves and a return of 6 percent on invested capital, as defined in the contract:

20 percent of the first $250,000.00 of such net operating earnings

30 percent of the next $250,000.00

35 percent of all in excess of $500,000.00

However, the amount contributed to the fund by the company shall not exceed 15 percent of the aggregate salaries and wages of the participating employees for the fiscal year in which such net operating earnings accrued to the corporation.

The company's contribution shall be made annually on or before the 60th day after the end of the fiscal year provided net operating earnings are available. In the event no such net operating earnings are available the company shall make no contribution for any subsequent period unless and until the deficiency has been made up and the company reimbursed.

RETIREMENT

An employee with a minimum of 40 years of service, may voluntarily retire from the services of the company at the age of fifty-five (55) years. The board of directors of the company may retire an employee at any time when it shall determine that he is unfit for further service by reason of mental or physical incapacity. When an employee reaches the age of sixty (60) years, his retirement shall become mandatory unless the company desires to continue the services of said employee and he shall consent thereto.

BENEFITS UPON RETIREMENT

Upon retirement the employee shall cease to be a member of the fund and his share of the fund as reflected on the books of said fund shall be invested for him as follows:

a. If married—in a joint and survivor annuity contract providing a monthly income for the life of the employee or his spouse, as long as either shall live.

b. If unmarried—in a monthly annuity contract payable for the life of said employee only.

c. Where, in neither of the above settlements, the employee's pro-rata share in the fund is, in the judgment of the trustee and advisory committee, sufficient to economically warrant the purchase of an annuity contract, such share may be invested or distributed in such manner or form as in their opinion will best carry out and accomplish the underlying purpose of the fund. They shall have the same discretion in other unusual or exceptional circumstances.

DEATH BEFORE RETIREMENT

An employee may designate a beneficiary, and may, from time to time, change such beneficiary.

In the event of the death of the employee before retirement, his full interest in the fund as reflected on the books of the fund will be used to purchase a monthly annuity contract for the benefit of the beneficiary, or may be invested and distributed in such other manner or form as determined by the trustee and advisory committee.

A Los Angeles company has an unusually complete employee security program of which the profit-sharing plan is but one part. In addition, the company has set up an insurance plan, a pension plan, a savings plan, and a relief and loan plan.

The funds accumulate in a trust account and are payable only upon the employee's retirement or if he should leave the company after 10 annual amounts have been credited to his account. Certain percentages of the funds accumulated in his name may be withdrawn should he sever his connections with the company before the 10 annual amounts have been credited.

Upon retirement, the employee has a choice of withdrawing his funds in cash, having them paid to him in annual installments not to exceed 11 in number, or the funds may be invested in an annuity.

There was a time when most companies favored the contributory type of pension trust. Either the employer "matched" the money paid into the trust by the employee, or set up the trust so that an employee who elected to participate in the plan had to make regular payments to the fund. Many insurance pension plans had that requirement.

However, this type of plan is not so popular as it was. Profit-sharing trusts now being set up are usually financed wholly by the employer. Experience with contributory plans has been unfavorable, due to the complication of administering a trust in which employees have a vested interest and are able to draw out what they put into the fund in a lump sum upon leaving the company. Employees sometimes are tempted to quit, if they think they need money, just to draw out their equities.

Chapter 23

INSURANCE PROGRAMS

G ROUP health insurance payments cover a good many of the
medical bills paid by United States families, but many companies are still too small to take out group policies. This difficulty is
being solved in some cases by grouping together the employees of
an entire industry, or a section of it. In New York, for example,
some 7,000 members of the painters' union are covered by group
policies financed by 600 painting contractors. The American Trucking Associations, Inc., working with Travelers Insurance Company,
has set up an industrywide insurance program for its members. The
employees of many small groceries are insured through a group
plan administered by Super Market Institute on a nationwide basis.

These programs usually include a nominal amount of life insurance and very often provide for payment of a weekly sum in the
event of prolonged illness. The cost of prolonged hospitalization can
take a large part of a year's pay, and that possibility weighs heavily
on the serious-minded employee. To relieve their employees of this
worry and the company of the responsibility of having to aid the
employee whose health fails, Eastman Kodak Company and others
have established complete health insurance programs.

"Broadly speaking," said an Eastman official, "we feel that people
do their work more effectively when they are relieved of worry and
anxiety. Medical care may be delayed if they haven't the money to
pay for it. But with prompt medical care they will recover more
quickly, lose less time."

Many employers already have programs that call for periodic
medical examinations, and over the past few years much has been
accomplished in the way of voluntary insurance plans, paid for by
the company alone or with the help of employees. In 1939, only a
handful of Americans in industry were covered by medical insurance; now over 40 million are protected. But many companies still
think of health insurance plans as merely fringe benefits and neces-

sary evils. Actually, experience proves they are one of the best investments in employee relations an employer can make.

The Internal Revenue Act of 1954 put the stamp of Government approval on employee accident and health plans. It allows employers to deduct cost of such a program from taxable income, whether it is insured or self-financed. Employees benefiting from the program also can escape tax, even on benefits running as high as $100 a week, when they are paid in lieu of compensation.

This change in the tax law has induced many employers to look more closely at the benefits of an accident and health plan, with sick pay of fixed amounts, for hourly rated employees. Noting the trend, alert unions have been quick to include accident and health protection among fringe benefits for negotiation. To round out the picture, insurance companies which specialize in underwriting industrial groups have stepped up their sales efforts. As a result, providing this type of protection is rapidly becoming standard practice.

Company Administered Insurance

Since the type of protection provided by industrial group insurance is usually for the term of a worker's employment with the company, some large employers operate their own insurance pool rather than pay an insurance company to administer the plan. They set aside reserves for this purpose, and make periodic payments corresponding to the premiums they would pay a stock insurance company. The entire cost of company-administered insurance is borne by the employer as a rule, although some plans, such as that of Swift & Company, are partly employee financed. While employers who administer their own insurance programs report paper savings, such estimates seldom consider the time executives and clerks spend on administrative details.

Another objection to company administered plans, even when the company picks up the tab, is the controversy which arises in settling claims. Employees feel that they have a right to expect certain benefits from the plan and feel abused if they do not get treatment as good as or better than some other employees. These situations cause bad employee relations. The independent underwriter, such as a well-organized company with agents in your community, is prepared to deal with these situations and is in a position to settle grievances without involving the employer. Most employers feel that while it may cost less to administer a group insurance program than to turn the job over to an outside insurance company, the benefits of the latter procedure far outweigh the savings of the former.

Experience With Group Insurance

Experience with industrial group insurance on the whole has been good. It rounds out the compensation plan by providing security which is greatly appreciated by the best employees—that is, those who are forward-looking and stable. Its pay-envelope value, therefore, is often greater than what the insurance costs the company. It tends to cut down turnover. Just as a union member hesitates a long time before giving up his union card, if by so doing he will lose the protection of his union insurance, so an employee hesitates to quit his job, even for slightly higher pay, if in so doing he cuts off his group insurance protection, or must lay out a considerable sum of money to convert his group policy into regular insurance. The longer an employee remains with the company the more value he attaches to these insurance benefits. This feature alone is considered well worthwhile by most companies, and is one of the reasons employers are willing to absorb a growing percentage of the premium cost.

Aside from the balance sheet value of company participation in employee insurance plans, employers today have a growing sense of responsibility for their employees' welfare. The one-time idea that an employer's obligation began and ended with the pay envelope has now disappeared. Rare indeed is the employer who does not recognize that not only has he an obligation to society, but that the business which he heads is held by him in trust for his *jobholders* as well as his stockholders. The public today judges a company by its employee relations, fully as much as by the dividends paid to stockholders. Indeed, the two phases of management are closely related. Since the very foundation of enduring employee-employer relations depends upon job security, an employment policy which protects the workers in the event of layoffs, sickness, or death has a very definite appeal, not wholly covered by wages.

Employees' Insurance Benefit Associations

In order to secure maximum acceptance for group insurance plans, some companies find it desirable to set up an employees' organization for that purpose. This plan overcomes the feeling some employees hold that the company is making a "commission" on the insurance. This is especially true where the entire cost of the insurance is levied against the employee and the company contributes nothing, except its buying power. However, even where the company assumes a part of the cost, it is often good strategy to let the employees supervise the collection and payment of the premiums.

The Employees' Mutual Benefit Association, in operation at the Reliance Manufacturing Company, is managed by a committee selected by the employees. This has proved to be an important factor in stimulating interest in group insurance, and, at the same time, giving each member the opportunity to voice any ideas or suggestions that might be of value to the association.

Members of the organization pay a nominal fee from their salaries for insurance. The company takes upon itself an expense twice the sum of all the fees put together to keep the organization in existence.

The hospitalization plan is operated to provide for any necessary surgical operations and countless phases of hospitalization; it even goes so far as to arrange for eye tests for those who need them, and to provide glasses for persons with faulty eyesight.

The office force, since it is the administrative body, keeps the Employees' Mutual Benefit Association in a sound financial condition.

Membership in the association is not compulsory, and the only requirement for entrance is a service record of six months or more. The fact that membership is voluntary did not split the employees, for every office worker at Reliance readily grasped the opportunity to obtain this protection. Adoption of this hospitalization plan has done a great deal to promote a more integrated and secure group of workers.

Because the association is administered by the employees themselves, the dominance of executive authority is avoided. The individual employee feels free to complain instead of restraining himself perhaps in the fear of offending an executive or an officer of the company.

Types of Group Insurance Policies

There are three general types of insurance which are covered under a group insurance plan. These are, aside from hospitalization insurance:

1. **Life, Total and Permanent Disability Insurance.** To provide income for an employee's dependents in the event of death; or to provide income for an employee who becomes totally and permanently disabled.

2. **Accidental Death and Dismemberment Insurance.** To provide an additional income for an employee's dependents in the event the death is accidental; or to provide benefits for an employee who is dismembered as a result of an accident.

3. **Sickness and Accident Insurance.** To provide an income for an employee who, as a result of a nonoccupational injury or nonoccupational sickness, is unable to work.

All of these benefits are available to employees at low cost, part of the cost usually being borne by the employer.

Under these group plans no medical examination is required, a feature which has a strong appeal to the older men in an organization who might be unable to qualify for regular policies. However, in order to take advantage of these lower group rates, insurance companies require that a stated percentage of all the employees (usually 75 percent) apply for the insurance. By the elimination of certain departments this requirement is not as difficult as it might seem. The cost to the company is not great, and, under some plans we have examined, whatever outlay may be required in getting the plan started may be recovered subsequently if the underwriting company pays dividends.

Benefits in Case of Disability

Group policies with reliable underwriting companies usually provide that in the event the employee becomes disabled and can no longer work, he will be compensated. Under Swift & Company's Employes Benefit Association plan, members of the association are eligible for low-cost group life insurance with variable death benefits. The annual rate of contribution for those under age 36 is $7.80 per $1,000 of insurance. Those over age 45 pay $15.60 per $1,000 of insurance. These are nonmedical policies, but disability is covered in the Swift plan as follows:

Full life insurance protection will be continued for a year during absences from work without pay on account of sickness or injury after age 45, whether or not the member continues contributions. If the member wishes, he may continue to increase his paid-up insurance by making contributions while absent.

Full life insurance protection will be continued for a year during absences from work on account of sickness or injury before age 45, if the member continues contributions.

If a disabled member receives salary payments or E. B. A. benefits, contributions will be deducted from such salary or benefits.

At the end of a year's absence due to sickness or injury, all insurance will terminate, except for paid-up insurance already purchased in the case of members over age 45. The member will then be entitled to the rights described under "Termination of Employment."

If, however, the member while insured and under age 60 becomes totally disabled and is thereby prevented from engaging in any occupation for compensation or profit, full life insurance protection will remain in force as long as he remains so disabled without further contributions on his part, provided the required proofs of disability are furnished. The first proof must be filed with the insurance company within 3 months after total disability has lasted 9 months. Subsequent proofs of disability must be furnished each year thereafter. If a disabled member over age 45 surrenders his paid-up insurance for the cash value, the amount of insurance continued under this provision will be the excess of the amount for which he was insured when disability commenced over the amount of paid-up insurance surrendered.

Swift & Company, like many other employers, offers (in addition to its employee benefit program) group privileges in connection with the Blue Cross and Blue Shield plans under a contract with Health Service, Inc., a wholly owned affiliate. Any employee, except casual and part-time workers, who has been in the employ of the company continuously for six months or more is eligible for this hospitalization insurance. Eligibility continues for 30 days after an employee becomes absent due to sickness or accident. The plan pays up to $10 for the first day and $3 a day for the next 60 days for each hospital admission. Five thousand dollars in extra benefits is paid in polio cases. Allowances for surgery are determined from a published schedule which is changed from time to time.

Benefits to Employees

When the company pays all the premium there is no conversion privilege as a rule. If an employee quits, his insurance automatically lapses. But where the employee pays the bulk of the premium, through a payroll deduction, he has the right to convert his group policy without medical examination into any of the regular policies customarily issued by the company (term insurance excepted) at the rate applicable to the employee. This depends upon age and the class of risk if he converts to industrial insurance.

The operation of such a plan, from the standpoint of benefit to the participating employee, is shown in the following schedules taken from the plan adopted some time back by the Caterpillar Tractor Company plant in Peoria, Illinois, and it is based upon the contract that company has with the Metropolitan Life Insurance Company of New York.

SCHEDULE OF BENEFITS—BASIC PLAN

LIFE INSURANCE

After 30 days' employment, the Caterpillar worker is automatically covered by a group life insurance policy in the amount of 200 percent of his annual base salary. There is no employee contribution. Additional insurance coverage is available to the employee in an amount up to 200 percent of base salary for which the employee's contribution is 1 percent of pay.

ACCIDENT INSURANCE

Insurance coverage for accidental death is provided on a 24-hour basis in an amount equal to 100 percent of annual base salary with no employee contribution. Accidental dismemberment coverage is provided for 100 percent of the annual base salary for the loss of two body members, and 50 percent of annual base salary for the loss of one member. This insurance is provided after 30 days' employment with no employee contribution.

From the first day of employment, the Caterpillar worker is covered by supplemental accidental death benefits which supplement state workmen's compensation death benefits payable so that the total is two times annual base salary. Coverage exists only while the employee is at work, while traveling for the company, or while in foreign service.

DISABILITY INCOME BENEFITS

Caterpillar employees disabled at work can count on continuation of 100 percent of their salary for the first six months of disability from the first day of employment. After 30 days of employment, disabled workers are eligible for monthly disability benefits of 50 percent of base salary until age 65, when pension benefits begin. There are no employee contributions to this coverage.

MEDICAL BENEFITS FOR EMPLOYEES AND DEPENDENTS

After 30 days' employment, Caterpillar medical benefits include 100 percent of hospital charges for room and board in a semiprivate room. For a private room, the plan pays the greater of (1) 80 percent of charges (maximum payment of $24 per day) or (2) the most common semiprivate room rate. The plan is not limited to any maximum number of days. Charges for other hospital services and supplies are paid 100 percent; also 100 percent of operating surgeon's fees and charges for general anesthetics and administration.

For the following services, 80 percent of charges are paid by Caterpillar group insurance: doctor's visits in the hospital, emergency first aid, laboratory expenses and diagnostic X-ray, and miscellaneous medical expenses such as doctor's home and office calls, medicines, registered nurse services, local ambulance service, etc., which exceed $80 per person in one calendar year.

Maximum benefits for the employee and each covered dependent are $10,000 per year and $30,000 per Caterpillar employment career.

Eligible dependents are an employee's spouse and an employee's unmarried children under 25 years of age provided they are not employed full time, not in the armed forces, and are principally dependent upon the employee for support.

Pregnancy benefits are paid in the same manner as for other disabilities if the pregnancy was not existent on the effective date of coverage.

EMPLOYEES' INVESTMENT PLAN

At age 21 and after one year of service, employees are permitted to purchase Caterpillar stock. Monthly deductions from salary are at the rate of from 2 to 6 percent of gross pay, as the employee chooses, and the company contributes 50 percent of the employee deductions. Stock is held in the employee's name by a trustee, and dividends are automatically reinvested in the plan.

RETIREMENT INCOME PLAN

The Caterpillar pension plan is based on a normal retirement age of 65, and retirement is automatic at age 66. The annual pension at age 65 is the greater of (1) one percent of the first $4,800 of annual salary, plus 2 percent of the excess of each year's earnings over $4,800 up to age 65, or (2) 1½ percent of the average annual earnings for the final 10 years, times years of service since age 30, less Social Security benefits. Early retirement is optional after age 55 with at least 15 years of service.

Group Hospitalization Insurance

Protection for employees in the event of an illness which requires hospitalization and surgical care is offered by many insurance companies, both stock and mutual, and by companies which specialize in that service alone. Before taking on a plan, the contract should be carefully checked to determine the kind of benefits which accrue to the employee and the conditions under which benefits will be paid or withheld. The plan most favored is where employees pay a fixed amount each month, and the balance of the net cost (which may vary) is paid by the company. If the policy is taken out with an insurance company, the benefits are usually paid in cash to the policyholder who makes his own arrangements with the hospital or surgeon. Companies specializing in hospital care usually have special arrangements with local hospitals to handle their cases, and pay the hospital and doctor direct, up to the amount of the contract obligation. Unfortunately, the cost of these specialized insurance policies has increased rapidly.

In a Dartnell survey covering the subject of life and health insurance for employees, it was found that nearly 90 percent of responding companies have some kind of hospital plan for clerical employees. Blue Cross accounts for 30 percent of the enrollment, with the company paying part of the insurance and the employee paying the other part. The First National Bank of Oregon (Portland), has a policy whereby all of the first $200 of expense in the hospital and 80 percent thereafter is paid by the bank. F. A. Riler, a vice-president of the bank, reports that surgical benefits are generally covered completely, though "we do not pay for doctor's office calls."

W. S. Corrie, former treasurer of National Gypsum Co., Buffalo, New York, reports a company plan whereby employees are allowed $18 per day for hospitalization, $600 surgical, and $270 for extras. The employee's entire family is covered.

At The Sorg Paper Company, Middletown, Ohio, the company pays all costs of hospitalization insurance. American Standard's Controls Division has a 50-50 payment system for hospitalization.

Commenting on the trend toward greater hospital and medical benefits for employees, one respondent, vice-president of a large midwestern utility, stated:

Since 1945 we have seen tremendous increases in employee benefits. Clerical workers have kept up well with employees who are unionized. It is our opinion that hospital and medical insurance has reached the point where it is almost a sure thing for any employee no matter where he happens to work. I further predict that by 1967 we will see even more benefits of this nature. We enroll the employee's entire family in the program and I understand this is a growing practice.

The important thing for management is to be sure employees realize the cost and importance of these benefits. The American worker is the most secure employee in the world and will continue to be so. We believe it is management's responsibility not only to provide these benefits but to make workers aware of their worth.

Insurance as a Reward for Service

Some employers use group insurance as a means of attaining certain objectives in employee relations. Aldens, Inc., has a plan whereby salaried employees' premiums will be automatically reduced on their 10th, 15th and 20th anniversaries with the company.

After six months of service, all employees are covered by $2,000 to $5,000 worth of life insurance without cost. Salaried employees may take additional insurance, with cost to the employee based on length of service.

"Catastrophe" Plans

Since it is in the major medical expenses that health insurance really counts—and where it now most often fails to pay the bill—this is the area of interest for many companies. Led by General Electric, many hundreds of employers have installed "major medical" or "catastrophe" plans to cover such diseases as cancer, tuberculosis, and other long illnesses. These plans are usually integrated with regular group medical insurance, which pays the first part of the bill. The employee pays the next $100 to $600, in somewhat the same way as he would pay for minor auto damage under a deductible policy. Anything over that (up to as much as $10,000) is paid by the insurance company. Premiums need not be prohibitive under such deductible schemes. At Sears Roebuck, departments are excluded from the major medical plan to keep costs down, and the premium runs to only 40 cents a month.

General Foods' Accident Plan

Today, many companies provide travel accident insurance for employees. General Foods recently updated this insurance to include personal coverage for employees who wish to pay a small premium and receive additional nonbusiness benefits.

Part I—Business Travel Coverage provides for an insurance payment in the event of dismemberment, loss of sight, or death within the 100 days following an accident which occurs at any time of the day or night while the insured employee is traveling (with certain exclusions) anywhere in the world, on the business of General Foods, or its designated subsidiaries. Personal travel which interrupts the continuity of any one itinerary of such business travel is considered business travel. There is no cost for this coverage.

Part II—Personal Coverage provides insurance for accidental death or dismemberment occurring at any time, at any place, and whether during business or nonbusiness hours (with certain exclusions).

Part I covers each regular employee as defined or described in the Personnel Administration Code of General Foods Corporation who has completed any probational period in effect at his unit. Part II coverage is extended to those individuals who are paid from a GF payroll office in the United States, its territories or possessions, or Canada, and who make application and pay the required premium. Cost is 70 cents per year per $1,000 of insurance with the total amount limited to the company's Schedule of Insurance.

The Schedule of Insurance has been broken into 29 separate earnings classes ranging from less than $1,200 to $100,000 and over. The amount of insurance ranges from $2,000 to $200,000 according to the class.

Payment under Part I is made under two separate circumstances. For death or loss of two members, sight of two eyes, or a combination of these, the payment for an accident other than in an aircraft is the amount of insurance for the employee's earnings class. In an aircraft accident the payment is the amount of insurance for the employee's earnings class with a minimum payment of $100,000 and a maximum of $200,000. The plan pays one-half for the loss of one member or the sight of one eye in an accident with a $50,000 minimum in an aircraft accident.

Payment under Part II is the same under all circumstances. The insurance amount is based on the employee's earnings class. Under no circumstances is payment made under both parts of the plan for the same accident.

Business Travel Coverage does not provide protection against certain hazards to which the insured employee may be exposed:

1. While engaged in commutation travel defined as transportation between his regular place of residence and any office, plant, building, boat or any other premises owned, rented, leased, chartered or operated in whole or in part by General Foods, except any such transportation the entire cost of which is borne by or chargeable to the employer, or

2. While in, on, boarding or alighting from an aircraft which at the time of the accident is (a) owned by the employee or operated by any member of his household, (b) operated by him, except an aircraft owned, rented, chartered, leased or borrowed by General Foods, or (c) used for crop dusting, sky writing or other listed types of flying.

3. While on scheduled vacation, layoff, excused or nonexcused absence, or in the armed forces of any country.

4. While on leave of absence except a medical leave that directly interrupts travel on the business of General Foods.

5. By intentionally self-inflicted injuries, suicide or any attempt.

6. By war or any act of war.

Part II of the coverage plan protects the employee while commuting, while on scheduled vacation, layoff or excused or nonexcused absences except while on military leave of absence or in the armed forces.

Personal Coverage also extends to a leave of absence but does not give coverage for suicide or war.

Part I terminates at the cessation of active employment. Part II terminates the last day of the quarter for which the premium has been paid. An insured employee may withdraw from Part II at any time, but he may not rejoin for one year after that termination date. Nonpayment of premium in advance automatically terminates coverage.

The insurance company underwriting the plan is Indemnity Insurance Company of North America, the home office of which is located at No. 1600 Arch Street, Philadelphia, Pa. The General Foods Insurance Division at the general offices is organized to handle all notices and claims direct with the insurance company, and the normal procedure is to have notice of any accident involving a possible claim under the plan transmitted through the personnel representative of the employee to the insurance division.

Tax Aspects of Health and Accident Insurance

Changes in the 1954 Revenue Code have given health and accident insurance policies a privileged status. Formerly, premiums paid by the company were taxable to the employee unless policies were written under group plans. Now company contributions to health and accident plans are not taxable to the employees that benefit from them. A Senate Finance Committee report says that, as far as the employee is concerned, exclusion from his gross income "is applicable regardless of whether the employer's plan covers one employee or a group of employees. Therefore, the premium paid by an employer on an individual policy of accident and health insurance for an employee will not be includible in gross income."

Company contributions, then, are excluded from the employee's gross income and constitute an "ordinary and necessary" business deduction. The employee's contribution, if he makes any, is deductible as a medical expense.

How about the taxability of the proceeds if the employee collects on his policy? The law says they are not taxable either to him or to the company except in whatever amounts are attributable to, but not more than, the deduction allowed as a medical expense in a prior year. Thus, if the medical expense and reimbursement took place in the same taxable year it is a simple matter of applying the reimbursement against the expenditure and figuring whatever is left over as a deduction.

Split-Dollar Insurance

Split-dollar insurance plans are most effectively applied to the rising young employee or executive, possibly between the ages of 30 and 45, whom management especially wants to favor. The company takes out a policy on his life, usually in $10,000 or $20,000 amounts, but sometimes as high as $100,000. The employee pays the full first-year premium himself because the policy has no cash value. After that, management takes the larger share, paying that part of the premium that is equal to the increase in cash value over the year. Once the cash value increase equals, or is more than, the premium or net premium (gross premium less dividends), the company pays all. This usually happens in about seven years.

The first-year payment can be a staggering one, especially if the face amount of his policy is high. Common practice is for the company to lend the employee the money, repayable over a period of a few years. After the first year, the employee's portion of the obligation can be handled easily enough by payroll deductions.

In the split-dollar plan, two beneficiaries are named. The company is beneficiary to the extent of the cash surrender value of the policy, the employee's beneficiary receives the balance. The company will always get back what it has put into the policy, while the employee's family gets the difference between cash value at the time of his death and the full amount of the policy. If the employee should die while the policy is young, his family stands to get more than if the policy ran its course.

Advantages of Split-Dollar Plans

Both employer and employee come out ahead. This is the point that insurance salesmen are hammering away at and why there is such fast-growing interest in split-dollar plans.

The employer loses nothing in the transaction except the use of his capital. It is true that he could invest and draw interest on the money he puts into split-dollar premiums, and in that sense he has a theoretical loss. There might be cases, too, where companies would be unwilling to make long-range commitments that could be embarrassing when more working capital is needed. But, if management is genuinely interested in showing its key employees and its "comers" what it thinks of them, if it wants to throw more chains around them to bind them fast to the company, a split-dollar life insurance plan can help to do the job, only at the cost of the interest lost by not investing the money elsewhere. Such companies look upon the split-dollar plan as another benefit that can help to keep a reservoir of junior executives to be trained for bigger things.

Chapter 24

EMPLOYEE HEALTH

I N a study of working conditions in 165 offices, Dartnell has found that the trend toward more employee benefits carries into the area of sick leave practices.

According to a vice-president of Jack & Heintz, a division of Siegler Corp.: "Pay for sick leave—or, particularly, accumulating sick leave days as is common in civil service—is a form of guaranteed annual wage and a costly fringe benefit. How far these items are going is hard to say but they introduce two principal evils: (1) Cost of fringe benefits, and (2) they are the kind of benefits which should be reserved for the office worker, otherwise we have no differentials, no compelling advantages to white-collar positions."

Trends in office payments seem to be moving from a rigid policy to one of deciding each case on its merits. The director of personnel relations for Nordberg Manufacturing Company explains his company's flexible policy this way:

"As criteria, we take into consideration length of service, previous attendance record, importance of position, and performance as to whether the employee is compensated for time. These criteria are used in determining how much and how long an employee will be compensated during sick leave. This applies to the salaried and office groups only."

Northrup, King & Co. operates on a "general policy" basis for the office as well as the plant. It is called a "proper attendance" plan, wherein no employee need lose pay for absences beyond his control. The idea is that sick pay is to protect employees against serious illnesses.

Out of 154 companies reporting sick leave plans, Dartnell found that 128 allow sick leave pay immediately after an office employee reports ill, four withhold the first day's pay, two wait three days, six do not pay for the first week of absence, six have a seniority schedule, and eight firms have no policy at all. The overwhelming majority, then, are liberal in this respect.

With only two exceptions, office employees are allowed full pay for sick time—for at least a portion of the time off. The exception is a self-insured plan which allows $100 a month up to a maximum of three months after three years' employment. A number of companies will continue paying an employee's salary at a reduced rate for a certain period of time. For instance, Ford Motor Company pays office workers $100 base salary plus cost of living for the first 21 days, 50 percent for the next 42 days. The Ford policy: "Leaves with pay are provided by the company primarily to afford salaried (office) employees additional security against sudden reduction in earnings due to sickness or other personal reasons, and employees are not to be considered as having an earned or vested right in them."

As to the effectiveness of sick leave policies, most companies seem well satisfied with present practices. These are a few of the many interesting comments representative company officials have made to us on the subject:

"In my opinion, a good percentage of employees abuse the sick leave privilege." (Food processor.)

"We have no sick leave policy, as such. We do have health and accident insurance to cover our office employees." (Metal products manufacturing firm.)

"Biggest concern at the moment is control of sick pay for office female help on salary basis. If absent more than five days, supervisor discusses trend. If more than six or seven days, office manager discusses and future time off is put on a 'no pay' basis. This tends to decrease the 'status' of 'salary workers.' We are considering changing nonexempt (employees) to time and hourly basis for better control." (Paint manufacturing firm.)

"We believe, to be truly workable, a sick leave policy for office personnel should be very flexible since no set of circumstances is the same as another. This also helps management control the employee who is trying to 'beat the system.'" (Oil company.)

Sick Leaves and Pension Plans

Tying sick leaves in with the pension plan is a practice followed by many companies. An Iowa insurance company in its most recent case, for example, allowed six months' sick leave credit to one of its employees who had been with the company for 20 years. The pension plan picked up where the sick leave left off, providing a monthly income for life under total and permanent disability.

A Georgia textiles manufacturer had something like that in mind when he said: "In the past our (sick leave) program has been informal, with employees generally remaining on the payroll during periods of illness. At the moment, we are considering formalizing our policies in this area, tying them in with our pension plan. Our pension plan is an individual policy contract with a waiver of premium provision in the event of permanent and total disability. Any employee qualifying under the permanent and total disability provisions of the pension plan would be retired at 40 percent of salary under the plan being considered. This plan would pay the cost of retirement until normal retirement age 65, at which time the pension benefits would take over—likewise 40 percent of salary. This plan would dovetail with the existing pension plan since the waiver of

---

ABSENCES

General Policy:

Generally speaking, any absence from work is without pay and subject to salary deduction or charge against vacation leave. However, to protect your earnings in the event you are absent because of personal illness or injury, serious illness in the immediate family, an acute emergency, or an important personal matter that cannot be handled outside of working hours, the company allows you to accrue sick leave credits on the basis of one-half day for each month of service.

Accruals are made and considered earned on the fifteenth of each month commencing with the first month following the month of your employment. *Sick leave is not to be regarded as time off to which you are entitled.* This policy is only to provide for employees who are actually ill or faced with serious emergency. An employee with a real sense of fair play should have no great difficulty in deciding when to make use of this privilege.

Accrued sick leave not used in one calendar year may be carried over to the next. The granting of sick leave is always at the discretion of your department manager and the personnel manager, who will satisfy themselves that the reasons are bona fide. Habitual absenteeism, unsubstantiated illness, poor punctuality record, and general unreliability will be deemed justifiable reasons for withholding sick leave. If it is determined that sick leave should not be granted, a salary deduction will be made or earned vacation leave will be charged.

The general sick leave policy of Eastern Mortgage Service Co., as stated in the employee handbook "Welcome."

premium provision in the pension plan would have kept benefits intact without additional cost to the company."

Sick Pay Formulas

One of the more popular considerations in setting up sick leave formulas is length of service. Many times it is the number of years worked that has a direct bearing on the number of days, weeks, or months during which full pay is extended. Sometimes a month's employment is worth a day of sick leave, sometimes it takes a year of service to entitle the employee to a week or month at full salary. These are some of the formulas we have found companies to be using:

Full pay for six months.

One year at full pay.

Three months at full pay, three to six months at half pay.

First 13 weeks at full salary, next 13 weeks at three-quarters salary, last 26 weeks at half salary.

One day for each full month of service, with a maximum of 13 weeks at full pay, next 13 weeks at half pay.

One month for each year at full pay.

One week for each year of service; can be extended at the discretion of the directors.

Full pay for three months, half pay for the next three months, with special consideration where the employee needs more time.

Continuation of pay is at the discretion of the president. We have never found it feasible to set up a rigid policy on sick pay.

After six months' employment, the first four weeks are at full pay, the next 16 weeks carry a minimum rate of $50 a week. This amount can be raised at the discretion of management.

Each employee draws $60 a week for 17 weeks under insurance program, with regular salary continuing from four weeks to a year depending on position and length of service.

Length of sick leaves are on a sliding scale from three weeks for three years of service to a maximum of 16 weeks for 10 years of service; special cases calling for exception to the 16-week rule are referred to the board of directors.

Top executives have four months' leave at full pay by contract; other employees' leaves, and extensions of top executives' leaves, decided on basis of length of service and position.

After six months' employment, full pay for 26 weeks for any single illness or in any one calendar year.

Full pay to a maximum of one year after 15 years of service.

Maximum of six weeks a year allowed for full pay; additional time allowed as the individual circumstances and estimated period of convalescence requires.

Sick leave is geared strictly to length of service without regard to rank of the affected employee. The maximum amount of time allowed at full pay is nine months. After that, half pay prevails indefinitely.

Sick leave time accumulates at a rate of one day each 30 days. A careful accounting is kept, and an employee who has not accumulated enough time may "borrow" against future earnings. If the employee is still with us at the end of five years, any "debt" he may have is forgiven.

HANDLING THE EXPECTANT MOTHER PROBLEM

Admittedly, expectant mothers have many problems. But they are increased, both for the mother-to-be and the employer, when she is an employee. What are office policies with regard to pregnancy among employees? Do most companies have a set and established policy governing such situations? What about maternity leaves of absence? To get answers to these questions and to review a comparable group of office managements' ways of handling this phase of personnel administration, Dartnell's editors asked nearly 150 compa-

---

ACCIDENT AND SICKNESS

1. The basic benefit of one day per month (maximum of twelve days per year) paid sick leave, as is now in effect, will be extended to cover all employees after one full month's service.

2. Credit for unused time for not less than one full day will accumulate as sick time credit for each employee.

3. With the completion of three full calendar-years' service, an employee may have the option of applying one-fourth of the accumulated sick leave time to his/her credit toward his/her regular vacation period.

4. Not more than five days of such additional vacation could be taken in any one year.

5. The balance of an employee's sick leave credit will remain intact to be used for either:

   a. Supplemental sick leave purposes, or

   b. To be used as a basis for retirement benefits upon reaching the age of 65.

Leading National Advertisers, Inc., sick leave policy as explained to employees. Unused sick leave time, under some circumstances, may be added to vacation time.

nies to state their views and experiences. The results of this survey follow:

Only slightly more than half (51 percent) of the responding companies have a set procedure for handling pregnancy among employees. A number of executives who reply negatively feel the company should consider a policy. The president of an insurance company says, "We think we must become more formal in our policies." He also expresses interest in the outcome of this survey.

How Long Expectant Mothers May Work

Among companies having an established policy in the matter of pregnancy among employees, the majority allow the worker to stay on the job until such a time as the pregnancy is physically apparent— provided she is in good health, regular in attendance, and able to do her work.

One respondent observes, "A lot depends upon the location of the work, regularity in attendance, appearance, and availability of replacement; these things really determine how long an expectant mother may work." Another office executive says, "We leave it to the discretion of her doctor, but after pregnancy is physically apparent she cannot work at a job where she meets the public." Following is a tabulation of replies:

Until condition is physically apparent, provided she is in good health, etc.	20 percent
8 months	3 percent
6 to 7 months	4 percent
6 months	17 percent
5 to 6 months	5 percent
5 months	16 percent
4½ months	2 percent
4 months	5 percent
At discretion of physician	5 percent
As long as she wishes	5 percent
Determined individually	1 percent

The personnel director of an insurance company in the Midwest says, "Employees upon reaching the fifth month of pregnancy are terminated. This is enforced generally throughout our office. Exceptions have (very rarely) been made in instances where a real hardship would be worked on the department, due to replacement difficulties—provided the employee's physical condition will allow her to work beyond the fifth month."

Termination Notices

Thirty-one percent of the contributing companies do not have definite policies covering termination notices for pregnancy. Another 22 percent set the termination date "as soon as the pregnancy is noted or reported." The industrial nurse-personnel assistant for Shampaine Industries, St. Louis, says, "As soon as the company is notified of the condition, written permission is obtained from a doctor allowing the employee to work until the beginning of the fifth month; date of termination or leave of absence is then set." Another St. Louis company leaves the termination date solely up to the employee.

Ten percent of the surveyed concerns give employees the regular two weeks' notice; 5 percent—3 months' notice; 5 percent handle termination dates on an individual basis; 1 percent—6 weeks' notice; 1 percent—2 months' notice; and the balance offer other explanations of policy. Typical of these are the following excerpts:

"Employee must submit written resignation stating reason as pregnancy. This must be done at least two weeks before the mutual date of separation has been agreed upon."

"Medical counsel at time of pregnancy is advised, with 30-day notice prior to a termination or leave of absence."

Maternity Leaves

Only 8 percent of the responding companies have a definite, written policy covering maternity leaves of absence. Of this group, one company permits leaves of absence only for employees who have been with the company five years or more.

While the great majority of offices have no written policy in the matter of maternity leaves, all office managers should make sure that practices conform with requirements of Title VII of the Civil Rights Act, which forbids sex discrimination.

The Dennison Manufacturing Company, Framingham, Massachusetts, grants a certificate of absence to permanent employees for a maximum period of six months. Though this certificate does not guarantee any job on returning to work within the period specified, every attempt is made to place the employee on a job equal to the one she held at the time of leaving. The employee serves the regular probationary period, after which, if still on the payroll, she is treated as though there had been no break in service.

Insurance and Hospitalization

Approximately 85 percent of the surveyed organizations provide some type of hospital insurance for employees. In many instances, the expectant mother must be covered by the insurance from 9 to 12 months prior to delivery before she can take advantage of the benefits offered, depending, of course, on the type of policy she holds.

Among the plans reported, most common is Blue Cross-Blue Shield. Others include Travelers Insurance Company's plan, Metropolitan Life Insurance Company, Prudential, Bankers Life and Casualty, Mutual Life Assurance Company, Hawkeye Security Insurance Company, and Industrial Insurance Company. Benefits of these plans vary. For instance, in one company's plan, the insurance pays a flat rate of $75 for the doctor attending the expectant mother, and $125 allowance for hospital and miscellaneous fees. Another company reports a 13 weeks' disability insurance plus $150 maternity benefit and miscellaneous hospital charges.

Fifteen percent of the participating companies state, "No coverage provided for pregnant employees."

Asked, "Does the employee maintain seniority rights while on leave for pregnancy?" 30 percent of the nearly 150 companies represented in this survey replied "no." Forty-two percent said they did maintain seniority rights, provided employees are not away "too long," or return "within a reasonable time."

Regardless of whether companies have policies covering maternity leaves, termination, seniority, insurance, etc., the majority are more than willing to have a former employee return to the fold. However, there are some "iffy" factors here. Rarely, according to replies, is a job held open until the employee returns. Efforts are made by most concerns to give the employee an equal type of work, but cannot assure that such a job will be open at the time she returns.

Several offices discourage hiring of mothers with infants. "Too many problems involved," is the general view of these companies.

Warner-Lambert Policy

At the outset, the Warner-Lambert Pharmaceutical Company states the purpose of maternity-leave policy: To protect the health of a pregnant woman while working and to provide an opportunity for her return to work, either on the job held at the time of leaving, or to another job for which she is qualified, without loss of service.

If an employee's position can be filled efficiently on a temporary basis or if other position coverage can be arranged, the employee qualifies for a leave of absence, provided she reports the pregnancy to the company medical department before the end of the third month, with a written statement from her doctor showing anticipated date of delivery.

If the employee's position can be filled efficiently only on a permanent replacement basis, she qualifies for termination-reinstatement status, provided she reports the pregnancy in the same time and manner.

The employee is required to stop work at the end of the sixth month of pregnancy, as calculated by the company medical department from the doctor's anticipated delivery date. The employee may be required to stop working earlier if her doctor or the company doctor feel conditions warrant earlier stoppage.

The employee may not return to work earlier than the completion of the sixth week following delivery. She must return with a written statement from her doctor that she is physically qualified to work, and must pass the company doctor's physical examination.

The employee returning from a leave of absence returns to her former position. An employee with termination-reinstatement rights is considered for any position available for which she qualifies. If no position is available, she is carried on recall, with priority over other applicants for employment on any job for which she qualifies.

Employee benefits which are suspended during the employee's absence but reinstated upon her return include participation in the retirement plan, long-term disability insurance, nonpregnancy coverage under the medical plan, savings and stock-purchase plan, sick leave, and seniority.

Group life insurance continues for 30 days after the employee stops work, and is restored immediately upon her return. Any vacation due is paid when the employee stops work, and vacation begins to accrue after the first full month of her return to employment.

Chapter 25

REST PERIODS AND COFFEE BREAKS

WITH millions of Americans now stopping work for coffee every morning, and the number growing every year, coffee breaks are posing some special problems to office and plant managers. One way to handle these problems is to overlook them; and many companies are doing that. Whether overlooked or not, they are still a matter of concern in many quarters.

Company officials have found careless planning and poor service can boomerang a coffee break into serious cost and service headaches. Avoiding such pitfalls requires knowledge of what the problems are, and what steps other companies have taken to overcome them.

How 141 Offices Handle Rest Breaks

Well over 82 percent of the companies face up to the "rest-period problem"—have a policy covering it in black and white, no hit-and-miss verbal order policy. Along these lines, one contributor, general office manager of a large trucking firm, says: "Since the coffee break has now become something of a national institution, the progressive concern has analyzed its trends and tried to keep step with others. After all, the idea of letting employees take a short rest and obtain refreshments isn't new, it was done back in Ben Franklin's day."

A morning rest period is allowed by 132 of the responding organizations. It varies in length, but 15 minutes is closest to being "standard." Here are the tabulated replies:

10 minutes	39 companies
15 minutes	85 companies
20 minutes	6 companies
12 minutes	2 companies

While they are not quite as common, afternoon rest breaks are growing and are part of the curriculum with a high percentage of the companies. We find 116 allow such rest periods and 23 say "No, we do not." Again, the 15-minute break is most common. Here are the results:

10 minutes	39 companies
15 minutes	73 companies
5 minutes	2 companies
12 minutes	2 companies

Asked whether employees are allowed to take breaks or go to vending machines at times other than those designated, 58 percent of respondents said "yes." Thirty-five percent replied negatively and another 10 percent said employees might go to "vending machines only." But the big question is how do these managements control abuses, see to it that employees keep the break periods within reason? Quite a few stress the honor system—don't use controls. Others leave the matter to supervisors, and still another group tries closely knitted time schedules. All work—up to a point.

The accounting office manager of The Pioneer Rubber Company, Willard, Ohio, reports thus on his firm's scheduling:

Our cafeteria is located on second floor of the building. Office periods are 9:50 to 10:20 a.m. and 2:45 p.m. to 3:15 p.m. Half of the office goes at one time, half the next. As a result, each group seems to control the other."

Some organizations, like Liberty Life Insurance Company, Greenville, South Carolina, have refreshment carts that travel through the offices at the scheduled break times. Coffee, milk, or soft drinks are thus taken right to the desks of employees—no other refreshment sources being available. The company official reporting this policy feels it has worked out reasonably well, too.

Since this is a rather broad exchange of views and experience, we feel readers will be interested in a selected series of comments on the matter of controls. They follow:

"We haven't had any problems with employees taking advantage of our rather informal program."

"No formal control policy—common sense covers excessive abuse."

"Definite time periods for each group of two men and two women are given."

"Break times are not assigned—as long as not too many people are gone at any one time. Each department makes sure all phones are covered at all times."

"We do not regard coffee breaks as rest periods. Personnel may go to the lounges or vending machines at the discretion of the department head."

"In the afternoon, one or two from each department usually get Cokes, candy, and so for., for the various personnel in their department; and these are eaten or drunk at desks while they work."

"Employee takes a break when his or her workload permits—no control has been established due to variation in the workload from one day to the next."

"We are a small organization (24 office employees); everyone takes pride in work accomplishment and no one seems to take advantage of privileges."

"The time of the break is at the option of the employee, except when departmental activities necessitate establishing a specific schedule."

Other comments follow similar lines—some using controls, some appealing to the employee's conscience and sense of fair play, others putting the matter up to supervisors. Perhaps the most succinctly put comment comes from an executive of The Alberta General Insurance Company, Edmonton, Alberta, Canada, who says: "Good responsible employees in a small office need little control or supervision if supplied with enough work." This firm's office of 26 employees allows two 15-minute breaks a day, feels "it improves employee morale," and describes the practice as "successful, at least for our firm."

Dartnell asked cooperating office administrators if there is any difference in policy on rest breaks between men and women. There is very little—only 13 companies answering affirmatively. For instance, of those answering "Yes," one firm, a woolen mill in Wisconsin, points to the fact that most men employees are either line or staff personnel and, as a result, have certain "extra" privileges. Another says the difference lies in the fact that women have more access to rest lounges than men. Still another respondent says the only difference lies in the location of the coffee rooms for male and female employees.

Most of the companies have a cafeteria, lunch or coffee room, or vending machines placed conveniently for employees—some 65 percent falling into these categories. Despite this, 61 companies out of the 141 joining in this exchange of policies allow employees to bring coffee, Cokes, or other liquids to the desks. Eleven companies have a coffee wagon which circulates throughout the offices during the rest periods, and 34 firms allow employees to leave the premises during the break. In this latter case, they are mostly companies having no vending machines, cafeterias, or other inside facilities for employees to get refreshments—mostly small offices with limited staffs.

The spokesman for a Pittsburgh motor freight firm explains the following policy: "Our company furnishes coffee and rolls—served each morning at employees' desks about 10 a.m. This is free to employees. At this time, each employee takes a five-minute break—in addition to our regular 15-minute break."

Firms with shorter working hours are less prone to extend the rest-break idea. For example, the manager of systems and offices, Supertest, London, Ontario, petroleum products company, points out: "Since our office hours are short (6¾ hours per day, five days a week) no break is given. Employees are allowed to go to vending machines any time under control of supervisors. They may drink coffee at their desks."

An interesting program is described by the senior vice-president of the Palmetto State Life Insurance Company, Columbia, South Carolina. He tells of a 30-minute "coffee caucus" held once each month. Employees plan and run the meeting and it is held in the company's training room and attended by company officers. Coffee, Coke, sandwiches, and cookies are served in an informal atmosphere.

The personnel manager, P T F Mutual Insurance Companies, Harrisburg, Pennsylvania, believes his firm (which has 400 office employees) has the break problem under pretty good control. He says, "By locating vending machines on each floor and having a coffee wagon come through each department, congregating has been practically eliminated. And our employees seem well satisfied with the system."

There are, of course, many other comments and descriptions of rest-break controls and policies. Some experiences are good, some woeful. But, on the whole, respondents are agreed, some sort of controls help avoid problems.

Advantages of Coffee Breaks and Rest Periods

Quickly summarizing responses, over 75 percent of the companies feel such breaks improve morale. Another 40 percent feel they tend to increase productive output. And some 45 percent say they help curb errors and mistakes by giving individuals a change of pace. One slightly embittered office manager says, "We couldn't lick 'em, so we joined 'em. Now we all drink coffee together." Here are some of the other comments passed along—all generally classified under the heading of "advantages":

"Creates a better atmosphere to work in, although we doubt they will get work done any better or faster."

"They give a certain 'lift' to employees—intangible but nevertheless there."

"The pace is fast in an adjusting office like ours, and these breaks certainly do refresh our staff."

"If morale is improved, it seems reasonable to expect that quality should be improved."

"They help new staff members to get to know others on a more informal basis."

"A good policy brings the 'break' out into the open instead of employees having secret meetings or sneaking refreshments in out-of-the-way places."

"While such breaks admittedly need watching, they do help build teamwork and take the pressure off, especially for those in confining or routine jobs."

"I believe everyone should take a short break occasionally—it takes the monotony out of things."

What's Wrong With Coffee Breaks and Rest Periods?

High on the list of management complaints about break periods is the one listed by nearly 60 percent of respondents—employees overstay their allotted time. Another 20 percent feel housekeeping problems are caused by paper cups, bottles, crumbs, etc.—all by-products of the refreshment break. And still another 23 percent point to the fact that conversations started during the breaks are continued afterwards—too much conversation follows them. Here is a selected list of "disadvantage" comments from participating executives:

"People tend to schedule work around the break time."

"Our biggest disadvantage—we lose 15 minutes of work per employee, twice a day."

"Too many are gone from each department at the same time."

"One break per day should be sufficient on company time."

"In my opinion, it is still a moot question who gets the coffee 'break'—employee or employer."

"Once allowed, it's hard to discontinue the practice."

"Such breaks cause a disruption of work for men who need the services of a girl who is on her break."

"We find it difficult to carry on business since there are no phones in the coffee room and outside calls for personnel (which are usually business) must be held until they return to work."

"This whole concept of coffee breaks has gotten out of proportion. It is our belief employees take advantage—that few of them take such 'breaks' at home on Saturdays and Sundays."

Suggested Controls for Rest Periods and Coffee Breaks

Like it or not, office management realizes that the rest period or coffee break is now an institution and has joined the ranks of vacations and holiday time-offs as far as employees are concerned. Time-study experts suggest that the selection of the proper length and frequency of rest periods is a complex matter, requiring research into the nature of the job and continuing study of output curves. A great majority of the firms using such periods have cut this particular Gordian knot by giving 10- or 15-minute recesses in the morning and afternoon. A few still give one single 20-minute break, but this is becoming less common.

Following are rest-period control methods used by typical reporting firms, with comments on the relative success of the practices:

Types of Business	Practice	Success
1. Insurance rating bureau	Supervisors are held responsible.	Reasonably good
2. Mechanical manufacturing	Schedules for each girl in the office—one group polices the next.	Very successful
3. Finance company	General observation only.	Partial
4. Hospital	Honor system—periodic checks by supervisors.	Good
5. Grocery chain	IBM clock signals start and end of break period.	Good
6. Electronics	Automatic time signals.	Fair
7. Warehouse	Periodic memos reminding employees that extended breaks hurt them and the company.	Quite effective
8. Paper box manufacturer	Coffee cart stays during break—leaves when it's over. Constant reminders to employees about time limits.	Fair
9. Appliance manufacturer	Department managers are responsible for employees under their supervision. No abuses allowed.	Good, but requires constant followup
10. Food processing	Cafeteria closed except during coffee breaks and lunch periods. Bells sound end of breaks.	Works well
11. Retail bookstore	Employees sign in and out on breaks. We try to encourage employees to control their own breaks.	85 percent effective
12. Auto parts distributor	Use of bulletins to employees—appeal to sense of fairness.	Quite good
13. Cartage and storage	We shift people between breaks to reduce the grapevine tendencies and the overstay habits.	Reasonably successful
14. Fire underwriting	We have 15-minute shifts with senior employees on the final shift. They see to it things move along.	Very well
15. Bank	Informal practice—let employees take breaks as needed as long as practice isn't abused.	Good

When Profits Are Involved

With the growing use of vending machines in business and industry, there is the matter of who gets the profits from sales to employees. While some concerns consider such mechanical feeders part of their cafeteria operation, applying earnings to cafeteria accounting tabs, others use profits from such machines mostly for employee benefits. For instance, a Dartnell spot check of 50 companies shows the following disposition of vending-machine funds among those who do not apply them to the cafeteria operation:

Profits used for employee recreation .... 9 companies

Profits used to finance employee clubs .... 7 companies

Profits used for employee welfare work .... 5 companies

Profits used for flowers and wedding gifts .... 4 companies

Profits used to finance company picnic .... 4 companies

Profits used to finance Christmas party .... 1 company

Profits used to finance veterans' club .... 1 company

Profits retained by company .... 1 company

What Is "the Solution"?

There seem to be three ways of facing up to the refreshment-break problem: (1) overlook it—hope it will go away; (2) live with it and try to handle it with the least amount of employee relations difficulty; (3) police it like a Nazi storm troop operation. Most of the companies contacted by Dartnell in readying this exchange of experience lean toward number two of the above choices.

Admittedly there are costs involved—obvious ones and hidden ones. Hidden costs are often the biggest headache. They include time lost from productive output. For instance, a coffee break that stretches out beyond reasonable time limits adds up to costly production time losses. A half-hour given over to the refreshment-break period each morning is a jolting expense.

To curb some of these expenses, progressive companies are seeing to it that time spent by employees going to and from the vending machines or cafeteria is limited—that these facilities are nearby and service is fast. Prime reason for the growth of vending-machine operations is their flexibility and adaptability to locations and areas.

Company officials have found careless planning and poor service can boomerang a coffee break into serious headaches. Consensus is that if service is fast and efficient, if breaks are scheduled and the schedule adhered to, management can live with the "break problem."

But, as we pointed out in the beginning of this report, you can't put your head in the sand and ignore the trend. Break periods (generally, two a day) are here and might as well be accepted. As one vice-president of office services concluded, "Arguing about the coffee break today is about as backward as refusing to recognize mechanization—both are part of the 1960's."

How Alexander Film Saves Man-Hours

One solution to the "fringe problem" of the coffee break is the use of the coffee cart, which brings coffee and related items to the employees. At Alexander Film Company, Colorado Springs, Colorado, two busy attendants and two little carts take care of 600 employees every working day. Everybody, including the company president, gets a chance to get his morning and afternoon lift from the cart which is stocked with food, cigarettes, and other merchandise, as well as the very important faucet-type thermos of coffee. The Alexander studio is spread over 18 acres, and getting to and from a restaurant in a reasonable length of time would be impossible for most employees. Even companies with a centrally located restaurant find that the coffee break tends to grow longer.

Many companies have found that the coffee-cart type of service saves hundreds of man-hours, not only in procuring coffee, but in trips to the commissary for candy and cigarettes. The cart is part of the commissary operation at Alexander. The commissary is owned and operated by two company employees. However, they pay rent for the use of the company building space and the facilities. In turn, the company places this money in an Athletic Association fund used by the employees for their sports and recreation programs.

Some companies find that it is economical to take bids from various caterers who then make the rounds serving employees coffee and rolls. Sometimes this service is free; in other cases the employees may contribute at regular intervals to pay for the service. Incidentally, the coffee (or tea) cart is widely used in European offices. In Dartnell's London office, tea is delivered twice daily by cart, once midmorning and at 3:30 p.m.; this practice is almost universal in British offices.

Coffee Vending Machines

Recently an executive of a large vending machine concern cautioned us to avoid the use of the term "coffee break." He argued that many employees don't drink coffee—prefer soft drinks, hot cocoa, or something else. However, like the word "Frigidaire" to refrigerators, "coffee break" has become the term widely used to describe the break or rest period.

Twenty-nine percent of several hundred companies surveyed feel that the use of automatic dispensing machines actually reduces lost time by employees at the rest period. Another 32 percent are doubtful that any time is saved and 17 percent feel sure no time is saved. Typical comments follow:

"Without vending machines our people would have to go to a cafe across the street, which would take more time."

"Good locations of machines will cut lost time even more."

"Employees stay near their work areas, whereas before they sat around too long in the cafeteria."

"We only have machines for office employees. If there was one established coffee break, they might save time. But we have no limit on access, so total saving is limited."

"It saves us lost time in elevator travel and service delays at the restaurant counters. We also have fresh rolls available."

"If you can't lick this coffee break thing you had better join it. Our three coffee dispensing machines have at least kept the thing under control."

Only a loose-leaf binder with weekly editions could hope to keep up with the "latest thing" in vending machines, but here is one popular type.

Courtesy, Rudd-Melikian, Inc.

Other comments substantiated the reasons quoted above. Prime feeling is that you can cut excessive to-and-from time if employees have machines handy and can use them at the rest break. However, the mere fact that you have such equipment doesn't guarantee time won't be lost unless some controls are exercised. In this regard, one concern reports a policy whereby the dispensing machines are controlled by lock and key and are only available during the specified break periods.

A New York publishing concern tells Dartnell's staff, "Coffee machines have been removed in our offices, due to employee disapproval. One machine is still retained for overtime workers, but we've replaced the others with an eating service."

What Vending Machines Sell

In order to get a more complete picture of the most commonly utilized type of automatic merchandising machines, we asked the office executives participating in this exchange of experience to list types of machines used in their companies. Below are the types of dispensing equipment used in 700 offices:

Soft or cold drink	80 percent
Candy (gum)	77 percent
Cigarette	66 percent
Coffee	62 percent
Milk	41 percent
Other	25 percent
Ice cream	20 percent
Hot soup or canned food	16 percent

Among "other" machines are such things as sandwich, pastry, peanut, Kleenex, stamp, and other types of machines.

Problems of Vending Machines

In order to get some views on the various headaches caused by vending machines, we asked participants to list their prime problems. Used bottles left lying around on the floor and on desks, and accumulated debris are the prime villains to vending machine users; over 50 percent complain that these are the biggest headaches.

Others listed are malfunctions of machines themselves, use of slugs by employees, breaking into machines, sour milk, cold coffee, liquid poured in wastebaskets, soiled floors near machines, bottle caps, and broken bottles. One respondent complained that "debris from pastry and doughnuts is causing roaches and bugs." Another says, "We are getting tired of refunding nickels and dimes to employees who lose them in the machines."

What to do about the problems caused by vending machines? Consensus among participants is that a constant campaign must be waged to keep the area clean and see that good service is forthcoming from the vendor. As one office manager summed it up, "Our biggest weapon to keep the machines and the areas around them in order is to threaten to take them out. We did once, and employees were not too happy. Now they do a better job of housecleaning."

Advantages of Vending Machines

It is interesting to note that even respondents who listed several complaints with vending machines also had some advantages to list. "Availability" and "convenience" are the two most commonly used words to describe the advantages of machines. Typical responses follow:

"It improves morale when an employee can purchase cigarettes, food, or a drink with a minimum of effort."

"These machines eliminate our need for a lunchroom or cafeteria facility, which has always operated at a loss."

"As a small company, we can't have a lunchroom. But thanks to these automatic machines, our employees can have seven varieties of hot sandwiches; soup, milk, and coffee. Our area isn't the best for outside eating and the machines assure good, wholesome food for our clerical employees who are mostly women."

"The operation is clean and efficient. Nothing is released until it is paid for and we have no food inventories to write off as we did with our cafeteria. Incidentally, we closed the cafeteria about a year ago, and replaced it with automatic machines. We have better morale and less headaches today."

Profits From Vending Machines

The employee recreation fund or social club, the Christmas party, the employee benefit fund for illness or death, and community charities are the most common recipients of the vending machine profits. One concern gives the profits to the United Fund, another to a local hospital, and still another to needy families at Christmas.

Small companies sometimes get no profits from machines. Since their volume of sales is so small, the vendor wants everything. The machines are solely a convenience to employees.

Respondents list coffee as the biggest single item dispensed by machines in their concerns. Second in popularity is assorted soft drinks; followed by candy, milk, and ice cream, in that order. Geographical locations and seasonal factors are to be considered, however. As one respondent indicates, soft drinks sell more in the summer and coffee more in the winter; but for the whole year, coffee leads.

Contributions to Employee Relations

Because many respondents took the trouble to elaborate on the matter of vending machines as an aid to better employee relations, we have selected a number of comments that represent majority thinking. Typical are the following:

"The potential is great. The vending machine company does the work, the company handles regulation. In this manner, expansion into fuller service can be judged and added to benefit of company and employee. Growth of the business has already caused vending machine companies to improve equipment materially. They have also added products to fit the needs of customers."

"We believe that the good outweighs the bad and that vending machines will be a morale-builder in the shipyard of the future. We plan, in the near future, to eliminate food service in the yard completely and install a complete vending machine operation that will serve soups, hot dogs, sandwiches, etc."

"It is hard to determine. The machines are taken for granted at the present time. They are located all over in almost all types of businesses, so there is little that they can do to promote employee goodwill or otherwise."

"In my opinion, a complete vending machine operation combined with an attractive seating area will eliminate a manual food service and its resulting cost. Machine service today is not the complete solution—perfection is missed— but we believe our Kwik Kafe operation is the forerunner to a better operation than our former cafeteria operation. A cafeteria is old-fashioned. It's a space-eater, expensive to operate even with a subsidy, and presents a continual source of gripes and groans from employees."

"Not much. Machines have now extended the 15-minute coffee break to more frequent breaks throughout the day. Some of our people drink coffee from the time they arrive at work in the morning until they go home in the evening— consuming anywhere from 6 to 10 cups a day. (Note: This includes me, too.)"

Chapter 26

VACATION POLICIES AND PRACTICES

E ACH year more and more office workers are getting more time off than before. The trend toward more liberal vacation periods which contributors to Dartnell's annual surveys have noted in other years still continues. The other trends of significance:

Staggering vacations throughout the calendar year.

Added vacation privileges for length of service.

Greater efforts to use the vacation allowance as an incentive by giving more time for good attendance, high productivity, and other employee accomplishments.

While vacation periods are getting longer, efforts are being made to give employees with greater seniority the benefit of most of the increases. For instance, adding an extra week after 15 years of service is becoming an accepted practice in many plants and offices. Companies realize that vacations (at least extra time added to the standard period) are good incentive material. One executive, general manager of a New Jersey metal products firm, comments, "Two years ago we started a policy that allowed employees with perfect attendance over a six-month period three extra days on their regular vacation time. The policy worked. In fact, we had well over 70 percent of our employees eligible for the three extra days last year. This year we hope to get up to 90 percent."

Vacation Allowances

Better than 50 percent of participating companies give employees two full weeks after one full year of service. A growing number give three weeks after 5 years of service. The greatest changes in vacation allowances deal with employees who have 10 to 20 years of service. The extra week or weeks are going to them. More than half the companies offer four-week vacations to long-service employees.

As already stated, many companies are using vacation time as an incentive by adding extra time for perfect attendance, high productive output, and other employee accomplishments. One executive reports a plan whereby employees who made suggestions that were accepted had the privilege of three extra vacation days over and above the monetary award the suggestion would normally carry.

The Northwestern Life Insurance Company has a program of "earned bonus days." If during 23 consecutive working days an employee has a perfect attendance record based on the time-card record, with no tardiness or absence for illness or any other reason, a half-day with full pay is granted. A form authorizing the "bonus day" must be obtained from the personnel department and the time selected must be approved by the employee's immediate supervisor to avoid the possibility of conflict with a department work load.

The employee, when taking a bonus half-day absence in the morning, must punch in for the afternoon's work before 12:45 p.m. If the half-day is taken in the afternoon, the employee may not punch out his time card until after 12:15 p.m.

A report from a large Midwest department store is of interest. Usually, retail stores find the slack summer months ideal vacation months. However, an officer of this company commented, "I personally feel that the civil service plans of government have been worked out with more equity and understanding than the average business, and I see a trend in that direction on the part of business. We plan to go from a zoned vacation period in the year to releasing people for vacations any time of the year they can be spared."

Many companies, like Jewel Tea Company, allow year-round vacation schedules. Jewel has encouraged employees to take winter vacations through bulletins issued to employees and the company's internal magazine which describes advantages of winter vacations. A Chicago electronics manufacturing firm encourages employees to take vacations before April 1 and backs up this suggestion with a $15 bonus for each employee who takes a winter vacation. Many breweries and soft drink bottling firms push winter vacations as the summer is the peak production period.

Policies of companies vary in handling the case of an employee who is called for two weeks' summer military reserve training. A Chicago publishing firm (which has a three-week vacation period for all employees after one full year of service) charges one week of the man's vacation against the training period, but pays a week's salary for the second week after deducting the amount he made for service duty. Other policies are either more or less lenient. One company puts it this way, "We give them the two weeks off with pay and let them have their vacation, too. After all, these boys are the ones we depend upon when an emergency breaks out."

Vacation Incentive Plans

A hunting trip to Africa, an around-the-world jaunt, a cruise to South America, an ocean voyage to Europe with a chauffeur and limousine waiting at the gangplank—and a maid for the ladies in the group—are some of the alluring incentive vacations being dangled before ambitious salesmen and other employees. One enterprising company is sponsoring a contest in which the winner and his wife may have a three-week trip to any spot in the Western Hemisphere— and that includes the South Pole! Philco Corporation, Philadelphia, Pennsylvania, one of the first users and biggest boosters of incentive travel, in its latest contest, offered a "Shangri-La Cruise" as top prize, giving the winner and his wife their choice of a vacation in Mexico, Hawaii, or South America.

The trips are especially attractive because they enable people to visit places that ordinarily would be out of their reach. Leaving the fun unspoiled, most companies pick up all the tabs for the winners

These girls enjoy swim at Cuernavaca, Mexico, during day spent there as part of a trip awarded them in a contest at a Boston specialty store.

TIPS FOR TRIPS

Harold H. Heisler, for several years in charge of the Travel Division of The E. F. MacDonald Company, offers the following suggestions to companies considering vacation incentive trips:

1. Limit the length of the contest—two or three months is best to maintain interest and enthusiasm.

2. Make it easy for as many people as possible to qualify for the contest on a point system instead of taking the top 10, and so forth. This gives everybody a better chance.

3. Include the cost of the trip in the quota so that the only out-of-pocket cost is the time lost. Allow enough money for all the incidentals, such as baggage transfers, tips, entertainment, so that you are really giving your prize winner an all-expense holiday.

4. Get the wives interested. Promote the contest to the wives at home so they will spur their husbands on and help them win. Be sure to include the wives on the trips, for a vacation for husband and wife is much more successful than when the prize winner goes alone.

5. Send literature or novelties to contestants at least once a month, but preferably every two weeks to keep their interest alive.

6. Publish progress reports frequently—unless a few winners get way out ahead so the others might be discouraged.

7. Award a large number of less expensive prizes, instead of a few costly trips, to spread the loot. If your trip budget is $5,000, for instance, it is better to give 25 winners $200 trips each, instead of five $1,000 trips. Or else, compromise with $200 trips for 20 people and two grand prize tours at $500.

and their wives, even taking care of porters' tips and travel insurance, and providing flowers for the women. Aside from souvenirs for relatives and friends, the lucky travelers could leave their wallets at home. This open-purse policy causes the employer no pain, incidentally. In most cases, these tastes of "the full life" raise their people's sights so that they go back to the job determined to work harder to earn enough money to take similar trips on their own in the future. The tours also foster loyalty to the company and establish *esprit de corps*. Philco reports that many of the same dealers win cruises year after year—its habit-forming—and gives incentive trips a large share of the credit for maintaining its leading position in the radio and television field.

HOLIDAY PRACTICES IN 280 COMPANIES

Average Is Seven Days

Seven holidays with pay appears to be the consensus of 280 companies reporting to Dartnell. This figure holds for the United States, both salaried and hourly paid, but it falls short of the number of holidays scheduled for Canadian workers. Across the northern border, indications are that eight holidays are on tap with many companies reporting nine or 10.

Indications are that wherever there are both hourly and salaried employees, the holidays granted are the same. As to be expected, six major holidays dominate in the United States. New Year's Day, Memorial Day, Independence Day, Labor Day, Thanksgiving, and Christmas are the universal holidays. Following in order are Washington's Birthday, Good Friday, Columbus Day, and Veterans Day.

The table below gives data covering 11 major U.S. holidays as reported by 265 companies with salaried employees and 200 companies with hourly paid employees. The total group of workers represented is slightly over 730,000.

Date (1966)	Holiday	Hourly	Salaried
*January 1	New Year's Day (Saturday)	195	264
*February 12	Lincoln's Birthday (Saturday)	8	7
February 22	Washington's Birthday	56	75
April 8	Good Friday	68	71
May 30	Memorial Day	185	232
July 4	Independence Day	197	261
September 5	Labor Day	200	251
October 12	Columbus Day	20	27
November 11	Veterans Day	41	58
November 24	Thanksgiving	198	260
**December 25	Christmas (Monday)	200	263

*Saturday. **Sunday.

Computing Holiday Pay

Of the 190 companies reporting on methods used to compute holiday pay for hourly employees, 156 stated they give eight hours' pay at the guaranteed rate. The next group of 25 companies indicated they pay for eight hours at the average earned rate. Nine companies say they pay an employee for the number of hours he would have normally worked on that day.

Some of the other formulas used in compiling pay data include:

"The average daily hours worked in the preceding normal work week."

"On the basis of average hours worked per day during the previous complete pay period prior to the holiday."

"Straight time for day-work employees and guaranteed rate plus 10 percent for incentive employees."

"Eight hours at the rate being paid on that day."

Some of the formulas and programs are more complicated where companies such as utilities or newspapers are reporting. As an example, the Biloxi-Gulfport *Daily Herald* normally publishes a paper every day. Christmas is the one full holiday off, and all hourly employees are paid a full seven hours.

All other holidays are considered half-day holidays for both hourly and salaried employees. This means that each employee is paid for three hours *plus* the actual time he works. An employee who does not work on a holiday does not get paid.

Of the 200 companies reporting on holiday pay for hourly paid employees, 121 state that employees must work the day before and the day after a holiday to be eligible for holiday wages. A total of 52 companies state that the employees must complete a probationary period to be eligible. A sizable number of firms have a policy that permits employees to be absent on one or both of these days due to illness or some other acceptable reason.

There are many individual policies covering this particular area. For example, Pitney-Bowes, Inc., Stamford, Connecticut, requires that the employee be in a pay status *either* the day before or the day after a holiday. Oneida Ltd. of Oneida, New York, has a policy that requires the employee to have worked *during the week of the holiday.*

A paper company requires a 90-day probationary employment period and two scheduled work days prior to and following the holiday. Several companies have policies that state that employees are entitled to, and paid for, a certain number of holidays. This means they collect whether or not they are present the day before or after.

Double-time pay for working on a holiday represents only 23 percent of the entire group reporting. Time and one-half is next in popularity and a newcomer in popularity, time and one-half plus holiday pay runs third. There were a total of 36 methods described for payment by the 280 companies. Here are the leaders:

Pay for Holiday Work	Number of Firms
Double Time	67
Time and One-half	35
Time and One-half plus Holiday Pay	27
Another Day Off	22
Straight Time	11
Triple Time	11
No Work on Holiday	20

Holiday on Saturday and Sunday

When a major holiday falls on Saturday, the majority of companies (169 out of 280 companies reporting) have the Friday preceding the holiday as the off day. Twenty-four companies pay employees for the extra day, 11 offer compensatory time, and 10 state that if the holiday falls on Saturday, it is observed on Saturday.

When a major holiday falls on Sunday the large majority of companies (257 out of 280) give Monday as a day off. In nine reports, the employee is given an extra day's pay for the week.

Most of those giving information state that the holiday falling during a vacation period will be treated as an *extra* day of vacation for the employee. In those cases where this practice is *not* approved, *the instructions are very definite* in spelling out the policy.

In compiling information on holiday practices it becomes evident that a *stated* holiday practice is by far the most effective. While some companies retain the flexibility of granting holidays according to work loads and/or the profit picture (such as the extra day at Thanksgiving) it is still more effective to let employees know exactly where they stand each year.

Policy statements (in the manual or in a bulletin board release) can be very simple, very direct and very clear. Here is a short but simple reminder from Illinois Mutual Life and Casualty Company of Peoria:

HOLIDAYS . . .

You can look forward to having six paid holidays each year. New Year's Day, Memorial Day (May 30), the 4th of July, Labor Day, Thanksgiving Day and Christmas. If any of these holidays falls on a Saturday, it will be observed on the preceding Friday; when it falls on a Sunday it will be observed on the following Monday.

You must work both the day before and the day after a holiday to be paid for the holiday.

This wraps up the entire program (except for vacations and leaves of absence), and these can be covered in a special policy item. Here is one way to include the section on holidays during vacation time:

"Your vacation is on the company's time; so, if a holiday should fall on one of your vacation days, you may add this time to your regularly scheduled vacation."

TIME OFF FOR JURY DUTY

Most firms have a set and established policy governing employee time off for jury duty. In every instance where there is a set plan, employees are granted the time off. The office manager, Allied Van Lines, Broadview, Illinois, pretty well sums up the views of these administrators with the comment, "We believe all employees should be encouraged to serve as a matter of civic responsibility."

However, while most agree jury duty is a responsibility to one's community, there are varying views among the executives as to how the allowance should be compensated. Following is a cross section of comments:

"We will pay full salary all the time an employee is away and encourage our employees not to shirk the duty."

"Time off is allowed when the person has properly been subpoenaed by a federal or state court."

"All employees to serve on jury unless it is impossible to replace them with temporary help or it is a peak season."

"It is accepted as an automatic excuse for absence—employees are paid the difference between jury compensation and regular pay."

"We do not interfere. The employee is advised to do what he needs to do. In exceptional cases of a seasonal peak or year-end audit, we have requested and obtained deferrals."

"Employee is entitled to the time off if he has one year or more service."

When an office employee is called for jury duty, the standard practice requires the individual contact his immediate supervisor or the personnel department, telling them of the call. A record is made of the dates involved and a copy is turned over to the payroll department for its record. Then the employee is usually granted an authorized leave of absence to fulfill his civic obligation.

The director of industrial relations, Callaway Mills Company, LaGrange, Georgia, reports: "The employee is given time off for the jury duty but makes it up on other dates. However, if he works overtime on other dates, he is still paid at time and one-half."

Most common practice among those participating in this exchange of management experience is to pay the employee full pay while he or she is on jury duty plus letting the individual keep the jury pay, too.

The industrial relations manager of an International Harvester Division in Chicago says, "Office personnel get full pay and keep the jury fee; factory personnel get the difference between the company wage and the fee." He also points out that factory employees are paid after they complete jury service. The assistant secretary, Lynch Corporation, Anderson, Indiana, explains that length of service is a factor in the determination of compensation. Generally, employees at Lynch get full pay and the jury fee, but, this executive says, "This may be limited on an extended leave, depending on seniority. Each case is decided on its own merits."

Only one concern, a Virginia company, charges the jury duty time off against regularly scheduled time off. The spokesman explains, "Jury duty is set the same as sick leave or vacation—it is allowed when called." All of the others answered "No" to the question of whether jury duty is charged against general time off.

In most instances the affected department "picks up the slack" when one of its members is called to serve on a jury. However, some concerns, like Lambert Company, Ltd., Los Angeles, use "extra" help that is already in the company and hire temporary help, if needed, from outside services. Some respondents point out that replacement is usually dependent upon the nature of the affected employee's duties—whether others are skilled enough to fill in, in the event of absence. If not, they use temporary help services.

Chapter 27

RECREATION AND ATHLETIC PROGRAMS

I T was getting on toward the close of another business day in an office in Morgantown, West Virginia.

The time was 7:30 p.m.—the year 1850. The manager had just posted a new set of "company rules" on the inside of the front door. Rule 6:

Man employees will be given an evening off each week for courting purposes, or two evenings a week if they go regularly to church.

Now, depending upon your understanding of the word, you could say this was an early example of recreational programs for business and industrial employees in the United States.

Things have changed. Today there aren't many provisions for "courting time" in recreational programs. You will, however, find an amazingly wide variety of other activities.

Don L. Neer, executive director of the National Industrial Recreation Association, says industrial recreation got its start in Peacedale, Rhode Island, around 1854. The Peacedale Manufacturing Company established that year a library "where Peacedale kids were taught singing on weekday afternoons and the company employees read by night."

Allis-Chalmers had its first employee picnic in Milwaukee on August 26, 1882, and started a rifle club in 1886. The following year, Bridgeport's Warner Brothers Company erected a clubhouse for its 500 employees. The first employee recreation association was formed, according to Mr. Neer, at the Metropolitan Life Insurance Company in 1894.

Sports, he says, entered the picture in 1866 when an Equitable Life Assurance Company baseball team beat the nine from Metropolitan Life to the tune of 42 to 18 on a sandlot.

To bring this history quickly up to more recent times, World War II, with its tensions and overtime work, provided the impetus that has pretty well established recreation, in its multitudinous forms, as a business and industrial way of life today.

It goes by a variety of names and diverse company executives are responsible for it. But, it may safely be said that recreation is a factor in the devices used by management in attracting and keeping loyal and contented work forces.

As Mel C. Byers, long-time employee service supervisor for Owens-Illinois, Inc., puts it: "I feel that recreation is one of the very few unnegotiable benefits that management can still give its employees and that it offers a better media for communications than any other method presently offered in industry." He adds the recreation program "has greater possibilities for building company loyalty with employees and family than any other media the company might select."

At Welch Grape Juice Company

The Employee Recreation Association of The Welch Grape Juice Company, Inc., Westfield, New York (WERA) has 375 members. Organized in 1954, WERA's typical yearly calendar offers a diversified choice of activities.

In its sports participation offerings, WERA has a golf league and clinic, water skiing instruction, bowling leagues, fishing contest, skeet and trap shooting, ice skating parties, and pocket billiards. To the sports spectator it offers pro football, baseball, and hockey games. Other WERA-planned events include Chautauqua operas and plays, "name band" dances, plant tours (a brewery and a biscuit manufacturer have been on the schedule), ice shows, Christmas benefit shows, card tournaments and bridge instruction, social dance instruction, and the Rotary-sponsored circus.

The year's activities are topped off by WERA with an annual banquet in May. Members hear an annual report and awards and trophies are presented. Dancing concludes the program.

The organization's membership fees are 50 cents annually. There is an annual contribution of "approximately $1,800" from the company.

Faultless Rubber

The National Industrial Recreation Association (NIRA) yearly presents the Helms Industrial Recreation Award to programs judged by a panel of specialists to be the best and most significant. A three-time winner in the 500-1,000 employee group is The Faultless Rubber Company, Ashland, Ohio.

"Our program centers around our recreation building," says Howard Honaker, recreation director. He explains the building "houses four bowling lanes, billiard tables, Ping-Pong tables, a dining room, shower and locker rooms for men and women, a television room, an exercise room, and meeting rooms. We also have a platform tennis court near the building."

A Boy Scout troop, junior bowling teams, and Little League baseball are included in the organization's youth activities.

Shell Started With Sports

A good many of today's industrial recreation programs had their beginnings when a few plant men got together to toss a ball around at lunch time and later organized a team to compete with industrial neighbors.

This is the way the Shell Development Recreational Association began. A dozen or so men from Shell's Emeryville, California, research center put a team together in 1939, entered the Berkeley Industrial League, and won the championship. By the end of that year, SDRA had added basketball, a children's Christmas party, and a Christmas dance for the 100 employees. Aside from other sports activities, in its early years the association had annual spring and fall dances, a yearly family picnic, and rifle, photography, gardening, chess, and stamp clubs.

The current menu of social, athletic, educational, cultural and recreational opportunities served up to the Shell people is widely diversified. These are some of the more popular activities:

Softball	Bridge club	Camellia show
Basketball	Chess club	Christmas dance—adults
Lob ball	Coin club	Christmas party—children
Volleyball	Skin/Scuba club	Spring dance—adults
Bowling	Stamp club	Fall dance—adults
Ping-Pong	Tennis club	Art/Photography
Golf	Judo/Karate club	Hobby show
Sailing	Travel program	Picnic
Fishing derby		Ski trips—water/snow

At Owens-Illinois

Most of these interesting facets of employee recreation can be found in the program of Owens-Illinois, Inc. O-I's organization for its people is known as The OnIzed Club. It was organized in 1934 to: (1) supply opportunities for cooperation in matters of common interest, (2) promote good fellowship, and (3) offer wholesome welfare, social and athletic activities to all Owens-Illinois men and women.

Each department elects its officers for one-year terms. Each department officer, except the secretary-treasurer is automatically a member of the four councils that govern the Central Club: executive, social, welfare, and athletic. Sometimes there is both a women's and men's athletic council.

There are not OnIzed Clubs at every one of the 87 Owens-Illinois units. Facilities and programs vary. Some clubs have their own clubhouses and others have clubrooms. There are three parks and two lakes, and other facilities range from a playground in conjunction with one plant to a vacant lot rented by the season. The general office OnIzed Club in Toledo has its own rooms within the skyscraper Owens-Illinois building.

"An Integral Part" at Jefferson

"We feel that our club and all that it has to offer is an integral part of the company operation and many of us are dependent upon the club for much of our social and recreational activities."

So says Charles L. Robinson, personnel assistant at the Jefferson Standard Life Insurance Company, Greensboro, North Carolina, in summing up the Jefferson Standard Country Club.

The Jefferson Club is situated on over 500 acres of land "in one of the most ideal sections of Piedmont, North Carolina." There is a large colonial type clubhouse, fully equipped for small or large groups up to 500. A kitchen, several private dining rooms, a ballroom, a recreation room and a snack bar are features of the house. Outside, there is a 4½-acre swimming lake, a 29-acre fishing lake, several smaller holding or filtering lakes, a playground and picnic area, bathhouse, picnic shelters and eight tennis courts.

In addition to all the activities associated with a "country club," the Jefferson program includes such events as children's Easter and Christmas parties, teen-agers' seasonal parties, dancing classes, Red Cross first aid classes, bridge lessons, art class, interior decorating and hobby shows. There is an employees' choral group, directed by a professional.

Battling the Paunches at Gates Rubber

"According to some medical authorities," says Lloyd Smith, 20-year recreational director for The Gates Rubber Company, Denver, "fatigue and tension are major complaints of a significant number of executives across the country."

Since 1911, when the company was founded, recreational activities ranging from baseball to stamp collecting have been encouraged and given support. The year-round program involves more than half of the 6,500 Gates employees and their families. It is conducted by a service organization, the Gates Fire Brigade, complemented by the Gates Sports Club.

NCR Has "Exceptionally Good Investment"

John Henry Patterson, founder of The National Cash Register Company, is credited with being "a pioneer in industrial organization and scientific management," according to a statue that memorializes him in Dayton, Ohio. At the turn of the century, he already was known as the "radical" who provided women employees with backs for their chairs and hot meals. Earlier, he had hired a "welfare director" to look after the human relations aspects of his business.

Today's NCR management places great emphasis on attracting and keeping outstanding people, and its recreational program has proved to be an exceptionally good investment in achieving these objectives.

There are two major recreational features at NCR. The oldest is the 167-acre recreation park, Old River, completed and opened in 1939. The facility includes a large swimming pool, picnic sites, children's playground areas and provision for sports.

Another facility is the NCR Country Club, which gives social membership privileges to over 6,000 NCR'ers. Another 2,000 play golf.

Athletics Rate High

As we've noted, a good many recreation programs got their starts in athletics for the more energetic company people. Athletics and sporting events still play a major role in company programs. Of the 20 leading activities sponsored by company members of NIRA, half are in the broad athletics-sports category:

1	Bowling	94%	10 Horseshoes	41%
2	Golf	93%	11 Fishing	40%
3	Softball	87%	17 Rifle, pistol	34%
4	Basketball	73%	19 Volleyball	29%
9	Table tennis	41%	20 Baseball	28%

Picnics take over as the most frequently sponsored event aside from athletics-sports. Picnics rank fifth (70 percent) among NIRA members and are followed by dancing, Christmas parties and movies, with 52 percent, 51 percent, and 44 percent of companies, respectively, sponsoring these events. The other nonathletic events in the top 20 are bridge, travel, chorus, handicrafts, photography and ticket sales.

Initiating an Employee Recreation Program

The first step in initiating an employee recreational program may be taken by management or the employees themselves. Whether the firm is large or small, the employees should be brought in on the ground floor, either by group or through chosen individuals who have shown outstanding leadership and hold the respect and confidence of their fellow workers.

A committee should be formed to set up the type of organization that would best suit your particular firm. A representative from management should be invited to participate on this committee. He can act as a liaison between the employees and management to interpret company policy and help where necessary in the work of organizing and administering the program.

To stimulate interest it is valuable to send to every employee an interest-finding questionnaire. With the information received from this questionnaire an outline of activities can be prepared.

In an employee-owned organization a considerable amount of time is consumed in administering the facility instead of the program. Employee organizations may find themselves involved in real estate, litigation, insurance, and tax problems and many business transactions which are far removed from employee recreation. This is not a total disadvantage as some members of the employee organization will enjoy making a hobby of the business administration.

Now it is evident that there are two distinct phases in recreation programs—the business administration and the recreation activities. The governing body then must be versatile enough to provide the type of recreation required for the employees and also to transact all related business. Obviously, it is mandatory that a highly competent, versatile, and ethical staff be retained to carry out the orders of the employee council.

Perhaps the most successful program could be achieved under a combination administration. With the company owning and administering the facility, the employee organization could concern itself solely with recreational activities.

Procedures for Setting Up Budget

(1) Determine the total revenue available from membership card sales and from company contributions if any.

(2) Determine the number of activities and the net cost of each. This should include an adequate reserve.

(3) If a deficit balance exists the number of activities or size of the activities should be reduced. If this is not feasible, additional funds can sometimes be obtained from special activities.

Chapter 28

CHRISTMAS BONUSES AND GIFTS

SLIGHTLY over one-half of the companies responding to a Dartnell survey covering the practice of giving Christmas gifts or bonuses to employees state they do give gifts. Approximately 45 percent of the respondents indicate that they have a Christmas bonus program.

Important facts gleaned from the survey include the following:

1. More companies give gifts of merchandise to employees than give cash.
2. More companies give Christmas gifts than give bonuses.
3. The majority of merchandise gifts to employees are in a price range under $20.
4. The majority of cash gifts to employees is under $20.
5. Better than two-thirds of the companies who pay Christmas bonuses to salaried employees give them over $100.
6. Approximately one-fourth of the companies who give a gift or a bonus give *both*.
7. Smaller companies (work force) are more apt to give gifts and/or bonuses than larger companies.

A substantial number of replies to a questionnaire revealed that the practice of a Christmas gift or bonus has been eliminated in favor of a profit-sharing plan or an increase in annual wages. Several respondents stated bluntly that former gift and bonus giving practices resulted in "trouble," "discontent," and "inequalities."

Some who have dropped monetary or merchandise gifts now give a party for employees and their families.

Cash Gifts to Employees

A total of 50 companies reported that they give annual Christmas "gifts" to employees in cash form. More than half indicate that the gift is under $20. Ten out of the 50 report that the gift is over $50.

Several have different types of schedules for cash gifts such as a week's salary.

A breakdown of the number of companies and the range of gifts in cash in shown below:

Cash Gift Range	No. of Companies
$ 1 to $ 3	3
$ 5 to $10	11
$10 to $20	13
$20 to $30	6
$30 to $50	3
Over $50	10
Other	4
Total	50

As closely as can be estimated, the typical Christmas cash gift is over $10 and averages out to about $25. A few companies indicate that the gift is a week's pay, but in most cases this is interpreted as a bonus on second thought. Several companies use the Series E bond as a gift.

Some of the gifts are distributed on a sliding scale based on years of service. One company starts with a $2.50 gift (cash) and this climbs to a top of $65. Incidentally, this same company gives a Christmas bonus on a similar scale.

There are some companies that give both a small cash gift ($5 to $50) *and* a merchandise gift. The latter is normally a turkey or a ham, but in some cases it is a gift from a catalog. One company gives a cash gift of $10 to $25 and includes the turkey, ham, or fruit cake as an extra.

More than one company generously gives a gift of $10 for each year of service to employees other than those in management positions. Another distributes cash gifts on the basis of the success of the business year and the employee's individual contribution. This company also has a profit-sharing Christmas bonus.

One company has been mailing a check for $25 to the employee's home with a brief year-end letter for 25 years. Another firm states that the Christmas gift is $1 for each year of service.

Merchandise Price Range

Of the 112 companies reporting the practice of giving Christmas gifts to employees, 62 said these gifts were in the form of merchandise. The price range indication is that 58 percent of the gifts are valued under $10 and 27 percent are in the $10-$20 range. The extreme case indicated by one company was for some gifts with price tags as high as $200. Four companies said the gifts had values over $50.

Value of Merchandise	No. of Companies
$ 5 to $10	36
$10 to $20	17
$20 to $30	2
$30 to $50	1
Over $50	6

As well might be expected the traditional turkey and ham lead the Christmas gift parade, although companies reported an imaginative variety of other gifts.

The range included fruit cakes, candy, food baskets, personal items, gift certificates, company produced items, a selection from a gift catalog, and in one case a color TV set for salesmen who increase their sales 10 percent.

Turkeys *and* cash came in for play in 10 reports, and cash and merchandise combinations were reported by 27 companies. One company provides employees with a selected gift item from the home country of the company.

The Annual Christmas Party

Still in existence, many companies reported these events as very special with steak dinners, dancing, and entertainment. Needless to say these were *family* affairs. No report specifically stated that a party was held for *employees* only.

The children are in the act as well. Several firms include them at the party and make sure that each one receives a toy or gift.

There were several cases reported where the hourly paid (factory) employees received the annual gift of merchandise while salaried or office help receive cash and/or a party. In several cases *only* the party was held for the office help, and this was costed out at approximately $15 per person.

The Christmas Bonus

Seventy-five of the 94 companies which reported giving a Christmas bonus stated they are distributed on a regular basis (annually, over long periods of time). Some 69 of these companies say that their bonus program is *not* based on profit alone, with 25 reporting that it is.

Exactly half (45) of the companies reporting how bonuses are determined stated that both salary and length of service are considered. Thirty firms reported that salary determines the size of the bonus and 15 companies said length of service determines the size. There were 47 companies that said the bonus size was determined on a graduated scale.

Better than two-thirds of the 94 companies indicating that they pay a Christmas bonus (or year-end) to salaried employees state that the amount is over $100. Slightly over 40 percent say the bonus payments range over $250, and over 15 percent present their employees with bonuses ranging about $500. Payments to hourly-paid employees range lower. About 50 percent of the companies pay $100 or less. Only three companies say they pay $500 or more.

The week of December 15 to 20 is far and away the most popular time for the payment of the Christmas bonus. The second most popular time is right at Christmas Eve, and the first week of December pulls into third place.

Several companies hold off the bonus payment until after Christmas, some distributing the bonus payment on the last working day of the year, and some making payment on the payday after Christmas. Several other companies indicate that the bonuses are paid in January or February.

Comments and Opinions

In the final analysis of the practice of giving Christmas gifts and bonuses to employees, management gave strong indication that the idea is either fully accepted or highly undesirable.

As a long-time practice in a majority of companies that do have the program, it is normally considered a good idea. Comments from some show a growing doubt, and others indicate they are looking for another way of paying an employee for loyalty and service.

To get the opinion across, here are some of the comments received:

"Christmas gifts or bonuses can be a 'dangerous' thing inasmuch as the employee learns to expect one to finance his Christmas spending. Should a company sustain a loss in any given year and pay no bonus, it could be very upsetting to employee morale."

"Gifts and bonuses are self-perpetuating. I would never advise that the practice be started because the potential gain is limited, and once the practice is started it is almost impossible to stop it."

"Our bonus payments have been increasing in size for the past five years. A bonus amounts to just another way of paying an employee, but it does allow a bit more flexibility in rewarding him for his progress."

"There is a question that the token Christmas gift may do more harm than good. There are complaints that the gifts are not suitable, that they give the impression of cheapness, etc. Bonuses, at least, are substantial and accepted in better spirit."

"We are not always sure that our employees consider their bonus in evaluating our salaries with those of their friends who work at other companies."

"We have taken a definite stand against giving or receiving gifts. We don't believe in giving gifts to employees because (1) there are unions in the shops, and (2) employees don't appreciate gifts, they prefer money."

"Bonuses must in some way be attached to salary or earnings. I'm opposed to a small company giving a bonus unless the recipient be fully aware of the relation of his contribution to profits. There is no Santa Claus!"

"Since the courts have ruled that any form of a Christmas bonus is considered a part of an employee's salary, we have discontinued this practice and taken this money and distributed it over the year, increasing weekly wages accordingly. We have found this to be a better and a healthier method of operating a firm."

"Bonuses are of doubtful value as motivation. Employees probably do not consider this a form of additional income when comparing employment and wages with those of other companies."

"We emphasize Christmas every day of the year by providing the best gift of all, the opportunity to advance with satisfaction, money, and power."

"We feel that a profit-sharing program during the year is more effective, and the only difference is that the bonus at Christmas is enhanced by a good dinner for employees and their wives or husbands."

"The cash bonus has never been profitable or workable for us. It just doesn't get the job done."

"Generally speaking, there seems to be a trend away from bonuses or gifts at Christmas time in our industry. This is probably brought about by changing employee-employer relationships and the practice of operating on a fiscal year rather than a calendar year from a bonus standpoint."

"A bonus or Christmas gift would upset our profit-sharing plan. It is our opinion that an award based on profit is much greater incentive than salary or length of service."

"We stopped giving a Christmas bonus because it created too much ill will."

"We gave a Christmas bonus but discontinued the program four years ago. The amounts varied and so did the complaints!"

"We have eliminated bonus and gift giving. The problem of equality-rate and individual performance raised such hell that management found it wasn't worth the trouble. Our annual wage is now the best in the industry, and this does the job."

"Gifts and bonuses are only effective the first time. Afterwards, they become a 'right' of employees and an 'obligation' of the employer."

Chapter 29

EMPLOYEE CREDIT UNIONS

CREDIT unions, which began in Germany more than a hundred years ago, have won favor with American employers because they make it possible for employees to obtain small loans for approved purposes without red tape and at a lower rate of interest than would be charged by the average small loan firm. Besides encouraging thrift, credit unions have enabled employees in financial difficulties with a number of creditors to consolidate their debts and make periodical payments to the credit union.

Take the case of Joe Smith, an amiable industrial employee on Chicago's South Side. He wanted his family to have the best of everything, including an automobile, a TV set, a refrigerator, and a merry Christmas every December 25. Early one year, Joe bought a number of things on time. Unfortunately, his payments weren't on schedule. Soon his wife was peeking through the shades every time the doorbell rang.

So Joe joined the credit union at his plant (that took only 25 cents and his signature on a card) and asked for help. The treasurer analyzed his case and recommended a $400 loan. That was paid to Joe's various creditors and Joe began paying the one consolidated bill he owed the credit union.

Eventually Joe paid off the final $5-a-week installment, but he's still handing the credit union the same amount each week. Now the money is going into a savings account. Joe's case is typical of the way a lot of fellows start saving. Then, when they borrow again, they may have the amount of the new loan more than covered by their savings.

In spite of opposition from small loan and finance companies which consider credit unions "unfair" competition and socialistic because of their cooperative nature, employers are encouraging employees to organize credit unions in the United States at the rate of 1,000 a year.

A list of companies with credit unions includes Allis-Chalmers, Republic Steel, Phoenix Hosiery, Land O'Lakes Creameries, Motorola, Kimberly-Clark, Swift & Co., Eastern Air Lines, Lockheed Aircraft, Shell Oil, Esso Standard Oil, Dow Chemical, National Cash Register, Kraft Foods, and many others. Among the largest groups of credit unions are those in the various departments of the United States Government in Washington.

What Is a Credit Union?

An official of the Credit Union National Association, Inc., Filene House, Madison 1, Wisconsin, to which most American credit unions belong, and which charters and supervises these undertakings on behalf of the membership, defines a credit union as a cooperative savings and loan membership association, not for profit. The credit union is organized within a specific group of employees. It is limited in operations to its members, and is managed by officers chosen by and from the group in elections in which every member, regardless of his holdings, has a single vote. The credit union performs three major services for its members, as follows:

1. The credit union is a thrift plan, supplying its members with a convenient system of savings which makes the accumulation of appreciable savings possible by establishing the habit of installment savings at regular intervals.

2. The credit union is a credit plan, as the accumulated savings are loaned to members of the group at normal interest rates for provident or productive purposes, thereby protecting members from the high-rate money lender in time of credit necessity.

3. Because the credit union is self-managed and deals only with its own members, it has far-reaching value as a means of popular education in matters pertaining to money management.

Credit unions are organized under either state or federal law, and, as the case may be, are subject to supervision and annual examination by state or federal authorities.

Encouraging Thrift Among Employees

To belong to a credit union the applicant must first belong to the group within which the credit union has been organized. Next, he must agree to buy at least one share, generally of a par value of $5, and pay for it with cash or at the rate of at least 25 cents per pay period. He may save in any amount he desires—25 cents, 50 cents, $1, $5, or $500. He may deposit $50 today and tomorrow withdraw that amount if he so desires. A shareholder may also make irregular deposits, at any time. Credit unions rarely set limits on the amount a member may hold in shares; usually they encourage him to save as much as possible.

The net result of the plan is to encourage systematic savings, and many members who have never previously been able to accumulate a savings account find that they can save easily in a credit union. The savings unit is usually small and the credit union operates for the maximum convenience of the member. Instead of the member going to the bank, the credit union comes to the member. Something of the practical aspect of the credit union is indicated by the story of the largest one, the Detroit Teachers Credit Union. Organized in 1926 by nine teachers, it now has nearly 13,000 members, with savings of $20 million.

When Workers Need Credit

The second function of the credit union is to create normal money credit resources for average workers. Until the credit union showed the way and proved conclusively by much experience that average workers are entitled to reasonable money credit, workers were left pretty much to the loan sharks when they needed credit. This problem became so acute that, to remedy it, the Uniform Small Loan Law was drawn up and enacted in many states. Originally this law permitted the licensed lender, who had agreed to conform to its provisions, to charge 3½ percent a month on unpaid balances or 42 percent a year of real interest. While this rate may seem high, it is low compared to rates charged by some unlicensed lenders. A railroad employee in a large Midwestern city once borrowed $30, paid back $1,080 in interest, and was then sued for the $30. Every usury investigation turns up innumerable cases of this sort, and the Uniform Small Loan Law did much to alleviate this unjust situation. With the passage of time, the original 3½ percent contained in this law has been reduced until now there is much lending at 2 percent a month by lenders operating in strict conformity with the law. Unquestionably, the Uniform Small Loan Law has done much good.

It is difficult for a layman to understand usury. But usury existed long before Christ drove the money changers out of the Temple. The borrower who goes to the loan shark generally has no other recourse. He needs the money. The lender he goes to will accommodate him. In that case, the rate is most often fixed by the greed of the lender and the need of the borrower.

The credit union enters this field and uses its money to make loans to its own members at rates of interest which never exceed 1 percent a month on unpaid balances. No paper or investigation or other fees are allowed. The 1 percent a month is the maximum limit, the actual rate being fixed by the board of directors of the individual credit union. One percent a month on balances is approximately 5.9 percent discounted.

In connection with the credit union maximum interest rate, the disposition of earnings must be taken into account. After 20 percent of net earnings (in most states) has been set aside in an indivisible reserve fund established to take care of an occasional bad loan, and after the relatively small expenses of the credit union have been paid, the balance reverts to the members as dividends on their savings in the credit union.

This does not mean, incidentally, that loans are only made to members who have substantial savings in the credit union. As a matter of fact, many times the employee fails to join until hit by an emergency requiring a loan. He must, of course, join and start paying for a share, but the fact that he has not hitherto belonged to the credit union does not disqualify him for a loan.

The purposes of loans vary. The laws provide that loans may be made for "provident and productive purposes." That has been interpreted to mean that there must be at least a reasonable chance that

This standard credit union loan application form is simple but comprehensive, and widely used.

the loan if made, will perform a real service to the borrower. Many loans are made to take care of bills incidental to sickness, surgical operations, dentistry, births, and funerals. All the normal family requirements at one time or another come within the scope of credit union loans service. Furniture, coal, automobiles and household appliances, insurance premiums, taxes and home repairs, education, and a thousand and one other financial problems of workers have been taken care of in credit union operations.

Credit Unions Educate Workers

The third function of the credit union is its most important function. Because a credit union must find within its own membership men and women to serve as directors, committee members, and officers, and because these officers come in close day-to-day contact with the money problems of the members, they develop a firsthand, intimate acquaintance with this mysterious thing called "money."

Anything mysterious causes the most alarm among the uninformed. For too long banking has been a mysterious thing and, as a result of sad experiences, not every employee has confidence in banks, in spite of federal guarantees and supervision. The credit union seeks to prove there is nothing mysterious about money; that money can be harnessed and made the willing slave of man rather than man a slave to money; that we have the hitherto unsuspected capacity to grapple with our own money problems and solve them.

We learn in the credit unions that usurious interest is not so important as a moral question as it is a common problem in economics. When hundreds of millions of dollars of the earnings of working people are paid out annually to high-rate money lenders, we learn how to subtract normal interest charges from abnormal interest charges and to determine for ourselves how much buying power is wasted in usurious money lending. Thus, the credit union seeks to supply its members with knowledge about basic economics. This education is one of the primary purposes of a credit union.

Credit Union Management

As has been noted, each credit union elects a board of directors, by and from the group, large enough to represent all subdivisions of the group and composed of men and women who can develop sufficient enthusiasm for the credit union that they will all be willing to work hard to make it a success. A credit committee, generally of three members, is also elected by and from the group. As the designation indicates, this committee passes on all loans and on all problems affecting loans, such as security. There is also an auditing committee (sometimes called the supervisory committee) of three members; this committee makes regular reports and audits and, in general, checks to see that the credit union is managed according to the rules. Incidentally, this committee usually has power to remove any director, officer, or committee member if the committee finds, from its audit, that such individual is unfaithful to his trust. If such removal is ordered, the committee is required to call a meeting of the members within seven days to pass finally on the removal.

The directors choose from their own numbers a president, a vice-president, a treasurer, and a clerk. Usually, the treasurer is manager. He and the other money-handling officials and employees are bonded. He is the most important cog in the credit union machine. An able treasurer will generally produce a good credit union if backed by an interested and industrious board and by committees which take their obligations seriously.

For the most part, credit union treasurers have not had prior accounting experience. The credit union bookkeeping system is relatively simple. Officials of more than 22,500 credit unions have mastered it. It is much more important that the treasurer be someone within the group who understands the everyday problems of his fellow workers than that he be a certified public accountant. It is important also that the board of directors and the committee members be rank-and-file employees who understand from personal experience the economic perplexities of the average wage earner with a wife and children to support.

Credit Union Supervision and Organization

The state credit union laws generally vest jurisdiction for purposes of supervision and annual examination in the state banking department. This department also determines whether or not a charter shall be granted to a given group. Examination is generally an annual affair and the state supervisory body may liquidate a credit union for insolvency.

Federal credit unions are supervised under the Federal Credit Union Act by the Bureau of Federal Credit Unions of the Department of Health, Education, and Welfare. In most states, the state-chartered credit unions are supervised by a division of the state banking department. There is practically no difference in operating methods and functions between state- and federal-chartered credit unions.

In most of the states and in the Canadian provinces there are leagues of credit unions, each in charge of a managing director. The Credit Union National Association, Inc., is composed of 60 leagues, including 45 state leagues, the District of Columbia league, the Hawaiian league, nine Canadian leagues, and three in Puerto Rico, Jamaica, and British Honduras.

The organization work of the Credit Union National Association, Inc., and of the state leagues is carried on as a disinterested, non-profit public service, without charge, direct or indirect, for any services rendered. Men and women capable of cooperating with any interested group to organize credit unions are available anywhere within the territorial limits of the United States. The national association also carries on an extensive correspondence with interested parties abroad.

Early History of Credit Unions

The first credit unions were organized in Germany by two eminent economists, Raiffeisen and Schulze-Delitzsch. The idea spread throughout Europe and from Europe to other parts of the world. Alphonse DesJardins, of Quebec, became interested in the plan about 1885, due to his contacts with the problem of usury as he went about his business as a newspaperman in Montreal. He studied the plan, contacting leaders in Europe for 15 years, and then in 1900 organized the first credit union on this continent at Levis, in the Province of Quebec. Edward A. Filene, of Boston, Massachusetts, first learned about the credit union while traveling in India in 1908. In 1909 he assisted the then bank commissioner of Massachusetts, Pierre Jay, in obtaining the enactment of a credit union law for Massachusetts. By 1921 there were 199 credit unions in the United States, in the three states which then had usable laws.

In that year Mr. Filene, in cooperation with Roy R. Bergengren, organized the Credit Union National Extension Bureau, with the objective of securing the needed laws and of organizing credit unions until the credit unions should become a national institution in the United States.

Between 1921 and 1934, Mr. Filene spent a million dollars of his own fortune to make this pioneering work possible. An office was maintained at Boston, Massachusetts; laws were enacted and the first 2,000 credit unions organized. By 1934 the work had proceeded to the point where it was possible to begin the organization of state leagues on a broad scale, a few leagues having by then been organized. In that year, the credit union leaders of the United States held a convention at Estes Park, Colorado, and organized the Credit Union National Association. In 1937, Mr. Filene turned all the work over to the association.

The national association also maintains a life insurance company, the Cuna Mutual Insurance Society, and a cooperative manufacturing company to provide credit unions with accounting forms, known as the Cuna Supply Cooperative. The official publication of the national association is *Credit Union Bridge,* a monthly which deals with credit union progress and problems.

Since credit unions were established they have made a real place for themselves in employee relations and are now a definite part of any human relations program. When well managed they are self-supporting and tend to reduce employee turnover. Certainly they make for better employee relations.

Employees flock to the headquarters of the East Hartford (Connecticut) Aircraft Federal Credit Union, one of the largest federal credit unions in the United States.

HOW TO ORGANIZE A CREDIT UNION

Anyone can organize a credit union. Select a group, preferably of 100 or more, with some common bond of occupation, association, or residence. Write to the Credit Union National Association asking for free literature and for contact with competent personnel to assist in the effort. This contact will be the managing director or field representative of the league. Talk with members of the group about the credit union. Find out from them the names of persons in the group who are leaders and capable of making decisions for the group. In occupational groups this will be the employer and possibly some of the employees in supervisory jobs. While these persons have no responsibility to the credit union and should not actively participate in its management, it is important to establish a spirit of friendly cooperation with them. They can help in many ways to make the operation more successful. In an associational group, it is the executive committee or similar body that guides the activities of the members. In a residence group, the heads of various civic organizations are the persons to contact.

Let us assume the group are employees of a business establishment. Arrange an interview with the owner or manager and the person whose name you received from CUNA. At this interview explain the credit union plan, answer the manager's questions, and ask him to arrange a meeting of a representative cross section of his employees —possibly 15 to 50 persons and not necessarily the entire group. The purpose of this meeting is to explain the credit union to those who will actually be most concerned when it is organized. Explain it in simple terms and answer their questions. Descriptions of the success of other credit unions in the same community are helpful. This is particularly effective if presented by some officer of the local credit union described. Following the question-and-answer period, ask the group for a show of hands on organizing a credit union. Under most credit union laws the required number of charter application signers is seven. If that number or more of the group favor organizing, ask them to sign the papers for charter application. Usually these must be notarized, so you should make sure in advance of the meeting that notary service is available.

From that point on, procedure varies a little under the various laws. In some states those present at the first meeting also elect a board of directors and the credit and supervisory committees from the group to be served, being careful to pick men and women of good standing and sympathetic understanding, who will probably join. Generally, however, the organization meeting is held later, after the application for the charter has been filed and granted. There is a fee paid to the state or federal government. These fees vary but are not large. At the organization meeting the board is elected and then the board meets and elects the president, vice-president, treasurer, and clerk from its own number. Meanwhile, the managing director has provided the required accounting forms, passbooks, ledgers, etc., and also the form of application for the treasurer's bond. He explains to the treasurer how the books are kept and generally opens them for him by starting to do business at the organization meeting.

Each person present joins on whatever basis he sees fit. Member "A" may, for example, buy a $5 share and make a first payment of 25 cents on a second share, on which he is going to pay 25 cents weekly. He also pays a 25-cent entrance fee. Member "B" may know all about credit unions and decide to take five shares from the beginning, paying in $25. Member "C" may pay only the entrance fee and 25 cents on the first share. And so it goes throughout the group.

Some credit union officers may hold regular jobs, handling loan and savings work on the side. In a small credit union only the treasurer is paid, and he may not get more than $50 a year. But the trend is toward full-time, fully paid management.

You can see why when you look at the size of some of these organizations. The 11,000-member group, Wabash Credit Union at Decatur, Illinois, has $12 million in assets, with outstanding personal loans of $7.6 million, and has 14 full-time employees.

Full information on credit unions, with up-to-date statistical data, can be secured from the Credit Union National Association, 1617 Sherman Avenue, Madison, Wisconsin. Similar information is also available from the Credit Union Leagues, which can be found in the principal cities of nearly every state.

When to Begin Loaning

As soon as the credit union has a few dollars, it starts making loans. For example, if there is $50 in the treasury at the end of the first day's business, the credit union is ready to loan all or part of that $50 to its members to meet their needs. It will be found that as soon as the employees know that the credit union makes loans, there will be plenty of loan business to keep the money working.

The plan is quite simple and the credit union plan will work well wherever the few fundamentals exist. The need and benefit of credit union services must be explained to the group. The members must be closely allied. Even the community credit union is limited to small towns where the prospective members know each other or can get acquainted easily. Finally, there must be a few men or women within the group who will become sufficiently interested to do the considerable amount of bookkeeping and other services involved.

Many scientific surveys—including a survey by the National Industrial Conference Board, Inc.—have highly commended the credit union from the viewpoint of its value both to the employee and to the employer. As far as the employee is concerned, the credit union gives him a chance to accumulate a financial reserve; it solves his short-term credit problems and he acquires an understanding about money by his participation in the management of his own savings.

As far as the employer is concerned, the credit union takes a small-loans problem off his hands which he is not usually too well qualified to solve. Primarily, the value of the credit union to an intelligent employer is a demonstration of qualities of leadership and management in his employees which he did not know existed.

Employers Report on Advantages

The experience of credit unions during the century of expanding credit union operations warrants concluding that the plan is sound and that a credit union operating in typical fashion performs a service of great value.

In *Studies in Personnel Policy, No. 42,* issued by the National Industrial Conference Board, Inc., and entitled "Employee Thrift Plans in Wartime," there is an interesting analysis of 84 typical industrial credit unions. In this study, the credit union is compared with various other thrift plans with some very thought-compelling conclusions. An official in a company employing 25,000 persons is quoted: "We feel that it is better for the employees to get their ideas . . . by the pooling of personal experiences rather than in paternalistic manner from the company or from outside sources not interested in the employees' welfare. Substitution of the credit union for a company loan program has been of great value to the company."

Another company reported: "The credit union has improved the working efficiency of employees who were formerly hounded by creditors and personal finance companies . . . It has improved the morale of our entire working force and has increased working efficiency due to the removal of financial worries."

The report notes that, "By and large, the credit unions withstood the depression years very satisfactorily. This statement is borne out by statistics compiled by the federal government and the National Industrial Conference Board."

Chapter 30

HANDLING OFFICE GRIEVANCES

HANDLING employee dissatisfactions and grievances in an office where there is no negotiated grievance procedure requires standard practice, a good knowledge of human relations on the part of supervision, and a smattering of the wisdom of Solomon.

Experience with grievance clauses in labor contracts will bear out the conclusion that, no matter how carefully the legal procedure is followed, if the human element in management is not proper and in good faith, the system will bog down.

Because the unsettled grievance is one of the best arguments for a work stoppage or slowdown, the importance of cleaning up accumulated grievances cannot be too strongly stressed. Accumulation of grievances is a potential source of danger at any time; during any period of union efforts to organize office groups, such irritations can give an organizer just the opportunity he is seeking.

Insofar as possible, therefore, action should be taken to handle employee complaints and dissatisfactions, whether real or imagined on the part of the worker, in as orderly and efficient a manner as possible. In addition, efforts should be made to ferret out the "gripes" which, although they may not have yet reached the grievance stage may, nevertheless, be symptomatic of serious internal unrest.

Griping is traditional with human beings—Americans in particular. This country started on the gripes of men and women dissatisfied with things as they were. Today we complain about the government, prices, traffic, transportation, politicians, and many other conditions. Anyone who served in the Army, Navy, or Marine Corps knows that griping was a 24-hour pastime. Labor gripes, consumers gripe, investors gripe—everyone, regardless of his position or situation, can find something to complain about with little difficulty. Much of our progress has come from being discontented with the way things are.

So long as employees grumble about things, management can find what is wrong and try to do something about it. If there are no gripes, conditions may go from bad to worse before management has an inking of the situation. Many companies use employee opinion surveys to allow workers the opportunity to state their views without fear of recrimination. The results are successfully used to improve company policies, employee relations, and overall administration.

One office manager, with a large Ohio insurance company, comments: "When grievances cease to accumulate in our office, it is a danger signal. Either supervisors are giving too much away or are too hard to approach."

Typical Office Gripes

Listed below are the 13 most prevalent grievances in 185 offices contacted by Dartnell. They are listed in order of popularity (if the term may be used here). Since many companies indicated several grievances as common, the percentages are developed from the responses of all. They are, in order of occurrence:

Wages	85 percent
Particular supervisors	80 percent
General working conditions	60 percent
Promotion policies	58 percent
Physical conditions	47 percent
Company policies	42 percent
Transfer policies	35 percent
Seniority policies	30 percent
Benefits for employees	28 percent
Time-off policies	25 percent
Fellow workers	23 percent
Transportation to work	18 percent
Lack of communication	10 percent

Others include poor food or service in the cafeteria. Many firms report continual checks on the number of employees using the cafeteria against the total number who could use it will reveal whether the feeding service is a success or not. If the percentage is low, the reason could be: (1) Prices are too high, (2) the food is poor in quality, (3) the food is unattractively served, (4) the service is poor, (5) the atmosphere is unpleasant, (6) the portions served are too small.

One good way to find out if any of these conditions exist is to try the cafeteria with these questions in mind. Another and better way used by many companies is to ask the employees point-blank why they don't like the cafeteria. The form shown below has been used successfully for this purpose.

If a company suggestion system is used, watch for lack of interest. It is another clue to employee gripes. When workers aren't sending in sufficient suggestions from certain departments and sections, something is wrong. It is time to check up before other symptoms begin showing up.

CAFETERIA SERVICE

We have noted recently that a great many employees prefer to eat elsewhere rather than in our cafeteria. We believe the food to be good, wholesome, and the portions reasonably large. The prices seem to be in line with other cafeterias in the neighborhood. As the more persons the cafeteria serves, the better we can buy on the market and the lower the prices to the employee, it is to our advantage—yours and the management's—to make the cafeteria a good place to eat.

Therefore, will you fill out the form below and return it without your signature tomorrow?

(a) Do you eat in our cafeteria? Yes.......... No..........

(b) If you do, have you found the food to your liking? Yes.......... No..........

(c) Is there sufficient variety? Yes.......... No..........

(d) Are the prices too high? Yes.......... No..........

(e) Are the portions of food large enough? Yes.......... No..........

If there are any other reasons why you do not eat in our cafeteria will you list them below in order that we may make a further check on the service and the food:

PLEASE DO NOT SIGN THIS FORM. DROP IT IN THE BOX AT THE LEFT OF THE DOOR AS YOU ENTER IN THE MORNING.

Only 60 percent of the reporting companies have a set and established policy or system for handling office-type grievances. Another 5 percent have no set policy, facing the problem when it comes up, and 35 percent have no policy at all. The controller of a Michigan auto parts manufacturing firm comments: "We used to let each section head handle grievances as they came up in his section, but there was so much variation in handling of similar problems, we worked out a formalized procedure three years ago. It has worked well and we at least are prepared to handle situations in a fair and equal way now, though we still haven't completely stopped grievances from accumulating."

Who Handles the Grievance?

Asked this question, the 185 companies that contributed of their experience answered as follows:

Immediate supervisor ....85 percent
Office manager (or assistant) .... 8 percent
Personnel department .... 5 percent
Director of industrial relations .... 2 percent

These percentages do not tell the whole story, however, since many companies report a step-by-step procedure designed to carry the complaint to its final conclusion. As one office manager said, "Office grievances are like returning inferior merchandise to the store. If the customer doesn't get satisfaction from the clerk who sold her the item, she goes to the buyer. If he doesn't come through, she'll soon be upstairs trying to see the president." Of course, one might add, progressive retailers use a standard system on returned merchandise just as progressive office management formalizes its grievance procedure.

Here are the methods used by officials of some of the reporting companies in the handling of office worker complaints and dissatisfactions:

Ordnance Research Laboratory, Pennsylvania State University. If she (the employee in question) followed the grievance procedure, she would contact her immediate supervisor. In practice she comes to the personnel office. I hear her story, check with the supervisor for his information, and call the offended worker for a separate conversation. After analyzing information with the supervisor, I talk with each clerical employee involved and straighten it out.

Liquiflame Oils, Ltd., Toronto, Canada. Office grievances are handled through the supervisor. The worker's supervisor handles it to his satisfaction or the employee has recourse to any of the company management committees. This company, with an office force of 50 employees, reports very few grievances because our active management level interest is the main deterrent.

U.S. Electrical Motors, Inc., Milford, Conn. Grievances are handled by the immediate supervisor. If not settled on that level, they can be taken to the department head and a member of the personnel department. If still not settled, they are referred to the commercial manager and personnel manager.

Gibson Refrigerator Div., Hupp Corp., Greenville, Mich. Each case is treated as individual—in most cases the persons involved would be brought together in the personnel office. The company has over 500 office workers and uses the honor system without setting up a list of "don'ts."

United Van Lines, Inc., Maplewood, Mo. If the situation comes to the attention of the department head, he will try to reconcile the problem. He will refer to personnel for assistance if he meets with resistance. However, we try to get the department manager to resolve the grievance with advice and consultation from personnel.

Pay Grievances

With so many of the prevailing grievances dealing with wage and salary dissatisfactions, a moment should be spent with some of the contributing factors. All employees (if they are ambitious) are anxious to be advanced to higher pay classifications. Some want this whether they are entitled to it or not. They present many and varied reasons why they should be advanced. Among their claims will be that their job classifications are incorrect and they should be receiving the wages of a higher classification. Or they may insist that they are doing work of greater skill and ability in comparison with other office jobs on which workers are receiving higher wages.

When grievances accumulate over job classification, time study rates, etc., it would seem that the whole rate setup needs, (1) an overhauling, or (2) to be properly sold to employees. Many managements seriously try to clarify the system of wage rates and job classifications. All ratings and classifications should be so clearly set up and explained to the employee that he can readily understand the difference between his job and the other fellow's job.

As long as an employee is confused about rates, there will be evidences of dissatisfaction on that score and grievances to be settled. Simplifying the system, clarifying and explaining it, and then selling it to the workers is very much part of management's job; and the better it is done, the less friction and the fewer disputes there will be.

Also high on the list of common grievances is the problem of complaints about certain office managers, submanagers, or other supervisors. Some years ago, J. C. Staehle, in charge of industrial relations, Aldens, Inc. (Chicago mail-order company), released an analysis of the 10 most common causes of employee discontent: These were:

1. Failure to credit employees when they make suggestions.
2. Failure to investigate and correct grievances.
3. Failure to encourage employees.
4. Criticism of employees in the presence of others.
5. Failure to promote from within the organization.
6. Failure to recognize and praise employees for good work.
7. Failure to grant wage increases when deserved.
8. Failure to ask employees for their opinions.
9. Failure to keep employees informed as to progress they are making.
10. Favoritism—deliberate or unintentional.

Top management must bear the brunt for some of these dissatisfactions, but the direct supervisor is responsible for the majority. When too many complaints about one supervisor pile up, it is a danger signal. They deserve investigation. Many progressive concerns, like Merck & Co., Inc., are developing office personnel development programs to equip office managers with the fundamentals of human relations as well as the technical aspects of their work.

Another prevalent grievance among office workers is dissatisfaction with working conditions in general. Such complaints are usually brought about by an accumulation of little irritations which, after a while, the employee merely boils into one big one—a general gripe about everything.

Here is the way a controller of a large publishing firm in the East puts it: "When a complaint about general working conditions arises, it puts the supervisor on a spot. He must draw out the real reason from the employee. Here is our method of handling such complaints:

1. Draw the employee out
   a. Talk with him in private
   b. Put him at ease so he can tell his story
   c. Be sympathetic and understanding
   d. Get him to restate his objection
   e. Hold back your temper
   f. Get all the facts and assure him you'll give him an answer.

2. Verify the conditions
   a. Investigate the things brought out
   b. Check with other people who may have information
   c. Be sure of company policy on the matter
   d. Check for other complaints along similar lines.

3. Report back to the employee as soon as you can
   a. Have your facts and answers ready
   b. If the employee is wrong, handle it tactfully
   c. If the employee is right, admit the mistake
   d. Don't be harsh—don't be domineering—don't be uncertain.

4. Learn from the grievance
   a. Make sure such a situation won't happen again
   b. Follow up with the employee to see that all is well
   c. Keep an eye open for other dissatisfactions.

"If a manager will do these things," the controller continued, "he will find it works on handling about every type of office grievance situation."

Explaining Procedures Change Cuts Grievances

Getting changes in procedures put into effect with a minimum of effort and time and a maximum of cooperation and acceptance can be a problem. The Prudential Insurance Company of America solved it by a carefully planned three-day training course for the girls whose work was involved. The girls were called into the home office and instructed in the new methods in one fell swoop. An added advantage of such a training program is that standard procedures which may have drifted off course may be straightened out.

Denis W. Menton, assistant sales manager, who helped set up the course, explains the program:

"This class was our first experience with this type of training and was scheduled because of some changes in our business procedures which we felt would be best transmitted to our field clerical help by calling them in for a three-day training class.

"Previously, these clerks were hired in the field and received informal training from clerks they may have been succeeding or from the salesman in charge of the office.

"Most of our group field offices are small units with a group salesmen and serviceman and one girl clerk as the staff. In the larger cities we do have multiple offices with several men and several girls. The girl in the smaller office, however, has very general duties: taking correspondence, filing, answering the telephone, etc.; and, in addition, has some technical jobs in calculating insurance rates and in making insurance proposals for our prospects. It was primarily the need for training in these latter jobs that led us to conduct this class. As far as the subject matter of the class, it was largely devoted to the preparation of proposals and a review of proper rate calculation procedures, although there was some discussion of general office procedures regarding filing and submission of reports to the home office.

"The girls were given, along with their invitation to the class, a written agenda, a listing of the girls that would be attending, together with the instructors for the class, and the instructions regarding transportation, hotel reservations, etc. We prepared in advance a field manual which included information on general office procedures, together with a complete write-up of material discussed during the class. These manuals were taken back by the girls to their offices and will be kept up-to-date by amendments whenever necessary.

"We tried to keep the meeting on an informal basis with plenty of time for discussion and questions and answers, rather than using the lecture approach. The girls do use automatic calculating machines in their rate work and the proper use of these machines was reviewed with them during the class.

"We do feel that this program was a success and have noticed since the class that there has been a definite improvement in the clerical work in the field offices and in the accuracy and completeness of the reports that they submit to the home office. It is entirely possible that we will have further programs of this sort in the future."

Providing instructions in written form in considered very important by most companies. Even a simple listing of procedures in mimeographed form is better than depending on memory. Since most grievances arise because employees are not properly informed, or at least feel they are not, Prudential's program serves the purpose well.

Some Case Studies

The case studies that follow are taken from actual office grievances passed along to Dartnell's editors. Each situation happened. The names of employees, supervisors, and companies were changed at the request of contributors.

The studies are made up in three parts. First, the situation as it happened; second, the action taken to remedy the grievance; and third, the results of such action. In some cases there is a fourth part consisting of additional comments by the contributor. For purposes of organization, the types of problems are listed under general headings:

COMPLAINTS ABOUT PHYSICAL CONDITIONS

The Case of Frigid Frieda

THE PROBLEM—Our office has unit-type air conditioners. Certain individuals constantly complained about the drafts from the units. They said they could not stand the cooling breezes. One girl made it a practice to get up from her work place and turn the unit off despite the majority feeling that it was not too cool.

ACTION TAKEN—The department head designated one person to take charge of checking temperatures at the various points throughout the office and adjusting the air conditioners accordingly. The prime complainant was called into the office by the department head where it was explained that turning the units off and on at random actually created drafts. She was given a choice of:

    a. Changing her seat to another location, or

    b. If she was still uncomfortable, she must realize that the office could not be rebuilt nor all of the other employees discommoded because of one person.

RESULTS—The girl did change her seat. Actually she still was under air conditioning, but felt a moral victory in having her placed changed. There have been no further complications. By explanation, firmness, and suggestion, a bad situation was brought under control.

Mirror, Mirror on the Wall

THE PROBLEM—The mirror over the washbowls in the women's washroom was arbitrarily removed by the maintenance department, on the rumored basis that certain girls using the mirror interfered with other girls wanting to wash their hands. There was a storm of protest and a petition was circulated demanding that the mirror be replaced.

ACTION TAKEN—The office personnel department, realizing the adverse effect upon personnel relations, took steps to have the mirror replaced, pointing out to management that the body of women employees could not logically be penalized because of a few possibly inconsiderate individuals.

RESULTS—Peace returned.

Lead Kindly Light

THE PROBLEM—One of our better typists, who has been with the company for 18 years, recently began complaining about the lighting over her work place. We had installed new lighting a year ago and were sure it was the best available for close clerical work. None of the other girls complained, but Jane kept arguing that she was getting headaches from the poor light.

ACTION TAKEN—When the problem reached the stage where the girl threatened to quit unless her lighting improved, we started to act. We now realize we should have shown interest in her problem sooner, but felt it was all in her mind and she'd forget about it. We started by using a lightmeter to check all the work places in the office. The meter reading showed Jane's lighting was equal to the average throughout the office. We showed Jane the reading which was very high and equal to the highest recommendation of the electric company. She still balked.

The office manager called Jane into his office for a private session and tried to draw out her feelings about other working conditions in the office. She seemed generally unhappy. Finally he hit upon a good suggestion. He told Jane to go to a doctor and have her eyes checked. It was agreed that the company would pay for the examination. She agreed to do this, although with inner reservations.

RESULTS—The examination revealed the fact that Jane needed new glasses. The headaches were caused by a weakness in her eyes, not the lighting. Inasmuch as we sent her to the doctor, we carried through and paid for the new glasses. She is perfectly happy and doing a good job today.

COMMENTS—This case proved to us that the things employees complain about are not always the real problem. It is up to the manager to help the employee discover the real cause of a grievance, and help her solve it. In this case we were fortunate enough to salvage an excellent worker that we might have lost. She now feels a new sense of loyalty and security within her company and it was well worth the cost.

COMPLAINTS ABOUT FELLOW EMPLOYEES

Religion Is One's Own Business

THE PROBLEM—We had a case of religious zealousness some time ago that really caused a disturbance in our office. One of the girls was distributing religious pamphlets and spent considerable time, during working hours, talking with other employees about her church. She was a loyal and conscientious employee, but was causing considerable resentment among other employees by her actions.

ACTION TAKEN—Upon receiving complaints from other workers, the supervisor had a heart-to-heart discussion with Mildred, the girl in question. He presented the problem to the employee in such a way that she realized her comments and passing out of religious literature reflected on the commission (a state civil service commission) as representing beliefs of the commission. The very basis of our Constitution was pointed out to the employee, showing that we are each entitled to our own belief and that we should respect the beliefs and religious convictions of others.

RESULTS—The girl is a good Christian, desirous of doing the right thing. Her honesty, loyalty, and conscientiousness were important factors in her acceptance of this constructive criticism. She has controlled her actions since and is getting along well with others.

COMMENTS—No company complains, or has a right to complain, about the religious beliefs of its employees. Very few do, either. But when the employee uses company working time to further religious activities, it is not Christian in the first place. "Render unto Caesar the things that are Caesar's and to God the things that are God's." Usually an employee of this type will see the point and refrain from such actions when she realizes she is not doing the work of God properly by using company time.

The Problem of "Papa's Little Helper"

THE PROBLEM—Jennie is secretary to the office manager, but is not responsible for the work activities of the other girls in the office. Around the office she has the reputation, among the other girls, of being "papa's little helper." Recently she complained to the office manager and to the general supervisor that three of the girls (whose work tied in with hers) were not doing good enough work and not working as steadily as she thought they should. She also told the girls and they resented her criticism and stopped talking to her. They, too, complained to the general supervisor. The office manager agreed with Jennie, since he listened to only her side of the story.

ACTION TAKEN—Since both Jennie and the three girls had complained to the general supervisor, he decided to talk separately with them. The girls were still resentful and wanted more concrete action. It took two talks to soften Jennie. The general supervisor even presented the girls' work records to show that they were not making excessive errors and were doing more than the required amount of daily work. To some extent this impressed Jennie. A cooling-off period of several days was allowed to elapse.

After the waiting period, the general supervisor called the four girls together for a discussion of ways to improve general clerical conditions in the office. No mention was made of the previous disagreement. Jennie and the other girls talked freely, with the supervisor and with each other. All seemed glad to have a convenient "way out."

RESULTS—Harmony was again restored. When opportunity permitted, the general supervisor reported the situation to the office manager and let him draw his own conclusions regarding his part in the affair.

COMMENTS—The disagreement was best handled by someone emotionally apart from the trouble. It was, of course, wise to talk to the involved parties separately. It was also wise to let the initial irritation die down. But the most important element was to achieve a solution that would save face for everyone. Note, too, the fact that the general supervisor provided a common basis for reconciliation by invention (the discussion of how to improve clerical operations).

Don't Be Half Safe

THE PROBLEM—Some time back three girls came into the office manager's office to complain about Helen Smart, another girl in the same office. They said working near Helen was very objectionable because the girl had a bad case of body odor. She was fairly new with the company, having been hired four months previously. All signs pointed to the fact that she did good work, was conscientious, and had a fine attendance record. The office manager had noticed Helen's problem, but had ignored it.

ACTION TAKEN—When the girls came in and reported their grievance, the office manager assured them action would be taken to help Helen realize her problem without hurting her feelings. He asked the girls to refrain from saying any more about it until he had a chance to act. They agreed to this request.

The office manager took the matter up in confidence with the controller of the company and the personnel manager of office employees. They agreed on a course of action. As a matter of good morale for office employees our company provides a luncheon meeting about once every two months. The girls are given a two-hour lunch period and are taken to a nearby restaurant where a nice lunch is provided and a presentation in the form of a film or lecture is given. This has been an effective morale-builder for our office girls for several years and they look forward to the luncheons. We decided to use the next luncheon to present a good film on personal hygiene, combined with a talk on the subject by our company nurse.

The nurse was tipped off about the condition, although the girl's name was not mentioned. She did a good job of covering hygiene, ranging from the importance of brushing one's teeth twice a day to personal habits of cleanliness. A little folder, or check list, was given each girl to help her in her personal hygiene.

RESULTS—The other girls made quite a point of talking about the program and the importance of the tips given. Helen joined right with them in these discussions and apparently took the hint. The other girls report the situation is no longer a problem and everyone is happier.

COMMENTS—Criticisms about personal appearance or such a personal thing as body odor are hard to handle with the person alone. She feels hurt and loses confidence. She also tends to resent such advice. We feel we handled this one well. Everybody gained something from the program, and Helen caught on without being singled out. We are very proud of the way it was handled. We kept everybody happy and helped a valuable employee improve her interpersonal relations by indirect effort.

COMPLAINTS ABOUT SUPERVISORS

The Self-Appointed Purchasing Agent

THE PROBLEM—A woman supervisor was in the habit of taking it upon herself to select and buy gifts for fellow employees for birthdays, sicknesses, weddings, and other occasions. After purchasing the gift and showing it to the other girls, she would tell each girl how much money she owed.

Last fall the climax was reached when the girls had to contribute about eight dollars within a period of two weeks without having any voice in the matter of gift selection or amount to be spent. In all fairness to this supervisor, we should say her intentions were the best, but she had been doing this for so many years that she little realized the resentment her actions had built up.

The office manager, fairly new in the organization, knew nothing of this situation until his secretary complained to him that the other girls had been told to donate three dollars each as a wedding gift. The girls were willing to give the three dollars each, but felt the gift should be purchased through the group.

ACTION TAKEN—The office manager, by discreet inquiry among the girls, found out that the facts were as outlined above and that a feeling of resentment had grown to tremendous proportions over the entire situation.

He talked with the supervisor and asked about the policy of buying gifts. He asked for suggestions on ways to improve the practice. She agreed to the idea of an employee fund to provide for such gifts. The girls agreed to this idea, too.

RESULTS—A questionnaire was made out for the girls to answer and add their comments. As a result, an employee fund was started, each girl giving 25 cents a week until the fund should reach an amount sufficient to take care of ordinary expenditures.

Two girls were chosen to collect the money and take care of selecting gifts with the approval of fellow employees. Each three months a different pair of girls handled the details. The girls now feel they have an equal say in the matter of donations and gifts.

COMMENTS—We feel it is the duty of the office manager to handle situations of this kind with the greatest amount of tact to see that the problem is solved to everyone's satisfaction, if at all possible. In this case it worked out just right.

Where Do I Stand?

THE PROBLEM—A grievance was received from Mary Jones, a project technical stenographer (in an ordnance research laboratory). She said, "I work hard, am inexperienced, I know, but all I get from my supervisor is criticism. I am really disgusted and would like a transfer."

ACTION TAKEN—The personnel director talked with Mary and asked her to cite examples of the type of criticism received. She cited several instances. Asked if the supervisor ever complimented her work, she said, "No." Asked if she would describe her work as poor, average, good, or excellent, she replied, "Good."

The information obtained in the interview was relayed by the personnel manager to the assistant director of the laboratory. The personnel manager also agreed to talk with Mary's supervisor.

In talking with the girl's supervisor it was learned that he was not familiar with her complaints at all. Asked if he ever complimented her, he said, "No." Asked about the quality of her work, he described it as good, the same way Mary described it. The supervisor agreed to talk the matter over with Mary.

RESULTS—Some weeks later, Mary returned to the personnel manager's office to report things were much better. Her supervisor had talked with her about the situation and she no longer wanted a transfer. She thanked the personnel manager for his assistance.

COMMENTS—Situations involving things the supervisor did NOT do are tougher to handle than things he actually did. In this case it was an obvious situation of lack of good communication from supervisor to employee. It might also be noted that most grievances come about for the same reason.

Look What I Did

THE PROBLEM—Our telephone company has had some interesting grievances over the years. One of the commonest gripes is held by the employee who makes a good suggestion and the boss takes credit for it. Recently, one of our girls suggested rearranging the names on the pigeonholes used for sorting the inter-office mail so that the line-up would agree with the route taken by messengers who deliver the mail. She complained to the office manager because her direct supervisor scoffed at the idea when it was presented, claiming it would take a while for the sorters to get used to the new arrangement.

Six months later, the supervisor changed the pigeonhole names, according to the employee's original idea, but passed it along as his own idea.

ACTION TAKEN—The office manager took the girl's statement, not promising direct action, but offering to look into the matter. He then called in the direct supervisor and told him the complaint, without mentioning the girl's name directly. The supervisor claimed he had thought of the idea over a year before, and had held back using it until he had worked the details out. He admitted talking with the girl in question, though he didn't remember which girl it was.

Since the situation could not be corrected at this time, plans were made for an office suggestion system. We now have one.

RESULTS—Our system is not elaborate, but very adequate for our office needs. We have suggestion forms and a working policy on handling and processing suggestions. No supervisor has any right to call a suggestion his if it has been turned in to the central suggestion box. It becomes the property of the person making the suggestion, and, ultimately, the company's when accepted and the contributor is rewarded.

COMMENTS—Suggestion boxes work if the system is right. They encourage employees to think of methods to improve their work and give them the feeling of security that their suggestion, if accepted, will receive proper recognition.

COMPLAINTS ABOUT TRANSFERS

Correcting the Negative Attitude

THE PROBLEM—Adams, a mature man, was transferred to the office from another unit. His attitude toward the organization and management was hostile. His training, background, experience, and performance indicated the possibility that he would be a better-than-average employee, if his attitude could be improved.

ACTION TAKEN—In a friendly, courteous, and helpful manner, the manager explained to him his duties, responsibilities, and opportunities. He was permitted to carry out his assignment without close supervision. When his performance was better than average or outstanding, he was complimented in a routine, matter-of-fact manner.

RESULTS—Instances of outstanding performances increased. Additional responsibility was given to him; his attitude began to improve and today his loyalty to the company is without question.

COMMENTS—Corrective action was determined after a careful study of the employee and the remedial measures were tailored to bring out his strong qualities. Little opportunity was afforded the man to practice a negative attitude. Corrective action must be fitted to the individual and the supervisor must exercise patience.

Life Is Easier in Herb's Department

THE PROBLEM—Recently Alice Brown, a typist in the billing department, registered a rather loud complaint about the company's transfer policies. Alice had been with the company two years, was a pretty fair employee, though she did have a spotty attendance and tardiness record. She complained to the office manager that she wanted to work in Herb Barton's department, because she liked the work that department did better than routine billing work. Barton is the head of sales correspondence. She had applied for such a transfer twice before but was not transferred because she could not be spared by the head of the billing department and there were no openings in the sales correspondence section.

ACTION TAKEN—Because we were shorthanded for typists we made a real effort to help Alice resolve her problem. Her record showed she had always been in a routine typing job and had no experience or training correspondence. When this was explained, and she saw the possibility of such a transfer was very remote, the real reason came out. It came out as a result of anger. It seems her friend, Cathy, worked for Herb and told of his easy way in handling company rules and regulations. The friend "rubbed it in" to Alice that her boss was a slave driver, that he went "by the book" too much, which Herb didn't do. As a result of this incident a meeting was held for all department heads. The particular case was not mentioned, but a standard operating and practice procedure was developed for all departments.

RESULTS—The incident brought out the fact that it was true that certain department heads "winked" at regulations and procedures, while others enforced them. We had no standard policy and employees were comparing treatment in one department with that in another. We now have a standard practice in all departments. Alice, though she doesn't realize it was her gripe that brought it all about, is still in the billing department and is contented. The friend is not "talking up" Herb's department any more because he, too, is going "by the book."

COMMENTS—We believe one of the greatest mistakes a management can make is to neglect to develop a standard practice manual for all supervisors and employees. We have eliminated many of the little jealousies and irritations that previously existed by working out such a manual.

GROUP GRIEVANCES

When Do We Eat?

THE PROBLEM—We recently discontinued the privilege of eating rolls, sandwiches, candy, etc., at the work desk. The reason for this decision was the amount of dirt, filth, and vermin caused by such practices. It also brought about a great amount of wasted work time. Adverse group opinion and feeling had been high as a result of this decision.

ACTION TAKEN—We still allow employees to drink coffee, milk, or a soft drink at the work place. We are planning a controlled coffee break and rest period and plan to make the recreation room available for such a rest period. We plan to explain the whole program, the reasons for the change, and the benefits of a planned program, to employees next week.

RESULTS—It's too early to tell, but we think employees will be better satisfied with the new setup. We have just completed an attitude survey which has helped considerably in planning employee services.

COMMENTS—If there was a mistake in handling this grievance, it lies in not planning the controlled break before stopping the old practice. In this way, we would have avoided the dissatisfactions that now exist as a result of stopping a practice that has been in effect for years. The moral of the tale is, simply, if you make a change in procedures or rules, make sure you explain why you are doing it and what it will mean to employees.

They Were All Unhappy

THE PROBLEM—Ours is a rather large life insurance company. In one department we had a group of dissatisfied girls with hidden grievances that only showed in attitude and morale. It was obvious that, as a group, they were very discontented but it was also quite difficult to find the basic cause of this dissatisfaction.

ACTION TAKEN—After careful planning on the part of the supervisors, a group meeting was called. During the course of the meeting each clerical and staff employee was given ample opportunity to express grievances and bring them out into the open. It took a bit of careful planning and tact to get the sessions started, but once the ice was broken, employees opened up and stated their gripes and offered suggestions.

RESULTS—The results of such meetings have increased morale in our office 100 percent. Excellent ideas have been developed and put into action. For example, staff itineraries are now posted, the filing system has been revamped, and dozens of other procedures have been made more effective through pooling our thinking.

COMMENTS—It takes an aggressive and alert system to eliminate grievances. They should be anticipated and acted upon before they have a chance to fester and grow into a mass grievance held by the majority of employees.

The Boss Keeps Looking Over My Shoulder

THE PROBLEM—Admittedly our offices are crowded. We need more space and are planning to add to the office some time next year. In the meantime, the cramped quarters in which we work have caused some rather ticklish interpersonal problems. For instance, here is one that happened not too long ago. A group of the girls asked for some time with the office manager. He granted the interview and the girls told him they resented the way the boss (the company president) was always looking out of the glass window in his office. They said he seemed to check who was at the work place and who was at the drinking fountain, etc. The girls also felt he made unnecessary trips through the office peering over the shoulders of workers to see what work they were doing.

ACTION TAKEN—Our president is a quiet, introverted type of man. He is serious and not given to much social expression. He also has bad eyes and cannot see beyond the glass in his office. His biggest failing is the fact that he doesn't bother to speak to the girls other than on business. The office manager told the girls he would see what could be done about their complaint.

He talked with me (I am vice-president) and we decided to tell the president about it. He was amazed to learn of the complaint, but did not resent the fact that the girls said it. Less than a week later, a venetian blind was installed in the president's office window. He also made less trips around the office and when he did, he either smiled at or talked with the girls.

Now everyone is happy, but it goes to show what little petty things can develop when you are in a crowded space.

COMMENTS—Many complaints like this could be avoided with a little preventive maintenance. In this case, the preventive maintenance would have been a little friendlier manner on the part of our president. Girls are rather sensitive—more so than men. They take things seriously that men might laugh off. Anticipating these sensitive points is very much part of office management's job.

SALARY COMPLAINTS

I Want More Money, Too

THE PROBLEM—We recently gave a series of increases in hourly rates on the basis of merit. One of the girls, with very limited ability, asked for a substantial raise in salary. She pointed to the cases of two other girls (both better-than-average workers) who received such increases.

ACTION TAKEN—The department head explained to the girl why she did not get an increase along with the others. Dissatisfied with this explanation, the girl went to the general office manager. He promised to review the situation. A little later he called in the department head who repeated the reasons that he had given the employee before. The girl has been with the company over a year, had had no increases since she started with the company, yet had been retained. As a result of this case, our company now has periodic merit reviews with employees to keep them posted on their progress and development. Incidentally, the girl was given a small raise and told the next one would be based on her improvement.

RESULTS—The department head resented the action by the general office manager, feeling he had gone over his head in dealing directly with the employee. He was correct in this feeling, but it was his lack of informing the girl about her weaknesses that caused the problem. The girl has improved tremendously in her work, even in the eyes of her supervisor who now feels she deserves another increase. He had just finished a periodic merit review. The form is on my desk now and says in part, "Jane _____ has shown more interest and willingness. Her work is much better, though it is still not tops in ability. I think she deserves the increase."

TIME-OFF GRIEVANCES

Weekends for All

THE PROBLEM—A number of resignations accumulated because of too-frequent assignment to weekend shifts. Our hospital was seeking a fair and satisfactory rotation of days off. Saturday and/or Sunday work, especially on the 7:00 a.m. to 3:30 p.m. shift was the big problem.

ACTION TAKEN—Our supervisor called a meeting and asked for suggestions regarding a solution to the problem. The employees, who eagerly participated in the meeting, unanimously agreed that each member would prepare a schedule covering a four-week period and develop a system of "days-off rotation" which would be fair and satisfactory. Seniority would not be considered an exemption qualification, since the group felt this would tend to perpetuate the problem of too-frequent weekend work for a few of the office clerks.

RESULTS—At the next meeting, the employees presented their "proposed" four-week schedules. Each schedule was discussed and its relative merits and weaknesses pointed out. Finally, the group selected a combination of three schedules. It was decided that a trial run of four weeks should be initiated before accepting the schedule permanently.

At the end of this four-week period, the group unanimously decided that the trial run had been a success and that the schedule should be installed on a permanent basis.

This new schedule permitted each office employee to work the same number of Saturdays and Sundays each month. In addition, it gave them the opportunity of knowing exactly what their days off would be on a week-to-week basis.

COMMENTS—A bad grievance situation was eliminated by allowing employees to solve the problem as a group.

A Gripe About Vacation Time

THE PROBLEM—An employee hired after January 1, and entitled to a one-week vacation, felt it was unfair that a fellow employee hired just prior to the first of January was given a two-week vacation. This was complicated by the fact that the other employee was on a leave of absence without pay for three months. Actually, as the first employee pointed out, their respective times on the job were almost equal. The complainant also added her feeling that she was a better worker than the other girl and had carried the load during the other's absence.

ACTION TAKEN—The problem was turned over to the personnel department by the supervisor of the two girls. The complainant was called into the personnel office where it was explained that neither quality of work nor a leave of absence, without pay, were factors upon which to determine vacation entitlement. The personnel director further explained that to penalize a worker for leave of absence would negate the privilege leave is supposed to represent. The company stood firm on the ruling.

RESULTS—It took some convincing, but finally the first girl realized her grievance was not based on sound and fair thinking. When she saw how such a decision, if it favored her request as originally presented, could very well have an effect upon her vacation status were she ever forced to take extra time off on a leave of absence, she went along with the ruling.

COMMENTS—All grievances do not have a "pat" ending where the company and the grievant compromise. When a matter of policy is involved, the company must stand firm. However, it is well to show the complainant where her grievance is off base.

The Why of Grievances

There is a common thread to all grievances. Something is lacking in communication, something that causes little annoyances and irritations to fester and grow underneath what might be an otherwise smooth-appearing surface. Just because grievances are not brought out into the open does not necessarily mean they don't exist. In fact, the company that claims "we have no grievances at all" is more apt to have a deluge of hidden gripes churning under the surface because opportunity has not been given to employees to bring them out.

If office employees are to be kept happy and contented, it will only be accomplished by managements alert to the dangers of accumulated grievances and willing to make determined efforts to establish better employee relations. Progressive-minded top managements are doing this by studying the types of complaints most commonly aired by employees, analyzing how they develop, and using varied techniques to prevent such problems from arising in the future. The trend toward established and standardized procedures for handling office grievances is growing. The use of office manuals is more prevalent today than ever before. Employee relations programs include new and better employee handbooks, company magazine features, posters, and letters to employees. Group meetings to solve problems and air gripes are part of the new trend. Use of employee opinion surveys, regularly scheduled merit-review interviews, employee counseling services, and selling of "fringe" benefits to employees are also component parts of the well-organized program.

While the handling of actual problems brought up by employees varies with the particular case, the nature of the business, and the working conditions, other contributing factors must be considered. The case studies, taken from actual office situations, are not offered as "pat" solutions. They are offered as exhibits of ways and means used by office managements to curb employee dissatisfactions.

Good communication keeps employees informed and up-to-date on company rules, regulations, planning, and procedures. It starts at the top and filters through the mid-management level to department heads, supervisors, and, ultimately, the employees. A short circuit at any level can spell the difference between successful human relations and a low level of morale. Office employees are not different from production, engineering, technical, or sales employees. Because they are not, as a rule, an organized group does not mean they are without the usual personal dissatisfactions and complaints. Successful handling of the problems of this large segment of American workers will pay off in great productivity, lessened turnover, higher morale, and—most important to most managements—satisfied and contented employees.

PENNSYLVANIA STATE UNIVERSITY
ORDNANCE RESEARCH LABORATORY

GRIEVANCE PROCEDURE FOR REGULAR EMPLOYEES AND FOR EMPLOYEES DESIGNATED AS PART-TIME

A. A grievance is defined as the claim of an individual employee, as well as a small group of employees, that his rights under announced rules and regulations or past practices have not been respected.

An employee can use this procedure without fear of prejudice to himself.

B. Any grievance to be considered under the following procedure must be brought up at Step 1 of the grievance procedure within one (1) calendar week of the time that the employee has knowledge of the act which is the basis for the grievance.

Since most grievances can be settled in conversation between the employee and his supervisor, a written grievance will not be considered by the University unless the grievance has first been discussed with the supervisor by the employee, and the supervisor has had two (2) work days to give an answer to the employee.

STEP 1

The employee shall put his grievance in writing on a form provided by the University. He shall make two copies and give them to his supervisor. A meeting is then held within the next two (2) work days of the request and is attended by the employee, his immediate supervisor, and the next higher supervisor. At this step, the employee may be accompanied by another University employee of his own choosing from his own department.

A written answer is given to the employee within two (2) work days of the hearing.

STEP 2

If satisfaction is not gained in Step 1, and the employee requests a Step 2 hearing, the employee and all supervisors concerned will meet with the dean or administrative officer and the director of employee relations within two (2) work days of the time the meeting is requested by the employee. At the meeting the employee may have representatives of his own choosing not to exceed six in number. A written answer will be sent to the employee within two (2) work days.

STEP 3

If satisfaction is not gained in Step 2 and if the employee requests a Step 3 hearing, a meeting will be held of all persons present at the Step 2 hearing plus a person designated by the President of the University. This meeting will be held within seven (7) days of the request by the employee and an answer will be given to the employee within seven (7) days.

STEP 4

If not settled at Step 3, the grievance may be referred by either party to a tripartite board consisting of one representative of the University, one representative of the employee, and a neutral representative chosen by the representatives of the employee and the University. After the hearing, the decision of a majority of the board shall be final and binding. The board shall apply and interpret existing rules and regulations to the case at hand.

The procedure prescribed herein when applicable shall be in lieu and to the exclusion of the procedure prescribed by the Act of June 30, 1947, P.L. 1183, as amended.

C. The employee can take his grievance to the next step of the grievance procedure if he is not satisfied with the results at any step.

D. If an employee gets an answer within the time limit at any step of the procedure and does not ask for further review of his grievance within the next four (4) work days, it will be assumed that he is satisfied. As a result, that particular grievance will not be considered any further.

E. An employee will not lose pay for any time that he is not on his job if his presence is required at any step of this grievance procedure. An employee will not be paid for any time that he is present during the processing of a grievance, if this time falls outside his normal working hours.

SAMPLE GRIEVANCE FORM

STEP 1

If you have a grievance, talk with your supervisor about it within one week of the time that you have knowledge of the act which is the basis for your grievance. Otherwise, your grievance cannot be brought up again at a later date.

If you feel that your grievance has not been settled satisfactorily after your supervisor has had an opportunity to give an answer to you regarding your grievance, make two (2) copies of this form and give them to your immediate supervisor. This will indicate that you want your grievance to proceed to Step 1 of the grievance procedure.

After your Step 1 hearing a copy of this form containing statements of your supervisor and the next higher supervisor will be returned to you. (Note to supervisor: After receiving the two copies from the aggrieved employee, make two additional copies. This makes a total of four copies. Write your answer to the grievance on all four copies and give them to the next higher supervisor. Note to next higher supervisor: Write your answer to the grievance on all four copies and distribute them as follows: Keep one copy, send one to your dean or administrative officer, send one to the aggrieved employee, and send a copy to the Director of Employee Relations.)

A complete statement of the University grievance procedure is available through your supervisor on request.

_____   _____

      Your name (please print)   Department

STEP (1) My grievance is:

_____   _____

      (Sign your name here)   Today's date

Statement of immediate supervisor:

_____   _____

         Signature   Date

Statement of supervisor at next higher level:

_____   _____

         Signature   Date

If you want to take your grievance to Step 2 in the Grievance Procedure, return this form to your supervisor. This must be done within four (4) work days from the time it is given back to you following your Step 1 hearing.

Chapter 31

OFFICE WORKER UNIONS

MORE than ever, organized labor is casting covetous looks at white-collar workers in offices, stores, plants, everywhere, and definitely stepping up recruiting efforts. While 2,500,000 white-collar employees are already organized, the unions are aiming at a target involving far larger objectives.

One of the softer spots for their initial efforts, the unions feel, is in plants where production workers are already organized and some of the white-collar people are also union members. The white-collar workers are ripe for union organization, is the ever-recurring statement from labor, and on that basis they are mapping their campaigns.

Unions are armed with plenty of ammunition. A point regarded as one of the most effective is the steadily narrowing gap between the wages of the white-collar employees and the blue-collar workers. Since the ratio of production workers to white-collar employees in industry is declining, unions also realize they must organize the white-collar group in order to maintain their status.

"It is only a question of time before your office forces are unionized," the late C. Wright Mills, associate professor of sociology, Columbia University, once told members of the Office Management Conference of the American Management Association. Professor Mills pointed out that the changing status of the white-collar worker was paving the way for unionization.

How Companies Are Meeting Office-Union Drives

One of the most informative one-day conferences on the broad area of office administration was sponsored by the University of Wisconsin's Management Institute. The conference was titled, "Office Unions—What's Ahead?" It was led by Elmore V. Knaack, industrial relations manager, tractor division, International Harvester Company, an "old pro," both in company negotiation and conference leadership. The result was a highly informative, objective appraisal of where we stand today in the matter of office unionization.

According to the Bureau of Labor Statistics, white-collar workers now form the largest group of the nation's labor force.

Unions such as the United Auto Workers are now aiming at the white-collar worker to offset the loss of blue-collar workers due to automation and advanced production techniques.

Three B-P's of Preparing Against Organization

Pointing out that there are actually three important areas of relationships to be considered, Knaack stresses the three B-P's of management obligation. The areas of relationships are: Management-Management, Employee-Management, and Employee-Employee. In each of these prime areas there can be one of the things—conflict or cooperation. The three B-P's are:

> —BE POLITE
> —BE PLEASANT
> —BE PROMPT

The management that communicates fully and frankly, is consistent in policy, works toward better employee relations, exercises its rights under existing laws, and has the courage to face organizers will fare better than the organization that does not meet these qualifications.

Knaack points out that white-collar organizers are not rough-and-tumble union agitators. They are usually well educated, informed, cultured, and go about their jobs with dignity. He adds, "They appeal by pointing out that members of the symphony orchestra you enjoyed so much last week are all organized. The pilot of that jet plane you took on your last flight is unionized. Movie and TV stars you enjoy belong to unions. Why shouldn't you?" When properly put, this makes a strong case. It isn't the old name-calling, funnybook type of approach used on rougher elements in the blue-collar field. It is geared for today's needs.

Automation and Mergers

High on the list of appeals used by today's white-collar organizers is automation—that relatively new word for an old, old practice, mechanized improvement. Unions will "protect workers from automation." They have given the word a dirty meaning. They will help the white-collar worker "keep from losing his identity" in this age of computers, data processing, and other major discoveries for more efficient business operation.

Another word that is being expressed with a curled lip is "merger." Unions are hopping on mergers. Prime reason they are effective is that a management, by process of merger, can get skills and know-how without having to develop it from within. It can diversify its operations without the many years and dollars spent in research and development. A lot of union officials fear this will hurt them—curb skill development of workers. From a company viewpoint—why train a worker to do a job when you get a man trained and experienced at it in the merger?

Benefits to White-Collar Workers

Unions say that economic benefits for blue-collar workers have increased 200 percent as opposed to a 68 percent increase for white-collar workers over a given period of time. The union organizer appeals in the following ways:

The steward can represent you to management more objectively.

By organizing you will end economic discrimination.

Promotion practices will be improved through seniority emphasis.

Grievances will be handled systematically—we'll go to bat for you.

Better hours, better holiday and vacation allowances.

More fringe benefits, like blue-collar workers have.

There are, of course, many other appeals used. But basically they are all aimed at the same objective—to make white-collar workers feel discriminated against and to show them that in number there is strength.

Obstacles to Unionization

The conference leader and group discussed some of the obstacles faced by unions who wish to organize white-collar workers. Five prime obstacles were listed as follows:

1. It is too costly to unite small companies for organization drives. Size of groups is a factor in organizing.

2. Many office workers fear that a union might separate them too much from management. These employees feel they will fare better with closer management contact as they now have it.

3. Strong influences of cliques within the office organization. For instance, secretaries consider themselves on a level above office boys, etc. Such

groups do not wish to be lumped together with workers they consider to be less skilled or important—the status factor.

4. The white-collar office worker doesn't feel identified with the "image" of the labor leader. Despite the charm, dignity, and mature approach of the white-collar organizer, many clerical workers still identify him as part of labor unions—a vague and not too appealing image to many.

5. The economics of white-collar organization are not conducive to rapid organization. For instance, the office boy may be taking an evening course in accounting and is preparing for that move upward. Many white-collar workers are developing themselves for bigger jobs and don't consider what they are doing today to be their final life's work.

Thus, the union organizer today faces in some instances a suspicious and at least semihostile group when he starts his campaign. This has probably been the reason that unions have been slower than many expected in getting white-collar organization off the ground.

Organizing Techniques and Procedures

What steps must the organizer take to get his organization campaign moving? Here are five considerations he must face for ultimate success:

1. The organizer must become an integral part of the community, get known and be identified as a local man.

2. He must get to know other union officials and organizers—develop these kindred souls for communication purposes.

3. He must face the issue that companies not having production unions are harder to organize than those already unionized in the shop.

4. He must rely on high-type letters and letterheads, be dignified in his efforts. Cartoons and abusive literature won't work in white-collar organization.

5. He must point to examples of organized white-collar workers—movie stars, pilots, musicians, etc.

Ways to Prepare Against Organization

Elmore Knaack cautions: "You can't buy a nonunion office. Giving more than the union offers won't hold off unionization. This has been proven time and time again. Don't try to buy labor peace." He adds, "Don't give any more in the face of organization threats than you are willing to give right now." Prime warning from this experienced industrial relations expert—BE CONSISTENT.

Knaack points out a case wherein an executive's secretary went on vacation. He decided to use a young typist in her absence. During the first day of work on her new assignment, the young typist mentioned that she had taken a course in shorthand and would try to take it for the executive. After a few days, she proved to be quite efficient. But, when the secretary returned, the girl was put back in the typing pool and never given recognition monetarily for her ability, even though the company was desperately in need of secretaries and advertising for them. A case of lack of consistency that too often occurs in white-collar dealings.

Here are 12 steps suggested by Mr. Knaack for those executives who wish to guard against the threat of office organization. These are areas where office management is frequently vulnerable for unionization arguments:

1. Develop a good rate and classification system for jobs. Have a good merit rating plan and see that it works.

2. Set up a wage or salary structure based on job differentials. Check to be sure wage spreads are adequate and uniform.

3. Know what your competition is doing. Are you in line with the business or industry?

4. Know your work schedules. Do they compare favorably with the area?

5. Compare fringe benefits with area business and industry. Review your holiday, vacation, and other benefit plans. Are you consistent?

6. Compare insurance, pension, and retirement plans. Will an organizer find yours are way behind the times?

7. Check such areas as safety, heat, ventilation, general working conditions and physical setup.

8. Do you have a system for recognizing seniority in the event of layoffs? Is it consistent and fair?

9. Do you have an adequate system for handling grievances—a way of reviewing complaints on down the line?

10. Do you hold meetings with supervisors? Do you get varied groups of supervisors together so that they can compare problems and ideas?

11. Do your supervisors and managers really know company policies? Are they consistent in interpreting policy? Do you have a policy manual?

12. Do you have real two-way communication? Don't wait for trouble to start communicating. Last year International Harvester sent 36 letters to each employee's home.

Summarizing, the University of Wisconsin conference again emphasized that there is no need to get frantic in the face of organization efforts. But with some preventive labor relations, office administrators can be ready to face the organizational efforts that surely will be coming in the next few years.

Seniority in White-Collar Contracts

Employers who follow the practice of promoting factory and service-department employees to positions in the office, will also find it advisable to have a clear understanding of the seniority rights of such transferred workers. It is desirable to have the seniority of white-collar workers on an *officewide* or a departmentwide basis, rather than an establishmentwide basis. This is in fairness to employees of the department who otherwise would lose their seniority to a newcomer. It also facilitates promoting the employee in the organization. In the case of sales employees, particularly, rigid seniority requirements may prevent a sales manager from removing a salesman who is not producing. If he is required to cut back the sales force on the basis of establishmentwide seniority, a recently promoted factory worker enjoying high establishmentwide seniority would have to be retained, while another salesman having more sales ability but less seniority would have to be discharged.

Independent Foremen's Unions

Dissatisfaction with company compensation policies which permitted workers under their jurisdiction to "take home" more pay than their supervisors, plus the fear that they would be laid off suddenly when labor cutbacks were required, resulted in a movement of foremen to organize into independent unions, even though the Taft-Hartley Act does not require employers to bargain with foremen, who are now regarded as a part of management. The National Labor Relations Board, prior to the passage of the Taft-Hartley Act, took the position in the Packard case that foremen could organize for collective bargaining if they elected to do so. The basis of this decision was a report by a special panel under the chairmanship of Dr. Sumner H. Slichter of Harvard University, which held that in many cases foremen had been deprived of their traditional management functions (such as the right to hire and fire) and were little better than "traffic cops." This decision was violently attacked by employers, especially those in mass production industries, as an infraction of management's rights and an appeal was taken to the U.S. Supreme Court. In a five to four decision the board was upheld on the broad theory that since foremen could not fix their own pay, they were employees under the terms of the National Labor Relations Act.

However, organized labor has long since, in the case of most crafts unions, won acceptance of its point that foremen and even owners in a craft represented by a union should carry a union card.

This is the so-called "clean hands" theory which restricts a union man from touching work that is not union made. The printing trades, building trades, textiles, mine workers, and numerous other unions all require working foremen to be union members in good standing.

Advertisements such as this in local newspapers have a wholesome effect on public opinion. They permit management to tell its side of the dispute in its own way.

Most employers in those industries are not averse to the practice, and in some cases employers find it to their advantage to have a representative in the union. They are very often able to block hot-head action.

While conditions are different in an industrial union, which includes all the workers in a plant, compared to a crafts union, which may take in only a few workers from a number of plants, there is a similarity so far as the foreman's dual relationship between the union and the company is concerned. Then, too, most crafts unions operate under union shop conditions, whereas in the plantwide unions the prevailing condition is often open shop, which means that a continuous membership campaign is being conducted by the union in the plant. Management wants to keep the foremen on its side, while organization work continues in a plant.

Much of the success unions have had in organizing white-collar workers can be laid at management's door. The average company goes to great lengths to determine, through opinion polls and employee attitude studies, what the workers think about management, what they want from management, etc. But, until quite recently, little or no attention was paid to the grievances of the white-collar worker. He was truly the forgotten man of employee relations. It is only natural that these white-collar groups, observing the success of rank-and-file unions in getting almost everything they asked for from management, should feel they might be missing something by not taking advantage of the right to organize extended to them by the Labor Relations Act, as amended.

TYPICAL OFFICE WORKERS' AGREEMENT

Article I

This agreement made this .... day of ...., by and between the .... Company (hereinafter referred to as the "Company"), and Local .... of the United Office and Professional Workers of America (hereinafter referred to as the "Union").

WITNESSETH:

That for the purpose of facilitating the peaceful adjustment of grievances, complaints, or disputes which may arise from time to time between the Company and its employees, the parties hereto agree with each other as follows:

Article II—Scope of Agreement

1. It is agreed and understood between the Company and the Union that this agreement is limited to and embraces only such matters as are specifically set forth in the agreement, and that all other matters shall be subject to further negotiations.

Article III—Union-Management Relationship

1. Mutual pledge of Union-Company cooperation for maximum production and efficient operation.

The .... Company and the Union in recognition of the need and possibilities of increased production through creative cooperation mutually agree to cooperate fully for harmonious relations, efficient office discipline, and maximum efficiency.

The Company recognizes the established rights, responsibilities and values of Management, and the specific rights of Management to hire and discharge its employees and to direct the working force subject to the grievance procedure as provided in this agreement.

The Union agrees not to coerce or intimidate any employee into joining the Union, and will discipline any member who is guilty of such coercion or intimidation.

The Union agrees further that it will not solicit Union members or carry on other Union activities on Company time or in such manner as to interfere with the efficient operations of the plant.

The Company recognizes the established rights, responsibilities and values of the Union and has no objection to its employees becoming members of the certified Union, responsible in conjunction with the Company for making and keeping this agreement. The Company specifically will not tolerate, on the part of its representatives, any discrimination or activity whatever against the Union, and will discipline any employee, who on Company time, carries on antiunion activity or who seeks, directly or indirectly, to interfere with the status, membership, or responsibilities of the certified Union.

In recognition of the National Agreement between Management and Labor for the peaceful settlement of all disputes, and of the reciprocal guarantees of no lockouts, strikes, or slowdowns, and in order to promote maximum production, these union-management relations shall continue for the life of this agreement.

Union Recognition

2. The .... Company recognizes and will deal with the Union as the sole and exclusive collective bargaining agency for the employees of the bargaining unit during the life of this agreement for the purpose of collective bargaining in respect to wages, rates of pay, hours of employment, and all other conditions of employment.

Membership in the Union

3. The parties hereto, having in mind established practices with regard to the inclusion of Union security provisions in labor contracts and believing that a stable and responsible Union is necessary in order to secure the increased production which will result from greater harmony between workers and employers, do now agree as follows:

1. All employees who, fifteen (15) days after the posting of the notices hereinafter referred to, are members of the Union in good standing in accordance with the constitution and bylaws of the Union, and all employees who thereafter become members, shall, as a condition of employment, remain members of the Union in good standing for the duration of the existing contract.

465

2. As soon as practicable after the date hereof, the Union and the Company will jointly post notices in the form hereto attached and marked Exhibit "A." Such notices shall be posted at not less than .... of the most public places in and about the Company property.

3. The Union shall promptly furnish the Company a notarized list of its members in good standing as of the fifteeneth (15th) day after the posting of said notices. Should any employee whose name appears on the list assert that he was never a member, or that he had withdrawn from membership prior to said fifteenth (15th) day, and should a dispute arise therefrom, or should a dispute arise as to whether an employee is, or is not, a member of the Union in good standing, such disputes shall be settled by the procedures set up in Article VII of the existing contract, entitled "Grievance Procedure," commencing with Step "2" and continuing, if necessary, through Step "5" and Section 4 of Article III.

4. The following shall be the procedure in cases where the Union desires the Company to enforce the provisions of the paragraph numbered 1 above:

   A. The Union will submit in writing to the Company cases of employees subject to termination of employment for failure to maintain membership.

   B. The Company will immediately investigate such cases and when it has done so and found that the employees concerned will be subject to dismissal for the reason stated, it will inform the employee at once, by written notice substantially like Exhibit B hereto attached.

   (a) That he is suspended for the period of two (2) weeks beginning with the date of such notice.

   (b) That during the two (2) week period such suspension may be removed by appropriate action on his part and/or on the part of the Union.

   (c) That if no such action is taken within the two (2) week period of suspension, his employee status will terminate at the end of such period and his dismissal at the request of the Union will become final and have the same effect as discharge.

   (d) That such dismissal will affect his rights under the Vacation Plan, Pension Plan, Savings and Extra Compensation Plan, Group Life Insurance Plan, Employees' Benefit Association and Hospitalization Plan, as provided in such plans.

   C. In all cases the Union will be given copies of the written notices referred to in the preceding paragraph.

Disputes

4. If any dispute arises under this article, it shall be settled in accordance with the provisions of the grievance machinery article of this contract, or if not so settled, it shall be finally determined by an arbitrator approved by the parties or designated by the Federal Mediation and Conciliation Service.

Article IV—Bargaining Unit

1. The bargaining unit recognized for the purpose of collective bargaining and represented by the Union is as follows:

All office, clerical, technical and professional employees of the .... Company but excluding the following. . . .

Article V—No Discrimination

1. The Company shall not discriminate against any person because of race, sex, political or religious affiliation or nationality.

Article VI—Representation

1. The Union shall designate a suitable number of department stewards, such number to be fixed by mutual agreement of the parties hereto. The Union shall choose two grievance committees, one to be known as the Office Grievance Committee to consist of seven (7) members and the other the Engineering Grievance Committee to consist of five (5) members. No one shall be eligible to serve as Union Steward or Committeeman unless he or she is an employee of the Company.

The Company will recognize and negotiate with said stewards and committees with respect to the adjustment of grievances as provided in the following article, but either party shall have the right to call in International Union representatives to assist.

Article VII—Grievance Procedure

1. During the life of this agreement, should any dispute arise as to the meaning, interpretation, or application of the provisions of this agreement, or as to the performance by either party of obligations imposed by this agreement, there shall be no slow-down, sit-down, stoppages of work, or strikes on the part of the Union nor shall there be any lockout on the part of the Company, but instead an earnest effort shall be made by the Union and the Company to settle such disputes in the following manner:

   1. In the event a grievance, complaint or dispute arises between an employee or affecting more than one employee and the Company, or any of its agents, such employees should refer such grievance, complaint or dispute to his or her department head or steward for adjustment. The grievance shall be reduced to writing on forms supplied for that purpose.

   2. If the dispute is not thus settled, such grievance shall be referred to the Office Grievance Committee or to the Engineering Grievance Committee as the case may be, which shall take such matter up for adjustment with the Industrial Relations Department at the next weekly meeting.

   3. If the dispute is not settled under Step 2, it shall promptly be taken up for adjustment between the Grievance Committee and the Works' Manager or the Chief Engineer as the case may be.

   4. Any grievance, complaint or dispute that cannot be settled in the three previous steps, shall be immediately referred to the Executive Officers of the .... Company for further negotiations and adjustment, provided, however, the Union shall have the right to call into such negotiations, Executive Officers of the United Office and Professional Workers of America, affiliated with the AFL-CIO or their designated representatives.

   5. If such a dispute has not been settled after the steps herein provided have been exhausted, then in order fairly to protect the interests of all concerned, it shall be submitted (within five days) to binding arbitration before a Board of Arbitration as elsewhere described in this article.

2. The Board of Arbitration herein referred to shall consist of three members, one of whom shall be selected by the Union, one by the Company and the third

by the two so chosen. In the event the two appointed members are unable to agree upon the selection of the third member within seven (7) calendar days after the aggrieved party has appointed its member, the Federal Mediation and Conciliation Service shall thereupon be requested to designate the third member whose services shall be without cost to either party.

The decision of the Board of Arbitration shall be final and binding upon the Company and the Union provided it is not in contravention of any Federal or State statutes.

3. The Company and the Union shall pay the salary, wage or fee of its respectively appointed member. All other expenses for hearings or meetings of the Board shall all be paid equally by the Company and the Union except that the cost of any stenographic service shall be paid by the party requesting such service.

4. The functions of the Board of Arbitration shall be of a judicial rather than legislative nature and such Board shall not have the power to add to, to disregard or modify any of the terms and conditions of this agreement nor shall such Board pass upon issues involving increase or decrease of occupational, group or general wage rates nor upon any issue involving the exercise of functions of management, meaning thereby those rights, duties and responsibilities which rest upon the management to direct the operation of the Company and its working forces. Such functions of management include (but are not limited to) the exclusive rights to:

1. Determine the products and schedules of production and the methods and processes of manufacture;
2. Determine the basis for selection, retention and promotion of employees for occupations not within the bargaining unit established in this contract;
3. Maintain discipline and efficiency of employees including the right to make reasonable rules and regulations for the purpose of efficiency and discipline;
4. Direct generally the work of the employees subject to applicable requirements of this agreement, including the right to hire, discharge or suspend employees for good cause and also to promote employees, demote or transfer them for proper cause, to assign them to shifts, determine the amount of work needed and to lay them off because of lack of work in accordance with the provisions herein;
5. Determine the number and location of the Company's plants.

5. The Union's Grievance Committee shall meet weekly with the Industrial Relations Department. It shall also meet when necessary with the Works Manager or the Chief Engineer to resolve grievances that are appealed to that step of the grievance procedure. Whenever either party is unable to meet at the time regularly scheduled, the meeting may be advanced or postponed according to mutual agreement.

6. Union representatives (meaning the stewards and members of the Grievance Committee) shall be afforded such time off without loss of pay as may be required for the performance of their duties as such representatives, namely:

1. To attend regularly scheduled meetings with the management pertaining to discharges and other matters which cannot reasonably be delayed until the time of the next regular meeting. Before leaving his or her place of employment, each representative shall give notice to his or her department head or other person designated for that purpose by the Works Manager, or Chief Engineer.

2. To make necessary legitimate investigations of employee grievances, provided the Union representative gives advance notice to his or her department head of the approximate amount of time to be spent, and provided the employee's absence will not seriously interfere with the normal operation of the department. The Company will not be required to pay Union representatives for time allegedly spent in investigating employee grievances in any case in which the privilege is abused by a Union representative who spends excessive amount of time, or who uses the time permitted for any reason other than making necessary legitimate investigations of employee grievances.

3. The Company will notify the Union in writing of any alleged abuses under this section.

7. Grievance Committee members shall be paid for time spent outside of their regular working hours in meeting with the management. Stewards shall be paid for time outside of their regular working hours only when called in by mutual agreement of the Grievance Committee and the management.

8. Whenever the management requests a Union representative to leave his job and confer upon Union matters, such representatives shall not lose pay for the time so spent. In case such representative works on the second or third shift and the management requests him to confer at an hour which requires him to make a special trip to the Plant, he shall be compensated at his usual rate for the time so spent.

9. The Union agrees that any grievance, complaint or dispute referred to the Grievance Committee will be presented to the Company for adjustment in writing and the Company agrees that its decision on any such grievances, complaints or disputes will be presented to the Grievance Committee in writing in accordance with the terms of this agreement.

ARTICLE VIII—SUSPENSION AND DISCHARGE CASES

1. In the event an employee shall be suspended or discharged from employment and believes he or she has been unjustly dealt with, such suspension or discharge shall constitute a case to be handled in accordance with the method of adjustment of grievances herein provided. Should it be decided under the rules of this agreement that an injustice has been done with regard to the employees' suspension or discharge, the Company agrees to reinstate him or her and pay full compensation at his or her prevailing rate for the time lost. The Company must be notified of a claim of wrongful suspension or discharge within three (3) working days after same occurs and the case shall be taken up promptly and diligent efforts made to dispose of it within five (5) working days. Upon being notified of his or her suspension or discharge it shall be the duty of the employee to leave his or her department and go to the plant employment office. The departmental steward affected or the Chairman of the Grievance Committee shall be notified immediately by the Company and given the opportunity to review such case with the employee and others before the records in the employment department are closed. The wages of the employee shall cease at the time of his or her suspension or discharge excepting in the case where it is later determined that the Company's action was not warranted.

ARTICLE IX—FUNCTIONS OF MANAGEMENT

1. It is agreed that the Company has the right to direct generally the work of the employees, to hire, discharge, or suspend employees for good cause and also

to promote employees, demote them, or transfer them for proper cause, to assign them to shifts with due regard to seniority and ability to perform the work, determine the amount of work needed, and to lay them off because of lack of work (in accordance with the provisions herein). However, no employee shall be discharged by the Company except for cause and none of the foregoing shall be used for the purpose of discrimination.

To enable the Company to keep its product abreast of scientific and technical advances, it is agreed that the Company may from time to time, and without reference to the rules of seniority set out in this agreement, hire, transfer, teach and assign duties to a small number, such number to be mutually agreed upon between the Company and the Union of technical men or others who, in the opinion of the Company, may be qualified to accomplish that purpose. It is understood that employees hired or designated to carry out this purpose shall not displace any employee of longer service on the seniority list.

ARTICLE X—WAGES

1. The Company agrees to make available to the Grievance Committee of the Union a list of the job classifications and rates of pay applying thereto of the occupations covered by this contract.

2. All hourly paid and salaried employees operating on second and third shifts shall receive ten (10) percent per hour over and above their hourly rates or salaried earnings in their respective classifications.

3. In the event an employee is assigned temporarily to a different classification such employee shall receive his or her regular rate for such classification, if it is the higher rate.

If as a result of reduction in force, an employee is transferred to a lower rated classification, such employee shall receive his or her then existing salary rate if such rate does not exceed the top of the rate range established for the classification.

If an employee is definitely transferred to a lower rated classification as a result of demotion, such employee shall be rated within the salary range established for such classification on a merit rating basis.

If an employee is definitely transferred to a higher rated classification, he or she shall be rated within the salary range established for such classification, on a merit rating basis, but not less than his or her already established salary rate.

4. Where inequalities are alleged to prevail in individual or group wage rates within the occupations covered hereby, the matter may be taken up through the Union representatives for adjustment and settlement under the procedure herein provided.

5. The management will furnish weekly a list of separations; new employees hired stating department and classification; transfers into the bargaining unit, within the unit and outside the unit.

6. The management will inform the Union representatives of cases of merit rate increases granted by the Company. In cases of rate increases granted as the result of bargaining with the Union, or because of grievances presented by the Union, the Company will notify the Grievance Committee before the affected employee is informed.

7. When an employee is assigned to a new or different job, he or she will be informed in advance of the rate of pay to be paid for such job.

8. Should either party in the future propose to again review the general wage rates covered by this agreement, a sincere effort will be made through collective bargaining to arrive at a satisfactory conclusion.

9. The principle of equal pay for equal work shall be applied without discrimination.

10. The Union having proposed, during the negotiations of this contract, to review the general wage rates covered by this agreement both parties agree that a sincere effort will be made through collective bargaining to arrive at a satisfactory conclusion.

ARTICLE XI—GENERAL WORKING CONDITIONS

1. The Company agrees that in the event it is necessary to work overtime on any job, such overtime shall be allocated as evenly as possible among the employees who perform such work. It is mutually agreed, however, that in each instance the employee must be qualified to do the job required by the Company.

2. Union representatives shall be given the opportunity to review all cases of layoffs before such layoffs are made effective.

3. For the sole use of the Union, the Company will erect and maintain a suitable number of bulletin boards throughout the Plant. The location of the same, as well as their number and size, shall be mutually determined. Such boards may be used for the purpose of disseminating information concerning meetings, elections, social events, and other affairs of general interest. Under no circumstances may they be used for advertising, for political matter, for distributing pamphlets or circulars or for propaganda of any sort. No matter shall be posted until it has been submitted and approved by the Works Manager or some person designated by him for that purpose.

4. Present practices with respect to rest periods and smoking privileges shall be continued.

5. Any female employee who becomes pregnant shall be allowed a leave of absence not to exceed a period of twelve (12) months. The Plant physician will determine when, prior to confinement, such leave of absence should commence and also when after confinement, such employee is physically able to return to work. If such female employee or the Union believes the Plant physician's determination is unfair, the question shall be submitted to the head of the Company's Medical Department for final determination.

6. When a job or operation is moved from one department to another within the plant, and is not otherwise altered, the employee holding such job shall have the privilege of transferring with the job subject to the seniority provisions set forth in Article XIII of this agreement.

7. Managerial employees shall not so long as they continue to have such status, perform the work of employees covered by this contract. However, managerial employees may in cases of emergency temporarily perform the work of an employee of the appropriate unit.

8. Time spent by Union representatives in negotiating labor contracts with the management, attending meetings or otherwise carrying on duties of Union representatives as permitted by management, will be counted as time worked in computing service and attendance records under the regulations of the Company's Vacation Plan and Extra Compensation Plan.

9. Whenever a physical examination or laboratory test has been made by physicians acting for the Company, a report thereof will be given to the personal physician of the employee involved upon the written request of such employee and his personal physician.

10. In the event that any employee who has been or may be promoted to positions not covered by this agreement is demoted, such employee shall lose no seniority rights, but the time spent outside the unit will not be credited to total service in applying the seniority provisions.

11. The company recognizes that there may be cases of legitimate illness and injuries which will necessitate the absence from work of employees covered by this agreement. The Company will pay salaried employees covered by this agreement for necessary absences from work due to such causes in cases in which such consideration is warranted based on the employee's length of employment service, previous employment attendance records, the individual's application to the job and in accordance with the general practice established heretofore. The Company agrees to work out with the Union a memorandum which will seek to make definite the Company's policy for the purpose of acquainting each employee with their rights under this section.

Salary-rated employees covered by this agreement will be permitted time off without loss of pay for compelling and necessary personal reasons in cases in which permission to be absent without loss of pay has been granted by the management prior to such absence, in accordance with the general practice established heretofore.

The provisions of this section will be applied without discrimination against any employee.

Article XII—Hours of Work, Overtime and Holidays

1. It is agreed and understood that under normal conditions regular operations shall be confined to five consecutive eight-hour days, Monday to Friday, inclusive, but it is further agreed that in cases of emergency, employees may be required to work Saturday and Sunday.

2. The regular daily starting and quitting times of employees covered by this agreement shall continue in effect except as may be required because of emergency conditions. Any contemplated change in the starting or quitting time of employees covered by this agreement will be discussed with the Union before being made effective.

3. Employees covered by this agreement shall have two consecutive off-duty days (normally Saturday and Sunday) in each workweek.

Employees covered by this agreement shall be paid salary compensation at one and one-half times the regular salary rate for work performed:

1. In excess of 8 hours in any one day, or
2. In excess of 40 hours in a workweek, or
3. The employee's scheduled first off-duty day in each week, or
4. Any of the following holidays when work is regularly scheduled for such holidays: New Year's Day, Memorial Day, Independence Day, Labor Day, Thanksgiving Day, Christmas Day.

Salary compensation at twice the regular salary rate shall be paid:

1. For emergency work performed on the holidays listed above when work is not regularly scheduled.

2. For work performed on the employee's scheduled second off-duty day in each week.

No employee shall be requested to take time off from work for overtime worked.

4. A day shall consist of twenty-four (24) consecutive hours from the time an employee begins the shift in which the work is performed. No employee will be paid overtime twice for the same hours and no day-shift employee shall be paid overtime and night premium for the same hours.

5. An employee called in to perform emergency work after his regularly scheduled hours of work have been completed, will be guaranteed a minimum of four (4) hours' work. If the work does not require the full four (4) hours it shall be the employee's prerogative to go home and be paid for four hours.

An employee called in to do emergency work on one of the holidays designated herein will be guaranteed four (4) hours' pay in addition to his regular salary for that day. If the emergency work does not require the full eight (8) hours, it shall be the employee's prerogative to go home after the emergency work is completed.

6. Scheduling of employees for Sunday work shall be confined to necessary work.

7. In all cases of absence, the employee must notify either the Department Head or the Employment Office before or on the first day of absence.

8. Employees covered by this agreement, not scheduled to work on any of the following recognized legal holidays shall suffer no loss of pay: New Year's Day, Memorial Day, Independence Day, Labor Day, Thanksgiving Day, Christmas Day.

Article XIII—Seniority

1. In case of increase or decrease of forces, where an employee is capable of doing the job, length of continuous service shall govern.

1a. Employees presently coming under the jurisdiction of this agreement who have been transferred in from the factory shall receive credit for the length of service employed in the factory. This, however, shall not apply to employees who may be transferred subsequent to the date of this agreement, whose seniority shall begin from the date of transfer.

2. In determining an employee's length of service for seniority purposes, computation will begin on the date the employee began work for the Company, and no deduction will be made for lost time due to any reason. However,

Continuity of service shall be broken when:

1. An employee voluntarily leaves the Company's employ.
2. An employee is discharged for cause and the decision is not reversed under provisions of Article VIII herein.
3. An employee fails to maintain membership in good standing with the Union and is discharged in accordance with Article III, Section 5 herein provided.
4. Due to layoff of an employee on the probationary list, a period of more than twelve (12) months has elapsed since the employee last worked for the Company.
5. Due to layoff because of no work of any employee on the seniority list, a period of more than three (3) years has elapsed since the employee last worked for the Company.

6. An employee who has been laid off because of no work fails to report when properly recalled within a period of five (5) working days. This five (5) day period may be extended providing a reasonable and satisfactory explanation is given for not reporting, but in every case the employee must report within fifteen (15) working days.

7. An employee fails to report for work at termination of a leave of absence or furlough.

8. Before new employees are hired, the management will give consideration to recalling longer service employees whose service is broken during the life of this agreement under the operation of (5) above.

3. The method set forth in this agreement for computing length of service for seniority shall be applied retroactively. However, it is mutually agreed between the Union and the Company that in computing service retroactively that layoffs of periods in excess of two (2) years, the employee will not receive service credit for the period in excess of two years of such layoffs but continuity of service will not be broken. Such methods of service computation will be in effect only for present employees.

4. Employees having less than three (3) months of service shall be considered probationary employees and will have no seniority rights, but when such rights are acquired, service shall date from the date the employee began work subject to provisions determining length of service as defined herein.

5. Employees having three (3) months of service and less than one (1) year of service shall be placed on their departmental seniority list.

6. Employees having one (1) year or more of service shall be placed on the office-wide seniority list in their respective divisions.

7. When it becomes necessary to decrease the force in any department, all probationary employees shall be the first to be laid off. Should further reduction in force be necessary employees having three (3) months or more but less than one (1) year of service, shall be laid off on a departmental basis. A longer service employee may replace a shorter service employee if he or she is capable of performing the work of the shorter service employee.

If layoffs are still necessary, the same shall be applied in the following manner:

An employee on the officewide seniority list will be transferred to replace a shorter service employee, provided such employee is capable of doing the work of the shorter service employee. For this purpose the longer service employee will be deemed capable of performing the work of the shorter service employee if the longer service employee does not require more than a three day break-in period to acquire the fundamentals of the position.

8. Employees whose services are to be terminated because of reduced manufacturing schedules will be given as much advance notice as possible, such notice to be not less than two (2) weeks, excepting in cases where the Government orders operations reduced or discontinued on less than two weeks' notice.

9. It is agreed that up to a maximum of forty (40) of the local officers, plant grievance committeemen and stewards of the Union shall be accorded a preferred seniority status subject to provisions hereinafter stated. In the event the working force increases or decreases substantially from its present number, the number of officers, committeemen, and representatives of the Union who shall have such preferred seniority status may be increased or decreased by mutual consent of the parties.

The right to designate the persons who shall have such preferred seniority status shall be vested in the Union, provided that the list at all times shall include employees in office and whose services are necessary for the conduct of the Union's business. Whenever the Union desires to substitute another person for one then having preferred seniority, it shall notify the Company in writing and thereafter the person whose preferred seniority has ceased shall resume his regular seniority. Preferred seniority status for those other than Union officers and Grievance Committee members, shall be restricted to the department wherein the designated employee is regularly employed. In no case shall the Company be under obligation to assign work, because of preferred seniority status, to a person who is not capable of doing the work available.

10. At each layoff, or recall following layoff, the Company may designate certain individual employees whose services are required under the special circumstances existing, and such employees may be retained in, or recalled to service regardless of their seniority. No such designation shall become effective until approved by the Works Manager or Chief Engineer upon agreement with the Union. The fact that an employee has been so designated shall not affect his regular seniority standing and he shall resume the same as soon as the special reasons in his case cease to exist.

11. The Company will furnish to the Union an up-to-date office-wide seniority and departmental seniority list every six (6) months, and from time to time will notify the Union of changes in those lists in order to keep them up-to-date.

12. It is agreed and understood that in the application of the seniority provisions of this agreement, the Engineering Department (Experimental and Product Design), and the Manufacturing Department (office and clerical) are to be considered separate divisions.

13. When filling positions outside of the bargaining unit, the Company will not discriminate against any employee covered by this agreement.

14. Seniority and qualifications shall be the governing factors in making promotions and transfers within the bargaining unit.

Article XIV—Vacations

1. All salaried employees covered by this contract shall be afforded vacations in accordance with the .... Vacation Plan for salaried employees. Such plan provides as follows:

1. When an employee has established a service period of six (6) months of employment and less than twelve (12) months of employment, he will be entitled to one (1) week's vacation; however, when he has established a service record of twelve (12) months or more of employment, he will be entitled to one more week or a total of two (2) weeks' vacation annually.

2. Vacation pay will be based on the salary in effect on date immediately prior to employee leaving on vacation.

3. Vacations may be taken at any time during the year; however, vacation schedules will necessarily conform to the requirement of the business. No vacation shall be taken for less than one week at a time, nor is it permissible to postpone a vacation from one year to another to waive vacation and draw double pay.

4. Employees entitled to vacation, whose services are terminated because of resignation, layoff, physical disability, discharge, or death prior to taking their vacations, will be paid vacation money for the vacation periods for which they are entitled. However, no such employee during any calendar year will be entitled to a vacation or vacation pay exceeding one week or two weeks depending upon his length of service. In case of death, the vacation money will be paid to the wife or family of the deceased employee.

5. Vacation pay will be determined on the normal five-day week. If employees are scheduled to work on the sixth day of their vacation period, they shall receive time and one-half for work performed on that day.

[Articles XV—XXI omitted.]

Chapter 32

INCREASING OFFICE PRODUCTION

THE typical classified ad for a clerical worker says, "Good working conditions, excellent starting rate, 40-hour week." The 40-hour week is still standard with over 80 percent of the companies responding to a Dartnell survey on working conditions in the office.

To be completely realistic about the meaning of the 40-hour workweek, it should be borne in mind that while the lunch hour is not included, in almost all cases the coffee break or rest period *is* included in the workweek figure. As one executive put it, "We say we have a 40-hour workweek, but that doesn't take into consideration the 15-minute coffee break each morning. If that is figured, we actually work 38 hours and 45 minutes each week, without considering the other rest periods during the day."

It is utterly impossible to be precise on the matter of the hours of the workweek. For, if you really want to be accurate, you must figure the time spent powdering noses, packing the pocketbook at the end of the day for the journey home, time spent while Mabel tells Lucy about her dream date Saturday night, trips to the water fountain, etc. If all these things were figured in, one company estimates, "You are lucky to get 30 hours of work in a week."

The following percentages show the average workweek of the 00 companies that contributed to the survey:

40-hour week	82 percent
37½-hour week	10 percent
38½-hour week	3 percent
Other	5 percent

When it comes to starting and quitting times, national averages are concentrated in two main groups—8:00 a.m. to 5:00 p.m. and 8:30 a.m. to 5:00 p.m. Well over half of the reporting organizations use one of these periods as the workday. A great majority, too, begin and end the day on the hour or half-hour. The geographical area, the size of the business, and the type of business enter into the picture, too, when considering the hours of the workday. For instance, it has been found that in cities of less than 10,000 inhabitants earlier starting and quitting hours are more common. In fact, there appear to be very few small-town offices that start as late as 9 o'clock. On the other hand, in large metropolitan areas many companies have a 9 o'clock starting time. An executive with a New York insurance firm explains this in his comments: "This is a big city and we have a lot of our help living in the outlying suburbs. As a consequence, we found that 8:30 was too early to start work and get them all here on time."

Quite a few offices report a policy of starting and quitting earlier in the summer months to allow employees more evening time. One Cincinnati company switched from 9 a.m. to 5 p.m. in the winter months to 8 a.m. to 4 p.m. in the summer. It worked well, too, according to a company representative. It is also interesting to note little change in working hours in the last decade. The only real difference lies in the trend toward a shorter workweek—but the daily working hours are similar.

Over half of the companies surveyed have no work at all on Saturday. In cases where there is work to be done on Saturday, it is most common to let the decision be made by the department head who is responsible for the flow. A number of companies have found it feasible to enlist volunteers for a skeleton Saturday work force when necessary. In other cases, a rotation system is used whereby all employees share the Saturday chores. One office manager who uses this policy said, "It works. Our people know a month ahead when Saturday work is coming up and they plan accordingly. We believe the volunteer system creates hard feelings."

Some companies still give the extra work to the most capable and deserving workers who are seeking a way to increase take-home pay. Seniority was not mentioned as a serious factor in determining who works on Saturday. The important consideration, according to most companies, is to make Saturday work a reward rather than a punishment. You can't keep employees after school if their work isn't done. Don't threaten them with extra work.

Lunch Periods

Better than 70 percent of the companies taking part in Dartnell's survey have lunch periods of one hour. Second most common lunch period is 45 minutes. This applies mostly to companies that are working less than a 40-hour week. A few companies report a 30-

minute lunch period; but the shorter lunch period is more common in large cities than in small towns, where most employees go home to eat.

One office manager has this to say on the subject of lunch periods: "I know that in our organization we have not given this problem the attention it deserves. Our lunch period is half an hour just because it has always been, but in recent years the changing character of the neighborhood in which we are located has made it very hard for the girls to get a decent meal in that length of time.

"Of course, a lot of them would settle for a sandwich and a bowl of soup or a cup of coffee no matter how long they had, but under our present system they have no choice. Knowing what we do today about the importance of proper eating habits in relation to productivity, we should certainly check up on the actual time it takes to eat a decent meal. I know that none of our executives can make it in half an hour."

A minority of companies have cafeterias for office employees only. A number of the larger companies have a general cafeteria available to all employees. About 80 percent of office employees eat outside of the office. Ten percent carry their lunch and eat somewhere in the office; the remainder eat in the cafeteria or lunchroom. Several companies report the use of catering services to bring in hot food at noon; others have vending machines which provide coffee, soup, hot chocolate, and small cracker sandwiches or candy bars.

ORGANIZING FOR MAXIMUM PRODUCTION

In the shop, any employee who found it necessary to work within a tolerance of one-thousandth of an inch, and didn't have the proper tools for measuring thousandths of an inch, would have such a high spoilage rate that he would be too expensive to keep. So the company usually makes available to those employees the proper gauges, micrometers, and other tools for accuracy. But that same company might conceivably require employees in its office to keep books by hand, write names over and over again, add up long columns of figures and make complicated calculations without benefit of the tools now available for doing such work speedily and accurately.

It is the duty of office management when mistakes occur regularly in a particular operation to find out if the reason for the mistakes might not be lack of proper tools as much as employee carelessness.

In offices where there is a lot of figuring to be done, a calculating machine will not only reduce the number of errors, but pay for itself in time saved. If books are kept in old-fashioned ledgers, consideration should be given to installing a mechanical bookkeeping system. Every time a name or a number is copied, there is the possibility of a mistake. Could mistakes be eliminated by using an addressing machine or duplicating orders from one master copy? In preparing sales analyses, an always-present danger area so far as mistakes are concerned, it might pay to install punched-card equipment. Management which fails to "tool up" the office for accurate and fast work must take the blame for many of the needless and costly mistakes that are the result of horse-and-buggy methods.

The Overtime Habit

While most of the loss that comes from paying overtime for doing work which should be done on regular time is due to time wasted or lost during the day, some of this, too, can be laid at the door of inefficient tools. Businessmen are too willing to say: "We have always done it that way, why change?" Instead of considering a proposed piece of up-to-date office equipment or appliance from the standpoint of what it might save in overtime, they regard it with a fishy eye, and treat it as an unnecessary expense.

Analysis shows that in departments where overtime has become a chronic habit, the introduction of timesaving machines and methods will usually put an end to overtime once and for all. There is a case where the company is actually paying for the needed equipment in overtime. Savings which the purchase of the equipment makes possible will cover its early amortization and greatly facilitate the work. It also improves the morale of the department. Unfortunately, overtime soon becomes a habit; and once employees get the habit they are not prone to break it. They find many reasons why they must stay after hours to get out the work. They like the extra pay. Giving them faster tools is one way to break the habit.

An overtime control system will automatically bring to the attention of the office manager or controller the amount of money paid out each month for overtime (the premium pay, not the base pay) by each department; or if the organization is small, to each employee. These reports tell top management which operations are bottlenecking production in the office, and show up inefficient department managers. If the department is understaffed, steps can be taken to add to the personnel. If the system or distribution of work is at fault, it can be corrected. If laborsaving equipment or appliances are needed, they can be purchased. The important thing is to have some means of finding the leaking faucets, so that they do not become permanent profit seepages.

Of course, excessive overtime is a direct reflection on the management of the department in which it occurs, on top management, or on both. Usually it has its roots in faulty organization. When the office is efficiently organized, with good supervision and the responsibilities of each executive clearly defined and understood, overtime is kept at a minimum.

The well-organized office today recognizes the ever-present danger of changing conditions and the effect these have on the work load of different employees. Studies are constantly being made to determine which employees have too much work, and which have too little work. This is done before overtime on any operation is necessary. Overloads can usually be corrected by a redistribution of work, and by the installation of appliances or systems which permit short-cutting the operation.

Breaking the Log Jam

Some years ago, Connecticut General Life Insurance Company adopted a night shift in the stenographic division as an experiment.

The plan called for several married women with excellent business experience and ability to come in at 5 p.m. and work until 10 p.m., transcribing and doing manuscript typing. The supervisor has commented, "The experiment has proved most satisfactory both from the point of view of the company and those who work on the night shift. Emergency help is always available for those departments and individuals who have occasional evening conferences. Also, any rush work which arrives late in the afternoon can be ready first thing in the morning."

The vacation season can set back office production, if all employees' work is allowed to pile up while they are away. If the vacationing person's tasks can be divided among the remaining workers, well and good. If not, it might be wise to call upon one of the services that supply temporary help to break vacation bottlenecks and level overloads during peak periods. In the long run, hiring outside help may prove more economical than paying employees overtime to catch up with their work.

Sun Oil Company has found that high school and college teachers make excellent vacation-time employees. Particularly, teachers with technical knowledge fit into specialized jobs without a great deal of job training. There is another bonus to this policy that pays off for firms like Sun Oil. Such programs make a modest contribution toward enriching the interest level of science courses in secondary schools and thus help attract more young men and women into science careers. The company has found that this effort does a great deal to enhance industry-education cooperation.

Arranging the Workplace

There are two working areas on a desk or bench for each hand. One is the "normal" working area; the other is called the "maximum" working area. The normal area over the desk top is the area which can be reached by the hands with the upper arms hanging vertically at the sides of the operator and the forearms extended normally. The maximum area is the area that can be reached with both the upper arms and the forearms extended all the way. Both areas are semicircular. The normal area is about 15 inches from the top to the edge of the desk and about 47 inches along the front edge of the desk. The maximum area is larger—about 20 inches from top to bottom and 60 inches across the front. If the most-used items are placed within the normal working area, and the less-used items within the maximum area, desk work is less fatiguing.

It will pay to undertake an educational campaign to teach employees the importance of proper desk organization. See that typewriters and calculating machines are located within the normal working area. Equipment such as numbering machines, paper clips, racks holding forms, etc., should be located within the maximum area. Periodical checks should be made of all office desks to see that they are properly arranged, that each desk contains the necessary conveniences, and that the drawers are clean and tidy.

Check the adjustment of posture chairs and height of desks. Posture chairs, one of the most important means of reducing fatigue in the office, should be adjusted for each employee and then tagged with the name of that employee. Desks should be adjusted to the correct height for the person working at them. The U.S. Government Printing Office, after a careful study, designed a desk which greatly reduced fatigue. Some of its features are:

1. Lower: 29 inches high instead of 30½ inches gives the operator greater comfort in doing the work.

2. Narrower by seven inches than the old desk makes depositing of papers in the compartments a less fatiguing job.

3. The light pearly-gray color is in harmony with ceiling and side walls and greatly reduces the factor of contrast.

4. At desk level is a container in which remittances for purchases are deposited. With the old desk this detail has been a misfit arrangement, confusing and time-consuming.

5. A conveniently arranged place for all things used in the work permits better housekeeping.

6. Locked drawer for personal use of the employee—a much-appreciated convenience.

In general terms, the special desk is fitted to the job, not the job to the desk.

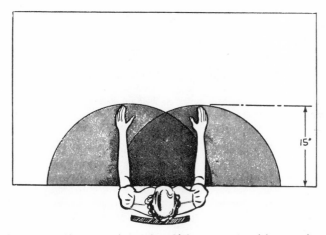

Minimum working area of desk in which most-used articles are placed

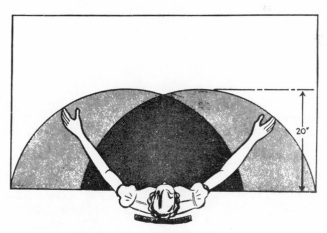

Maximum working area of desk in which less-used articles are placed

The desk is 44 percent smaller than the old one. Add to this the space saved because of production increases, and the economy in floor space is better than 50 percent.

How Nationwide Insurance Developed an Hourly "Call-In" Clerical Pool

Overtime work may put extra money into employees' pocketbooks by increasing the weekly paycheck, but it also adds to their fatigue and inconvenience. Nationwide Insurance Company, Columbus, Ohio, uses an "hourly call-in program" that keeps the organization's employment division in touch with former employees. The idea is to use them as a source of help when clerical demands become excessive and permanent personnel is pushed with too much piled-up work.

An executive of Nationwide described the plan as follows:

We have the "hourly call-in" program well under way. It helps many of our departments that have a lot of overtime work. While it does add extra dollars to the employee's paycheck when he works beyond the regular hours, overtime is a source of inconvenience and fatigue, too. From a company standpoint expense-wise, time-and-a-half is costly and not economical—affecting us eventually profitwise.

Our employment division prepared a list of former employees who were willing to come back to work on an hourly call-in basis. For these purposes, three general categories have been established at different hourly rates. They are:

1. Specialist
2. Typist
3. General Processing.

All terminating employees are asked:

1. Their interest in part-time work
2. Their availability for such "call-in" work
3. Amount of time they will have available
4. Type of work preference.

Another point—there are no fringe benefits to be handled and the average "Call-In" straight-time salary is less than that of a full-time permanent employee. Thus, expense reduction is important, including the fact that no time-and-a-half cost is involved either. The company spokesman reports that there has been very favorable cooperation and acceptance by supervisors, indicating their satisfaction with the expense reduction.

An old saying to the effect that "absence makes the heart grow fonder" is poorly received by most managements today. "Better late than never" is another tired bromide that has fallen into oblivion as companies seek to improve bad employee attendance records in this day of competitive markets, high wages, and growing union demands for more.

Everyone loses when an employee is off the job or loafing on it. Out of 200 working days in the average office year, the equivalent of 40 days are lost, so far as production is concerned, because of vacations, absenteeism, tardiness, illness, visiting, and plain everyday loafing. In the case of vacations and legitimate illness, there is not much that management can do. It is a part of the cost of operating an office. Persons doing repetitive work must have a change of pace and an opportunity to relieve the monotony of their lives. Since we cannot all be free from common colds, and other indispositions, some loss of time is inevitable. According to a U.S. Department of Labor survey, illness was responsible for nine times as much absenteeism as conditions on the job.

There is a growing practice, started by the U.S. Government during the last war, to allow employees two weeks' "sick time" with pay in addition to two weeks' vacation. The theory is that it is unfair to those who take care of their health, or are fortunate enough to be born healthy, to be penalized by having to stay on the job while their less-robust associates stay home to nurse a real or imaginary illness. However, with the prevailing shortage of clerical workers, and especially stenographers, most companies are slanting personnel policy toward rewarding those who stay on the job, without penalizing those who become ill.

The cure for the absence and tardiness problem, according to a great many executives, is not rules and regulations but common sense. One official says: "It involves a study of causes, a sincere effort to remedy faulty situations, and the segregation of chronic offenders." He further states, "It is far better to reward and recognize employees who have good attendance records than to punish those who stay home without good reason, or without getting permission first."

How 162 Companies Handle Tardiness and Absence

"Absenteeism and tardiness only become problematical in cases where company rules alone are expected to control them. Conscientious concern about the problem at the time of employment, explanation of the importance of good attendance and being to work on time, followup by supervisors—all will keep absenteeism and tardiness at a minimum. Generally, however, you can't expect the supervisor to have more than 50 percent of the enthusiasm that management puts forth, neither can this manager expect a greater amount from his people." This comment, made by the director of personnel, Porcelain Steel Buildings Company, Columbus, Ohio, pretty well points up the whole concept of attending controls.

Well over 80 percent of the companies joining in this Dartnell exchange of management practice and experience have an established policy governing absence and tardiness by employees. Only 24 companies in the group indicate they have no set policy.

The director of personnel of a Philadelphia insurance company describes his company's system as not being "formal," but controls are left in the hands of first-line supervisors. By general definition, this would appear to be a formal policy, since responsibility is placed.

We asked participating executives to list what they find to be the most common causes of absenteeism in their concerns. The results are quite diverse, showing that absenteeism has many sources. Here are the tabulated replies of the 162 cooperating organizations:

Sickness (real)	44 percent
Sickness (imagined or feigned)	33 percent
Home problems	32 percent
"Don't care attitude"	25 percent
Transportation problems	23 percent
Drinking	12 percent
Poor supervision	11 percent
Accidents (home or on job)	8 percent
Other	4 percent

Listed among other reasons are "lack of training in self-discipline and personal habits," female problems, illness of children, farming, and "looking for another job."

Seventy percent of the concerns find the absence rate is higher among women than among male employees. Twenty-three percent feel it isn't and 6 percent are not sure.

Interestingly enough, only 34 percent of the companies feel the tardiness and absence rate of new employees is greater than that of workers who have been with the company a longer period of time. Fifty-six percent don't feel this is so and another 10 percent aren't sure. An actual figure taken from an analysis of the rate was passed along by the personnel director, Tung Sol Electric, Hazleton, Pennsylvania, who reported that the absence rate among new employees is 1 percent as compared with 2.3 percent among older employees. On the other hand, the executives of a number of companies, including The London Assurance Group, New York City, and the Pennsylvania Farm Bureau Cooperative Association, stress the fact that their experience shows older employees to be more reliable and conscientious.

A Catholic nun, administrator of a large hospital, feels there is a definite indication that difference in age among women employees is a factor. The sister points to greatest absences among younger married women.

Systems for Controlling Tardiness

Below are reported a sampling of methods used in handling the tardiness problem in surveyed companies:

"Reviewed by personnel. More than seven times tardy in one month—warning; third time and future occurrences—three days' suspension."

"Employee is sent home if a substitute has been placed on his job that day."

"Supervisors handle the matter."

"Morning sign-in books are promptly picked up at each division by 8:45—lateness is charged against the tardy employee."

"Verbal warnings: then written one which states that next offense will result in time off and the following offense can mean discharge."

"Four or five warnings—then dismissed."

"IBM listing of all absences, including salary costs. All reasons sent to supervisors periodically for discussion with individual concerned—chronic cases discharged."

"Example set by supervisors. Discussion with employee on tardiness—results recorded in personnel folder."

"We have no system of control. We do maintain records, hoping it will motivate employees to be on time."

"Attendance and punctuality only stressed to new employees as being important for job advancement and personal growth in the company."

"Three times tardy unexcused in a 90-day period makes employee subject to discharge."

"Daily report form used. Second offense in one week—talk between supervisor and employee. Purpose is to understand causes and help the individual, if possible. A record of what transpired is maintained in personnel record."

"We 'forgive' the first 15 minutes in any week. When it is exceeded, we dock the employee."

"We have something a bit unusual and unorthodox. When a tardy employee enters the department, cowbells, whistles, and howls greet him. Very effective."

"We take periodic spot checks. Extreme cases can get a day off without pay—even two days off. Chronic offenders discharged."

"We penalize the tardy employee by deducting the coffee break. He must fill out written form."

"Permit 14 minutes' tardiness a week. If employee is 15 to 29 minutes late, he loses 15 minutes' wages; if 30 to 44 minutes late, 30 minutes of wages; and so forth."

"We have had more success with sugar than we have with vinegar. We reward good attendance and try to counsel with offenders. We have no major problems, either."

All in all, Dartnell finds 53 percent of the companies let supervisory personnel and/or the personnel department handle the situation. Seventeen percent dock employees' pay, and 30 percent use other means of controls, such as listed in the above comments.

Methods for Controlling Absenteeism

The problem of absenteeism is a major concern of office executives in 73 percent of the cases reported. Deductions in pay, sick leave, or vacation pay are made in 8 percent of the situations. Other means of controlling absenteeism are as follows:

"Daily absentee slips, giving reasons for absences, are made out by foremen; recorded in personnel records. Habitual absenteeism is subject to disciplinary suspension and ultimate discharge."

"Three unexcused absences in one month liable for discharge."

"Nurse checks after one day's absence."

"Supervisory control—sick pay program provides pay for illnesses supported by a doctor's statement."

"Written note required explaining reason for absence. Monthly report of attendance and lateness of each department submitted to managers and executives."

"Verbal warning, written warning, and then time off."

"Thirteen weeks of perfect attendance—no absences, no tardiness—earn a bonus day to be taken off during the next 90 days. Not accumulative."

"We allow seven days a year of short-time absence, then a warning is issued pointing out that continued short-time absences can mean discharge. Merit increases are held for six months when warning letter has been sent—no second warning is given."

"Salary increases withheld in chronic cases."

"Counseling helps reduce chronic cases. We try to see what the trouble is— maybe it is an illness that needs treatment or a mental attitude. We have found a patient and human approach to these things helps."

"Twelve days a year are paid for on unused sick days. After this there is a deduction from pay."

"Maintain weekly reports on each employee according to reason for each day of absence. This information is translated into a quarterly report by our data-processing center. The report indicates rate and days lost per person per year for each department and branch. Management keeps individual departments and branches informed of absentee rate as compared to overall bank absentee rate."

Policies on Prolonged Absenteeism

Seventy-eight percent of the firms have a policy governing cases of extended absence. Here is the way they break down:

Given leave of absence .... 28 percent

Taken care of by personnel department
or department head .... 8 percent

Each case handled individually .... 14 percent

Set time limit for absences—must be
complied with or employee is subject to
dismissal or other disciplinary action .... 21 percent

Other means .... 8 percent

Examples of stated policies are shown below:

"People who have excessive leaves of absence have their records reviewed with an interview by personnel and department head periodically."

"Personnel can apply for leave of absence. Employees who are not on leave of absence but who have an excessive absentee record are either reassigned or terminated—two weeks may be considered excessive."

"Only prolonged absence is recognized as illness. Absence due to illness, if prolonged, is recognized as sick leave—maximum duration, one year."

"If employee is absent five consecutive workdays without notifying employer, this is considered a 'quit' or voluntary termination. If shorter unauthorized absences occur frequently, employee is counseled and may receive a warning."

"Each case is considered on its own merit and is so evaluated. Our group insurance plan administration procedures control most cases. If malingering is suspected, company and insurance doctors are called in—if proven, employee can be discharged."

"Three days without notifying the foreman, medical office, or personnel, rates a termination. After one week's absence, even though employee reports, a personal check is made by personnel and medical department. The findings determine the decision."

Controlling Absences—Awards Vs. Discipline

Forty-seven percent of respondents feel "strong company rules" are vital in controlling the absence and tardiness rate, and 92 percent feel the key to such controls lies in good supervision. While it is growing in acceptance and is more prevalent than 10 years ago, only 16 companies indicate they use incentives for attendance. Most common of these is the bonus day off, for good attendance. At The Dartnell Corporation, for instance, we have for some years had a policy whereby an employee having two months of perfect attendance, with no absence or tardiness, gets a "bonus day," that is, a day off with pay during the next two-month period. This can be taken at any time with approval of the department head, but bonus days cannot be accrued. Others have similar policies.

Owens-Corning Fiberglas Corporation has plant "perfect attendance" dinners and a company spokesman describes them as "fairly effective."

Who Punches Time Clocks?

When Dartnell recently asked a number of companies "Who punches time clocks?" 70 percent of the respondents said plant em-

Absence - Lateness

Because so many of your fellow employees depend upon your work to do their own, and because the activities of the Club and Exchange require prompt attention, we know you will cooperate by being on the job regularly and at the proper time each morning. The other employees in your department or office will appreciate it, and your own work will not pile up. Of course, everyone is ill at times, and we would not want you to come to work if you are so seriously ill that it would endanger your health or the health of others. If you find it necessary to stay home, or if for any reason you are going to be late, it is requested that you phone your supervisor as early as possible so that your work can be distributed to other employees for that day.

If you are absent or tardy too frequently, your supervisor can only feel that you have lost interest in your work, and will have to indicate this on your record. If you remain away from work for three consecutive days without reporting or giving your supervisor any reason, the Company has no other choice than to assume that you are no longer interested, and your name will be dropped from the payroll the same as if you had quit.

For the good of the other employees, and to safeguard you from returning to work before you are entirely well, every home office employee who is absent be-

Pages from the employee handbook of

ployees, 40 percent included office employees, and 15 percent said no one. One executive, clarifying his statement, said, "In our company, we have a policy whereby all nonsupervisory personnel punch the clock."

Those who feel that time clocks are resented by employees and are a source of low morale may be surprised to learn that 60 percent of the respondents reported that employees "accept clocks and there are no problems involved." Twelve percent reported that clocks "were not well accepted." One respondent, apparently of the "do as we say and not as we do" school of thought, commented, "We sell them

---

cause of illness is requested to report to Health Service the morning of his return whether he has a doctor's certificate or not. Your supervisor will discuss Health Service visiting hours with you.

Funerals

In the event of death in your family, you will be given time off with pay on the following basis:

1. For members of your immediate family (your parent, brother, sister, spouse, child)—time off from the day of death through the day that the funeral takes place. (Not to exceed three days unless approved by the Department or Division Manager.)

2. For other near relatives (grandparent, uncle, aunt)—time off for the funeral only.

If, for any reason, you believe an exception should be made to the above rules, please discuss the matter with your Department or Division Manager.

Holidays

New Year's Day, Memorial Day, 4th of July, Labor Day, Thanksgiving Day, and Christmas Day are the paid holidays. In the event that a holiday falls on Sunday, the following Monday will be observed as a holiday.

The Automobile Club of Michigan

(time clocks) but do not use one." A spokesman for Bell & Howell reported that "our engineering personnel especially did not like to punch clocks."

W. C. Follendorf, budget manager of the Great Lakes Carbon Corporation, commented that, "Our plant has been in operation for 35 years. Time clocks were installed July 1, 1956—no reaction from employees." The director of a special service division of a large hospitalization insurance group said, "I do not believe there is marked objection to punching time clocks by personnel in our organization."

Henry A. Carlile, office manager of Allied Paper Bag Division, observed, "We have been operating with time clocks for over 25 years. New employees are oriented to this system when hired."

Making Clocks Acceptable

Few companies have programs designed to make time clocks acceptable to employees. "Why should we?" asked one executive. "The employee contracts to work a specific number of hours for a specific amount of pay. All the time clock does is control that agreement for both the employer and the employee."

Most commonly used timing device is manufactured by International Business Machines Corporation. General Time Corporation, Cincinnati Time Recorder Company, Lathem Time Recorder Company, and Simplex Time Recorder Company are also mentioned as manufacturers of preferred timing devices.

Should the timecard system be abolished? Very definitely not, according to respondents. Even executives representing firms which do not use timing devices see no reason for eliminating them from our industrial scene. One executive, a strong supporter of the "honor system," states, "We don't use timing devices (except for time-pieces), but I'd feel insecure if they vanished from the earth. We'll use the honor system as long as our employees play the game squarely, but we'll use timing devices just as soon as they show signs of abusing the privileges they now enjoy. I should add that I don't expect them to abuse that privilege since we have enjoyed it for better than 18 years."

Using Job Enlargement to Attack Absenteeism

It has been already said that one way to lessen the problem of absenteeism is to attack the boredom that attaches to some office jobs. One solution is to give closer supervisory attention to all the details and ramifications of the job to see if it cannot be made more interesting. Another way is through job enlargement.

Dwight G. Baird, a prominent business reporter, recently described how the principle of job enlargement was used at The Detroit Edison Company to combat job boredom. Here are excerpts from Mr. Baird's report:

The Detroit Edison Company serves more than a million customers. Its offices are equipped with modern machines of many kinds. It employs the mass-production technique, including an adaptation of assembly line procedures. In the customer billing department, over 100 employees each day bill more than 30,000 accounts, handle more than 2,000 service orders daily, and maintain a file of names and addresses of all customers. Much of this work is necessarily routine, repetitive, and monotonous. The punched-card system of billing is used, and billing records flow from operation to operation, gradually accumulating information in much the same way as parts are built into a finished product on an assembly line in a factory.

Up until about three years ago, the management just assumed that it had attained the ultimate in high production and low cost by mechanizing and specializing. Then it began to realize that while specialization and the mass-production technique have many notable advantages, they also have disadvantages. Both the advantages and disadvantages are well known. The advantages admittedly are too great to renounce. But the disadvantages, too, are great. Such being the case, couldn't something be done to eliminate or at least to mitigate the disadvantages?

There seemed no way to eliminate the tedious and monotonous billing operations, so the company began looking for ways and means of relieving the monotony and boredom induced by highly repetitive, one-operation jobs. It adapted such improvements as more frequent rest periods and music played over the public-address system for 15 minutes of each hour. But while such measures did provide more frequent breaks and did relieve the tedium to some extent, they did not eliminate the monotony and boredom of the work.

"Then," said J. Douglas Elliott, superintendent of the customer billing department, "we became aware of the indirect costs related to the many monotonous jobs we had, and of the fact that many of our people were capable of performing tasks beyond those on which they were employed. The rudest awakening came when we were made aware of the fact that to reduce costs, we had overspecialized some of our tasks to the extent that we had actually increased costs by creating many needless or duplicate operations."

To correct this condition, Detroit Edison began making experiments which gradually developed into a definite program of job enlargement . . . so far restricted to the billing department. In doing so, it has had three objectives in view: (1) To reduce job monotony, (2) to utilize employees' intellectual capabilities to a greater extent, and (3) to decrease the amount of specialization where it has created duplication and increased costs.

Job enlargement does not imply the creation of more jobs or different jobs, Mr. Elliott said. It does not increase costs, or if it does, it should be abandoned. It does not conflict with work simplification. Detroit Edison has a work-simplification program as well as a job-enlargement program. It also has an employee suggestion system and pays adequate awards. Job enlargement has brought some wage increases, but they have been far more than compensated for by increased production and reduced costs.

Specifically, job enlargement in Detroit Edison's billing department has resulted in these benefits, Mr. Elliott said:

Increased employees' responsibilities, utilizing their abilities to a greater extent.

Reduced monotony and boredom, replacing them with interest in the work.

Cut absenteeism 15 percent or more in some work groups.

Cut overtime in half where the activities of some entire work groups were enlarged.

Eliminated the need for additional personnel by abolishing several unnecessary jobs and operations, in spite of an increase of 5 percent or more in the volume of the work.

Reduced the number of job classifications.

Cut one day off the schedule for setting up new accounts.

"Here's a formula," Mr. Elliott said, and wrote on a scratch pad: "A headache plus lack of interest in the job equals an absence; the same headache plus an interest in the job equals an attendance.

"An actual survey of 78 work groups which we made revealed that the absence rate of employees in groups whose work was highly repetitive was 20 percent higher than in groups whose work was only moderately repetitive or nonrepetitive."

Detroit Edison has applied its job-enlargement program to workers, work groups, and supervisors. A few examples will suffice to illustrate what has been done in this respect.

On one operation, a girl formerly operated a machine, another girl checked her work, and a third took totals and balanced the operation. Now this operator rotates on four types of machines, checks her own work, and balances her operation. Her work has variety and interest and her skill has broadened. She is a more valuable employee for all of these reasons. Formerly, if she made a mistake, she might feel inclined to overlook it because she knew her work would be checked by someone else. Now she checks her own work and if she makes a mistake, she stops and corrects it and also corrects the cause of the mistake. While a spot check is still made, she knows that if she lets a mistake pass it will go to the customer and she will be responsible for it.

There are three machine work groups. The work flows from machine to machine within and between these groups. As a result, there were many specialized machine jobs within each of the work groups. Such a high degree of specialization began to take its toll in low employee morale and in lack of flexibility. One machine-job classification in each work group was established and each operator was required to perform any job in the group. The supervisor assigns them to any task necessary. Such free movement of employees promotes teamwork, affords variety, eliminates boredom, and so is a factor in increasing efficiency.

Past-due statements are run on tabulating machines, but some typing is required. Three typists formerly typed all day long, and one of the rotating machine operators ran the machine all day long. Typists were supposed to help the operator run the machine, but there was a tendency not to do so. A fourth typist was added, the machine operator was assigned to other work, and the four typists now run their own printing machine. Each spends about one-fourth of her time on the machine, which is a welcome relief from typing. A recent increase in the volume of this work has been absorbed without additional help.

At the group level, one group formerly maintained a customer address file which contains over 1.7 million punched cards. They filed the cards, assigned account numbers to new customers, and performed other routine duties. A second group, consisting of key-punch operators and checkers, set up the cards and other records from service orders received from customers.

Activities of these employees were enlarged by establishing two new groups, each of which became responsible for all of the duties formerly performed by both of the other groups. One group now does the key punching, filing, checking, and maintenance jobs for half of the file and the other group does the same work for the other half of it.

The two supervisors soon discovered that both old groups had been duplicating one another's work to a considerable extent. This was particularly true of the checking on one another's work. Now each group is responsible for its own checking and the duplication has been eliminated.

Each new group has nine clerical jobs. These were studied with a view to enabling each employee to perform several tasks instead of only one. As a result, seven of the job classifications were reduced to three.

Before the change was made, one group was usually behind schedule. Overtime was common. The management had about decided to hire more personnel to eliminate overtime and keep the work on schedule. But soon after the change was made and the duplication of work was eliminated, both new groups caught up with their work and have since been able to keep up with it without the addition of new personnel; overtime has been reduced to less than half of what it was previously.

In another case, a machine specialist was employed to set up machines, assist in making minor repairs, run down and study the cause of machine errors, and coordinate the servicing of machines with the repairmen. The first-line supervisors of the three work groups performing machine operations referred machine problems to this specialist. They were not required or expected to understand the machines, make changes, and work with repairmen.

This specialist's job was discontinued and his duties were added to those of the three affected supervisors. They required some training, but they now are operating their groups more efficiently than ever before. They know more about the machines and they have a new interest in their jobs. As they are better acquainted with their own work than the specialist ever was, they have been able to make some valuable suggestions. And they don't have to wait for the specialist to wire a new plugboard for them. They also save production time by coordinating the servicing of their machines directly with the serviceman rather than having to work through a third party.

As a result of such changes, some employees have been upgraded into higher pay-rate classifications. That, too, is pleasing to the employees, but how does the employer benefit?

"Well, consider the example of the regrouping mentioned previously," Mr. Elliott said. "Disregarding such benefits to the employer as improved morale and increased job interest when an employee gets a raise, we still saved money on the change. We didn't have to hire additional personnel."

Chapter 33

QUALITY CONTROL IN THE OFFICE

FINDING a better way of doing work in the office is the natural goal of an office administrator. Saving time and money in the department will benefit management, but at the same time these gains should benefit the employees as well. Today, the office manager knows he is responsible to the people who must do the work as well as to the company. Perhaps this is the key to the ready acceptance of new systems and techniques which can improve both work output and working conditions.

Simplifying office procedures is a good place to begin the job of improving quality. The office manager has hundreds of sources willing to sell him machines, equipment and systems that will speed work without burdening employees. But, first the administrator should know where the need exists.

Whether the responsibility for administrative efficiency rests with a committee, with a continuing department, or with the office manager himself, it is important to analyze periodically the work being done by each employee. Such analysis differs from the so-called *job* analysis which concerns itself with who does what, whereas *work* analysis is concerned with most efficient use of an employee's time. It affords a basis for establishing reasonable standards for clerical production, and locating inefficient operations as well as work overloads.

Making Work Analyses

One of the large manufacturing corporations of the country, for example, has a department known as the "Office Methods and Equipment Division," which makes continuous studies to determine ways of reducing administrative costs in the office. Employees are required to fill out a form daily for six days stating just what they do with their time during the period.

A company spokesman describes the work analysis process this way:

"With this data available we determine the loading of each employee in a given department or unit. The mass of data from the analysis forms is broken down into appropriate and useful classifications. These various subdivisions are studied; tentative production norms are established and variations from these norms are investigated.

"Actually, when we begin these studies we don't know what we will find; it is important to begin with an open mind and no preconceived ideas of what methods a department should use.

"The 'work analysis sheet' plays an important role in our study of the data accumulated on the analysis form. It is on this that the variations I referred to earlier show up. By this time, the analysts of the methods department have become extremely familiar with the operations and procedures of the department being studied. They have a good idea of the time needed for many or all of the department's operations. They may suggest revisions in some of these procedures based on their knowledge of motion-economy techniques.

"There recently occurred a good example of a variation which, when investigated, led to an important saving. A worker had indicated on the analysis form that it had taken her about 300 minutes to do a filing job which, from our knowledge of standards required for such work, we felt could be finished in no more than 20 minutes. One of the analysts went to the worker and asked, quite tactfully of course, about the operation. It was immediately apparent that the worker was quite efficient but that the operation was needlessly complicated.

"The worker went to a stack of forms (the 300 minutes had by no means finished up the job), took one off the top, walked 20 or 30 feet to a shelf containing a number of loose-leaf binders, selected one, returned with it to a desk, unlocked the binder at a selected page, inserted the form, locked the binder, and returned it. That completed the operation.

"All this was required to file a relatively unimportant form in numerical sequence in binders. The operation was changed considerably: The form was redesigned so that it is now filed in a standard cabinet. The binders are no longer used. The operation takes less than a tenth of the time formerly required.

"Studies of one department will naturally frequently lead into other departments. Recently an analyst investigated a department and found that its employees did not know why they were receiving a copy of a certain operating form from the billing department; each day they had to file away a large pile which, once stored, was never referred to. The analyst went to the originating department, told its supervisor about the unwelcome and unnecessary copies, and the latter had the procedure immediately changed to eliminate this waste of time and paper.

"When the survey and the study and investigation of its findings have been completed—it can be easily seen that the time required will vary considerably from survey to survey—the analysts write a joint report with only the essential ideas in it. This report is given to the supervisor who originally requested the survey. It is divided into two general sections:

1. Corrections which have been made.
2. Corrections which should be made.

"This second section does not necessarily consist of recommendations of the analysts which have been turned down. In many cases, the time is not appropriate to make the corrections—a more appropriate time frequently occurring when we make changes in models.

"The supervisor now has a fairly definite idea of his departmental assignments and the standard time required to do each of these. In setting standard times, our only aim is to try to find out what constitutes a reasonable day's work by employees who come up to company standards. We pay very well, require applicants for office positions to pass job-sample tests (55 words per minute for typists is a typical pre-employment requirement), and expect our employees to do their share. A further example of this liberal policy is that if the hourly standard is 100, the daily standard is not 800, though we have an 8-hour day, but 700. We make allowances for rest periods, and personal time.

"Surveys reveal from time to time that changes should be made in the general administration of the department as well as individual job procedures. If, for example, a worker frequently lists 'waiting for work' on the analysis form, it is obvious that some correction should be made."

"Upgrading is based on job performance and employees are moved to a higher classification when they are able to do the work required. This is an important reason why our departmental and section supervisors keep records of individual production. We have encountered a little resistance on this score but when we demonstrate that no sound and accurate estimate of manpower requirements—upon which are based requisitions for additional employees—are possible without such records, we never have had any further trouble."

Work Measurement in the Office

No formal attempt to measure work of clerical employees is made in three out of four companies, a survey finds. Seventy-six percent of 5,000 companies sampled by the Administrative Management Society answered "No" to the question: "Do you use any type of clerical work measurement?"

The basic problem of office administration, according to the association, is to see that employees do an acceptable or outstanding job at lowest possible cost. Work measurement is a means of determining the relative efficiency of the clerical office worker by comparative analysis of such things as:

1. Variation in volume of work from one employee to another doing the same job, or from one time to another for an individual employee.

2. The time and number of people it will take to do a projected office job whether the job has been done before or not.

3. The improvement or loss of clerical time and quality of work resulting from a change of method or system.

While unit output of a production worker in a plant is fairly simple to determine, attempts to establish the efficiency of the clerical worker have lagged because of the difficulty, complication, and expense of measuring clerical office functions.

Clerical work measurement, the survey finds, increases in direct proportion to company size: Fifty-nine percent of companies with over 5,000 office employees use some type of work measurement, and only 13 percent of the companies employing one to 10 office workers do so.

Larger companies have an advantage which explains their more extensive use of work measurement: Their office workers are more specialized and stay on one type of work, so that work volume can be measured more easily. Then, too, the task of measurement of worker productivity is spread over a larger number of workers, and can be done at a lower per capita cost.

Size of companies included in this survey ranged from those having from one to over 5,000 employees in the office. Almost half of the companies surveyed, however, employed 11 to 100 office workers.

Aldens Error Control System

In large offices where there is considerable paper work to be done, and the possibility for making mistakes is an ever-present problem, it is possible to set up a system for controlling the quality of the work. One such system which has been in operation for some years is that used by Aldens, Inc., a Chicago mail-order house. The system sets up a sampling unit for each operation, and requires periodic tests to determine the percentage of errors. The sample used is 100 work units. The advantage of using a sample unit of 100 is that the error ratio contained in the sample is easily computed and scored. Scoring is done by means of wall charts, which are maintained on a monthly basis for each department. A solid line (or plastic ribbon) extending across the chart shows the goal for the month.

Two forms used in connection with this Aldens system which are important to its successful operation are the data sheet on which the inspector reports the results of his sampling, and the analysis sheet. The first form provides data on the number of units of work inspected on each operation, the number and description of the errors found, and the operator who is responsible. Before it is sent to the control desk for analysis, it is signed by the department manager, the supervisor, and the trainer. This is done so any kinks can be ironed out and corrected before the data sheet is turned in. The second form is an analysis or recap sheet maintained by each section. It is made out each week for the previous week by the section manager, and shows the percentage of errors in relation to the work done

499

Form Used in a Work Analysis Program

ANALYSIS OF WORK

Name...

Department...

Operation...

Date...

Symbols	Explanation

Interruption Symbols

1. Telephone
2. Errand (explain)
3. Washroom

4. Waiting for work
5. Instructions
6. Late

7. Luncheon

Overtime Worked

From........................to........................Total Min........................

Daily analysis form is used to evaluate work of office personnel and simplify administrative operations. Forms are completed by each employee at the close of the day and sent to a central department for summarizing and control purposes. Work abbreviations shown opposite are on the reverse side of the form.

Form Used in a Work Analysis Program (Cont.)

ABBREVIATIONS FOR COMMON OFFICE OPERATIONS

ASSISTANTS, SUPERVISORS

AA—Analyzing reports
AB—Assigning work, giving instructions
AC—Checking work, explain
AD—Dictation to dictaphone
AE—Dictation to stenographer
AF—Dictation to typist, direct
AG—Discussion, explain
AH—Preparing reports
AJ—Reading correspondence, literature
AK—Writing copy
AL—Writing memos (handwritten)

STENOGRAPHERS

BA—Memory file tickler
BB—Receiving dictation
BC—Typing from dictaphone dictation
BD—Typing from shorthand notes
BE—Typing letters, telegrams, memos from handwritten notes

TYPISTS

CA—Addressing envelopes
CB—Filling in forms or form letters
CC—Proofreading (two persons)
CD—Typing cards
CE—Typing lists
CF—Typing manuscripts or reports (handwritten)
CG—Typing manuscripts or reports (typewritten)
CH—Typing orders (stationery, purchase, advertising, sales, etc.), requisitions, etc.
CJ—Typing stencils for mimeograph
CK—Typing tabular reports

CLERKS

DA—Looking up information
DB—Alphabetizing
DC—Sorting material to be filed
DD—Filing material in
DE—Transferring files
DF—Removing from files
DG—Adding—hand
DH—Adding—machine
DI—Computing—hand
DJ—Computing—machine
DK—Invoicing and billing
DL—Checking bills and invoices
DM—Balancing (trial balance, balance sheets)
DN—Profit and loss statements
DO—Entry, original (cash book, journals, etc.)
DP—Hand posting
DR—Machine posting
DS—Make checks
DT—Arranging stock
DU—Counting and listing (inventory)
DV—Withdrawing stock

MISCELLANEOUS

EA—Opening and assorting mail and packages
EB—Picking up or delivering items from or to other depts. (indicate if route delivery)
EC—Attending or operating mechanical conveyers
ED—Switchboard operation
EE—Cleaning equipment
EG—Repairing equipment

An important factor in the program for analyzing office operations is a complete set of job abbreviations. These are printed on the back of related forms, so that all who use them will have the same understanding of the terms.

in the section. The information is taken from the quality control work sheets each day. It puts the finger on sections having a high percentage of errors, and provides the section manager as well as the department manager with a yardstick by which the quality of the work in each section can be measured and compared.

While the system is used in all departments of the business, it was first introduced into the office as a means of controlling clerical errors. Clerical work performed in Aldens general offices includes the following operations, all subject to errors:

1. Open envelope, remove contents, verify remittance, apply cash impression to order blank.

   Error possibilities: Total remittance incorrectly; apply wrong cash impression; fail to transpose customer's name and address from postal money order or personal check when information is missing from order blank and envelope.

2. Read order to see whether any phase of transaction will not be handled in regular mail-order process. If so, apply special rubber stamps, make abstracts on special requests, inquiries, and complaints.

   Error possibilities: Fail to handle special phase of transaction.

3. Record order on customer's index stencil; show date received and amount. Imprint stencil showing customer's name and address on shipping label and order.

   Error possibilities: Record order on wrong stencil; show incorrect date or amount; imprint wrong stencil on shipping label and order.

4. Pull entry "ticket" for each catalog number ordered; circle size, color, and quantity wanted.

   Error possibilities: Pull wrong tickets; circle wrong color, size, or quantity

5. Schedule order for shipment. A machine operation showing time, aisle, section, and bin number in shipping room where order will be packed.

   Error possibilities: Switch tickets and send order to wrong customer.

All of the above activities are under statistical quality control. Applications have also been made on key-punch operations in the general offices and on the freight and express routing activities.

Reporting on the results of this control system, an Aldens executive said:

During the years statistical quality control has been used in our general offices, the combined error ratio has been reduced by 67.6 percent.

In one clerical department, the order reading, where we originally had only one chart, we found we needed a still further breakdown by order classification, such as cash orders, no-cash orders, and credit orders. Accordingly, we now have charts on all of these separate activities.

A few years ago, statistical quality control was introduced into the credit department, where charts are now maintained on posting-checking operations, credit approval, follow-up typing, files, and related activities. Comparing three

```
                                                    Sheet No._____
            ALDENS  QUALITY  CONTROL
                         Data Sheet

Department _____ Date _____ Inspector _____

    Operator No.                 Units of Work Inspected

_____    _____

_____    _____

_____    _____

_____    _____

_____    _____

_____    _____

                         Description of Errors

                                                        Operator
        Error No.                                       Responsible

_____    _____    _____

_____    _____    _____

_____    _____    _____

_____    _____    _____

_____    _____    _____

_____    _____    _____

_____    _____    _____

_____    _____    _____

_____    _____    _____
```

When you complete the inspection of 100 work units, post the number of errors found on your control chart immediately. If an error is serious or repetitive in character, call the matter to the attention of your supervisor at once. This worksheet to be circulated to and initialed by the following:

Department Manager _____ Supervisor _____ Trainer _____

F1053

months of one year with the same three months of the preceding year, combined error ratios for all credit department activities were reduced 37 percent.

The manner in which data is obtained for the control chart on the filing operation may be interesting. Before sign-out of work is made to file clerks, duplicate stencil impressions showing customer's name and address are removed from the papers. After 100 names have been accumulated and the papers filed, a look-up is made to see whether they were filed correctly.

Aldens QUALITY CONTROL
ANALYSIS SHEET

Section_____   Week Ending_____

Operator												
Date												

UNITS OF WORK

Total												

Operator												
Catalog No.												
Color												
Size												
Quantity												
Price												
Stamp												

TYPES OF ERRORS

Total												
% Errors												

Entries should be made on this recap sheet daily, with data taken from
your Quality Control work sheets of the day previous. This report to be
made in duplicate and the original sent to your Department Manager
each Monday, for the week previous.

_____
Section Manager

While every well-managed office has some method of controlling errors and getting rid of costly mistakes (so far as is humanly possible), the process can be speeded up by establishing error ratios for each department, or each operation, making monthly samplings of specific operations and then posting the result for all to see. Such a practice tends to (1) keep the organization mistake-conscious, (2) show up lax departmental management and sloppy supervision, and (3) locate weaknesses in methods which may be causing recurrence of the same type of mistakes.

One thing a supervisor must understand is that every personality has been formed by countless influences over a period of several decades. Remolding is an impossible task, but people can and do change in some respects, and it is the manager's job to help them adapt to the work situation. Many characteristics, attitudes and work habits are superficial enough to be susceptible to change.

Broadly speaking, the blame for recurring errors in office administration rests on the shoulders of management. It is beside the point to say they are due to carelessness of employees. Who picked the employee who made the mistake? Who trained him? Who supervises him? If mistakes have become a chronic occurrence, the solution may be found in breaking down the operation in five ways: (1) Selecting and training employees who are temperamentally fitted to do their work accurately and well; (2) improved procedures and systems, with the necessary modern tools to keep down the percentage of error; (3) working facilities conducive to doing painstaking work; (4) competent supervision; (5) a control system which will keep every employee aware that should he make a mistake it will count not only against him, but hurt the entire department and all his fellow workers.

OFFICE PRODUCTION STANDARDS

Establishing standards for different types of office work has been hampered by the varying conditions of the work. For instance, it is hard to rate stenographers because one man may dictate rapidly, while another will compose his letters slowly or may have more interruptions. However, those companies that have made the effort to set a criterion for each job have been well repaid. The standards give each employee a mark to aim for and an incentive to improve her speed and accuracy. When work standards are tied in with salary administration, they can serve as a merit-rating plan.

Knowing what output to expect from each person on the staff not only helps in scheduling work but also spotlights those who excel— and should be rewarded—and those who need more supervision or better organization of their time. Billions of dollars are wasted in this country every year through inefficient and ill-directed methods of office management. A National Office Management Association survey showed that 25 percent of the total salaries paid to all office employees in this country is for "wasted time."

Besides classifying employees, standards enable the office manager to schedule and dispatch work the same way the factory manager does. The following examples illustrate how two companies determined standards and the resulting benefits.

A Chicago mail-order house, after trying several unsuccessful methods to speed work through the stenographic department, put in a "schedule clerk" to plan the work for all the stenographers. The output of that department increased 18 percent immediately.

No correspondent was allowed to dictate more than 10 letters to a stenographer at one time. If he had more letters, he called for another stenographer. As soon as a stenographer finished taking dictation, she reported to the schedule clerk. Thus the schedule clerk could plan to best advantage, by being in touch with each girl six to eight times a day.

When the stenographer reported to the schedule clerk at, say, 9:30 a.m. after taking 10 letters, the clerk stamped the correspondence: "Letters must leave department at 10:30 a.m." Experience has shown that 10 letters could be expected in an hour, at average speed. However, the stenographer was given five minutes' leeway. If she finished the letters later than 10:35 a.m., the clerk asked for an explanation and accepted a valid excuse. The clerk noted the facts whenever work was returned more than five minutes ahead of or behind schedule. These records go to the department head each day, so that he can tabulate them and use the information in deciding upon rates and promotions.

Another company made a motion picture of operations that were repeated daily. Analysis of the movie enabled the company to eliminate waste motion. In comparing two typists, the company found that one produced twice as much work as the other. Although the fast typist was only 6 percent quicker in typing, she was quicker in getting ready. However, the slow typist was faster in cleaning up. When the good points of both typists were combined, their speed improved. The new method was standardized, and all the other typists have been taught to use it.

FATIGUE AS A FACTOR IN OFFICE PRODUCTION

"Four o'clock fatigue" has long been a problem in offices. In the case of female employees, it is especially acute because young women today are often more concerned about their figures than they are about their health. As a result, dieting lowers their resistance and they tire easily. When they are fatigued, not only the output of their work suffers, but mistakes occur which can be very costly. Apart from a general educational program, there is not a great deal that office managers can do to improve this particular situation.

A common cause of "four o'clock fatigue," however, is failure on the part of office workers to get a good night's sleep. Too often they stay up until the small hours of the morning, and report for work with only two or three hours of sleep. Naturally they become fatigued. If persisted in, this loss of sleep can seriously undermine a person's health, making him an easy victim of disease. While an employer may not dictate how his employees spend their time after working hours, much can be done by education. When office workers realize that they cannot "burn the candle at both ends" night after night and expect to enjoy good health, and when they realize that most colds and health breakdowns are the result of insufficient sleep, they will, if they are sensible, do something about it. Another approach to this problem is through good-natured posters, or cartoons in the office bulletin, which poke fun at people who think they can work all day at their jobs in the office and then stay up most of the night being good fellows.

There is another wide-open opportunity to reduce afternoon fatigue by encouraging employees to enjoy a good breakfast before coming to work, and having something more than a Coke and a cheeseburger for lunch. Many authorities contend skimpy breakfasts are one of the principal causes of poor health and fatigue among white-collar employees. Some employers seek to raise the resistance of employees to fatigue by providing hot luncheons at cost, especially if the office is located in a district where there are no good restaurants.

Not all the factors that make for "four o'clock fatigue" are controllable to the same extent, but many are. Foremost among these is noise. Some experts insist that noise is not fatiguing, and offer as proof the fact that in metalworking plants punch-press operators and others get so used to noise that they feel lost without it. They also point out that there is little or no difference in the production and lost-time records of shop workers engaged in noisy operations than in operations where there is little noise. But punch-press operators or jackhammer men don't have to concentrate as an office worker does. Any person who has to think amid distracting noise, soon tires, develops headaches, and is more prone to nervous breakdowns.

Dr. E. Lawrence Smith, famous neurologist, determined that noise at a level of 60 decibels or more has a decided effect on digestion. The decibels are easy to understand when comparisons are made. For example, an ordinary conversation averages 40 decibels. Normal noises in a business office will combine to create a noise that measures 50 decibels. A noisy office often hits 70 decibels.

The rustle of leaves in a gentle breeze measures 18 decibels. A whisper 5 feet away amounts to 25 decibels. That loud radio next door probably registers 65 decibels or more. An automobile horn blasted at you from a distance of 10 feet jumps the count to 120 decibels, hurts your ear, and probably makes you angry.

Occupational deafness is becoming more and more common. As our cities become noisier, there's more deafness among road builders, bus and taxi drivers, and traffic policemen. Organizations of employers and insurance groups now are analyzing this hazard and are beginning to develop control techniques.

Procedures include study by physicists of the actual and potential noise levels in big industrial plants and a careful study of an employee's hearing before he is assigned to a section of a plant where noise is loud and continuous.

In offices using tabulating and recording machines, a certain amount of noise is inevitable. It can be minimized by placing such equipment in a soundproof room, and deadening the sharpness of the noise inside the room. The A. B. Dick Company, now occupying a modern office on the outskirts of Chicago, Illinois, met the problem by acoustical ceilings and walls, and, in addition, carpeting the floors and air conditioning the room so that it could be tightly closed. Glass partitions in rooms of this type are usually made of Thermopane glass, which is far more effective than single-thickness glass for keeping noise from penetrating into other departments of the office.

If the expense of acoustical ceilings and walls, or laying carpets on the floors, would seem to be high in relation to possible savings, a test area may be established (say a room in which there are a number of typewriters or other sound-making machines) and soundproofed as an experiment. Carefully check increased production, and then decide how much can profitably be invested in noise reduction. In the same way make a test of noiseless typewriters versus standard machines in private offices, or in open offices where noise might disturb employees working near them. Felt pads under typewriters also keep down noise, and they are relatively inexpensive.

Music at Work

The use of music in office and factory has undergone certain changes in technique and approach since the day in 1876 when John Wanamaker installed a small organ in his Philadelphia store and invited employees to start the day with hymns and favorite songs.

Background music system from 3M Company features small audio unit which transforms any wall, ceiling, desk, or other flat surface into a speaker providing nondirectional sound over the entire surface.

The advances have been chiefly on the technical side, and today piped-in music is accepted as an important part of employee relations (and increased productivity) in many a company.

"It is impossible to measure any speed-up in productive output traceable to music programs," said one executive, "but we can say in the new departments, before music is provided, we have definite demands from employees to put it in. If a breakdown occurs during the day, we usually have requests from employees to get the system back in operation."

Companies using music at work are generally agreed that it reduces the midmorning and midafternoon drops in productivity, and the treasurer of one organization said that the tardiness rate dropped sharply after the inauguration of a period of music at the beginning of the day. On the other hand, one office manager with another company stated, "We have experimented for several months with a sound system but have decided to eliminate it because of disagreements among employees over the type of music desired and whether or not any music at all should be provided." Those companies which use music at work report better success with instrumental music than they do with vocal recordings.

Bad Vision Cause of Mistakes

According to the National Society for the Prevention of Blindness, the eyesight of 40 percent of the employees in our offices and plants may not be good enough to enable them to do their work speedily and accurately. This conclusion was based on vision tests made by examiners of the society in small plants in the Baltimore area. In that checkup the percentage of employees who failed to meet their job visual standards ranged from a low of 39 percent to a high of 46 percent. Job standards used were those developed by the Occupational Research Center of Purdue University. These visual-skill tests make it possible to compare the seeing ability of each employee with minimum visual requirements found necessary for accurate performance on the job. Bad vision affects the quality of work in so many ways that the desirability of vision tests is self-evident. Mistakes may be the result of inability to read figures quickly, or headaches which contribute indirectly to careless work and general indifference about mistakes.

A vision-measuring machine could be brought into the office (and also into the plant for that matter) to determine how many employees need glasses. Workers found to have adequate vision for their jobs are so notified; those found to have defects are advised to obtain a complete eye examination from a qualified doctor; those with visual deficiencies which are not correctable are assigned to jobs consistent with their visual capacities. Since the vision of most people can be corrected to meet the requirements of their jobs, few readjustments are usually necessary.

A regular quarterly inspection of office lighting should be made by a qualified person using a light meter. Most public service companies will provide this service, or the company maintenance man can make the check. Very often the only thing that is needed to bring the light up to the required standard is washing the fixtures and putting in new bulbs. If incandescent lighting is still being used, the use of fluorescent lighting from concealed fixtures should be considered. Fluorescent lighting, unless properly installed in fixtures which shield the eyes from glare, can aggravate eyestrain. Savings in electricity should, over a period of years, liquidate the cost of the better light. Offices should be floodlighted to avoid spotlighting of desks, which produces eyestrain.

Ventilation as Fatigue Factor

In climates where there are prolonged periods of warm and humid weather, it usually pays to install some sort of air-conditioning equipment. There is some objection to air cooling by office management men who contend it gives employees colds and contributes to absenteeism. This is due, however, to the improper use of the equipment and keeping the room temperature too low in relation to the outside temperature. It has been found, for example, when an office is kept at 70 degrees, when the temperature outside is 90 to 100 degrees, the change is too sharp when employees go outside the office. However, if the room temperature is just enough below the outside temperature to make working comfortable, no harm results.

The relation between temperature in a working area and humidity likewise affects fatigue. The New York Ventilation Commission made a report (published by E. P. Dutton & Co.) in which it was shown that when the temperature of the air is approximately 80 degrees and the relative humidity is 86 percent, the working capacity of the body is reduced about 25 percent. On the other hand, air that is too cold and too low in humidity also has a harmful effect on the human body and predisposes it to colds and other acute respiratory infections. These ailments cause an alarming loss of time among the employed.

Generally speaking, the atmospheric conditions that are most comfortable to the body are most conducive to work and good health. The fact that the temperature was varied from 68 to 75 degrees without obtaining general satisfaction, in all probability is due to too low humidity. Even when the atmospheric air is at 80 degrees and the relative humidity is very low, the body may not be comfortable. But, as a rule, a temperature of 65 degrees with the proper humidity makes an entirely satisfactory atmospheric condition. When the outside cold air of winter is admitted to a room and warmed, it expands and the relative humidity is markedly decreased. In fact, outside air (which has the proper humidity for its temperature) when heated in a room becomes so dry that it attacks everything containing moisture, even furniture. This throws a definite load on the human body, in its attempt to moisten the air before it reaches the lungs, and even attacks the skin in a good many instances to the point of being partially responsible for "winter itch."

The temperature that has been found best for the human body from the standpoint of appetite, working capacity, and comfort is approximately 68 degrees F., when the air is properly humidified. The proper relative humidity for this temperature has been found to be approximately 40 percent.

DEVELOPING CUSTOMER-CONSCIOUSNESS

In most businesses, courtesy and regard for the customer's needs are essential to success. But employees are human beings, too, who sometimes get up grumpy in the morning; who are too busy and become short-tempered; who find the customer pretty irritating at times.

Large amounts of exhortation *may* help make angels out of everybody who has any contact with the customer—whether in person, by phone, or letter—but a light touch puts the point across more effectively and less painfully.

Reproduced on the following pages are excerpts from a booklet, "We're Giving Out Samples," put out by Southern Pacific Lines. It's a cheerful and well-done piece. However, it was not expected to do a complete job, but is merely one item in a continuing campaign to improve employee attitudes. K. C. Ingram, assistant to the president of Southern Pacific, said: "When first we tackled the problem of getting employees to be polite to customers, it soon became evident that an employee would not be a good public contact person if his morale was bad. Next, we found that morale depends on the boss— depends on the quality of supervision given the employee and the relations between the employee and his supervisor.

"Out of the job relations training provided by the government during the war, Southern Pacific developed a twofold program of human relations training for (1) officers and supervisors all up and down the line and (2) public contact employees. The human relations training is done chiefly by the conference method because we found that participation of the persons being trained was necessary if we were to get their interest and open their minds to receive the training."

The conclusions we have reached in dealing with the problems of public and employee relations are, briefly:

1. **Morale is a prerequisite to public relations training (and to good teamwork in production and selling as well).**

2. **Morale begins at the top and flows down, through good human relations.**

3. **Participation (the conference method) and creation of desire are essential to bring about changes in attitudes.**

4. **Communication involves the whole field of human relations.**

5. **Once morale is established, all forms of communication should be used.**

Dartnell's "Customer Contact" booklets and films are used by a large number of companies for the purpose of increasing customer-consciousness of employees who meet the public.

SAFETY IN THE OFFICE

While time loss as a result of on-the-job and off-the-job accidents by office workers is not as great as in the plant, it is still a possibility that should not be overlooked.

In addition to taking the usual precautions of posting signs at changes in the floor level, lighting dark passageways, and providing wide aisles where mailbags and other bundles are less likely to cause employees to trip and fall over them, Allied Paper Corp. has included its office departments in its regular safety educational program, which was worked out in cooperation with Allied's insurance company. Its aim is to make safe working as much a habit as good production. By making employees safety-conscious *on* the job, it automatically keeps them safety-conscious *off* the job. As far as office production goes, it does not matter a great deal whether the accident happened on the job or at home, if it means the employee must stay away from the job and slow down the group effort.

In addition to the usual safety meetings of supervisors in the office as well as the plant, a safety contest to emphasize good housekeeping often helps. In order to rate each department, a monthly inspection is made. At Allied Paper Corp. it is called the "Skull and Bones Contest." The department with the lowest housekeeping record for the month receives the Skull and Bones banner which it is required to display until passed to another department. The department which has the best housekeeping rating is given a green safety ball (a large green rubber ball), and any department which wins the award for three consecutive times wins for each member of the department a free ticket to a current sports event.

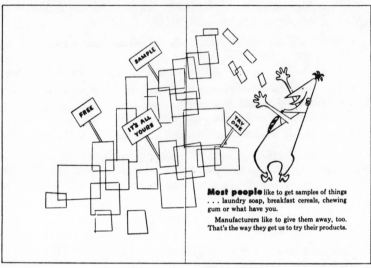

Light touches in Southern Pacific booklet help

Safety Committees

A weakness of many safety programs is that they depend too much on the worker reading something. As every office manager knows, the average worker seldom reads anything he doesn't have to read,

Competition is getting a whole lot tougher these days. We can't hope to compete with air travel when it comes to speed, and most buses can get people from one place to another somewhat cheaper.

Where we can beat em is in comfort. *WE HAVE THE EDGE WHEN IT COMES TO RELAXING TRAVEL* ... lots of room to move around, shiny new dining and lounge cars to go to, private rooms to sleep in.

IT'S OUR JOB TO PROVIDE THE PERSONAL ANGLE. We all like to be friendly, but sometimes it takes a little extra effort to avoid being short and abrupt.

A conductor with a heavy train to work, a passenger service man with a dozen matters on his mind, a waiter trying to get meals served quickly in a crowded dining car ... all have moments when they have to bite their tongues to keep from sounding curt or unfriendly.

People can ask the darndest questions, particularly when you're in the middle of something.

Some of their questions may sound silly, and the answers quite obvious, but a lot of our patrons don't know much about trains and may be riding one for the first time.

DON'T SPOIL THEIR IMPRESSION OF S. P. WITH A CRANKY ANSWER. . . . .

Trips are pretty complicated for most people. They have enough to think about just stopping the paper and leaving a note for the milkman.

A little careful planning on our part can go a long, long way. Try to tell them everything you can about their trip well in advance ... what to do, where to go, how much to pay ... everything!

An agent with a good eye for details can make a lot of friends for himself and for the company.

to remind employees of good customer relations.

unless it is exciting. Most safety literature is not exciting. On the contrary, it is dull and uninteresting. The National Safety Council and others have prepared motion picture films and sound-slidefilms on safety which may be rented. But there is still room for improvement in safety educational methods.

The usual approach to the problem is through safety committees, which are set up largely for enforcement, as well as for educational purposes. The committees are composed of employees who have shown an interest in safety work. Their job is to meet periodically with the safety director, or members of his staff, for the discussion of safety problems. While they function as an advisory committee, in reality they are an educational committee, carrying the safety program of the company to their fellow workers. The success of the committee plan depends on three things:

1. Wide-awake chairmen who supply strong leadership.

2. A definite program of action to follow through.

3. Necessary aids to carry out their program.

The committee plan alone is not the answer to accident prevention in an office, though. The most important factor is the supervisor, and frequent meetings should be held with supervisors in a continuing effort to not only make *but keep them* safety-minded.

SUGGESTED SAFETY REGULATIONS

1. Report all accidents, no matter how slight, whether they result in an injury or not, to the dispensary immediately.

2. No running.

3. Wear no visible jewelry—while working.

4. Wear shoes strapped or laced, medium or low heel, foot entirely covered.

5. Use no cups or glasses made of breakable material.

6. Enter the elevators *slowly* and *orderly.*

7. *Walk carefully* and *slowly* on the stairs. Hold on to the hand rail.

8. Observe warning signs.

9. No *unauthorized person* is permitted to touch switch boxes or other electrical equipment.

10. "Horseplay" is forbidden.

11. All material or equipment must be placed solidly on the floor.

12. *Keep aisles, stairways, exits, and fire equipment* clear of obstructions.

13. Keep floors *clean.*

14. *No eating* permitted in other than designated places.

15. *No spitting.*

16. Keep water fountains, washing fountains, and wash basins *free of refuse.*

38 OFFICE HAZARDS

1. Broken glass should not be placed in wastebaskets. If bottles or other pieces of glassware have been broken, it is suggested that this material be folded or packed in heavy paper and the package should be marked "Broken Glass" and placed alongside the wastebasket at the end of the day so that the person removing wastepaper will not be cut accidentally.

2. Individual upright filing cabinets should be secured to prevent overbalancing. Single cabinets should be secured to the floor or the wall, and when there are two or more they should be fastened to each other.

3. Linoleum covered office floors when wet or highly polished may present slipping and falling hazards, especially for girls wearing high heels. These hazards on stairways are particularly dangerous.

4. The tension of springs on self-closing doors is frequently too great, thereby causing the door to close rapidly and strike the employee passing through or someone entering the doorway.

5. Splintered parts of desks and chairs should be dressed or taped to prevent damage to clothing.

6. Paper spike files have always constituted a distinct office hazard and most companies have discontinued their use altogether.

7. Desk drawers, file drawers, and desk slides carelessly left open very often cause serious injuries when a person inadvertently stumbles over one of them.

8. The overcrowding of files, desks, etc., should be avoided to prevent falling material.

9. The use of pins to fasten papers frequently results in minor injuries which may easily become infected. It is considered a good practice to use clips or staples and to discontinue the use of pins.

10. Walking through aisleways or working places with pens, pencils, knives, or scissors in the hand is a hazard which is recognized and prohibited in a number of companies.

11. Loose wastepaper or discarded catalogs or magazines on floors may cause slipping and create fire hazards.

12. Pencil sharpeners which protrude beyond the ends of desks are accident hazards.

13. Loose electric outlet plates may result in short circuits and cause shock through contact with them.

14. Small card index files, when placed on top of large correspondence cabinets or near the edge of cabinets, desks, bookcases, etc., easily overbalance and may fall when two or more drawers are pulled out.

15. Quite often fatigue, lighting, and ventilation are factors which tend to create accidents.

38 OFFICE HAZARDS (Cont.)

16. Running or hurrying while opening the doors in hallways may lead to an accident if another person is opposite the door.

17. Defective electric cords for dictating machines, desk lamps, and adding machines create fire hazards.

18. Sheet metal sockets on lights adjacent to plumbing and other equipment where grounds are involved may cause shock through contact.

19. Thumbtacks on floor or in chairs.

20. Loose electric fan blades and defective fan guards.

21. Protruding radiator valves, riser plugs, and steps to fire line valves present leg bumping hazards.

22. Loose linoleum or carpeting.

23. Extension cords for lamps, electrical equipment, and telephones on the floor, across aisles or in other areas where employees have occasion to walk, create tripping hazards.

24. Unauthorized and improperly supervised electrical connections.

25. Exposed moving parts on the Addressograph, Mimeograph, bookkeeping, and tabulating machines, and other power-driven equipment.

26. Oily rags, stacked newspapers, or other printed matter containing ink may cause spontaneous combustion.

27. Elevators should be operated only by responsible employees who have been fully instructed in their use.

28. Pens placed on desks when pointed toward one create a possible puncture wound hazard when reaching forward to pick up something near it.

29. Tilting backward in a swivel chair with the feet elevated.

30. The closing of disappearing typewriter desks without using the handle provided for that purpose constitutes a hand-pinching hazard.

31. Going through revolving doors too quickly.

32. Material precariously stacked on top of lockers, filing cabinets, and other high objects.

33. Weak spring tension adjusting bolts on swivel chairs may break and throw the occupant with considerable force.

34. Unnecessarily sharp burrs on edges and perforations of metal filing cabinets and lockers.

35. Matches placed in stand with the heads exposed.

36. Carelessly discarded cigarette butts.

37. Highly inflammable material or liquids stored in lockers or closets are fire hazards.

38. Lifting loads improperly or lifting too heavy loads.

Chapter 34

MEASURING EMPLOYEE PERFORMANCE

IT is not unusual for a good employee to quit his job because he feels his boss plays favorites. Since he doesn't happen to be one of his supervisor's fair-haired boys, he considers his chance to get ahead with the company to be slim indeed. He isn't an apple polisher, and his spirit of independence rebels at having to curry favor.

Supervisors, being human, often do have their favorites, and both the company and the less-favored employees suffer as a consequence. To place employment and recognition on a merit basis as nearly as possible, the more progressive companies rely on some sort of periodical audit or rating of employees. The rating is done by supervisors and executives who are familiar with the work each employee is doing, and who are therefore in a position to judge objectively a person's present and potential worth to the business. Such plans are known as merit-rating programs and are an important factor in salary administration.

Every supervisor is continually evaluating the performance of his subordinates. He may do it consciously or unconsciously; he may do it regularly or sporadically; he may do it informally or by means of a formal procedure. In whatever manner he does it, the important thing is that he does it. He cannot avoid it.

Each supervisor must, at frequent intervals, make important decisions concerning his employees (e.g., promotions, transfers, pay increases, layoffs, etc.). In reaching these decisions, he must rely heavily upon the evaluations he has already made. Hence, whether or not he is consciously aware of it, a supervisor is constantly employing some sort of "merit rating" and the correctness of his actions depends upon the quality of these "merit ratings."

In very small organizations management is able to maintain a close personal relationship with every person, and an informal system for evaluation (i.e., merit rating) of its personnel may, quite conceivably, be entirely satisfactory. On the other hand, as a company grows and enlarges its operations, the informal approach to the problem of evaluating employees becomes inadequate. Even when the supervisor realizes the need for periodic evaluation of his employees, his other responsibilities often interfere with the completion of such performance reviews.

There are many dangers in this. First, it may result in overlooking good employees who will eventually leave the company because they have not been afforded sufficient opportunity to develop. Second, it may result in the promotion of the wrong person. Third, it can result in a serious morale problem because the employees may gain the impression that their superior is not interested in their welfare. These and similar conditions which exist in many companies are among the basic causes of low productivity, high personnel turnover, and constant employee dissatisfaction. Hence, a formalized merit-rating program which is designed to assure prompt and proper consideration of each employee is the next thing to an absolute necessity.

Realistic Standards

Realistic standards for a sound merit-rating program are based on these factors:

1. *It must be as simple as possible.* Merit rating need not be a complex procedure; rather, it is far more desirable that the system be relatively simple and based on principles which are fair and fully understood by all involved. There should be a minimum of red tape. Both the instructions and the procedure should be simple and straightforward. Also to be avoided are procedures which require the supervisor to consider the behavior of his employees in unnatural terms (e.g., abstracting out of a person's "ambitiousness" or "cooperativeness" rather than considering the person as a whole).

2. *It must give, where possible, both quantitative and qualitative measures.* This means that the procedure provides a measure of where the employee stands in relation to the other persons on the same job and also gives a measure of why he has that standing—what his strong points are, what his weaknesses are, what his potential is, where he needs help, and so on.

3. *It must be flexible* so that special or temporary factors which may be affecting the person's performance will be investigated thoroughly and so that the permanence of their nature can also be evaluated. Rating forms which make use of only certain predetermined categories such as "Initiative" or "Dependability" fail to meet these criteria.

4. *It must be thorough.* A hurried, superficial rating is worthless. The very nature of the rating procedure itself must require the supervisor to explore fully every aspect of the employee's job performance. This means that any rating procedure which is susceptible of misuse (e.g., the hurried checking off of categories) must be avoided.

5. *It must provide definite control over personal biases and prejudices.* Everyone has certain personal prejudices which may unfairly influence his ratings. Yet few merit-rating procedures provide any definite controls to prevent these biases and prejudices from creeping into a supervisor's evaluations. Mere warnings about such sources of error during a training period are not enough; *on-the-spot control is necessary.*

6. *It should provide,* whenever possible, *for two or more independent evaluations of each employee.* When ratings on any given person are obtained not only from his immediate supervisor but also from the next highest man in the chain of command, there is less chance for important factors to be overlooked or for a biased evaluation. Furthermore, multiple ratings serve to broaden each manager's knowledge of his subordinates and to bring to his attention areas where he lacks complete information.

Objective Appraisals

Many a rating plan has failed because the employees were rated subjectively by their superiors. Of course, as William R. Howell, industrial engineer, explained, it is natural to do so because for years we have been making up our minds in a subjective way. We select the food we eat, the clothes we wear, even our friends, because they satisfy us. For the most part, we are seldom called upon to decide things objectively.

Consequently, the supervisor or department head who is going to rate others must reverse his way of thinking. He must learn to judge the employee according to his actual abilities and performance rather than according to his, the rater's, conception of them.

One way to get the employee rating plan off on the wrong foot is to use terms which are not clearly defined. For example, the term "initiative," may mean one thing to one department head, be defined in another way by some other department head, and still mean something different to a third department head. These terms must be clearly defined and explained in a conference with those who are going to do the rating. Once these terms are selected, defined, and explained, the rater should be able to maintain a reasonably objective attitude.

Another spot where the rater may find himself becoming subjective is in determining the degree of each attribute the employee may possess. Is employee "A" a poorer or better man on production than employee "B"; is employee "C" better than both or just better than "B"? In order to help the rater decide such matters, the rating guide should be so set up that the process of determining the degrees of each quality or attribute will require little or no subjective thinking on the part of the rater.

Another common fault in the administration of merit-rating plans is that the person doing the rating takes a critical attitude in grading the employee. The best rating technique is to strive sincerely to help the employee advance himself with the company. The following suggestions for conducting a counseling interview in connection with a formal merit-rating plan are from a manual prepared by the Pillsbury Company:

1. Arrange to talk to the employee when interruptions will be at a minimum. Neither of you should feel rushed.

2. Be sincere so that the employee will have confidence in you and feel that you are really interested in his welfare. Your attitude can make or break the success of the whole rating program.

3. Make a definite appointment ahead of time with the employee so he realizes the importance of the meeting.

4. Conduct your counseling interview where you will not be overheard—in a private office, if possible.

5. Explain thoroughly the rating program and what can be accomplished for his good and the company's.

6. Talk frankly about each factor. With the exception of the back page, let the employee see the form and where you have placed your check marks.

7. Mention good points as much as you do the poor ones. Let him know *why* he has a good rating or a poor rating.

8. Be open-minded. If you find that a rating is wrong, admit it, and change it.

9. Record what you told the employee and what his reactions were, at the close of the interview.

Merit Rating and Job Evaluation

Once a job-evaluation program has been installed is it necessary to set up a merit-rating program? Not necessarily, but it is highly desirable to do so.

Merit rating is important in rounding out the salary plan because it rates the *employee on the job,* whereas job-evaluation rates only the *job.* All people are not equal in ability or capacity to do a good job, so some method is necessary to set up an impartial rating of an employee's ability to handle the work of his present position and to determine his potentialities for a better one. Merit rating answers this problem.

What will merit rating accomplish that cannot be achieved by job evaluation? First of all, it helps to improve employee morale because it develops a feeling of confidence in management—makes the employee feel that management is interested in his future. From this standpoint alone, such a program will prove its value to the company. Other benefits a company can receive by means of a rating program include the following:

1. It helps to select employees for promotion.
2. It helps to develop supervisors.
3. It provides a training tool.
4. It helps to determine layoff procedure.
5. It provides a basis for personal counseling.
6. It provides a way of giving employees recognition.
7. It is an aid in determining salary increases.
8. It stimulates more careful interviewing procedure by executives.

One of the important phases of employee rating is the selection of factors. This is a list of those factors which show up in most merit-rating programs:

Quality of Work	Adaptability	Dependability
Quantity of Work	Job Knowledge	Attitude

Other factors often included are: Attendance, originality, loyalty, initiative, and cooperation. Some factors are objective and some subjective. Such factors as accuracy, quality and quantity of work, and attendance are all objective. They are the factors which can be uncovered by reference to the personnel records. There is no guess-work about them. Such factors as attitude, adaptability, and original-ity are subjective, however, since they must be left to the discretion, judgment, and observation of the supervisor. Thus, while consider-able information going into the merit-rating records will be factual, there must be, nonetheless, heavy reliance upon the judgment of the supervisory group. It is important, therefore, that this group be thoroughly and carefully trained in all phases of rating procedure.

Merit Rating at the Pillsbury Co.

To get an accurate knowledge of an employee's capacity, the Pills-bury Company uses a carefully tested merit-rating system which covers rank-and-file employees. The aim of the plan is to transfer people who may not be promotable in their own department to an-other department where they will have a better opportunity to grow. In this way, it has been found, turnover can be held to a minimum and employees given every opportunity of fully developing their abilities.

The following checklist was developed at Pillsbury for rating both nonsupervisory and supervisory employees, the rating being done periodically by the supervisor. The employee's performance since the last rating is used as a basis, and those doing the rating are cautioned not to allow themselves to be influenced by former ratings.

I. Quality of Work—Accuracy

How would you rate this individual with respect to the quality of the work he turns out, the neatness and accuracy evident in the job he does?

—1. Careless worker. Tends to repeat same type of errors.

—2. Work is sometimes unsatisfactory because of errors or untidiness.

—3. Usually turns out acceptable work. Not many errors.

—4. Checks and observes his work. Quality of the finished product can be relied upon.

—5. Work is of highest quality. Errors extremely rare, if any. Little wasted effort.

WHAT DO EMPLOYEE RATINGS DO?

Employee ratings give you a chance to:

1. IMPROVE MORALE by letting the employee know that his supervisors are sincerely interested in his progress.

2. KNOW YOUR PEOPLE by bringing into focus your opinion of each employee. You know specifically why you are satisfied or dissatisfied with the employee's performance.

3. COUNSEL WITH EACH EMPLOYEE in order to discuss frankly the work he has done. The hardest part of supervision is to tell the person what he has done wrong—to criticize him. Employee ratings can be a helpful guide for this discussion.

4. UNCOVER MARGINAL PERSONNEL by evaluating each phase of the employee's work, point by point. Marginal employees are costly!

5. PLAN FOR THE FUTURE by strengthening each employee's better points and outlining a program for improvement of his chances for added responsibilities.

II. Quantity of Work—Speed

How would you rate this individual with respect to the speed with which he works? Is he a fast worker who turns out a large amount of work, or does it take him an unusually long time to complete a job?

(Do not consider here the quality of the work produced. Whether the individual is fast and accurate, or fast and inaccurate, you are to rate the *speed and volume* factor only.)

—1. Exceptionally fast worker. Turns out large volume of work. Keeps up on assignments even when load is heavy.

—2. Gets his work done promptly.

—3. Works at moderate speed. Occasionally needs encouragement. Good output on repetitive work.

—4. Tends to let work pile up. Has difficulty keeping up on regular assignments.

—5. Volume of work done is unsatisfactory. Slow.

III. Does Employee Learn Quickly?

—1. Brilliant and keen mind coupled with eagerness to learn.

—2. Quick to grasp new ideas and methods.

—3. Learns satisfactorily.

—4. Learns new methods and procedures by excessive repetition; needs guidance.

—5. Slow in learning even simple procedures; needs constant guidance.

IV. Does He Assume Responsibility?

—1. Does not accept responsibility or takes responsibility which is not justified.

—2. Assumes responsibility without necessary qualifications or seems to have ability but does not adequately utilize it.

—3. Assumes responsibility only on matters in his own sphere of activity.

—4. Takes full share of responsibility in keeping with good judgment.

—5. Takes more than his share of responsibility in keeping with good judgment.

V. Is He Thorough—Reliable?

—1. Extremely careless; makes many mistakes; seriously lacking in dependability.

—2. Work of uneven quality, ranging from good to poor.

—3. Does what is expected of him; sometimes requires followup.

—4. Very industrious; requires very little followup.

—5. Extremely reliable; consistently does an excellent job.

VI. Attitude Toward Job

—1. Is enthusiastic about type of work; sold on organization. Criticism of constructive nature and in keeping with good judgment.

—2. Happy on job; is satisfied with organization.

—3. Seems to be satisfied with job and organization.

—4. Shows little interest in either job or organization.

—5. Is disgruntled on job. Not in accord with policies of organization.

VII. How Does He Cooperate?

—1. Outstanding ability to work with people on all levels; inspires cooperation; maintains *esprit de corps.*

—2. Cooperates willingly; obtains willing cooperation from others.

—3. As necessary, cooperates with others and secures cooperation from others.

—4. Has some difficulty working harmoniously with others.

—5. Poor attitude in dealing with others.

VIII. Does He Make Decisions?

—1. Lacks self-confidence; extremely reluctant to commit himself.

—2. Slow or reluctant to make decisions or makes decisions on matters for which he is not qualified.

—3. Makes necessary decisions only on matters in own sphere of activity.

—4. Makes decisions based on sound reasoning.

—5. Makes timely decisions based on sound reasoning. Creates confidence in his ability.

IX. Is He Analytical?

—1. Needs constant guidance; "cannot see the forest for the trees."

—2. Needs guidance; often confused as to relative importance of factors.

—3. Satisfactorily analyzes data and for the most part gives proper emphasis to each factor.

—4. Alert. Correctly weighs important factors.

—5. Extremely keen; has outstanding ability to pick out and emphasize important factors.

X. Has He Imagination?

—1. Vivid imagination; visualizes future possibilities and methods.

—2. Active imagination; keeps a step ahead of current problems.

—3. Satisfactory. Visualizes his own and others' situations.

—4. Visualizes only immediate situation. Does not relate his activities to others.

—5. Lacks imagination. Sees only the obvious.

XI. Does He Organize?

—1. Confused with detail; attempts to do it all himself.

—2. Often fails to properly apportion work and authority. Frequently lacks time for important matters.

—3. Ordinarily gets things done; usually delegates assignments to qualified subordinates.

—4. Gets things done; successful in apportioning work load and authority.

—5. Does first things first, correctly evaluates what can and should be delegated, shifts authority as well as responsibility.

XII. Is He a Good Teacher?

—1. Outstanding ability to evaluate and develop subordinates; builds men.

—2. Good appraiser and developer of men.

—3. Recognizes strong or weak qualities in subordinates; usually develops subordinates.

—4. Usually overlooks strong or weak traits in subordinates; seldom makes an attempt to develop subordinates and/or tries to develop persons not qualified.

—5. Fails to appraise or develop his men.

XIII. Does He Recognize Ability in Others?

—1. Apt to claim credit for all good work performed by his employees; seldom commends employees for good work.

—2. Overlooks giving credit to others except when it is brought to his attention.

—3. Usually fair in recognizing good work of subordinates.

—4. Gives credit where credit is due.

—5. Gives timely recognition of subordinate's work to both outsiders and the employee.

XIV. Promotability

How would you rate this individual with respect to his potentialities for future growth in the company? Does he seem to have attained his limit of development, or does he show evidence of a capacity for advancing beyond his present job level?

—1. Very good potentialities for advancement. Tends to raise level of job he now holds. Alert to opportunities for improvement.

—2. Fairly good possibilities for promotion. Eager to learn and to assume greater responsibility.

—3. Becoming more valuable on present job with increased experience, but may not go beyond present level.

—4. Very limited capacity for growth.

—5. Would not consider him for advancement beyond his present level. Tending to slip back instead.

The Patterned Merit Review Procedure

Rating through the supervisor is coming to be a popular and effective way to do it. When a rating expert, in the person of the office manager or a representative of the personnel department, works directly with the supervisor, the final rating is bound to be much truer and fairer than if the untrained supervisor had done the job alone.

The following is a suggested outline of the interview which takes place between the supervisor and the rating expert or interviewer. While the interviewer is at liberty to adapt the approach to his own personal style (and, in fact, is encouraged to do so), it is essential that the conversation cover each of the indicated areas of discussion.

It is important to note that the interviewer's sole purpose is to guide the discussion to be sure that the proper procedure is followed and also to be sure that all important areas are explored. The interviewer should never interject his own views. He is not evaluating the employee; he is merely giving the supervisor a frame of reference.

The interviewer should have a list of all the employees under the jurisdiction of the supervisor to whom he is talking. He should also have a 3- by 5-inch card for each employee bearing only the person's name and job title. He will also need a patterned merit review form for each employee to be discussed; he records the supervisor's comments on this form as the conversation progresses. Patterned merit review forms, prepared by Dr. Robert N. McMurry, management consultant, are available from The Dartnell Corporation.

I. Obtain a Ranking of All the Employees on a Given Job Who Are Under the Superior's Direction.

A. *When Rating Less Than Eight Employees on a Given Job*— The supervisor is given the cards and is asked to check through them to insure that all of his employees on the particular job have been included, that all the employees who are included are actually under his supervision, and that no employees who have different jobs are included. Those workers who have not been on the job long enough to have demonstrated their qualities and abilities (probably a minimum of three months) should not be rated by the supervisor until the next rating period. In those cases where the supervisor has less than eight employees on a particular job under his direct supervision, he is asked to take the cards and arrange them in accordance with their rank from best to worst, as he considers them. (This can be handled with a question such as: "Disregarding seniori-

POINTERS ON MERIT RATING

1. Top management must approve the plan and be interested in making it a success.

2. Supervisors and employees alike must be sold on the purpose of the merit-rating plan and that management intends sincerely to use it.

3. Rating forms should be flexible and adapted to particular companies, types of operations, and work.

4. The plan should be only a part of a complete employee and supervisory development program.

5. All ratings should be considered only indicative, not final.

6. Thorough training is necessary for supervisors and other raters.

7. All ratings should be discussed with employees by raters.

8. Provisions should be made for appeal from ratings.

9. Ratings should be reviewed at regular intervals. Programs must be kept to some sort of a regular schedule.

10. The forms and the whole plan should be kept fluid, changeable to meet conditions, and liable to constant improvement.

11. Ratings should be validated by comparison with performance of others on the job rated.

12. All raters should know the person rated.

13. Interviews with employees should always be private, and ratings should not be discussed with those not connected with the administration of the program.

14. All raters should be familiar with every factor and definition of the factors in the rating form.

15. An inaccurate rating is worse than no rating at all.

ty, who is your best employee on this job?" "Disregarding seniority, who is your worst employee on this job?" "Disregarding seniority, who is your next-best employee on this job?") After the supervisor has placed the cards in order of rank, the representative then marks the appropriate rank order on the reverse side of each card.

B. *Rating Eight or More Employees on a Given Job*—In those cases where the supervisor has eight or more employees on a particular job, the first part of the procedure is exactly the same as that outlined above. The supervisor is asked to check through the cards for the reasons outlined under "A" above. However, to facilitate the ranking process, he is usually asked to select the best 25 percent of his employees, the poorest 25 percent of his employees, and (in those cases which would warrant further discrimination) the second-best 25 percent and second-poorest 25 percent.

1. Assuming the foreman or office manager has 12 employees on a given job, the first phase of the ranking could be handled with a question such as "If you were allowed to retain only three of your men on this job, disregarding seniority, which three would you keep?" The personnel department representative then marks a "1" on the reverse side of each of the cards selected.

2. In a similar manner, the supervisor is next asked to indicate his three poorest men on the job; i.e., disregarding seniority, the first three men whom he would release, were he forced to do so. The cards of these employees are then marked with a "4" on the reverse side.

3. In a similar manner, the supervisor is then asked to select his three next-best men whose cards are marked with a "2" on the reverse side by the interviewer. (A likely question for this is: "If you were allowed to keep six people on this job, disregarding seniority, which three others would you select in addition to the three you have already chosen?")

4. In the same way, the supervisor is then asked to select his three next-poorest men; the reverse sides of the selected cards are marked with a "3" by the personnel department representative. (A sample question for this choice would be: "If you had to lay off six men on this job, disregarding seniority, which three other men would you lay off besides the three you have already indicated?")

NOTE: This procedure is called, and *is* literally a forced distribution. It is absolutely essential that the supervisor designate his subordinates according to the prescribed categories in order that each employee can be ranked in terms of his group as a whole.

II. Determine the Exact Job Duties of Each Employee.

NOTE: Steps II through VI are all to be completed on one employee before proceeding to the next employee. As representative begins Step II, he should record the ranking (which he put on the reverse of the card) on the form following "Ranking of Employee Compared With Others on Same Job."

Despite the fact that a foreman may, for example, consider all assemblers' jobs to be the same, it is very important that the personnel department representative has a clear picture of each man's duties and responsibilities. The personnel department representative should determine whether there are any unusual working conditions, physical requirements, or any unusual aspects of the job which may actually make it different from other jobs bearing the same title. This information should be recorded on the patterned merit review form during the interview.

III. Obtain the Supervisor's Education of Each Employee (including strong and weak points).

NOTE: It is quite natural to expect the rater's favorable and unfavorable comments will be interspersed. The interviewer does not interrupt; he merely records the information as it is obtained: He must, however, be sure that the supervisor explains all points fully.

The supervisor is asked to describe (in his own words) the individual employee's strong points. Since this usually results in a generality such as "He's a good man" or "He does a good job," the interviewer should require the supervisor to substantiate his statements. He should determine in what way the employee does a good job. When the supervisor has given his views in full, it may then be necessary for the interviewer to inquire about specific aspects of the employee's performance which have not been covered. In the same way, the supervisor is asked to describe the employee's weak points.

IV. Determine Past and/or Contemplated Action Concerning Each Employee.

A. The supervisor is next asked what he has done to help this employee develop.

B. The supervisor is also asked what he plans to do to assist the employee.

V. Determine Promotability of Each Employee.

The supervisor is asked whether he feels that in the light of the man's strong and weak points, the employee would be eligible for promotion, disregarding seniority, to a position such as supervisor if such an opening were available. The answer is recorded on the form and the interviewer asks the rater to substantiate his answers. The interviewer should determine what size and type of group the supervisor feels the man could handle, how well he would be able to do the work planning and scheduling, and how well he could manage subordinates, how soon he could be promoted (that is, does he need more experience in certain areas on his present job, or some specialized training before being promoted).

In the same manner, disregarding seniority, the supervisor should be asked to indicate whether he feels that the employee could be given a more difficult job.

VI. Obtain an Overall Rating on Each Employee.

In the course of this planned conversation the supervisor has been called upon to consider very thoroughly the strong and weak points of the employee. As a final summary of the supervisor's opinion of the employee being discussed, the interviewer should get the supervisor to make an overall rating on the performance of the man.

With the facts on the employee clearly in his mind from the detailed discussion just concluded, it should be possible for the supervisor to make a fairly accurate overall rating of each man. However, the supervisor should be allowed as much time as he may need to make his decision.

The rating should be done on the basis of a four-point scale, as follows:

> 1—Outstanding
>
> 2—Above Average
>
> 3—Below Average
>
> 4—Unsatisfactory

The rating should be recorded on the form by making a check mark in the appropriate space.

VII. Obtain a Reranking of All the Employees on a Given Job Who Are Under the Supervisor's Direction.

After all the employees have been discussed (according to the procedures outlined in notes under Step II), the supervisor should once again be given the 3- by 5-inch cards bearing each man's name and Step I is repeated. The supervisor should be instructed that he is completely free to change his mind. The interviewer should be careful not to influence the supervisor's judgment, either with regard to the rankings or with regard to the discussions which have been held concerning each individual employee. The new rankings should then be entered on the form following "Reranking of Employee After Discussion."

NOTE: The 3- by 5-inch cards for any employee whose job is considerably different from the jobs of the other employees should be removed before the reranking is done.

VIII. Secure a Second Independent Evaluation of All the Employees Where Possible.

The same procedure should be used, if possible, to obtain merit reviews of the same employees by the next level of supervision. This should be done on page 3 of the patterned merit review form. It is essential that page 2 be folded under so that second rater will not be influenced by the first rater's statements.

IX. Resolve Any Discrepancies in Evaluations by Joint Discussions With Raters.

When the interviewer has completed the second review, he should compare carefully the two interviews on each employee. In those cases where serious discrepancies occur, the interviewer should arrange for a meeting of the two supervisors and himself to clarify the situation and determine the factors which actually affect the case. The interviewer must realize that there will be a strong tendency for subordinates to agree to adapt their evaluation and rankings to those of the higher ranking supervisors. This is to be expected, of course, because most people do not consider opposing their superiors as being profitable. The points on which the two disagree should be discussed fully. After all points have been considered, the two raters should be asked to give new overall ratings in order to reach agreement. If, after such a discussion, the two raters still cannot reach an agreement, and each has satisfactory reasons for his opinion, a notation of this situation should be made on the form.

A Small Company's Experience With Rating

Anchor Casualty Company, now the Agricultural Insurance Company of Watertown, New York, used a simpler type of review form called "General Merit Review" to rate some 175 employees engaged in clerical operations. Supervisors were given one hour of training in the use of the form. Anchor reported that the principal benefits derived from its plan were that it served to make supervisors more aware of employee progress, more conscious of their employees. Most of the other companies Dartnell's editors have interviewed have said approximately the same thing.

To many office managers and personnel directors, the fact that merit-rating plans caused supervisors to start thinking about their people in terms of abilities, performance, and possibilities for promotion is sufficient justification for the whole plan.

Anchor reported on the other side of the picture that there was a poor correlation with merit-rating results and test scores on employees, resulting in a "halo" effect. This was laid to "definite prejudice in favor of older employees" shown by supervisors, a condition reported by many other participating firms.

Further details of the Anchor plan are included in the company's instructions to supervisors as follows:

To: All Supervisors

From: Personnel Department

Subject: Instructions for Merit Rating

This Merit-Rating Blank is designed to measure the individual employee's growth and value to the company. Before assigning a rating for each trait read carefully the description of that trait. Always compare the employee being rated relative to other employees in your department. Then indicate your rating for that trait by placing a check mark in one of the boxes.

Why do we use Merit Rating?

Estimates of people are built up unconsciously; when a person is asked for an opinion regarding another person he frequently realizes that he has an opinion already formed. These opinions are of little value in personnel situations because the terms unfortunately are quite relative, and mean very different things to different individuals. General impressions of this sort are likewise apt to reflect prejudices. This is the reason for trying to obtain estimates in a more scientific and standardized fashion.

What are the values from Merit Rating?

It educates both the rater and the rated. The rater observes the employee more closely if he is required to rate him occasionally. The supervisor tends to become conscious of his employees. The natural tendency is to devote attention primarily to the employee as a whole or to some outstanding aspect of the employee. Merit Rating teaches the supervisor to judge him with reference to different traits and to consider each trait separately.

It is extremely important that you discuss the Merit Rating with the employee. The employee will not know what sort of a job he is doing or what his status is unless you discuss his progress with him. Employees will readily take to constructive criticism.

Merit Ratings for new employees must be completed at the third-month and six-month periods. All other employees will be rated at least twice a year. You will be notified in the weekly supervisors' meetings about forthcoming ratings.

Revlon's Merit-Rating System

The merit-rating plan of Revlon, Inc., is designed to measure the performances of some 300 employees and consists of both a direct and an indirect form of rating. Executives are rated by the direct form. However, no form has been developed for positions at the professional level.

Salary increases are dependent upon the employee's showings on these forms and employees with high ratings are kept in mind for promotions. A rating form is completed on each employee before any scheduled pay increase.

Revlon considers the following factors in determining the promotability of employees: Ability to learn, dependability, accuracy, quantity of work, and job knowledge. All these factors are taken into consideration on its merit appraisal forms. Revlon reports further:

"The personnel department, a supervisor, or an administrative head may suggest a promotion for an employee. Agreement to promote usually is decided between the administrative head, supervisor, and the personnel department. Merit appraisal scores, attendance records, punctuality records, etc., are taken into consideration. All these factors play a part in reaching a decision to promote someone.

"Particular attention is paid to merit-rating scores obtained by employees who hold second-line positions in a department. The indirect rating form in this case is used as a counseling aid in an attempt to develop leadership."

In Revlon's indirect rating method, the indirect form is made up of a series of items (five or six items in a grouping) ; in making the appraisal, the appraiser writes the letter "M" in front of the statement that is most descriptive of the employee's performance. The rater then writes the letter "L" in front of the statement that is least descriptive. For each group of items there should be one "M" and one "L."

Wherever possible either the supervisor or a member of the personnel department discusses the ratings with employees, and an administrative head or a member of the personnel department discusses ratings with the supervisor. Under the Revlon method, supervisors rate all employees under their jurisdiction. Administrative heads rate all supervisors in their respective departments. Training in the completion of merit-rating forms is given during supervisors' meetings.

In most cases the supervisor discusses the rating results with his people. The cases of problem employees are referred to the personnel department for the purpose of skilled counseling.

A Revlon official says:

"In cases where merit-rating forms have indicated that an employee falls short in the quantity of work, particular effort is directed to attain fuller utilization of such employee's services. In some cases, a noticeable increase in the amount of work completed has been achieved.

"We believe that our merit-rating plan is a big help in the general overall development of all of our employees. We consider our indirect form to be a fairly objective measuring instrument.

"We consider one of the advantages of our merit-rating plan is that it has given us a more objective procedure in evaluating our employees. Although the program is timely and costly, we believe the results obtained are fully worthwhile. One of the prominent disadvantages is the difficulty in getting all employees or all supervisors to believe in the merit-rating plan. A few of these feel that merit rating should be more objective and until it is so, should not be used."

Standard Oil of California Aims at Development

The Employee Appraisal and Development program of Standard Oil Company of California is directed primarily at employee and supervisory development. Ratings are made once a year in all departments of the company, covering approximately 30,000 employees.

The plan is used secondarily for promotion purposes where the major consideration is an experience record of various positions and assignments held by the employee in the past.

A Standard official explains: "Maximum utilization of manpower is achieved mainly through good supervisory training. However, the rating plan in many cases has enabled us to steer an employee into types of work that best utilized his talents.

"A good rating plan adequately justifies the time and cost involved. When properly used, its effect on human factors and fellowship is entirely beneficial. Disadvantages can creep in if supervisors lose sight of the importance and objectives of the plan.

"Rating is done independently by two or more supervisors sufficiently familiar with the employee's performance to rate him. The results are then consolidated on one sheet and discussed with the employee by his immediate supervisor. Training in rating has been done through supervisory meetings usually conducted by a staff employee thoroughly familiar with the plan.

"Employee counseling is frequently based on ratings, principally during the discussion of the rating with the employee.

"A limitation in any rating plan is the accuracy of the appraisal. For this reason, we urge raters to supplement the ratings with explanatory notes. Also for this reason, we use the plan primarily for the purpose of employee development.

"Rotation in various jobs and assignments, particularly management personnel, is used as far as practicable to broaden experience and in turn maintain a supply of people qualified for vacancies as they occur."

INTERSTATE FINANCE CORPORATION PERFORMANCE ANALYSIS

INTRODUCTION

Improving Performance Is an Everyday Function

In your capacity as a manager of a group of Interstate employees, you are naturally interested in seeing that each person in your office is continually developing in terms of efficiency and performance. In exercising this normal supervisory responsibility you will have almost daily occasion for discussing with employees their progress or failings. Most of these discussions will be unplanned and casual and will be concerned with little items on which employees need assistance or helpful criticism.

Periodically We Have Written Performance Analyses

In addition to this more or less routine type of review of the progress and problems of your employees, the company has provided for a periodic formal review and analysis of the performance of all your employees. This program is designed to insure that a comprehensive and systematic review and appraisal is made of the work of each employee at least once a year.

Purposes of the Performance Analysis

The appraisal is recorded on the company's performance analysis form and serves three major purposes:

1. Primarily this rating is designed to provide a good systematic analytical review of the employee's performance. On the occasion of these analyses your major objective is to let the employee know exactly how and where he stands in terms of what is expected of him. Upon the completion of each performance analysis, the employee should know in detail the things he is doing well and where he needs to improve, so that he can do a better job and ultimately increase his worth both to the company and to himself.

2. These analyses provide progress reports to your supervisor as well as the personnel department and gives them an insight into how well, in your opinion, your employees are progressing. They serve as the basis for approving the recommended advancement of employees in the Career Progression Plan. Performance analyses help headquarters officials and district managers to do overall personnel planning; such as, promotions, transfers, relief managers for vacation periods, etc.

3. Performance analyses serve as the official basis for awarding good salary increases to deserving employees.

Problems Involved in Performance Analysis

There are many types of performance analysis plans; all of them have certain advantages and disadvantages when compared to others. In many instances performance analyses have failed to operate satisfactorily in actual practice even though they were considered to be sound in theory. In these instances the programs fell short of the desired goals because of the human shortcomings of the individuals who did the rating. The raters failed to be objective and realistic. In some instances raters were so strict and demanding that no one could receive a satisfactory rating and others rated everyone too highly. In other instances personal feelings, bias, and prejudices were permitted to creep into ratings. In too many instances ratings were prepared too hurriedly and without enough thought.

While realizing that there are many ways in which a performance analysis program can fall short of its objectives, Interstate is a firm believer in the fundamental principle underlying performance reviews: "If a person is going to improve, he needs to be told wherein he should improve, and he ought to be given some real help as to how he can do better than he has been doing."

Like most worthwhile things in life, getting the best out of them takes a bit of doing on our part. Getting the real values out of a performance analysis program is not an easy thing. The manager who waits until the last minute, fills out a handful of performance analysis forms in 10 minutes, hands them to employees, and asks if they have any questions is putting nothing into the program and certainly won't get much out of it.

Performance analysis is difficult because, among other reasons, it involves a process in which one human being (who is inherently subjective because that is the nature of people), attempts objectively to rate the subjective qualities of another human. Another reason that performance analysis plans cause difficulties is that the rater's opinion should be conveyed to the person being rated if that person is to profit from the analysis. When this is done, the good objectives of the program sometimes backfire because the individual being rated flares up or sulks over what he feels is undue criticism.

This brings us to the fact that many of us do not like to be criticized; objectively, subjectively, constructively, destructively, or in any other way. Yet this does not mean that a certain amount of criticism, including self-criticism, isn't good for us. The problem in most cases seems to boil down to how to talk over people's shortcomings with them and get them to want to do something about them, even where we can't get them to like being confronted with their weaknesses and failings.

In this chapter you will find some useful information to help with problems of this type and the policies, procedures, and forms which apply to Interstate's performance analysis program.

Types of Performance Analyses

Interstate maintains two types of performance analyses. Both types of analyses are designed for a special purpose and to report specific performances. They are: (a) new employee 30-day ratings; (b) performance analyses.

New Employee 30-Day Rating

It is important that a new employee knows how he is progressing; so in addition to the almost daily reviews by the department head or branch manager the 30-day rating is provided to give the employee a systematic review of his progress to that point. Since at this stage of an employee's development it is not possible to make a very precise and accurate rating of his abilities, this form requires only a simple evaluation. This rating is to be used for all new employees in the branches and in headquarters as well.

Performance Analysis

The performance analysis is designed to rate all employees regardless of job or length of service. This form will be forwarded to the branch manager or other supervisor by the personnel department.

Basis for Rating Performance

In rating the performance of any employee you should use as a basis the entire rating period. It is important in arriving at a fair and accurate rating that you avoid making your decision predominately upon the basis of the employee's work during the last few weeks or months before the rating. To do this reliably, it is necessary that you maintain some sort of simple record on each employee's progress and performance so that at the time of the rating you have a brief history of each employee's accomplishments and failings over the entire rating period.

How the Performance Analysis Fits In

In our selection procedure, we evaluate certain basic personal characteristics of each applicant through the use of tests. We attempt to hire those people whose characteristics will give them the best possible chance to like our business and succeed in it. Through the use of the performance analysis we will continue to evaluate those characteristics, and others, in each employee as he performs his assigned duties. Therefore, through careful review and study of an employee's test scores and performance analyses, an unusually reliable composite picture of that employee will appear. We will know many of his likes and dislikes, personality traits, and strong points and weaknesses. This knowledge will be of great help in the placement and promotion of personnel.

Organization of the Performance Analysis Form

To accomplish the objectives outlined in the previous paragraphs, the performance analysis form has been devised to accurately help measure and report the performance of all employees.

The employee will be rated on each factor listed and along a scale measured from zero (0) to six (6). By circling the appropriate number in the scale under each factor listed, the rater will rate the employee on each factor. The rater must be familiar with the explanation of each of the numbers in the scale and what they mean. This information is to be found on the first page of the analysis form. The following is a further explanation of the numbers in the rating scale:

0- When the rater has no knowledge of an individual's performance of any factor, or if any factor does not apply to the individual, the rater will so indicate by circling the zero.

1-5   The numbers one through five indicate the quality of an individual's performance, with the number one indicating superior performance, the number five indicating a low level of performance, and the numbers two, three, and four indicating the levels of performance lying between the two extremes.

6-   The number six indicates a level of performance which is too high, or the possession of characteristics which would tend to make him unsuitable for the position he holds. For example:

He may be too intelligent for his position.

He may possess too much leadership ability to be satisfied with his job.

The performance analysis form is divided into four parts: (1) basic factors, (2) general factors, (3) principal duties, and (4) summary and conclusion. Each of these parts must be completed, each factor rated, and all questions answered. Raters should use the space for comments for clarifying information on each factor.

Part I—Basic Factors

The letters A through J identify the 10 basic factors over which each employee will be rated. The rater must be certain to rate the employee over each factor only as it is related to the job which the employee is performing. For example: In rating a BA 1 on factor B—*Job Knowledge,* we know that at the BA 1 stage of training the employee's job knowledge is not very great and yet he could be rated average or above because he knows what he should know as a BA 1.

The following information on each basic factor is designed to help you as a rater:

A. *Personal Characteristics*—Much of the impression which we make on others depends upon personal characteristics, such as appearance, physical characteristics, health, and personal habits. In view of the job which the individual is performing consider the following:

Is he always neat in appearance? Is his appearance pleasing?

Is there anything about him physically which would handicap him in the performance of his duties?

Is his health good? Is he frequently off from work because of illness? Does he complain of something bothering him?

Are his personal habits good?

B. *Job Knowledge*—This factor pertains only to the possession of job knowledge, skills, and abilities which are necessary to the job which the individual is performing. Do not consider the ability to use them. Consider:

How thoroughly has the individual absorbed the training given?

Do his skills conform with the requirements of the job?

Does he have the ability both mentally and physically to perform the job?

C. *Adaptability*—One of the primary duties of education and training is to teach an individual how to use the education and training and adapt it to meet different situations. Consider here:

How rapidly does the individual learn?

Can he adapt his education, training, and experience to meet different situations?

Can he understand difficult problems?

D. *Interest*—Interest in one's job is of primary importance in determining success or failure. We are inclined to do well in those things in which we are interested. Generally, the higher our interest the better job we do. Consider the job the individual is performing as a whole, and not specific parts.

Does he appear to be interested in his job?

Does he gain satisfaction from performing his duties?

Does he do only enough to get by?

E. *Motivation*—Consider here the energy, drive, and initiative which the individual shows in the performance of his duties.

Is he a self-starter?

Does he have to be pushed?

F. *Independence*—All of us are dependent upon others to varying degrees. Some of us are relatively freethinkers, and others of us prefer to follow along with the thoughts of others. Consider here:

Does he think for himself?

Does he accept the suggestions of others too readily?

Is he able to think through a problem and arrive at a logical and decisive conclusion?

G. *Temperament*—In this factor, consider the ordinary day-to-day problems. Also consider:

Is he moody?

Does he show excessive irritability?

Does he lose his temper?

H. *Objectivity*—Consider the individual's ability to be objective with himself and others. Consider:

Is he willing to accept the responsibility for errors and mistakes?

Is he frank and straightforward?

I. *Self-Confidence*—In the course of our everyday duties, we face situations which place us under pressure of one degree or another. Consider here:

How well does he hold up under pressure?

Is he excitable?

How much self-confidence does he demonstrate?

J. *Standards*—All of us, in one way or another, set standards of performance for ourselves and others. Consider:

Is he a perfectionist?

Are his standards too low?

Does he expect more from others than he is willing to do?

Part II—General Factors

The eight general factors are identified by letters K through R. They should be completed in the same manner as the Basic Factors. Here again the rater should be careful to rate the employee only in relation to the job which the employee is performing.

K. *Company Relatedness*—Loyalty to the company is a good indication of a satisfied employee. An employee who considers himself an important part of the company is much more likely to do an outstanding job than one who is just performing his duties for a pay check. Consider here:

To what degree does he relate himself to company policies, objectives, and problems?

What is his attitude toward the company?

Does he consider himself an important part of the company?

L. *Personal Relations*—"Friendly Financing" is Interstate's motto, and it can be accomplished only by friendly people. Consider how well the employee gets along with his fellow workers and the customers. Consider here:

Is he tactful?

Is he considerate of others?

Does he have a genuine interest in people?

Do people like him?

M. *Operating Judgment*—The training and experience one receives while working on a job are calculated to progressively increase his operating judgment in the daily problems which arise within the realm of his responsibilities. Consider here:

Does he weigh all factors of a problem?

Can he arrive at a logical and decisive conclusion?

N. *Ingenuity*—We all possess creative ability to one degree or another, but it must be stimulated by a desire to want to do a better job and to have a more efficient operation. Consider here:

Does he make suggestions?

Has he submitted an idea to the suggestion committee?

Is he inclined to get into a rut and stay there?

O. *Persuasiveness*—In our everyday dealings with other people, we are constantly selling something—ourselves, ideas, opinions, and, of course, in some instances, tangibles. Consider here:

Can he put an idea across?

What do others think of his ideas and opinions?

P. *Leadership*—Leadership is the ability to lead and direct others toward established goals. Consider here:

Does he lead or push?

Can he stimulate others to do their best?

Does he provide a steadying influence necessary for a smooth operation?

Q. *Administrative Ability*—The ability to plan, organize, and supervise the flow of work in an efficient manner is indication of administrative ability. Consider here:

Are his instructions to others clear?

Is he able to get the job done within prescribed time limits and with a minimum of confusion?

Do bottlenecks occur frequently as a result of his planning?

R. *Training Effectiveness*—This factor is reflected in the job knowledge of the employees supervised by the individual being rated.

Does he conduct regular training sessions?

Is his training material well prepared?

Does he develop trainees to maximum efficiency?

Part III—Principal Duties

The principal duties are listed in each employee's job description. The rater lists the principal duties in Part III of this form in the same order that they appear in the job description. After he has listed the duties, the rater will then rate the employee's performance of them, using the same method he used in the previous two parts.

Part IV—Summary and Conclusion

This part, in most instances, is the most important of the four parts of the rating. Here the rater will sum up the various qualifications of the employee and in his own words tell what he thinks of the employee's overall performance. Each section must be answered.

A. *Write a brief paragraph giving an overall summary of the employee's job performance.*

In the first three parts, the rater has torn the employee apart and rated him on each part. Now the rater should put him back together and look at him and his performance as a whole. This paragraph should tell how the rater feels toward the employee's overall performance.

B. *What are the employee's principal strong points?*

Here the rater should write a brief summary of the employee's strong points.

C. *What are the employee's principal weak points?*

Write a brief summary of the employee's weak points.

D. *Considering the overall job performance, this employee is evaluated.*

In this section the rater circles the number above the evaluation which best describes the employee's overall job performance. The rater should be careful to rate the employee's performance as a whole. The comments portion of this section should be used for clarifying or qualifying.

E. *On the basis of your observations, what is the employee's potentiality for future advancement with the company?*

The rater places a check mark in the space which best indicates the employee's potential.

F. *For what jobs, and when, should the employee be considered in the future; or if on the career progression program, is trainee ready for advancement?*

If the employee is not on the career progression program, the rater should consider what jobs he can handle in the future and when he will be ready for advancement. If the employee is on the career progression program, the rater should indicate whether or not he is ready for advancement to the next training grade.

G. *What can or should we do to help employee improve where weaknesses are indicated and to prepare for advancement?*

The rater is to indicate here what steps should be taken to improve the employee's job performance.

H. *What can or should employee do to improve or prepare for advancement?*

The rater is to indicate what the employee can do to improve himself.

I. *Is the employee entitled to a salary increase, and what amount?*

In this section, the rater is to indicate whether or not the employee is entitled to a salary increase and the amount of the increase.

J. *Summary of review with employee including employee's reaction.*

After an analysis has been completed on an assistant manager or a branch assistant, the branch manager must discuss it with his district manager either in person or by phone before the discussion with the employee. All others may be reviewed with the employees immediately. The rater has to pay particular attention to the employee's reaction and after he has completed the review with the employee, the rater is to write a summary of the review and the employee's reaction to it. The discussion of the analysis with the employee is more fully covered later.

Disposition of Performance Analysis

After the performance analysis has been reviewed with the employee, the rater will forward it to the personnel department. It will then be reviewed by the district manager (in the case of a branch employee) or by the rater's immediate superior (in the case of a headquarters employee), and his comments entered thereon before the form is returned to the personnel department, where it will become part of the employee's permanent file.

All Employees Will Receive Performance Analyses

All employees of Interstate and subsidiary corporations, except the top executives, will receive performance analyses. The analysis is to be completed by the immediate superior of each employee.

Performance Analyses of Headquarters Department Heads, Supervisors, and Regional and District Managers

All headquarters department heads, supervisors, and regional and district managers shall be reviewed in December of each year providing that they have served at least six months in the capacity held in December. In the event an individual has not completed six months' service in a supervisory or department head capacity, a performance analysis is to be conducted for the first time at the discretion of his immediate superior and the personnel department and thereafter in December of each year.

Performance Analyses of Branch Managers

Branch managers shall be reviewed by their district managers upon completion of 12 months' service as a branch manager with Interstate or subsidiary company and annually on the anniversary date of promotion to branch manager.

Notification When Rating Is Due

It will not be necessary for the branch manager or department head to originate performance analyses. The personnel department will forward the form to the branch manager or department head 60 days in advance of the employee's performance analysis date.

Transfer and Return From Leave of Absence

If an employee is transferred without promotion from one department to another or from one branch to another, his performance analysis date will not change. In the event his next review falls within 60 days after his transfer, his former supervisor or branch manager will complete the analysis form and forward it to the personnel department. It will then be forwarded to the employee's new supervisor or branch manager, who will discuss it with the employee and then return it to the personnel department. If the performance analysis date of a transferred employee should occur after 60 days following the transfer, the normal procedure will be followed.

An employee who returns from extended leave of absence (medical, military, etc.) will be reviewed six months from the date of his return and annually on the anniversary of his employment with Interstate.

THE PERFORMANCE ANALYSIS INTERVIEW

BASIC PRINCIPLES FOR SUCCESSFUL CORRECTIVE INTERVIEWING

Plan the Interview

If you have maintained a simple record of each employee's achievements and shortcomings over the last six months, planning and conducting the interview will not only be simpler, but the interview itself will be more objective. Make a list of all good points and weak points about the individual's performance. This will be extremely helpful to you in the interview and will go far toward insuring that you don't miss or omit important points.

Don't Plan to Cover Too Much

As Rome wasn't built in a day, employees can only improve a little at a time. If you try to accomplish too much in one rating interview you are likely to accomplish little, if anything. All employees can develop further. There is no one who cannot improve in some respect. With each employee, pick the one or, at the most, two things that you feel are the top priorities. Cover these well and let the other things go until the next time. We can't eat enough at one sitting so we won't need food for a week, and we can't sleep 48 hours consecutively and then go without sleep for six days. The same is true when discussing improvement with employees. Failures or mistakes that have accumulated over a six-month period cannot be corrected immediately. Furthermore, too much criticism at one time is very likely to make the situation look hopeless to the employee, or at the very least discourage him seriously because he feels he is almost worthless in your eyes.

Take the Employee to a Private Place

Be sure you are out of earshot before you discuss with any employee his performance analysis. If you criticize him in any way in the presence of others you immediately will have a hard time to get him to cooperate. If possible, discuss the rating at lunch or in the evening after work.

Avoid a Formal Atmosphere

Do not go about the performance analysis interview as though it were a grim occasion. It is serious only in the sense that you want to do a good job of it. But taking a very serious attitude may in itself destroy your chances of getting the best results. Take a friendly and affable approach, but be systematic and thorough in covering all the points you think are important.

Conducting the Performance Analysis Interview—The Nondirective Approach

The nondirective interview is one in which the interviewer guides and manages the interview, but does not dominate it. It is an approach in which you give the person you are interviewing a somewhat free rein to talk. You don't try to "control" the interview rigidly, but you do manage it. You try to steer the other person along the right path and get him to arrive at the right conclusion or decision on his own power.

The nondirective interview is particularly valuable when discussing an employee's performance with him. Presumably, if he is an average employee, he has some performance problems. Very often the most important key to getting a solution to the problems is to maneuver the employee into finding the right answer himself. The individual differences inherent in you, the employee, and the problems to be discussed make it obvious that each interiew will be different from each other interview. There are, however, certain basic steps that should be covered when you are discussing a performance problem with any employee. There are no fixed things that must be said, but there are definitely good and poor ways of saying things. You will find on the following pages a discussion of a basic nondirective interview chart which you will find helpful in planning any corrective interview.

You will also find a listing of key phrases which tie into a nondirective pattern chart. Together these will help you understand the successful corrective interviewing. Careful study of these techniques will be of great help to you.

IMPROVEMENT INTERVIEW CHART

As indicated on the following chart, any discussion of a performance problem can be divided, for discussion purposes, into four parts:

    I. Setting the Stage

    II. Getting the Other Person's Reaction

    III. Considering What Should Be Done

    IV. The Result

In general, a well-conducted performance analysis interview will include all these stages, although, of course, normally the discussion will shift back and forth, to some extent, from one stage to another. The improvement interview chart will not mean a great deal to you until you have studied it and gone through it a time or two in conjunction with the list of key phrases provided with the chart.

The List of Key Phrases

You will find on page 548 a series of 12 phrases, each numbered for identification. *The numbers of those phrases relate to the same numbers on the Improvement Chart* shown nearby.

The purpose of these phrases is to suggest to you the approach to your statements. While you would not necessarily use exactly the same phrase as the one suggested, you should use a similar starting phrase with the same general meaning.

THE PERFORMANCE ANALYSIS INTERVIEW

The Improvement Interview Chart

(Corresponding to the Key Phrases)

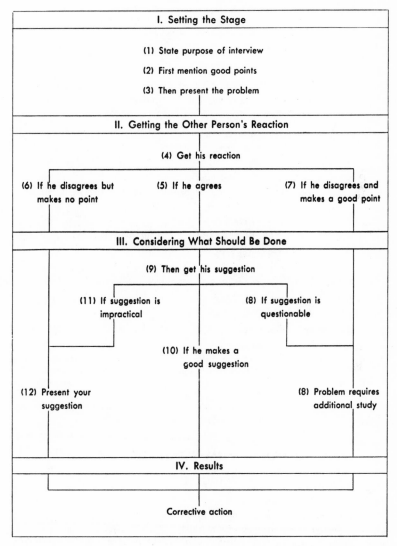

I. Setting the Stage

(1) State purpose of interview

(2) First mention good points

(3) Then present the problem

II. Getting the Other Person's Reaction

(4) Get his reaction

(6) If he disagrees but makes no point

(5) If he agrees

(7) If he disagrees and makes a good point

III. Considering What Should Be Done

(9) Then get his suggestion

(11) If suggestion is impractical

(8) If suggestion is questionable

(10) If he makes a good suggestion

(12) Present your suggestion

(8) Problem requires additional study

IV. Results

Corrective action

Numbers in parentheses refer to corresponding key phrases in the text.

1. *State Purpose of Interview*
   Key Phrase—"I want to talk to you about your work.............................."

2. *First Mention Good Points*
   Key Phrase—"There are a number of things you have been doing well......."

3. *Then Present the Problem*
   Key Phrase—"I think you can do a better job than you are doing on............"

4. *Get His Reaction*
   Key Phrase—"Do you agree that's pretty much the situation.......................?"

5. *If He Agrees*
   Key Phrase—"What do you think we can do about it................................?"

6. *If He Disagrees But Makes No Point*
   Key Phrase—"Nevertheless, the fact remains that................................"

7. *If He Disagrees and Makes a Good Point*
   Key Phrase—"I'm glad that you told me those things, it puts a different light on it.."

8. *Problem Requires Additional Study*
   Key Phrase—"Let me give this some further study, and we'll talk about it again later.."

9. *Then Get His Suggestion*
   Key Phrase—"What do you think we can do about it................................?"

10. *If He Makes a Good Suggestion*
    Key Phrase—"I like your idea and I think it will work............................"

11. *If Suggestion Is Impractical*
    Key Phrase—"Frankly, I don't think your idea will work because.............."

12. *Present Your Suggestion*
    Key Phrase—"What do you think of this plan.......................................?"

To review a most important point: The main idea behind the nondirective performance analysis interview, as illustrated by this chart and these phrases, is to get the employee to come up with the right solution of his own performance deficiency. *Your own greatest problem is to discipline yourself not to tell the employee what he should do about it.* Withhold any suggestions you may have until you are completely convinced that the employee cannot arrive at a good answer. Then, and only then, make your suggestions.

EXPLANATION OF IMPROVEMENT INTERVIEW

I. SETTING THE STAGE

State Purpose of Interview—(1)

Naturally, before you begin discussing a performance analysis you should tell the employee what you are going to be talking about. There is a tendency among some employees in a situation of this nature to engage in a considerable amount of preliminaries. Some like to begin by talking about topics of unrelated but general interest such as the weather, baseball, news topics, etc. However, there are probably as many or more advantages in simply getting down to the business at hand, with as little waste motion as possible. Usually, in situations of this type the employee has a pretty good idea as to what the interview is about and extended preliminaries are not of particular value. Open with a simple statement in your own words, beginning something like:

Key Phrase—"Ed, I want to talk to you about your work.."

First Mention Good Points—(2)

In a performance analysis interview it is, of course, highly important to comment favorably on the employee's good points, and there is some advantage in doing this in the beginning of the interview. This helps get the discussion off to a friendly open-minded start. If you withhold your favorable comments until after your criticism you run the danger of having your praise look like "buttering-up." In other words, it may appear that you are using the praise as a form of apology for having been critical.

Key Phrase—"There are a number of things you have been doing well................"

Then Present the Problem—(3)

As indicated in the section "Don't Plan to Cover Too Much," it is usually better to isolate one, or, at the most, two items on which the employee needs most to improve, and concentrate on these. If you try to cover too many points the employee tends to become discouraged and even resentful. Start with just one problem and begin your discussion of it something like this:

Key Phrase—"However, I think you can do a better job than you are doing on.."

You have now stated the purpose of the interview, you have praised the employee for some of his good work, and have stated an important problem in terms of his performance—you have set *the stage* for getting the employee's reaction to your view of the problem.

II. GETTING THE OTHER PERSON'S REACTION

Get His Reaction—(4)

It is important to bear in mind that no matter how sure you think you are about the problem, the employee may be able to make points in his defense that may change your view. In any event, the course of action you decide on, or eventually agree upon, may be strongly affected by the employee's attitude and statements about the problem. At this point, check the employee's reaction, see if he agrees or disagrees with your thoughts on the situation.

Key Phrase—"Do you agree that's pretty much the situation................................?"

If He Agrees—(5)

If the employee's reaction is one of agreement on the problem, you are ready to move into stage III of the interview—considering what should be done.

Key Phrase—"What do you think we can do about it................................?"

If He Disagrees But Makes No Point—(6)

After you have stated the problem and asked the employee's opinion about it, he may say he does not agree with you, but offers no sensible reason for his position. He may argue around in circles, talk emotionally about the matter, but offer no real reasons to support his disagreement. In such cases, the disagreement is probably based on emotion rather than facts, and therefore, for all practical purposes should be treated as agreement.

Key Phrase—"Nevertheless, the fact remains that..."

You are now ready to consider what should be done about the problem. In other words, if the employee has agreed with your view of the problem, or disagrees but makes no point, you are ready to consider what should be done about it.

On the other hand, if the employee disagrees with you about the problem and raises a good point that requires further investigation or consideration, you should bring the interview to a close, and, if desirable, have another interview after you have had an opportunity to give the problem additional study.

If He Disagrees and Makes a Good Point—(7) and (8)

If the employee disagrees with you about the problem and raises a good point which you had not considered, you will probably want to give the problem further study. In this case, you would bring the interview gracefully to a close and perhaps take the discussion up again sometime after you have had a chance to get additional facts or to give the situation some further thought.

Key Phrase—"I'm glad you told me these things, Ed, it puts a different light on it.."

Key Phrase—"Let me give this some further study and we'll talk about it again later..."

III. CONSIDERING WHAT SHOULD BE DONE

Then Get His Suggestion—(9)

In considering what should be done to correct the performance problem be sure to start out by trying to get the employee to think out the answer. Restrain any tendency on your part to jump in and say—"Here's what we think you'd better do..."

Key Phrase—"What do you think we can do about it......................................?"

If He Makes a Good Suggestion—(10)

If the employee comes up with a good suggestion, one that you like and think is practical, accept it. You have achieved a corrective action as your result, and the interview can be brought to a close.

Key Phrase—"I like your idea, Ed. I think it will work..............................."

If Suggestion Is Not Practical—(11) and (12)

The employee will not always be able to make a good suggestion. Sometimes he will have none at all; in other cases, for one reason or another, his suggestion will be impractical. If one suggestion isn't good, try to get another. If none of his suggestions are good, then, *and not until then,* state *your* suggestion.

Key Phrase—"Frankly, Ed, I don't think your idea will work because...................."

Key Phrase—"What do you think of this plan..?"

If Suggestion Is Questionable, Problem Requires Additional Study—(8)

In some cases the employee will make a suggestion that requires further study on your part. It may be one that will cause you to want to think about it some more. In these cases you can go back to:

Key Phrase—"Let me give this some further study, and we'll talk about it again later.."

By way of review: After getting the employee's reaction to your view of a performance problem, you ask him for his suggestion as to what should be done to correct the situation. If he makes a good suggestion, that is acceptable to you, you have achieved your results—corrective action.

On the other hand, his suggestion may be one that you are not sure about, and you may want to drop the matter until you can give it some further study.

Finally, he may not be able to make a suggestion acceptable to you, in which case you will want to tell him why his idea is not practical. If you cannot get a useful suggestion from the employee, then you will have to make a suggestion of your own—which again will be the result, or corrective action, which was the purpose of your interview.

Always Remember That You Are Trying to Help the Person to Improve

Remember throughout the entire procedure of performance analysis and review that you have but one purpose in mind based on this fundamental principle:

IF A PERSON IS GOING TO IMPROVE, HE NEEDS TO BE TOLD WHEREIN HE SHOULD IMPROVE, AND OUGHT TO BE GIVEN SOME REAL HELP AS TO HOW HE CAN DO BETTER THAN HE HAS BEEN DOING.

Chapter 35

OFFICE MANUALS

EXECUTIVES of more than 100 companies have been asked by Dartnell's editors to contribute from experience they have accumulated while developing and using office manuals in their respective companies. One of the questions asked has to do with the basic fundamentals of effective office manuals. These are the five points most frequently mentioned by respondents to the questionnaire circulated by The Dartnell Corporation:

Top Management Support. No office manual—procedural, organizational, policy, or training—can be effective and successful unless backed by top management. To justify the time, money, and hard work which a good manual requires, the manual must be followed by employees and supervision. It will not be followed unless the *authority* is there.

Provision for Revisions. Because of the rapidly changing picture in office procedures, the manual must be so set up that allowances for frequent changes in content can be met. This means, not only designing the manual so it can be changed when necessary, but also setting up a system for making such changes in order that they will actually be made when required. A loose-leaf binding will make the job of revising easier.

Analysis of Dissatisfactions. Since most manuals come into being because some dissatisfaction exists regarding the way things are being done—or not being done—all dissatisfactions should be carefully considered to insure that the final job will improve procedures.

"Policing" the Manual. Enforcing of policies is one of the most important parts of the whole undertaking. Even after receiving a manual embodying the latest methods and backed by a directive from top management, employees may persist in outmoded, inefficient methods. To avoid this possibility, the procedure of the manual should be set up so that any deviation from it would automatically be revealed. Where this is not possible, periodic examinations will insure compliance with procedures outlined in the new manual.

Employee Acceptance. Experience has shown that when a new or revised manual is introduced with some formal training—classroom type preferred—it gets wider and quicker acceptance from the employees who will use it. Time spent in such training may mean the difference between failure and success in the presentation of the new manual.

Justifying the Cost of a Manual

There are as many reasons for office manuals as there are types. The following comment of a business systems consultant indicates the important uses:

1. The manual with a system of getting approvals and clearances for each procedural instruction is the best and quickest device for getting uniformity of operation.

2. A well-administered manual will guarantee continuity of action as well as place responsibility for performance.

3. In the case of organizations with multiplant or multioffice operations, a manual provides adherence to one plan throughout the entire organization. This is particularly true in the case of cost-conscious corporations which limit traveling.

4. Any good systems manual can also be used as a training device to help explain a job to a new employee.

5. Because it is actually a job description, a manual can be very helpful to management in recognizing and evaluating a job. This is especially true in the case of companies with only rough job titles such as "clerk," "clerk-typist," and so forth.

6. It eliminates the tendency of employees to be secretive about a job and to monopolize a set of job skills, thereby increasing their bargaining leverage.

7. A manual preserves details of former procedures which the company no longer uses. Sometimes a company will return to an old procedure—resuming production of an old item is just one of the many possible reasons—and a manual can serve as an invaluable guide, if not as an exact model.

A. F. Bortz, assistant secretary, Lord Manufacturing Company, advises making haste slowly in setting up a company manual of procedures. "The success of a procedures manual," Mr. Bortz told an American Management Association conference on office management, "will be judged in the end by its effectiveness and not by the rapidity with which a large mass, or we might say 'mess,' of writing is turned out in the first flush of enthusiasm in undertaking the project. The old adage that haste makes waste has never had a more pertinent application."

Mr. Bortz cited 14 advantages of reducing procedures to writing. Procedures manuals:

1. Formalize all operations of the company.
2. Facilitate communications.
3. Can be used as training and personal development media.
4. Clarify or establish policies.
5. Insure coordination and eliminate duplication of effort.
6. Mean uniform interpretation of policy.

7. Establish reference sources.
8. Define responsibility and authority.
9. Preserve policies even though personnel change.
10. Strengthen supervision.
11. Insure work simplification.
12. Establish control of forms.
13. Strengthen employee relations.
14. Establish control points for cost analyses.

Two prerequisites are absolutely necessary to insure success in a procedures manual program, according to Mr. Bortz. They are a policy manual, or at least a statement of policies; and an organization manual, or at least an organization chart.

Responsibility for the procedures manual sometimes is centralized —in a separate administrative department, in the president's staff, or as a function of the office manager or controller—and sometimes is decentralized. Mr. Bortz prefers the former arrangement because more time is likely to be given to the job, coordination is easier and conflicts can be minimized, and all departments can be kept on the same timetable. The procedures-writing unit also should have control of the use of the forms.

Other suggestions which will make for a successful manual include the following: Make the manual readable, both in writing style and in physical layout. Use flow charts where sequences of steps and operations are involved. Adopt a classification and coding system that facilitates filing and reference and makes it possible to insert additions. A comprehensive index is a "must." Review the manual regularly to make sure it is kept up to date. To get full cooperation from all personnel, enlist the active support of top management, let as many people as possible participate in the preparation of procedures, use the conference technique in installing the manual, and provide assistance in educating personnel where needed.

Some Typical Flaws of the Office Manual

How *not* to do an office manual is, of course, as important as how to do it. Those companies that have put out an office manual are in the best position to avoid some of the usual mistakes. They know where their manuals are weak or where they have been hard to use because of poor arrangement, lack of clarity or conciseness.

In examining the manuals distributed by companies in various lines of business, the following faults are found to be repeated most often:

1. Poor arrangement, making it difficult to find specific subject matter.
2. Too large, bulky, or heavy for day-to-day use.

3. Too abstract—fail to get down to "brass tacks."

4. Too complex and wordy.

5. Fail to follow step-by-step job procedure.

6. Hard to read because of:
   a. Poor type.
   b. Poor production.
   c. Wrong type of paper for process used.
   d. Poor layout.
   e. Faulty or indistinct illustrations.
   f. Insufficient use of white space.
   g. Too many "unbroken" pages of type due to too few heads and subheads.

7. Fail to fit the jobs of the employees who are to use them. (This is due to inadequate job study before the manuals were written.)

8. Out of date—obsolete.

Most of these faults are, of course, due to hasty and/or inadequate planning. Some of them are due to the fact that the writer (or committee) responsible for preparation of the manual did not familiarize himself with the various jobs in the office. In some cases, the writer has simply failed to put himself in the position of the user. He has failed to comprehend the employee's lack of "word understanding" or to envision the worker's attitude toward his job. In other words, he doesn't make the employee *want* to learn how to do the job in the correct manner.

If the person responsible for planning the office manual will put himself in the place of the user, the manual should be easy to read, of convenient size, well arranged, and simplicity itself. It is important to remember during the planning of the manual that, no matter how good a job you may do in "selling" the employee on using the manual, if it isn't clearly and concisely written, attractive and easy to use, the "selling" job won't pay off.

Tailoring the Manual to Fit the Company

Unless the manual is tailored to fit the needs of the company, it is unlikely to be as effective as it should be. If there is any one job in a office which should be tailor made, it is the office manual. No one pattern can possibly fit all companies, even those which are in the same line of business. The manual should vary depending upon the size of the company, its field of operation, and whether its operations are centralized or decentralized.

Very large companies, because of their extensive operations and great number of employees, usually find it advantageous to employ separate manuals for different divisions of the company or individual sections for large departments within the company. Often, desk sheets for the individual employee or small groups may be necessary.

Whether the manual is to contain general company information such as operating policies, history, and general characteristics of the company; whether it is to be an office rule book covering methods of paying employees, holidays observed, etc.; whether it is to be a straight secretarial manual or a standard practice instruction manual; the office manual must be tailored to fit the needs of the company and/or the user.

This is not to say that you cannot use a basic office manual as a guide in the preparation of your own manual. If some company has set up a particularly good office manual and you have an opportunity to use it as a guide, well and good. However, it is best to consider it only as an aid in formulating your own manual to cover *your* procedures, policies, and operations.

What Is an Office Manual?

Whatever its definition, we know that the concept of an office manual varies greatly from one company to the next. One may set up a book of rules and regulations for employees to follow and call it an office manual. Another may plan its manual as a training or instruction book, while a third may look upon the office manual as simply a correspondence handbook for the stenographic department. A company may also call its office manual a "job manual" and write it as a guide for supervisors to spell out the requirements of various jobs, to provide written work procedures, and to set up a work-flow chart.

An insurance company calls its office manual, "A Manual of General Agency Operations"; a manufacturer in the East gives its office manual this title, "Orientation Manual for Office Employees"; while a drug manufacturer calls its manual an "Office Practices Manual."

Whether it called by one of the above titles or termed a "Supervisory Manual," "Personnel Policy Memoranda," or "Credit and Collection Training Manual," the office manual is a good example of the "put-it-in-writing" principle. Once all essential information for the guidance of employees is put in writing, the supervisor's job is simplified. The manual makes it unnecessary for constant repetition on his part in assigning jobs or in specifying correct procedures.

The Job or Functional Type of Manual

One of the most widely used manuals among companies today is the "functional" or "job" manual. This type of manual can be most helpful to personnel administration, inasmuch as it contains a general description of duties for various clerical jobs. Such a manual is particularly useful in job evaluation, in making estimates of manpower requirements due to changes in production, and as an aid in salary administration.

A functional office manual may be one overall office manual covering several clerical jobs; or it may be confined to one activity, such as that of the stenographic department.

After it has been decided to prepare a job manual, and the person or committee has been appointed to handle preparations, one of the first steps is to "sell" the supervisors on the procedure. Once supervisors are sold on the potential benefits, the next step is to secure the cooperation of the workers. Supervisors should check with their workers to gain insight into what may be wrong with each work procedure. To simplify the checkup, a list of questions about the job should be prepared and the supervisor should go over this list with each employee working on similar jobs. The questions should cover step-by-step procedure on the job, equipment and materials used, records and forms maintained, filing procedure, and storage facilities, if applicable.

Answers to questions like these may eliminate unnecessary steps in the procedure followed; suggest the use of more suitable equipment or elimination of faulty equipment; bring out the proper use of materials and whether such materials are easily accessible; and show if files can be properly maintained and used under the present system.

Questions for supervisors to ask employees will vary according to the job specifications and operations. As jobs are analyzed, questions pertinent to their operation will present themselves. The main idea is to get the cooperation of the employees in setting up the best job procedure. Such help is not to be taken lightly, for who should know what is wrong with present procedures better than the one doing the job?

Job Analysis as a Basis for the Manual

Should the standard procedures manual be based on the way the job is being done, or on the way it should be done? Few companies use manuals merely to embody existing systems. They prefer to analyze present methods or procedures in order to find the *best* way—the way which eliminates useless operations and insures employees learning from the start the right way to do the job.

The amount of analysis which precedes preparation of the manual depends upon the size and complexity of the operation being studied. One procedural manual may outline just the details of a single, simple operation; while another may describe a large area of responsibility, possibly covering an entire department. An excellent tool for analyzing detailed clerical operations is the job-breakdown technique, which is an accurate, concise, understandable organization of facts, in writing about the one best way to perform each operation making up a job. Actually, it is a road map of an operation which will serve as a guide for the worker and make it practically impossible for him to get lost along the way.

Job breakdown, according to one well-known company, enabled it to eliminate useless operations, prevented teaching new people wrong or useless methods, and paced the flow of work through the office.

While making these job breakdowns is a comparatively simple process, it takes time. However, for a company with divisions and branch offices throughout the country, job breakdowns more than pay their way, because they standardize and correlate procedures throughout the organization and they make it easy for local management to train new employees.

The Single, Simple Operation

Many office workers are paid for doing the same job day after day. They expect—and usually receive—increases in wages for doing this job. It is only fair to establish work standards for the job, and it is necessary to measure the work and arrive at the best possible method for the sake of the employee as well as the company.

Work Simplification and the Manual

While in most cases job breakdown techniques are sufficient preparation for the office manual, there are some instances where a different approach is necessary. This is especially true today when such tremendous changes are taking place in office procedures—new automatic equipment for one thing.

If a general review of analysis of office procedures has not been made in some time or if costs seem to be unduly out of line, an office methods study may be indicated. This is particularly true during a period of spiraling costs in labor, materials, and equipment.

Primarily, the office methods study is an important part of the cost-reduction program, but equally important is the fact that it will lead to improvement in office methods and thus speed up production and improve efficiency. Among other things, the office methods study should aim to improve distribution, improve office layout, simplify paperwork and improve the use of existing equipment. It should also suggest areas where more automatic equipment could be put to work.

The Work-Flow Chart

One test of planned work assignments is the work-flow chart. If a chart is drawn to show how the work moves through the unit, important errors in procedures will show up clearly. Such a chart will spot any unnecessary movement of the work or any inadequate arrangement for work stations and equipment.

If procedures in the department are rather simple—a mail or messenger service unit or a central filing unit, for example—the work-flow chart can usually be prepared by the supervisor or department head himself. However, if many operations are involved in the unit, the job is best turned over to the drafting department.

The chart or map may indicate the actual area involved, drawn to scale, with such items as desks, tables, chairs, files, counters, and machines or other equipment in their proper location. These items are generally indicated by symbols—squares, ovals, circles, triangles, etc. The work itinerary is plotted by means of dots or dashes with arrows showing the direction of the flow. If these lines of operation tend to overlap or double back, there is need, of course, for reorganizing the work stations so that the most direct line of operations will obtain.

Before including the work-flow chart in the office manual, it is a good idea to prepare a temporary chart to pinpoint what is being done. With this temporary chart to work from, bottlenecks or snags in the flow of work will be spotted. To make certain that every procedure along the line is being included in this temporary chart, it is a good idea to check with each worker in the department. Once the pattern of work is set down on paper, the system can be analyzed for gaps or overlaps, and revisions can be set up to secure more efficient flow of work.

After these work sheets or temporary work-flow charts have been analyzed and corrected and a more efficient system has been devised on paper, it may be necessary to rearrange the department to take advantage of the new system. All this should be done before the system is written up for the office manual in any sort of finished form.

The Policy Manual

A number of companies have found it expedient to issue a special policy manual for the executive and/or supervisory groups. Such policy manuals are not common, for, as a rule, the analysis of existing policies and the preparation of a manual amount to a full-time job. Management may also feel that such a manual has a tendency to make supervision too inflexible. A policy manual could have this effect, *if* it were set up strictly as a rule book, rather than as a guide toward better supervision.

Why should a company go to the trouble of putting its policies into writing? First of all, it means—or should mean—the end of fuzzy thinking about policies, because the minute policies are put down on paper they must be defined.

Putting policies into writing also means that some clear thinking has to be done to formulate company policies so that they will be understandable by both supervision and rank-and-file employees. It means, too, that some decisions have to be made at the management level about keeping old policies on the books or dropping them. Many old policies, meaningless as they now stand, must be redefined and given proper emphasis. Possibly, this is the best thing about writing a policy manual—the chance to clear away the debris of unnecessary, inadequate, and obsolete policies that have been cluttering up the books for many years. Even if the company got nothing else out of preparing a policy manual, this result alone should be worthwhile.

Another important result of putting policies in writing is that supervision will have a uniform code for handling workers. No one needs to explain what such standardization in handling discipline, methods, and instructions can mean to a smooth-functioning department and to good employee morale. As indicated previously, the supervisory group must understand that such written policies are to be used as guides—each case of employee discipline or instruction is an individual problem. For the supervisor to handle every situation in the same way can only result in lowered morale of the department. Rules or policies can never take the place of common sense!

What should such a manual include? First, it should include simple, basic procedures in relation to employees. This means policies covering new employees, their orientation and placement on the job; employee attendance; pay and promotion; overtime; pay checks (deductions, etc.); and all other areas relating to the employee's behavior or conduct on the job, as well as his pay, his health, and his welfare.

Second, the manual should include policies that cover departmental practices. This may be a large section, depending upon the number and types of jobs in the various departments. Besides step-by-step work procedures, the manual should clarify policies relating to work flow, use of forms and records, materials and equipment, work schedules, and costs.

Third, the policy manual should deal with relations with other departments. This section should clarify those policies which will smooth the way for teamwork among departments and the various levels of supervision. What these departments may be, and how closely the supervisors must cooperate, depends upon the type and size of the business. Even in the smaller business, however, such a section should not be omitted from the manual, for lack of definite policies in this area of operation can mean a serious bottleneck in production.

If You Have a Union

Unions in offices are not yet so widespread that they need to be considered in preparation of the office manual. However, some of the large offices—in insurance, for example—have been organized in the East. In such cases, management has to take into consideration the union agreement in preparing the policy manual for supervisors.

Practically all policy manuals for supervisors in plants conform to the policies and procedures recorded in the union agreements existing in those plants. Any policy manual in use in a shop or plant will, therefore, suggest a pattern to follow. The main factor to consider is that the company policy manual will not be at variance with policies established by the union agreement with the company's office workers. It is, therefore, important to check the one against the other before it is put in final form, to see that the policies conform in all details.

To insure acceptance of the policy manual, management may have to go a step further and hold a meeting or two with union representatives to sell them as well as the supervisors on the use of the manual. In fact, it might be worthwhile to get the approval of the union representatives before the manual is printed in its final form.

WRITING AND PRODUCING THE MANUAL

In the last few years, there has been quite a different approach in handling employee publications. Booklets, manuals, magazines, informational leaflets, and other forms of communication have not only become better written and edited, but also more attractive and truly informative.

The office manual of former years was probably written in an old-fashioned style, rather than the simple, direct form being used today. The simple, direct style means elimination of ambiguous phrases, excess wordage, and long unwieldy sentences. The writer may have to break down the job page by page in rewriting the manual in order to eliminate these outmoded sentences. He must also watch for dated expressions or cliches.

The company may find a person on its staff who can write simple, effective prose. If so, it will not be difficult to change the old manual to one with a concise, lucid, direct style of writing. If an outside consultant is used for this job, the person in your company responsible for the overall job should watch the copy style carefully to make certain the revised manual will not carry over the old-fashioned faults of the previous edition.

A simple, direct style of writing is not easy to achieve; it cannot be reduced to a set of rules. However, there are a few basic principles which can help to keep the writer on the right track:

1. Use the "command" style as opposed to the indirect style. As a rule, indirect sentences are long and involved; the reader loses interest quickly when this style is used. In the "command" style, the writer gets action.

   Examples:

   > *Indirect*—All applicants are treated with every courtesy, even when they are unsolicited and no immediate opening exists.

   > *Simple Command*—Treat all applicants courteously, even if they are unsolicited and you have no immediate opening.

2. Make it personal. Don't be afraid of you, we, they, our, your, or any word that will let the reader know you are talking to him. Referring always to "the company" and "the employee" sets up too formal and rigid a pattern.

3. Use the obvious, natural expression. Track down all ponderous phrases and convert them to crisp, lean expressions. Why say "in the event that," when "if" does the job?

4. Trim the fat. Excess words that merely repeat what you have already told the reader weigh down any manual. Many a four-line sentence can be cut to two or less by this method. By doing a little rewriting, you can end up with a third fewer words—and the reader will understand you better.

5. Use active verbs. Build your sentences around active verbs. Pick out the word that describes the action you want your reader to take; build your sentence around that word. Try to stay clear of any form of the word *to be; to be* usually deadens a sentence. (Use of active verbs ties in with principle 1, the "command" style.)

6. Shorten your sentences. Sentences in employee or office manuals should not run more than 17 to 20 words. One sentence of 39 words is about 70 percent harder to grasp than three sentences of 13 words each—the same number of words, but a world of difference in readability. Remember: The short, simple sentence makes for readability—and understandability.

7. Interrupting phrases. Many sentences are long because they include numerous phrases. These phrases interrupt the reader's thought-flow. It is better to break such sentences up into shorter ones.

8. Paragraphing. A paragraph is built around one single point, and has a simple three-step progression: (1) Statement of point, (2) elaboration of point, (3) conclusion of point. All one has to do is to determine what the main point is, state it briefly, tell all you need to about it, and then conclude it. Watching for key ideas when writing will give you natural, effective paragraphs.

These are only a few of the high spots. There is much more to writing clear, lucid prose than these eight principles. But these precepts will do for a starter and, if they are followed, the manual is bound to be improved.

The "Playscript" Technique

When writing a manual requires much description of job procedures involving several workers or departments, good use can be made of a modified script-writing form such as is used for plays and radio or TV shows. This technique is aptly called "playscript." It identifies, in step-by-step sequence, each worker responsible for each particular part of a job. For instance, the procedure to be followed in taking a new employee into the company would be written like this:

1. *Hiring supervisor,* after preliminary interview, asks prospective employee to fill in employment application card. Supervisor fills in company "New Employee" form with copies for personnel and accounting departments. Supervisor then directs new employee to personnel department.

2. *Personnel clerk* checks employment application form, obtains information which may have been overlooked, opens department file for employee, then sends employee to accounting department with that department's copy of "New Employee" form.

3. *Accounting clerk* has employee fill in payroll and Internal Revenue withholding forms, then sends employee to insurance department.

4. *Insurance clerk* obtains necessary information from new employee for company insurance policy, and gives employee copy of insurance plan folder. Employee is then directed back to personnel department.

5. *Personnel clerk* gives employee copy of booklet, "Welcome to Our Company," and assigns department guide to take new employee for a brief tour of the plant, ending in the department of the hiring supervisor.

This "who does what and when" technique makes procedure writing easy. And, when each participant in the action is identified, it becomes difficult to cover up lack of procedure knowledge with vague ambiguities. Another benefit of the playscript method is that it often reveals contradictory or unnecessary steps in procedures.

Responsibility for the Job

Before tackling the job of writing the manual, it must be clearly understood not only how the manual will be used but, also, who will use it. Will the worker use the manual? Will it be for the supervisor only? Will the same manual be used by both worker and supervisor?

In the case of job or functional manuals, the supervisor should have a complete loose-leaf manual covering all the special jobs for his department. Each employee will have his own manual, relating to his specific job. We believe, however, that he should be able to see the supervisor's manual, if he wishes, so he may understand more about the job ahead. Thus he can better prepare himself for the next step up.

The answer to the question, "Who is responsible for the job of preparing the manual?" depends upon the type of manual to be written and the facilities and/or talent within the organization for handling this sort of job.

In some companies, delegating this responsibility will be a minor problem, if it is a problem at all. For example, companies which have established work-standards divisions or work-simplification departments are ideally set up to do a good job—especially on the type of manual concerned with job functions or procedures.

However, where such departments have not been set up, the personnel department provides the ideal "climate" for the preparation of the manual. Often the manual can be improved by making its preparation a joint responsibility of the personnel department and the office manager, for example. Or, the personnel department and the systems division may assume this responsibility.

One of the advantages in setting up a committee to handle the job is that it brings representatives of several departments into the picture. Such a committee may consist of the personnel director, office manager, and public relations or advertising director; or the office manager, training director, and systems coordinator.

When facilities for preparing a good manual are lacking, the company is well advised to turn to an outside organization. The firm's advertising agency can often handle the job or suggest someone able to do so. Many management consultants will also handle a job of this sort and, if they work closely with the company's own executive group, the result can be an excellent job.

One company official has this to say about the problem of deciding who should be made responsible for the manual:

Management consultants can do a good job of preparing office manuals because they can bring new and unprejudiced attitudes to the solution of tiresome problems. Moreover, they are usually trained in the techniques of preparing written procedures and manuals. But most important of all, the use of an outside consultant assures that the job *will* be done and this is by no means always the case when a supervisor is made responsible.

When a company uses an outside consultant, it is necessary to make sure that the entire problem is studied and that the manual will not be a superficial and incomplete job.

When a member of the organization is assigned the job of preparing a manual affecting a number of other departments—and this is frequently the case, since few departments operate in a vacuum—it is wise to keep the authorship as anonymous as possible.

Companies employing one or more people whose responsibilities include or consist of methods and systems analysis will naturally assign to this group the responsibility for many of their manuals.

A few companies make the supervisory group the key to the preparation of the manual. In these cases, individual supervisors are made responsible for collecting the essential information. Then the actual job of writing the manual is turned over to someone in the advertising or personnel department who has the ability.

Whether the training department, the supervisory group, the systems division, the office manager, a special committee, or an outside organization is responsible for the job is not so important as that the job gets done.

Determining Size and Format

The most popular size for office manuals is 8½ by 11 inches. This holds true for printed manuals as well as those produced by Multigraph or Mimeograph. One reason for the popularity of this size is, of course, ease of production. Other reasons:

1. This size is less likely to be lost or carried away than a smaller-size manual, such as pocket-size.

2. It is generally more adaptable to extensions, revisions, and additions.

3. If there are several volumes to the manual, the 8½- by 11-inch size stands better on the bookshelf.

4. Many manuals, especially·procedural and organizational, have loose-leaf covers and the 8½- by 11-inch size is a popular one and easy for binderies to furnish.

5. Examples of letterheads and office forms generally conform to the 8½- by 11-inch size and, therefore, can be bound in or pasted on blank pages without a change in size.

It is well to plan the size and the number of pages of the manual far in advance, so you won't end up with a bulky book. Too bulky a book is difficult to use. If the job turns out this way in spite of advance planning, the following steps can be taken to achieve a more usable size:

1. If typewritten, some of the copy may be reduced photographically and be reproduced in smaller size by the offset process.

2. If printed, some parts may be set in smaller type, although care should be taken to make the type legible.

3. Lighter paper stock may be used, but too light a stock will not stand constant handling.

4. Study the book carefully to see if some subject matter cannot be dropped or if there has been duplication of information, forms, etc.

Economies of Production

Often the production process used is that generally available in the office—Mimeograph, Multigraph, offset printing. The choice of production process involves not only the cost, however, but also whether illustrations are to be used, the number of copies required, and so forth.

If illustrations are to be used, offset or printed processes usually give the best results. It is also important to decide upon the type of paper, because illustrations are naturally more attractive if a good grade of paper is used.

When a substantial number of copies of the same manual are required, printing by letterpress or offset will be most economical. These methods of production are easy on the readers' eyes, and the copy can be kept standing for the reprints so often necessary in large organizations.

In checking costs, it is well to remember that the cheapest is not always the most economical; the most expensive not always the best. A very useful manual may actually be one without illustrations, simply bound or stapled, printed clearly with plenty of white space, and without the expense of added color. There is more to a good office manual than meets the eye!

Illustrations are being used more freely than ever before in employee publications. Carefully selected illustrations help to make an office manual more inviting to the employee using it.

Generally speaking, a variety of illustrations makes for a more attractive manual. The use of a few cartoons, some photos, a map, or an occasional chart will result in a much more interesting manual than one where photos or drawings alone are used.

The use of humor is fairly widespread in today's manuals. Clever cartoons either in black and white or color do add "spice" to what is often factual and dry reading matter. However, good taste dictates that such cartoons be selected with care, and it goes without saying that any emphasis upon race or color be avoided.

Since revising the manual is not an overnight job, keeping all the details of the production in hand takes a bit of doing.

So, to expedite the job and at the same time to keep the details in mind, it is well to follow a plan. One good method used by many companies in preparing printed matter is to set up a worksheet which will chart the whole procedure, step by step. Such a worksheet will vary, of course, depending upon the type of publication being prepared. By and large, however, it should show the operations involved, the person responsible for each operation, the dates that work in various areas has been completed, dates the copy has been revised, cost involved (estimates), and so forth.

A Prize Winner

Dartnell editor Marilyn French conducted a contest to find a good secretarial manual. The winner was Mrs. Bernice C. Koegel, secretary at Bell Telephone Laboratories, Inc. Here is what she had to say:

"The most effective type of secretarial manual is a hard-covered, loose-leaf book to hold the standard 8½- by 11-inch sheet in order to facilitate easy removal and addition of pages. A plastic cover is preferable for easy cleaning. The manual should be separated into numbered sections for quick reference.

"A manual should not only be considered desirable, but also necessary to any office worker to ensure the least confusion on proper procedures and handling of work upon the inevitable absence of a secretary from time to time. It should be arranged with simplicity in mind for the frequent reference by others who may have to attend to her work during her absence. Do not overload the manual with unnecessary detail, but be precise and thorough in listing and describing all duties and procedures.

"A section on polite and efficient telephone techniques, good grooming and manners will serve as a reminder that a woman's appearance and actions reflect not only her own capabilities, efficiency and neatness, but also that of her superior whom she represents.

"Also, in line with personal appearance, there should be a paragraph to serve as another reminder—that of appearance of work. The importance of appearance and quality of work leaving a woman's desk can never be overemphasized. The neatness and appearance of correspondence establishes a first, and sometimes a lasting, impression on customers as to a company's attitude in dealing with them as well as the impression of the quality of product or services rendered."

On pages nearby is a sample of an index for a secretarial manual that was prepared by Mrs. Koegel. Included are items that can be useful in any office position, which may be modified to suit the particular type of business. The important thing is that all areas are covered.

An Eye on the Future

Since the majority of office manual users are on the distaff side, here is still another feminine view of a combination handbook and manual that will encompass the basic needs. The ideas are those of Helen P. Mitchell, personnel secretary at Moore's Super Stores, Inc.

"An office woman's manual in loose-leaf form would be durable and could be kept up to date economically. It should be small enough to slip in and out of desk drawers easily, perhaps 5½ by 8 inches.

"Beginning with a history of the company and its operations, her handbooks should contain an organization chart for a better understanding of her position and the position of her immediate superior. It can serve as a guide for the direction of interoffice communications.

"Since today's working woman is bearing part, and often all, of the family financial burden, a feminine view of the 'fine print' concerning what the company offers her in the way of insurance, pension, retirement and/or profit-sharing plans should be made available.

"Again, with an eye to the future, she should be given an idea of the positions available to women with the necessary qualifications, job descriptions, and beginning and maximum wages for these positions. Holidays, vacations, leaves of absence, overtime, and sick leave should be explained.

INDEX FOR A SECRETARIAL MANUAL

INDEX FOR A SECRETARIAL MANUAL (Cont.)

This index for a Secretarial Manual was compiled by supervisors of the Service Operations Division of Bell Telephone Laboratories, Inc., and submitted by Bernice C. Koegel.

"A section containing examples of the preferred forms for letters, memorandums, information bulletins, etc., should be provided together with a listing of reference books (English usage, encyclopedias, dictionaries), company manuals on products or services, and their location. Procedures for obtaining office supplies should be noted.

"An explanation of the company's preference in dress could be included. If there are regulations concerning behavior, employer-employee or employee-employee relationships, these, too, should be listed in order that there may be no misunderstandings which might embarrass the employee or the company. Office hours, lunch and coffee breaks, and regulations regarding personal phone calls and visitors should be clarified.

"Employee committees and their functions, recreational facilities, company-sponsored sports leagues, parties, picnics, company publications, and her participation in these activities should be outlined.

"And throughout her handbook there should be stressed a positive attitude, an encouragement for her to become not only an efficient, productive part of the company, but also a welcome and wanted person in an organization that offers her opportunity, security and friendships."

Keep It Up to Date

The key to the successful office manual is that it serves the immediate needs of the employee. Today's emphasis on work simplification, automation, human relations, and better employee communication has truly outmoded many of the books in use.

Bringing the manual up to date can also serve as a painless way of introducing work measurement into the office. If employees are made aware of the reasons for the study (to update the manual) and if they are asked to cooperate and participate with suggestions, they will be less hostile when their work is scrutinized. They probably will have good ideas as well.

The office manual can be the keystone of employee communication if it is properly written and "sold" to the employee. Management's approach must be informative, factual, and helpful. If there is a new and better way of doing something, it must be made available to the employee.

1. What purpose is manual to serve?
(Check one or more)

A. To inspire and stimulate office workers ......

B. To inform and instruct on office rules ......

C. To provide guidance on office methods or the job ......

D. Other:.......................... ......

2. What audience is manual to reach?
(Check one or more)

A. All new office workers ......

B. All old office workers ......

C. Special group workers ......

(Name:..........................)

D. Other:.......................... ......

3. What type of manual is best?
(Check one)

A. General office manual ......

B. Induction manual ......

C. Special training manual ......

D. Job Manual ......

E. Combination of........and........ ......

4. Who will prepare the manual?
(Check one or more)

A. V.P. in charge of office management ......

B. Personnel director ......

C. Office manager ......

D. Advertising director ......

E. Advertising agency or management consultant ......

F. Work-simplification committee ......

G. Other:.......................... ......

5. How many volumes should there be? ....

6. What size is preferable?
(Check one)
A. 8½x11 ......　　E. 9x12 ......
B. 5 x 6 ......　　F. 11x14 ......
C. 6 x 8 ......　　G. Other:..... ......
D. 7 x10 ......

7. What subjects will we want to include?

1. Abbreviations	......	40. Mailing lists	......
2. Accounting procedures	......	41. Mailing procedures	......
3. Adding machines	......	42. Manual revisions	......
4. Addressing envelopes	......	43. Manufacturing policies	......
5. Administrative policies	......	44. Money orders	......
6. Advertising policies	......	45. Office equipment care	......
7. Air mail	......	46. Office rules	......
8. Alphabetizing	......	47. Order handling	......
9. Banking procedures	......	48. Organization chart	......
10. Business letters	......	49. Organizing work	......
11. Cablegrams	......	50. Patent information	......
12. Calculating machines	......	51. Pending correspondence	......
13. Callers, receiving	......	52. Personnel policies	......
14. Carbon copies	......	53. Postage pointers	......
15. Card indexing	......	54. Postal zones	......
16. Carrying out instructions	......	55. Precision in work	......
17. Cash accounts	......	56. Promptness hints	......
18. Claims, handling	......	57. Proofreading	......
19. Collection procedures	......	58. Property, care of	......
20. Credits, handling	......	59. Purchasing procedures	......
21. Cross-referencing	......	60. Record keeping	......
22. Daily routine	......	61. Routine procedures	......
23. Department relationships	......	62. Rubber stamps, using	......
24. Dictating machines	......	63. Rush procedures	......
25. Duplicating machines	......	64. Sales department data	......
26. Enclosures, handling	......	65. Service department	......
27. Envelopes, addressing	......	66. Shipping department	......
28. Errors, preventing	......	67. Sorting methods	......
29. Executives, names of	......	68. Stock room information	......
30. Filing procedures	......	69. Supplies, securing	......
31. Follow-up work	......	70. Technical information	......
32. Form letters	......	71. Telegram procedures	......
33. Forms, office	......	72. Telephone rules	......
34. History of company	......	73. Ticklers, using	......
35. Indexing	......	74. Traffic department setup	......
36. Information, securing	......	75. Typewriters, care of	......
37. Inquiries, answering	......	76. Typing tips	......
38. Job descriptions	......	77. Valuable papers, protecting	......
39. Legal department setup	......	78. Vault, care of	......

PLANNING CHART

8. What type of binding is best?
   (Check one)

   A. Saddle stitch   ......
   B. Side wire stitch   ......
   C. Bookbinding   ......
   D. Ring loose leaf   ......
   E. Patent loose leaf   .....!
   F. Other:........... ......

9. How many pages do we want (estimated)?
   (Check one)

8	40	72 ......
16	48	80 ......
24	56	100 to 200 ......
32	64	200 or over ......

10. What paper stock for body?
    (Check one or more)

    A. Eggshell   ...... G. Machine finish ......
    B. Calendered   ...... H. Gravure   ......
    C. English finish ...... I. Bond   ......
    D. Supercalendered..... J. Offset   ......
    E. Enamel   ...... K. Card   ......
    F. Uncoated book...... L. Mimeograph   ......
          Other:......................... ......

11. Shall we thumb-index the manual?   .....

12. What production process shall we use?
    (Check one or more)

    A. Letterpress ......   D. Mimeograph ......
    B. Offset   ......   E. Multilith   ......
    C. Multigraph ......   F. Other:...... ......

13. Shall we use illustrations?   .....

14. If illustrated, what kind should we use?
    (Check one or more)

    A. Line cuts (drawings)   ......
    B. Halftones (photos)   ......
    C. Offset (multilith, etc.) ......
    D. Actual prints of photos ......
    E. Color plates   ......
    F. Lithography   ..•....

15. What technical devices should we add to give greater effectiveness?

   ....
   ....
   ....
   ....
   ....
   ....
   ....
   ....
   ....
   ....
   ....

16. What plan shall we use to distribute the manuals?

   ....
   ....

17. How shall we "sell" the manual to employees; to supervisors?

   ....

18. How often shall we revise the manual?

   ....

19. Remarks:.......................................
   ....
   ....
   ....

REVISING THE MANUAL

Before getting into the problems involved in writing the revised manual, here are some of the primary steps essential to planning the work. Following is a list of questions which will suggest the type of decisions someone has to make:

1. What is the purpose of this manual?
2. What employees or group of employees will use it?
3. Who will prepare the manual?
4. Who will have the responsibility of keeping it up to date?
5. How often shall the manual be revised?
6. Will it be necessary to reconsider all office procedures before revising the manual?
7. Shall the manual differ in size from the previous edition?

To facilitate making the decisions, it is well for the committee or individual in charge of the revision of the manual to be able to refer to a planning chart. The "Office Manual Planning Chart," shown on following pages, will be helpful.

How to Collect and Organize Revision Material

Allowing for revisions at scheduled intervals presupposes that someone has been placed in charge of a file where new or changed material may be stored in properly labeled folders until ready for use in a new edition.

This person should also be the one to see that the new or revised pages are entered in each employee's manual. Experience has shown that you cannot hand correction pages for a manual to employees and expect them to make the changes or insertions. Too often, they put off making the changes and the corrections become lost or mislaid. The only way to guarantee that manuals will always be up to date is to place someone in charge of inserting or changing material. Even then, further checking is usually necessary.

One company which has a well-planned program of handling its office manuals turns over to the standard practice division the responsibility for keeping a revision folder on each manual. Material is filed in these folders for inclusion in a particular manual at its next revision. Most of this material is prepared in bulletin form. In every instance the material covers items on which decisions have been made. Thus, at revision date it is not necessary to go into a huddle to get decisions on changes. This helps to expedite the revision procedure, for time is not taken for investigation, presentation of facts, and decisions at this point.

A Midwestern company handles the revision problem as follows:

We have a regular schedule of revisions for our manuals. The frequency of revision depends upon the type of manual. Some must be revised weekly, some quarterly, some semiannually, and some annually. The standard practice division is responsible for keeping a record of the revision dates and for seeing that the revisions are made according to the schedule.

We try to follow the practice that it is better to have a few manuals that are up to date than many manuals, of which none are current. Also, we have adhered to the policy of preferring only a few pages in a manual and having those pages up to date rather than having 100 pages with a number of them obsolete.

"Home Office Employees' Handbook" is presented in a small (5- by 7½-inch) dark-green leather loose-leaf notebook, which facilitates adding or removing sheets when additions or changes are made.

The handbook is a product of the personnel division and a review sheet is circulated monthly to each department head in the personnel division in order that changes and additions may be suggested at that time. Rather than issue each revision individually, we accumulate two or three, thereby preventing the addition or removal of sheets from becoming a chore to employees and possibly lessening their interest in it.

"Selling" the Manual

It is one thing to prepare a good manual; it is another to get it used, and used properly. This is one of the toughest jobs in the preparation of the manual and, therefore, it is the one job that is likely to be bypassed. It takes time and thought and preparation to "sell" supervision on the manual—to insure the right attitude toward its use. When this step is not taken, however, it is easy to understand why the supervisor looks upon the manual as a straitjacket or even an alibi for dodging the blame when something goes wrong.

Many situations will occur which have to be handled with common sense. If the supervisor uses the manual as an alibi or crutch, he will fail in developing his judgment and in maintaining control of his department. As one management man put it, manuals are like budgets—a means to an end and a guide in the operation of the business. *The manual is no substitute for good supervision.*

To secure acceptance and understanding of personnel, there is nothing like *participation*. Let a man participate in a project and he will make it *his* project; he has accepted and approved it! Companies which have enlisted the help of supervision in preparing the manual usually have a well-rounded program of employee relations. They realize that all projects which have the backing of supervision also gain ready acceptance by rank-and-file employees. Usually the

HOW KOPPERS COMPANY REVISES ITS "MANAGEMENT PROCEDURES MANUAL"

A manual of this type to be of maximum value must be kept current with changing conditions and requirements. The control section's interest and responsibility in this connection is to set forth a method by which manual revisions may be originated and to edit, publish and distribute all such revisions.

The following method of reporting procedure revisions as these affect the procedure manual is outlined for the guidance of all concerned.

PROCEDURE:

1. Source departments should currently report to the control section in writing all procedural revisions already authorized by them which in any way alter or add to the existing procedures manual. Similarly each source department should periodically review its section of existing procedures as recorded in the manual.

    a. Each such advice to the control section should refer to the procedure number requiring revision and include a suggested draft of the revised procedure.

        1. If of a minor nature, only specific paragraphs affected need be rewritten and reference should be made to such paragraph numbers of the existing procedure.

        2. Major changes may necessitate a complete rewriting. (Extra copies of procedures may be obtained from the control section to be used as work sheets.)

    b. When desirable to add a subject not already covered in the manual this may be done by drafting such necessary data in its entirety following the general format of other manual subjects. Obviously no reference other than "new subject" can be indicated for the advice of the control section.

    c. All manual revisions resulting from advices so received will be edited by the control section and resubmitted to the source department for final approval before revision sheets are printed.

2. All staff departments and operating divisions affected by procedures originated by other units should also periodically review procedures as presently recorded in the manual and proceed as follows:

    a. All changes suggested by such review should be referred to the appropriate source department, furnishing data necessary for revision.

    b. Source departments should review such suggestions for changes and, if approved, they should be furnished to the control section in the same manner as outlined herein under paragraphs 1-a to 1-c inclusive.

    c. If the unit suggesting the change, and the source department have some disagreement concerning the procedure, the questions in dispute should be referred to the control section.

plan for obtaining participation by supervision includes bulletins and meetings. A bulletin to supervisors announces the beginning of the project and the importance management places upon supervisory participation and help.

Following this announcement, there are at least three meetings. The first explains, briefly, why a manual is necessary, what it will include, and how it will be used. The meeting should then be thrown open to discussion so that as many ideas as possible may be "tossed into the pot."

Second, after the outline has been developed and overall policies have been decided upon, there should be a discussion meeting to eliminate the "bugs." Finally, when the manual has been completed, there should be another meeting to clarify any problems or queries. This meeting should be held as soon as possible after the manuals have been distributed to supervision and before copies are turned over to rank-and-file employees.

One company follows up these meetings with a specially prepared form to secure recommendations regarding inadequacies in the manual, omissions, or faults. This form, which is distributed to supervision once every six months, insures to some extent the use of the manual as well as the building of a file of revision material for subsequent editions.

If cooperation with supervision is handled adequately, it also helps to improve the attitude of the supervisor toward his job. He feels he is more a part of management and responsible for some of the policymaking generally relegated to the "top brass."

By spreading meetings and bulletins out during the development of the manual, by making them interesting and informative, management not only gains the good will of the supervisor, but, at the same time, invaluable help in preparing the manual as well. Supervision *should* have a real contribution to make to the manual; if it doesn't, something is wrong with the selection and training of the supervisory personnel.

After the Manual Is Distributed

A number of companies admit to having failed to follow up the distribution of the manual to see that it is being used properly. Of course, when a new employee has his orientation interview with the office or the personnel manager, the manual is presented to him and explained to some extent. Some companies go a bit further than this and also see that the supervisor again explains the manual to the worker. Usually, however, the employee is on his own after he

CHECKLIST FOR INDUCTION MANUALS

I. *What is the publication planned to do?*

A. Answer routine questions about the company:
1. When it was established...........................
2. Who established it; describe the circumstances...............
3. Where it was established........................
4. Why it was established..........................
5. What it manufactures...........................
6. Number of employees...........................
7. Number of plants or branches.....................
8. Names and titles of executive personnel...............

B. Tell employees about their job:
1. Describe duties of the job.......................
2. Tell whether job is permanent or temporary...............
3. Tell how rate of pay for job is determined...............
4. Tell how employee's time is recorded.................
5. Tell how payment is made and on what day...............
6. Tell what holidays are observed....................
7. Give rules for punching time cards..................
8. Whom to notify when absent from job.................
9. Tell how to collect pay when leaving the organization.......
10. Tell how company will help employee save money...........
11. Tell about chances of advancement..................
12. Give rules for personal conduct while on the job...........
13. Tell about the need for badges and passes and other
    identification insignia.........................

C. Tell employees about health and safety:
1. Give right and wrong rules with illustrations for
   doing things...............................
2. Tell employee what to do when he has an accident or
   one happens to employee working with him............
3. Introduce the company physician and his staff; tell
   what their duties are..........................
4. Describe medical and hospital services of the company......
5. Tell employee about personal cleanliness..............
6. Tell employee about nutrition.....................
7. Tell about need for proper rest...................
8. Give employees suggestions for wholesome relaxation
   while off the job............................
9. Give rules for health and safety...................

CHECKLIST FOR INDUCTION MANUALS (Cont.)

D. Tell employees about benefits accruing from job:

1. Describe pension and retirement plans...
2. Describe bonus plans...
3. Describe sickness and accident benefits...
4. Describe hospitalization plans...
5. Describe stock buying or profit-sharing plans...
6. Describe awards and cash prizes for suggestions, attendance, safety, production, etc...

E. Tell employees about miscellaneous facilities available to them such as:

1. Cafeterias ....
2. Car pools...
3. Public transportation services—routes and schedules...........
4. Parking lots...
5. Check cashing service...
6. Shopping services...
7. Help in securing places to live...
8. Savings bank plans...
9. House magazine...
10. Plant recreation facilities...

F. Tell employees about their jobs and future with the company:

1. Tell about company's future plans...
2. Tell what such plans will mean to each employee...............

G. Tell employees about company policy:

1. Describe the company's reputation abroad—what it stands for...
2. Describe the service and manufacturing policies with regard to quality, future expansion and growth, and satisfaction on the part of the customer...

II. *How should the information be presented?*

A. Format:

1. Size ....
2. Number of pages...
3. Number of colors...
4. Self-cover or separate cover...
5. Type of binding...

CHECKLIST FOR INDUCTION MANUALS (Cont.)

B. Basic design:

    1. Straight text treatment.. ....

    2. Straight text with occasional pen and ink sketches................ ....

    3. Text plus use of pictorial charts and graphs............................ ....

    4. Text plus use of photographs.. ....

C. Possible illustrative material:

    1. Photographs of men at work.. ....

    2. Photographs of plants and offices.. ....

    3. Pictures of products.. ....

    4. Pictures of products in use.. ....

    5. Photographic trip through the office and plant........................ ....

    6. Pictures of junior and/or senior officers.................................. ....

    7. Pictures of recreational and other employee facilities............ ....

    8. Chart of main steps in manufacturing process........................ ....

    9. Chart showing departmental organization................................ ....

    10. Chart of production by products.. ....

    11. Chart showing end uses of products.. ....

    12. Map showing location of company plants, offices, etc............. ....

    13. Floor plan maps of the plant.. ....

    14. Pictures showing social benefits enjoyed by employees......... ....

    15. Reprints of company advertising.. ....

    16. Reprints of company trade-mark (s).. ....

    17. Photographs of employee activities (sports, social, etc)....... ....

    18. Chart showing interdepartmental relationships...................... ....

    19. Flow charts of work passing through the office
        and/or plant.. ....

    20. Pictorial statistics of company operations.............................. ....

    21. Photographs of safety devices and their use............................ ....

    22. Pictures of new machines and tools.. ....

    23. Pictures of typical employees.. ....

III. *How should the booklet be distributed?*

    1. At the plant.. ....

    2. By mail.. ....

    3. With accompanying letter.. ....

    4. With return card to acknowledge receipt................................ ....

    5. With name of individual employee filled in on cover
        or elsewhere.. ....

receives the manual. As one office manager says, "Frankly, I would say that we are a bit lax on following up the program."

The Tennessee Valley Authority "sells" the manual to employees in various ways. For example, all employees are invited to suggest revisions, and scores of suggestions are thus coordinated. TVA also holds refresher classes among all divisions in the regular training program. A monthly bulletin, *Office Oddments,* proves effective in suggesting uses for the manual. It also offers a means of keeping employees posted on changes and rules interpretations.

Not as much "selling" effort is required in handling stenographic or secretarial manuals as there might be in the case of policy manuals. The very nature of a stenographic manual makes it an essential —almost a daily—aid to the employee. Letters must be standardized, and, therefore, the employee must follow instructions in her manual. All that is essential, as a rule, is to go over the manual with a new employee on her first day at work. Any followup can be made by her immediate supervisor, who is in a position to answer any questions and to insure compliance with company rules and regulations.

Chapter 36

GETTING OUT THE CORRESPONDENCE

THE continuing spiral of inflation has sent the cost of the average business letter zooming upward. In the first analysis of such costs, made by Dartnell in 1953, the average figure was $1.17. Today, the same business letter would cost around $2.50. These figures are based on an annual survey of 8,000 companies, coast to coast, and statistically weighed.

The yearly increases are due primarily to increased labor costs: salaries of secretaries and of the executives who dictate letters, and wages for nonproductive labor, which add to overhead costs. Other influential factors are the upward surge of material costs and increased postal rates.

In 1953, the average salary of a good sales correspondent was about $75 a week. Today, his salary is generally about $150 a week. In 1953, one could hire a stenographer with at least two years' experience for a starting salary of $55 in big cities or $40 in one-industry communities. Today, the latest Administrative Management Society survey figures show, the average stenographer is paid $94 a week. Wages paid mail-room and file clerks have also increased.

A shortening of working hours in many offices continues. However, Dartnell's latest study of working conditions in offices shows over 65 percent of offices working a 40-hour week, 10 percent a 37½-hour week, and smaller percentages working 38½-hour weeks or less. Saturday work is rapidly becoming a thing of the past in most lines of business. Exceptions, of course, do exist among businesses which must retain Saturday hours due to their type of operation—dealing with the public, retail operations, etc.

Building cost is another item that has increased steadily. Space rentals in office buildings are up and annual rentals per square foot of space are at all-time highs.

According to the Dartnell study, the cost of an average business letter (one side of the letterhead—i.e., 200 words—or approximately a cent a word) can only go higher. Not only business costs but also the continuing reduction in the buying power of the dollar can be calculated to increase the expense of each written communication.

While it is quite true that the increase in cost of a single business letter as shown in this new Dartnell study is not in itself startling to some people, when you multiply it by the thousands of letters that the average business sends out in the course of a normal year, it becomes a cardinal part of the budget.

On the chart accompanying this text, subscribers will find some estimates of possible savings, based on the Dartnell study. The figures represent savings made by various companies that have come to grips with this item in the budget, thus making substantial savings without impairing the present effectiveness of their business relationships.

Whittling Down Costs

Savings of from 10 to 20 percent of what a company normally spends for business communications can be made easily if the various

Automatic typewriters can save a great deal of time, expense, and effort in turning out large numbers of individually typed letters. This Auto-typist can type up to 150 words a minute, yet can easily be stopped by simply pressing a control button for the insertion of a special paragraph.

AN AVERAGE LETTER COSTS $2.49—WHAT DOES YOURS COST?

Cost Factor	Average Cost	Your Cost	Ways to Cut Cost Factor
DICTATOR'S TIME Based on a salary of $150 a week and an average of 7 minutes for each letter.*	$0.42		Encourage shorter letters, increase use of dictating equipment, develop form letters when possible.
STENOGRAPHIC COST Based on a salary of $94 a week and an average of 20 letters a day, including taking dictation.*	0.94		Centralize stenographic and typing department, use automatic typing when possible, use advanced transcribing equipment and techniques, develop efficient style manual.
NONPRODUCTIVE LABOR Time lost by dictator and stenographer due to waiting, illness, vacations, etc. 15 percent of labor cost.	0.20		Consider pool operation, use form letters when possible, use telephone control at dictating time, use outside services.
FIXED CHARGES Overhead charges such as depreciation, rent, light, interest, taxes, pensions, and other costs. 45 percent of labor.	0.61		Review space use, study equipment available for greater efficiency consider number of employees needed.
MATERIALS Stationery, carbon papers, typewriter ribbons, pencils and other supplies.	0.07		Investigate better quality supplies, consider in-plant letterhead and envelope printing on office printing equipment, check sources of waste.
MAILING COST First-class postage (20 percent airmail), gathering, sealing, stamping, sorting and delivering to post office.	0.15		Study latest metering and mail systems, control use of airmail.
FILING TIME File clerk's time, cost of filing equipment, cost of supplies, etc.	0.10		Investigate new filing methods and systems, develop planned retention program, centralize filing to cut employees.
TOTAL	$2.49		**YOUR TOTAL**

*The salary listed for the dictator is based on an average between a sales correspondent and someone in sales or managerial capacity. Top executive salaries are excluded. The stenographer's salary stands between a senior stenographer's and secretary's wage. You can achieve more accuracy by using your own labor cost factors.

factors which affect their cost are analyzed *separately.* Such a study would include not only business letters as we think of them, but all communications a business has with customers; suppliers; municipal, state, and federal agencies; outside consultants; employees; stockholders; consumers; and the public at large. The factors to be considered include:

1. The time of the correspondent or executive who dictates the letter or bulletin, or carries on the telephone conversation.

2. The time of the stenographer (in establishments which do not use dictating machines) to whom the communication is dictated, including nonproductive waiting time, etc.

3. The time of the typist or dictating-machine operator who types the communication and prepares it for mailing.

4. The time of the supervisor or dictator, as the case may be, who checks the letter before signing and mailing.

5. The cost of the stationery on which the message is written, including the prorated cost of the supplies used and wasted.

6. The cost of transporting the message—messenger, postage, telegram, telephone, as the case might be.

7. The time of the filing clerk who must file the communication and the reply, call it up for further action if need be, and transfer it to an inactive file when the time comes.

8. The proportion of the general expense properly chargeable to the dictating, typing, mailing, and handling of communications; such as the wear and tear on typewriters, dictating machines, taxes on office space occupied by typists, etc. These items usually amount to about 100 percent of the cost of labor and supplies used.

In studying how various companies have cut the cost of their business communications, the best results seem to be obtained by a two-way approach to the problem: (1) Getting rid of frills, waste, and lost motion; and (2) improving the tone and effectiveness of communications, especially business letters, so as to make more friends for the business. The company that overdoes economy in its communications, such as using cheap stationery and letting letters go out with inked-in corrections to save retyping, makes a poor impression on prospects.

In reducing communications expense, there are many small economies which, added together, can effect great savings. The following ideas have worked for others and they may suggest ways you can trim the cost of correspondence:

1. Centralize purchases of stationery.

2. Stop rewriting names, addresses, and amounts by using mechanical writing devices. Call in systems men from companies that make name-writing and addressing equipment to get their recommendations.

3. Check your mailing room for efficient computing scales and postage metering machines, laborsaving folding and inserting and collating machines.

4. Keep mailing lists "alive" by weeding out dead names, fringe prospects, and incorrect addresses. Get out a clean-up mailing at least once a year.

5. Have cylinders or discs picked up at intervals to spread the transcribing department's work more evenly.

6. Compose standard form paragraphs which answer most of your routine correspondence. Number the paragraphs and indicate which ones to use on the letter to be answered.

7. Type the carbon copy of each reply on the back of the original letter instead of using second sheets. This system saves paper and halves the filing time. Further, the copy cannot be detached and lost.

8. Where there is extensive correspondence with the sales force, use comment slips instead of dictated letters.

9. Sort mail to branch offices and mail each batch in one omnibus envelope to save envelopes and postage.

10. Let mail-room employees fold letters and enclose them in envelopes, instead of having stenographers or secretaries stop to do this.

11. Use government postal cards to acknowledge orders and give shipping date or other information. These can be partly printed.

12. To speed replies when asking for information and to eliminate follow-ups, enclose a self-addressed envelope and ask the recipient to jot his reply on the bottom of your letter and return it.

13. Have part-time or mail-room employees come early to open and distribute mail before correspondents arrive at work.

How MONY Got Better Letters at Lower Cost

Believing that every postage stamp represents an investment in good will among its 1 million policyholders, and that when people write letters they want prompt answers, Mutual of New York recently announced 98 percent of the 156,000 letters it received during a single year were answered within three days. While such speed is enviable in itself, it represents only one phase of a letter-improvement program that has saved an estimated $85,000 a year and has also bettered customer relations.

Management's thinking about the program was explained in a statement by a MONY executive who indicated that "Most companies maintain contact with customers through letters. If those letters are not courteous, to the point, and helpful, then, of course, the company stands to lose good will. Further from an operations viewpoint, planned letter writing through the use of guide material certainly reduces clerical time and help, typing, and dictation—all of these effect considerable savings."

MONY began emphasizing the importance of letters as good-will builders after it surveyed policyholders back in 1941. The survey was conducted by Clifford B. Reeves, senior vice-president, who was then in charge of the letter program. Mr. Reeves discovered a chronic complaint of customers was that letters were too complicated to understand and frequently did not seem to answer the question. Often answers were delayed, and occasionally a policyholder felt he had to write again "for an answer to the answer." There were also signs of a lack of sympathy for the customer's problem and a tendency toward officiousness in the letters.

As a result of the survey, MONY started a campaign to "keep it simple," on the theory that people tend to mistrust things they do not understand. The company wanted customers to have a clear picture of their rights, privileges, and responsibilities. A program was set up with these objectives:

1. Systematize correspondents' methods.
2. Improve the quality of the correspondence.
3. Speed the flow of replies to letters.
4. Reduce the cost of producing letters.

An expert interviewed department managers to learn their special problems. Then he reviewed the letters being written and held discussions with home-office letter writers. A set of 125 guide letters was prepared to cover the main types of customer requests received in any agency office. Along with tips on how to "humanize" letters, these guides gave the writer a choice of language and eliminated timeworn and repetitious phrases. True to claims made for them, the sample letters enabled correspondents to double their output and at the same time saved from 20 to 70 percent in stenographic time.

A similar manual was prepared for use by the home-office staff, and later on a Correspondence Section was organized in the Policyholders Service Bureau (now the Service Division of the Office Operations Department). This section answers directly all letters received in the home office which contain several questions. Previously, such letters had been routed from one person to another until all the information was obtained. Now requests for answers to different parts of a customer's letter go to the various departments involved simultaneously, which saves a good deal of time.

Setting up this correspondence section also enables the company to keep a time-study record of all the letters received. When this practice was started, more than half of the letters received took six or more days for a reply. After 18 months, only 7 percent of the total correspondence was held more than five days. The following year, 73 percent of all letters were answered within three days, 26 percent in four or five days, and 1 percent took six days or longer. Six years later, 96 percent of the letters were answered within three days, 3 percent in four or five days, and 1 percent in six days or more.

These time-control records are kept for 21 departments and divisions, showing the date inquiries are received and the date they are answered. Monthly tabulations of these records, which go to all company officers, have brought about three important benefits:

1. They create a healthy, competitive atmosphere among various divisions.

2. By disclosing chronic tardiness in some sections, they pinpoint areas where management can take steps to improve work-flow.

3. They keep employees aware of the power of the simple letter to create and maintain good will among MONY's policyholders and other correspondents.

Even though a peak of answering 98 percent of its mail in three days has been reached, the insurance firm is not content to rest on its laurels. The letter program has enjoyed the support of top management from the beginning, and many methods have been devised to keep the 1,000 letter writers interested and enthusiastic. For example, a weekly news bulletin contains tips for correspondents like: "Don't open your letter by slamming the door in your reader's face." The consultant reviews carbon copies of all letters, holds monthly clinics, and trains new people to handle correspondence. MONY constantly looks for letter-writing ability in new employees and gives them every chance to develop this flair. Good letter writers receive pats on the back via the house organ and congratulatory notes from the executives.

Customers are not the only ones who count; field underwriters come in for their share of attention, too. MONY has explained to home-office employees that their letters to underwriters should follow the same principles used so successfully to keep customers' good will. In a bulletin, the company pointed out that "if we unintentionally antagonize an insured, he may switch his insurance to another company. Then we would probably lose one or two contracts. But suppose we rile or discourage one good productive agent, and he resigns and goes with another company. This can easily result in the loss of 30 to 50 contracts he probably would have sold for us over the year. And that can really hurt."

Currently, the bulletins prepared for letter writers are stressing the danger of becoming smug and complacent about the project,

and articles in *MONY Folks*, Mutual's house organ, remind correspondents of the benefits gained so far: "The enthusiastic response
from men in the field whose selling jobs you have made easier;
thousands of complimentary letters from policyholders; and a favorable public reaction that has been expressed in increased business
and company prestige."

THE QUALITY OF LETTERS

One company that realizes the harm a carelessly worded letter
can do is the Tandy Corporation. This Fort Worth firm has found
that it pays to review each of the 100 letters that leave the home
office every day. About 90 letters are okayed on the spot. The remaining 10 are redictated. Charles Tandy, chairman and company
president, feels that if 10 percent of the letters to customers do a
poor selling job, the company may lose 10 percent of the business
it has spent good advertising money to develop. The cost runs high
to develop each customer for this mail-order leathercraft firm;
Tandy does not want to alienate him with a botched inquiry reply.

"Under pressure of time," says Mr. Tandy, "even an excellent
letter writer occasionally turns out a letter which antagonizes or
disappoints the customer. Then the manufacturer loses the customer
—and usually he never knows why."

Mr. Tandy considers the customer with a complaint the most
valuable of all. "The fellow who thinks enough of your service to
kick, probably will stay with you for life if you straighten out the
matter to his satisfaction."

Sparking Interest in Correspondence

Getting everyone to cooperate in a letter-improvement plan to
insure its success can be handled several ways. The company magazine can help to create acceptance for a letter-improvement program.
At Continental Companies, the *Family Circle* digested the essentials
of the letter-writing course to be conducted by Mrs. Evelyn Couni-
han. To whet correspondents' interest, the magazine provided a quiz
so that everyone could rate his own letters, and a list of overworked
phrases to avoid. Letters by "Willie Wordy" and "Kenneth Conciseness" contrasted the long and short way to get the same idea across.

To keep employees interested in making their letters build good
will, many companies supply them with newsy bulletins. These bulletins usually illustrate good letters and take bad ones (unidentified)

apart to show where they went off the track. News of how others are improving letters keeps interest alive.

Letter-writing contests are conducted by many companies in an attempt to improve the quality of their correspondence. In some contests, however, the entrants only number those who believe they have a chance to win because they feel their letters are already of high quality. At The Gates Rubber Company, Denver, a contest has been developed which in effect makes an entrant of every employee who writes letters, assuring maximum benefits from the event.

Carbons of all letters written in a particular department go into a bound chronological file every day and the file is read by the department head and several supervisors. Knowing each letter will be inspected tends to keep letter-writing quality high. Awards are given for the best letters and there are opportunities to counsel with those whose letters show they need it.

Dave Large, letter counselor, describes a recent contest as follows:

The program was for our mechanical sales department (industrial, automotive, hardware, export).

Each month, on several unannounced days, we had transcribing save carbons of all letters of correspondents in the group.

From these samples we chose an award letter and three honorable mentions.

In our written announcement of winners, we discussed our reasons for selecting them.

There were two permanent judges: Dave Large, letter counselor; Charles Korsoski, assistant sales manager, mechanical sales. A different person was chosen each month as the third judge.

Many qualities were looked for in judging the letters. These included fast-moving openings, logical sequence of ideas, mustering of specific facts along with restraint in giving claims or opinions, skill in developing the "you" slant, simplicity and naturalness of expression, positive rather than negative phrasing, and closings which encouraged action or emphasized the basic idea of the letter.

While quality of composition was considered important, we counted as even more significant the *substance* of a letter—the resourcefulness shown in developing ideas. Closely related to this was the question of whether the writer had recognized what the true purpose of his letter should be.

The award winner received a cash prize, and had his name engraved on a letter award plaque. Each month this plaque hung in the sales division of the current winner. The division which had the most winners during the year gained permanent possession of the plaque.

Awards were made right in the sales department, with various department heads offering congratulations while *Progress News* took pictures. Pictures and news of the awards appeared in the next issue of the magazine.

You can see from this explanation that no letters were "entered" in the contest. Instead, correspondents knew that any letter written on any day might come under the eyes of the judges.

Because we sampled "working" letters, we did not expect the "polish" possible with a specially prepared contest entry. But we did find that most of our letters do a commendable job of carrying a straightforward, satisfying message to our customers and to our salesmen.

Five Tests for Better Letters

John R. Mayer offers these five yardsticks for measuring letter effectiveness:

1. *Sentence Length*—As most people know, interesting reading requires a variety of sentence lengths. Too many short sentences in succession are monotonous, and too many long ones are confusing. But in business writing it is especially important to avoid long sentences, for it is easier for a reader to grasp ideas one at a time than in groups of several. However, what constitutes a "long" sentence cannot be judged simply by the number of words. A 40-word sentence dealing with just one idea, or two ideas that are very closely related, is not necessarily too long. On the other hand, an 18-word sentence that tries to express several only slightly related ideas may be entirely too long.

To be on the safe side, it is wise to be suspicious of any sentence longer than 20 words. The simplest way to shorten such sentences is to break them up into two shorter ones, or to remove unnecessary words.

2. *Too Many Passive Verbs*—Perhaps you are one of those writers who has drifted into the practice of taking a weak stand on every other statement they make. You may feel that you will appear more objective, or at least more formal, if you are not too positive about what you say. And you may accomplish this by using passive instead of active verbs. For example: "It is believed," instead of "I (or we) believe"; "Application should be made to," instead of "Make your application to"; "The attached memoranda are submitted," instead of "We submit the attached memoranda."

Of course, a particular circumstance will sometimes make necessary the use of a passive verb. But this usage tends to be habit-forming and spreads throughout your style. As a result, your writing loses much of its force and becomes far less convincing than it might have been.

3. *Too Many Unfamiliar Words*—Do you feel that if your writing is dominated by simple, well-known words it will sound a bit childish? Some businessmen do. But there is nothing especially mature about being obtuse in what you say, and nothing childish about making your meaning crystal-clear. This is particularly sig-

nificant in business writing, which should transmit thoughts clearly and concisely.

The practice of using uncommon words is not confined just to long and complex words of general meaning, but includes vocabularies developed by each profession. Many words habitually used by engineers cannot be understood by most accountants, who in turn have their own vocabulary with which to confuse readers in other professions. Of course there are occasions where exactness of meaning requires a word of this kind, but all too often a writer uses such a word mostly to impress the reader with his professional standing.

If your reader is to clearly understand what you write, try always to prefer the simple word to the complex one.

4. *Unnecessary Words*—If you were given the job of selecting a staff for a particular function, chances are you wouldn't dream of assigning four men to a job that required only two. Yet you may be one of those writers who persist in using 10 words instead of five.

Unnecessary words not only help to confuse the reader, they also add to the time he must spend in reading your message.

5. *Words of Vague Meaning*—No matter how carefully we choose our words, it's never easy to tell other people exactly what we have in mind, for words do not always mean the same thing to different people. For instance, what is a "high" salary? To some men it may mean $25,000, while to others it may mean $15,000 or less. Other words and terms are even more indefinite, more abstract. Such words as "policy," "procedures," "conditions" can mean a host of different things to your readers because these words do not create a tangible picture. Most of the time it is both desirable and possible to avoid such vague words by using others that are more concrete.

These five most common defects are not the only ones found in business writing, but they are certainly the most important. If you can avoid them in your writing, you will have licked the major problem.

Off to a Fast Start

Cameron McPherson, well-known letter-writing expert, offers this advice:

The first five lines in a business letter make it or break it. When we sit down to dictate, we assume that because what we have to say is important or interesting to us, it will be interesting and important to the person to whom we are writing. Actually, that letter will be in competition with a hundred other letters for the recipient's attention.

That situation was not always so, but, as figures show, in the last five years the mail delivered to the average business establishment has more than doubled. Today, getting through the morning mail is a chore businessmen want to put behind them quickly. Executives have developed the habit of "sizing up" a letter and deciding whether to read it or toss it aside, according to what they see in the opening.

It is in the first few lines of your letters that the person to whom you are writing meets you. It is there the "climate" in which your letter will be considered is established. If you touch a live nerve, if you create the feeling that you are writing about a matter of importance to the reader, you will be on your way.

Among the facts of life that some of us never learn is that in order to get off to a good start in letters, or in personal contacts with people, we must talk *with* them and not *at* them. Don't try to tell people anything—especially don't try to tell them what they may already know.

When you are starting a letter, use your imagination and seat the person you are writing to just across the desk. Then in your mind, observe his reactions to what you are trying to say. This will help as you try to write your letters in friendly fashion.

So to get the best results from the letters you write, come to the point quickly. Don't depend upon trick approaches to get attention. Cleverness in letters may cause the recipient to think the fellow who wrote to him is a very clever young man, but a clever opening seldom creates a favorable climate. Rather endeavor to establish yourself as a kindly sort of person, with a deep interest in helping your friends with their problems.

Then touch that live nerve—make the recipient aware that you know his problem and want to help him. If he is a businessman and is interested in profits, let him hear the cash register jingle. If he is interested in prestige, put him in that picture, well up in front, but do it quickly. Don't wait until the last paragraph. Your reader may never get that far. If he is interested in security, then make it clear that this is your reason for writing.

Commonplace, stereotyped openings are all too common in business letters. The whiskers that marked the letters of a decade ago may have been shaved off, but too many letters are still unimaginative and commonplace. A slight twist of the wording, the "you" rather than the "we" approach, a fresh way to say the same old thing will give sparkle to an otherwise dull letter and put it on top of the pile.

Checking Mistakes

Mistakes cost money that no company can afford, but that is not all. If allowed to become a habit, the *esprit de corps* of the office suffers. Employees grow careless and shiftless.

There are many facets to the problem of getting rid of mistakes in correspondence. The first and most important step to insure accuracy is the refusal by management to condone mistakes. One Chicago company, for example, will not permit any letter to go into the mail on which an erasure has been made. It must be rewritten. Stenographers are not even furnished with erasers. This might seem to add

---

How to Figure THE FOG INDEX

STEP 1—*Count the number of words in a group of sentences.* Then divide the total number of words by the number of sentences. This gives the average sentence length of the passage.

STEP 2—*Count the number of words of three syllables or more per 100 words.* Don't count words that are: (a) Capitalized, (b) combinations of short words (such as "bookkeeper" and "butterfly"), (c) verb forms made into three syllables by adding -ed or -es (like "created" or "trespasses"). This gives you the percentage of hard words in the passage.

STEP 3—*Total the two factors just counted and multiply by 0.4.* This gives you the Fog Index.

	Fog Index	Reading Level by Grade	*By Magazine*
	17	College graduate	
	16	College senior	(No popular
	15	College junior	magazine
	14	College sophomore	this difficult)
Danger Line	13	College freshman	
	12	High-school senior	*Atlantic Monthly*
	11	High-school junior	*Harper's*
	10	High-school sophomore	*Time*
Easy-	9	High-school freshman	*Reader's Digest*
Reading	8	Eighth grade	*Ladies' Home Journal*
Range	7	Seventh grade	*True Confessions*
	6	Sixth grade	*Comics*

Try this "Fog Index," developed by Robert Gunning, on letters, memos, and reports. It won't be long before you'll be able to tell at a glance the good writing from the bad. (From "How to Take the Fog Out of Writing.")

needlessly to the cost of writing letters, but it tends to make stenographers and typists accurate, not only in their typing but in whatever else they do. When they have completed their "boot training" in the stenographic department, and are promoted to secretarial positions, what it cost to make them painstaking pays dividends.

Some persons are by nature careless and inaccurate. If those traits are strongly entrenched, they will never make painstaking workers and should be given work suited to them. For example, sales or sales promotional work which requires people who are creative, rather than painstaking in detail, is a good place for people with a high degree of imagination. Imaginative men and women seldom work out well in clerical work. On the other hand, people lacking the so-called creative abilities often have aptitudes for desk work and working with figures.

How to produce quality correspondence consistently is a problem for many businesses. Often it is an organization's most important contact with the general public. American Tobacco Company has improved the quality of its letters by routing them through a proofreading division. Other benefits of the checking are the saving in translation costs and the time saved in typing technical reports.

Ten college graduates with English or journalism majors check the work of 85 stenographers for perfect appearance and composition. They read transcribed letters and form letters for errors in grammar, punctuation, and spelling. They edit for coherence, and check letters against a file to be sure that addresses, dates, and references are correct. When errors are found, the checkers submit corrected suggestions to the correspondents for approval, on separate slips of paper.

Proofreading has also eased the recording burden considerably for technical men who often are eager to get facts down on paper without regard to grammatical form. Their reports are edited before the work is typed in final form.

Most of the American Tobacco Company girls know French, Spanish, German, or Italian, so they are able to handle the company's translations, which formerly were done by an outside service. The proofreaders also check stencils, statements, etc.

Certified Professional Secretaries

The lack of office standards prompted the formation of the National Secretaries Association more than a decade ago to raise the standards for secretaries. Chief among its projects has been its Institute for Certifying Professional Secretaries. Members and other secretaries who pass a 12-hour two-day examination receive CPS

Section 10: RULES FOR PUNCTUATION

Do you see the difference in meaning between—

1. "All of your switches, which were defective, have been returned."

2. "All of your switches which were defective have been returned."

If the difference is not immediately clear to you, read both sentences aloud, pausing after the commas in the first. Notice that the use of commas in sentence 1 makes the sentence say, "All your switches were defective and all have been returned." The omission of commas, in sentence 2, tells the reader, "Only those of your switches which were defective have been returned." (As a matter of fact, there are better ways of wording the sentence; the two examples given here are merely to show what a vast difference in meaning can be made in the same sentence by including or omitting commas.)

Here is another example of how punctuation can alter meaning:

1. I called your representative a chiseler, it is true; and I am sorry for it.

2. I called your representative a chiseler; it is true, and I am sorry for it.

Punctuation is a means to an end, not an end in itself. The one and only reason for the use of punctuation marks is to make the meaning of the words more easily understood. Therefore the one ultimate test for all punctuation is:

"Is this comma (or other punctuation mark) needed to make the meaning clearer?"

If it is, put it in. If it is not, leave it out. .

Some typists sprinkle commas, as with a salt shaker, wherever they pause in their typing, or wherever the dictator has paused to take a breath. Others leave them out entirely. There is a happy medium for the use of commas, as well as of other punctuation.

Following are some memory-refreshers which will help you become more adroit in making your punctuation clarify the meaning of the letters you type.

But remember, while the rules and examples given in the following pages will help you settle disputed or doubtful points, the ultimate test for all punctuation is:

*"Is this punctuation needed to make
the meaning of the words clearer?"*

Two sample pages from the Dartnell Correspondence Manual. *This manual, with pages permitting company personalization, is used by several hundred concerns.*

SPELLING

GENERAL RULES FOR COMPOUNDING:

1. Avoid the hyphen if at all possible.

2. Use two words without a hyphen if the intended meaning is perfectly clear.

3. If the meaning is not clear through the use of two separate words, write it as one solid word unless this obscures the meaning, makes the word hard to read, or confuses the pronounciation.

4. Then, and only then, use a hyphen.

NOTE: Observe carefully the difference in the meaning made by the hyphen in such words as:

re-create *and* recreate

re-cover *and* recover

re-count *and* recount

Cooperate, Co-operate; Coordinate, Co-ordinate: Authorities are about equally divided on whether these words (and others where *co-* is followed by an *o*) should be written solid or with a hyphen. Business usage favors the simpler form, *cooperate,* etc.

-ei, -ie: Remember the old spelling-book rule from schooldays?

I before E
Except after C
Or when sounded like A
As in *neighbor* and *weigh.*

Chief Exceptions: Neither leisured foreign counterfeiter seized the weird heights.

Final Consonants: One of the few rules which do not have so many exceptions as to make them worthless is the following:

Monosyllables and words
accented on the last syllable,
ending in a single consonant
preceded by a single vowel,
double the final consonant
on taking a suffix beginning with a vowel.

The only common exceptions to this rule are words ending in *x* (which is never doubled) and the following four words:

gaseous   gasify   inferable   transferable

certificates. These tests include dictation, transcription, grammar, accounting, economics, management aspects, office practices, business law, general clerical, judgment, and office problem situations.

To help ambitious women pass the examination, institutions like Northwestern University, the University of Michigan, Hunter College, and the University of Denver have set up review courses varying from 10 to 18 weeks. Masterco Press has published a book, *Business Theory for Secretaries,* with an outline for study.

By proving their qualifications for top-level secretarial positions, many CPS certificate holders have received promotions.

Dartnell Letter Manuals

There are many good books available, for the guidance of secretaries and others who write business letters, on such subjects as use of punctuation, proper abbreviations, improvement of spelling, and so forth. One of the most widely used is the Dartnell *Correspondence Manual,* now in its fifth edition. This spiral-bound manual is designed not only to lie flat on the user's desk but also has blank pages for letterheads, envelopes, memo forms, and other similar material, permitting companies to "personalize" the manual for their employees. Other Dartnell letter manuals in use by office administrators include *Tested Sales Letters* and *Credit and Collection Letters.*

Trim, compact design and simplicity of operation are emphasized in the Recordak Starlet Reader. Motorized starting, stopping, and direction of film travel are controlled by a single lever. Film loading, focusing, and fine-scanning controls are also within finger-tip reach at operator hand level. Only 16 seconds are required to advance or rewind a full 100-foot magazine or roll of microfilm.

Chapter 37

CENTRAL DICTATION AND STENO POOLS

ONE of the most effective ways to cut the cost of transcribing
business letters is to group stenographers and transcribers in a
central pool, instead of assigning them to various posts throughout
the offices. This system increases production, distributes the work
more evenly, saves space, reduces overhead, and makes it possible for
one person to supervise all the transcribers. Even relatively small
companies benefit from establishing pools.

Employers Insurance of Wausau (Wisconsin), cites its dictating
department as a good example of the effects achieved under a standardization program. At the home office in Wausau, all dictation is
done on 200 Dictaphone machines. Some fieldmen use Dictaphone
equipment in their cars, and similar machines are used in the 88
branch and service offices throughout the country. The same standardization, incidentally, is found in file cabinets, posture chairs,
desks, and other equipment. When employees are transferred from
one branch to another or to the home office, there is little adjustment
for them to make as far as methods and equipment are concerned.

Some organizations that have used steno and transcribing pools
for years continually look for ways to improve their usefulness. The
Baltimore & Ohio Railroad, for example, wanted to insure quicker
service in tracing freight shipments. Requests about the location of
shipments frequently accumulated on the desks of trace clerks because of the pressure of their other duties. Meanwhile, stenographers
who type and dispatch the telegrams answering these inquiries waited
for work. At intervals, dictated cylinders from all the dictators would
converge on the transcribers, creating peak loads that meant further
delay and overtime.

Finally, B & O replaced wax-cylinder dictating machines with a
telephone-type dictation system. Eleven telephone dictating stations
and two central recorders were installed. Now, the trace clerks dictate
replies as soon as they receive inquiries. Their words are recorded

on a plastic disc on one of the central recorders, and the stenographer transfers the disc to a transcribing machine and replaces it with an unused disc. The system provides a steady work flow, eliminates peak loads as well as the need for extra help, and speeds the replies. In addition, the railroad saves about $200 a year in messenger time needed to shave and deliver wax cylinders.

Network dictation has proved a boon for a Chicago insurance agency, too. G. A. Mavon & Company discovered that most of its dictators did not have enough correspondence to warrant individual machines. Sharing machines with several dictators was clumsy and delayed correspondence. Then Mavon tried the Edison Televoice system. Each man has a dictating station at half the cost of conventional machines. After a month, two girls were transcribing the work formerly done by several secretaries.

Maryland Casualty Company's Oklahoma City office is another convert to the network system of dictation, using seven phone stations and one transcribing unit. One operator transcribes an average of 7,000 words a day, and the letters from all departments are uniform in appearance.

A 16-phone Televoice system replaced 14 individual dictating instruments at Mutual Benefit Life Insurance Company, Newark. Besides saving 42 percent on original cost and maintenance, Mutual has given its claim examiners the fastest dictation service they have ever had.

RUNNING THE STENO POOL

There are many ways in which a good supervisor can act as "liaison" between the dictators and transcribers. She can schedule the work so that no transcriber is overburdened, and she can give the dictators a reliable estimate of how long a job will take. Where possible, she can split a task among several girls so that it will be finished quickly. When necessary, she can tactfully relay any fault a dictator may find to the girl who made the error.

One supervisor kept the work flowing smoothly and settled the problem of whose dictation should be transcribed first by numbering the cylinders in the order received. In emergencies, the supervisor would get the permission of the other dictators whose work had come in earlier to give priority to the rush job.

Another transcription department head urged dictators to send their discs to the pool in the morning while her typists were still fresh and not rushed. As a result, a sales correspondent who rearranged her work to dictate when the morning mail had been delivered noticed an increase in sales due to the prompt response.

How Employers Mutual Runs Its Stenographic Pool

Employers Mutual has had a pool since its early days. Policies regarding stenographic work have resulted in an efficient setup that gets the work out—and pleases both dictators and those in the pool. There are over a thousand employees in the home office located in a complex of three modern buildings. In the stenographic division, 14 women do the typing and 20 operators transcribe for 362 dictators. In addition, the pool takes care of Teletype and Western Union messages to and from branch offices.

Mrs. Lorraine Blieding, stenographic supervisor, describes the Employers Insurance operation as follows:

"There are at present more than a thousand employees in the home office. There are 362 employees dictating regularly and their work is done in the stenographic department by 20 dictaphone operators or transcribers. There are 12 secretaries who work for the president, three senior vice-presidents, nine vice-presidents and 20 assistant vice-presidents, managers, and specialists.

"There are 68 employees assigned to the stenographic department and they are as follows:

1 Supervisor	14 Typists
12 Secretaries	1 Xerox operator
2 Assistant supervisors and dictaphone operators	6 MTST operators (magnetic tape Selectric typewriters)
1 Dictaphone proofreader	1 Multilith operator
4 Copywork proofreaders	4 Communication operators
20 Dictaphone operators	2 Switchboard operators

"Most of our dictation is done by telephone recording. Seventeen Telecord recorders are used. Two of the machines are used for Teletype and Western Union messages exclusively. Executives and managers are assigned individual dictating machines and each department has one machine to be used for long reports or after working hours when the Telecord equipment is turned off.

"We also use magnetic-tape Selectric typewriters for producing our safety and health confirmation letters and elevator reports. We had anticipated an increase in production with a decrease in typists, plus a monetary saving. Actually, we were soon experiencing a 30 percent increase in work—over 100 percent increase in production with two less people and a monetary saving of three times as much as we had anticipated! We are at present making studies to use additional machines for other work applications.

"The Teletype, Western Union, and WATS communication is done in our communication room supervised by stenographic services, because of the necessity to coordinate the communications. The stenographic supervisor also was appointed technical advisor to the branch stenographic departments.

"Procedure and form manuals are issued to the branch offices from the home office. All the people trained for the various jobs are trained in the stenographic department, and in addition new dictators are also trained here before they start to dictate. This procedure is also followed in our larger branch offices. With this standardization and uniformity in dictating procedure, it makes it convenient for employees transferring from one office to another.

"It is also the responsibility of the stenographic department to train employees for our branch offices. We hope that with the greater availability of people from our small surrounding communities, it will be simpler to train them here and transfer them to our branch offices than it is for us to hire people in our branch-office locations.

"The stenographic department also conducts a training program as a service to our other departments. This training is for job applicants who have a low typing speed with great accuracy. The program is for one week, and its purpose is to increase the typist's speed so as to qualify her for one of our other departments which asks for part-time typing, writing checks, rough drafts, etc. The secretaries are supervised, trained, and promoted by the stenographic supervisor."

Morale in the Central Typing Pool

Because forming pools has "mechanized" correspondence and lessened the personal contact between dictator and transcriber, maintaining good employee relations is more difficult and at the same time more important. Relations with employees have a direct bearing on morale and turnover.

A company employing 200 stenographers made a survey to learn why so many quit. Chief among the causes reported were the dictator who insisted upon repeated revisions of his dictation and the chap who thought a stenographer was an errand girl. Those who stayed any length of time disliked being considered part of the office furniture by many of the supervisors and complained that some of these men never bothered to find out the stenographers' names.

Tools Save Transcribing Time

To sustain the advantages gained by speeding the dictator's work, it pays to equip each transcriber properly. Posture chairs, functional

A good worker deserves good tools. This Olivetti Underwood electric typewriter is one of many modern machines which make the secretary's job easier. Modern productivity levels cannot be achieved on old, stiff, inadequate machines.

typewriter desks, sound-deadening typewriter pads, and good lighting make the work easier and help the stenographer to accomplish more.

For neat, uniform appearance and increased production, an electric typewriter is a good investment. In fact, one company that had trouble getting enough typists switched to electric typewriters and found that four girls could do the work which previously had required five. It does not take long for a typist to become accustomed to an electric machine.

Copyholders are timesavers as well as aids to accuracy. Remington Rand's Line-a-time saves an estimated $87 a machine each year. A lucite magnifier has been designed for use with Rite-Line copyholders for fine print or copy that is hard to read. Abbott Laboratories, Ohio Brass Company, and Socony Mobil Oil Company, Inc., are among the users of Liberty copyholders, which hold copy in full view at sight level. A Dareda revolving bookstand holds dictionaries, directories, catalogs, and other large books at the right level for copying or reference.

SUGGESTIONS TO DICTATORS USING REMOTE CONTROL STATIONS

Butler Manufacturing Company

Your Televoice Secretary must listen to your dictation. When your dictation is clear and concise, your Televoice Secretary can do a good transcribing job for you. It is just as easy to make good recordings as poor ones. A good recording will help her to write your letters promptly and properly, and to produce letters you will be proud to sign.

PREPARING TO DICTATE

1. Notice your Televoice instrument to make certain that the line is not in use before picking up the handset. If the busy light is on, wait until the circuit is free.
2. Pick up the handset (busy light will come on).
3. Hold handset to ear in customary telephone position.
4. Press switch in handset to start the recording disc. Release switch to stop disc.

NOTE: Do not stack work but dictate as the need arises. Your Televoice system is similar to a party line—only one person can use it at a time. When you have a letter to write, pick up the phone and dictate it; then hang up promptly so that the line may be used by someone else. To promote efficiency, plan your letter before you pick up your phone—look up needed information, jot down an outline, make any necessary decisions about policy—then you can dictate without hesitancy.

DICTATING TECHNIQUE

1. Identify yourself.
2. Instruct the secretary, if necessary, as to type of letterhead and extra carbon copies required. A file copy will always be made.
3. Dictate the letter. Spell all names, addresses, and any words which are unusual or which may be misunderstood by the operator. Indicate trade names which require capitalization when they occur in the body of the letter.
4. Enunciate clearly and distinctly.
5. Dictate periods, beginning of new paragraphs, quotation marks, and parentheses.
6. Hang up at the end of each letter, or depress the hang-up switch for a moment. This punches a hole in the operator's index slip to indicate the length of the letter.

PLAYBACK

Press button on the phone while listening. (Do not press talk-switch in handset.) The playback will give you the last 20 or 30 words you have dictated.

SUGGESTIONS TO DICTATORS (Cont.)

CORRECTION

Press talk-switch in handset, say "correction," and while still holding talk-switch depress the button on phone base momentarily. (This punches a hole in the operator's index slip so that she will know where to expect the correction.) Give instructions and continue dictation.

RUSH LETTERS

Ordinarily it is not necessary to indicate that certain letters are rush because all of your dictation will be transcribed and returned to you within a few hours. However, letters dictated which must be mailed at a specific time should be called to the attention of the operator or the Secretarial Department Supervisor when that may be advisable.

WARNING SIGNALS

Occasionally someone's dictation will come close to the end of the usable space on the Televoicewriter recording disc. The recorder gives the following audible signals in your receiver to notify you when this occurs:

Ticking Sound—you have one-half minute more of dictation time left. Finish the paragraph you are dictating, then hang up the phone. As soon as the busy light goes out, indicating that the operator has put another disc on the recorder, pick up the phone and resume dictation.

Steady Tone—you have used all of the available space on the recording disc. Hang up at once. As soon as the busy light goes out, pick up the phone and resume dictation.

INTERRUPTIONS WHILE DICTATING

If interruptions are momentary, hold the phone for the moment, then go on dictating. However, interruptions may occasionally take your time to the extent that holding the line will not be fair to the others on the line. In such cases do not hold the line but ask the operator to hold the part of the letter dictated or to make a rough draft of it for you, if that will help, until you can complete the dictation; then hang up.

SAMPLE OF DICTATION

"This is George Smith speaking—an air-mail letter, please, with a carbon copy to John Doe—to Thomson—spelled T-h-o-m-s-o-n—Hardware Company—Hardin—spelled H-a-r-d-i-n—Oklahoma—attention Mr. Samuel Thomson—subject Butler-Built Steel Buildings—Gentlemen—Thank you for your recent inquiry about Butler-Built Steel Buildings—period—We are glad to enclose our catalog illustrating the various sizes and types of our buildings which are currently in production—period—paragraph— A variety of windows and doors—correction window and door arrangements can be had with these buildings as you will notice in the literature— period—paragraph—Send us a simple pencil sketch of the layout you have in mind and we shall promptly give you a detailed quotation with any suggestions that occur to us which may help you in your plans—period— Cordially yours"

Carbon copy sets are a boon to busy stenographers. Carbon Paper Pac Company suggests letting clerical help load the one- to nine-copy carbon sets to increase the output of higher paid stenographers and secretaries. Remington Rand's Beautyrite carbon paper saves typing time because it enables a typist to make 20 legible copies on an electric typewriter.

A paper or plastic recording sheet in the Vanguard makes it possible to send dictation in duplicate to a branch office or to an associate, complete with personal voice inflections and tones. A coated 8½- by 11-inch sheet is placed in the recording machine, together with an inexpensive sheet. After dictating, the original recording can be mailed as a sound letter, and the duplicate kept as a file copy.

Where the volume of correspondence is large, it pays to place dictators in rows and install a conveyor belt down the righthand side of each row of desks. The desk worker places any papers, dictation recordings, etc., on the conveyor, and they are immediately carried to the rear of the office where the central transcribing department is located. A clerk is on hand to take the papers off the belt and distribute them to the proper desks.

Steno Pool Trends

The pool has not, in most cases, replaced the private secretary. Top executives still rate "a girl of their own." However, there is a trend

Soundscriber's "200" BIC portable dictating machine weighs only six pounds and is powered by standard flashlight batteries. It is designed to fit all dictation, interview, and transcribing needs, and may be slung over the shoulder; carried by hand or in a briefcase or suitcase; or stowed in the glove compartment of a car or in a desk drawer. The microphone and mailable discs all fit into the self-contained carrying case.

to the use of machines, even so. As Robert N. Stewart, office manager of Butler Manufacturing Company, says: "Only department heads are assigned secretaries, but they are encouraged to use dictating machines, and many of them do. (A secretary does not necessarily use shorthand.)" Certainly, with the high cost of secretaries these days, it's more economical to save time with machines. Standard practice in many companies is to train the secretaries to take over the routine correspondence, have machine-dictated letters transcribed in the pool.

In other companies, assignment of secretaries, stenographers, or machines follows the order of rank. Such as: Executives are assigned secretaries, others in management are assigned stenographers, full-time correspondents are assigned machines.

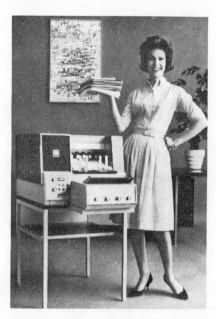

Microfilming of office records is often added to the duties of members of the stenographic pool. This Remington Rand microfilm camera will photograph both sides of a document simultaneously at the rate of 125 paper feet a minute. The camera is no bigger than a portable television set and can be fed by hand from one position, or automatically by a document feeder that will handle stacks of mixed documents.

In another case: "Secretaries handle various assignments in addition to dictation—decision is made primarily on nature of work with consideration to confidential material and to a limited extent on position held by dictator."

Following are some of the specific answers to specific questions on steno pool operation given by companies taking part in a Dartnell survey:

What Were the Reasons Behind Your Decision to Have a Pool Arrangement?

More economy, better supervision, more production..

Economy and effective filling of marginal manpower needs.

Timesaving.

Handle greater quantity of work.

Cut costs, improve efficiency, purchase new equipment.

Relieved departments of having individual secretaries as well as reallocation of work load.

Departmental overstaffing with underqualified stenographers; production peaks.

Ability to turn over more transcription at less cost and with less help.

To reduce number of secretaries and typists.

Full use of facilities of the system will save time spent by secretaries in taking dictation.

To increase efficiency of operators and be able to train various girls on all office typing.

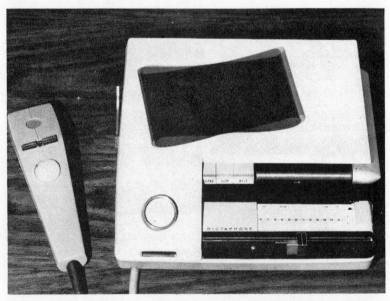

Less space than a letter is consumed by the Dictaphone Model/7 Time-Master. The smaller, lightweight unit is highly automatic. It was designed for Dictaphone by the Raymond Loewy—William Snaith, Inc., organization.

Need for general office assistance.

To provide typing facilities for areas too small to employ typists. To handle peak or overflow work. Training area for stenographic and secretarial help.

Reduces number of personnel needed. Distributes work more evenly so that all girls are busy an equal percentage of time.

To obtain the most efficiency out of a group of stenographers. To obtain more flexibility and more centralized supervision.

Too many secretaries and stenographers were being used only part time by men who *thought* they needed full-time girls.

What Were the Chief Reasons Behind Resistance to the Pool Setup?

Status, lack of understanding, and an unwillingness to cooperate brought about by poor selling of the plan.

Taking secretaries away from executives they liked to work for.

Dictators didn't like the idea of using machines.

Some difficulties in getting executives to dictate to machines. Machines require better dictators than secretaries do.

Dictators not used to machines, matter of prestige having their own private stenographers.

Dictators objected to losing personal convenience and prestige. Girls thought they lost their individuality.

Fear of loss of control and speed; fear that a pool cannot understand problems of other departments.

Lack of prestige. All secretaries like to feel they are assistants to busy executives.

Each supervisor prefers to have a girl that he can refer to as his secretary.

One or two dictators preferred a stenographer, or thought they did.

Loss of personal stenographers, prestige, and resistance to change.

Girls like "their own job."

How Did You Overcome Resistance to Central Pools?

Management directive.

Still working on this problem. Top management is behind it, however.

Decision made by top management and machines assigned to dictators.

Slow—must gradually be educated to machine dictation.

Time and education.

By demonstrating advantages over period of time.

Demonstration on a small scale that fears need not exist. From there we'll continue to expand.

We didn't. Some resigned, others were transferred. After we hired new ones for pool steno jobs, the resistance stopped.

Only partial.

The president of our company was strong for the change.

Management directive.

Pool jobs reclassified to the senior grade. More salary.

Do You Consider Your Pool Successful? On What Do You Base Your Estimate?

Increased production due to spreading of work as in the case of a large job. Uniform typewriters (same make) cut costs. Part-time people conscientious, usually older than the regular girls.

Less personnel needed. Efficiency and production greater in that same girls work with necessary reports, etc., and all are familiar with same.

Savings in both money and time. Stenographers are more flexible and efficient.

Savings the first year gave us a substantial profit on the investment.

Direct supervision of each girl's work provides for scheduling each one's time to better advantage; fewer girls needed, which effects a financial saving; increased production and efficiency.

Efficiency. Also having available a source of stenographers familiar with basic operations of the company.

Mainly savings in personnel and at times its production and efficiency.

Without the pool we would need 50 percent more stenographers or typists trained in transcription.

Efficiency, ability to handle work load of many people on several floors with concentrated effort. Full utilization of labor and supplies.

Efficiency in time and equipment investment; uniform supervision of personnel; flexibility in handling varying work loads.

Savings and efficiency. Pool would be better than adequate if girls with better training could be found.

Efficiency; provides for general training program for new employees; promotion made to departmental jobs.

Comments by Participating Companies:

All positions in department are evaluated, with minimum and maximum rates. We have junior typists, senior typists, junior transcribers, senior transcribers, and two assistants to department supervisor. Promotions are within the department. Our particular type of organization uses few girls in other departments, therefore promotions are not available outside the transcribing department. (A trade organization.)

Pool has been in operation only 10 months. Greatest problem is keeping trained girls. When operating for a three-month period with few changes, the pool proved very successful; but when girls leave, the problem of training causes a considerable backlog of dictation to be built up. Greatest backlog is two days; we have been able to give four-hour service when pool is up to strength and trained. (Scale and food machinery manufacturer.)

Our stenographic pool, which we call our Ediphone department, is made up of carefully selected persons who are encouraged to think of themselves as group secretaries, not just typists. They learn the problems of the several dictators assigned to them and are encouraged to correct obvious errors in dictation and to produce a superior product. (Insurance managers, mortgage loans.)

We just completed a thorough study of our correspondence and typing activities to uncover any areas in need of change and to find out if we can economize in our handling. We also desired complete information regarding our total work load to determine the possibili-

The electronically glued multicopy system known as Stub-Flo, developed by Hamilton Autographic Register, permits high-speed data processing or typewriter operations with up to five interleaved carbons. Used in typewriters, these forms eliminate the need to tear off each page after it is typed.

ties of centralizing much dictation so that a high quality may be maintained. We are now in the process of making the changes which were determined to be advisable. (Insurance, hospitalization.)

The central stenographic pool has worked very well at our company because the executives were behind the program from the inception. The standards for the type of work to be released by our stenographers are very high; but we think that each letter or memo represents the company, and each one should be perfect as far as spelling, neatness, and grammar are concerned. (Heating and air conditioning equipment.)

Most instructions to pool personnel are oral. These consist of: progress report on assignments, general information on office practices and procedures, local and corporate organization, personal appearance and behavior, product familiarity, safety and good housekeeping, and care of equipment. (Food processor.)

The steno pool under survey is not a general pool in the sense that anyone in the company in any department can forward work to it. The pool is under the supervision of the accounting bureau and will do work for other departments only if work coming from the accounting bureau is slack. (Electric protection.)

Chapter 38

THE SECRETARIAL MANUAL

THE importance of letters in business is demonstrated by the fact that the majority of functional manuals are devoted to jobs concerned with letter writing. These secretarial or stenographic manuals have come a long way from the little black books passed out to stenographers and typists in the past. Colorful covers, illustrations, and good layouts and indexes have made these manuals more attractive, more readable, and more useful.

Montgomery Ward's Secretarial Manual

A secretarial manual unique in arrangement is that prepared for the secretarial force of Montgomery Ward & Company, Chicago, entitled *Your Letters, Miss!* This is a die-cut job, spirally bound in bright blue, red, and white. Because of the die-cut arrangement, the index is on the outside of the manual, which has stiff covers. All the reader has to do is to open to the section indicated on the cover. This manual, too, is easy to read because of the good typography and generous use of white space.

On a following page is a sample of instructions from *Your Letters, Miss!* Note the generous use of white space, the good typography and arrangement of the text for easy reading.

While spirally bound manuals open more easily than those which use brads and slide fasteners, this type of binding is advisable only when there are likely to be infrequent changes in procedures or policies.

Few secretarial manuals cover the secretary's job more thoroughly than the one prepared by the Minnesota Mining & Manufacturing Company, St. Paul, Minnesota. All the policies and routine procedures which go along with the job are presented in careful detail—detail which is easy to understand and follow.

The manual is divided into several sections covering such essentials as: Letter-Writing Procedure, General Procedure (handling

CAPITALIZATION

CAPITALIZE

First Words (of a sentence or direct quotation)
He wrote, "Refund the money."

Proper Nouns—Names of persons, places, races, rivers, languages, departments, organizations, business firms, and trade names.

Jim Cauley's watch is a Bulova.

The Export Department sponsors classes in Spanish.

Montgomery Ward & Co. is located at the Chicago River.

Proper Adjectives (an adjective derived from a proper noun)

Her Canadian beaver coat is brown.

These are Irish linen tablecloths.

Refer to the New York style center.

Days and Months

Sunday, Monday, Tuesday, Wednesday

January, February, March, April, May

Holidays

Labor Day is always on Monday.

Armistice Day is November 11.

DO NOT CAPITALIZE

The second part of an interrupted quotation
"I," he asked, "you mean me?"

Common Nouns—The name of a member of a class or kind

The boy bought a wristwatch.

He is a merchandiser in the department.

Our company is located at the river.

Proper Adjectives that by common usage have lost association with the proper noun

chinaware, manila folder, morocco leather, roman type, india ink

Seasons

spring, summer, autumn, winter

The word *day* when it is not a part of the name

Thanksgiving day was cold.

They arrived Christmas day.

Sample page from Montgomery Ward's, "Your Letters, Miss!"

cables and wires properly, use of the telephone), Classifications of Mail, Company Products, Address List. Since this 8½- by 11-inch manual includes many forms and illustrations and each section has its own index, the material bulks rather heavily. The manual is loose-leaf so additions may be made whenever necessary.

One of the most attractive—and most modern—of secretarial manuals is *Right From the Start,* used in training stenographers and secretaries of the West Penn Power Company, Cabin Hill, Greensburg, Pennsylvania.

Spirally bound, in blue covers, with main dividers in a complementary color, and thumb indexed, this training manual has achieved a friendly style without the sacrifice of dignity or seriousness of the job. Wide margins of the 8½- by 11-inch pages, plenty of white space, and clear illustrations have made a readable, easy-to-use book.

The organization of the material in West Penn's manual is particularly effective. The three main sections—Stenographic, Secretarial, and Forms—enabled the writer of the manual to keep related facts together and thus make the manual easy to use. The section devoted to "forms" is the unusual feature of this manual. In most manuals, the essential forms are scattered throughout the text; this method makes it much easier for the employee to use the manual as a quick-reference guide.

Putting the Emphasis on Human Relations

Both in the writing of secretarial manuals and in their distribution, management must depend on an appreciation of human relations. It does little good to spend time, effort, and money on a secretarial manual if in the end it affects the employee the wrong way. Nor does it do any good to prepare an excellent manual and then make no attempt to present it properly to the people who are going to use it.

To see how the human relations element can be made to serve, look at the booklets prepared for the secretarial group of the General Electric Company. They are attractive in every way—colors used, typography, illustrations, copy style. And they are written from the standpoint of the user.

These booklets are five in number: *Strictly Personal, Your Manners Are Showing, Secretarial Skill, Strictly Business,* and *English Know-How.* The entire set is held together with a band bearing the title, "For Women Only . . . Especially Those Who Want to Get Ahead." With the set of booklets is a little sheet, "Memo to the Boss," which reads as follows:

Dear Boss,

The booklets which are enclosed with this note were prepared for the use of your secretary. We hope that the material contained in the booklets will help your secretary to improve her effectiveness on the job.

Before you present the booklets to your girl, you may wish to examine them yourself. It's just possible that you may find procedures described here with which you do not agree. While these are the practices most widely accepted and followed throughout the company you may have a perfectly good reason for not desiring to adopt any one of them for use in your bailiwick. You are the boss.

These booklets may also help you to understand the problems of your secretary, to review with her any local variations in these practices, and to explain the reasons for your decision. We know that if you will do this she will cooperate and accept your directions.

She is trying to do a good job—to be your strong right arm. If she is new to the business world—or to her present assignment—these booklets should help you in giving her technical guidance and personal counsel. She will always appreciate your guidance in her efforts to help keep your office and work running smoothly and efficiently.

Employee and Plant Community Relations

The booklet, *Strictly Personal,* covers use of make-up, suitable clothes for the office, cleanliness, personality. *Your Manners Are Showing* explains how to answer the phone correctly and covers courtesy and good manners in the office. *Secretarial Skill,* as its title indicates, includes helpful hints on taking dictation and suggestions on special secretarial functions. *Strictly Business* explains the procedures which make for a smooth-running office; describes the duplicating processes; gives filing facts; covers supplies, mail handling, and housekeeping hints. *English Know-How* is a handy collection of tips on dividing words, spelling, punctuation, grammar, correct use of titles, and abbreviations.

Revising the Manual

Once a company has decided to bring its secretarial manual up to date, it finds it is not faced with a serious or time-consuming problem because much of the material in the manual is of the "rule-of-

BUTLER MANUFACTURING COMPANY
SECRETARY'S MANUAL

STRICTLY PERSONAL TIPS TO STENOGRAPHERS
(FROM THE PRUDENTIAL INSURANCE COMPANY'S MANUAL)

1. Keep your personal appearance neat and businesslike, and not theatrical. Avoid extreme styles of clothing, startling hairdos, long brilliant fingernails, and heavy application of vivid cosmetics.

2. A word or two of greeting when you sit down to take dictation is a proper courtesy, but long conversations are distracting to a dictator when he is planning his letters.

3. Do not appear impatient while you are waiting for dictation. The tapping of a pencil or a foot is annoying. It is best to sit quietly with your hand and book in position to take notes.

4. If the dictator interrupts his dictation to answer the telephone or to talk to someone else, read the last several sentences in your notes so that you will be ready to read them back to him without hesitation upon his request when he is ready to resume dictation. If you have time, read through the whole letter, putting in punctuation marks and correcting poorly written outlines.

5. If you fail to hear what the dictator says, ask him to repeat the missing words while they are fresh in his mind, rather than waiting until he reaches the end of the letter.

6. If the dictator lets you work from his file, be sure to return it with all papers in order.

7. Treat your dictation confidentially, and do not discuss the subject matter with other employees.

thumb" kind. Generally speaking, revisions mean checking to see that the latest letterheads are used as illustrations, that forms shown are those in current use, that letter styles and instructions conform to modern day usage, and so forth.

One company faced with a revision job selected an employee in the standard practices division and instructed him to make up an outline of all the items management wanted to pass on to stenographers as guides or standards in the handling of stenographic work. The list, compiled from the old manual, included descriptions of how to set up a letter properly on the company letterheads, the various salutations to use, the standard complimentary close, correct phrases, and other routine stenographic requirements. From this outline, the various chapters of the revised edition were set up and passed on for use by the employees affected.

After these stenographic instructions had been in use for a while, a few questions or problems came up which could not be answered by the manual. These questions and problems were filed for future editions and revisions. This procedure recognizes the fact that even though the manual may be revised, it can still be more complete, and arrangements must be made for further revisions at a future date.

In order to make revisions as easy as possible, each manual prepared by this company has a standard plan of layout, consisting of title page, authorized distribution page, foreword, table of contents, index, text, and exhibits. Each manual is broken down into chapters, and each chapter carries its own breakdown of page numbers. Thus, the number of chapters in a particular manual can be expanded as needed and pages may be added or taken away from any individual chapter without affecting the page numbers of the other chapters.

This tryout system provides a good method of developing a really comprehensive manual for stenographers. By setting up the manual on $8\frac{1}{2}$- by 11-inch pages and putting them in a loose-leaf binder, it is easy to make additions when usage shows the manual to be inadequate. If the first try is mimeographed, it will run into very little money. Later editions can be run on letterpress and dressed up with illustrations.

Following is the introduction to the Butler Secretary's Manual:

"This manual is prepared in order that our Secretaries, Stenographers, and Typists may find it easier to learn and use our Company's standards relative to their work. It is not intended to supplant standard reference books but to supplement them.

"A copy of Dartnell Corporation's *Correspondence Manual and Transcribers' Handbook* (pages illustrated in Chapter 36), and a copy of an approved dictionary are made available to each stenographer. These books and other reference books, as well as this manual, should be diligently studied and used toward making our stenographic work and typing as nearly perfect as possible and to conform to our Company's standards.

"Each letter and any other piece of typewritten material you type represent our Company, and also represent you. It is to our mutual advantage that this representation will be highly creditable. Attractive, well-typed letters reflect high quality of performance and products. Smudged, poorly typed letters, on the other hand, give a poor impression.

"You will use your initials and the initials of your dictator on all letters you type, and on all other typewritten material, unless otherwise directed. Your initials may well be considered your personal trade-mark. Let them always be the mark of good workmanship in which both you and our Company can take pride.

"Keep your Secretary's Manual as well as other manuals and reference books which may be assigned to you in good order so that they may serve you well. Become expert in their use. A good workman is known by his tools. He keeps them in good condition and does good work with them.

"Pages three and four illustrate our standard form for letters to other firms or persons outside our Company. Page five illustrates our standard form for Intra-Company letters. You will please observe the instructions contained in those letters and in the following pages of this manual."

HOW TO PRODUCE AN EFFECTIVE MANUAL

The secretarial manual has been generally found to be one of the most useful tools for increasing secretarial efficiency, and thus reducing office operating costs in relation to productivity. A specialist in this area is Miss Marilyn French, editor of women's publications for The Dartnell Corporation. These publications include secretarial booklets, and *From Nine to Five* monthly bulletins for white-collar girls. Miss French is coauthor of the Dartnell *Correspondence Manual and Transcribers' Handbook*. She was secretary to J. C. Aspley, the founder of Dartnell, and is a past president of Lake Shore Chapter of The National Secretaries Association (International) in Chicago.

Miss French, after a special study of secretarial manuals, points out that a company needs such manuals (1) if it has a large number of secretaries and stenographers, (2) if it has many executives, (3) if it has several brands, (4) if it has diverse products and lines or peculiar terms, (5) if it has numerous departments, (6) if it uses a variety of letterheads and forms. Even medium-sized and smaller companies have found a manual worthwhile, for it offers many benefits, among which are—

1. Policy on correspondence, telephone procedure, and other means of communication is set down in compact reference form;
2. Employees know what is expected of them and how their work should be done;
3. All letters and forms are handled in uniform manner;
4. Information about company executives, branches, products, etc., is at the employee's fingertips;
5. Training time for new employees is reduced;

6. Supervision is easier because the manual covers most questions;

7. Work is simplified by outlining the best procedure for each job;

8. Job analysis is automatic, because procedures must be studied so that they can be described accurately and clearly;

9. Outmoded practices and unnecessary forms are brought to light.

One company found an additional advantage: When it had to re-establish a discontinued procedure, this was done quickly by re-surrecting the proper pages from an old manual.

Physical Appearance

Packaging the material is important. The manual doesn't have to be flossy; it should look businesslike and neat. Bulky, unorganized manuals are licked before they start, and they usually wind up in the bottom drawer of the desk.

About half the manuals are spiral bound so that they lie flat on the desk when open. Loose-leaf binders are also popular. A few manuals consisted of information sheets stapled together. The pages of these were mimeographed or were reproduced on a spirit duplicator.

Standard size is 9 by 12 inches. Most of the manuals are multi-graphed or offset printed; although a few, run in large quantities, are letterpress. White paper predominates, while special sections may be printed on yellow paper to stand out. In large manuals, colored dividers separate the sections.

Clear printing, plenty of white space, and subheads to break up the pages and for easier reference, make a manual attractive and readable. Illustrations may not be necessary, although some manuals use line drawings or charts to play up important points.

Getting Specific

Companies with problems peculiar to their business put special instructions in their manuals. For example, a manufacturing firm includes a glossary of technical terms. Others show code words to save money on telegrams. And the *Secretarial Development* manual used by Southwestern Bell Telephone Company devotes the largest of its 15 sections to telephone procedure and courtesy. Equally important as the contents is the way in which the material is presented. The instructions must be clear and complete in order for the secretary to follow them.

Obviously, the manual should be written by someone who is thoroughly familiar with company procedures and who can express them clearly. Large companies assign this "manual labor" to a special staff. In the smaller firm, the steno-pool supervisor or a secretary with seniority, often the chief executive's assistant, may compose the manual. Usually, the steno-pool supervisor has a secretarial background and a flair for teaching. Since she knows the work and how to explain it, she is a good choice for the job. She also knows which points are most confusing to her girls and need more explanation.

To make sure that the manual is easy to understand, one office manager asked a beginning stenographer to set up sample letters and forms by following the directions in the first draft of the manual. Her efforts and the questions she raised guided him in rewriting some of the material.

He explained, "A senior stenographer or secretary would have known the right way to do these tasks by experience. I felt that if a beginner could follow the text, it would be clear to all." He intends to use the same idea whenever he adds new material.

Whatever the format, the first few pages often determine whether the secretary will want to read the entire book. Most manuals begin with a brief explanation of their purpose designed to "sell" them to the user. This device is effective if it's written from the "what's in it for me" angle.

A simple list of contents for quick reference is a "must." Basic as that may seem, there are a few manuals that omit this feature. If you want your employees to find the treasure in the manual, you should give them the "map."

What to Include

One rule of thumb for what to include in the manual is: "What does a secretary need to know in order to do a good job here?" She needs to know your company's correspondence style; information on executives and titles; departments and duties; information of branches and their key people; company products and brand names; telegraph, telephone, and Teletype procedure; frequently used technical terms; preferred abbreviations. Sample letters, memos, and forms should be included; they are better guides than detailed instructions.

Some secretarial manuals go further. These include company rules, personality pointers, reminders on grooming, office etiquette, hints for getting along with the boss and co-workers. These suggestions will get a favorable reception if they are written in friendly style. If company rules appear in the general employees' handbook or welcome booklet, the manual can skip them.

Getting People to Use the Manual

Several office managers have complained that no matter how good a manual is, they have trouble getting employees to use it. "The easier you make it to use the manual, the more successful you'll be," advised one office manager, who did the following:

1. Listed the contents and page numbers;
2. Put the most frequently needed material in the first section;
3. Printed each section on a different colored paper for quick finding;
4. Ran a complete index in back, which took several pages;
5. Put all sample forms and letters in one section, instead of scattering them throughout the manual;
6. Cross-indexed instructions to the sample letters by page number.

He added, "The office supervisors know the manual from front to back, and we politely refuse to answer any question covered in it. We tell the girls, 'That's in your manual on page . . .' "

Other companies presold the manual and insured its acceptance by holding meetings among supervisors. Their suggestions and ideas were incorporated in the manual, which gave them a sense of participation. After the manual was printed, each supervisor was asked to call his employees together and explain the manual's contents and special features. Both supervisors and employees are urged to submit questions and suggestions to make future editions as clear and simple as possible.

Keeping the Manual Up to Date

Many companies start out with good manuals but find it hard to keep them up to date. Normal turnover and promotions will make some of the "who's who" lists obsolete. A merger, new products, centralization, decentralization, branch or division moves, policy changes also outdate the materials.

For this reason, loose-leaf binding seems best, because pages can be rewritten, added, or deleted. One office manager solves the next problem—getting employees to insert new material, by collecting outdated pages when he distributes revisions. "I wait while each secretary takes out the old pages and substitutes new ones. The most complete information won't do any good unless it's in the proper place. This takes time, but it saves a lot of errors and confusion."

Another office manager found a different solution. "I ask several employees to cut stencils for revised pages. They absorb the new directions while they type masters and run off copies, and their interest is aroused." When a secretary or stenographer is waiting for work, he suggests, "If your manual isn't up to date, why not do that now."

How Southwestern Bell Uses Secretarial Development Manuals

Southwestern Bell Telephone Company, Oklahoma City, Oklahoma, has a "Secretarial Development" manual used by the personnel department. Miss Frances Koop, personnel training assistant explained, "The manual sets up the pattern and material for a program designed to assist the secretary to increase her overall effectiveness."

All 65 secretaries have received this training at various times. Classes are limited to 12 secretaries for better "audience participation." It takes six days to cover the material—either a full day once a week for six weeks, three days a week over a two-week period, or two days a week for three weeks. Fifteen main topics are discussed, with emphasis at each meeting on "Job Planning and Organizing." Each secretary develops an individual job plan that dovetails with her duties.

This manual is a complete leader's guide. It outlines various phases of each main topic, shows when to ask questions, how to keep the discussion on the track, when to pass out related material, which points to emphasize.

Chapter 39

HANDLING THE MAIL

$\mathbf{F}$AST opening and distribution of the daily mail makes it possible to answer incoming letters the same day, and customers appreciate the fast service. Many large companies have laid out their offices to facilitate the flow of mail. At Crowell-Collier-MacMillan, the mailroom shares its space with the cashier's section of the accounting department. This is convenient because much of the incoming mail contains stamps and money for service items advertised in its magazines. Mail clerks remove the remittances and pass them on to the cashier. A messenger takes the service requests to the company's mailing service bureau near the post office.

Government Employees Insurance Company, Washington, D. C., also has planned its office layout according to the routing of mail. The mail department on the first floor opens the mail and sends it to the second floor, where it is verified—by a master index, as to policyholder—classified, indexed, and routed to the proper division or regional area.

Conveyors transport the mail at Lever Brothers' glass skyscraper in New York; at Minnesota Mining & Manufacturing Company; and at Smith, Kline & French, Inc. At the 3M company, the mail is automatically deposited on the various floors, where it is picked up for distribution to various departments.

At The Upjohn Company Portage plant, mail is transported in several ways—in large brown envelopes carried by messengers, in carts similar to those found in supermarkets, or via a small electric truck which takes care of delivering packages and large bundles of mail to various points in the big plant.

Incoming Mail

What is the most efficient system of handling incoming mail? Should an executive or a mail clerk open the mail? Is it important that executives get their mail first thing in the morning?

These questions have come up, at one time or another, in most offices. There have been cries of anguish because personal letters were opened, because an executive thought somebody else was getting letters which rightfully should have been delivered to him.

In trying to get an answer to these questions, a number of companies of various sizes have been questioned to see how they handle the problem. In general, the pattern seems to run something like this: In larger offices, an individual picks up the mail early in the morning. It is sorted, usually by clerks who are supervised by somebody with a little more authority than they have. Letters addressed to an individual are not opened, but mail addressed to the company is opened by machine.

Most companies time-stamp their incoming mail, and several firms hold on to "empty" envelopes for a prescribed time for reference if something is missed or there is some question about a name or address. The opened mail, together with the unopened correspondence, is then delivered to the executive or to his secretary. It is generally the executive who decides whether or not his secretary will open his personal mail.

Mail for The Borden Company of New York City is picked up at the post office early in the morning by an independent carrier service and delivered to the Borden mailroom before 8 a.m. The mailroom staff opens and sorts the mail by department, and delivers it in carts to 48 delivery points in the 23-story headquarters building. Desk-to-desk distribution is handled by the department itself. The first delivery is around 10 a.m. Departments wishing mail earlier may send an employee to the mailroom to pick it up.

Envelopes opened in the Borden mailroom are kept for one week. This is because the envelope may provide clues to the time and place of mailing or the full address of the senders of occasional "problem mail."

The type of mail-handling system used depends upon the size of the company or other influencing factors. In many cases, an executive has the responsibility, but other employees will actually carry out the details of a company's system. For instance, the Intertype Company, Brooklyn, gives the mail-handling responsibilities to the assistant secretary. The manager of the mail department sorts incoming mail, but he turns over all mail addressed to individuals to the assistant secretary. This executive inspects the "personal" mail and turns back to the mail department manager correspondence which comes from vendors, branch offices, or similar sources. This mail is then opened with the regular company mail. The correspondence that appears to be personal is distributed unopened. Intertype's executives arrive at their offices rather early, but the mail department gets an even earlier start. Mail is on their desks when the executives arrive.

Officers at First Federal Savings and Loan Association, New Haven, Connecticut, also get their mail early. In this case, the mail is on the desks before 9 a.m. each day. First Federal deposits all empty envelopes from incoming mail in a special receptacle so that they can be easily checked for missing items, if necessary.

In many cases, a mail-handling system must be tailored to meet special needs. The City Public Service Board of San Antonio, Texas, opens all envelopes of mail remittances (from gas and electricity customers) by machine—but leaves them in the envelopes for the cashiers to handle because of the importance of mailing date and address. These mail remittances are addressed to the organization and not to the attention of any specific department or particular individual.

The Thomas-Diggs Company, wholesaler in Sacramento, California, has its own special procedure. The mail it receives from the East usually contains only factory invoices or details concerning orders or shipments. This eastern mail is placed in one pile and sorted according to departments. The factory invoices are then run through a dating machine and the company thus has a record of the date the invoice arrived.

Murphy & Rochester, Inc., Odessa, Texas, has its own special mail-handling system, because of the complexities of its small business (insurance, real estate, and mortgage loans). An executive normally handles the mail under the general insurance portion of the business. It is important that he keep up with what is happening on each individual policy, and considerable detail work is therefore necessary.

In the real estate and mortgage loan department, the secretary handles the mail, for she can expedite much of this correspondence without having to consult an executive.

The size of a company naturally influences the mail-handling procedure, as in the case of National Bank of Commerce, Pine Bluff, Arkansas. The officers' mail is distributed unopened, and a vice-president opens the general mail with one of his assistants. Each officer opens his own mail and distributes it.

Citizens Finance Company, Grand Junction, Colorado, has its mail opened by the president and general manager. In fact, the president says, "I am one of the old fogies who still believes that the head of a company should have something to do with the opening of mail. During all my years of being in business, I have made it a practice, when I am home, to go to the post office and get the mail and then sit down and open it. In this way, I can keep my fingers on the pulse and know about what is going on in the different departments. When I am out of town, my assistant manager gets the mail and he follows through practically the same procedure."

Speeding Mail Distribution

Businessmen often complain that it takes longer for an interoffice memo to travel across the hall to the next office than it does for an airmail letter to fly across the country.

In an age of heightened communication, with nobody-knows-how-many-millions of letters, memos, notes, or forms asking for immediate action every day, any delay in mail distribution can be a pressing problem—and the bigger the company, the bigger the problem.

The Esso Research and Engineering Company, largest United States petroleum research firm, is faced with the task of distributing

Mail girls at the Eastman Kodak office building prepare to start on their rounds.

mail regularly to at least half of its 2,400-plus employees in four separate New Jersey offices in the Elizabeth-Linden area (another 100 employees are in the company's New York City headquarters offices).

To streamline the distribution of mail—which includes some 650,000 pounds of incoming U.S. and overseas mail a year—the research firm tackled the problem from three different directions through a current companywide study of all operations.

One step was to begin overhauling a system of central and subsidiary mailrooms. At one company site, the Esso Research Center in Linden, mail had been handled to a large degree by separate company divisions operating from their own mailrooms. Consolidation of the mail system resulted in a central mailroom that handles the whole job, and freed three smaller mailrooms for other productive use.

Step two was to buy a fleet of 17 specially constructed mail carts not unlike the grocery carts used in supermarkets. The top "basket" of each cart is equipped with labeled folders so that mail can be sorted as it's picked up, rather than returned to a mailroom for sorting. In many cases, a piece of interoffice mail is distributed to an addressee along the same mail route a few minutes after it leaves an office. Seven of these carts are being used at the research center; the others are in use at other company installations.

Similar carts for pickup and delivery of mail are providing improved all-around mail service at Eastman Kodak Company's general offices in Rochester, New York.

Nearly one-half million pieces of intracompany mail and incoming and outgoing post office mail (excluding parcel post) are handled each month by these offices.

The lightweight mail carts, which recently replaced the leather mailbags worn with a long leather strap over the shoulder, enable mail girls to handle a greater volume of mail and with greater convenience than under the old system.

The amount of mail that formerly could be carried was limited because of the relatively small size of the mail pouch and, of course, because a particularly heavy delivery or pickup of mail might be burdensome to the mail girl. So much more room is provided in the carts that incoming and outgoing mail from company departments can be handled with ease.

This has also helped to reduce greatly the number of special trips to a particular department to handle mailings of extraordinary volume, as well as making it possible to reduce the number of regular mail trips required a day.

The carts are easily maneuverable, and no difficulty has been experienced in rolling them on or off elevators and through aisles in offices or other departments. The top rack is used for mail being delivered; the bottom rack is for mail pickups.

Reducing Mail Costs

Steadily rising postage costs are causing companies with even moderate-sized postage bills to critically examine the way their outgoing mail is handled. Savings made there might conceivably offset much, if not all, of the increased expense.

Although many companies report the installation of efficient machinery and equipment to improve mail handling, a close-up study of their systems reveals the adoption of a great variety of simple devices and methods which can be used by others.

For example, a look at the mail-handling system of National Family Opinion, Inc., probably the biggest volume customer of the Toledo Post Office, uncovers eight cost-cutting ideas:

1. Reliable part-time help is used to eliminate occasional idleness that is the plague of many mailroom operations. The company employs only seven full-time people in the mailroom. In a typical week, the mailroom put in 440 work hours, half by full-time help and half by the part-time "bench strength." Idle hours eliminated save thousands of dollars a year.

2. Proper scheduling of jobs so they are ready when people are. Expensive "get ready time" is saved.

3. When an assembly line is used in getting out a large mailing, one side of the table is kept clear to facilitate the feeding of materials to the workers, thus avoiding the congestion so usual on mail tables.

4. Using automatic staplers cuts stapling time 30 percent. One person can complete the stapling of 2,000 double postcards an hour, as compared with 500 stapled by hand.

5. Timesaving equipment such as postage meters, tying machines, envelope openers, label wetters.

6. Different slogans printed to the left of postage marks on return mail speed sorting of about 10,000 pieces a week. About 20 dies, ranging from "Support Your Local Red Cross" to "Employ the Handicapped," are each used about once a month to identify a prepaid piece. Sorting by slogan eliminates the checking of each return piece for subject matter.

7. Cut the time involved between the hour a job enters the mailroom and the time it moves out. Idle mail ties up traffic.

8. Watch the weight of outgoing pieces. Recently, a postage saving of $600 resulted on a 10,000 mailing by advance planning that made it possible to eliminate one page.

How Sorting Table Helped Upjohn's Mail Service Problem

A problem every company must face is that of its mail and delivery service. The Upjohn Company of Kalamazoo, Michigan, has helped this challenge with a unique modern system. The hub of activity in the mailroom is an "ultra-efficient" mail-sorting table. From the center of the circular table, one employee sorts the mail into separate bins for a number of different routes.

Each mail messenger uses a cart. Mail is sorted into a big file folder in each cart for delivery along the route. This method eliminates carrying heavy folders of mail and putting them down at each stop. In order to use this cart method, a hydraulic lift was installed for moving the cart between floors. It takes 30 seconds for the platform to move to the desired level.

There is an hourly delivery and pickup servicing 12 buildings and 1,000 people. All the buildings are connected, so that messengers need not go outside any building. Parcel delivery and pickup service are handled by a man, while the mail messengers are girls.

Upjohn also uses this mailroom as a center for preparing U.S. mail for the post office and assists on other types of work such as envelope stuffing, special typing jobs, providing temporary replacements for secretaries. The mail messengers eventually transfer to office jobs throughout the company.

According to The Upjohn Company, use of these improvements makes the handling of mail and parcels less burdensome, in addition to making it possible to offer faster and more efficient service. Equally important—people who work in the mailroom are proud of the efficient way they can provide delivery service.

The Illinois Bell Telephone Company uses a battery of high-speed inserting machines in the mail division, and a labeling machine which can label up to 10,000 pieces of mail an hour.

Outgoing mail for Chrysler dealers is assembled from all departments at the central mailing department and placed in a single envelope for each dealer. A pigeonhole board is used to collect the mail for each dealer. The "boardmail" plan effects big savings in postage.

Chrysler reports the use of a conveyor belt system for collating uniform mailings that must be sent to all dealers. At the end of the belt, finished envelopes are sent to the metering machine located in the central mailing department on the floor below. About 800,000 envelopes are metered a month.

Mail going daily to branch offices of Friden, Inc., is sorted in bins that have been arranged alphabetically by the principal cities.

A small compartment of each bin carries preaddressed envelopes and labels for each branch for quick handling of mail. Each bin is labeled to indicate cities to which mail is to be sent airmail and cities which are reached by regular mail overnight—an easy way to save postage.

The new building of Automatic Electric Company is well equipped with various modern devices for speeding the handling of mail, including handy Chesley mail carts and a 39-station pneumatic tube system.

Westinghouse uses a variety of devices on wheels in addition to light-duty carts and heavy-duty push trucks for loaded mail bags. To cover long distances around the plant, tricycles are used at Kansas City and electric scooters at Columbus. At South Philadelphia, a station wagon makes deliveries and pickups.

The company spends more than $4,000 a day for postage, and

Versatility has been built into the later models of mailing machines. This type of machine can be used for stamping, postmarking, sealing, and counting letters up to 150 a minute; for check signing; for backstamping incoming mail; or for sealing envelopes without metering.

Courtesy, Pitney-Bowes, Inc.

the metering system is watched carefully for opportunities to cut postage.

These are just a few of the money-saving and mail-speeding ideas reported by various companies. Most executives in these companies agree that there are plenty of opportunities for improvement any time and that constant vigilance is necessary to spot the opportunities and take advantage of them.

MAILING ROOM EQUIPMENT

Steadily rising costs of labor in the mailing room have made it imperative that facilities for getting out promotional matter quickly and efficiently should be modernized. Hand-addressing, sealing, stamping, and sorting are no longer economical and are now done by machinery. Even gathering, a tedious operation, is now done mechanically in mailing rooms where large quantities of the same type of mail matter are handled. Such equipment should be the best.

Many addressing or mailing departments prerun envelopes or labels for all branch offices, salesmen, dealers, or other groups which receive mail regularly. These labels or envelopes are kept in special racks, and as the mail reaches the mailing room the contents are sorted into racks which already contain a supply of preaddressed envelopes or labels. This plan speeds the work and tends to level out peaks and valleys on schedules, because the addressing can be done at times when the staff is not busy.

Selection of mailing and addressing equipment can be done intelligently only after a careful analysis of every kind of mail handled in the organization. Salesmen for the office appliance companies are usually well informed and no one should hesitate to call them in for consultation and help.

Addressing Equipment

At present wage rates for white-collar help, hand-addressing is usually too costly for any consideration. It is both too slow and too inaccurate. Hence, machine-addressing is a "must."

Basically, there are two types of addressing jobs. The first, and most important, is the addressing job which must be done over and over again. In this category is the list of employees for mailing house magazines, announcements, etc.; then there is the list of dealers, wholesalers, or customers. Add to this the list of salesmen, manufacturers' representatives, fieldmen, branch offices, agents, or others who receive regular mailings.

The second type of addressing job involves the special mailing, in which a list, large or small, is addressed perhaps only once or twice a year.

For the regular weekly or monthly mailing, the addressing machine, working from pre-cut or pre-embossed metal plates is the thing to use. It is usually the cheapest in the long run.

Whether metal plates are used, or the paperlike stencil variety, depends upon the frequency of use, the value of each name, and the investment which seems justified.

Address stencils are made on a regular typewriter with a special attachment. These stencils are mounted in a card frame and may be used over and over again.

Metal address plates are embossed on a special machine for the purpose. Such plates have a very long life, and may be used over and over again without appreciable signs of wear.

The post office now requires all direct mail to bear the recipient's full zip code number. Your local postmaster will help you zip code your entire mailing list.

Addressing machines are available for either kind of nameplate in a wide choice of models, ranging from the simplest hand-operated machines on up to fully automatic, high-speed models which handle a tremendous variety of work.

For really big operations there are addressing machines which print from a roll of paper and print an entire label, insurance premium notice, or bill, inserting items such as premium amounts automatically.

Equipment required in an addressing department are the stencil-cutting or embossing units, the addressing machines, and cabinets for the address plates.

Hand-powered portable Addressographs save many hours of tedious typing in smaller offices, where power equipment is not needed.

JOB DESCRIPTION FOR SUPERVISOR
OF MAIL DEPARTMENT—KRAFT FOODS

GENERAL DUTIES:

Under the general office manager and office manager, directs the personnel who are engaged in the following work:

Incoming mail	Informational service to all divisions and departments
Outgoing mail	
Inside messenger service	Outside messenger service
Acting as receptionist	Housekeeping
Preparing advertising material for mailing	Petty cash fund

Assume full responsibility for the foregoing activities, train employees engaged in such work, schedule the work and arrange the hours of attendance, prepare (or supervise the preparation of) periodic reports with respect to the activities and employees as required by the office manager, plan the work to be performed, determine that each operation is being performed efficiently, maintain adequate housekeeping arrangements and perform such other duties as required by office management.

SPECIFIC DUTIES:

Training:

a. Initiate training programs for each class of employee (pages, messengers, mail clerks, etc.).

b. Instruct each new employee in his or her duties, responsibilities and privileges.

c. Assign personnel and ascertain that they are familiar with their duties.

Mail:

a. Ascertain by frequent checks that the incoming and outgoing mail service is being maintained.

b. Schedule the receipts of mail from the post offices, making certain that mail is gotten promptly from the post offices and that it is received promptly in the mail department.

Page Services:

Arrange for adequate page mail delivery and pickup mail delivery (at least every 30 minutes). For the first mail delivery in the morning, a sufficient number of pages should be scheduled for arrival at 7:45 a.m. Frequent independent checks of the pages' operations by the supervisor or assistant supervisor is eminently desirable. Special page assignments, where messages or material are to be taken from one department to another, should be arranged whenever required.

Messenger Service:

Schedule and maintain a regular messenger service to approved points outside the building. Special messenger assignments may be arranged whenever available personnel permits.

JOB DESCRIPTION FOR SUPERVISOR
OF MAIL DEPARTMENT

SPECIFIC DUTIES (Cont.):

Special Duties:

Whenever relief personnel is required for such assignments as acting as cigar stand clerks, as floor receptionists and similar special work, a mail department employee considered competent shall be directed to assume such duties.

Informational Services:

Information relative to classes of mail, airmail schedules and postal service information should be currently obtained and furnished to any Kraft employee requiring such information. The *U.S. Postal Guide* and periodic supplements is one source.

Selection:

After weighing all factors, select the person in the mail department with the proper qualifications and recommend such person to other departments where a person is required to fill a more highly skilled position. Among the factors to be considered are:

a. Seniority in the department and in the company.

b. Technical qualifications.

c. Personal qualifications.

RESPONSIBILITIES:

Discipline:

Maintain proper work habits, particularly when personnel is in the department, but also in messenger assignments, cautioning personnel with respect to unnecessary visiting, especially when absent from the department on assignments.

Cash:

Since a petty cash fund is maintained, frequent counts of such fund should be made and adequate safeguards adopted. Personnel who handle cash, checks, transportation tickets, postage and meter media should be cautioned as to their responsibilities.

Equipment:

Arrange for the procurement of scales, postage meters, envelope cutters, page carriers, mailbags, etc., as required. Make certain that such equipment is used more effectively.

Punctuality:

It is of the utmost importance that the supervisor be punctual in attendance and insist on the same punctuality from all members of the mail department. This is a service department, and therefore it must be borne in mind that many of the activities of the business depend to a great extent on the prompt receipt of their mail.

For regular mailings it is customary to address labels or envelopes in advance, have them ready when the contents of the mailing—letters, magazines, catalogs, or folders—arrive.

Folding Machines

When an office folding machine is purchased, it should be the best available. It will pay in the long run. There is nothing in the way of office appliances that will waste so much time, cause so many work interruptions and headaches, as a folding machine that only folds when the spirit moves it. The trouble with most office folders is that they depend upon rubber rolls to pick up the sheet and feed it into the machine. They work all right so long as the rolls are kept roughed up. But they soon become slick and slippery, failing to pick up the sheet or, if there is too much static electricity in the air, the sheets are apt to cling together and jam the folder.

The roll-fed office folder is useful in small offices where most of the work to be folded is of the same size, as, for example, standard-sized two-fold letterheads. But if the range of work varies, and it is necessary to "set up" the folding machine frequently for different folds and different kinds of paper stock, it is well to buy a folding machine of the type used in commercial binderies. It usually feeds by suction, and is far more dependable. This type of folder is now available in small sizes.

Gathering and Mailing Equipment

There are still offices which lay out work to be gathered on a long table, and the gatherer assembles the brief, or whatever it might be, while walking back and forth. In most commercial shops the gathering operation is speeded by placing the "pickups" on a rotating table, which is slowly turned by a motor. Several girls sit around the table and pick up the sheets as it turns. The most up-to-date method of gathering stapled materials for mailing or other purposes is an electrically operated collator.

When a company's direct mail is well standardized, with long runs of the same piece, there are automatic gathering and sealing machines for the work. These machines, operating on the principle of a gathering machine used in a commercial bindery, automatically pick up most enclosures; stuff them into the envelopes; and seal them ready to stamp, sack, and mail. These machines are expensive, so, unless a company has long runs, they should not be purchased. They take too much time to set up and adjust. But once adjusted and kept going on the same mailing, they will gather, insert, and seal thousands of pieces of mail an hour, tirelessly day in and day out. While there are several good sealing and stamping machines on the market, most mail users today meter their mail and depend upon that equipment for these operations. The latest metering machines are fast, reliable, and pay for themselves several times over in stamp savings, advertising benefits from special indicia, and labor. Not many modern mailing departments use adhesive stamps for the run of their outgoing mail. However, when adhesive stamps are called for, affixing machines which operate like a numbering machine save postage and time.

Sorting and Tying Direct Mail

There are many opportunities for savings in the way the mail is handled after being sealed and stamped. In the case of large metered mailings, where it is not necessary to cancel adhesive postage stamps, delivery will be greatly expedited if it is tied into packages by cities, and then sacked by train routes. Mail thus treated will usually go right out as soon as it lands in the post office. Otherwise, under the prevailing practice of handling "slow" mail, it may lie around the post office several days until someone feels inclined to sort it. For this operation the well-equipped mailing room should have a good tying machine, and enough racks to hold four to eight mail sacks during the sorting. If the sizes of the mailings are not sufficient to use sacks (supplied upon request by the local post office) a wall sorting rack can be constructed with pigeonholes for each of the 50 states and the principal cities.

How Combined Insurance Modernized Its Mailroom

In line with this Chicago-based company's tremendous growth and consequent physical changes, radical improvements have been made in the methods of handling the mail. A study of the situation showed two main factors needed modernization—fast. General confusion was caused by:

1. Too much individual walking around.

2. Too many piles of paper scattered about.

Mail was sorted by the simple method of people reaching into the mailbags and coming up with their own separate supplies of mail. These were opened, read when necessary, and distributed into separate piles for future distribution. Thus, a single category of mail could find its duplicate in front of any one of five or six people. Sorting the mail was a major problem.

One member of the firm's systems and procedures department and the supervisor of mail and transportation went to work on this issue. They designed a machine, consisting of three conveyor belts, fed by three men sorting the mail. Each belt carried a different category of mail to three different drop-off spots.

It took some 10 days to draw up the plans for the machine and they were given to the company's maintenance department for construction. One of the maintenance crew had previous experience in building conveyors and he helped considerably in making the machine possible.

The top belt of the machine carries the cash—usually recognizable in remittance envelopes. The middle belt carries mail specifically designated for a certain individual or department. The bottom belt totes the miscellaneous mail—usually addressed only to the company in general. Wherever each belt drops off its load, there are people to receive it. Each load is then broken up and distributed into the mail cases placed on top of the counters, in front of each seated person.

Combined employees call the machine "The Mailiac." It has an electric motor and speed can be controlled from one to three feet per second, depending upon the load of the mail. Company spokesmen estimate that the new company-made machine will cut in half the time spent in handling the mail and that the new setup will be able to handle the expected increases in mail over the next five years.

Naturally, as in any operational changes, there are bound to be some adjustments needed—on the personal level. But, according to information given Dartnell, the Combined Insurance mailroom group is "very level-headed" and has quickly adapted to the new and better way of handling the mail. Traffic to the mailroom has been reduced and the entire area is less crowded, thanks to "Mailiac."

In offices where many packages are tied, easily operated machines like this one are great savers of time and labor.

Chapter 40

RECORDS MANAGEMENT

R ECORDS are the tools of management, the memory of the organization, and the sources of many kinds of information. Often, though, full advantage is not taken of them. The greatly increased volume of business records in the past few years has become a burden to some companies. But the wise use of retention and disposition schedules, forms control, and other approaches to sound records management, has made it possible for many more companies to trim their files down to no more than the essentials.

All Dartnell studies show that companies trying to reorganize their files generally begin by stating the objectives of the proposed program. Here is an outline of a typical program:

1. Establish retention periods for each kind of company record so that records are destroyed promptly when no longer needed, but never prematurely.

2. Divide retention periods into three stages—active, semiactive, and inactive —through one or more of which each record passes.

3. Provide some device so that departments from which records are transferred are always given the opportunity of final approval before records are destroyed.

4. Establish a simple procedure for withdrawing records from storage and returning them for refiling, and for following up and retrieving delinquent returns.

5. Organize a system that will "police" the movement of records through the files and ensure observance of established retention periods.

6. Assure that a history (where stored, when, how, and by whom destroyed) of every record transferred to noncurrent storage is automatically provided as a by-product of the indexing procedure.

7. Establish "security files" by proper use of microfilm and other methods from which to replace lost, stolen, or misplaced documents such as engineering drawings and other vital records.

High Cost of Keeping Records

Arthur Barcan, executive director of the Records Management Institute of New York, says, "In the United States today, we are creating and keeping more than 8,500 pieces of paper for every man, woman, and child. United States business is long overdue in substituting professional techniques (of records management) for 'just plain hunches and common sense.' "

For many companies, finding a way out of the paperwork jungle which has grown up during years of operation will require the guidance of a skilled consulting firm, declares Robert A. Schiff, president of National Records Management Council, Inc. (Naremco).

"Every year American industry pays a stiff price for its vigorous growth—in dollars, time, and efficiency," says Mr. Schiff. "A tangle of paperwork and cumbersome office procedures hamstring executives with semiclerical routines—robbing them of important time to manage and to think creatively. Paperwork excesses divert supervision time, manufacturing productivity, and sales effort.

"Despite the earnest efforts of industry and government, the paperwork snarl increases. The reason is clear. Our swiftly developing technology and our expanding economy continue to make business operations infinitely more complex. The result is a greater volume of business machines and more paperwork—and a phenomenal rise in clerical and administrative overhead.

"More people, mechanization, and canned methods have not solved our paperwork problems. Advanced office systems, individually engineered for cost reduction and efficiency, require creative thinking, professional objectivity, research facilities, and tested experience. These are the factors which a professional records-management consultant can provide."

Company Filing Practices

Some of the recent trends in company filing procedures are toward shorter retention periods which are established after an examination of company needs; centralized files with low-cost storage for necessary, but infrequently used, records; and specific controls for preventing the creation of unnecessary records. Progress of this type is being made under a number of different organizational setups; in some, the office manager is responsible, in others, the controller, in others a staff officer such as a records administrator or company archivist. In the most successful cases, however, the records program is placed at a high enough level in the organization to permit it to function as an overall program and to have the benefit of top-management decisions, planning, and support.

Does a records-management program pay off? To this question, now being asked by top management in many companies, answers like these have been given:

The custodian of records for Westinghouse Electric Corporation reports that his company saves $200,000 a year in filing costs with its program. The company has been able to destroy more than 120 carloads of useless records and move more than 300 carloads from the main offices to central archives where storage costs are much lower.

A records inventory permitted a foundry and machine company in East Chicago, Indiana, to cart away 35 truckloads for burning.

The Sun Oil Company has been able to discard more than 1,000,000 pounds of records over a three-year period.

These examples, dramatic as they are, list only the mechanical advantages of a destruction schedule. They do not reflect the greatly increased operating efficiency of filing departments which companies are reaching by sound records management. Moreover, records management is not limited merely to destruction of records as they become obsolete. The first step in any permanent program has been called "records birth control," controlling record-making and standardizing forms. And there are possibilities for great savings in many other approaches to the general problem.

Such savings are by no means limited to large companies. Proportionate reductions have been made by companies ranging in size down to the very smallest, whose experience has proved to them that the solution to the filing problem is not confined to the great corporations. The same principles and techniques apply to all companies, regardless of size.

Office executives who are running their filing departments on the old "catch-all" basis will be interested in these results of studies made by the National Records Management Council:

Of the records of the average company, less than 10 percent must be kept indefinitely or permanently; another 20 percent must be retained in office space to meet current operational needs; approximately 30 percent can and should be transferred to less-expensive storage space; approximately 35 percent, the balance, can be destroyed.

ORGANIZING A RECORDS PROGRAM

Agreement among records administrators and other authorities as to definitions of important terms and the wisdom of setting objectives does not carry over into the area of assigning responsibility for the overall records program. There is, however, general agreement in respect to some aspects of the organizational question:

1. A proper place on the organizational chart is vital to the efficient operation of the program.

2. While records administration is not a top-management function, the nature of the records problem is such that it is an overall function. It should, therefore, be not more than one step removed from top management which alone should make the policy decisions.

3. The creation, administration, preservation, and destruction of records are not separate problems, but different aspects of the same problem. This fact should be remembered when setting up the organization to administer the records program.

There is wide variation in organizational structures among companies whose programs are found to be outstanding for efficiency.

A compact motorized file like this requires less than 17 square feet of floor space and offers push-button filing for fast and efficient mass record handling. No record is further than three seconds away from the file clerk's fingertips, as this device brings the records to the file clerk by the shortest route without waiting for the trays to complete a full cycle.

In some the controller is responsible, in some the legal department, in some a specialized department with no other responsibilities, in others the office manager. The most successful programs, though, have one quality in common: The records administrator has over-all control.

Today there is a new awareness of the need for professional records management as a legal safeguard. With government subpoena powers over business documents being applied more vigorously than ever, missing records and gaps in documentation can result in serious implications arising out of a government inquiry into the conduct and operation of a company.

Only through an effective information control system can a company protect itself against this possibility. The time to prepare is *before* government investigation is launched. The "office of record" concept, providing complete documentation of all files, is an excellent safeguard in the event of subpoena.

RECORDS MANAGEMENT PROGRAM

The following functions should be considered in any well-rounded records management program, according to the Hoover Commission Task Force report:

1. Management of correspondence.
2. Control of reports.
3. Control of administrative issuances.
4. Control of paper forms.
5. Control of paper work procedures.
6. Microfilming.
7. Mail service control.
8. Files control.
9. Records retirement.
10. Records storage.
11. Reviewing requests for space and equipment for records.

Marathon Oil Company Plan

Many companies use the committee approach. One of these is Marathon Oil Company, where this procedure is followed:

Our records disposition committee, which became the nucleus of our company records management program, was appointed by the board of directors in 1944. In a resolution by the board of directors the committee "was delegated the responsibility of acting upon all questions involving the retention or destruction of company records." The committee, in conjunction with its staff agency, the forms and records disposition department, is accomplishing its function through the establishment of formal records disposition policies and security procedures.

These are communicated to those company personnel concerned through the media of records disposition policies manuals as well as written records security procedures.

The records disposition committee consists of managers of procedures research and data processing; office services; corporate records; auditing; banking; supervisor of forms and records disposition department; attorney, administrative services; a forms analyst; and tax attorney; the latter two being staff members. The committee is responsible to the controller.

The committee does not meet regularly, but is called into session at the request of the chairman as the need arises.

In considering a specific disposition policy, normally all of the investigation is completed before the committee meets. This work is conducted by staff analysts assigned to work for the committee. Following formulation of a policy, it is reviewed by the legal staff; the committee then considers the policy for approval. In this manner the work of the committee is limited to a review of factual data and consideration of the recommendation of persons concerned with use of the specific document. Requests for a disposition policy may originate with department heads, the records center, or any other interested party.

Records Disposition Form: In setting up a disposition policy the preliminary work includes a discussion with the department head or other supervisors using the record, and in some cases with an attorney. For example, when our company established a disposition policy on stock certificates, the matter was discussed at board level. In a limited number of cases specific statutes or regulations provide a guide for action. In the majority of cases the decision is a matter of judgment applied to the specific facts. As each item is considered, the data are entered on a records disposition policy form with the reasons underlying the decision reached. (We found we could not dispose of old records without creating new ones.) These forms, when approved by the committee and signed, become the official disposition policy. Each disposition policy covers all copies of multiple-copy forms.

Manual: After the retention periods have been established, it is necessary to make this information available to those who are to use it. In our case we prepared a records disposition policies manual which contains nearly 2,300 disposition policies. The manual serves the following purposes:

1. The name of the record becomes the official name for standardization of nomenclature.

2. The distribution of each copy of the record is shown.

3. When required, the filing basis is prescribed. This provides standardization and assists in preparing records for transfer to the records center.

4. When it is considered advisable to have valuable records transferred to the general office records center, the period after which they are to be transferred is indicated in the manual.

5. The retention period is shown in years. Records to be retained *permanently* are indicated by "P," and those which may be destroyed at the discretion of the custodian, upon serving their current purpose, are indicated by "C." Records with a "C" retention period are not transferred to the records center.

6. If the record may be filmed, this is so indicated in the manual.

Conserv-a-scan, electronic hard-copy data storage and retrieval system of the Supreme Steel Equipment Corp., selects single folders or groups of file folders upon signals from a keyboard or punch cards or tapes. Scanning heads search the file shelves at the rate of 100 inches per second, and the wanted folders are thrust forward to permit easy manual retrieval. Best of all, the folders may be returned at random to any available opening, since the scanners will find them again instantly.

RECORDS DISPOSITION POLICY

TITLE OF RECORD

DISTRIBUTION

FILING BASIS OR COMMENTS

DESTROY

To Be Held Records Center | Record | Micro Film

FORM NO.

DISPOSITION POLICY AS SET FORTH HEREON FORMALLY ADOPTED

BY RECORDS DISPOSITION COMMITTEE IN THE MEETING OF:

SECRETARY _____ NEW _____ REV.

DEPT. _____

SCHEDULE: _____ RETENTION PERIOD: _____

Form 2768 Rev. 2-65

Marathon Oil Company's records-disposition form

In order to carry out the program, a committee representative has been appointed in each of the field offices, and it is his duty to administer the policies outlined in the manual. This includes distribution of the manual as well as supervision of the filing, transfer, and destruction of records.

Correspondence: In discussing this program with others, one of the first items mentioned is correspondence. Of course, correspondence is too broad a subject to be covered by a simple blanket retention policy. We have placed the burden on each writer-recipient to sort his correspondence files annually, so only that with some permanent value is retained. Periodically a bulletin is sent out to all supervisors as a reminder. That may seem like "passing the buck," but it has prevented the wholesale transfer of correspondence files to storage. In some departments all correspondence is rubber-stamped, providing spaces for the department head to immediately classify it for temporary or permanent retention.

Records Center: A program for the selective disposition of records is not complete without an efficiently operated records center. As previously indicated, our company has such a center in the general office, which is the final repository for original copies of most of our basic records which are no longer needed for current reference in departmental files. Records are filed in cardboard cartons of uniform size, in the proper filing series, and labeled to show series designation, box number, type of record, and date to be destroyed. Records can be withdrawn under a procedure similar to that used by libraries. A complete index of each series of records is made at the time records are placed in storage, and the index is noted when records are destroyed. Records subject to destruction are listed on a destruction authorization form which is reviewed by the originating department and the secretary of the committee. Records of secondary importance, or duplicate copies of multicopy forms, reports, and statements which are not transferred to the records center, require no additional destruction authorization. This includes all documents with a short term disposition policy in the manual and most of the records in field offices.

Our procedure has resulted in a substantial reduction in the volume of old records, and in improved filing, classification, and control of paper work. Many of the original permanent retention policies have been reduced to a set number of years, and all established policies are constantly being reviewed.

Any company wishing to set up a formal records program would do well to consider Marathon Oil Company's committee system. Among other things, this is a safeguard against the temptation to leave a system alone indefinitely, once it has been established. This can be dangerous, as Marathon Oil has realized.

THE INVENTORY

Companies that have successfully reorganized their records programs agree that no general housecleaning should be attempted until a reasonably accurate survey has been made of the existing records. This, they admit, is a painful and unwelcome task, but, at the same time, one well worth doing.

The inventory consists of a physical count of the contents of filing cabinets, boxes, and anything containing records. Once the count has been made, the records problem will assume more manageable proportions. About 35 percent of the average company's records, according to the findings of the National Records Management Council, can be destroyed immediately. A records inventory brings other advantages. It discloses duplications; it helps decide questions of centralization vs. decentralization of files; and it provides the facts needed before a judgment on the feasibility of microfilming can be reached.

Mrs. Vera A. Avery, well-known filing consultant, describes what can happen during the course of a records inventory:

"Obtaining a records inventory can be a quick and inexpensive process—certainly it is the only safe and accurate basis on which to construct a disposal program, and it has the additional advantage of helping to get control over all the records, both inactive and current, as well as pointing up defects in current records procedures, and finally an inventory will reveal additional records accumulations which can be scheduled for disposal.

"In the average company, impatience will be evidenced at what looks like additional delay on disposal, but far better this delay than a costly destruction. There is no change possible once the record is destroyed. You can't 'undestroy' records.

"This hypothetical case illustrates the value of an inventory of records in a disposal program.

"Form X is a quadruplicate form which is required to be made in every branch and field office of an organization to cover the reporting of a certain type of transaction. The transactions have a long-term implication and therefore some record of each transaction must be retained for an undetermined period, probably permanently. The originating branch retains one copy of Form X and sends the other three into the main office. Here is surely a place for a reduction in the volume of records—at least a two-thirds reduction and probably three-quarters.

"You are assigned to reduce the volume of accumulated records in this hypothetical corporation without benefit of a records inventory. The first encounter with Form X is in Department A where it is interfiled with a great deal of temporary material and interoffice memoranda of no value and where the bulk has already been transferred to storage because the personnel in Department A indicate that they seldom use the record beyond the past two years. The cost of extracting Form X from the bulk of the temporary and valueless material, and the fact that the file is not complete except for the past two years, indicate that this copy of Form X is not the one for permanent retention and so you authorize the destruction of Form X file after two years.

"Next, Form X is found in Department B—here it is kept in good orderly arrangement and is complete for all years except for the fact that the forms covering a certain specialized type of transaction have not been included and have been transferred to Department C. In Department C it is found that they have systematically been destroying these records at the end of a period 12 months after their closing action. This destruction in Department C, prohibits the reconstruction of a complete file of Form X by combining the files of Department B and Department C and therefore the files for both departments are authorized for destruction 12 months after the close of each transaction.

"Eventually you come to Department D, but as Form X was merely used by them to compile statistical summaries and analysis, they have been regularly destroying that copy of Form X at the close of each reporting period. This information is more than a little disconcerting for it means that there is not one complete file of the form remaining in the headquarters office. But then there is that copy in each field office and that, after all, is the copy which should be retained according to good archival practice.

"You dismiss the matter until such time as the field offices are visited. Then as Offices Nos. 1, 2, 3, and 4 are visited you find all is well, they have complete and orderly files of the Form X's that they made out and you give them instructions then and there that they must never destroy their files of this Form X. Your plan is to eventually consolidate all field office files of Form X into one complete record, though this is going to be a bit difficult for Offices 1 and 2 have the form filed chronologically, Office 3 by the customers' names and in a yearly breakdown, while Office 4 has filed the forms by the customers' names in one ever-expanding file.

"Then you visit Office 5 and find that they have only a portion of the Form X relating to their territory for it is a new office made up of a portion of the territory formerly assigned to Offices 6 and 7.

"Office 6 has thrown out all of the Form X prior to the formation of the new Office 5, though no authority for this destruction was ever given. The individual who did the destruction is no longer with the company to give a report on his reason for the destruction —though it was probably based on the assumption that with three copies going into the home office they would always be able to rely on that source of information whenever any reason for reference to the forms was required.

"For Office 7 the story is nearly the same—and so on down the line of all field offices—so in short you are ending up with no one complete record of this basic reporting of the business of the corporation.

HOW RESPONSIBILITIES ARE DIVIDED

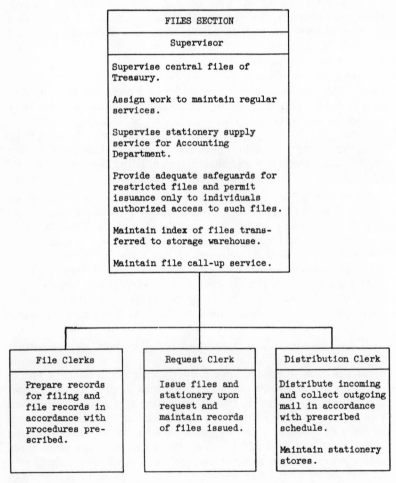

Organization chart, showing personnel responsibilities of one company's files.

"But you say now: 'I would have found out about those other copies of the Form X before I authorized the destruction of the forms in Department A.' Yes, I heartily agree that that is the method to follow, but that is just why I am arguing for an inventory— only, an inventory of one item (as Form X) at a time is doing it the expensive way. Whereas a real inventory of all records before any destruction occurs and used as the basis for decisions on destruction would mean an early decision on which copy of Form X is to be retained, that is, which is to be the 'record copy.' Such a decision would not only permit the destruction of all other copies, but would mean that they could be destroyed just as quickly as the immediate use of them has been fulfilled, thus permitting the release of valuable space and filing equipment in the department and offices where they formerly were retained.

"If the inventory seems a herculean task—just recall this hypothetical case and if necessary get the help of additional staff or outside agencies; but do not attempt a disposal program or to get disposal decisions without the inventory as a basis for such decisions."

An example of mechanization to speed order handling: A 24-inch, 2-row manual rotary for holding acetate jackets containing 8-channel punched tape. Jackets will hold tapes up to 7 feet in length, numerically filed by order number and indexed by grease pencil. When pulled for billing, the order number is wiped off with a dry cloth and the jacket is reused. Rotary will hold about 8,000 feet in tapes.

Courtesy, Acme Visible

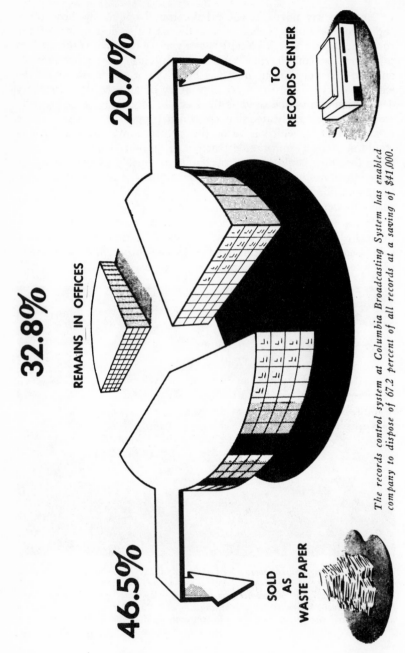

20.7%

TO
RECORDS CENTER

32.8%

REMAINS IN OFFICES

46.5%

SOLD
AS
WASTE PAPER

The records control system at Columbia Broadcasting System has enabled company to dispose of 67.2 percent of all records at a saving of $41,000.

SELECTING FILES PERSONNEL

Training of filing employees is limited by the caliber of the employees themselves; companies which assign substandard workers to the filing department will find it difficult to improve matters by training, however extensive it may be. The desirable qualifications for records personnel are these:

1. A basic knowledge of records system and procedures.
2. Knowledge of the organization—its structure, functions.
3. A sympathetic ear and a pleasant personality. Tact and diplomacy.
4. Good health. Frequent absenteeism will impair operations. Good eyesight and hearing.
5. Supervisors need the following additional qualifications:
   a. Ability to organize work and to train all employees in systematic habits.
   b. Ability to develop performance standards and analyze employees' performance to make sure that jobs are being handled efficiently.
   c. Ability to develop and modify procedures and systems. Ability to make decisions.

Job-sample tests developed at the Admiral Corporation have proved useful. The speed and accuracy with which these tests should be completed will vary with the needs of the company; useful standards can be obtained by giving the tests to your present filing employees whose abilities have already been demonstrated on the job. The scores and speeds of applicants can then be compared to those made by your employees. Examples of Admiral's tests are on pages 654-656.

MICROFILMING

More companies are putting their records on microfilm. This is particularly true of larger companies. Court decisions upholding the legal admissibility of microfilm records have led to increased use of filmed files.

One of the important advantages of microfilming is stressed at the Meredith Publishing Company:

"The principal advantage we have gained from microfilm is the saving of floor space. We think, however, that look-up on complaints, etc., may be slightly faster with the microfilm than with the regular files of orders."

Full Potential Still to Come

Sophisticated data processing equipment is forcing the use of microfilm records in large companies. The combination punched

---

THIS IS AN ERROR CHECKING TEST

You will cross off with a line thus \ all of the figures that are not the same as those in the first line. Then put the total number of errors in the space provided.

Example: 19876   198₿₿   2   errors

		ERRORS
17421	17421	....
93986	93968	....
12390	12390	....
48502	48520	....
15838	15838	....
14837	13748	....
30586	35068	....

THIS IS A NUMERICAL TEST

The figures in the left column are to be put into numerical order. Start with the highest figures and list them down to the lowest.

10940	....
4512	....
4252	....
5926	....
4315	....
1474	....
11566	....
7784	....
4238	....

THIS IS A COMPARISON TEST

The names, cities and states may differ in the second column. Check the errors with a line / thus.

Paul Nacon, Memphis, Tenn.	Paul Macon, Mempris, Tenn.
Martin French, Evansville, Ind.	Martin French, Evensville, Ind.
J. Homa, Birmingham, Ala.	J. Homa, Birmingam, Ala.
Molly Beard, Tampa, Fla.	Beard Molly, Tampa, Fla.
Warren Grand, Boise, Idaho	Waren Grant, Boise, Iidaho
M. R. St. Clair, Minneapolis, Minn.	M. R. St. Clair, Minneaolpis, Minn.
M. K. Needleman, Jackson, Miss.	M. K. Needelman, Jackson, Miss.
Charles Willhite, Norfolk, Va.	Charles Willhite, Norfolk, Va.
Louis Macek, Portland, Oreg.	Louise Macek, Portland, Oreg.
W. H. Dryer, New Orleans, La.	W. H. Dryer, New Orleans, Ala.
James Smith, Denver, Colo.	James Smith, Denver, Colo.

ARRANGE NAMES IN ALPHABETICAL ORDER

Julius Clayton ....

Edward Sugg ....

Nora Huber ....

Calvin Courtney ....

E. N. Lefkowitz ....

Theodore La Drew ....

Frank Bond ....

Gilbert Cohen ....

Helen Faulkner ....

J. John Schaser ....

Joseph Schasser ....

David Conners ....

Sylvia Schwartz ....

P. I. Paul ....

Paul Schock ....

Daisy Craig ....

Frances Neger ....

Francis Miger ....

Dorothy Kessler ....

Inez Rothman ....

Catherine Burk ....

K. Leone Martin ....

Catherine Burke ....

Marie Naughton ....

J. Paul Craige ....

ARRANGE ACCORDING TO STATE AND CITY

Philadelphia, Pa. ....

Decatur, Ill. ....

Lansing, Mich. ....

Audubon, N. J. ....

Fort Worth, Tex. ....

Peoria, Ill. ....

Kenmore, N. Y. ....

Detroit, Mich. ....

Dallas, Tex. ....

Chicago, Ill. ....

Kingston, N. Y. ....

San Francisco, Calif. ....

Milwaukee, Wis. ....

Princeton, N. J. ....

New York City, N. Y. ....

Cleveland, Ohio ....

Parsons, Kans. ....

Sullivan, Mo. ....

San Antonio, Tex. ....

Iona, Mich. ....

Austin, Tex. ....

Belleville, Ill. ....

card and microfilm record is necessary to maintain some kind of visual approach to the information. Very new units, like the Stromberg-Carlson 4400 system, are capable of producing microfilm documents at a rate of 50,000 pages per eight-hour shift. Retrieval of this data is entirely automatic and practically instantaneous, and it is possible to eliminate both magnetic tape recording and any printing on paper.

It is obvious that this system, which reduces a storeroom of paper to a file drawer of film, is a far cry from the simple microfilming of documents intended to be a permanent record. Need is the only criterion for investing in any type of operation, and there may be no magic solution available.

Preparation of records for filming adds to the expense of the process. This frequently involves removing folders and clips and may include arrangement of disordered material and provision of a filing system. The following questions can serve as a check list for office managers who are investigating microfilming with the thought that it might be put to good use in the records program:

1. Are the records worth preserving on film?
2. Will the total cost of microfilming and subsequent use of the film be less than the cost of preservation and use of the original document, including space costs?
3. Can the records be so identified on film that they will serve as legal substitutes for the originals?
4. Are the records of such a type that it is possible to film them?

While the existence of microfilm dates back almost to the invention of photography, its full potential is yet to be realized as an instrument of business, science, industry, and government.

Its greatest handicaps have been (1) a lack of understanding of what it can do, (2) slow development of equipment for simple and economical utilization in business, and (3) reluctance on the part of some microfilm users to let the system do its best work for them.

Since the introduction of America's missile program, however, microfilm has made a great deal of progress. With the race for control of space came the need for faster methods of reproducing, filing, retrieving, printing, and shipping millions of engineering drawings, specifications, and other data around the world.

Microfilm was the answer, and the military services, National Aeronautics and Space Administration, prime contractors, subcontractors, and even our allies in NATO adopted it as the swiftest, most economical method of communication. So tremendous were some of the systems installed by these organizations that microfilm was viewed by many prospective users as a luxury only a business as big as the Government could afford.

The important point is not whether your business is large enough, but whether it will lend itself to filmwork. If you are thinking of going into microfilm, it would be well to ask whether it will: (1) save money, (2) save labor, (3) save time, (4) improve accuracy, (5) increase efficiency, (6) replace hand methods.

Next point to consider is how much space will it save? Microfilm has the advantage of reducing a document to 1/40th of its original size, yet on a reader-printer it can be enlarged to full size or larger depending on the equipment.

Western Union Cuts Costs With Microfilming

Microfilm is cutting clerical and billing costs at Western Union while improving customer good will.

Eastman Kodak increased the microfilm file capacity of its Recordak system by 700 percent with the addition of a Dekafilm accessory. The foot-long, plastic microstrip holder shown here can hold up to 10 strips of 16 mm. microfilm instead of the single-strip capacity formerly available.

To speed lookup of vital zip-code data, Eastman Kodak's new "Zip-O-Matic" directory uses a rigid plastic holder containing a strip of 16mm. film. All filmed images for the directory are contained in an access file. A pointer puts the searched-for zip code on a screen.

Formerly, the telegraph company retained all telegrams in its files for six months to meet regulatory requirements, and also for use in preparing monthly statements. This caused a huge storage problem.

While searching for a solution to the problem, the company discovered that a microfilm copy of each telegram would meet all requirements. Western Union decided to install the Reliant Microfilmer, manufactured by the Recordak Corporation, in many key offices.

With microfilm billing, the messages (sorted alphabetically and chronologically by customer) go to the billing clerk along with preaddressed statement sheets. She simply drops each telegram into the microfilmer feeder and posts the charge on the statement form. Then the telegrams are mailed to the customer along with his abbreviated statement.

Customers receive the original messages with the complete text, and can easily check the charges and allocate them to the proper department. Further, they have a choice of destroying the telegrams or incorporating them into the proper correspondence file as proof that the message was sent, a precaution which might well be important to a specific contractual agreement. And if there is still some question, Western Union offices have a microfilm viewer which permits quick examination of any message desired.

For Western Union, the elimination of descriptive billing means as high as a 50 percent saving in billing time. A clerk formerly able to bill only one cycle a day now bills two.

Previously, some customers requested that telegrams be sent to them for checking. The refiling of these telegrams in the Rochester, New York, office, for example, consumed about 25 hours each month. This operation is now completely eliminated.

Another saving is in filing cabinets and floor space. The microfilmer photographs 14,000 telegrams and statements—equal to a stack of telegrams 10 feet high—on a single small 100-foot roll of 16mm. film.

How Simplicity Pattern Company Does It

The records essential for successful operation of the largest clothing pattern company in the world reach enormous proportions. For one thing, the company line includes around 700 different styles in as many as 1,800 different sizes. Around 16,500 accounts are billed every month and involve from 150,000 to 175,000 pieces of media. But records retention at Simplicity Pattern Company, Inc., has been developed into a smooth-working microfilm system—for both active and inactive records.

Simplicity was formed in 1927 to offer women who sew patterns which could readily be understood and applied as a simple, economical guide for transforming cloth into a finished garment.

During the years that followed, sound business policies, coupled with consumer acceptance of the company's products and services, served as groundwork for continuous expansion. Simplicity Pattern currently maintains two factories and four branch offices in the United States, a factory and branch in Canada, and similar organizations in England and Australia. A few years ago, a subsidiary was formed in Germany. Annual sales volume is $12 million.

"The accumulation of records during the company's history was enormous," Chief Accountant George J. Klein has said. "By the end of World War II, we had reached the point where we felt as though the beams were bulging with cardboard storage boxes. Moreover, frequent reference was made to data in storage, and too much time was required to locate and refile material. We decided that the best answer to our records retention problems was microfilm.

"Transforming documents into tiny images on microfilm immediately began to relieve the situation; however, our program did not really mature and become an integral part of our accounting system until we installed the latest Burroughs microfilming equipment."

Under the current program, all accounts receivable and posting media—the 150,000 to 175,000 monthly items—are microfilmed on a daily basis. The original media is sent to the customer and the microfilmed copy is retained as the company's permanent record. The preparation of accounts receivable records is done on three Burroughs cycle billing machines, equipment similar to that used by department stores.

"Although we understand that cycle billing at the commercial level is quite unusual," Mr. Klein said, "the plan works very satisfactorily for us and has eliminated the month-end peak loads. About 11,000 of our accounts are handled in 16 cycles, and the remaining customers are billed on a month-end basis."

In addition to the accounts receivable records, canceled payroll checks are microfilmed on a monthly basis. Both sides of checks are filmed simultaneously and then are placed side by side on the film. The checks are then destroyed and the microfilmed copies become the company's record.

Since much of the export activity requires extensive and numerous record work, an important part of the program includes the filming of export files.

The procedures are handled with such ease and rapidity that the equipment also is available for other jobs.

"All film," Mr. Klein said, "is filed in two nine-drawer cabinets. We estimate these cabinets will adequately house the records for seven years of activity. This is the legally required time for retaining most of the records, then the film is destroyed."

A simple filing system makes it possible to locate quickly any microfilmed document. Each roll of film is numbered by sequence in the filing cabinet. The subject of media on the film is cross-indexed onto a master record in the form of a three-ring binder, and this becomes the reference for locating any microfilmed item. Though dissimilar material may be on the same roll, any document can be located immediately.

Three microfilm readers are in use at the company. One reader is kept in the adjustment department, so that analyses of accounts may be made directly within the department. The second reader is kept in the bookkeeping department, and is used primarily for making facsimile records requested by customers or by other departments within the company. Facsimiles are prepared directly inside the reader, without the use of a darkroom. The third reader also is kept in the bookkeeping department for general use.

"Since we first began our new microfilming program," Mr. Klein said, "we have been able to eliminate one employee, increase speed, and reduce film costs nearly 75 percent."

Simplicity first installed two recorders and had two operators microfilming one side of documents on a 16mm. film. The current program calls for one operator with one recorder handling a greater volume of work and, when required, simultaneously filming both

The Recordak Magnaprint Reader provides push-button projection of records stored on microfilm. Within seconds, a print of the record is printed and delivered to the operator. The unit handles 16mm. and 35 mm. roll film, but new accessory units can accommodate film magazines, aperture cards, film jackets and Micro-File Filmcards.

sides of documents in 8mm. images. Where 7,000 to 7,500 items originally were filmed into a 200-foot roll of film, 13,000 items are now filmed on a 100-foot roll.

"And I am certain that as we gain further microfilming experience, we shall find new and broader applications which will increase the efficiency of our accounting activity," Mr. Klein said. "After all, a primary function of accounting is to prepare records for future use— as information for guiding management decisions or as evidence for supporting claims—and microfilm is a fast, accurate, simple method for retaining these necessary records.

When information from a production order is needed, jacket containing microfilm is located and copy is made on enlarging printer.

Saving Storage Space at The Foxboro Company

The Foxboro Company of Foxboro, Massachusetts, solved the problem by microfilming and storing the half-million production records it must keep for 30 to 40 years in a few filing cabinets. Moreover, a simplified filing system has made it possible for this manufacturer of custom-built recording instruments to maintain the file of vital records with a minimum of clerical expense.

These records are essential to keep because they contain detailed information needed for filling repeat orders, occasional repairs, and parts replacement. In addition to instrument specifications (which are complex because each instrument is engineered for the customer's individual requirements), the production orders show serial numbers, types of instruments, and their applications. Any or all of this information may be needed at the main plant in Foxboro, or at affiliated plants in Montreal, Canada; Redhill, Surrey, England; Soest, The Netherlands; Arras, France; Mexico City, Mexico; Tokyo, Japan; Melbourne, Australia, or at one of the six factory branches or 53 sales offices in the United States.

In their original form, tens of thousands of the oldest of these records once occupied many thousands of feet of valuable space.

Because the instruments are designed for long service, a Foxboro Company production order must be kept for a very long time. So production orders dating as far back as 1938 have to be maintained in the active files, and that's where the actual measure of their old system versus the new gives a graphic picture of microfilming as a time-, space-, and money-saver.

Only the most current production orders are kept for a while in their original form. Those for the first 30 years of the company's existence are stored on microfilm reels in a fraction of the storage space formerly required.

The production order records from 1938 to those considered current (three years back, in most cases) are filed in 3- by 5-inch Filmsort jackets. In each of these are the facsimiles of 33 order-and-specification sheets.

For the microfilmed records covering a period of 45 years, the microfilm department uses five feet of floor space for filing purposes. The unfilmed records and order correspondence for only three years require several shelf files that occupy 50 square feet of floor space. That means that 45 years of microfilmed records are housed in one-tenth the amount of floor space taken up by three years of original documents.

Because of the size and complexity of a typical Foxboro control system in a chemical or petroleum processing plant, such production orders frequently remain in the "active" stage for several years. They are then microfilmed and the facsimiles are inserted in the jackets.

Even now these film records, totaling 50,000 to 60,000 a year, must be within easy access. In fact, between 150 and 200 a day are required for quick reference by engineers in the service or production departments.

Before the production orders were microfilmed, five girls were required to keep up with the demands for reference copies. Now the microfilm reels and jackets are processed, filed, pulled, copied, and refiled by two operators.

And because it is less expensive and more efficient, photocopies that need not be returned are made up as production order records are requested. And because they are exact copies of the original documents, there are no chances of error in transcribing and no need for checking or proofreading.

Setting up a microfilm operation need not be complicated. Equipment of varying prices and types is available. Should your business be large enough, the most practical, efficient, and economical method is to buy or rent cameras, either 16mm. or 35mm. depending on the documents involved.

If the operation is not of sufficient size to justify camera and filmwork, microfilm service companies are available, in most major cities, which sell film, cameras, and other supplies, and also process film, make duplicates, and do microfilming on a job or contract basis.

One example in which a microfilm service company is of particular benefit is in microfilming old records while current records are being filmed on a daily or weekly basis. On the other hand, a camera and operator may be required for only a few hours each month, in which case the service company may be hired to do the whole job on a continuing basis.

Film can be stored in rolls, just as it is returned from processing, but the most efficient method is unitization. This consists of collecting microfilm copies pertaining to one subject, person, or project into one or more cards or jackets. The cards or jackets may be kept together in a deck and may be sorted and retrieved by hand or by machine.

Filmsort aperture cards are available in various shapes and sizes, the most common being the familiar tabulating cards with apertures provided to accommodate either 35mm. size frames or 16mm. frames. Film frames can be unitized with the aperture cards by means of hand mounters or semiautomatic mounters designed for this purpose.

Each card can be coded for instant automatic or hand retrieval. It also provides space for other pertinent information. For some systems, especially files in which records are needed in only one location, acetate jackets form a satisfactory method for preserving the microfilm frames.

With the addition of a film storage cabinet and drawers for filing the aperture cards, the system is two-thirds complete. Final step is the addition of the reader-printer, which offers the opportunity of taking more than a look—you can take a copy in a matter of seconds.

With these elements, (1) photography, (2) processing, (3) filing films by unitization or acetate jackets, and (4) installation of a reader-printer, a microfilm operation is ready to roll.

Whether your operation involves big business or individual enterprise, the installation of a microfilm system is only the start toward more savings and higher savings if the system is utilized to its fullest extent. By assessing the seven major categories of both passive and active microfilm application any business can determine how to accrue the greatest benefits and savings. These seven categories are:

Duplicating. Speed, low cost, and long life all contribute to the use of microfilm for the recording of vital statistics and technical information that may have to be quickly and economically duplicated many times over a period of years.

Consolidated filing. Here microfilm is used because of its low cost and its capability of making large files more useful by consolidating complete records in a reduced size with current papers. Examples are the filing of medical records and personnel records. Because the files are consolidated, access to information is faster and easier.

Retrieval. Because large amounts of information can best be stored in a small volume on microfilm, and a given item found rapidly by machine sorting of film in card form or rapid scanning of indexed reels, the use of microfilm for rapid retrieval of information is steadily becoming more important.

Copying. Microfilm is used by banks, retail stores, and other businesses for the rapid copying of checks, sales, and statements. It is used because it is the fastest and least expensive method of copying a large number of documents.

Publishing. Microfilm is used for the low-cost, high-quality publication of rare books, research theses, and periodicals.

Preservation. Microfilm is used to record valuable files of newspapers, engineering drawings, and other documents because paper cannot stand the wear and tear of years of use.

Storage. Experts say 40 percent of what is being kept in most offices should be destroyed; however, low costs of recording and storage are prime features of microfilm for keeping vital corporate records.

How Microfilming Is Used in Billing

In many offices, microfilming is being used increasingly for reducing posting time. Billing clerks in retail stores, for example, post only the totals of sales checks, credits, and returns on the bill. No description is needed because all these items—including the simplified bill—go out to the customer after being microfilmed. With some of the newer microfilm cameras, up to 500 items can be photographed in a minute.

Chapter 41

THE PRINCIPLES AND RULES OF FILING

MANY companies make extensive use of filing manuals. One company explains:

"We have found manuals very useful for several reasons. They make training of new employees much simpler and more complete than our previous 'by word of mouth' system. Our filing manual is valuable for reference purposes for types of work which occur infrequently or when a regular employee is ill. Another advantage of our manual is that it permits us to maintain standard procedures despite widespread operations."

Job breakdown techniques form the basis for compiling filing manuals in a number of companies. The typical approach to the problem is to have each operation of the department broken down by the files supervisor and an experienced worker. Differences between the two breakdowns are reconciled in a meeting conducted, preferably, by the office manager's staff.

Training at Shell Oil Company is typical, and here the filing manual is the most important training aid. Most of the instruction is given on the job by the files supervisor or some other experienced employee. Manuals are prepared by the methods and statistics department for each of the major administrative divisions of the company. Following are a few typical pages:

PRINCIPLES OF FILES MANAGEMENT

What the Files Are

No business office can do without files. Files are the storehouse of the information which an office needs to operate smoothly. Files contain the documents which tell the day-to-day history of the business. They are the memory of an office, and, just like the memory of a human being, the office memory is useful only when it can retain facts in an orderly manner and produce them when they are needed.

The devices which are used in filing, such as the index of the files, the sorting mechanisms and even the cabinets housing the records, are all part of a system which permits the memory of the office to function quickly and accurately.

THE PRINCIPLES AND RULES OF FILING

Files Employees Serve Others

No memory can be made to work without the aid of a brain. The brain which supplies intelligence to the office memory is composed of the combined efforts of the people who work in the files. They provide the judgment which selects the right storage place for the records, from which it can be produced upon demand. They select the correct record from its storage place when it is needed, replacing it with another record to show the whereabouts of the one which is in use.

Above all, the files personnel who make the office memory function intelligently always keep in mind that a memory is useful only when it serves the other people who work in the office. Only if they get good service, cheerfully given, is the Files Section doing its job well.

High-quality service from the Files Section to the remainder of the office saves valuable time in the operations of the department as a whole. Each file clerk is a link in the chain of activities which constitutes the accomplishments of the office. High-quality service means accuracy in the marking and filing of records and neatness in labeling, splitting of folders and arranging papers in folders. Neatness in the appearance of folders and of their contents encourages others who handle them to keep them orderly. Clean labels are more legible than soiled labels. Neatness also means keeping the tops of desks and cabinets clear.

A good file clerk handles all requests for records and information in a courteous, businesslike manner. Clerks and supervisor alike are alert to opportunities for supplying new or improved services to the rest of the department, thus increasing the worth of the Files Section. Each clerk has the opportunity of becoming a good-will ambassador by answering requests promptly and pleasantly.

STANDARD FILING PRACTICES

Increased efficiency will result from the proper use of the tools provided for filing employees. For example, all papers should be processed with the aid of a rubber finger. Sorting devices should be used to effect the grouping of a large volume of records into filing order. All filing material should be stored in file cabinets. Unfiled records should be on the top of the file desks, or in the sorter. They should be stored overnight in a clearly labeled file drawer. No files should be stored in the file clerk's desk.

Counting the Volume of Work

Everyone likes to know how much he or she has accomplished after spending considerable time on a certain type of work. This knowledge enables him to measure his own output at various times as well as to compare his productivity with the output of others performing similar tasks. It also enables supervisors to plan work ahead and to divide it up equally among the employees. For these reasons, a tally count of the work accomplished should be standard practice in the filing organization.

Maintenance of the Files

Folders should be reviewed regularly and new folders made up when necessary. When folder thickness exceeds ½ inch, the contents should be divided and new folders made. Miscellaneous folders should be checked and individual folders prepared for all names which have four or more letters filed.

The scoring at bottom of folder should be used to form a base for expanded folders. Restricted records should be kept in locked files.

Typing and Attaching Labels

To ensure ease of locating a specific folder it is important that uniformity of labeling be observed. The folder tab should not be written on. Standard gummed labels should be typed according to the specifications below and centered on the folder tab. Typing should start one space down from the center crease of label and two spaces from the left margin. Solid capital letters should be used and abbreviations avoided unless title is too long for the label. The year of the record should be typed on the upper right-hand corner of the label. The label should be folded along the center crease; the gummed side moistened; the center crease should be pressed to the top edge of folder tab; and the label smoothed down from the top.

Standard Indexes and Folders

File drawers should be indexed with fifth cut metal tip pressboard guides. The main guides should be in the first position, secondary guides in the second position, and special guides in the fifth position. Records should be enclosed in manila folders with triple scored bottoms and center position tabs in one-third cut. Records that are not filed in folders, such as cards and sales invoices, may use the center position for tertiary guides if necessary. Outcards will be inserted to the extreme left in the fifth position.

This general outline can be adapted to any sequence of file, as follows:

Sequence	Guides			Folders
	Main	Secondary	Special	
Alphabetical....	A-Z	Finer break-down of letters (AC, AN)	Outcards Common names Large active accounts	Individual name Miscellaneous
Chronological...	Year or months	Alternate months	Outcards	Alphabetic Date Location
Geographical....	State	Town or city	Alphabetic in large cities	Street address
Organizational..	Major groups	Departments or sections		

Conditioning Records for File

Remove all pins and clips and staple where necessary. Repair torn or worn papers with mending tissue. Mount small papers on standard size sheets. Reinforce worn punched holes with gummed reinforcements.

Collection and Distribution of Records

File material should be collected from all section file boxes at least once each day. The volume of work to be filed will determine the frequency of collection trips and a definite collection schedule will be adhered to.

Upon receipt of records in the files section, the distribution clerk will sort them into file groups and deliver each group to the file clerk assigned to that file.

Call-Up Procedure

Records which are requested for future reference will be indicated by the letters C.U., the call-up date and the requester's name in the upper right-hand corner of the top sheet of the record. (Instructions to the effect should be issued by the Office Manager.)

The file classifier will circle the C.U. date with a red crayon and list a description of the record on an Outcard (form SR-1698-1). A small check will be placed inside the red circle to indicate to the file clerk that the call-up has been recorded and that the papers may be filed in their regular folder. The Outcards will be filed in a call-up file in chronological order.

Each morning the file distributor will remove the call-up cards which have fallen due and distribute them to the file clerks who will remove the records called up and leave the Outcard in place of the records withdrawn. Records will be delivered to the requesters each morning.

Charge-Out Procedure

For general use, the Outcard (SR-1698-1) will be filed in place of the record withdrawn from file. On the card will be listed the title and date of the record, the name of the requester and the date withdrawn from file. Upon return of the record to file, the Outcard will be removed, the file description crossed off and the card kept for re-use.

In some instances, where requesters are not adjacent to the file section, a written request form may be used (SR-698—File Requisition). This form is filled out and sent to the File Section. Upon receipt of this file requisition, the file clerk will pull the desired record, replacing it with the requisition mounted on a heavy pressboard out-guide. The record is sent on to the requester.

When the record is returned to file, remove the Outcard and destroy the file requisition.

Use this file requisition when telephone requests are received.

Sorting Records

In order to facilitate filing of records into their proper sequence in the file drawer, the file clerk will arrange the records into filing order. The use of alphabetic sorting devices with the appropriate number of dividers for the volume of work to be sorted will increase the speed of handling quantities of records.

Standard sorters may generally be secured with 25 divisions, 50 divisions or multiples of 50. To determine the necessary number of divisions the average number of records handled at a time should be divided by 10 to 15. Should the resulting figure exceed the number of folder headings, the figure should be revised downward to that number. Generally speaking, fine sorting of records behind each divider may be accomplished most efficiently when quantities range from

GENERAL FILING PROCEDURE

DAILY ROUTINE

STEP 1	Distribute call-ups each morning.
STEP 2	Go to call-up tickler file and remove Outcards for all call-ups due.
STEP 3	Go to file and remove requested record, leaving Outcard in its place.
STEP 4	Deliver charge-outs to requesters.
STEP 5	Mark and file all new records received the previous day.
STEP 6	File returns after each collection.
STEP 7	Fill requests for records as they are received, notifying requester when records cannot be located or when they are already charged out.
STEP 8	Distribute the day's reading copies after the last file collection.
	Hold aside reading copies received during the day.
	At the end of the day, attach a distribution slip to the top and staple all together.
	Distribute to interested senior personnel.

WEEKLY ROUTINE

STEP 1	Check files for records charged out for more than a week.
STEP 2	After returns have been refiled on Tuesday morning, check drawers for files outstanding for more than a week, and list.
STEP 3	Request return of files that are no longer being used. If files must be held longer, request approximate date of return.
STEP 4	Mark charge-out card with estimated due date and recheck the following Tuesday after this due date.

Shell Oil Company's manual enumerates the duties of the file clerk

10-15 pieces. Sorter divider labels should conform to the filing system. A straight alphabetical breakdown should not be used for geographical or organizational files.

After fine sorting is completed the clerk will count the number of pieces to be filed and record the amount on a daily tally sheet.

ALPHABETICAL SORTING PROCEDURE

Steps	Action Taken
1	Drop records behind appropriate dividers (topical, geographical or straight A-Z)
2	When primary sort is complete, hand-sort contents of each divider into strict filing order.
3	Where there is more than one record for the same name or location, arrange in date order with latest date on top.

In most cases, the sorting of records numerically may be accomplished more quickly by the following system of hand sorting, since there are only 10 primary divisions used.

NUMERICAL SORTING PROCEDURE

Steps	
1	Sort numbers by digits starting with the extreme right and moving a column at a time to the left.
2	Sort by units column into 10 piles (0-9).
3	Place groups in numerical order with the highest number on top.
4	Repeat this process using the next column to the left each time until all the columns have been sorted.
5	After the last column has been sorted, reverse the pickup of the group so that the highest number is on the bottom and the complete pile is now in strict numerical order.
6	This process can be stopped at any column if it is decided that the time spent in sorting is not balanced by the time saved in locating the record. (i.e., D-1 Invoice filed by last 3 digits.)

HOW TO MAKE

TROUBLE	SOLUTION
Too many filing places?	Try centralizing files under one supervisor. Use roving clerks if some departments insist on keeping certain types of information themselves.
Everybody a file clerk?	Centralize authority with responsibility. Allow only designated persons to use files except in emergencies.
Do you have a definite plan to follow?	Start a filing procedure manual and then *use* it! Don't depend on snap judgment or the opinions of others. When a problem arises, make a ruling, then write it down.
Does your system fit the way material is called for?	Study the possibilities of using subject, geographic or numeric, as well as alphabetic filing for certain specialized materials.
Are files disordered; show no particular plan or arrangement?	Pick a ready-made, engineered system that best fits your needs. Adjust it if necessary as time goes on. Your stationer carries several systems and can work one out to suit your needs.
Are drawers jammed too tight?	Allow at least 4 inches of working space in files, at least 2 inches in card files. Space is not as valuable as working time.
Do you have to finger too many folders before you find the right one?	Have an index guide for each inch of active drawer space or each 6-8 folders. This averages out about 25 guides per drawer for best efficiency.
Same trouble with card files?	Have not more than 30 cards to a guide in an average reference file; not more than 20 in an active or growing one; and definitely not more than 10-15 to a guide in a posted record file, such as a ledger.
Do bulging folders slow down your filing speed?	Have not over 25 sheets per folder for best efficiency; not over 50 at the maximum.
Do papers pile up in the "miscellaneous" folders?	Give a customer his own folder after his sixth letter to you. If that doesn't work, you need a larger number of divisions in your index.
Is it hard to find papers in the miscellaneous folder?	Be sure to file papers alphabetically by name first, then by date, with the last date on top.
Too many Johnsons, Smiths, Nationals?	Use special name guides for frequently occurring names of individuals, firms, states, etc.

YOUR FILES SMILE*

TROUBLE	SOLUTION
Are guides in good condition?	Replace broken guides. Use reinforced tabs in the active file. Use angular tabs for easier reading. Use tab inserts for greater versatility and less expansion expense. Use edges of guide and not the tab when pushing contents of file.
Are folder tabs readable and in good condition?	Use gummed labels; they strengthen and beautify as well as add legibility. Use reinforced tabs where reference is frequent. Use a good grade of paper for active files—it pays!
Do your folders get lazy and sag down out of sight?	Stop misfiling and extra time waste with stiffer folders. Use scored or bellows folders for better expansion. Use suspended or hanging folders for active files.
Some individual folders too full?	Make a special name guide for the individual then put a set of period or chronological folders back of the guide, one for each anticipated 30 papers for the year.
Do your folders wear out too soon?	Use at least an 11 point folder for frequent usage out of the file, 14 point or pressboard for heavy use. Save space yet add strength with double tabbed folders.
Is old correspondence slowing up the filing of current paper?	Transfer old material at least once a year, oftener if necessary. See if some types of correspondence need be filed at all.
Is file storage using up valuable floor space?	Check use of 5-drawer cabinets, side-opening cabinets, or shelf filing. Establish a destruction plan. Consolidation of files can help.
Have trouble finding material called for before it is filed?	Use sorting devices and sort immediately on arrival. Keep in the sorter until ready to index.
Does getting the papers into the final folders take too long?	Use sorting devices to completely arrange the papers. Saves walking and fumbling time and reduces errors.
Are you a one-armed paper handler?	Use filing shelf to free both hands for filing. The stool is another handy device to ease fatigue.
Have trouble finding missing papers or cards?	Keep track of removed papers and cards with out-guides or folders. You are always responsible unless you have facts to back you up.
Did your files keep pace with your progress?	Check size of alphabetic breakdown to see if it is adequate. Check type of alphabetic breakdown to see if it matches need and fits customer name patterns.

Courtesy National Stationery and Office Equipment Association

After approval by the Department Manager having jurisdiction over such records, the original will be forwarded to the custodian of Storage Files. The duplicate will be held in the department pending receipt of the records.

Upon receipt of the request, the Storage Files Custodian will insert the date in the space provided. The date files are released will also be noted. The requested records will be pulled from file and replaced by out-guides. Form S-1714-2 will then be filed in the custodian's charge-out file arranged by department and date of request. Strict follow-up for return of records held more than thirty days will be maintained.

Disposal of Records

The prompt and orderly disposal of storage files upon expiration of their retention periods is an important objective in releasing space and keeping storage cost at a minimum.

The storage custodian will remove the Storage Files Transmittals (S-1714-1) from his destruction call-up file when the retention period of records has lapsed, and will dispose of the records as indicated thereon.

When disposal of records has been effected, the storage custodian will indicate, on the first and third copies of form S-1714-1, the manner in which records were disposed of and the date. The custodian and a witness will sign both copies. Copy 1 will be transferred to the custodian's Terminated Records Binder in chronological order. The third copy will be forwarded to the originating files section. Upon receipt of this copy the file custodian will remove copy 2 from the master binder and destroy it, replacing it with copy 3. Copy 4 will be placed in the Terminated Records Binder and a destruction notation will be made next to the record in the Register of Storage Files Transmittal Numbers (S-1714-5).

STORAGE OF INACTIVE RECORDS

In order that the Records Protection, Retention and Destruction Program may be carried on successfully, a system for controlling records sent to dead storage is necessary. A storage files custodian should be appointed at each storage location to assume full responsibility for the protection and retention of those records. It will be the responsibility of the file supervisors to prepare records for inactive storage in conformance with the following procedures.

Processing Files for Storage

ELIMINATING TEMPORARY RECORDS

All extra copies of records, newspapers, magazines and periodicals in file, as well as all draft copies, will be removed.

Informational copies of reports received from other departments will be retained in the active files until they have served their purpose, then destroyed.

REMOVAL OF SALVAGEABLE MATERIAL

Salvageable material will be removed before packing records in storage cases. Records will be removed from loose-leaf binders and placed in regular file folders. Storage binders will be used where permanent binding is desirable and records will not be microfilmed. Metal or celluloid tipped pressboard folders will be replaced with regular file folders. File guides and indexes will be retained for active files. Out-guides will be left in place to indicate charged-out records.

Chapter 42

RETENTION AND STORAGE
OF RECORDS

THE benefits of a reorganization in the records department do not become evident until the first batch of records is tossed out. This should not take place until the records have been inventoried and the findings of the inventory have been analyzed. There are many companies that have developed forms to get better control over the actual disposition of the records.

There are, of course, other dispositions to be made of inventoried material beside destroying it. What happens to this remaining material should be decided by the legal and operating needs of the individual company. There is serious danger when one company adopts the retention schedule developed by another organization—an example of "one man's meat being another man's poison."

The problem of establishing retention dates based on legal requirements is not a difficult one: Check the state and federal laws and examine your records with these in mind. For companies in interstate commerce there is one more step: Determine the statutes of limitation for the states in which you do business.

Retention information based on these legal requirements is a fairly clear-cut matter; the influence of operating needs on the retention schedule is not. The following paragraphs outline one company's approach to the problem of retention dates; it is typical of the methods used by many others:

A. A records retention system to be workable should be:

1. Simple.

2. Flexible—decisions are made on a variety of factors requiring judgment and appraisal, rather than on the basis of sharply drawn definition.

B. The important elements affecting records preservation policies and the periods for records retention are:

1. The statute of limitations.

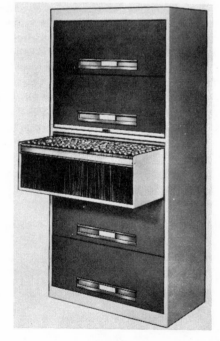

Above, lateral files are offered for the convenience of the modern office by Steelcase. There are add-on storage cabinets. At the right, a filing system by Supreme Steel Equipment Corp. provides effective filing space for almost every fraction of its 30-inch width due to a new, invisible suspension device which eliminates suspension slides.

2. The regulations of governmental agencies.

3. Recognized historical value.

4. Sound business judgment.

ROUTING	STORED DOCUMENT REQUEST
Purchasing & Service	Please use separate form for each type of request, and submit each in duplicate.

Requested By _____ Date _____

☐ DESTROY ☐ STORE ☐ REMOVE FROM STORAGE ☐ REPRODUCE ☐ Photostatic Copies

Description of Document (Title, Form Number and Quantity)	Date of Document		Document Number	Present Location	*Storage Location
	From	Through			

APPROVALS:

DESTROY
Authorization for Destruction _____ Date _____
Method of Destruction _____
Destruction Certified by _____ Date _____

STORE
Purch. and Service Section Supervisor's Approval for Storage _____ Date _____
Purchasing and Service Section Clerk Certification of Storage _____ Date _____

RETURN FROM STORAGE
Signature of Receipt of Requester _____ Date _____
Returned to Storage by Purchasing & Service Clerk _____ Date _____

REPRODUCTION
Purchasing & Service Section Supervisor's Approval for Reprod. _____ Date _____
Order Placed for Reproduction--Purch. & Service Clerk _____ Date _____
Order Received and Given to Requester--Purch. & Service Clerk _____ Date _____
*Completed by Purchasing and Service Clerk

A multipurpose records-disposition form

677

Date _____

_____
(Name of Bank)

SCHEDULE OF RECORDS FOR DESTRUCTION

Item No. in Schedule	√	Description of Record	Form No.	File No.	Date of Record		Location
					From —	To —	

Authority is requested to destroy the records described above.

_____
(Name of person in immediate charge of records)

Examined and approved:

_____ Signature

I hereby certify that the records described above have

been destroyed by _____
(Indicate manner disposed of)

_____
(Name of person destroying records)

_____
Date

A form like this one makes it possible to maintain control over disposition of records and establish responsibility for their destruction at the same time.

C. The following are four classifications often applied in grouping records for retention purposes:

1. *Class 1 or Vital Records*—These records are irreplaceable and include records which offer direct evidence of ownership, franchises, minute books, deeds, journals, and ledgers.

2. *Class 2 or Important Records*—These are administrative instruments and include reports, statistical and cost studies, and the great bulk of accounting records supporting current operating routines.

3. *Class 3 or Useful Records*—These are records frequently used and currently available, but their loss will not seriously handicap business operations.

4. *Class 4 or Nonessential Records*—These records have no long-term value and are eligible for immediate destruction.

D. In classifying records into retention groups consideration should be given to:

1. Possible future value.

2. Legal value.

3. Possible interference with operations.

4. Relations with the public or customers.

5. Relations with governmental agencies.

6. The problem and expense of replacement in case of loss.

7. Availability elsewhere of identical copies.

8. The extent to which the same data summarizes or is summarized by other records.

9. The degree to which the record provides essential details.

E. Records may be further classified into file groups for reference purposes as follows:

1. *Active Files:* These files should include only records to which relatively frequent reference is made.

2. *Semiactive Files*—These are files which contain records no longer in the "Active" group but which should be retained within the office premises area for occasional reference.

3. *Inactive Files*—Records included in these files are to be retained permanently or for a specified period and are seldom used for reference purposes. Inactive files would be placed in the Records Storage Warehouse.

It is often unwise to rely entirely upon one department head's judgment when establishing retention and destruction schedules. He sometimes has distorted ideas of the importance and frequency of use of certain records. An accurate check can be made of the frequency of reference to records by having file clerks tabulate the requests. An earlier Dartnell study of this problem disclosed that when one company compiled such a tabulation for several months and analyzed the data, it discovered that 91 percent of the requests were for material less than six months old; only 1 percent was for material older than a year. Some companies take what they call a "calculated risk" in destroying some records; they get rid of records whose lack in the years to come may cost the company money. This decision is, of course, not made until all the facts, pro and con, are tallied up, and until the cost of retaining the particular record far outweighs all possible losses which could result from not having it.

Flexible Retention Schedules

Disposition schedules should function continuously and as automatically as possible. Companies that delay disposition until file cabinets are overflowing often discover to their sorrow that the job is too big to be handled without a major effort on everyone's part.

Retention schedules should be characterized by a flexibility that will allow them to conform to the changes that experience indicates necessary from time to time. It is important that some device be set up for recording this experience—to show that some records will have to be kept for a longer time, others for a shorter time.

Unfortunately, establishing a well-coordinated retention schedule does not in itself insure that a company will have safe, economical, accessible, and efficient records. The program has to be policed. As an official of the General Tire & Rubber Company said a few years ago:

Our main experience with our retention schedule is that it must be constantly policed. Two years ago when this function of our company was placed under my supervision, I started a house-cleaning campaign and disposed of over 50 tons of old records which could have been thrown away had our manual been followed. We again reviewed our old files this spring and secured approval from our Legal Department to shorten our requirements on some items and were able to dispose of a great many more old records.

Specific Record Groups

The following summary of typical record groups includes an explanation of the factors to watch in setting a retention period for each type of record. The list was prepared by the president of The National Records Management Council, for publication as a management aid for small manufacturers by The Small Business Administration.

Accounting, General (journals, ledgers, trial balance). Journals and ledgers mean different things to different companies. The general ledger, as the basic summary accounting record, is usually retained permanently. The subsidiary journals and ledgers are required only for internal administration and need be retained only through periods of actual use by the accounting department, auditors, or top management. Trial balances are working papers that need be retained only through final audit.

Accounts Payable (general canceled checks, canceled payroll checks, vouchers). While canceled general checks may be retained for the number of years defined in each state's statute of limitations (average of six years), some companies keep payroll checks for only two years. Canceled payroll checks can create a volume problem. The greatest activity is in the first few weeks after issuance, and usually falls to next to nothing after the first year. Vouchers are always a bulk problem. Rather than keep them all for six to 20 years, breaks can be made between plant vouchers (retained permanently), operating vouchers (retained for an average of six years), and petty cash vouchers (retained for an average of one to two years). This holds for originals only. Further breaks might be made by dollar value. It pays to limit retaining copies of these vouchers for a minimum number of weeks or months.

Accounts Receivable (billing copies of invoices, credit-memo invoices, accounts receivable ledger). Management's chief concern is in the unpaid invoices. Paid invoices—particularly large-volume, small-dollar-value items—may often be disposed of within six months to two years. Most complaints on payment or amount of payment are received within this period. Equally important is minimum retention of any invoice files that duplicate the basic record (arranged by customer or by invoice number). Only those invoices connected with items of new design or the first item of a patentable product require long indefinite retention. The accounts receivable ledger, as a basic summary of credit sales, need be kept only so long as it is a ready index to invoices or total daily sales. Where there is no other summary of sales, it may be useful to retain it indefinitely for historical purposes.

Legal (contracts, copyrights, patents, trademarks, suits). Copyrights, patents and trademarks are usually retained permanently. Contracts are more often kept for six years after expiration, but when renewed annually are generally kept for shorter periods. Records on lawsuits are typically kept for six to 10 years after settlement. Bulky work papers and routine notes connected with contracts and suits should be cleaned out as soon as the matter is legally completed.

Payroll (earnings records, payrolls, pension records). The basic legal requirements are: (1) Internal Revenue Service—four years for earnings records (Federal Insurance Contributions Act and Federal Unemployment Tax); (2) Department of Labor, Wage and Hour Division—three years for payrolls, two years for earnings records; and (3) the Department of Labor, Division of Public Contracts—four years for wage and hour records. Pension records are usually retained permanently and may often serve as the earnings record as well.

Personnel (applications for employment, attendance records, time clock cards, employee history records, personnel folders). Where a company maintains both employee history cards and personnel folders, the history cards may be destroyed within one year after termination of employment. An exception to the latter might be the top executive personnel data. Employment applications should be kept only for jobs or persons where the company anticipates action in the near future. Attendance records, time clock cards, and related data should be handled as a package: where this information is summarized on project or payroll records, the bulky initial records may be discarded within one to six months.

Production (job tickets, maintenance records, operating reports, production orders). Job tickets and production orders are really only of value in processing the order through the factory or when the customer raises questions on delivery or quality. These points come up in the initial months after shipping. Actual production orders are the only ones that warrant retention beyond one year. And of all the records for one order (e.g., job ticket, shipping ticket, bill of lading) only one need be retained in the original. Most information is repeated from one form to the next. Maintenance records are usually retained for the life of the equipment on which the data are compiled. Monthly operating reports on production are valuable up to two years. Annual operating reports should be kept permanently for historical and management purposes.

Purchasing (bids, purchase orders, receiving reports, purchase requisition). Purchase orders should be broken down into categories for retention purposes: major equipment, expendable supplies and materials, and the like. Major purchase records, particularly where specifications are included, might be kept for six years. Routine items may be cut to three years and still stay within legal requirements on proof of local purchase and on records of use for tax purposes. Purchase requisitions need be retained only until the items are received—since the data are covered on the purchase order. Receiving reports are usually supporting documents for the accounts payable vouchers and are retained accordingly. Bids are kept after a contract is let out only so long as management wants them for post-audit purposes, and so long as purchasing agents may need them as references for the next contract where the services or items may be identical, or nearly so, for the same service or items.

Real Estate (deeds, leases). Deeds, rights-of-way, and easements are usually retained permanently; leases for six years after expiration. If leases are renewed annually, they may be kept only for the current year plus one.

Sales (correspondence, customer orders, salesmen's reports). Sales correspondence on deliveries, acknowledgments, bids, and so on, need only be kept at the most 30 to 60 days for possible answer and followup. Policy letters should be segregated and retained permanently. Customer orders in sales departments are only copies of accounts receivable files and should be kept, if at all, for minimum periods. Salesmen's reports on individual sales, and expenses, are important only for immediate review. They warrant keeping for only a few months.

Secretary (annual reports, by-laws, minutes of stockholders' meetings, canceled stock certificates). The first three items are usually kept permanently. Canceled stock certificates are not governed by any federal legal requirement (except for regulated companies) and may be destroyed at the discretion of the company. However, most firms keep a formal certificate of destruction.

Tax (purchase-and-use tax returns, state and federal tax returns). Regulations on purchase-and-use taxes usually state that a city must announce its intentions to act on a company's returns within three years. There is no limitation, however, in case of fraud. The same holds true of state and federal returns. The purchase-and-use tax statements are usually retained for three years. State and federal returns, being more involved, are retained at least six years, often permanently. Work papers may be destroyed within the minimum periods.

Traffic (bills of lading, freight bills, packing lists). The only legal requirement on these items is on "order, shipping, and billing records"—Department of Labor, Wage and Hour Division—for two years. However, there is rarely need for more than one official record to cover any one shipment (see also preceding section on "Production").

Preparing Records for Storage

Some companies, particularly larger ones and those located in expensive office buildings, have established outlying records centers in low-cost buildings or areas. One consideration here is the possible historical use of the records to be stored. Company rules and policies, for example, that were in effect during World War II will provide valuable guides to follow in the event of another war. Then too, it sometimes happens that a company must revive a practice which has not been in use for a number of years; the memory of some office "old-timer" is all the company can lean on.

Many companies retain historical material by sampling a certain part according to some established plan. Some save 10 percent by selecting every tenth record, destroying the rest. Others use certain key days of the month or letters of the alphabet.

The Oxford rotary sorter is designed to handle large volumes of paper work while the clerk remains seated.

Courtesy, Oxford Filing Supply Co.

Western Electric Company has followed the procedure outlined in the following paragraphs for more than 15 years. The company finds it a simple and economical method of indexing and filing inactive records. It is eminently satisfactory from the point of accessibility. N. R. Frame, former secretary, says of the system: "It enables us to store any kind of records in any quantity from any organization with no risk of error." The description that follows originally appeared in "The Folder," a publication of Records Management Association of New York.

Employees preparing records for storage shall carefully analyze all binders, folders and loose papers. Insofar as practical, the following shall be done:

1. Records shall be reviewed to determine whether they belong in the group classified "General" for which mandatory periods of preservation are established by the secretary, or whether they belong in the group classified "Routine" for which retention is determined by organizations having jurisdiction.

2. Papers having no value as records such as extra copies shall be removed and destroyed, and records for which prescribed periods of preservation have expired shall be removed and authorized for destruction.

3. For most economical storage heavy binders, folders, index sheets, fasteners (including paper clips) which constitute unnecessary bulk shall be removed or replaced with less bulky items which can be made to serve the same purpose (i.e., heavy binders may be replaced by kraft folders; many thin folders may be combined into a single folder; contents may be removed from folders and filed loosely in stapled sets; Acco or other bulky fasteners may be replaced by wire staples).

4. Rubber bands deteriorate in storage and shall be replaced by paper bands to eliminate risk of confusion which may be caused by physical breakdown of files.

5. Papers constituting a file or subject segregated by means of paper bands, or folders, or fastened together in stapled sets shall be plainly labeled to indicate the divisional file reference number and other description of records, including date or period covered.

   Card records expected to be used infrequently for reference shall be arranged in banded sets in such a way that they can be conveniently placed in storage boxes. Custodian of the record room shall be consulted for method of packing and labeling since these vary with the size and nature of the records.

6. Records so prepared shall be placed in kraft storage envelopes (9 inches high, 12 or 15 inches long, 4 inches expansion), and the filled envelopes shall then be placed in storage boxes approximately the same size as the envelopes. (The boxes, which are marked with temporary numbers on the outside, are used for convenience in transporting records to storage.)

   Upon arrival in the record room, the envelopes and their contents are removed from boxes and placed in metal transfer cases. Pressboard tabbed guides are used to mark the beginning of each storage unit (see Par. 7d) which may consist of one envelope or many envelopes of related records. All records contained in one storage unit shall be scheduled for destruction at the same time.

   In order to facilitate the handling, storage, withdrawal and refiling of inactive records, the subdivisions within a storage unit (i.e., folders, binders, banded sets, etc.) shall be arranged in organizational file sequence and each of the subdivisions shall be assigned a number in sequence beginning with the numeral 1 for the first subdivision at the front of the first envelope in the storage unit, and continuing through the last subdivision in the last envelope of the storage unit.

7. For each storage unit four copies of a form entitled, "Index to Records in Secretary's Organization Storage at General Headquarters" shall be prepared in typewritten form showing:

   a. Subdivision number, with complete description of records contained in each subdivision, including period covered;

   b. Records Schedule—i.e., information indicating whether records are classified "General" with applicable paragraph number of Secretary's Direction which covers such records and which specifies period of preservation established for them, or "Routine" with period of preservation established by organization having jurisdiction over the records involved;

   c. Name of organization having jurisdiction, and name of person responsible for sending records to storage;

   d. Date period of preservation expires as computed from date of records (see item a, above) on basis of records schedule (see item b, above);

Custodian of the record room examines all records reviewed for storage to ascertain that all instructions regarding preparation for storage have been complied with, and then assigns a storage unit number which is a combination of (1) prefix letter indicating size and type of container in which records are to be stored; (2) year records are consigned to storage; (3) accession number in series beginning with 1 for each storage container group; (4) suffix letter combination indicating name of general division having jurisdiction over records sent to storage.

Example: C-56-1236-GA—indicates the 1236th unit filed in correspondence size transfer case for the year 1956—sent by Comptroller's Organization.

This method of assigning storage unit numbers enables the custodian of the record room to fill up transfer cases (and shelves where used for oversize records) solidly without regard to kind of records or sending organization, thus eliminating guesswork and wasted facilities which ordinarily result when storage space is allocated to the various organizations or according to type of record involved.

8. Storage unit numbers are stamped on pressboard guide tab (see item 6), on each subdivision within the unit, and on all copies of the Index form referred to in Par 7. One copy of the form is filed by the records clerk in a centralized file according to divisions sending records to storage, arranged by unit number within the divisional groups, and one copy is returned to organization sending records to storage. Other copies used for followup.

9. Requests for records from storage are made on special salmon tabbed requisitions which serve as "Out Guide." The only information required for locating records in storage is storage unit number and subdivision number. (By using this method records clerk avoids the necessity of familiarizing herself with labeling idiosyncrasies and filing systems of a hundred or more file clerks in the various organizations—theoretically she doesn't even have to know what has been sent to her for storage.)

Protection of Records Is Vital

In major disasters such as floods, cyclones, tornadoes, etc., more than a few businesses have lost all their records, with far-reaching catastrophe resulting from the blow. Particularly in the case of a smaller business without cash reserves, funds for reestablishing the operation are very difficult to obtain when there are no proper records of earnings. Insurance payment is questioned because no evaluation of the extent of damage is possible without current and correct records.

Even large companies often do not properly protect their vital records, and small concerns fail more frequently because they are sometimes prone to operate on a more casual basis. A case in point concerns a businessman who manufactured automotive devices and who was, unfortunately, the victim of a severe flood. A substantial part of his loss was destroyed or damaged inventory ($35,000), and records. An outside financial specialist had to be brought in to make estimates and analyses of the company's sales and normal inventories, with the usual ratios in effect in the automotive trade. If the owner had been able to produce proper inventory records, he could easily have substantiated his inventory losses. Failure to maintain these records and store them in a safe place required the financial specialist to devote much high-priced time to his estimated verifications of the flood loss.

PROTECTION OF RECORDS

Type	Description of Records	Protection Required
CLASS I "Vital Records"	All records essential for the re-creation of the business including those which may be used as a basis for loans or collections, immediately after the fire.	Fire-resistant safes or vaults with protection comparable to the maximum fire hazard to which records may be exposed.
CLASS II "Important Records"	The reproduction of which may be obtained, but at considerable expense.	Fire-resistant safes, vaults, or certified record containers commensurate with the exposure hazard.
CLASS III "Useful"	Loss of which would be inconvenient but which might be readily replaced.	Uninsulated steel filing equipment.
CLASS IV "Nonessential"	Material which has outlived its useful life.	Should be destroyed to reduce fire hazard.

According to fire insurance practice, only records which can be re-created from other sources are considered acceptable risks. Remington Rand Div. estimates that proper equipment can save 70 percent of insurance rates.

Another case involved an aircraft company which sustained a heavy loss, also a result of floods. Unfortunately, master blueprints and specifications for plane production were lost and serious interruption of operations resulted. The cost of reproducing the necessary thousands of drawings and specification records was very high. Moreover, only a rough estimate of their replaced value could be made. The loss on account of production problems and delays in delivery of finished units ran into large figures. If a second set of blueprints and specifications had been deposited in a safe, dry vault located on high ground out of reach of floods, the company could have been back in production almost immediately, and could have saved much good will and thousands of dollars. Moreover, it would

Computer tapes begin to lose information when temperatures reach approximately 150 degrees F. This Mosler Safe Company Tapeguard unit has been tested to withstand 2000 degrees F. temperatures for as long as four hours with the contents remaining below 150 degrees F.

not have been necessary to lay off large numbers of employees because of the work interruption.

Tax considerations also make it vital, for documenting statements of earnings, to keep records. If a followup investigation shows that a businessman has consistently failed to maintain proper records the Internal Revenue Service may hale him into court on a charge of willful negligence. Penalty for this misdemeanor is a fine of $10,000 or one year's imprisonment, or both—plus the court costs.

How 234 Companies Protect Vital Records

The Dartnell office-management research staff has had an increasing number of requests for current information on records protection. Therefore, we compiled an exchange of management experience in protecting vital records.

Proper record protection should be of concern to all companies—large or small—in all types of business and industry. In the case of smaller organizations without cash reserves, funds for reestablishing the operation are difficult to obtain after a disaster when there are no proper records of earnings. Large companies often do not protect their vital records properly, operating on too "casual" a basis. Aside from the need for such information, there is a need to have tax records in order.

Larger concerns, particularly those located in expensive office building space, have a preference for using records centers in low-cost buildings or areas. But, whether the firm be large or small, there is general agreement that a system for protecting records should be developed.

Of the 234 companies joining in this Dartnell exchange of management experience, 41 percent store their records in burglarproof, fireproof vaults, 10 percent use fireproof steel files or cabinets, and another 13 percent have fireproof storage rooms. Other storage areas mentioned include archives buildings, basements, banks, special record rooms, branch offices, and one bombproof shelter.

Sixteen percent of the respondents have guards protecting records. Thirty-five percent have a sprinkling system that is set off automatically in the event of fire, and a number of others have an alarm system.

Classes of Fireproof Safes, Files, etc.

Nearly 74 percent of the firms have point-of-use protection for daily records. Sixty-seven percent report their safes or storage areas bear a classification of the National Board of Fire Underwriters.

These ratings range from one hour (the most prevalent reported) to four hours. The four classifications are:

CLASS A —these units protect documents up to four hours in fire temperatures up to 2000 degrees Fahrenheit.

CLASS B —units that protect for two hours up to 1850 degrees Fahrenheit.

CLASSES C
AND D—each protects for one hour up to 1700 degrees Fahrenheit. Class D units are not required to meet impact tests Classes A, B, and C must meet. Impact specifications assure that the cabinets won't spring open if they fall several floors to the basement if floors should burn through.

Experience With Damaged or Destroyed Records

Most of the participating companies (63 percent) have been fortunate enough never to have had records damaged or destroyed in the past. But among the others, 12 percent have had flood losses; 8 percent, fire losses; and several report theft and decomposition losses.

We asked the 234 executives included in this study, "If fire swept through your building tonight, would you be out of business, hard-pressed to recover, or protected?" Here is what they said:

Out of business—12 percent

Hard-pressed to recover—27 percent

Protected—61 percent

One controller admitted, "We'd be in a helluva shape even though we are protected." Others stressed the fact that recovery would be a tedious and time-consuming process.

Asked to make any supplemental comments they deemed pertinent to the subject at hand, many contributors have added statements to the information already given in this survey. We have selected a number of these as representative:

"Our records storage is certainly far from adequate, the situation being complicated by the fact that we maintain several separate plants and are quite crowded for space in general."

"All areas where records are in daily use are fully sprinklered. Numerous other related precautions are taken, too. Buildings are of the most fire-resistant construction. We have adequate fire department protection. Buildings are patrolled by our own employees and/or building and patrol service people."

"We have found our records-protection program to work most effectively as part of our records-retention program. This provides operating units with a single document indicating retention and protection requirements. It also assures that vital records volume is kept at a minimum."

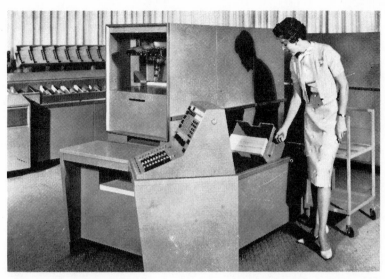

Modern electronic data-processing equipment like this helps cut expenses by saving thousands of hours of clerical time. ABOVE: Burroughs B251 Visible Record Computer shows results of advanced production and design techniques. Completely solid-state, it has over 4,400 transistors and magnetic core memory.

BELOW: The General Electric 225 Information Processing System puts microfilm to work for inventory control and record keeping at the Martin Company in Denver, Colorado. Paperwork costs have been slashed.

"We take microfilm pictures of all our daily charges and credits. Statements are microfilmed before mailing. Two prints of each roll are developed. One is stored in our main office and another in the branch office. Mortgages, deeds, and other important records have all been photostated and placed in a branch safe. As for vital records, we feel we are quite safe. Everyday invoices and papers of communication are not as well covered, however."

"We are a small company. Originals of agreements with authors and editors are protected in our safe. Accounting ledgers and records are placed in a vault at night. Accounts receivables are kept in a fireproof, locked file. Loss of manuscripts is insured."

"Most of our problems are with Canadian statutory regulations—different government offices require records kept for longer periods of time. Also, we have just completed our greatest growth and our records-retention program is out of date."

Respondents agree—offices are run on papers. Paperwork can become a monster or a tamed pet, depending upon the system involved and the care given it. With a sensible system of filing, protecting, and disposing of paperwork, companies have a strong tool in combating rising office costs. As one respondent summed things up, "The fewer records you have, the better they are maintained and protected, the faster you'll find the ones you need."

In some companies the mail and file operations are combined under the same operating supervisor. When this is done, care must be exercised to see that the files are not neglected, since the urgency of mail-room activities has a tendency to sidetrack the filing operations. A daily production report showing outstanding backlog on the files is usually sufficient to keep this situation from getting out of hand.

HOW TO FILE PAPER TAPES AND CARDS

A practical method for filing and finding punched paper tape or edge-punched cards is an important feature of any system of mechanizing data processing through the use of these coded media. Every minute saved here contributes to the purpose of applying automatic writing and reproducing equipment.

Generally speaking, record filing and finding represent one of the most expensive and time-consuming jobs of the office. The purpose here is to suggest a number of methods and devices that are employed in many offices to simplify the handling of tape and cards.

Punched Tapes—Characteristics: There are two special problems peculiar to tape handling: (1) identification; and (2) that arising from the physical character of the paper tape.

The only tape normally self-identified by a typed interpretation of code punching is the "chadless" tape produced by a typing reperforator, part of a Teletype system. Otherwise, an essential element in operations is some other means of positive tape identification.

While special tapes of various widths are available, the most common standard widths are:

11/16 inch—Five-channel general communications tape

7/8 inch—Five-channel or six-channel

1 inch—Seven-channel or eight-channel.

This discussion covers five-channel tape unless otherwise indicated, but the methods of filing can be applied to others in most instances.

Tapes are supplied either in rolls or flatfolded in various length folds. Feed holes are not preperforated in tape. Tape is impregnated with an oil for added strength and resistance to wear—although at least one company manufactures a nonoily tape claimed to be as tough as the impregnated variety. The "bleeding" effect on any paper with which the tape is in contact for any time must be considered.

Temporary Filing of Tapes: Punched tapes may be held temporarily in one of several ways depending on circumstances.

1. *Butterfly Fold.* The tape is wound in a Figure 8 on two fingers of the operator's hand. The same side of the tape is always faced toward the hand at the crossing of the 8 in the winding so that the concentric layers are flat against previous layers. Once wound, the tape can be held simply by a clip at the cross of the 8 and can later be unwound from either end without twisting or rolling.

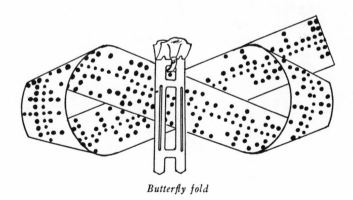

Butterfly fold

2. *Slotted Rack.* Wire communication companies provide slotted racks for location near the machine into which tapes may be slipped

without folding or rolling. Such racks can also be made by practically any carpenter shop and will provide a satisfactory method for holding a limited number of tapes which are to be reoperated in a reasonably short time.

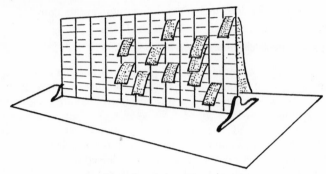

Slotted rack for tape strips

3. *With Form.* Tape originally furnished in flatfolded form, and short lengths of rolled tape, are often merely clipped to the form to which they relate, the rolled tape being folded as little as possible for this temporary handling.

Permanent Files—Flatfolded Tape: Filing of punched tape for longer periods presents the additional requirements of identification and a more compact storage space for each tape. In general, the tape is held in one of two ways: flatfolded or rerolled. The rerolling, of course, applies to rolled tape only, although rolled tape is often manually folded by the operator after perforating.

Tapes can be flatfolded manually or mechanically. Mechanical equipment is either electrical or hand-powered. Tapes can be filed flatfolded as follows:

1. *Within Folded Form.* Based on the fact that a form is normally typed at the time a tape is punched, the simplest method of handling the associated tape is to place it within a folded form. Yet this does not entirely eliminate the possibility of separating the tape from the form which identifies it. Filing the folded forms also requires care. The forms must be folded in such a way that identifying information remains prominent in the file.

Parallel vertical slits in the form, located so as not to interfere with printing, can be used to hold the tape more firmly by threading the folded tape through them. Addition of a horizontal perforation between the slits will permit the breaking of a tab out of the form (after it is typed) to make a notch for holding the tape.

A folded-over portion of a form might be joined at the sides with a hand stapler to form a permanent pocket.

2. *Identification Envelope.* Continuous envelopes or envelopes on a carrier sheet for continuous feed on the writing machine provide a very satisfactory answer to many tape filing requirements. The envelope, providing a secure pocket, is itself typed as a proof copy of the form and/or an identification of the tape contained. For customer record or item description tapes, handling directions can also be preprinted. Envelopes normally are a heavy stock which resists tape oiliness. They are easily handled and filed.

3. *File Folders.* Ordinary letter size folders die-cut to expose identifying information on the form accompanying a tape provide a convenient method for filing both folded tapes and documents together. They are easy to handle and suitable for standard filing equipment.

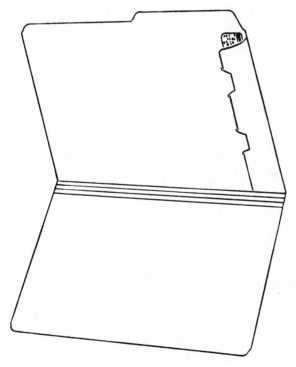

File folder (letter size or smaller) with tuck-in-flap pocket

Folders with clear acetate shields over the die-cut opening are available, as are gummed pockets for the tape which can be attached to the file folders.

Folders are manufactured with flaps which fold and tuck into die-cut locks in the folder to form a tape pocket.

4. *File-Card Holders.* Several types of holders with fold-over or flap construction provide means for tape filing and finding in card size file equipment. A pocket or slot or notched end for wrap-around holds the tape. The holders can be inserted in typewriter for typing identification data.

A combination file card and tape holder may be designed particularly for use where the posting of a card record is required with each reuse of a tape.

5. *Slotted File Cards.* Holders of the fold-over or flap construction type are available with slotted holes at bottom to hold them in place on retaining rods in rotary or other visible file equipment. Tapes can be quickly and easily inserted or removed from pocket or slot without removal of the holder. Identifying information can be typed on the face of holder.

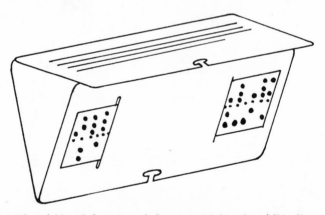

Three-fold and flap types of slotted-card holder for visible files

6. *Slotted Panels.* Plastic panels which fit standard size filing cabinets (approximately 11 inches wide by 8½ inches high) are provided with slot-type pockets by vertical ridges spaced slightly farther apart than the width of a tape. When flatfolded tapes are laid in the slots, a second facing panel holds them in place. Identification of the tape is by labels pasted at the top of each slot, by tabs on the panels, and by dividers between the panels.

Equipment of this type has varying numbers of slots depending on the width of the tape to be filed. There is available a slotted plastic file leaf with a transparent acetate cover over the slots.

7. *Celluloid and Flexoline Board.* A strip of celluloid folded so that one side is slightly wider than a tape and one side is slightly narrower, provides a very effective clip that completely encloses a flatfolded section of tape. Tape is firmly held by such a strip but can easily be slipped in and out when desirable.

For identification, labels may be added or the surface of the celluloid may be roughened permitting writing or typing to adhere. The stiffness of the celluloid will hold the strips in a Flexoline type board and a number may be filed side by side with each one immediately visible.

8. *Binders.* Standard three-ring binders with polyethylene expansion envelopes can be used to store flatfolded tapes. Each filler has 14 pockets for folded tapes, seven on each side of the plastic page.

Other flatfolded tape handling methods of varying value include:

a. Pliofilm or plastic bags—often used in conjunction with other filing to keep oily tape away from printed records.

b. Pigeonholes—varying in size for filing tapes alone or tapes

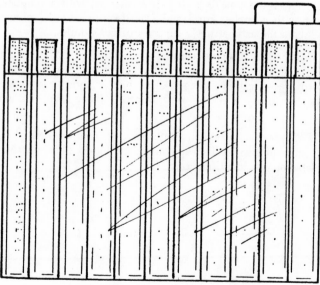

File-size plastic panel with slots for tapes

and printed records together. Requires labeling of individual slots and usually must be made individually.

c. Time card racks—for filing one or two permanent record tapes per slot.

d. Ordinary envelopes.

Rerolled Tape Storage: Tape is normally rerolled when long strips are to be reoperated in their entirety. However, shorter strips may be filed and handled conveniently by several methods. (Regular "chad" tape can be rerolled starting with either the front end or the back end of the tape. However, chadless tape from a reperforator, because of the small tabs, can be rerolled starting with the front end only.)

One method of rerolling tape is by the use of an ordinary pencil sharpener with an axle in place of the cutting heads. A rewinder for 35 millimeter film can also be used in much the same manner for rerolling tape. The communications companies can also furnish a spring drive rewinding unit, which will rewind the tapes as the documents are being transmitted. Rolled tape can be filed as follows:

1. *Tray-Drawer Files.* Rolls of tape can be stored in a regular three-drawer file cabinet which has been modified to accept 30 trays. Each tray has 150 pins (10 pins across the width and 15 pins in depth). After the tape is rolled, it is marked with a number, held compact with a rubber band and placed on one of the pins in the tray. Such a file cabinet has a capacity of 6,000 tapes.

2. *Plastic Ring.* A ring formed of a plastic band approximately one inch wide, with a diameter great enough to enclose the rolled tape provides effective storage. Clear plastic permits tape which is also typed (as by a typing reperforator) to be identified without labels.

3. *"Pillboxes."* Individual pillboxes or compartmented plastic trays will hold small rolls for convenient filing. These methods require labeling for identification.

Chapter 43

FORMS CONTROL AND DESIGN

A DARTNELL survey of the methods used by representative
companies to prevent the duplication of business forms and
the inefficient design of those that are actually necessary, makes
several conclusions obvious:

1. Control of the number of forms a company uses requires that
the responsibility for approving all new forms be placed in one
department.

2. It is necessary to devote special attention, "policing," to prevent department managers possessing reproduction equipment from
running off their own forms. This is equally true of unauthorized
purchases of forms from suppliers.

3. A forms program will not begin to make maximum yields
until the problem of designing efficient forms has been solved. In
other words, it is not sufficient to control the number of forms but
the quality as well.

4. A well-planned program of forms control can yield dollars-
and-cents savings quite out of proportion to its cost.

If one general statement can sum up the attitudes of most of the
companies surveyed, it would probably be, "Forms control is a headache—and a very expensive one it can be, too." For forms control,
like records management and similar administrative responsibilities,
can be forgotten only at the risk of having the situation get completely out of hand.

Centralized Control

It is easy to understand the reason why there is so much insistence
that the authority and responsibility for *all* company forms be placed
in one department. Anything less than that is no control at all. The
office manager in many companies has control over forms. Compa-

nies with methods and procedures activities frequently give this section the control over forms, reflecting the close relationship between forms and procedures.

Not all companies, though, have placed the design of forms in the same department that exercises control over them. Some manufacturing companies, for example, take advantage of the design experience of their industrial draftsmen; other companies use the art sections of their advertising departments.

Normal purchasing procedures do not have to be radically altered to get tight control over forms. The personnel of the forms-control section of some companies are authorized to conduct their own purchasing activities. But, if no purchase order for forms can be issued without permission of the purchasing department, neither can one be issued without clearance through the forms-control unit. Companies with duplicating machines have discovered that control is harder to get. Department heads who have their own duplicating equipment are understandably reluctant to get permission from the forms-control unit for a short run of "one little form." But it is at just such points as these that the situation gets out of hand. Here again it is not necessary to place control of all printing and duplicating equipment in the hands of the records people. However, this group should approve all requisitions for forms.

Sometimes there are justified objections to centralized control of forms: One is that rank-and-file employees may feel it is impossible to suggest a change in a form, or to recommend a new one. To avoid this, and to take advantage as much as possible of "on the spot" experience, many companies have appointed one employee in each of the line departments to serve as go-between for the forms unit. This plan has many enthusiastic adherents.

When a company whose control over forms has been only informal decides that tighter control is necessary, it may very well ask: "Where do we begin in organizing a forms program?" Answers to this and related problems can be found in this contribution from the office methods and procedures staff of the Caterpillar Tractor Company:

"The primary function of the forms-control section is to subject all of the office forms used by the company to a constant review and analysis to determine that, as tools in the hands of clerical workers, they are efficient and accomplish necessary work. When analysis indicates that a form is not efficient, it becomes the task of the forms-control section to redesign the form so that it will be. Similarly, should a form appear to be requiring unnecessary work, the forms-control section is expected to take steps to eliminate the form from supply.

"In order to carry out its primary function, the forms-control section has access to every form used by the company. This was accomplished when the division first became operational by requesting every department within the company to send to the forms-control section three copies of every form used. These copies were then used to establish three separate files as follows:

1. Numerical file by form number.

2. Alphabetical file by the department using the form.

3. Functional file by the function performed by the form.

"The forms thus filed were not intended to be subjected to analysis in themselves but were gathered merely to implement the method by which such analysis was to take place on the proper occasions for it. The next step was to require that the forms-control section review all requisitions for the printing of forms before the requisitions could be filled. Since a copy of the form must accompany the requisition, the section is not only able to take up each form on an individual basis but to prevent the possibility of new forms being designed and stocked without the knowledge of the section. This particular approach to analysis of forms, i.e., as they are requisitioned, has two distinct advantages. First, it is simple. It is entirely self-regulating to the point where in the course of one year the section has been able to take up for analysis every form used in the company. The second advantage is one of timing and costs. Analysis of a form at a time when the supply is at a minimum means that—should it become obsolete through redesign, replacement, or elimination—there will be a minimum on hand to scrap.

"The manner in which the forms-control section functions is understandingly simple since simplification is the basis for its existence. As requisitions are delivered to the section, they are placed in the hands of a forms analyst whose duty it is to carefully scrutinize the form to determine the following:

1. *Is the form properly designed?* This is a broad question covering a variety of things and has been the subject of complete articles and even books. No attempt to outline form design principles will be made here. The forms analyst is aided in this phase of his work by various reference publications and through frequent contact with manufacturer's representatives.

2. *Is the information entered on the completed form available on some other form or report?* This is a particularly important question since duplication of effort adds nothing but cost to the operation of the company. The answer may be found in either the functional or the departmental files mentioned earlier. By comparing the form being analyzed with other forms performing a similar function, it is often possible to eliminate one or the other. This not only reduces costs by the cost of the form and of the labor involved in its completion, but may also increase the value of other forms by extending their usage over greater areas.

3. *Can this form be combined with other forms?* Here again reference is made to the functional and departmental files. Combined forms result in reduced form costs.

FORM NUMBER	TITLE			
USED BY	PURPOSE			
FINAL DISPOSITION	ESTIMATED YEARLY CONSUMPTION	MAXIMUM STOCK	MINIMUM STOCK	

SPECIFICATIONS:

ORDERS

DATE ORDERED	QUANTITY	UNIT	PRICE	PRINTER

One way to keep track of forms is to set up a simple card system like this

"As these items are taken under consideration by the forms analyst, he also makes certain routine checks of both the form and the requisition. For one thing, he compares the quantity being requisitioned with the past usage as shown on the requisition. Should the form be a new form or a revised form, he makes a record of it so that, when printing has been completed, copies may be secured for inclusion in the section's files. After the form and the requisition have passed the scrutiny of the forms analyst, they are delivered to the section supervisor for his approval. Here again the form is subjected to at least some further analysis before being released for procurement."

The Forms-Control Section

The standard organizational pattern among companies Dartnell has studied is to make the forms department responsible for *all* the company's forms. The success of such a plan depends to a large degree upon the skill with which the forms-design people do their work, not to speak of their skill at human relations. But it is not completely a matter of professional skill and personality. Some companies have found it wise to make provisions for improving the liaison between the forms section—whose work is essentially a staff or "service" activity—and the departments with which it works. The American Enka Corporation uses the following policy procedure:

AMERICAN ENKA CORPORATION

Policy and Procedure Circular No. GM-3

Forms-Control Program—Requisitioning Forms and Other Printing

1. Purpose and Scope
    a. The purposes of this circular are:
       1. To revise and restate the company policy in respect to the forms-control program.
       2. To establish uniform procedures for control and requisitioning of all forms used by the company.
       3. To rescind and replace Policy and Procedure Circular GM-3.

2. Objectives of Program

    The objective of the program is to effectively use well-designed forms as a means of presenting information in a concise way to conserve time and effort.

    In addition, the forms-control program insures:

    a. That all existing forms are periodically reviewed and that proposals for new or revised forms receive proper consideration.

b. That needed forms are so designed as to best facilitate the purpose they are intended to serve.

c. That standards as to sizes, types, paper, and other specifications are developed and maintained.

d. That forms are produced and distributed economically.

e. That unnecessary forms do not exist, and that the total number of forms is kept to a minimum.

3. RESPONSIBILITY FOR CARRYING OUT THE PROGRAM

a. The office service section of the controller's department provides a forms-design service, maintains a complete alphabetical and numerical file of all the company forms and reviews existing forms and proposals for new or revised forms for the purpose of carrying out the objectives stated in paragraph 2 above.

b. In carrying out the above responsibilities, the office service section of the controller's department will conduct necessary studies, independent of or together with the staff and operating departments, and will make appropriate recommendations regarding the consolidation, elimination, or simplification of existing forms, or the need for a new form. Such recommendations will be presented for concurrence to the department having responsibility for the form prior to making any change.

Top-Management Support

The obvious need for some sort of centralized control is closely related to another important aspect of the matter: The need for top-management support of the forms-control program. One company contributing its experience to Dartnell's survey has had an interesting experience along this line. The company's president issued an order establishing the forms program and assigning responsibility over all forms. A few months later the company print shop turned over to the forms-control unit a reprint requisition for a highly individualistic memorandum pad; it came from one of the company's top executives who had been using it for some time and was quite proud of it. The forms-control unit, because the company had a standard memorandum form in use, did not approve the requisition. The executive took the requisition to the president who, after a considerable amount of heated discussion, upheld the decision of the forms-control unit. The executive in question now uses the standard form and the company still has control over its forms.

All the management directives in the world, no matter how high the source or how vigorously supported, will not get the maximum efficiency from a centralized forms-control program. It is clear that the forms unit itself has to make audits and spot checks to make sure that the provisions of its program are being generally followed.

FORMS CONTROL AND RECORDS MANAGEMENT

Many of the advantages of a records disposal program may be lost unless control is exercised over the development of new records. In general, all new forms should require the approval of the person responsible for records administration. This is necessary to prevent the duplication of existing forms and to plan, at the beginning, for the eventual disposition of the form. This is what one office manager has said about the problem:

When we reorganized our filing department, one of the first things we did was to study all the forms in use, or in supposed use; many of them were simply gathering dust in the office supplies storeroom.

We were able to eliminate many of them immediately. Others we were able to consolidate; this saved us space both in the storeroom and in the files.

We studied each copy of the forms required in our operation and then assigned appropriate retention periods. Now, the most important copy of the form has the longest retention period; the other copies are destroyed at an early date.

An executive of a New York brokerage house described the steps his company has taken to coordinate forms design and records administration: "A study of the number of forms we had in stock amazed us. We estimated before the survey that we had about 150; an inventory revealed more than 1,100. Further study permitted us to lower this number to 600, and the figure will get smaller. This alone has given us twice the storage space we had before."

"Planned Parenthood" for New Records

Another conviction shared by many companies is that records administration must not be limited in scope and operation merely to records disposition; a records program to be fully effective must have some control over form design and related activities. This control does two things:

1. It prevents the making of unnecessary records and the duplication of already existing forms.

2. By planning the eventual disposition of records *before* they come into existence, it assures that new forms are designed with sound records-management principles in mind; it also guarantees that the process of disposition will be as automatic as possible.

The following contribution by Mrs. Vera A. Avery, Chicago filing consultant, makes the need for coordination between forms design and records administration very apparent:

It is obvious that any achievement, however small, which is made in getting a control on records at the time of, or before, their creation, offers at least a threefold saving—and is thus to be preferred over the savings accomplished by a records disposal program. Even more evident is the fact that working on disposal only is like trying to fill a bucket with a hole in it.

I do not mean to imply that we are going to solve the records problem by prohibiting the creation of records, and even less do I believe that the records personnel should take over the functions of form design or forms control—but they must get acquainted in these fields so that they can talk their language and thus be able to contribute their specialized "know-how." Here are some practical illustrations of what can be done in this field by the records people when and if they are qualified:

1. They should be able to suggest to the forms design people (or in the smaller organizations to the individuals who are likely to design forms) that the selection of the quality and color of paper should be based on the length of service and type of service of the record. In the case of a department-store sales check where the maximum life of the form is only 30 days under a system of "cycle billing" and microfilming, the durability of the paper is a negligible factor—the cheapest paper available is permissible, but the color should be selected for the clearest reproduction on the microfilm. On the other hand, if your record is one for permanent retention, or one which during its lifetime is frequently or constantly handled, the paper quality must be selected with this purpose in mind.

2. Size, too, is a factor to be given consideration—not after the stockroom shelves are loaded with a year's supply of Form A-602-B, but before that form gets off the drawing board. The size of the form is of special interest to records people because of the fact that size governs the ease or difficulty of handling the form in the mailing, sorting, and filing processes—and that in turn governs your office costs. The size also governs the filing equipment needed. If the form is made up on legal-size paper, are there legal-size file cabinets available? Is the form to be interfiled with regular correspondence—if so, the legal-size form will require a special folding process on each item filed—that means *more expensive filing.* On the other hand, if the form is set at a 3- by 5-inch size, and is to be included in the letter-size file, the chances are your file clerk will glue or staple this form to another piece of letter-size paper before she files it—and look what that does to filing costs: Add time to glue or staple—add over 100 percent increase in filing space consumed.

    Size is also a very important factor in microfilming costs—so, if you know in advance that Form A-608 will be microfilmed, or can get a decision on this point in advance, the planning of the form can be done with an eye toward keeping the film costs at a minimum. Remember, in figuring microfilming costs, there are some very special criteria and indexes to follow. Your records manager is, or should be, expert in these matters, and, if you fail to take advantage of that knowledge, there are apt to be expensive mistakes.

3. The actual placing of the information on the form vitally affects the filing and handling costs. The records people should review forms in advance of their printing, to see that as far as consistent with other factors of good design, every possible aid in design is given to facilitating the handling and filing of that form because that is where costs, though hidden, really lurk. Here is a case history example of what can,

and did, happen when the records people were not consulted in the matter of the creation of records:

A form design expert, or rather, a whole group of such experts were called in to design a series of forms which were to be the working tools of a large enterprise. There were, as I recall, approximately 15 different forms in the series—each serving a special need for the recording of information. All were designed to be mailed out, and when filled in and returned to the originating officer, were to be organized into a data and reference file with a probable life of 5 to 10 years—and would serve not only as the "heart" of this particular office, but of the entire enterprise.

The forms when completed were really compact and eye-satisfying—what is more, I understand that a work-simplification expert had been consulted and the forms were actually designed to facilitate distribution—that is, with one or two folds they were inserted in a window envelope so that no special addressing was required, and the addressee's name and address was typed on the form to facilitate reading when it was returned. Everybody was very happy over the plan, and congratulatory back-slapping was indulged in.

The mailing was accomplished with great success, and, as time went on, the forms were being returned in such quantities that a filing problem developed. At that point, I was brought into the picture. It looked like just a simple job of estimating the number of clerks, the time and equipment required, and the setting up of a simple sorting and filing procedure. I determined immediately that the forms would be filed in letter-size cabinets (they were 8 by 10 inches) in letter-size folders with 50 to 95 to a folder—but the next step in my analysis turned up a hornet's nest.

The most direct method of filing was by a certain address which was inserted when the form was filled out. Any other method, i.e., by name—and there were at least two and usually three names on the filled-out form—would require a master index system to the address. The cost of such a master index was prohibitive, aside from the fact that it was totally unnecessary if the direct method of filing was used—that is, filing by the reference address. And where was this reference index—the address? There was the hornet's nest. On about 20 percent of the forms it was in the lower right-hand corner—on 50 percent in the upper right-hand corner—and the balance had the address inserted in various places in the body of the form. What is more, there were other addresses inserted on the form so that it was actually necessary to read a lot of fine print to determine which address to use—at least until the position of the address on each form was memorized. When you consider that all these forms were to be interfiled in the same file, you can perhaps have some small idea of what the initial filing costs were going to be—not to mention what refiling costs would be on the refiling of such items as were pulled out daily for the operating program.

I brought this situation to the attention of management, at the same time offering my solution—i.e., that as forms came into the office—in the mailroom if possible, certainly before their first sort—the reference index (that is, the address by which they were to be filed) be circled with a red pencil. That one simple and relatively inexpensive operation solved part of the problem—the balance of it is just an additional cost that the organization is paying every day in the increased costs of operating their reference files, and that they will continue to pay as long as the organization exists and uses that reference file—this cost results from the increased time that it takes the file clerk to adjust her eyes to a continuously changing spot on the form when she is filing, when she is looking up a reference, or when she is interfiling. As against this cost, there was the time saved in initial mailing out of the form, and the saving of a file consultant's fee in the design of the form.

4. Let me give another case history relating to the creation of records. This is, I suspect, one that many companies have already met and solved in any one of several ways. I am giving it here, therefore, not so much as an example of method, but to point up the fact that the records people must get their influence extended to the creation of records—and please note I say influence. I do not recommend, or even imply, that they take over the field.

This case history concerns the extra copies of letters, reports, and memoranda that are made and used in every organization. The ease with which extra copies can be produced these days has brought us closer than ever to the "paper peril." The carbon manufacturers, the paper manufacturer and distributor, and the typewriter and duplicating equipment manufacturers are all improving their products to permit organizations to make extra copies of each and everything that is recorded, and advertising repeatedly calls attention to the fact that a company can have extra copies at practically no extra cost.

That the advertising is effective is evidenced by Mr. X's prelude to dictation. "Take a letter to Mr. Best Customer with a copy to Mr. Credit Manager, copy to Mr. Production Manager, and a copy to Joe (my assistant)." The letter is duly transcribed, and it is after this that the real costs on these extra copies begin to mount—and that's what the advertisers didn't tell you. It costs just as much to classify, sort, and file each of the extra copies as it costs to handle the one official file copy of the letter. Filing costs on Mr. X's letter to Mr. Best Customer could conceivably be three times greater than is necessary.

The solution to this problem of filing costs must be at the source, or, rather, at the time of creation: Adopt a special color or form for all of these extra copies and instruct all stenographers and staff that copies on that particularly designated paper are extra copies and can be discarded —i.e., thrown in the wastebasket. The ideal solution is to print on the paper selected for these extra copies this very fact—that it is an extra copy of a letter *which is on file,* that it is supplied for informational purposes only, and *that it not only can but should be destroyed as soon as noted.*

Begin With a Survey

For companies just beginning a forms control program, the disorder, profusion, and unexpected discoveries can only be matched by the contents of a schoolboy's closet. The question invariably presents itself: "Where do we start?" While is is difficult to make specific recommendations, many companies begin by making a survey, form by form. They generally have developed a questionnaire which is sent to all users of forms. Sometimes this is done when a requisition for a new supply of the form is presented. During the early stages of a forms program, some effort has to be made to prevent the production of a lot of forms which will soon be superseded. In the meantime, the information gathered by the forms questionnaire is tabu-

```
F-634-R                    FORMS REQUEST
                                          DATE _____
                                     DATE NEEDED _____

  O                - NEW OR REVISED FORM -

FORM NO. _____ TITLE _____

  ☐   PERMANENT   PROJECTED YEARLY USAGE _____  SIZE OF FORM _____
  ☐   TEMPORARY   INITIAL NO. REQUIRED   _____  TYPE OF PAPER _____
                                                     PAPER COLOR   _____
CHARGE DEPARTMENT _____    NUMBER/PAD   _____
REQUESTED BY _____    CARBON ? ?   _____
                                                      PUNCHED _____ HOLES _____ SIDE
APPROVALS:                                          (  )  TYPED
                                      FORM IS TO BE (  )  WRITTEN
  _____                          (  )  BOTH
       (DEPARTMENT HEAD)               IF TYPED, _____ LINES PER INCH

  (SYSTEMS DEPARTMENT)
_____

                        - OBSOLETE FORM -

FORM NO. _____ TITLE _____
REASON FOR OBSOLETING: _____
DISPOSITION OF FORMS IN STOCK _____
REQUESTED BY _____
  O
APPROVALS:

  _____         _____
       (DEPARTMENT HEAD)              (SYSTEMS DEPARTMENT)
_____

DATE _____ FORM # _____         DATE _____

QUANTITY _____ FORM SIZE _____   TO: _____

PAPER TYPE _____ COLOR _____

PADDED ( ) NO ( )YES _____/PAD       THIS IS TO NOTIFY YOU THAT
CARBON ( ) NO ( )YES _____/PAD
PUNCHED( ) NO ( )YES ___HOLES___SIDE    FORM # _____ ENTITLED _____

CHARGE DEPARTMENT _____

DATE NEEDED _____      HAS BEEN PRINTED AND IS

OTHER: _____      AVAILABLE IN THE STATIONERY

                                        DEPARTMENT.
  O
  _____

RETAIN ORIGINAL
```

A systematic study of the need for a new office form will help to eliminate unnecessary ones before they can be published.

lated and analyzed. When this is done, it is possible to start making long-range plans and policies.

Some companies make a formal analysis of a form before it is adopted, whether it is a new form or a revision of an existing form. B. E. Duke of Reed International, Inc., reports the following procedure:

REED INTERNATIONAL, INC.
All Divisions

SUBJECT: FORMS CONTROL	INDEX:	1075
	ISSUED:	3-29-67
	REVISED:	
	EFFECTIVE:	4-4-67
	NAME:	G. L. Major
	PAGE: 1	

PURPOSE: To provide a procedure for processing all requests for new forms, revisions to existing forms, and/or obsoleting forms.

PROCEDURE:

SECTION RESPONSIBLE	ACTION
GENERAL	The "Forms Request" (F-643-R) form will be used to request a new form, a revision, and/or the obsoleting of an existing form. All form numbers will be assigned by the systems department. Also, *all forms must be approved by the systems department before they can be ordered or printed.*
INDIVIDUAL MAKING REQUEST	1. Complete the "new or revised form" section of the forms request when requesting a new form or revising an existing form. When obsoleting a form, complete the "obsolete form" section of the forms request.
	2. Obtain approval of department head who will be charged for new or revised form. If form is to be obsoleted, obtain approval of department head who originated the form.
	3. Attach either a draft of the new or revised form or a copy of the obsolete form to the forms request and forward to the systems department.

REED INTERNATIONAL, INC. (Cont.)

SUBJECT: FORMS CONTROL	INDEX:	1075
	ISSUED:	3-29-67
	REVISED:	
	EFFECTIVE:	4-4-67
	NAME:	G. L. Major
	PAGE: 2	

SECTION RESPONSIBLE	ACTION
SYSTEMS DEPARTMENT	4. Review the request. Upon approval and priority establishment by the divisional controller, document the flow of all new or revised forms. If the request is not approved, return to the individual making the request stating the reason the form cannot be printed or ordered at this time. Forward the approved request to obsolete a form to the staff assistant.
	5. Assign a form number to all new or revised forms and enter on the forms request.
	6. If the master is not attached and the form is to be printed in our print shop, draw a master.
	7. Forward the forms request with an attached master and/or copy of the form to the staff assistant.
STAFF ASSISTANT	8. Determine the action to be taken. If the form is to be printed in our print shop, complete the applicable information below the perforation on the "forms request" form. If the form is to be ordered outside, process in the usual manner.
	9. If form is to be printed in our print shop, tear off the instructions at the perforation, attach master and forward to the print shop. File the "forms request" by date.
	10. On all forms, complete the applicable information on the "addition/deletion of form' (F-861-R) and forward to the stationery department.
PRINT SHOP	11. Print form as per instructions and file the master.
	12. Tear off the notification section of the instructions, date, sign and forward to the individual shown on the form.
	13. Forward all forms to the stationery department unless otherwise instructed.
STATIONERY DEPARTMENT	14. Receive the "addition/deletion of form" (F-861-R) from the staff assistant.
	15. Follow the instructions shown on the form.
	16. File all "addition/deletion of form" blanks by number.

Some companies make periodic surveys—once a year or so—of their administrative forms. Others survey their forms each time they are reordered. Most companies carry out a survey of all forms before organization or reorganization of their forms units.

How Gamble-Skogmo Coordinates Form Design

Many office executives with experience in form design and control take pains to point out that no forms program should set its sights merely on controlling the *number* of forms; controlling the *quality* of forms is no less important. These companies make extensive use of the techniques of work simplification. One of them is Gamble-Skogmo, Inc., where the systems and procedures manager gives this description of his company's extensive forms control program:

The following organization, policy, and procedure is used by Gamble-Skogmo to control its 1,500 active forms. We believe our system prevents the duplication of existing forms and the inefficient design of those that are actually needed.

The systems and procedures department is responsible for the control of all Gamble-Skogmo forms. This department is responsible to the controller and is composed of three sections:

1. Forms control   2. Policy manuals   3. Work simplification

A new form cannot be printed or an old form revised or reordered without the approval of the forms control section. Our general purchasing agent and our own print shop will not honor any such requests unless approved by the forms control section.

To control forms drawn by individuals for specific individual uses which are run on department duplicating equipment, the following procedure is used to "police" such activities: All operators of duplicating equipment have permanent instructions that an extra copy must be run of any form duplicated and forwarded weekly to the systems and procedures department for review.

FORMS CONTROL SECTION—RESPONSIBILITIES AND ROUTINE

I. *Files, Indexes, and References*

    A. A master numerical list for all forms is maintained. This list is used to assign new form numbers and as a cross-reference for locating form titles.

    B. A form subject file, arranged alphabetically by form titles, is maintained. This file is used when reviewing form requisitions, to prevent duplication or to find a similar form which may be used, and as a cross-reference for locating form numbers.

    C. An individual file folder is maintained in numerical sequence for every form in active use giving the complete history of the form since its inception: Originator, department, authorization, purpose, distribution, filing and storage, printing specifications, current suggestions for improvement pending reorder, sample copies of the original form and all revisions, etc.

CUTTING FORMS*

Paper is usually purchased in large sheets, the sizes of which are standard with all paper mills. Consequently, these mill sizes must be cut to the dimensions of the individual forms. In order to avoid waste, the dimensions of a form should be even fractions of the standard mill size. For example, a form 8½ by 11 inches can be cut evenly 8 times from the standard mill size 22 by 34 inches, but a form 9 by 12 inches cannot be cut evenly from this same mill size; 316 square inches would have to be thrown away as waste. This waste may amount to thousands of dollars a year.

II. *Routine for Handling a Request for a New Form*

A. A form requisition is prepared by the originating department with a rough copy of the form attached.

B. The form requisition is sent to the forms control section where it is processed as follows:

1. A thorough investigation is made as to the necessity of the form.

2. A search is made for duplication in a similar form which may serve the purpose.

3. If the new form involves new, or a change of, procedure it may be passed on to the work-simplification section for study and recommendation.

4. If other departments are affected, those departments are contacted and approval obtained.

5. When approvals have been obtained from all concerned, a sample copy is given to the form designer for finishing.

*From Prudential Insurance Company's Forms Engineering Manual

6. The form is then sent to the purchasing department for ordering.

7. If a form is not approved by the forms control section, an appeal can be made by the originating department to the controller.

III. *Routine for Handling the Reorder of an Old Form*

The forms control section is advised by memo from the purchasing department that the minimum stock has been reached. This memo is processed as follows:

A. The history file is "pulled" and a review of the form, and any pending

HANDLING AND FILING FORMS*

HANDLING	FILING
	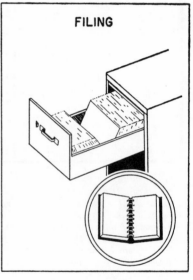

The manner in which the form is handled should determine to a large extent its size and shape. A long narrow form is to be avoided when it can be readily replaced by one which is more nearly square. Forms that are filed or clipped together should be the same size, since it is much easier to handle a case composed of many sheets of paper all the same size than a group of forms of varied sizes. Small slips of paper are likely to become overlooked or lost and therefore should be made larger when of sufficient importance, even though it requires using more paper.

If the form is to be filed in a cabinet, binder, or other similar storage place, its size should conform to the size of the equipment in which it is to be housed. Unless this is considered at the time the form is designed, it may be necessary to purchase special filing equipment. Allowance should be made if the form is to be inserted in a folder or pouch before being placed in the file, and when file guides are to be used, the depth of the form must permit the index tabs to be visible. In considering the size of forms bound in post binders or books, allowance should be made for binding margins.

*From Prudential Insurance Company's Forms Engineering Manual

suggestions, is made. The originating department is contacted and the following questions asked:

1. Is it necessary?

2. Can it be eliminated?

3. Can it be combined with some other form?

4. Are all copies necessary?

5. Are all captions and columns necessary?

6. Is the system, or mechanics, which surrounds the form as efficient as it should be—should the work-simplification section be asked for a survey on possible improvements to increase production and dollar savings?

B. If the form can be discontinued, a form requisition is prepared and proper approvals by all concerned obtained by the forms control section.

C. If the form is to be reordered "as is," memo is merely "OK'd" by the originating department and the forms control section and automatically reordered by the purchasing department.

D. If changes are to be made, a form requisition must be prepared and handled as a new form.

IV. *Form Audits*

The forms control section receives regularly from the purchasing department a list of slow-moving forms. The originating department is contacted and the following questions asked: Is the form still in use? has any procedure or policy been changed? was the quantity ordered too large? etc.

V. *Form Instructions*

A form instruction sheet is prepared for each form, showing a reduced illustration of the form and any additional or special instructions needed for its use. The form instruction sheets are released to the field and filed in three-ring binders.

Revising Forms

When the forms program is under way, provision must be made to accumulate the ideas on improving forms which turn up in one way or another. Many companies make a file folder for each of their forms, number the folders to correspond, and keep them in a filing cabinet. They can be used to collect all the information about the form and also to keep a life history of it—dates or reorders, quantities, revisions, and all other facts of possible use or interest.

Some companies accumulate forms information on cards. One such organization outlines its process this way:

"All stationery and printing is purchased by one person. This person is responsible for the review of all forms at time of reorder, working with the various department heads in a serious effort to reduce the number of forms, improve their design, and reduce printing costs.

"Such a program has been, with us, a continuing process. We first had to establish adequate records to review the forms as they came up for reorder. At time of reorder each form is studied for possible grouping with another similar form for economy of printing.

"Sizes are altered to cut out without paper waste. IBM electric typewriters are used to prepare paper masters for Multilith printing of internal forms. Some forms are eliminated or combined with others. Many are changed for better appearance or to reduce operations in their preparation.

"In order to establish records for buying of stationery and printing we decided it was more expedient to call a form by a number instead

PROCESSING FORMS*

MACHINES	MAILING
	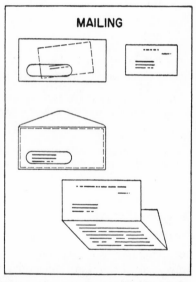

Any form which is to be filled in by typewriter, bookkeeping m a c h i n e, IBM tabulator or similar device, must meet the size requirements of the machine. We must consider not only the size of paper to be inserted but also the maximum width of the writing line. Adequate space should be allotted for a gripper margin.

Forms sent through the mail should conform to the size of the envelope in which they are enclosed. This is especially important in the case of window envelopes. In such cases the form should slip into the envelope easily and yet be snug enough to prevent any material except the name and address from showing through the window.

*From Prudential Insurance Company's Forms Engineering Manual

of a name. All departments operate on an expense budget, stationery and printing being an item for each. All existing forms were collected, grouped by departments, and assigned departmental numbers. Whenever feasible these numbers with the department abbreviation were printed directly on the form itself for ease of identification.

"Next a scrapbook was made for each department and the forms were pasted in this book in numerical order; a master list by name and number pasted in the flyleaf. At this time we had just finished setting up an improved Kardex purchase record and one of the two cards used for this record was used for printing records as well. One of the cards was prepared for each form showing on the visible portion the name of the form, departmental abbreviation and number. The cards were then arranged in the tray by department and numerical order within the department.

"The card has two index tabs, one red and one green. When an order is placed the green tab is moved to the month of order and remains there until the order is delivered when it is returned to the neutral area. These tabs then serve as an "on order" file for monthly followup of undelivered orders. At time of delivery the red tab is moved ahead nine months to serve as a signal for reorder. This allows three months for checking inventories, revising forms, securing proofs, etc. Also, in case of a faulty estimate of yearly consumption, sufficient leeway is established for reorder on a rush basis. To this card is posted data at each time of reprinting showing invoice date, purchase order number and date, quantity ordered and printing costs. Since we have a commercial printing company as a subsidiary in our own building, few of our jobs are done on the outside and little vendor data is required."

The office manager of a large dairy products concern describes how his company uses a loose-leaf book as a form information file:

Requests for new forms or the reordering of forms in use are all referred to me. All key personnel are instructed to suggest to me any new form that would improve the current record. If after giving consideration to the suggestion (this includes conference with our accountant and review of the job for which it is intended), it is found to contain sufficient merit, a printer is called in to assist in setting up the form.

All forms are given a form number which is printed on each by the printer. A loose-leaf book is kept at my desk with a separate page for each form we use. To each of these pages is glued a copy of one form with a protruding tab identifying the form by number. These numbers are run in consecutive series for easy reference. In the front of the book is an index by form number and description of the form. Accompanying each page is a small ledger sheet on which is recorded date of each purchase, name of supplier, quantity ordered, price paid, and a column for notation when an order is placed and the quoted price.

A few years ago we began the manufacture of powdered milk. This necessitated a whole new series of forms. I made a trip to the nearest plant whose operation most nearly corresponded to our contemplated operation. They gave us a complete set of their forms which we tailored to our individual liking. Incidentally, we have not seen fit to make a change in any of these forms since the first printing.

To keep our forms most practical, each time a reorder of any form is made I confer with the individual using this form to determine whether or not improvements can be made. The quantity to order and a price that sounds reasonable is determined by referring to the little ledger sheet in my book which reveals the quantity used in a given time and the price paid.

Functional Filing

The problem of forestalling the design of one form when another already exists to serve the same purpose is one which every forms-control program must solve. The standard solution is to compile a functional file in which forms are listed according to the department and the job they do. Thus, when a requisition for a new form arrives, the forms unit first checks the functional file; if this reveals nothing of any use, work can begin on the design of a new form with reasonable assurance that it is actually needed. As several companies have pointed out, an added advantage of making one department responsible for forms is that its personnel becomes acquainted with all the forms in the company and can supplement the cold facts of the functional file with personal knowledge based on their experience.

The Trane System

Forms control is an important procedure for a firm like The Trane Company, manufacturing engineer for air conditioning, heating, ventilating, and heat-transfer equipment. John O'Donnell reports that three departments—the controller's staff, advertising production, and the purchasing department—are involved in Trane forms control.

The originator of a new or revised form is required to submit a draft of the form and a printing requisition to the forms-control section of the controller's staff, together with written justification for the new form or revision of an existing form. This material must be approved by the originator's department manager.

The forms-control section of the controller's staff consists of a forms analyst and a secretary. They are responsible for assigning form numbers, form design and standardization, analysis for possible combination or elimination of duplication, elimination of unnecessary forms, and maintaining a forms-control register and book of samples of current forms.

Upon receipt of recommendations for a new form, the section checks for possible duplication of an existing form, and analyzes the possibility of combining the new form with another current form. If necessary, the section consults with the originator.

Production Steps

If the new form or revision is approved, the printing requisition is routed to the advertising-production department with a draft of the new form.

The advertising-production department is responsible for the printing, binding, and stocking of forms for which they have the capacity and equipment to reproduce. If the department plans to print the form, members prepare the necessary artwork, make plates, print, bind, or package and wrap, and stock the new form.

If it is determined that printing is to be done on the outside, the draft and printing requisition are routed to the purchasing department, which will obtain quotations from printing vendors and issue a purchase order. Some very special forms are controlled by the data-processing division.

Forms Review

The Trane Company maintains a continuous review of all forms. When the stock quantity of any form is exhausted, departments using it determine whether it should be reprinted as is, revised, or discarded. There also is a year-end review of all forms.

Control and review has been successful in bringing a number of common forms together. The success of the Trane system is best measured by the fact that in 1960 the number of different forms was 1,420. By the end of 1966 the number of forms had been reduced to 986. The number of forms is easily determined at the end of any month through plus and minus adjustments on a perpetual inventory record.

Numbering System

A two-digit activity control number is assigned to each activity or function of the company. Individual base numbers are assigned in sequence to each form. For example, all accounting department forms are controlled by the activity prefix 11, and the first accounting department form would be numbered 11.01.

Forms Can Be Ordered Jointly

Several companies report that they are able to cut office costs by making a study of their forms to determine what forms can be ordered in groups. An official of the American Chicle Company tells how it is done in his company:

"We centralize our forms control in the office manager's department and clear the design, the ordering, and the inventory control through that department. We have found if we can control to a reasonable extent the number of new forms that are introduced we can make definite headway in the improvement, consolidation, or elimination of our existing forms. We require that all new forms be thoroughly reviewed as to purpose, design, quantity on order, etc., before they are finally approved.

"Insofar as efficiency in the ordering of forms is concerned we have earmarked all of our approximately 1,000 forms inventory cards to show all other forms which can be ordered in combination. We also try to arrange insofar as possible that those forms which can be ordered in combination, reach an order point at approximately the same time. Considerable savings in printing costs result and the frequency of review is reduced."

Ford Motor Co. endeavors in every way possible to help vendors reduce their costs by giving careful study to such details as kinds of paper and ink, ream sizes, size of runs, and combination runs. They know which sizes cut without waste and they invite vendors to make combination runs of their work with that of other customers where doing so will effect economies for the vendor.

Principal features of the company plan are that it provides a means for taking price advantage of the company's total forms requirements. It establishes a basis for "make or buy" decisions by providing accounting locations with a vendor's unit prices by size of form and by quantity. Nonrecurring preliminary costs, such as composition, are separately identified so that such costs may be immediately dealt with and prevented from entering or remaining in unit prices. A basis for cycle releasing (on a multiple line item basis) of forms on a package plan, blanket order contract is established with resultant savings in shipping and other handling costs. The plan furthers standardization and uniformity of forms by making price, in itself, an incentive to the use of standardized forms.

A Complete Forms Program

The following comprehensive forms control and design program was developed by A. T. Kearney & Company, management consultants, for one of its client companies; it is shown here through the cooperation of the consulting firm.

Purpose of Procedure. The purpose of this procedure is to outline methods for greater standardization in record and report forms, improvements in their design, and uniformity in their sizes to better fit our office practice and to reduce the cost of paper work to the extent that this is possible. To obtain this result these steps are being taken:

1. Responsibility for reviewing all record and report forms and approving requisitions for their purchase, or requests for reproducing them in our own office, is placed with the secretary-treasurer.

2. Form numbers are to be systematically assigned to all forms.

3. A central file of all forms is to be maintained by the secretary-treasurer or his representative.

Numbering of Forms. Effective at once, all record and report forms to be printed outside or to be reproduced in this office are to be assigned our own serial form numbers by the secretary-treasurer. The assignment of new form numbers shall proceed just as rapidly as reprinting or reproduction takes place.

In assigning these form numbers, the letter "A" prefixed to a form number indicates Finance and Accounts Division; "P" indicates Personnel Division; "S" indicates Sales Division; "M" indicates Manufacturing Division; and "R" indicates Purchasing Division.

Approval of Requisitions. All requisitions for the purchase of printed record and report forms are to be routed to the secretary-treasurer for review of the design, size, and content of the form, for assignment of form number, and for approval before purchase.

All requests for the reproduction of record and report forms in this office are to be routed to the secretary-treasurer also for his review of the design, size, and content of the form, assignment of form number, and approval of the request before reproduction takes place.

The purchasing agent is authorized to purchase printed forms only after the approval by the secretary-treasurer.

Central Form File. To assist in his review of the design, size, and content of forms, and the assignment of form numbers, the secretary-treasurer or his representative is to maintain a central form file.

A folder is to be maintained for each record and report form, in which will be filed the latest copy of the form.

From time to time he will insert in these folders any suggestions received or originated relative to possible improvements in the form, its design, its size, its content, or any other suggestions presented which will be helpful in improving the form.

As forms come up for reprinting or reproduction, the secretary-treasurer or his representative draws the related folder from the file and checks carefully any information at hand relative to possibilities of changes in design, size, or content. He makes changes and improvements in copy for the printer as agreed upon.

Each folder is filed by form number on the basis of the new serial numbers assigned to the forms.

Design of Forms. The design of record and report forms is very important from the standpoint of indicating the data required, use of the paper surface, and indicating the sequence in which information should be entered.

There are various principles which may be applied in form design. The simpler form designs are usually best, and these may be described very briefly as follows:

1. *Boxing*—Under this plan, the entire surface of the form is "boxed" in, with most of the printing to show the data to be inserted entered in the upper left-hand corner, or at the top of each "boxed" area. If this plan of design is followed skillfully it makes better use of the form surface than any other plan; and provides, as well, a good appearing record and report form, and one easily used by the clerical force.

2. *Lines*—This plan of designing forms provides for the use of lines chiefly as a basis both for printing the information required, and the entering of the data. In other words, the instructions and data are entered on the same line level. This is the most common plan of preparing forms. Its effectiveness depends chiefly on the order in which data is provided for, and the extent to which the printed information describes the data required. This plan also provides for wide margins generally, and if the content of the form is set up in a congested manner it is more difficult to enter the data than in other plans of design. This plan, however, is satisfactory where skillfully used, and where care is taken not to waste space, or to set up the form "too close."

3. *Headings*—In designing forms, headings are used commonly to call attention to the information areas in which data is to be entered. Usually, the headings occupy considerable space, and sometimes result in wasting paper surface. If used carefully, however,

they help make a good-looking form and facilitate entering and reading report data.

4. *Columnar Design*—Often it is helpful to adopt the columnar idea so that information may be entered in columns. This type of design is particularly applicable to the tabulation of figures, where this is the form of information to be transmitted or recorded.

5. *Spacing*—Spacing is important for both appearance and use. Typing requires spacing in multiples of one-sixth inch. Handwriting requires one-fourth to one-third inch between lines.

As a general rule, neither of these methods of form design will be used exclusively. The method of design depends chiefly on the use to be made of the form and the type of information to be recorded on it. Skillful application of these principles in form design should result in improved design, economy in paper, and greater simplicity in clerical operations, regardless of the method chosen.

Size of Forms. The size of record and report forms is of particular importance because any failure to use standard sizes results in paper waste and increased cost. Some of the standard paper sizes are as follows:

Papers	Papers	Index Bristols
17 by 22 inches	22 by 34 inches	$20\frac{1}{2}$ by $24\frac{3}{4}$ inches
19 by 24 inches	24 by 38 inches	$20\frac{1}{2}$ by $28\frac{1}{2}$ inches
17 by 28 inches	28 by 34 inches	$25\frac{1}{2}$ by $30\frac{1}{2}$ inches

Standard sizes, therefore, of record and report forms which can be cut from standard sizes of paper sheets are as follows:

Paper Forms	Cards
$8\frac{1}{2}$ by 7 inches	3 by 5 inches
$8\frac{1}{2}$ by 11 inches	4 by 6 inches
$8\frac{1}{2}$ by 14 inches	5 by 8 inches
11 by 14 inches	6 by 9 inches
11 by 17 inches	8 by 10 inches

Care is to be exercised in the design of record and report forms so as to select the standard size for the record or report which will accommodate the data which must be shown on the form.

The form should not be larger than absolutely required. It should be large enough, however, to accommodate the data to be shown. It should have the dimensions indicated above.

Designation of Copies. While great convenience often results from the use of colors for different copies of record and report forms, colors should be used only in a very limited way. The cost of colored paper is, as a rule, greater than for white paper, and very often the same result in convenience can be obtained through designating different copies of forms by printing copy numbers, such as: Copy 1, Copy 2, and Copy 3 on the copies of the form, as required. This may be done by over-printing or direct-printing as each situation will permit.

Where, however, it is of extreme importance that each copy of the form shall be identified and used in a particular manner, and the use of the form is so important that the extra cost is justified, colored paper with a special color for each copy may be used.

In any event, it is the duty of the secretary-treasurer to keep the number of copies of each form to a minimum, and so far as possible for ordinary purposes, to avoid the use of colors.

Grades of Paper. Many factors enter into this important subject such as cost, longevity desired, severity of handling, ink absorption, and appearance required. Sometimes a saving of as much as 15 to 30 percent can be made in paper cost by appraising all factors. A careful appraisal of factors should be made in selecting paper for each form.

Purchase of Printed Forms. The purchasing agent will make no purchases of record and report forms from outside sources except on the basis of an approved purchase requisition, such purchase requisitions carrying the signature of the originator and the approval of the secretary-treasurer indicating that the copy for the form has been reviewed, the form number assigned, the quantity wanted checked, and the purchase authorized.

Reproducing Forms. All requests for the reproduction of record and report forms in this office will be routed to the secretary-treasurer for review and approval before the reproduction work is done. Forms are not to be reproduced except on the approval of the secretary-treasurer so that matters of design, size, content, form number, and other factors will have careful attention.

Suggestions. All suggestions for changes in form design, size, or content should be written in memorandum form and forwarded to the secretary-treasurer, together with the form now in use with corrections noted. He will file them in his central form file, awaiting the time when the record or report form is to be reprinted or reproduced. At that time he will give definite consideration to the suggestions, confer further with the parties concerned in the use of the form, and make such changes in design, size, or content as may seem necessary.

Copies for Central File. When printed forms are received, the receiving clerk will see that a copy of the form is sent to the secretary-treasurer.

When forms are reproduced in this office the clerk reproducing the form is required to forward one copy to the secretary-treasurer.

FORMS DESIGN CHECKLIST

NECESSITY AND USE

	Yes	No
1. Does the form duplicate existing standard forms you use?	....	....
2. Can an existing form be adapted for the same purpose?	....	....
3. Is the use of the form justified; i.e., will it get work done more quickly, more accurately, and more economically?	....	....
4. Can this form be consolidated with other forms?	....	....
5. Can some other form be eliminated?	....	....
6. Have actual users of the form, through all phases of its flow, been consulted for suggested improvements, additional requirements, and possible elimination?	....	....
7. Has everyone responsible for policy and procedure involved approved the form?	....	....
8. Will the wording of the text be understood by all users?	....	....
9. Is all recurring information printed so that only variable items are to be entered?	....	....
10. If serial numbering will aid in identification, has space been provided for numbering?	....	....
11. Is the necessity for a letter of transmittal eliminated?	....	....
12. If the form is to be mailed, and a window envelope is to be used, has the form been designed so that only the address box will be visible?	....	....
13. If routing, handling, or other instructions can be printed on the form, is it so designed?	....	....
14. If a written procedure for the use of the form is necessary for efficiency in its use, has it been written?	....	....
15. If copies of the form are required, is the number of copies justified?	....	....

ARRANGEMENT

	Yes	No
16. Does the form, by title and arrangement, clearly indicate its purpose?	....	....
17. Has the form been tested to ascertain if the spacing is adequate for entries by hand, typewriter, or office machine for which it is designed?	....	....
18. If the form is to be typed, are items arranged horizontally when possible, for speed in accomplishment?	....	....

FORMS DESIGN CHECKLIST (Cont.)

	Yes	No
19. Are the more important items prominently placed near the top, if practicable?	....	....
20. Are there items of major importance necessary for sorting and reference, and if so, have they been placed near the upper right-hand corner?	....	....
21. If the check system can be used to provide information or definite answers, has it been used?	....	....
22. Is the form designed to take data from, or pass data to, another form, and if so, do both forms have the same sequence of items so that quick and accurate transfer of data can be effected?	....	....
23. If the form is to be sent from one person to another, are proper spaces for "TO" and "FROM" provided?	....	....
24. Is there proper space for date, signature, and form number?	....	....
25. Have adequate margins been provided for binding, filing, and office machine limitations?	....	....

MACHINE USE

26. Have you tried it on the machine for register?	....	....
27. Is space sufficient for maximum postings?	....	....
28. Will arrangement allow for a minimum number of tabular stops on the machine?	....	....
29. Will continuous use require round corners?	....	....
30. If form will be posted over and over, does the grain on paper stock run up and down so that it will not curl in the tray?	....	....
31. Can the form be filed and guided in such a manner that it can readily be posted by machine?	....	....

SPECIFICATIONS

32. Is the method of reproduction proposed the most practicable?	....	....
33. Is the proposed size right for inserting in file folders or binders, as well as in office machines?	....	....
34. Is the quality and weight of the paper proposed appropriate for the number of carbon copies to be made, the handling of the form, and its permanency?	....	....
35. If colored paper is proposed, is it necessary in order to expedite handling of the form?	....	....
36. If the form is to be reproduced after entries are made, are the paper and ink used both for printing and for entries suitable for the method of reproduction desired?	....	....
37. If the form requires one or more copies, can all copies be printed from the same type or plate, without change?	....	....

COMMON FORMS DESIGN STANDARDS

As Adopted by U. S. Government Agencies

As an aid to agencies in developing their own standards for the physical aspects of forms, the following pages contain standards that have been selected from those now followed by many Government agencies. The list covers seventeen characteristics found adaptable to standardization. A large agency may wish to develop more explicit criteria in the light of its own circumstances and to expand on the number of different items covered as it gets under way, so that specialized classes of forms—form-type form letters, accounting forms and others—may have specific criteria for their design.

Such standards should be applied by the initiating unit when drawing a rough sketch of the form to be submitted with the forms requisition, and by the forms-control staff in reviewing the request and sketch or in making up a new design, as well as in making any necessary adjustment of specifications before forwarding the requisition for duplicating or printing.

1. CUT FORM SIZES

Any size that can be cut from 32 by 42 inches without waste, particularly sizes 3½ by 8, 4 by 5¼, 8 by 10½ and 16 by 10½ inches.

Normal file card sizes: 3 by 5, 4 by 6, 5 by 8 inches.

Post card sizes: 3¼ by 5½ inches.

Considerations:

a. Avoid crowding content;

b. Conform to dimensions of storage and filing facilities (i.e., legal size, letter size, etc.) ;

c. Fit to standard office machines for fill-in (i.e., typewriter, bookkeeping machine, etc.) ;

d. Fit to standard-size envelopes.

2. PAPER WEIGHT AND GRADE

Operating unit ordinarily should specify one of the following four:

Mimeograph	36 lb. (basis 17 by 22)*
Card	180 lb. (basis 25½ by 30½)*
Sulphite	32 lb. (basis 17 by 22)*
Bond (25 percent rag	32 lb. (basis 17 by 22)*

More precise specifications may be made by forms-control office. Variations permitted on special justification.

Selection should be based upon:

a. Handling requirements;

b. Writing method;

c. Number of copies to be made at one writing;

d. Length of time the form will be retained;

---

*Dimensions refer to sizes on which weights are based; not necessarily to sizes stocked by the agency. (See Standard 1.)

COMMON FORMS DESIGN STANDARDS (Cont.)

 e. Printing requirements (i.e., printing on two sides, by a given process, etc.) ;

 f. Filing and storage space requirements (affected by thickness of paper).

(Writing quality, erasing quality, durability, opacity, and thickness may be checked with the Government Printing Office.)

3. COLOR OF PAPER

Specify color only when needed for emphasis or for more efficient filing, routing or sorting. Reduce the need for colored paper by use of sorting symbols, bold headings, heavy ruled lines or other devices when possible. Exceptions permissible for specific organization or operating requirements.

4. COLOR OF INK

Specify other than black ink only when fully justified by volume and increased efficiency in use of the form and when the more economical possibilities of colored paper are inadequate. Two colors should be avoided except under extreme justification.

5. IDENTIFICATION AND HEADING

Heading may be centered across entire top of form or centered in space to the left of any entry boxes in upper right. (Upper right should be designed for file or other ready-reference entries if needed.) Within space decided upon, arrange generally as follows:

 Form number and issuance or revision date—upper left corner.

 Agency name and location (if needed)—upper left (under form number) or top center (depending on its importance in use of form).

 Form title—center of top (under agency name and location, if that item is centered). Use conspicuous type.

 Bureau of the Budget number and expiration date, for Federal report forms —upper right corner.

Exception: Run identification across bottom of vertical-file card forms unless needed for file-reference purposes.

6. INSTRUCTIONS

Well-designed forms require few instructions other than captions and item headings. When required, instructions usually should—

 a. Be set in two or more narrow columns rather than full-width lines.

 b. Be listed as numbered items rather than in paragraph style.

 c. Be placed as near items to which they apply as possible (unless length would detract from effective layout.)

When instructions are segregated on form, they should be placed—

 a. At top right or top center, if concise and applicable to the whole form.

 b. At bottom, if that will make possible more economical use of space.

 c. On reverse, if no space available on face.

COMMON FORMS DESIGN STANDARDS (Cont.)

7. ADDRESS

If name and address are inserted on form by agency prior to mailing, position of name and address should be suitable for window-envelope use. Forms requiring return to an agency should be properly identified as provided under Standard No. 5.

Forms intended for use in window envelopes must conform to postal regulations, which in general provide that nothing other than name and address, and possibly mailing symbol, shall appear in the window. The form must fit the envelope to avoid shifting of the address. Standard-size envelopes only should be used. *Post Office Department Schedule of Award of Contracts for Envelopes* is the guide to standard envelope sizes.

8. PREPRINTED NAMES OR FACSIMILE SIGNATURES

If form is to be stocked for continuing use, personal name or signature of official may be preprinted only on special justification or by legal requirement (to avoid having large numbers of forms made obsolete by change of officials). Preprinting of titles only or the use of rubber stamps or automatic signature inscribers are alternatives to be considered.

9. FORM ARRANGEMENT

    a. Align beginning of each writing space on form vertically for minimum number of tabular stops.

    b. If box design is used:

        1. Serially number each box in its upper left-hand corner;

        2. Start caption in upper left-hand corner, to right of number, leaving fill-in space below caption;

        3. Draw box size to provide sufficient space for fill-in.

    c. Place essential information where it will not be obscured by stamps, punches, or staples, or be torn off with detachable stubs.

    d. Group related items.

    e. Include "to" and "from" spaces for any necessary routing.

    f. Provide for use of window envelopes, when appropriate, to save additional addressing.

    g. To the extent practicable, provide same sequence of items as on other forms from which or to which information is to be transferred.

    h. Arrange information for ease in tabulating or transferring to machine punch cards, if those are involved.

10. CHECK BOXES

Use check boxes when practicable.

    a. Place check boxes either before or after items, but all in the corresponding positions within any line series.

COMMON FORMS DESIGN STANDARDS (Cont.)

b. Avoid columnar grouping of check boxes if possible, because of poor registration when carbon copies are required. Place check boxes before first column and after the second column when there are two adjacent columns of questions.

11. MARGINS

Printing Margin. Printed all-around borders usually should not be used since they tend to increase production problems and costs. In any event an extra margin of ⅜ inch or not less than 3/10 inch from edge of paper should be allowed on all four sides for gripping requirements in printing and as a safety margin for cutting. No printing—neither border nor text—should be permitted in that space.

Binding Margin. For press-type fastener, side or top, 1 inch; for ring binder, 1 inch (printing permitted but no fill-in within these margins).

Fill-in Margin. Top typewriting line, at least 1⅓ inches from top of paper if possible. Bottom typewriting line, not less than ¾ inch from bottom. Hand fill-in permissible above or below these lines.

12. SPACE REQUIREMENTS FOR FILL-IN

Typewritten—10 characters to the horizontal inch to accommodate both elite and pica typewriters;

Three fill-in spaces to the vertical inch, each space being double typewriter space.

Handwritten—⅓ more space horizontally than for typewritten fill-in;

Three spaces to the vertical inch, each space double that of typewriter space.

13. RULINGS

a. Use heavy 1½-point or parallel ½-point rulings as first and last horizontal lines, between major divisions, and across column headings.

b. Use ¾-point rulings across bottom of column headings, and above a total or balance at the foot of a column.

c. Use hairline rulings for regular lines and box lines when no emphasis required.

d. Use ¾-point rulings for vertical subdivision of major sections or columns.

e. Use leaders as needed to guide eye in tabular or semitabular items.

14. SIGNATURE AND APPROVAL DATE

Single handwritten signatures usually go at bottom right of last page. Allow ½ inch (three single typewriter spaces) vertically and three inches horizontally.

Two handwritten signatures, normally left and right at bottom of last page.

Space below ¾-inch bottom typewriter margin generally reserved for handwritten signatures and dates.

COMMON FORMS DESIGN STANDARDS (Cont.)

15. TWO-SIDED FORMS

a. Two-sided forms ordinarily should be printed head to foot (top of front to bottom of back), especially if top-punched for binder use.

b. If punched in left margin for binder use, two-sided forms should be head to head.

c. Three- or four-page forms (one sheet folded once) should be head to head throughout if open-side style, and head to foot if open-end (so that, when opened for use, head of third page follows foot of second page).

d. Head-to-foot open-end forms are preferable for machine fill-in.

e. For multipage forms, separate sheets of proper page size should be used instead of larger sheets folded to page size, unless the larger sheets can be cut economically from standard paper sizes and run on standard printing or duplicating equipment.

16. PRENUMBERING

Use prenumbered forms only if accounting or control is required for each form or document. Place number in extreme upper right corner.

17. PUNCHING

For standard press-type and three-hole ring binders:

Distance from edge of paper to center of hole should measure $\frac{3}{8}$ inch;

If two holes are punched, for press-type fastener, the distance between centers should be $2\frac{3}{4}$ inches;

If three holes are punched, distance from center to center of adjacent holes should be $4\frac{1}{4}$ inches.

See GPO guide for slotted, square, or other unusual punching, if necessary.

Chapter 44

CONTROLLING OFFICE SUPPLIES

OFFICE managers are well aware that the potential for waste of office supplies is tremendous and that it can run to staggering amounts of money that go down the drain. Efforts to reduce office waste are never-ending. They take many ingenious forms and are often designed to appeal to the emotions of employees and to their loyalties, in addition to their reason.

Paper Savings

Serious consideration should be given to the grade and weight of paper stock used for all stationery, forms, reports, memos—every piece of paper printed for communications use inside and outside the office. Several companies, under the impression it is better quality, are using heavier paper than necessary in stationery and mailing pieces, thereby running up their first-class postage bill. When several pieces are to be mailed in one envelope, substantial savings can often be achieved by using lighter weight paper. A number of companies have found this a source of hidden costs worth investigating.

There are many companies that are using higher-priced paper than necessary on forms that will be kept for only a few months. For legal papers, for records that will be retained for many years, a good rag paper is usually considered best, but sulphite bond of standard grade serves admirably for letterheads and all forms and reports that have a relatively short life. A competent printer can suggest the kind of paper that serves each particular purpose best and most economically.

To keep a pencil in his hand and make marks on paper—even if it is merely "doodling" as he talks—is as natural to almost every businessman as drawing his breath. If no other paper is handy, he usually snatches a piece of the company's best stationery from his desk drawer, or uses the most expensive printed form in the office. This needless waste can be prevented by providing scratch pads of cheap paper. For this purpose many firms use discarded forms that have one side blank for scratch pads, having them cut if necessary into convenient sizes and then made into pads. These inexpensive scratch pads can be supplied to every desk.

To save both paper and time some companies print up small memorandum forms for use in routing papers, letters, reports, magazines, etc. The messages are suited to various purposes: "For your file," "Please handle," "See me on this," or whatever fits the case. Supplying cheap scratch and "memo" pads to every desk can cut down the misuse of expensive stationery and printed forms.

SURVEY OF CONTROL METHODS

The buying, storing, and controlling of the numbers of items needed to operate any office can cause an office manager many a headache. A recent Dartnell study of how eight companies handled these annoying problems brought forth many worthwhile suggestions. Among these eight firms the annual investment in letterheads and envelopes, pencils, typewriter ribbons, and other office needs runs from $40,000 to $2,500,000.

The Liquid Carbonic Division of General Dynamics Corporation spends from $40,000 to $60,000 a year to buy 110,000 letterheads, 700,000 envelopes, 100,000 checks, 80,000 decals, 2,500,000 forms, 400,000 tags, 280,000 labels, 42,000 business cards, and so forth.

A mail-order concern with an annual budget of $250,000 for such items, figured that in a year its stores, offices, and mail-order plants in 50 states use enough staple and paper-clip wire to fence in the state of Texas. If made into one piece of wire, the straight pins used annually by its 165,000 employees would be long enough to fasten New York to Los Angeles and Seattle to Miami.

All the companies surveyed check constantly to keep the supply bill from growing bigger. Their methods should be helpful to other companies interested in economy and efficiency in handling business stationery and other office supplies.

How Sears Controls Printed Business Forms

At its national headquarters in Chicago, several thousand people in more than 50 buying and staff departments deal daily with the problems of Sears' mail-order plants, stores, catalog sales offices, foreign subsidiaries, and stores in Central and South America.

Control of printed forms is essential for economical handling of the many operating reports required, and this policy has proved valuable:

A request for a special form is referred to the general purchasing office for approval. The purchasing office tries to obtain the most suitable printed form and, if possible, to create a form that more than one department can use.

When the initial stock of a form is gone, the requesting department and the general purchasing office check it against policy and handling changes. A form may be revised or dropped if it is no longer needed or if another type would serve better.

Sears' constant study of office supplies has also whittled their cost. For one example, the company has adopted one-time carbon snap-out units for letters. More copies can be made at a time, handling and rehandling of carbon paper is eliminated, and a lighter weight, cheaper carbon can be used and economically discarded.

Illinois Bell's Stationery Committee

Economy and efficiency in purchasing also go hand in hand at Illinois Bell Telephone Company, which operates in some 360 Illi-

At The Upjohn Company in Kalamazoo, Michigan, the annual distribution of some 20 tons of paper, 5 million envelopes, 50,000 pencils, and 85,000 file folders is handled on a carefully inventoried basis.

nois communities and two counties in Indiana. Western Electric Company—the purchasing, manufacturing, and distributing arm for the Bell System—procures the office supplies, chiefly on a contract basis from thousands of suppliers, and stores them.

In a year, IBT spends $1,750,000 on supplies. Its 42,000 workers use 25 million envelopes, 10 million forms, 250,000 letterheads, 50 million paper clips, 20,000 ball-point pens, 50,000 pencils, and 1,000 quarts of ink annually. Most expensive item in stock is a three-pocket leather brief case; most expensive in quantity used is mimeograph paper.

Illinois Bell's stationery committee, with representatives from all departments, has the authority to stock, revise, or discontinue items or forms, with the approval of the department involved. Each month, this committee meets with Western Electric stock maintenance people to review stock conditions, submit requirements for new items, and so on.

Field forces order their supplies on a monthly basis from Western Electric to reduce handling, packing, and delivery expense. Each office or division keeps its own supply room or cabinets—with capacity for a month's requirements. Control and disbursement of such items are left to the local supervisor.

How Liquid Carbonic Handles Supplies

W. C. Hunt, supervisor of the stationery and mailing department, reported on Liquid Carbonic Division's system for purchasing and storing office needs. Twenty 12-foot bins hold forms, form books, stationery, envelopes, advertising material, and so forth. Each item is numbered and identified by a tag on the shelf. The tag tells "amount to order" and "order point."

When stock reaches the order point, the tag is pulled and three copies of the form are given to the supervisor. He fills a "want slip" and sends it, with the three copies of the form, to the purchasing department. After getting competitive bids, the purchasing department places the order and sends a copy to the stationery department. Delivered supplies are checked in by the receiving department and sent to the stationery department, which rechecks and shelves the supplies and marks the identification tag accordingly.

Each department requisitions supplies on a stationery requisition, typed by the person responsible for its supplies. The branch office manager or department head signs the requisition and forwards it to the stationery department. The stock clerk fills requisitions for main office departments and delivers them on Wednesdays. Branch requirements—carbon paper, folders, pencils, clips, erasers, forms that do not show a branch address—are packed and shipped each day.

For forms that show the branch address, each branch lists its expected needs for six months on a "semiannual report of stationery" card in April and October, and returns it to the stationery department. The quantities are tabulated, and want slips are sent to the purchasing department to order the forms. Suppliers ship envelopes, shipping tags, express and parcel post labels, and so forth, directly to each branch.

Upjohn Company's Central Storeroom

Some time ago, The Upjohn Company, Kalamazoo, Michigan, solved several problems by moving its office supply room into a larger, more central area. The results are faster service, better overall efficiency, quantity discounts from consolidated buying, and elimination of separate storage areas in each department.

The storeroom contains everything from "the lowly rubber band and paper clip to safe, silent, rubberized doorknob cushions to avoid static electricity shocks." A punch-card system is used by the supply department to record distribution of all supplies and stores.

Purchasing System at Egry Register

An Acme visible record system forms the basis of stock control by The Egry Register Company. Items are carried on individual stock-record cards, grouped by account numbers to help the cost department distribute the cost each month for accounting purposes.

Egry keeps a minimum balance on each item. When this point is reached, the stock-record clerk puts a red signal on the card to tell the stockkeeper to reorder. He prepares a purchase requisition stating quantity, description, and delivery date for each item. The quantity ordered depends upon usage, price, breakdown, and delivery schedule.

From this requisition, the purchasing department writes the order on a two-part, six-page form and sends the original copy to the vendor. The department files the second copy alphabetically by supplier, and the third copy by purchase order number for handy cross-reference.

The receiving department files the second three-page section alphabetically by vendor. When supplies are received, this department pulls the receiving report from its file, fills in the quantity received, date, signature, and any pertinent remarks.

Then the cost department gets the top copy of this set and holds it until the invoice is received from the purchasing department. On receipt of the invoice, the cost department posts the proper stock-record card, stating the date received, quantity, purchase-order number, and cost. The second, or audit, copy is sent to the purchasing department which removes its copy from the open file to complete its records. The third copy is filed alphabetically in the receiving department for reference.

How Prudential Fills Requisitions

The Prudential Insurance Company of America employs 154 people in the supply division at Newark, New Jersey, which serves eight regional offices (including one in Toronto) and 1,500 field agencies. (Regional offices purchase some materials directly.) F. S. Quillan, senior vice-president, describes the procedure:

Ordering offices mail requisitions at regular intervals—from one to five weeks. Most items are picked from stock, which occupies 184,000 square feet of space. Stationery items bearing an office address are ordered as requested from the printing plant or through the purchasing department from outside manufacturers. The printing plant produces 70 percent of the forms used.

Packed in corrugated cartons, consignments are shipped by freight, express, United Parcel Service, or mail to field and regional offices. Supplies ordered by the 7,300 employees in Newark are taken by truck to the home office four blocks away. Supply division personnel deliver these items to office areas.

Prudential stocks 15,000 supply items. In a year, the division filled 17,000 scheduled requisitions and about 40,000 special requests. (Special needs are requisitioned by phone, telegram, letter, or special form.) Branches received shipments totaling 4,500 tons; trucks delivered 3,300 tons of supplies to the home office.

Bell & Howell's Hints for Economy

Bell & Howell spends more than $200,000 annually for stationery and supplies used by its 3,800 employees. In 12 months, the company uses 500,000 letterheads of seven types and 1,200,000 envelopes of 16 varieties. Bell & Howell prints from 10 to 15 percent of the 700 different kinds of forms needed.

S. W. Knabe, director of purchasing, has offered six hints on wise purchasing:

1. *Estimate Annual Requirements.* "We estimate our annual needs, taking added sales and personnel into consideration. These requirements are grouped to fit their availability from our suppliers."

2. *Competitive Bidding.* "We send a list of our annual requirements to from three to six vendors for bids, with samples when necessary. We set a time limit for receiving bids, and ask for prices and samples of alternative items with lower costs, in addition to the items listed."

3. *Negotiation.* "We analyze all quotes and consider the alternative suggestions. Then we negotiate with the top vendors until we decide on all items."

4. *Blanket Orders.* "After selecting a vendor, we issue a blanket order for our annual needs, subject to special terms and conditions regarding price revision, quantities to be released, and the amount of stock the vendor should hold for immediate delivery when requested."

5. *Releases Against Blanket Orders.* "These releases are made via a special form."

6. *Cost Reduction Dockets.* "Buyers must submit dockets for every cost reduction they achieve. (Blanket orders have effected many savings in cost.) The number and amount of cost reductions buyers make help us considerably in rating their effectiveness."

WASTE AND PILFERAGE

Most companies feel that some control must be established to prevent the waste, excessive use, and outright theft of stationery, pencils, Scotch tape, and similar necessities of the office. This was revealed in a Dartnell study of the administration of office supplies in 37 selected companies. No companies, however, reported that the situation with them was desperate or that they had to take elaborate steps to get control of the problem. The prevailing attitude is that excessive "leakage" of office supplies is likely unless anticipated, but that the problem does not demand the use of highly organized systems, heavy vaults, and the other devices used to protect costly negotiables, for example.

Contributors to the study reported several basically different procedures by which they get maximum use of their office-supplies dollar. One of these systems is based on a central stockroom. A typical plan of this type is described by an official of the Connecticut Hospital Service:

All miscellaneous office supplies are maintained in a central stockroom in a locked cabinet by the office service department. Necessary supplies are requisitioned once each week by operating departments and staff secretaries. The supplies are delivered to them by office service department personnel. Thus operating personnel do not have routine access to large supplies of such items.

Periodically we review departmental requisitions to insure that usage is reasonable, and when reordering we analyze the period of time our supplies have lasted compared to previous usage.

Each department has at the most a week's supply of any one item on hand. Any misuse or theft would be readily noted by the supervisor, since he would have to initiate an emergency requisition and fully explain the reason for this.

A standard feature of the stockroom system is the use of requisitions and some provision for preventing the withdrawal of supplies without requisitions. Generally this requires that the supplies be kept in a storeroom which can be locked; the services of a supply clerk are also needed. In a small company the salary for a full-time clerk is out of proportion to the savings involved. One solution found by many companies is to keep the storeroom open only a few hours a day and to assign the job of clerking to an employee who has other duties.

A procedure developed by the American Abrasive Metals Co. is described by R. J. Pere, controller, as follows:

Within the past year we have instituted a regular stockroom procedure on all office supplies. Prior to that time the supplies were kept in the open and employees were permitted to help themselves, presumably to cover their office needs only.

Our procedure now calls for keeping all office supplies in locked metal cabinets. Each employee makes out his own requisition at a fixed period (before 9:30 a.m.) each day to cover his needs for the immediate future. This system is still haphazard to the extent that no check is made of who is ordering what supplies, and every employee is permitted to requisition almost anything without a department head's approval. There is, however, some psychological control in that employees requisitioning stationery know that the office boy, who handles the stockroom, can keep mental track of their usage. Presumably they would be hesitant to make it obvious that they were taking stationery for their own needs. With the haphazard system of control that we had previously, it is difficult to estimate just how much effect this has had on reducing petty pilferage. The feeling is, however, that there has been some progress all along these lines.

Other companies which contributed their experience to the study have discovered that periodic analysis of the filled requisitions can help to keep the situation under control. One of the organizations which does this is the Golden State Mutual Life Insurance Company. Golden State reports the following automated procedure for handling office supply needs of a number of divisions:

Our present system of supplying, storing, and shipping office supplies through an automated system away from our home office also provides us with a periodic usage report which is checked to determine if ordering by different districts and divisions is out of line based on past ordering practices and business activity.

When supply orders are received, they are also checked before the order is placed for reasonableness of the amount ordered, based on size of unit and past orders.

Distribution of the cost of office supplies to the using unit is also done through our automated system, which is a built-in check on oversupplying or petty pilfering.

Similar steps were reported by an official of the Dennison Manufacturing Company:

In checking with our office supply department, we find that there are no indications of petty thievery. Supplies are requisitioned as needed by the various offices and these requisitions show that the quantities being used are not above normal. Undoubtedly, the occasional pencil, rubber band, a few paper clips, or other small items are found in pockets when employees arrive at home. However, we feel sure that such happens through forgetfulness rather than with any intent to steal since the consumption of supplies is not excessive.

Our supply procedure is checked periodically and, as far as we can determine, no evidence of unauthorized or excessive requisitioning has been brought to light.

Employees who take any packages or bundles out of the factory at noon or night must secure a "Personal Package Slip" from the foreman or supervisor who signs it after checking the bundle or package. These slips are collected by the gatemen when employees leave.

Some companies, in addition to reviewing requisitions, make inventories from time to time of the material which has been withdrawn. The Iowa Mutual Insurance Company is one organization which does this. A highly placed executive has this to say about the problem:

All we do to prevent petty thefts of office supplies is to control the quantity requisitioned from our supply department for use in the individual departments. The most frequent abuse is that of ordering too large a quantity of small supplies, which creates small subsidiary supply departments in each department if not controlled. Occasional checks are made of the supplies on hand in each department and if there is too large a quantity it is pointed out to the department manager and the excess supplies are returned to the company supply department.

In our company supply department all items that might be useful to be taken home, such as paper, pencils, etc., are kept in locked supply cabinets and dispensed by supply clerks by requisition only.

It is the opinion of some companies that tighter control of office supplies can be obtained if some sort of fairly scientific consumption norms are determined and if variations from these standards are investigated. This is the prevailing view on the subject at Cargill, Inc.:

We have made studies of the actual usage of all types of office supplies in each department of the company, and problems are referred to the departmental supervisors for closer control of distribution of supplies. Petty pilfering may well be more prevalent than is realized, and such studies should indicate at least the size of the problem involved.

We would not favor posters or other printed matter or a campaign of any sort among employees in general. It would seem more advisable to attack such a problem through directly increased control of distribution of supplies at the source.

The company's thinking about theft or waste of office supplies is reduced to three main points at Interstate Finance Corporation, expressed as follows:

1. Make it a point of issue and thorough understanding in the orientation procedure for new employees.

2. Inaugurate some type of incentive plan for managerial and department head employees. This does much to make the manager or department head cost-conscious. It will help to keep him on his toes to prevent pilfering or any other activity which might result in lower profits.

3. If such a situation does exist it can best be controlled by the key people in each department, such as the department head.

PERSONAL PACKAGE

THIS PACKAGE CONTAINS ONLY PERSONAL GOODS BE-LONGING TO ME.

_____
EMPLOYEE'S SIGNATURE

APPROVED:

_____
FOREMAN OR SUPERVISOR

DEPT. ....

No. 43171

The supervisor or foreman at Dennison Manufacturing Company issues this slip to the employee after checking the contents of his package.

PURCHASING ECONOMY

In buying office supplies, real economy is usually realized by buying better quality. Take, for example, paper clips, staples, and other types of office fastenings. No doubt a few cents per box can be saved by buying inferior clips. But charge against this apparent economy the time wasted by office workers in finding papers that have worked loose and disappeared, throwing out bent clips, untangling papers that have become caught, to say nothing of the resulting irritation, and the purchasing *plus* soon becomes a *minus*.

Better quality clips give value beyond the increase in price. A good clip is stronger; its finish, galvanized in the better quality, lasts longer. There are no burrs where the wire ends are cut; burrs catch and tear paper.

So also with staples. In the manufacture of the better grades, rigid inspection assures quality. Broken or imperfect strips are rejected, points are clean-cut and even, without burrs.

In wasted time alone, a poor pencil may cost several times the price of a good one. Better pencils have a smoother lead that speeds writing; they do not break as easily. Add the extra sharpenings due to broken leads, the uneven wearing, and other defects of the inferior pencil, then contrast this with the time saved, the longer life, the far more satisfactory service of the quality pencil, and one can see that quality is economy, here.

High on the list of office supplies that call for quality as a vital consideration is the pencil sharpener. A good sharpener which doesn't break points or shred wood always pays for its initial higher cost, in the long run.

In far too many cases, pencil sharpeners are kept in use long after they should be discarded. A sharpener in bad condition naturally wears out pencils faster. And it's a rare office where pencil sharpeners are kept in good mechanical condition. Oiling and brushing are essential if a pencil sharpener is to render proper service.

An economy measure often overlooked when purchasing looseleaf binders is that a less expensive model will serve satisfactorily as a transfer or storage binder, while it is economy to select a sturdy heavy binder for active use.

Where offices buy pens for employees, utility is the important factor and today it is possible to get a pen in a very moderate price bracket which writes well and gives excellent service. Prestige lines offer pens which present a more attractive appearance, but where utility is the prime factor, it is not necessary to buy expensive pens.

On the other hand, better quality in carbon paper and typewriter ribbon—in fact in all inked ribbons—increases the cost of the individual letter so little, and gives such vastly greater satisfaction, that the higher quality is the wiser choice. If a stenographer is taught how to use her supplies properly, she will get more wear from the higher quality paper and ribbons, and this decreases the cost per letter. Tests, plus an analysis of their results, will decide what typewriter ribbons and which carbon papers prove the most economical for the special conditions that exist in every office.

Storing Supplies

Another economy measure, and one which should be carefully studied, is selection of the type of storage equipment and methods that provide proper care and protect the utility and life of a product.

Inks, for instance, must always be stored upright and kept from freezing. Numbering machine and check protector inks should never be used with rubber stamps, as the oils will deteriorate the rubber. Conversely, stamp pad inks should not be used with numbering machines; they will clog the mechanism. Different inks should never be mixed; the chemical reactions are likely to result in an unusable compound.

Rubber bands are an item that must be stored carefully to assure longer life. Since the heat, sunlight, oil, and ozone in air are deleterious to rubber, rubber bands should be kept out of direct sunlight. The ideal storage place is a dark, cool spot. Although science has developed resistors to combat the effects of air and other natural enemies of rubber, the stock of rubber bands should be rotated or moved so that the latest order received is placed behind those on hand.

In purchasing filing supplies, there are two costs to be considered —the initial cost and the operating cost. Experts have figured the whole problem out on accurate percentages. If a file that costs a few dollars more saves as little as 48 minutes of the filing clerk's time in a year, the extra feature or features in the higher priced file has cost you nothing. Beyond the 48 minutes, additional time saved is a profit on your slightly higher investment. And of course the cost of filing equipment and supplies is insignificant when compared with the value of the correspondence and records they protect.

Heavier, stiffer folders that won't sag down out of sight save time and pay for their slight additional cost very soon. Gummed labels, besides greater legibility, add strength and improve appearance. As to guides for the file drawers, the major requisite here is durability; throwing the contents of the files back and forth as they are worked puts a great strain on the guides. While manila guides can be used for transfer files which have very little "traffic," files which are constantly used should have guides of fiber, pressboard, index bristol, or similar heavier materials. The construction of the tab and rod projection also calls for careful consideration. Here again where there is hard usage quality items pay dividends.

With the almost limitless variety of filing cabinets available today, a good deal of thought is needed to select the most efficient type for the particular purpose. Substitute drawer inserts are available that can turn one standard vertical unit into a complete filing system for the small business. Where any reasonable quantity of records is involved, though, drawer inserts are more expensive in first cost and in space than a regular cabinet especially made for the records. To illustrate: A standard height cabinet using two drawer inserts in place of a letter drawer only provides eight drawers, whereas a regular 3- by 5-inch card cabinet of the same height will take care of 10 drawers. And a standard invoice file provides five drawers instead of four, at the same height. Economy in space is best served by the purchase of cabinets especially made for the type of records to be housed.

A good file will cost, say, $15 more than one of inferior quality. When this difference is amortized over the life of a file (which experts put at 10 years), it is readily apparent that the better quality is the wiser buy.

The basic and obvious economy in the purchase of office supplies and equipment is realized through having only one or two sources of supply. When the right supplier is found, this invariably proves an excellent money- and time-saver, with the additional benefit of getting something extra in the way of courtesy and attention.

HOW TO SELECT THE RIGHT PAPER

There are a number of ways in which a company can save money by thoughtful buying of office stationery. But there are also a number of dangers in starting a general economy drive. Saving a few dollars on stationery can lose the company hundreds of dollars in increased labor costs, poor customer relations, lost sales, and waste.

With the typical business letter costing nearly $2.50 and with stationery only about 2 cents of that cost, it is obvious that to reduce the quality of stationery is no way to start an economy drive. If *all* stationery could be eliminated, only 2 percent of the correspondence costs would be saved.

What to Consider

Standardizing on paper grades best suited for each office requirement results in economy. The quality of the paper used in the office
is determined by many factors in its formula and in the method
and quality of its manufacture. Since the office manager is usually
less informed in these areas than he might wish to be, he must trust
his stationer or printer to judge the qualities for him, and it is
important that the supplier be chosen with care.

The weight of a paper is an important factor in its "wearability"
and "feel." Letterhead stationery is commonly 16-, 20-, and 24-
pound weight. There is more than weight to be considered, though.
There are the factors of permanency, strength, erasability, opacity,
texture, color, and reasonable cost. These are all features which the
paper supplier can describe and demonstrate on request.

Paper used for correspondence ranges from 100 percent sulphite
to 100 percent rag content depending on the use and appearance required. Normal correspondence is not held long enough to make the
difference in wearing qualities too important. For this reason, the
largest volume of correspondence is written on either No. 1 sulphite
or 25 percent rag paper. Where the life of the paper is indefinite,
where the paper is subject to heavy wear and abuse, and where
quality and rich appearance are important, papers with higher rag
content are used.

Routine memos and notices that have short lives and are not
given rough handling may safely be written on the less expensive
grades of paper.

Letterheads may be engraved, embossed, printed, or lithographed.
The engraved letterhead is considered the acme of good business
taste, and 100 percent rag bond paper should be used with it. To do
otherwise would be like wearing a diamond tiara with a sports en-
semble. Beautiful results, however, can be obtained by a good printer
who uses other imprinting media on good bond papers.

The letterhead paper, envelope, and blank sheets for second and
succeeding pages should always match. This is just as important in
business correspondence as it is in social writing.

For Permanency

Every business has certain records which have permanent value
for all practical estimates of time. Examples of these records include
articles of incorporation, contracts and agreements, leases, wills,
minutes of board meetings, patents, and product specifications. Although improvements in paper production methods have increased

the life of all papers, only the 100 percent rag papers can be safely relied upon to last indefinitely.

The difference in cost between the paper used in routine correspondence and a 100 percent rag content paper may be as little as $1 a ream. No thinking person will risk the safety of an important document which may be worth thousands of dollars just to save one-fifth of a cent on the cost of the sheet of paper on which it is written.

Lightweight bond papers are commonly used for airmail letters. The lighter weight was originally chosen to save weight, but an additional important value is achieved by the attention airmail stationery commands. It invites preferred handling and preferred attention. Matching airmail envelopes should be used, of course, for without the distinctive decoration of the envelope, much of the desired attention value is lost.

For Carbon Copies

Carbon copies are important business records. They may be kept for only a short time until the original copy returns for permanent reference; they may be kept for reference because the original will not be returned; or they may be used as originals to send information to several different persons. The quality of paper, matched to the use and permanency required, runs from the cheapest newsprint to 100 percent rag content.

Carbon copy paper is light in weight, commonly 7-, 8-, 9-, 11-, and 13-pound. The lighter weights produce a greater number of legible copies at one writing and take up less room in the files. Carbon copy paper is known by various names, including manifold, onionskin, and second-sheets. The term "manifold," is generally applied to any lightweight sheets that are used where a number of copies are to be made at the same time.

Onionskin is generally used for more important filing and mailing copies; manifold sheets of various colors are used to help in getting faster routing and proper filing of reference copies. Second-sheets are the heavier grades and are usually yellow. Although they may be of sulphite, they more usually consist of inexpensive newsprint, suitable only for temporary records. Cockled paper resists smearing of the carbon and reduces slippage in the carbon pack, but smooth-finish paper makes a clearer impression.

Ten Points for Improved Protection Against Burglary

In studying the question of plant protection, the editors consulted, among other experts, the plant security officers of the Stewart-

Warner Corporation. The following points were listed by J. B. Vottero, of that company, as a useful checklist for office executives concerned with security:

1. Establish strong controls of safe combinations and keys with the fewest number of employees possible. Also change combinations and locks immediately as conditions require.

2. Unlock cash registers, if in use, and open cash drawers after removing contents, at close of business. Use your bank's night depository for excess currency, especially over weekends or holidays. Insist on full and complete deposits on each banking day.

3. Safes strong enough to withstand assault, well anchored so as to delay or prevent removal, and well lighted overhead in a conspicuous place, are advisable.

4. Exterior doors should be constructed to withstand assault with heavy bars. Strong locks should be key operated from outside and inside, especially overhead doors through which losses can easily occur.

5. Windows accessible for entry but not regularly used should contain heavy wired glass, screens, or bars, and should be securely locked from the inside. Skylight windows should be of a wired type with heavy bars across the opening and kept locked.

6 An adequate inspection of premises including autos, trucks, and boxcars should be made at each closing time to detect anyone in hiding, watching particularly for juveniles who often assist in and commit some burglaries.

7. Strong lights at entrances and exits, on loading and unloading docks, over tool cribs and shop supplies, finished goods warehouses, parking lots, etc., will often discourage breaking-in and occasionally assist in detecting those involved.

8. Maintain friendly liaison with the local police department, soliciting advice on matters of burglary prevention. If and when a burglary is detected, call the police or the plant guards but allow nothing to be touched until finishing the preliminary investigation.

9. Remain alert to the possibility of a burglary being an inside job. Obtaining personal history reports and current credit standing of those suspicioned, will be of aid. Lie-detector tests should prove valuable (check union contracts; some prohibit this).

10. Perimeter trips of the property should be made periodically to detect any condition that might permit a burglary to occur.

Chapter 45

OFFICE COSTS AND BUDGETS

OFFICE managers, perhaps more than most executives, are on their toes when it comes to saving time and money in their departments. They are constantly on the lookout for better ways of doing the work of the office. As a result, office management in America is far ahead of any other country in the world today. Perhaps the very fact that office management is so receptive to new systems and techniques is one reason for the amazing innovations which are constantly being made to simplify the paper work of business.

The three principal areas for seeking ways of cutting office costs are (1) men, (2) methods, and (3) machines. These are sometimes called the "3 M's of Management" and any program aimed at controlling office expense must fully explore each of these areas.

F. P. Hagaman, former controller of Esso International, told this to an American Management Association conference some years ago:

An operating budget that is soundly established and properly used can be a valuable tool in creating awareness of conditions and trends. It gives a basis of comparison and consideration of the various elements of the business that should be known and understood. Perhaps the greatest service the budget renders is to give management at all levels an opportunity to think of its plans—its future program—in advance. It should be used as an agency for coordination and comparison, but, without cost analysis and trend analysis, without study of cost variations from normal, budgetary control may be very incomplete. The word "budget" has been defined as "originally a loose bundle." I suspect that many budgetary procedures are very loosely handled, whereas proper administration is of the utmost importance. The *Reader's Digest* some time ago had something to say about budgets which has been much quoted since. "A method of worrying before you spend as well as afterwards."

One of the advantages of budgetary procedure comes from forecasting in advance desired results as a sort of reference standard and the setting up of an incentive to "beat the budget." Where the preparation of the budget is by the supervisor responsible for performance it becomes "his budget." Without this incentive the budget often becomes a form of administrative report to be "beaten" or reconciled by use of favorable variations from standard conditions. The proper preparation of the budget under the partnership arrangement between manager, supervisor, and worker will defeat this undesirable reaction, and thus any kind of a budget under these conditions will be one of the useful tools of control.

There are several natural requirements for sound budgeting which are hardly different from the requirements for many other management projects. Those which occur to me as being of major importance are the following:

The budget must be based upon a perspective of the scope of activities during the advance period being budgeted. This includes projection of work loads, effective seasonal demands, etc.

Each budget item must be subject to revision for major changes, and the planning of the budget should be based on well-planned methods of revision.

Obviously, the budgeting process must anticipate comparison with actual results, and provision for comprehensive analysis of variations should be made in advance. This emphasizes the need for retention of all data leading up to the preparation of budgeted figures for such later comparisons.

The budget should naturally follow organization lines on the basic premise of conforming to the division of authority and responsibility.

A major part of the budget plan should cover arrangement for followup of variations both to serve the purposes of future budgets and also to see that undesirable conditions are corrected.

How to Achieve Cost Control

The fundamental rules, which are of great importance to success in cost control objectives, are to:

Recognize the worker's stake in the objective. If management cannot develop the worker's philosophy of maximum productivity to a high level, cost control techniques will not substitute.

Use the first-line supervisor of the smaller groups of workers. The immediate boss must lead, teach, and preach a high standard of craftsmanship and productivity to the working personnel.

Bring the supervisor and the worker into partnership with management. Keep them informed. Do not put management's objectives on one side and the worker's on the other.

Live this philosophy in spite of the contrary influences coming up in all forms at all times.

Set up the motivation for reaching cost control objectives on the part of both the supervisor and the worker.

Provide the facilities—the proper office organization and functional relationship, the equipment, the systems, and working conditions.

Help the supervisor and his workers in the development of all of the measuring devices, standards, cost comparison techniques, efficiency rating methods, etc., which he and his workers can believe in.

Set up the machinery for progress reporting to all concerned, so that the path to the target can be visualized by the lowest worker. Give open publicity to purpose and plan in all phases of cost control. Recognize accomplishment.

Budgeting Direct Labor Expense

Labor expense in the office is one of the items that grows bigger every year. Indications are that it will continue to do so. The surprising thing is that more is not being done to control and plan for the money that is spent for clerical work. Why this is so has always been somewhat of a mystery. It may be that other areas of expense appear to offer greater opportunities for control, or perhaps "office costs" have been thought of as a stepchild not considered worthy of the kind of care exercised on materials or other members of the expense family. Whatever the reason, it is a problem deserving of forthright and serious treatment.

It is a strange paradox, but companies that do a splendid job with their manufacturing costs often give their clerical expenses a quick once-over. In many instances, these costs are charged off to a catch-all like general overhead or something similar, and that is about all that is ever done with them. This is an easy way to dispose of the problem, but it is an expensive way to run a business.

And, it need not be so. Something can be done to control and regulate the dollars spent on clerical work.

This is not a problem that has suddenly come to light, but is one that has been with us for a long, long time. With conditions as they are today—with costs going up, and competition increasing—it is important now more than ever before, to know not only what happens to the dollars that are spent for clerical work, but to set up a way to keep them from getting out of hand.

The ever-mounting importance of this area in the overall cost of doing business is almost startling when we see how the number of men and women engaged in office work has grown over the past few years. Food for thought too is the probability that this number will continue to grow even in the face of the savings that will result from the electronic machine age which we are now entering. So the problem is not a little one, but a big one becoming even larger.

Clerical activity can be controlled if it is planned for well in advance.

The underlying principle in this kind of thinking is that management at all levels needs to know where it is going, how it is going to get there, and when it starts off in the wrong direction. This kind of programming, or budgeting, is the key to the successful control of costs, clerical or otherwise. The plan must be kept simple and realistic. It must be complete and tailored to fit specific situations and conditions—halfway measures are not good enough.

The profitability of controlling costs through budgeting has been demonstrated enough times in other areas of expense to indicate the worthwhileness of a similar approach to clerical work. Most everyone will admit that some kind of "clerical budgeting" would be valuable if a way could be found to do so successfully and economically.

Recognizing Principles

With budgeting and control of direct labor in the factory the accepted rule rather than the exception, it is only natural that we look toward ways of applying the same kind of engineered principles of cost control to clerical labor.

In the field of clerical expense, just as with factory direct labor, there are two simple but basic principles that apply in a budgetary control program:

1. Direct clerical labor and supervision must be related to definite quantities of measured work.

2. Responsibility for each item of expense must be assigned to a specific individual.

The prerequisite to carrying out these two principles is the existence of a good organization structure and the desire and personal backing on the part of the top individuals in the company. The company that has this kind of interest, along with a sound organization plan, has taken the first step on the road to an adequate control of clerical costs. Many well-conceived plans for controlling costs have foundered because of a lack of drive in the top job, or because of a poorly defined organization. Unless these two conditions exist, it is a complete waste of time to install any kind of a plan to control expenses.

The Tools for Planned Control

A program designed to control direct labor and supervisory expense in the office requires that future activity be planned in advance and that a way be devised to keep track of how the program is carried out. To do this, three things are needed:

1. Standard costs (a knowledge of what the work should cost).

2. Actual costs (a knowledge of what the work is actually costing).

3. A comparison of the two (this is the variance, or the difference between standard and actual costs, and represents that part of the expense which can be controlled).

This kind of control program is built around the philosophy that the main concern of management should be with the profit that has not been made, rather than with the profit that has been made. Or, putting it another way, management should be concerned with the amount of money that has been spent in excess of what should have been spent to get out the work.

The key factor in this approach is to determine, first of all, what the work should cost; and then, knowing this, build plans for future activity around these standards.

Briefly, clerical work standards are best developed by following accepted time-study practice. This means making detailed outlines or descriptions of each step in a clerical procedure and determining a time factor for the various operations. Measurement can be made in a number of ways. One is to prepare procedure flow charts using symbols representing the major types of clerical work. The ones most commonly used describe work as falling in one of five categories: Receiving, examining, taking action, transporting, and filing. These symbols are connected by lines to show the work flow, and are accompanied by a running account of every operation performed by an employee or group of employees.

In this fashion, a detailed, comprehensive procedure chart is prepared for every item of clerical work that is done. If the charts indicate that no changes should be made in the procedure, then the work is ready for the calculation of time factors. In many instances, though, the mere fact that pencil is put to paper and a job is described in writing, will point out a number of things to do that will simplify present procedures. This is a by-product of work measurement that is sometimes overlooked but which an alert supervisor can make very profitable.

With the procedure flow chart completed, standard unit times are next developed. The goal here is to determine a fair and reasonable time factor for each of the operations on the chart. The fairest and most accurate time values are obtained by splitting the different steps into their component parts and timing each part separately. There are several ways to do this. The two most common are by direct observation of the work or by applying elemental data previously developed. Now, with standard times set up, standard direct labor unit costs can be calculated for each type of work by applying the appropriate hourly rate. This gives us, then, the basis for the standard costs, which is the first essential in a program to budget and control clerical activity.

Projecting Clerical Work

In actual practice, preparation of a clerical expense budget begins with a projection of how much work is expected to be handled in the coming year. Sales forecasts, service requirements, company programs, and other factors that might affect the workload are considered. This is best done by taking each organizational group in the company and setting up its workload budget separately.

A good way to start is to prepare a workload projection in tabular form, showing the amount of work in terms of standard man-hours per week that a clerical section is planning to produce during the next calendar year. The summary following is an example of one where the quantity of work in terms of standard hours is stated for each of the 52 weeks in the coming 12 months for a particular clerical section. It can be set up to show the probable frequency of occurrence, i.e., daily, weekly, and so forth, or whatever other arrangement is most usable. In any event, the first step is to figure out in advance what is going to be done and then get it down on paper in as much detail as possible.

The most common reason (or excuse) for *not* making up such a list is that "we don't know what is going to happen next week, or next month, let alone 12 months from now." This, of course, is right if the possibility is considered of looking into the future and predicting correctly down to the last penny what is going to happen. But this is not the case. What is needed for those in charge of the work, using all the information available to them—plus a little ingenuity— is to plan in advance for the activity of their group.

Now, with an itemized list of the work planned for the coming year, it helps to take the data and make a graph of the projected workload. This chart shows graphically the expected workload in terms of standard man-hours for each of the 52 weeks in the coming year. It is useful in many ways, but, most important, provides a "picture" of plans—easily appraised at a glance—and when every department is completed, there is available a composite picture of all the clerical operations in the company.

An example of such a workload projection for a typical section handling clerical work is shown on the graph headed, "Projection of Work Load."

This graphic outline, in addition to showing how the expected workload will be distributed throughout the year, forms a convenient document for the recording of the amount of work as it is actually produced. It is helpful likewise in determining staffing needs *in advance,* and for scheduling and making other plans to take care of that part of the anticipated workload which can be counted on as definite.

Converting to Dollars

Once the variety and quantity of the work expected to be processed during the coming year have been determined, the next step is to convert these standard man-hours to standard dollars. This is done by taking the standard man-hours previously calculated for each item of work and extending it by the applicable standard rate. The addition of these standard dollars for the 52 weeks gives us the total direct labor expense at standard to be budgeted for the coming year. With the direct labor portion calculated, the direct expense budget for clerical salaries and related expenses of the section is completed by adding to it:

1. The cost of direct supervision.

WORKLOAD PROJECTED FOR A CLERICAL SECTION

(Coming Year)
Standard Hours of Work Each Week of the Year

Item of Work	1st Week	2nd Week	3rd Week	4th Week	49th Week	50th Week	51st Week	52nd Week
1. Preparation of operating statement	13.7	12.9	11.6	2.0	11.9	11.6	12.0	21.6
2. Preparation of invoices	13.2	12.8	11.9	11.7	12.0	11.4	11.6	11.2
3. Verification of invoices	1.1	.8	.4	.4	.6	.4	.9	.3
4. Preparation and distribution of mail	9.6	7.2	5.2	5.8	4.7	5.6	5.2	4.2
31. Correspondence	13.9	12.6	11.7	11.4	12.0	11.8	11.4	11.0
32. Control of inventory reports	4.3	3.7	2.6	2.2	2.4	2.2	2.0	1.8
33. Debit and credit posting	2.6	1.8	.9	.6	.7	1.4	1.9	1.3
34. Payroll	4.2	4.2	3.1	2.9	1.7	2.0	3.2	2.7
35. Filing	2.4	1.9	1.4	2.5	2.7	3.2	3.0	2.4
Standard hours of work per week	455.9	393.9	200.9	248.8	241.6	225.2	295.0	190.4

2. The hours that will be paid for and not worked (these are vacations, holidays, illness, and similar allowances).

3. Supplies and materials.

4. Overtime.

The summary following is an example of a direct expense budget covering the work expected to be handled by a particular group throughout the coming year. The direct labor, which represents the bulk of the budget, is for the work shown on the workload projection graph.

Budgets similar to this are prepared for all sections and can be combined to form divisional, departmental, and, finally, an overall master budget for all the direct clerical expense in the company.

SUMMARY OF BUDGETED DIRECT EXPENSE

The Coming Year

ITEM

1. Direct supervision

    Supervisor $7,200

    Assistant supervisor (part time) 2,400

    $ 9,600

2. Direct labor (at standard) 33,176

3. Hours paid for but not worked

    Vacations $2,781

    Holidays 1,572

    Illness 1,248

    5,601

4. Supplies 1,425

5. Overtime 1,688

    $51,490

The Variable Expense Budget

In addition to making a summary of direct expenses for the coming year, it is good practice to set up a variable budget to show what the direct expense will be for each item at various levels of activity. This can be done for each 10 percent variation, covering a range of anywhere from 40 to 120 percent of capacity as figured at standard. The spread will depend on the degree of fluctuation that can be expected in the work of the section, and will probably vary from group to group.

This variable or flexible budget (as it is sometimes called) is built up work-item by work-item for the standard hours necessary to handle the volume or quantity of work at various levels of activity. In practical practice, the standard hours of direct labor required are divided into two general groups:

1. The standard hours required to handle the work that is *constant* month after month and is not affected by changes in volume.

2. The standard hours required to handle the work that *varies* from month to month in proportion to the volume.

The hours of work at standard for the various levels of activity are converted to standard dollars by multiplying these hours by the applicable rates. The other items can be worked out by formula, using the hours of direct labor as a basis. For example, the amount of supervision will depend on the number of direct labor hours that

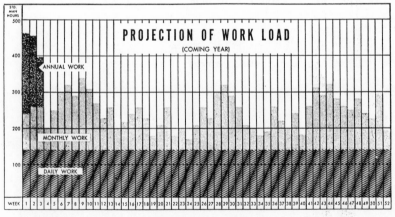

A forecast of the workload for the coming year, even though only approximate, helps the office manager prepare for peaks and valleys.

must be supervised. Perhaps the ratio will be, in some instances, one supervisory hour for every 15 clerical hours, or it may be as low as 1 to 5 depending on the particular work situation under consideration. There is no pat formula for this, but it is possible to set up general criteria for various kinds of work.

Referring to the basic principles of budgetary control already mentioned: (1) That of relating clerical labor and supervision to definite quantities of measured work, and (2) the assignment of specific items of expense to a particular individual, the value of setting up a flexible budget can be appreciated. The supervisor of the section is made, by this device, completely responsible for the expense items appearing on his budget. There is no way for him to shift responsibility to another. This puts him in business, so to speak, and places him in a position similar to that of being the owner of his own business.

The Position of the Supervisor

With a flexible budget such as this, the head of the section is accountable for the number of dollars he spends and the goods or services he provides for the money. If he spends more than he should, he ends up in the red. This sense of proprietorship is made possible through the simple expedient of: (1) Placing a dollar value on work turned out, (2) making a specific individual responsible, and (3) setting up an easy-to-use variance report. And, just as important, the supervisor has before him an incentive for doing a good job which will be reflected in dollars and cents. Its aid as a stimulus to advance planning of future activity is unmatched.

The report of a group's activity in this manner is, to all intents and purposes, a profit-and-loss statement. In fact, it is sometimes more effective to substitute the term "profit and loss" for the more high-sounding term "variance report." In any event, the budget, and the monthly statement of activity in dollars and cents, "puts the supervisor in business."

The budgeting of clerical work is a challenging assignment for management. It is a basic process of control because it permits management to retain control, yet centers responsibility for the expense of clerical work in the hands of those who administer the details.

Chapter 46

OFFICE BUILDINGS AND LAYOUTS

ONE does not have to go through too many speculative office buildings to realize the concessions necessary when occupying space in most rented offices. The ceilings are low, the electric service may be inadequate, and the elevator service and floor loadings are planned to handle minimum loads. In some cases, there are no underfloor ducts or steel reinforcements, so that it is impossible to improve the situation. Air conditioning and lighting are compromised so that they can be included in the advertised package. The freight elevator, loading, and car parking facilities are either omitted or too costly. Lastly, the buildings are generally built on the core concept.

The core-type office building is one where the elevator, stairway, shafts for mechanical services, toilets, and such are in the center of the floor plan, and a corridor around these services leads you to the office space which is usually 20 to 30 feet in depth. This permits the floor space to be divided up into smaller units for rental, giving each tenant independent access to building services.

A building of this type is often unsuitable for a large corporation. The 20- to 30-foot deep space does not permit grouping of large departmental units, or allow for the compactly planned office space which is possible when the office is planned on three or four floors of large, open-floor-type building.

A most important factor in office building space planning is the module used in regulating proportions. It is a fallacy to use a 3-, 3½-, or 4-foot module for windows and continuous glass windows, since it is too costly to coordinate the office lighting and air conditioning on a module smaller than 8 to 10 feet. Furthermore, the space administrator has a much easier job of apportioning the space when there is less choice in the size of private offices. The continuous glass window, even when used with treated glass and canopies, breaks down the economical modular principle for the space administrator. There are also added costs for cooling and heating the area.

Office in the City Skyscraper

Nowadays, the main reason a firm chooses a large city for its location is so that it will be convenient to related businesses, transportation, or its branch offices. Availability of office personnel, shopping, banking, and transportation are no longer major advantages of a city location.

Functionalism is the keynote in today's skyscraper

After having been located in a city for a long time, a company will often find its executives and general office personnel so scattered that moving out of the city would inconvenience three-fourths of its employees. Some cities, fortunately, do not present this problem to the corporation. For example, they might have industrial activity to the south, industrial housing to the east, and a river to the west. The white-collar residences, main highways, and transportation to the north then make a natural setting for the office to the north of the city on adequate acreage.

Today's city office buildings are mainly of the core-type plan. When a corporation builds on city property, it is too costly to have expensive property remain idle for future use. So space planned for expansion is usually rented. This practice restricts the entire building planning. Therefore, high ground values, high taxes, and related problems of city real estate make the office in the city skyscraper one where concessions are made that are often costly to the office efficiency and overhead.

Leasing Space in the Office Building

In all relations between the tenant and landlord, it is wise to use the services of a competent lease broker, a real-estate lawyer, and an office-planning architect. Their fees are inconsequential when compared with the many savings in time and money that can be brought about in the original leasing negotiations and during the term of the lease.

The office space lease has many typical clauses, and there are many standard forms of leases, but several essential factors to check upon in leasing of space are:

1. *Amount of Space.* The total area leased should be calculated as summarized in "Standard Method of Floor Measurement of the National Association of Building Owners and Managers."

2. *Space Description.* A reduced floor plan, or plans, should be marked to show the location of the office space agreed upon, and the plans made part of the lease.

3. *Rental.* The rental figure can best be checked by comparing it with other quotations for similar space and terms in the neighborhood, allowing a variance of 10 to 20 percent.

4. *Length of Lease.* Office leases normally commence on May 1 and expire April 30 of any year. Loft leases commence on February 1 or May 1. Considering the inconveniences and cost of moving, and a nominal period to live out any investments in floor covering and miscellaneous installations in the preparation of office space by the

tenant, a lease of five years should be a fair term for offices of approximately 15,000 square feet or less, and 10 to 20 years on larger areas. Longer leases with renewals, or even options on ownership of the building, should be considered by larger tenants.

5. *Expansion, Contraction, and Termination.* Arrangements should be provided in the lease for expansion through options on additional space, contraction through rights to re-lease or sublease, and termination through right to cancellation by compensating the landlord for alterations and loss until re-renting of the premises.

6. *Services.* Agreement between landlord and tenant as to services that the landlord is to give the tenant, and those the tenant is responsible for, should be made a part of the lease.

7. *Alterations.* Before signing the lease, the tenant should arrange for working drawings and specifications clearly describing what partitions, doors, electricity, plumbing, heating, ventilating, air conditioning, painting, and building standard alterations he expects of the landlord, and have them included in the lease, together with unit prices, in order to make adjustments as the work progresses, or during the term of the lease.

Any alterations the tenant proposes during the term of the lease should be approved by the landlord before the work is undertaken and paid for by the tenant.

8. *Miscellaneous.* The new tenant should try to favor installations of machines, materials, and services that have already been established in the building. Typical of these are water coolers, fans, towel service, building signs, and electric current.

Repainting of the leased premises should be done every three years and be referred to in the lease.

9. *Copies of Leases.* It is customary to prepare three copies of leases, one each for the landlord, tenant, and broker (a fourth where states require registering of leases).

The typical office lease has many standard clauses of restrictions directly and indirectly imposed upon the tenant, but the tenant can further investigate whether his organization tenancy is affected by the following restrictions or rules and regulations.

a. Buildings built for offices, stores, lofts, factories, or warehouses are often occupied by other tenants than the type for which they were originally designed, due to changes in neighborhoods and tenants of the buildings. It is wise to check any original and current restrictions.

b. Restrictions imposed by local zoning of business functions should be studied.

c. Local building department, labor department, and fire department rules and regulations should be investigated to determine their effect upon the proposed use of space.

The landlord usually requires that the tenant check with his building engineer before making any special installations such as air conditioning or electric machines, because electricity, water, and steam capacities in a building are not always adequate for the desired installations.

An Office in the Suburbs

In the suburban setting, one can build with fewer municipal restrictions on height, shape, materials, and zoning. Property values permit the purchase of large tracts of land which enhance the structure and give the employee a sense of pride in the firm for which he works. The visitor is also favorably impressed.

Locating offices in suburban sections is one of the truly American trends. The stature of the office worker is improved to its fullest, since he becomes a property owner—a car owner—and thus a more fraternal participant in the interests of his company and job, community, and country.

The hustle and bustle of the big city is lost in the semirural setting, and the office worker's personality is entirely different, due to the absence of tension formerly caused by traffic jams, crowds, competition, and higher costs of living.

The Home Office Building

Elements of importance to the office—beyond the normal considerations in the construction of a new office building—are planned flexibility of space, adequate building maintenance conditions, and provision for growth.

The amount of window office space, general office space, and storage space required for present and foreseeable expansion of an organization, and typical architectural and mechanical conditions of a building can be well planned for by an architect experienced in office layout requirements (or an architect and an office layout consultant working in collaboration).

These men are the interpreters of the problems of the office. They create the solution, supervise the work to completion, and are on hand when preplanned growth is to be undertaken. This relationship extends over a period of many years, if not indefinitely. The architect should coordinate the physical elements of the building with the functional requirements of the company.

Care should be taken to make physical surveys of the site, such as test borings and analysis of electric power, steam, gas, plumbing (water and sewers), telephone facilities, roads, sidewalks, and municipal limitations of the property. Transportation and shopping centers should also be investigated.

The architect should be given a free hand in investigating these conditions, and if he has not contemplated making these analyses, he should be urged to do so. He should be given a free hand in the selection of electrical, plumbing, heating, and structural engineers, and any further consultants he may deem necessary for the success of the office building.

The choice of the building contractor may be questioned by the owner. Additional qualified bidders can be added to the list of bidders, if desired, since as long as the plans and specifications of the office building have been completed, the choice of building contractor would effect no change in the project. An architect's and owner's representative (clerk-of-the-works) should be on the premises to check the construction as it progresses.

Several of the more important factors in the construction of an office building are:

1. *Number of Floors.* Where size of the property does not limit the area of a floor, it is wise to limit the horizontal distances from 100 to 200 lineal feet. An escalator, ramp, or stairway of a 15-foot rise to the next unit of space above or below, can be used up to five floors.

2. *Type of Construction.* Considering the constant changing of office layouts and the use of heavy machines and safes, files, and equipment, fireproof steel frame or reinforced concrete construction is believed most suited to modern office buildings.

3. *Shape.* Since the office is a combination of window, general office, and storage space, the shape of the building usually evolves from these requirements, limitations of the site, imposed design, and office functions.

Considering functional planning to arrive at the shape of the building, one would assume storage space being located in the basement, window office space provided by shape of corridors and offices on either side, and general office space of long beam span units of space.

4. *Orientation.* The private offices should face north or east, and the general offices south.

5. *Flexibility.* Window mullions in private office areas should be planned on 10-foot centers, in order to build 10- and 20-foot-wide private offices. Column spacings from the window wall can be 20 feet deep, in order to provide 20-foot-deep private offices. The column spacing for general office areas for proper planning of general office layouts can be 27 or 35 feet. Practical optimum dimensions for general office areas are usually within the range of 27 to 35 feet.

6. *Expansion.* Foreseeable expansion in private offices can be provided for by spare offices, conference rooms, or large offices that can be cut in two as new ones are needed.

Expansion in general offices can be provided through general office areas which are large enough to allow for future expansion, arranged more comfortably to suit today's needs.

Provision can be made for the growth of a building by planning additions to the building, or by adding additional floors.

The office in the rural community has many advantages over its counterpart in the big city, including ample parking space.

7. *Mechanical Facilities*. Electric light and power, heating, air conditioning, plumbing, and special devices such as underfloor ducts and intercommunication comprise the mechanical facilities of an office building. Electrical devices which will be added from time to time will require additional power, and this should be provided for when the building is planned, by providing spare electric service facilities.

8. *Services*. Cafeterias, car parking, recreation rooms, rest rooms, first-aid rooms, and similar employee service facilities should be provided for in original planning. Too often they are forgotten, and then provided for later at the expense of valuable office space.

9. *Maintenance*. Adequate storage for cleaning materials, locker room facilities, mechanical service access, and storage require coordination with maintenance people during the original planning.

Office Planning Standards

Every corporation has different ideas as to the size of private offices and the amount of space required by office workers in general office areas. It is the architect's responsibility, aside from basic functional requirements, to compromise these ideas with established space standards before his recommendations are accepted, in order to arrive at the total amount of space to rent or build.

In a new building project, the column spans and window modules can be planned to satisfy the final agreed-upon standards. On the other hand, if the office must be planned in an existing building, these standards must again be compromised to comply with existing space limitations. This problem is encountered mainly in private offices, the size of which is affected by the column spans and window modules.

Who Uses Private Offices?

While it was quite true two decades ago that the private office was pretty much solely the status symbol of the top executive only, such is not the case today.

According to a Dartnell survey, 278 companies replying, all executives and department heads have private offices in 41 percent of the companies. It is "top executives only" in only 35 percent, while 24 percent have offices for all executives, whether they be labeled "top," "middle," or something else. Among "other" executives having private offices in the surveyed concerns are personnel managers, research and production personnel, claims adjusters, supervisors, office managers, and so forth.

Most office departments are today enclosed—58 percent by partitions, 24 percent by some sort of railing arrangement, Thirty-four percent are not enclosed at all, with the executives sitting out in the open. In the general offices of the Atlantic Coast Line Railroad Company, Jacksonville, Florida, most departments are enclosed by partitions, but interiors of some of the larger departments are open. This is typical of quite a few of the larger offices reporting.

Acoustical Treatment

Respondents admit it is very difficult to measure the cost of noise in an office in dollars, but they agree that it is probably much greater than they realize. As a result, an increasing number of offices have been treated acoustically to lower noise. As a matter of interest, subscribers may find the results of a study made by Aetna Life Insurance Company worthy of consideration, since it bears on the noise problem. Before moving into new offices the company made a careful study of the effect of noise on productive output. After it had moved into its new quarters, the walls and ceilings of which were treated acoustically, the study was continued. Results were as follows:

—Noise level was reduced by 14.5 percent.
—Errors were cut 29 percent for typists, 52 percent for office machine operators.
—Employee efficiency increased 8.8 percent.
—Employee turnover decreased 47 percent.
—Absences decreased 37.5 percent.
—Personnel requirements were lowered nearly 10 percent.

Among the 278 offices included in the Dartnell survey, almost 60 percent are treated acoustically throughout the office, 24 percent in certain sections, and fewer than 20 percent not at all.

The most popular place to treat for noise seems to be ceilings—80 percent doing the job there only. Some 12 percent treat walls and ceilings acoustically. A few respondents mention carpeting as a factor in their acoustical treatment program. Still others mention the use of anti-noise enclosures for certain types of office machines that are inclined to be distracting when operating. There are now companies specializing in the manufacture of such specialized acoustical equipment.

Lighting the Office

Fluorescent lighting is by far the most common type of office lighting. The prime advantages of fluorescent lighting lie in its lower cost of operation, nearly shadowless lighting, less heat, and more attractive appearance.

One respondent, controller of a Detroit insurance company, suggests it is good business (helps to hold down cost, too) if a bulb or lamp replacement program is put into effect. This saves changing bulbs individually as they wear out because bulbs are changed on a mass production basis. This system is used at Chicago's huge Merchandise Mart and an official estimates it saves $4,500 a year. The mass change is scheduled at a time when 80 percent of the bulbs' expected life has expired.

Another tip—clean fixtures give better light, assure more accuracy in clerical work, reduce fatigue. A regular cleaning schedule for lights and fixtures is used by a number of the companies. It is considered part of their good housekeeping program.

Desks and Tables for Working Space

Desks are used for working space in 30 percent of the offices, but a combination of desks and tables are used in the majority of companies, 67 percent. Most common arrangement provides clerical workers with a desk and/or a table, depending upon the nature of the work. Many companies provide secretaries with a desk plus a work table placed in such a position as to allow ready access to either by merely turning around in her swivel chair.

Square Footage Per Person

We asked the 278 participating office executives to estimate the square footage allowed each person working in the office, including the desk and chair. Those who chose to make such estimates varied quite a bit. Following is a tabulation of replies by numbers of companies:

6 to 10 feet	12 companies
20 to 30 feet	38 companies
35 to 45 feet	50 companies
46 to 49 feet	6 companies
50 to 60 feet	22 companies
65 to 75 feet	12 companies
80 to 90 feet	16 companies

Other estimates range from 100 square feet to 500 square feet per employee. However, the methods of arriving at estimates vary, accounting for the extreme difference in figures. For example, some respondents figure the actual space needed for each clerical worker in his or her immediate area. Others take the size of the entire office area and divide it by the number of employees to arrive at the square footage per employee. One authority with whom Dartnell editors checked suggested the following formula for space assignments:

Supervisors	100 square feet
Interviewers	80 square feet
Clerks	65 square feet

These figures are, obviously, quite susceptible to variation according to type of business, but are considered to be a fair average for the usual general office.

Drawing Up the Plan

A little mechanical drawing experience is handy in making office layout drawings but it is definitely not necessary. The basic tools and supplies of the draftsman will make the work easier, however. Here is a practical selection for beginning a layout project:

1. Drawing board	5. Compass
2. T square	6. Shears
3. Ruler or scale	7. Thumbtacks or masking tape
4. Triangle	8. Supplies: pencils, pens, ink, eraser, etc.

Let's assume that you have made your rough drawing on graph paper. It is already in proper scale, so all you have to do is to make a clean tracing of it.

Square up the drawing on the board with the T square, then tack or tape it to the board. Place a sheet of tracing paper over the drawing and fasten it to the board. With pencil and T square, draw in all horizontal lines, starting at the top and moving to the bottom of the drawing. Draw in all the vertical lines with T square and triangle, starting at the left and moving to the right.

You can prepare the complete layout in this manner, including the placing of the equipment. If you plan to use the templates or scale explained later, however, you will merely draw the physical layout of the space, then use the templates or scale to place the equipment.

Using Layout Templates

Although the equipment may be drawn directly on the layout, templates are frequently used to show the position of the equipment. Their advantage is the ease with which changes can be made.

The templates are printed on paper or cardboard, showing the desk, chair, and other types of equipment in the same scale as the layout drawing. In some cases, the templates are die-cut to simplify their use. If not die-cut, the templates are cut from a sheet by scissors or sharp blade.

Templates are sometimes furnished by manufacturers with a coating of adhesive on the back. Like adhesive tape, they can be moved about repeatedly. Where coated templates are not available, the same convenience can be had through the application of a strip of double-coated adhesive tape to the back of the template. This can be done before or after cutting out the template.

Rubber cement is most frequently used to apply templates which are not already coated. It permits removing and resetting without harm to the template or layout, especially if cardboard templates are used.

If many changes are contemplated, or if several plans are desired, an acetate sheet can be laid over the space layout. The templates are attached to it rather than the layout. This protects the layout, makes changes easier, and allows several alternate plans to be made without redrawing the layout.

The chair and the desk are often shown on the same template, especially in the ¼-inch and larger scale drawings. The template may show the serial number of the equipment, the name of the occupant, and similar information. Symbols are added for lamps, electrical outlets, telephones, and buzzers to show where they will be needed.

To avoid unnecessary labor and time in the preparation of several layout possibilities, photostats may be made of one layout, then the templates rearranged for another plan and another photostat made.

Template Layout

It is during the conference with department heads concerning office layouts that the template layout is most helpful. The template layout consists of an outline plan of the proposed space, done on the scale of ⅛ or ¼ inch to one foot, mounted on a composition board to which can be fastened miniature reproductions of equipment and machinery prepared from information gained in the original survey.

The template provides a simple, speedy method for considering the various possibilities of equipment arrangement. When the proper location of equipment and machinery is decided on, the templates can be fastened in place. Various colored templates can be used, such as yellow for present equipment, green for new equipment, and blue for locations provided for future expansion. Partitions are indicated by strips of paper cut to scale, bearing the symbol of the type of partition it represents. The template layout has proved to be the best method of working out the problem for large open areas.

Design of Interiors

Every corporation has a distinct personality which can be expressed through the design and decoration of reception rooms, board room, private offices, and general office atmosphere.

Reception rooms are sometimes decorated with exhibits of company products and personalized to the extent that a company trademark or some sculptural symbolism is part of the decoration of the room.

WHEN TO REVIEW THE OFFICE LAYOUT

No organization should be constantly interrupted with changes just for the sake of change or to keep some specialist earning his salary. On the other hand, the present layout should be reviewed whenever some of these changes occur:

1. When there is an increase or decrease in personnel.
2. When flow of work is changed by new procedures.
3. When more working space is required.
4. When work piles up at one station while others wait.
5. When work is lost in transit.
6. When employees complain of lighting or ventilation.
7. When employees appear to have difficulty in passing about the office.
8. When overcrowding of personnel or record storage is apparent.
9. When buying or replacing equipment.
10. When there is a change in organization—new personnel, new authority, and responsibilities.
11. When alterations to the space are to be made.
12. When there are lease difficulties.
13. When functions have been added or taken away from the section.
14. When a balance of the sexes changes radically.
15. When certain persons have received promotions.

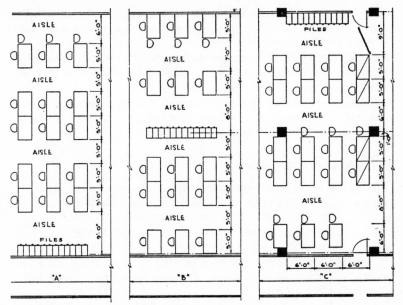

This office area has desks close together, for each individual has only 65 square feet

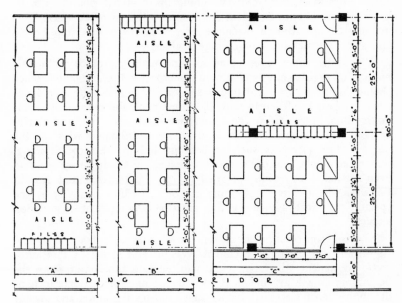

When each person has 80 square feet of space, there is more room around desks

Board rooms, like reception rooms, are sometimes decorated with related company motifs, such as trademarks or symbols, and maps or murals showing geographic location of plants or markets. The design of furniture and accessories is contemporary or traditional, suggesting the character and personality of the executives and the business.

Private offices sometimes go to extremes expressing an executive's personality, although the present trend for flexibility in layout limits these intimate details to pictures and colors.

Designing for Automation

More and more offices are considering the installation of the automatic units necessary to effect a vast timesaving with this new, swift, accurate way of handling integrated data processing.

Such installations, however, are not accomplished with the mere wave of the magic wand. The proper placement of this new office equipment with regard to efficiency, worker comfort, and many other important factors has become a new and important responsibility of today's office architect.

A typical office automation installation, although often involving 11 or more mechanical units weighing up to 40,644 pounds, can be housed, generally, in less than 8,000 square feet of office space. This includes a supervision and maintenance area, the power supply area, and sufficient metallic tape storage shelves.

With office space rates at an all-time high, the office architect's method of approaching space requirements for the automated office should be an arithmetical one based on the number of employees needed to work efficiently with the equipment, the number of automatic units, individual weights, electrical loads required, and refrigeration elements needed. These must be coordinated with all the normal office elements such as heating, lighting, air conditioning, underfloor ducts, and other factors. Space can easily be wasted and even spoiled if a carefully planned approach is not executed. And in this area, the architect's planning can be aided immeasurably by the specific technical advice of the automatic equipment installation experts.

Flooring construction alone will now necessarily take on a new significance to the office architect. Weight and stress of this automatic equipment will have to be worked into the layout from the beginning, as will arrangement and size of underfloor ducts to handle the maze of electrical wiring that pulsates the automatic master brain and its many electrically controlled appendages.

Modern office automation has to be figured from the standpoint of acoustics, room temperature, lighting, and the new setup in utilities necessary to operate these mechanical office brains. Some of the current equipment is water cooled via a refrigeration system. Obviously, the architect in laying out such an office will have to consider the installation of refrigeration equipment and what effect it will have on room temperatures all year around.

This consideration leads him directly to air-conditioning specifications based on the size of the equipment and its effect on normal office temperatures. Heat, light, and power loads necessary to operate automation equipment are within the planning province of the office architect.

It is not exactly like being catapulted into a never-never land, because a number of installations of these systems have already been made. Planning and layout architectural experience has thus been gained as a result of automating offices like those of one of our major electric companies which is now using office automation for payroll, accounting, material control, production line balancing, and budget and sales analysis.

One insurance company says it is highly unlikely that the insurance field in general will be able to keep up with the continued demand for services without introducing electronic data-processing equipment to handle the heavy amount of paper work which future expansion will bring.

The very nature of the business of transportation organizations involves a great amount of detail. For example, a large railroad network now has electronic office equipment processing a billion pieces of paper work per year in record time.

A normal operating cost of $200,000 for paper-work preparation has been shaved down to $15,000 for a branch of the military with the use of automation. Certain offices of a national insurance company, burdened with detail, became streamlined in data delivery after studies proved that automating the offices was economically sound.

A steel corporation has proved that the accurate calculation of this machinery now makes data processing possible in areas which were never before susceptible to such applications. And a government office, with a stock inventory of almost a million and a half spare parts, reported that a system of office automation performed 40 to 50 times faster than a punched-card machine method.

Let's take a closer look at just one appendage of a typical automation setup. A high-speed printer alone coordinates its part of the job with four units: Printing, tape, power supply, and memory.

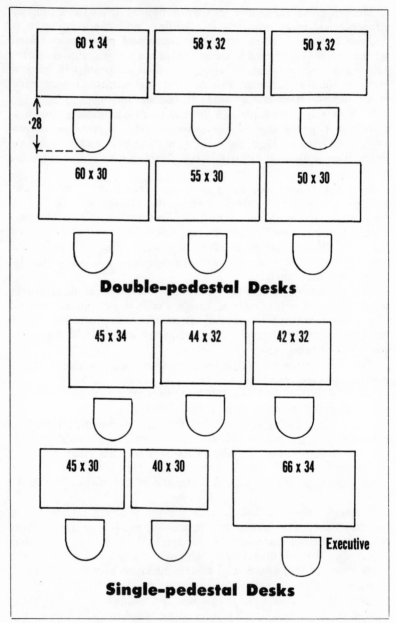

Double-pedestal Desks

Single-pedestal Desks

Scaled at approximately one-fourth inch to the foot, templates made from

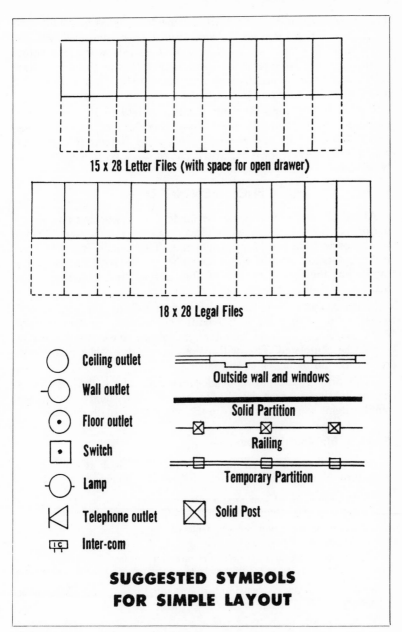

15 x 28 Letter Files (with space for open drawer)

18 x 28 Legal Files

◯ Ceiling outlet

◯ Wall outlet

◉ Floor outlet

▢ Switch

◯ Lamp

◁ Telephone outlet

Inter-com

Outside wall and windows

Solid Partition

Railing

Temporary Partition

⊠ Solid Post

SUGGESTED SYMBOLS
FOR SIMPLE LAYOUT

these drawings can be used to simplify the problem of making office layouts

These units are incorporated within the housing of one unit, and consequently there is a great space saving when compared with the usual number of people needed to perform this work. But, quite naturally, other considerations come into the space picture as a result of automation installations that have to be dealt with by the architect in the interests of best layout.

Layout for the automated office can only be based on functional, modular space planning. New floor construction considerations, added refrigeration, and electrical wiring for functional equipment can only be allowed for if the arithmetic of office space is methodically followed.

OFFICE MOVING DAY

Although smaller moves can be made during working hours, any major upheaval is more economically carried out between Friday after closing time and Monday morning. This usually involves overtime payments for some employees who are needed to assist in the move, but the lower amount of lost clerical time will more than make up the difference.

When a space becomes available, as much of the construction work as possible, including partitions, railings, fixtures, wiring, floor coverings, cabinets, counters, telephone lines, and decorating should be completed. This will make moving day easier and greatly reduce the adjusting time and labor.

With proper planning and adequate floor plans, the installation of the lighting fixtures, telephones, annunciators, buzzers, fans, and similar items can be made before the desks are actually in place.

Steps in Making the Move

Before you move to new quarters take a good look at your present furniture. You have to make one of three decisions:

1. You can move all your present furniture to the new office. Then you will have the same degree of efficiency or inefficiency and obsolescence.

2. You can repair and refinish damaged pieces, replacing those that are beyond economical repair.

3. You can trade in all the old furniture and buy new. The new furniture can be delivered to the new address, saving moving trouble and expense.

You must make a decision on one of these three alternatives. Choose the one that will be the most profitable.

Here are nine steps to be followed in planning an office move:

1. Appoint the moving committee.

2. Develop a set of instructions. Instructions will carefully outline the moving timetable; tagging and marking plan; how various types of articles will be handled. Make definite assignments to committee and record date started and date completed.

3. Prepare a scale plan for each department. Make sufficient copies for committee members at both old and new site for help in checking in and out. Show direction desks are facing.

4. Assign code numbers to major equipment on new layout plan. This will include desks, tables, cabinets, etc. All equipment used by the same person can be given the same code number.

5. Tag or mark major equipment with proper code number. This will facilitate placement in the proper location on the new site.

6. Box all loose supplies and records and code. Use same code as desk on which the box will be placed at the new location.

7. Make arrangements for all required maintenance and installation crews. In addition to the movers, elevator operators, carpenters, plumbers, electricians, janitors, telephone installers, and similar help will be needed.

8. Assign checkers and information personnel at both new and old locations. They should be thoroughly briefed on the plans and should be supplied with copies of the new layout with code numbers of locations.

9. Check the new quarters carefully just before the move. Some important details may have been overlooked or not performed.

Here are some ideas contributed by those who have had experience in moving their offices. By following their advice, you may save yourself both time and trouble.

1. Have employees remove personal property from desks before moving day.

2. Take special precautions with ink and similar liquids. Better throw them out than ruin records and supplies.

3. Do not fill boxes higher than rims. Then they can be stacked safely.

4. Take special precautions with business papers and records. Their loss could be quite expensive. Better put them in separate boxes or containers, coded for their return to the proper persons, and placed under the responsibility of one employee or committee.

5. Assign colors to the various sections on the master layout plan. Use the same colors for marking or tagging the equipment going to those sections.

6. Move stock, transfer files, and heavier equipment before or after the regular furniture to avoid confusion and cluttering in the passages.

7. Typists will frequently object to giving up a typewriter they are familiar with. It doesn't take much extra effort to tag the machines so they go back to the same users.

8. Use printed tags, gummed labels, or china-marking pencils for coding equipment and boxes. Be sure that markings will not come off during the move.

9. Mark off the floor area with chalk in the new location to show where the equipment will go. Use the coding system. Arrows to show direction equipment faces will help the movers. Carpenter's chalk lines will aid in lining up desks and aisles quickly.

10. Heavy equipment, like safes, will require special movers in most cases.

11. Save moving expense by trading in old furniture and having the new furniture delivered to the new location.

12. Use the publicity value of your move. Give the story to local newspapers, business papers, trade papers, community papers. It's good public relations!

Here is a checklist based on principles of good office layout. Use it to check your present layout.

PEOPLE

.... Are employees in front of, or at least around, their supervisors?

.... Are employees using the same machine grouped together?

.... Are employees adjacent to the files or references they use most frequently?

.... Are occupants of private offices placed so they can see the door?

.... Does the general office force have access to outside windows?

.... Does every employee have direct access to an aisle wherever possible?

.... Do those employees who carry on frequent interviews have additional space allowance for the visitors?

.... Are there adequate and convenient rest room facilities?

.... Is there a lounging area for employees during rest periods and lunch?

.... Is the air conditioned for proper temperature, humidity, and circulation?

.... Do employees have enough light, and is it glare-free?

.... Are the colors and decorations conducive to comfortable working?

.... Is the office free from distracting noises?

.... Does the reception room give a favorable impression to visitors?

EQUIPMENT

.... Is all the equipment efficient and attractive, or should some be replaced or renewed?

.... Is the equipment adequate for each worker? Would another type of desk be more efficient for certain employees?

.... Could smaller, space-saving desks be used for some operations?

.... Could a modern, executive conference desk substitute for a desk and table in the private office?

.... Do typists have a left-pedestal typing platform wherever possible?

.... Do all workers have chairs that are fully adjustable for correct posture?

.... Are desks facing the same direction wherever possible?

.... Is there enough space between desks to prevent crowding and disruption?

.... Have you considered five-drawer file cabinets to conserve floor space?

.... Are the two-drawer file cabinets by desks really necessary? Can file drawers be substituted in the desk instead to conserve floor space? Could a four-drawer file be substituted for two 2-drawer files?

.... Are counters equipped with file drawers, cabinets, and shelves?

.... Are there enough telephones for those who use them frequently?

.... Is heavy equipment against walls or columns?

.... Has surplus equipment been returned to stock?

.... Are electrical outlets adequate for the mechanized equipment?

PAPER WORK

.... Does the majority of work flow with a minimum of backtracking?

.... Is transportation distance at a minimum?

.... Are related units near each other?

.... Are smaller units between larger ones where the work flow permits?

.... Are individuals receiving frequent visitors located near the main entrance?

.... Are the service sections near the departments that use them most?

.... Are there efficient sorting trays and fixtures to speed up the transfer of working papers between operations?

.... Is the work brought or passed to the worker whenever possible?

.... Are valuable business records protected adequately from fire and theft?

SPACE

.... Is space adequate for efficient production, comfort and appearance? Could it be reduced without sacrificing these elements?

.... Have you utilized a single large area instead of several small parcels whenever possible?

.... Does the space have a minimum of offsets and angles?

.... Are private offices kept to a minimum?

.... Could railings and conference or committee rooms be substituted for private offices?

.... Could modular or unitized furniture be used to substitute for partitioned offices and to save space?

.... Are private offices placed so that they allow a maximum of light and ventilation for adjoining outer offices?

.... Are the partitions movable whenever possible?

.... Have you used file cabinets to separate units where practical?

.... Does space allow for peak loads rather than minimum requirements?

.... Have you left some space unassigned for later expansion or adjustment?

.... Are there enough rest rooms, drinking fountains, to minimize unnecessary walking?

.... Are aisles wide enough for the traffic?

..........Are the aisles wide enough for vault trucks and other carriers?

.... Are there two exits to rooms housing a group of employees?

.... Are the coat lockers near the exit for least disturbance?

.... Have you considered location of utility outlets, swing of doors, space for opening drawers?

.... Have clear openings been substituted for doors whenever practical?

.... Are doors placed so they leave long lengths of wall space?

AIR CONDITIONING

In most areas where competition for good employees is intense, air-conditioned offices are considered a necessity rather than a luxury.

There have been many reports on the value of air conditioning in improving employee morale, eliminating fatigue, and so forth. At Interstate Securities Company, Kansas City, Missouri, employee efficiency increased 20 percent as a result of air conditioning, according to a company spokesman. Similar improvements are reported by other companies.

Air conditioning also is reported to assure a company of more working hours, since there will be no short working days because the temperature has soared.

Some users report that office machines run more smoothly and require less maintenance and repair when they operate in air-conditioned offices. Keys and parts do not stick because of dampness, and carbons smudge less.

All in all, the case for air conditioning is a strong one and the fact that a great majority of offices now use it is ample evidence of its worth. It has been estimated today's figure of average of 90 percent compares with 45 percent of offices being air conditioned in 1948 in areas where this is suitable.

LIGHTING IN THE OFFICE

Lighting is one of the most important parts of the physical environment in the office. It not only serves the seeing function for a specific work task, but also provides the means for making the office a pleasant place to work. Both of these elements are critical in the operation of the office—the task must be seen quickly and accurately for optimum productivity and the surroundings must be stimulating and interesting without being glaring and distracting.

Lighting the Seeing Task

Few people realize the scope of laboratory research that has been conducted in the field of seeing over the past few decades. These investigators have discovered a great deal about how we react to light and what our needs are for everyday seeing. It has been known for some time that we see faster, more accurately, with greater clarity, and with less energy when there is more light on the task. The problem has been in determining just how much light is needed for a task at a given level of seeing performance.

Recent work has produced some answers. It was found, for example, that for a given reading speed, 76.5 footcandles were required for a sample of shorthand; 133 footcandles for a typed fifth carbon copy; 589 footcandles for a poor reproduction from a copying machine. This data has been used by the Illuminating Engineering

An average illumination of 150 footcandles is achieved in the large general offices of the Airport Parking Company of America. The central office bay is lighted by large louvered elements in the second-floor ceiling and by 4-foot-squares of prismatic fixtures in the low ceiling under the mezzanine balcony.

The footcandle reading in the general office of the Sacramento Municipal Utility District is 150. It comes from Columbia four-lamp panels spaced 18 inches apart in the ceiling. The area is 60 by 150 feet under a 10-foot ceiling.

Society to develop recommendations for the minimum footcandles to be used in various areas. These are shown below for office areas. They are based on research, but are modified by economics—the cost of lighting compared with the benefits to be derived from the lighting.

OFFICES	FOOTCANDLES
Cartography, designing, detailed drafting	200
Accounting, auditing, tabulating, bookkeeping, business-machine operation, reading poor reproductions, rough-layout drafting	150
Regular office work, reading good reproductions, reading or transcribing handwriting in hard pencil or on poor paper, active filing, index reference, mail sorting	100
Reading or transcribing handwriting in ink or medium pencil on good-quality paper, intermittent filing	70
Reading high-contrast or well-printed material, tasks and areas not involving critical or prolonged seeing such as conferring, interviewing, inactive files, washrooms	30
Corridors, elevators, escalators, stairways	20

Because the research has only been done for one speed of reading and only with the normal eyes of young observers, these values are rather conservative. Also, as lighting costs decrease due to more efficient light sources, and as salaries and wages increase, the economic picture indicates the need for having more than just a minimum amount of light.

Lighting for Comfort and Atmosphere

While footcandles on the task are important, the means of supplying them are just as important. In fact, if light fixtures are glaring or if room finishes are too dark, more footcandles will only accentuate visual discomfort.

The IES, again backed up by research, can guide us in this area of lighting quality as well as the lighting quantity discussed above. Their recommendations for light reflectances of room surfaces are shown below:

RECOMMENDED SURFACE REFLECTANCES FOR OFFICES

Surface	Reflectance
Ceiling finishes	80-92%
Walls	40-60%
Furniture	26-44%
Office machines and equipment	26-44%
Floors	21-39%

These values are derived from laboratory research that has determined which brightness conditions are comfortable and which are not. In addition, practical experience in offices has shown eyestrain can be reduced when dark desk tops are lighted, or when glaring light fixtures are replaced with low-brightness lighting systems, or when some other condition of unbalanced brightness is corrected.

The restrictions on room-surface reflectances are not necessarily restrictions on providing interesting decor. Very dark rich colors that violate these restrictions can be used on small areas that will occupy less than 10 percent of the view, or for an entire wall if it will not be in anyone's continuous view.

How Much Does Office Lighting Cost?

The cost of lighting for the office involves principally the fixtures and their installation and the cost of electricity to operate them. It also includes items such as the cost of fluorescent tubes, the labor cost to replace them, and the cost of cleaning the fixtures periodically. A total cost of lighting would have to include all these things and can be stated as generally amounting to approximately 50 cents per square foot per year for 100 footcandles of good-quality lighting. It can be more or less than this depending on the electricity rates, labor rates, and other local conditions. For levels of lighting other than 100 footcandles the cost would change proportionally except for extremely low or extremely high levels.

It is interesting to compare the cost of lighting with the other costs of an office. On a square foot per year basis, salaries and wages might range from $40 to $50; office furniture and equipment, about $2.50; office supplies and communication services, about $4, and rental for the space anywhere from $2 to $10. The total cost for an office operation, then, might range between $50 and $65. If the amount spent for lighting were increased from 25 to 75 cents, and if this would increase productivity by only a small percent, or slightly reduce employee turnover, or attract a better class of employees, then it can be seen that the amount spent on the total office will probably be enhanced by an amount far exceeding the cost of the lighting.

Gains in office productivity are very difficult to measure. However, two surveys made by the U.S. Government under well-controlled

Lighting for the general office of the Central National Bank of Chicago comes from 5- by 8-foot recessed units using F40/WW lamps. The footcandle reading is 135 throughout the office, 60 by 60 feet in area. The ceiling height is 10 feet.

conditions showed increases in production of 3.5 percent in one case and 5.5 percent in the other. In industry, where productivity is much easier to measure, it is not uncommon to find increases on the order of 10 to 20 percent resulting from better lighting. This would indicate that improvements of this magnitude are possible in the office.

Whenever there is any question about whether or not a lighting system is effective, an electrical consulting engineer can be hired to make a survey and then make suggestions for improvements if any deficiencies are found. Free advice can probably be obtained from the local electric utility. They will take footcandle readings and might even draw up plans for suggested relighting.

Seven Ways to Get the Most Out of Your Lighting

1. *Use Fluorescent Lighting*—As most modern offices attest, fluorescent lighting has become the main source of office light in recent years. This is because the fluorescent tube produces three to four times as much light as the incandescent bulb for the same power consumption.

2. *Check Those Light Bulbs*—The life of an incandescent bulb is rated at 750, 1000, or 2000 hours, depending on its type. Most fluorescent tubes have a rated life of 12,000 hours; others are at 9000 hours. Both incandescent bulbs and fluorescent tubes decrease in light output as they burn, so it is wise to have the illumination measured to see if it has fallen below its proper value, which would indicate that the bulbs or tubes should be replaced even though they have not burned out. Set up a schedule for changing, and investigate the labor costs involved—it is usually cheaper to replace all the tubes or bulbs at once than one at a time as they burn out.

3. *Keep Fixtures and Bulbs Clean*—Dirt and grime can cut down on the illumination by as much as 25 percent. This is particularly true if indirect fixtures are used. In many instances, fixtures are only cleaned at the same time office cleaning or decorating is done. In such instances, waste occurs due to dirty bulbs and fixtures which have in the meantime accumulated the grime. Set up a cleaning schedule that takes into account the dirt conditions in the office. Cleaning twice a year may be required where windows are opened; only once every year or so where there is a filtered air system.

4. *Use Light-Colored Walls and Ceiling*—Dull room finishes aid in reflecting light without causing glare. Pastel shades are best to use, since the proper wall color has an importance beyond the effect it may have on illumination and electrical current consumption. It also affects the employee psychologically. An eye-appealing decor, in proper color contrast, provides an emotional lift not provided by a drab and shabby working atmosphere. See table of reflectances listed earlier.

5. *Use Proper Wattage and Voltage*—It is important that bulbs are of proper wattage for the system. An incandescent bulb burned at a higher-than-rated voltage will give off increased light, but the natural life of the bulb is materially reduced. If the bulb is burned at less than the

rated voltage, current consumption is reduced out of proportion to the savings rendered. Fluorescent light output and life are not as sensitive to improper voltage as incandescent, but low voltage may not permit the tube to start; high voltage may overheat the ballast and cause it to fail.

6. *Discourage Auxiliary Lighting*—Auxiliary lighting on desks and drafting boards can be wasteful and a nuisance. General overhead lighting will usually be more economical and more comfortable to work under. If, of course, proper illumination is not provided from a general lighting system, auxiliary sources of illumination must be utilized. Do not use very bright localized lighting with low levels of general lighting, however. Eye fatigue is the usual result. It is possible to waste significant electric current in an effort to produce sufficient illumination by auxiliary lighting.

7. *Turn the Lights Out*—In days gone by it was common practice to lay the responsibility for turning out the lights on one particular employee. Today, however, that practice no longer exists. It is estimated that current consumption can be reduced from 5 to 15 percent by an educational program to turn off unnecessary lights. Most frequent violators, studies show, are persons in private offices. Get the word around—electrical current costs money.

OFFICE DECORATION

Color in Offices

The experiences of many companies are proof of the efficient psychological influence of colors in offices and factories. No more gray uniformlike monotony, but colorful surroundings even in small shops and offices. There is no reason to go to the extreme. Unusually colorful surroundings may be pleasant to the eye, but it is a wise technique to let them be passive in order to avoid competition with the job.

The idea that colors on the red side of the spectrum are warm and stimulating, while the opposite blue-green colors are relaxing and cool, is accepted as basic knowledge by color experts. If a room seems particularly cold in the winter, it can be made to feel warmer by the use of "warm" colors in the paint scheme. Colors based on yellow—ivory, cream, orange-yellow, buff, and creamy yellow—are the warm colors commonly used in homes. Application of such warm colors to the walls will make that formerly cold room much more comfortable for future use.

When the interior of a New York bank was changed from a faded yellow to light blue-green walls and white columns, officers and employees of the bank agreed that the interior seemed larger and definitely felt cooler in summer. And, so says the report, "women tellers were prettier against the new background."

"Color sells production," is a new slogan in business and industry. *Fortune* magazine has compiled a number of opinions of business and industrial users of color. Eaton Manufacturing Co. felt that a "20 percent reduction in absenteeism is directly traceable to the new color plan." Continental Can Co. reports that a new color scheme has reduced eyestrain and physical fatigue.

Art in the Office

Michael H. Levy, former chairman of the board of The Federated Brokerage Group, lists several reasons why good art can and should be extensively used in office decoration. As he puts it:

"First, is improvement in office appearance. But, it's more than that. Fine art in an office creates an atmosphere which goes beyond the mere sleekness of modern furniture and other decorative paraphernalia. It suggests a company's depth and personality as well as improving its external appearance.

"Second, is the development and improvement of artistic tastes which the businessman finds increasingly useful in everything from office design to advertising layout.

"Third, good art in an office affects the people who work and visit there. Employees derive greater job satisfaction and pleasure. Moreover, this new interest is conveyed to visitors who are stimulated to remember and speak of a company long after their visit. We learned this from a questionnaire which we distributed to all callers. Among the questions was, 'Did you find our art interesting? Dull? Jarring?' We got nine "interesting" replies for every "jarring," and no "dulls" at all.

"Fourth, we've found that our paintings and sculpture are constant conversation pieces. Of course, every piece of art does not necessarily receive universally favorable comment. But, whether our art pieces are criticized or admired, there's no doubt that they help 'break the ice' and create an informally stimulating atmosphere for our guests.

"Finally, the businessman could do well to approach art in a relaxed, easy, and understanding way. This approach could not only contribute to his own satisfaction and development, but also extend these advantages to the millions of office workers who don't have the opportunity or the inclination to visit art galleries. It can be the businessman's privilege to close this gap between the gallery and the office.

"But, how does a company start its 'art program'? Perhaps the answers to some of the questions which were asked of me can tell you that:

"1. *Isn't office art expensive?* Not necessarily—particularly if you consider the cost of an ordinary lamp or rug. A variety of good subject matter is available in most cities at prices as low as $25. A broader selection of fine originals can be found in the $100-$150 range. And from a tax standpoint, of course, the expenditure *can be amortized over a 10-year depreciation period* just like any other furnishing.

"2. *Can paintings be rented?* Yes. Many galleries rent wide selections of art and charge about 10 percent of valuation for a three-month period, with a reduced sliding scale thereafter. Incidentally, this fee can usually be applied toward the purchase price.

Mr. Levy's executive offices are designed for comfort and efficiency. The abstract paintings and sculpture stimulate the imagination and add interest.

STANDARDS FOR CLEANING OFFICE BUILDINGS

The standards appearing below, and on the pages following, were established by the General Services Administration as a guide to determining staffing and equipment requirements in office buildings operated by GSA. They are based on the experience of the Public Buildings Service in Washington, D. C., and other cities. To apply the standards to a particular building, the entire work load is figured (square feet of floors, number of windows, etc.) and the number of man-days is then divided into day and night forces.

Job Description	Performance	Equipment	Qualifying Factors	Production Per Man-Day	Normal Frequency in Work Days
FLOOR SCRUBBING WITH POLISHING MACHINE	Place cleaning agent on floor and agitate with machine. Pick up dirty solution and rinse. (Floor swept by zone cleaner.)	1. Floor scrubbing machine 2. 2-compartment mop tank and wringer 3. Dust pan and brush 4. Three mops 5. Rags and steel wool 6. Cleaning agent 7. Hair sweep 8. Electric water pick-up in lieu of mop (optional)	15″ divided wt. (rotary) polishing machine 15″ concentrated wt. (rotary) polishing machine	20,000 sq. ft. 20,000 sq. ft.	Main floor corridors daily Secondary floor corridors every 5 days Other space as required
FLOOR SCRUBBING WITH POWER SCRUBBING MACHINE	Machine applies cleaning agent to floor, agitates it with revolving brushes and picks up dirty solution with vacuum device, rinsing optional. (Floor swept by zone cleaner.)	1. Power scrubbing machine 2. 2-compartment mop tank and wringer 3. Dust pan and brush 4. Two mops 5. Rags and steel wool 6. Cleaning agent 7. Hair sweep 8. Hand squeegee 9. Gum scraper 10. Garden hose (5′ length) 11. Measuring cup	Machine covers strip 26″ wide	25,000 sq. ft.	Main floor corridors daily Secondary floor corridors every 5 days
FLOOR MOPPING	Sweep and then place cleaning solution on floor and work with mop. Pick up dirty solution and rinse as required with mop.	1. 2-compartment mop tank and wringer 2. Two mops 3. Cleaning agent 4. Gum scraper 5. Hair sweep		20,000 sq. ft.	Main floor corridors daily Secondary floor corridors every 5 days
FLOOR WAXING	Mop or scrub, apply new wax, polish. (Floor swept by zone cleaner.)	1. Dust pan and brush 2. Floor polishing machine 3. 2-compartment mop tank and wringer 4. Three mops 5. Cleaning agent 6. Gum scraper 7. Rags and steel wool 8. Mopping unit for wax 9. Wax, spirit or water emulsion	15″ divided wt. (rotary) polishing machine 15″ concentrated wt. (rotary) polishing machine 16″ cylindrical drum polishing machine	5,000 sq. ft. open area 3,000 sq. ft. office area 8,000 sq. ft. open area 3,500 sq. ft. office area 5,000 sq. ft. open area	Every 66 days

Job Description	Performance	Equipment	Qualifying Factors	Production Per Man-Day	Normal Frequency in Work Days
FLOOR BUFFING	Polish the floor to remove traffic marks without applying additional wax. (Floor swept by zone cleaner.)	1. Polishing machine 2. Steel wool (hand pad)	15″ divided wt. (rotary) polishing machine	40,000 sq. ft. open area 30,000 sq. ft. office area	Every 22 days
			15″ concentrated wt. (rotary) polishing machine	40,000 sq. ft. open area 30,000 sq. ft. office area	
			16″ cylindrical drum polishing machine	40,000 sq. ft. open area 30,000 sq. ft. office area	
FLOOR SWEEPING	Pick up loose paper and trash, sweep, clean telephone booths and dust surfaces that can be reached while standing on the floor. (Usually assigned to zone cleaner.)	1. 24″ hair sweep 2. Dust pan	Open space	50,000 sq. ft.	Daily
RUG VACUUMING	Vacuum rugs with domestic, portable, or central vacuum machines.	Vacuum machine or vacuum hose and tools for central system	Closely grouped rugs	80 (12′x15′)	Daily
STAIR CLEANING	Sweep, dust, and scrub.	1. Broom 2. Bucket 3. Scrub and deck brushes 4. Rags 5. Cleaning agent 6. Gum scraper	Sweep and dust Scrub	60 flights (floor to floor) 20 flights (floor to floor)	Daily Every 5 days
HIGH CLEANING	Clean lights, transoms, pipes, high files, and dust venetian blinds and other objects high enough to require the ladder and too high for zone cleaner to reach while standing on the floor.	1. Ladder 2. Buckets 3. Cloths 4. Radiator brush 5. Vacuum cleaner 6. Cleaning agent 7. Wall brush 8. Push broom 9. Dust pan		10,000 gross sq. ft. floor area	Every 66 days
TOILETS, CLEANING AND SERVICING	Empty waste containers, fill soap dispensers, towel and toilet paper holders. Clean fixtures, sweep floors and mop or scrub as required.	1. Mopping unit 2. 12 qt. bucket 3. Mop 4. Radiator brush 5. Hair sweep 6. Toilet brush 7. Scrub brush 8. Gum scraper 9. Rubber gloves 10. Cleaning agent 11. Cloths 12. Polish 13. Toilet supplies		80 fixtures (Wash basins, water closets, urinals)	Clean daily Service as required

Job Description	Performance	Equipment	Qualifying Factors		Production Per Man-Day	Normal Frequency in Work Days
LOBBY AND CORRIDOR POLICING (Includes adjacent stairs)	Sweep up scraps of paper and cigarette butts. Mop wet spots, keep jardinieres presentable.	1. Long-handled dust pan 2. Long-handled dust brush 3. Cloths	Main corridor		300,000 sq. ft. of corridor area	4 times daily
			Secondary corridor		300,000 sq. ft. of corridor area	Daily
LOBBY CLEANING	Sweep, mop, dust, polish metal, and clean glass.	1. Hair sweep 2. Mops 3. Gum scraper 4. Cloths 5. Metal polish 6. Chamois	Main (Large)		16	Daily
			Secondary		32	Daily
ENTRANCE CLEANING (Outside)	Sweep, police, clean glass and push plates. (Snow and sleet are removed by special work crews detailed from regular cleaning force.)	1. Broom 2. Hose 3. Cloths 4. Metal polish 5. Dust pan 6. Chewing gum scraper	Main		16	Twice daily
			Secondary		32	Daily
PAPER AND TRASH COLLECTION	Paper is bagged or boxed by zone cleaners and placed in corridors for the trash man to collect and take to trash room.	1. Twine for bags 2. 4-wheel push truck for bagged paper 3. 4-wheel box push truck for collecting loose paper			600,000 sq. ft. gross area	Daily
WINDOW WASHING	Windows washed inside and outside.	1. Safety belt (when needed) 2. Counter brush 3. Sponge or cloth 4. Chamois 5. Scraper 6. Sill pad 7. Cleaning agent 8. Bucket 9. Squeegee 10. Stepladder	Double hung 2-pane 4'x7' Double hung 4-pane 4'x6' Double hung 8-pane 3.5'x5.5' Double hung 12-pane 2.5'x5.7' Double hung 16-pane 4'x6' Industrial 20-pane 4'x7' Austral Casement 6-pane 6'x7'	60 55 45 40 35 30 35 35		Every 22 days
ELEVATOR CLEANING	Scrub, wax, and buff floors, dust interior of car, polish brass.	1. Hand truck 2. Two mops 3. Radiator brush 4. 14" hair sweep 5. Dust pan and brush 6. Dust and scrub cloths 7. Cleaning agent 8. Mopping unit 9. Short stepladder 10. Steel wool 11. Wax 12. Metal polish 13. Polishing machine (small)	Passenger elevator		25	Daily
			Freight elevator		25	Every 5 days

Job Description	Performance	Equipment	Qualifying Factors	Production Per Man-Day	Normal Frequency in Work Days
ESCALATOR CLEANING	Sweep treads and risers, remove gum, wipe tread and risers and polish metal fittings.	1. Bucket 2. Radiator brush 3. Dust pan 4. Wood gum scraper 5. Rags 6. Metal polish 7. Wedge		20 flights (floor to floor)	Daily
VENETIAN BLIND WASHING (In Place)	Venetian blind slats are washed in place. Tapes and cords are dry cleaned with stiff brush. Dusting is done by high cleaners and not considered part of the job.	1. Stepladder 2. Bucket 3. Cloths 4. Radiator brush 5. Cleaning detergent 6. Dust pan	4' wide 8' wide	16 8	Every 252 days Every 252 days
LAWN MAINTENANCE	Mow lawns and sweep adjacent sidewalks.	1. Mower 2. Clippers 3. Broom 4. Gum scraper 5. Rake 6. Edger 7. Baskets	Grass cutting (in season) Sidewalk sweeping	100,000 sq. ft. of grass area 100,000 sq. ft. of sidewalk	Every 5 days Daily
GARAGE AND DRIVEWAY CLEANING	Police, sweep, and mop or scrub.	1. Broom 2. Hose 3. Mops 4. Deck brush 5. Scrubbing machine 6. Mop tank 7. Scraper		50,000 net sq. ft.	Police daily, sweep every 5 days, scrub every 22 days
JARDINIERE CLEANING	1. Shine funnel, clean exterior, rinse container and refill (liquid type). 2. Remove soiled sand, clean opening and exterior, replace soiled sand with fresh sand (sand type).	1. 52-gal. tank (1 side screened) 2. Bucket 3. Cuspidor brush 4. Cup (Sieve if sand is used) 5. Rubber gloves 6. Rags 7. Sand, if used 8. Disinfectant		100	Daily
UTILITY WORK	General duties, truck helper, move light pieces of furniture, etc.			1,000,000 gross sq. ft.	Daily
EXTERMINATION (Insect and Rodent Control)	Paint and/or spray infected areas with insecticides—Bait for rodents.	1. Spray machine 2. Rubber gloves 3. Insecticides 4. Baits 5. Paint brush		16,000 gross sq. ft.	Every 66 days
ZONE CLEANING	Sweep corridors, empty ash trays, empty waste baskets, sweep or vacuum offices, mop floors, and dust all rooms and corridor space within reach while standing on the floor, clean wash basins and private toilets. Clean phone booths and drinking fountains in assigned zone.	1. Mops (treatment optional) 2. Cloths 3. Dust pan and brush 4. Radiator brush 5. Cleaning agent 6. Toilet brush 7. Hair sweep 8. Corn broom 9. Vacuum machine 10. Container for cigarette butts and ashes	File space Storage space Office space	Up to 50,000 net sq. ft. floor space Up to 100,000 net sq. ft. floor space 14,000 net sq. ft. (Plus adjoining corridor)	Daily Depends on type of storage Daily

"3. *What should my first step be in securing art for my offices?*
See a reputable art dealer—preferably one who has serviced other
business firms. You can probably find one by contacting your local
art association or your university art department.

"4. *What type of art should I look for?* Art which reflects the
personality of your particular business. For instance, a modern
mobile might seem a bit out of place in certain conservative New
England law firms founded in the days of the Boston Tea Party.
On the other hand, a classical portrait by one of the Renaissance
masters might appear a bit stuffy for a young, quick-moving advertising agency. That's why our art is both abstract and realistic—
to mirror both our youth and also our belief in the methodical, business way of thinking required in the insurance field.

"5. *Will art increase my gross volume?* Probably not. True, art
in the office can tone down a hectic business day and create a pleasant
atmosphere for employees and clients, but I don't believe it can be
evaluated in terms of money. The enjoyment and warmth which
good art can provide the businessman, however, seems to me sufficient recompense for the relatively slight effort and expense.

"6. *Do you predict a greater future for office art?* Yes. Burton
Cumming, director of the American Federation of Arts, sums it up
this way: 'To their eternal credit and profit, American businessmen,
in greatly increasing numbers since the war, are beginning to discover the value of putting art to work within their organizations.' "

Chapter 47

COMMUNICATIONS SYSTEMS
IN THE OFFICE

IN THE small business office, two partners can communicate with each other across a double desk, or, by raising their voices, talk across the hall from their private offices. If they want to tell a client of a decision, one of them can write a letter.

Office communications become increasingly complex, however, as a business grows beyond the one-man or the partnership stage. Large corporation offices are complex beehives of electronic communications systems, and even relatively small business organizations are making increased use of elaborate telephone systems, teletypewriters, pneumatic tubes, closed-circuit television, and similar devices.

Intelligent Use of the Telephone

With the cost of an average business letter nearly $2.50, it is often less expensive and more convenient to answer a letter or make a request by telephone—unless a written record is necessary. Many nearby cities can be reached by telephone for less than it costs to dictate, have typed, and mail a long letter. And telephone calls are answered immediately, while a letter is subject to unforeseeable delays.

Besides speed, telephoning has the advantage of more personal contact than a letter, if each call is handled properly. Ruth M. Roemer, receptionist at Republic Steel Corporation for many years, has made a study of how the telephone can boost sales. Here are some of her pointers on the type of equipment and the setup needed:

1. Enough trunk lines so that callers are not discouraged with a constant busy signal.
2. Accounts properly distributed among the clerks as to telephone call load so that reaching an extension is not delayed.
3. A paging system that will facilitate completing calls if the office is large and people may be away from their desks.

4. Teletype machines or long lines to plants or warehouses that service orders, especially in highly competitive lines.

5. A switchboard operator who is free from other duties to give prompt and friendly service.

Since the operator speaks to everyone who calls an office, she needs the ability to handle people and help them intelligently. To insure good telephone service, large city telephone companies conduct PBX schools to train and place operators and maintain lists of substitute operators who will work when a regular operator is ill, vacationing, or on leave of absence.

Using Phone Recording to Cut Clerical Loads

It is too often true that a business office seems to operate at its minimum efficiency during a period of maximum sales production. As the back orders pile up, the clerical situation becomes even more complicated and critical; invoicing, checking, and packing are slowed down. The telephone trunk lines are flooded; customer calls are delayed and added to a long waiting list. Desk-hopping brings relief in one spot, while office routine bogs down in another. Overtime piles up, casting shadows over the profit pages of company ledgers.

To the harassed executive trying to forget the chaos of past peak seasons while his ulcers signal the approach of another one, solutions may present themselves. But they are usually price-tagged too high— "Get an $800,000 mechanical brain," "Increase the size of the staff," or "Call in an outside service."

E. S. Buckler, Jr., general manager at McCarthy-Hicks, Inc., Baltimore wholesale beverage house, once had these peak season headaches twice daily. He could anticipate the first one early in the morning and the second in midafternoon when his salesmen, in all parts of Maryland, began telephoning in their orders.

Looking for a possible leveler of these peaks, the McCarthy-Hicks staff checked various recording machine systems, hoping to find a method to take care of the overflow of telephone calls and stabilize or even reduce the extra work falling on the switchboard operator and the clerical personnel.

After looking over a number of suggested systems and testing several of the most promising, a system was installed which helped to relieve those peak-rush headaches. It also has the necessary requisite of fitting into the existing office setup.

In operation, a salesman calls in to give his order. The switchboard operator plugs the call into any of six active special jacks connected

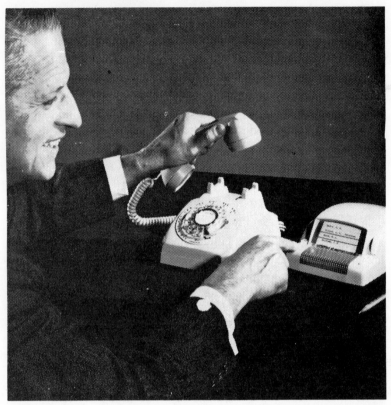

New equipment is constantly being developed to expedite voice communications. One example is the Magicall unit, by means of which telephone customers can dial any phone number by simply pressing a button. A companion unit to the dial telephone, Magicall is an electronic dialing instrument which operates quickly, accurately, and automatically.

The Electronic Secretary telephone-answering set answers the telephone in the absence of the secretary and takes the caller's message on a recording tape.

Among the many long-distance communication services offered by Western Union is the coast-to-coast Public Facsimile Service between major cities. Customers can send any written or drawn material up to 7 inches by 9 inches via this equipment. The operator (above) has placed on the transmitter drum a piece of material which, at the push of a button, will be sent coast to coast in 6 minutes. The received copy (illustrated at the right) is an exact "picture" of the original.

to electronic recorders. She notes the exact time and tells the salesman to go ahead.

As the salesman dictates his orders to the recorder, a light above the switchboard jack blinks intermittently with his voice. When the light at the switchboard stops blinking, the operator checks to be sure the salesman is through and then disconnects the line. At present, four McCarthy-Hicks salesmen can record their orders simultaneously, but two additional machines can be plugged into the system at any time.

Since the salesmen know their orders are being accurately recorded no matter how rapidly they talk, the average call-in—according to a survey of actual recorded orders—takes only 21 seconds of recording time. This figure is all the more surprising because salesmen handle 128 separate items.

Sales force reaction is summed up by the men themselves: "The automatic order recording system is beneficial because it is faster and more accurate, helps us make better call-ins, and adds to our selling time. When there are errors, they are usually our own. There is no waiting on the telephone, and this system has helped us correct our mistakes in order writing and call-ins."

Another benefit realized by the sales staff has been the addition of a very strong selling point—faster customer service. With the new system, the current day's orders often are filled before the salesmen return from their daily rounds, and orders are usually on a truck for delivery within 24 hours after being taken.

Installation of the system has effected a 60 percent savings in time, and has created a dramatic drop in overtime and cost of invoicing. Yet no additional workers were employed, no extra work was added to the present staff's output, and no disruption of office routine occurred. Work proceeds in an orderly, even, but swift, flow with less errors.

In the room where the recorders are located, employees work without annoyance from the equipment. A bell signal indicates when the recording medium needs replacing; but usually before this happens, the recorded material has been removed and is in the process of being transcribed.

A preprinted order form, duplicating that from which the salesman dictates his order into the recorder, is used by the transcriber who jots down the salesman's orders. In a test, a total of 84 were taken from transcribers to order pads in 35 minutes—25 seconds per order.

TWX

The Bell System teletypewriter is much like an ordinary typewriter in appearance and operation, and just as easy to use. The service combines the advantage of rapid two-way communication with the permanency of the written word. Messages typed on one machine are instantly and accurately reproduced on any other teletypewriter to which it is connected.

Typed information may be recorded in two ways. It may be recorded on a continuous paper roll, 8½ inches wide with characters spaced 10 to the inch and with lines either single- or double-spaced. Or it may be recorded on continuous multicopy business forms. Teletypewriters can be equipped with sprocket feed to keep the forms in accurate alignment.

While the manual teletypewriter prepares copies of the message or order on both sending and receiving machines, the automatic teletypewriter provides, in addition to manual sending by use of keyboard, the means for perforating tape which, when fed through the associated transmitter, automatically sends the message at the maximum speed for which the service has been designed.

"TWX does for the written word what telephone service does for the spoken word," say the manufacturers. Numbers are found in the TWX directory, calls are established quickly, and communication is two-way.

Private teletypewriter service provides direct and exclusive communications across the room, across the street, or across the country. The private Teletype system connecting branch offices with the Maytag Company's home office, for example, has been expanded to include 16 of the 18 Maytag major distribution centers across the nation. At the same time, the system was divided into an eastern and a western circuit, with the eastern circuit beginning and ending an hour earlier than the western circuit.

TIMING THE TELEPHONE CALL

Before	9:00 a.m. or after 5:00 p.m.	Builders and contractors
Between	9:00 a.m. and 11:00 a.m.	Physicians and surgeons
	1:00 p.m. and 3:00 p.m.	
	7:00 p.m. and 9:00 p.m. (some)	
Before	9:30 a.m.	Dentists
Before	10:00 a.m. or after 5:00 p.m.	Bankers and stockbrokers
Between	10:00 a.m. and 11:00 a.m.	Housewives
After	10:30 a.m.	Business heads, executives, merchants, store heads, and department heads
Between	11:00 a.m. and 2:00 p.m.	Lawyers
Between	1:00 p.m. and 3:00 p.m.	Druggists and grocers
After	3:00 p.m.	Printers and publishers
Between	4:00 p.m. and 5:00 p.m.	Chemists and engineers
Between	6:00 p.m. and 7:00 p.m.	Professors and schoolteachers (call at home)
Any time during day but avoid Jan. 15 to April 15		Public accountants
Any time after Tuesday		Clergymen
Call at home		Government employees, small-salaried salespeople

---

Northwestern Mutual Insurance Company compiled this time schedule for salesmen as a guide to the best time to phone prospects to arrange an interview. The schedule, based on the experience of many agents, can be adapted to other lines.

HOW TO COUNT AND CHARGE FOR TELEGRAMS

The following practices are observed in determining the number of chargeable words in domestic telegrams to all places in North America.

1. One address and one signature are free.

2. Dictionary words from the English, German, French, Italian, Dutch, Portuguese, Spanish and Latin languages are counted as one word each, irrespective of length. Any word or group of letters not forming a dictionary word in any of these eight languages is counted at the rate of one word for every five letters or fraction of five letters.

3. Proper names in any language are counted according to the way they are normally written. Examples:

    United States—2 words - North Dakota—2 words - New York City—3 words

4. Abbreviations are counted at the rate of one word for each five letters. Examples:

    1b—1 word - AM—1 word - PM—1 word - NY—1 word

5. Personal names are counted in the way they are normally written. Examples:

    Du Bois—2 words - Van Dyke—2 words - Van der Gross—3 words Vandewater—1 word

    Initials, when separated by spaces, are counted as separate words but when written together as J.O.R. in the case of J.O.R. Smith, they are counted at the rate of one word for each five letters.

6. Punctuation marks, such as period (or decimal point), comma, colon, semicolon, dash or hyphen, parentheses, question mark, quotation marks and apostrophe are neither counted nor charged for, regardless of where they appear in the text of the message.

7. Except for the punctuation marks enumerated in 6 above, the only additional signs that can be transmitted in domestic messages are: $, &, /, #, ' (for feet), and " (for inches). These are counted in accordance with paragraph 8, following.

8. Groups of figures, including the signs mentioned in paragraph 7, and mixed groups of figures and letters are counted in accordance with (a) and (b) below:

    (a) In messages between points within the United States and to points in Mexico and Alaska, such groups are counted at the rate of one word for each five figures (including signs), and letters. Examples:

12345 (5 characters)	1 word
#78694 (6 characters)	2 words
$25.05 (5 characters, decimal is punctuation)	1 word
B&O (3 characters)	1 word
AB12479 (7 characters)	2 words
12-3/4 (5 characters, hyphen is punctuation)	1 word
1st (3 characters)	1 word
107 1/4-1/2 (hyphen is punctuation)	3 words
(WAC) (Parentheses are punctuation)	1 word

    (b) In messages between points in the United States and points in Canada, and Saint Pierre-Miquelon Islands, each figure and sign is counted as one word, and each group of letters written together is counted at the rate of one word for each five letters or fraction of five letters. Examples:

BC-AD (4 letters, hyphen is punctuation)	1 word

Courtesy, Western Union

Five distributor organizations have joined the system to permit the transmission of fast, written communications between Newton, Iowa, and the various distribution centers. Expansion of the system bears out the fact that this direct, private wire Teletype is an important step in providing Maytag dealers with speedier and more complete service than ever before in meeting the ever-changing conditions of today's markets.

Operation of the system, known as "TADS" or "Teletypewriter Automatic Dispatch System," is through means of tape punched by an operator at each office or the Newton control center. Tape is placed on the sending equipment and messages are sent as an office is "searched." The automatic system "searches" offices in a regular sequence until it finds a transmitter which has a tape in it. At the conclusion of transmission from an office, the next office in sequence is searched. This procedure takes place simultaneously on each of the two circuits.

CARRIER SYSTEMS

Getting orders out to customers the same day the order is received presents a problem to every company, especially those having multiple-story plants. The time lost by messengers running up and down stairs between departments is not only costly, but it slows shipping schedules.

To break this bottleneck, more and more companies are installing conveyors like those in use at the Westinghouse plant in Pittsburgh. It is part of a program to speed the routine flow of paper work, cut costs, and improve customer relations.

The belt conveyor was installed to expedite order shipping. It is part of the company's methods-improvement program. The conveyor is equipped with sending boxes into which the order forms are placed on an upper floor. The shipping memo is whisked to the packing area in the company's East Pittsburgh warehouse. It is then taken by a stock man and the order is filled, shot through to the loading dock, and shipped. Transportation is only a matter of seconds.

While this is going on, the bill of lading is put in the sending box of the conveyor on the third floor, where it is carried to the first floor loading dock.

While expensive to install, the new method saves the company thousands of dollars every year. Other companies use pneumatic tubes to expedite incoming orders, and there are other devices. But all have the same purpose—to expedite filling orders.

Usually conveyor and related systems are overlooked when planning new office facilities, or management reasons "if we really need it we can always install it." But the economical time to provide for the rapid transmission of orders and other work papers, even in the case of one-story plants, is when the plant is being built, as Westinghouse did.

The reason for making the conveyor system a part of the original office plan is that it has a bearing on the arrangement since it affects the flow of work.

Pneumatic tubes help make for top efficiency in the recently built offices of the Vapor Heating Company. The company occupies a $2 million plant in Niles, Illinois. The tube system delivers and returns requisitions and messages to and from 15 different stations throughout the plant. Altogether, there are four miles of tubing in the system, and the farthest station is 400 feet away. It is estimated that without this tube system, some 20 people would be continuously going and coming with orders.

Papers travel from the third floor to the loading dock in matter of seconds.   *Conveyor speeds orders to warehouse stockroom for filling and shipping.*

A pneumatic tube system can always be added after the office has been built. One supplier has a "do-it-yourself" kit available to companies that want to buy a tube system at cost. Complete instructions are given for laying out the equipment which connects points up to 130 feet apart and allows messages to go through the tubes at a rate of 200 feet a second.

Two Tons of Mail a Day

One of the tallest skyscrapers in New England is the 26-story home office of the John Hancock Mutual Life Insurance Company.

Here the company has over 5,000 employees, who are served by the fastest elevators in the region, and who have the largest office cafeteria facilities in the area at their disposal. In this completely air-conditioned building is also to be found the world's largest electric stairway installation in any office building.

While the building is identified with a number of superlatives, one of the most efficient features of the home office is its mailing system. Using this system, 1,500 pounds of incoming mail can be cleared out of the mail room in 14 minutes. Half a ton of interoffice correspondence is distributed daily, and a ton of outgoing mail is handled. It is estimated that two tons of mail travel over the system during the course of a day's work.

The system includes three Lamson conveyors, which extend from the mail room in the basement straight up to the eighth, 15th and 26th floors. There are also dispatching and receiving stations on each of the 26 floors. In addition, another Lamson conveyor serves 11 floors of the adjacent Clarendon Building.

Through an ingenious interlocking system, all mail, interoffice memos, and supplies can be moved from any floor in the home office to any other floor in the office. Mail can be dispatched to the mail room from any floor, or from the mail room to any of the floors. When one of the Micarta conveyor boxes is routed to the adjacent building, an electric eye switches it automatically to an interlocking horizontal conveyor system which starts the box on its way to the fourth vertical conveyor.

The actual handling of the mail is quite easy. For example, on one floor there are three mail stations, each having a receiving chute and a sending chute. If an employee wants to send mail to another floor, he simply places the tray of mail in the sending chute, sets a dial on the wall to indicate the proper floor, and away the tray goes. The trays are controlled by the dial system, and also by electric eyes which react to the different colors of the trays.

When the tray arrives at the proper floor, the mail is distributed by another employee. The only "leg work" required with this system is distributing the mail on each floor; all transporting of mail between floors is handled by the conveyor system.

INTERNAL COMMUNICATION

Toll telephone costs have been reduced about 25 percent by George B. Carpenter & Company through the use of separate "inside" or "automatic" telephones.

The inside phones enable Carpenter executives to finish their long-distance telephone calls faster by calling for information needed right then. Too, executives have to make fewer "call-backs" to correct poor guesses or errors. More business can be settled in one single telephone call.

Carpenter also estimates that the overall employee working time saved by the internal communications system amounts to as much as 20 percent.

Another saving accomplished with the system is in inventory investment. Instead of using a conventional stock-recording system, Carpenter controls all inventory with P-A-X telephones. Loudspeakers serve warehouses and stockrooms, and anybody at any P-A-X telephone can dial the number of any loudspeaker and ask, "How much No. 24 Seine twine have we?"

The warehouseman near the twine shelf looks at his count, turns toward a P-A-X microphone (which may be as much as 100 feet away), and calls out the desired information.

Carpenter's entire inventory of 15 million pounds of merchandise, turned over annually, is handled in much the same way. It is estimated that an inventory investment of $750,000 is reduced 20 to 25 percent with the internal communications system.

While Carpenter's type of business is ideal for a separate inside telephone system, most businesses will find such a system of great help. Carpenter is essentially a buying and reselling organization and nearly every outside call requires some checking of accounts, credits, and inventory. With the separate telephone system, the necessary information can be obtained quickly.

The P-A-X system is a series of regular telephones connected to a completely automatic switchboard—entirely independent of the regular "outside" rented telephone service. These systems serve from 10 to several thousand phones, freeing the regular switchboard operator from handling internal calls.

Luria Brothers & Company saves money using inside telephones. Its monthly telephone bill of about $1,500 includes considerable long-distance telephoning. The saving effected by the use of inside telephones is estimated at about 19 percent of this monthly cost.

Geo. T. Schmidt Company, employing 100 toolmakers and highly skilled engravers, has also found that a P-A-X system saves money.

J. K. Howe, executive vice-president, stated that six minutes out of every hour—or 10 percent—was a very low estimate of the time lost by almost everyone in walking back and forth to exchange information. With the P-A-X system installed, about $12,000 a year is saved in the office organization alone.

One manufacturer has turned out a system built especially for small offices, handling two to five stations. Using no batteries or tubes, the device operates on power that is supplied from a little boxlike unit that measures 3 by 5 inches and stands 3 inches high. This is plugged into a regular 110-volt electric outlet. The telephones—up to five of them—connect from the box by a wire that can run under carpets or be glued to walls. The only tool needed to install the system is a screwdriver. Phones have four push buttons for buzzing each of the others.

Closed-Circuit TV

A recent development in the area of industrial communications is a televised meeting, which can be viewed simultaneously by groups in a network of cities. The American Management Association thus televised an actual labor-management contract negotiation meeting over a closed TV circuit, which was seen by more than 1,800 members. This medium has also been extensively used to introduce new products and advertising campaigns. The facilities for closed-circuit televising of the American Telephone & Telegraph Company now are available in more than 300 cities. Large-screen color TV is the next important development and should greatly add to the value of the medium.

Closed-circuit TV has many advantages in stockholder relations, since it permits the shareholders in strategic points to feel that they are participating in a stockholders' meeting. At least they have the opportunity to see the management team in action and to observe any product demonstration that might be held in connection with the meeting. Advantages of closed-circuit TV are as follows:

Minimum Loss of Time. Dealers and salesmen travel only short distances locally to attend conferences. Major executives don't have to travel from city to city. Time for organization and rehearsal is reduced. (About 3 hours of rehearsal is required for an hour show.)

Entire Audience Can Be Reached Simultaneously. Each person in the audience gets the message firsthand and at the same time. This arrangement has particular advantages in competitive situations and where spontaneity is important.

Interruptions Are Eliminated. The speaker's pace is undisturbed by late arrivals or talking in the audience. Compact presentation eliminates the need for luncheon or other breaks.

Message Gets Complete Attention. Top management, in person, makes announcements. This technique still is appealingly novel. The audience can see and hear better. Message is fresh.

Program Can Have More Than One Point of Origin. Participants and action can be in different cities.

Permanent, Reusable Film Can Be Made. Film recordings can be made for additional sales meetings. This record also permits better planning for future conferences.

Cost Is Comparatively Low. Average multicity (20 or more) network show costs about $2,000 per city including all expenses involved in origination, transmission, and projection. A second hour increases the overall cost by about 25 percent.

The compact television camera is placed in a specific location for whatever observation application is required. What the camera sees is relayed by wire to television receivers or monitors in a central control room. The control room may be from 500 feet to several miles from the camera and of course may be used to coordinate the observations of a battery of cameras located at strategic points throughout a given installation. RCA has made hundreds of such installations for production control, surveillance, dangerous observations, improved business services, materials handling, product demonstration, property protection, sales and merchandising activities, training, and teaching. In all applications closed-circuit television contributes greater speed in coordinating operations, increased efficiency of manpower, and important savings in time and dollars. Perhaps the best way to illustrate these contributions is by describing some actual installations.

At the Provident Institution for Savings in Boston a TV installation is enabling the bank to complete cash withdrawal transactions in a matter of seconds, which speeds up service to customers and saves thousands of dollars annually. The TV system provides a vital link between tellers and the bank's central signature files, and has introduced unbelievable speed in the flow of necessary information. Four TV cameras are installed in the signature department and individual TV receivers are located in each of 17 tellers' booths. A teller requiring signature verification to complete a withdrawal transaction requests the information by depressing an inquiry button as he enters the account number to post the transaction. In seconds, the signature card is placed under the TV camera and flashed to the receiver of the requesting teller. In other words, television makes it possible for the teller to obtain the information necessary to speed the account in a matter of seconds.

RCA has used industrial television in its own plant operations for teaching operators an intricate assembly problem. The assembly operation, performed by a specialist, is projected by television to receivers in front of the various operators. Via TV they can observe the method easily and watch how it is to be done. By simply following the leader on television, the assemblers can complete complex components in time to make deadlines. This successful application makes it clearly obvious that television can put a new meaning into on-the-job training and group education.

Steps in Preparing a TV Presentation

First decide exactly what you want the presentation to do—in other words, set up a target. Too many presentations lack direction. They just amble, without going anywhere.

The next step is to list all the points you can think of which should be communicated to the viewer, to open his mind for your message.

Assemble ample material about each point. Support generalities with specifics, and vice versa.

Build entire presentation around key point. Develop points in logical sequence, dramatically. Use group headings.

Write the story simply. Use "talking" words and phrases which the average person would not hesitate to use. Develop continuity among various sequences in which material might be used.

Start with an arresting statement or question that promises real advantage. Appeal to as many senses as possible.

Be sincere. Undersell your points rather than oversell them.

ELECTRONIC SYSTEMS

"The constantly growing number of applications for intercom in all types of offices, and in industry generally," predicts a manufacturer of such equipment, "indicates that in the very near future businessmen will recognize their need for intercom just as they today recognize their need for typewriters. More and more businessmen are recognizing the fact that it is as economically unsound to run their offices without an intercom system as it would be to answer their mail by longhand."

The benefits of intercom in business offices are many. It increases the productive time of all personnel by permitting people to talk instead of walk when they need information to make decisions, answer customer questions, and handle routine office business requiring communication between departments.

The reduction of telephone bills is another benefit. Intercom eliminates many call-backs forced upon office personnel when they cannot get information from other departments while on the telephone with an outside call. Telephone overtime charges, brought about by slowness in getting needed information from other departments, also are reduced.

Fast Service at Olson Transportation

Speedier customer service and reduced operating costs are the sequel to installation of a two-way radio system at the Chicago terminal of Olson Transportation Company.

A Parke, Davis Engineering Division receptionist handles an encoder which sends either an individual code to a particular receiver or, in case of emergency, can send out multiple signals for key supervisors to report in by telephone.. More than 80 such Pagemaster units are now in use by Parke, Davis in several of its plants.

The system provides a 15-watt RCA Carfone-450 base station and 75 Carfone-450 mobile radios in Olson trucks operating out of the Chicago terminal on local pickup and delivery.

The base station, remotely operated from the terminal dispatcher's office, is located five miles away atop the Lincoln Tower Building, in the heart of Chicago's downtown business district. The lofty installation of antenna and transmitter provides the Olson company with radio coverage throughout the Chicago metropolitan area.

"The two-way radio system," John A. Ebeling, vice-president, said, "is enabling us to provide customers with faster, improved service. The continuous contact between dispatchers and drivers enables us to service sudden, last-minute shipments, to decrease lag time between order and pickup, and to provide customers and drivers with information and assistance from terminal to point of pickup. We estimate that radio-control gives us the equivalent of 10 additional trucks on the street.

"Prior to radio, our drivers were required to phone in for information or shipping instructions. This system is particularly trying and time-consuming in large traffic-congested cities, since it involves locating a phone, finding parking space, and leaving cargoes un-attended. The elimination of phone-ins, we estimate, saves the Chicago terminal over $10,000 a year in phone tolls."

Pocket-Size Receivers at Parke, Davis

To permit speedier contact in case of emergencies, Parke, Davis & Company has equipped key personnel with pocket-size electronic receivers.

The handy page system ensures almost instant contact with any individual carrying one of the receivers, regardless of his whereabouts in the main laboratories of the Detroit pharmaceutical firm. These laboratories cover a square area with sides one-quarter of a mile in length, and they consist of 60 buildings with a total floor area of 38 acres.

Individuals equipped with the receivers have special code numbers which are on file at the page system switchboard. When one of the individuals can't be reached by telephone at his desk, the interplant number of the page system is dialed and the message is given to the operator. She then dials the man's code number.

The Pagemaster units, carried in the pockets of Parke, Davis engineers buzz when the encoder calls.

The man, who carries the receiver in his pocket, hears a buzz and contacts her at the switchboard for the message as soon as possible.

Milton Moore, utilities engineer for Parke, Davis & Company, often tours the area. He says the page system is particularly handy when a person is outside and (in prior times) difficult to contact.

"Our key maintenance, service, and engineering people, and the safety engineer (70 in all) are equipped with receivers," explains Peter Kenyon of Parke, Davis' electronic section. He says the system "gives us a mobile service and maintenance force that can be contacted almost instantly, if necessary.

"Exclusive of scientific or laboratory apparatus, the buildings here contain some 5,000 individual pieces of machinery. The economy of avoiding machine downtime is obvious," Mr. Kenyon notes.

Electronic Longhand

A means of communication designed to transmit handwritten messages from one point to another is provided by TELautograph's Telescriber system. It is made up of two or more Telescribers which can transmit and receive messages electronically. The equipment is connected by a wiring circuit.

Electronic longhand systems have many applications. One such, in operation at The F. & M. Schaefer Brewing Company, insures prompt action in truck placement and loading. With it, handwritten truck changes, cancellations, and additions in the loading sequence can be issued to an uploading area and a dispatch area to more efficiently handle the palletized loadings.

One of our leading hospitals uses the system to eliminate losses from late charges. The central business office is integrated with all departments so that patients' charges can be transmitted, accumulated, and posted. In this way, a complete statement is ready for any patient at the moment of discharge. Recordkeeping and guest charges at hotels and restaurants can be handled the same way.

In manufacturing industries, electronic longhand finds uses in job progress reports, timekeeping data, payroll accounting, material requisitioning, and other activities that are all coordinated to one central point to simplify accounting procedures.

New Developments

High-powered intercommunications systems with transistors and printed circuits are now available for use in offices, plants, schools, and other institutions. It is estimated that using printed circuits reduces wiring costs by 50 percent. The advantages of transistors are that they require less power, less maintenance, produce less heat, and thereby assure longer life for the unit.

Wireless intercommunication is becoming more popular and practical than ever. One supplier, for example, has perfected a device as simple to install as a lamp or a radio. It can be located wherever there is a power outlet and can be readily moved from place to place. Providing all stations on a given system receive power from a line fed by a common meter, they may be located at considerable distances from each other, often up to several miles. The intercom can be used with two or more stations, with all conversations heard by all stations in the system. A "Silent Watchman" permits a station to be locked in "transmit" position for a continuous listening arrangement. Additional stations can be added to the system at any time.

In another electronic system the nerve center is a master station which enables the user to call and converse with others at other master stations, and receive calls from a combination of up to 10 staff, or reply, stations. Calls from staff stations can be registered and held at the master station until answered. A call to the master station is announced by a soft chime and a signal light indicating which station is calling. Any number of masters, staffs, amplified reproducers may be added to the circuit.

No special wiring is required with the IBM portable paging units. They can be plugged into AC power outlets at convenient locations within a building. Both audible and visible signals are received, which makes effective paging possible regardless of the noise level or distance for stationary signals. Code signals are assigned to personnel, and special signals may be sounded to indicate the reason for paging, such as "telephone call," "visitor," or "customer waiting."

Providing "personalized service," a low-frequency radio paging system alerts paged staff members anywhere within the plant or building without anyone but the person being paged being aware that a message is being transmitted. The system consists of a selector console, an FM transmitter, and the radio receivers. Up to several hundred persons per system can be paged individually with new channels being added as needed.

Selective Ringing Telephone Systems

A line of selective ringing, centrally supervised telephone systems is now in use for private intercommunication in a number of company offices. Controlled from two styles of master phones, a single system may have as many individual telephones or substations as may be desired.

Wall-type handsets are installed either flush or recessed. Two styles are similar to conventional handsets while a third is a desk-type phone.

Communications take place between the master phone and any substation or from one substation to another through the master phone. A system can be installed in conjunction with a master clock signaling system, using the same buzzers for telephone signaling. Master phones can be installed with the signal distribution panel.

Another feature of these systems is a two-position "intercom" control switch. This sounds a buzzer when calls between substations are completed, and restores buzzer operation for call-in to the master station. Wall phones are equipped with either a hook switch for operation or an optional press-to-talk button. Desk phones have a conventional cradle hook switch.

Since these systems are the "common talking" type, only one pair of twisted wires is required to connect all phones.

A special unit, operating at 115 volts, 60 cycles, 1 ampere, provides 6 to 9 volts d.c. power for talking circuits. Full-wave rectified output is heavily filtered to eliminate system hum.

Telegraphic Services

The teleprinter is used over short distances where traffic is light. Its signals go directly over the telegraph line to a similar printer at the other end of the wire. Installation of thousands of these printers in offices of Western Union customers has, in effect, added that many direct-wire offices to the telegraph system. As messages are sent back and forth, transmission is practically instantaneous.

In many business offices the telephone is both a telegraph office and a Western Union charge account. It is only necessary to call Western Union, dictate the message to the operator, and ask that the charge appear on the telephone bill.

The Timken Roller Bearing Company in Canton, Ohio, was one of the first private industries in Ohio to be connected to Western Union's high-speed switching center in Cincinnati. With this electronic telegraph system, Timken operators use a teleprinter to send wires directly to the Cincinnati switching center where they are automatically relayed to any part of the country. Telegrams sent to

Wall handset is heart of Executone, Inc., mutichannel page/reply system. Voice of caller originating a page call is amplified throughout building. The person called goes to nearest Executone station and by lifting handset is in immediate two-way conversation with the caller. Amplifier is cut out, making conversation private. Conference calls also are possible.

the Timken Company Canton office from any Western Union office in this country are transmitted to the switching center. A push-button selection relays the message promptly to the receiving machine at the Timken office.

This modern telegraph system is so highly mechanized that message travel within the nationwide network is almost completely automatic. It sends messages from point to point electronically, needing only a minimum of personal supervision or regulations. The telegraph transmission is done by perforated tape. A telegram reaching a switching center is received as a pattern of electrical impulses. In a "reperforator" at the switching center this pattern is translated into an arrangement of small perforations on the paper tape. By push-button selection on the control panel, the message is quickly routed through the switching system to its destination.

Facsimile Telegraphy

Desk-Fax, a facsimile machine on the desk of the businessman, provides a direct connection with the nearest telegraph center. With it, it is possible to send and receive telegrams instantly in "picture" form by merely pressing a button. A tiny electronic "eye" scans the telegram and flashes an exact picture of it to Western Union. The same machine receives telegrams with equal simplicity.

Another type of electronic facsimile system has been developed to flash Pullman and reserved-seat coach tickets from one railroad station to another and provide them almost instantaneously to customers at the counter. Facsimile duplicates of tickets are delivered in eight seconds, while the originals are miles away at the main office.

Western Union also leases private facsimile telegraph systems, called Intrafax, for use within customers' organizations to provide fast intracompany communication. The device transmits letters, orders, requisitions, drawings—all kinds of documents—with photographic accuracy. It will reproduce a standard 8½- by 11-inch form or letter in less than three minutes. It will send 300 typed words a minute, more than twice the speed of the world's fastest typist.

Intrafax requires no photographic, chemical, or drying preparation at either the sending or receiving end. Original material is laced directly on the machine (about the size of a typewriter), and a button is pushed to start transmission. The material is received ready for instant use through Teledeltos, a dry, electrosensitive recording paper.

Private Wire Systems

In recent years, Western Union's leasing of private wire networks has grown to major proportions. Examples: Civil Aeronautics Administration weather reporting service linking airports: General Services Administration network linking government civilian agencies in 53 major cities; "Bank Wire" which links large banks in all parts of the Nation; networks connecting offices of U. S. Steel, General Electric, United Air Lines, and many other large organizations; networks for the United States Armed Forces. One Air Force network serves over 200 stations and uses 200,000 miles of telegraph circuits. The use of private wire systems by industry for centralized control of decentralized operations (integrated data processing) is resulting in even wider demands for such systems.

Offices requiring fast, direct, two-way monthly exchange of a large volume of words between large cities may use Western Union's telemeter service. The company installs two teleprinters at both ends so messages may be sent and received at the same time. All words sent are registered on a tiny wordmeter. For a flat monthly charge, a total minimum of 25,000 six-character words may be used.

Chase Brass & Copper Co., Waterbury, Connecticut, has leased an 8,000-mile private wire system from Western Union to flash messages between its offices and plants in 27 cities and 19 states. The network interconnects Chase offices as far west as Dallas, Kansas City, and Minneapolis, and as far south as New Orleans. It is equipped with teleprinter machines, each with a speed of 3,900 words an hour. Messages are typed by operators, producing a perforated tape. The coded tape speeds through an automatic transmitter at 65 words a minute. At their destination the messages are received automatically in page form, ready for instant use. A special feature of the system is a selector which automatically equalizes the use of the circuit between all stations and provides complete and continuous utilization of the equipment and circuit capacity.

Office Automation by Private Wire

Western Union private wire systems are providing a growing number of businesses with the specialized communication facilities needed to link operations at widely separated points. In addition to regular administrative communications, all types of statistical data can be sent, by means of punched tape or cards, over the specially engineered private wire systems which Western Union leases to industry and government. At destination, the data are reproduced automatically, ready for instant processing by business machines and electronic computers.

Because of the wide variety of electronic business machines and computers, and the differing requirements of companies, a private wire system must be tailored to suit individual needs.

The telegraph company offers a wide variety of specialized equipment for use in business automation systems. Such equipment may include sending and receiving teleprinters, automatic transmitters, switching apparatus, tape perforators, automatic numbering machines, data sorters, storage units, selectors, and other special devices that make possible a system best adapted to each customer's needs.

International Services

Today, all the continents of the world are interconnected by a vast network of submarine cables. Western Union operates more than 30,000 miles of ocean cables. All parts of the world are reached via the Western Union cable system and its connections.

Western Union has tripled the capacity of its transatlantic system through the use of deep-sea cable amplifiers. The new amplifiers are producing additional maximum-security channels for lease to the military and other departments of the government, and for business and social use.

Details on economic use, coding, and so forth, in international cables will be found in such special publications as *The Dartnell Correspondence Manual,* and *The Dartnell International Trade Handbook.*

Chapter 48

SELECTING OFFICE FURNITURE

TREMENDOUS strides have been made in designing well-planned, sound, architectural office interiors, and at the same time, well-designed high quality, contemporary office furniture has been introduced to fulfill the functional needs of the individual offices rather than the "monumental" needs of the organization or an individual. Today's office is much more human and informal than before, and it calls for furniture in kind. Designs that reflect this sensible attitude work well with the environment, fostering a harmonious relationship between the exterior, the interior, and the work at hand, and at the same time providing a fitting background for the personality and individualism of its occupant.

Says Jens Risom, a New York City designer:

"I find it difficult to imagine an executive who can justify a completely traditional office if his overall goal is to run an up-to-date organization using the very best and most modern equipment, manufacturing methods and machinery, providing the public with the most modern products and up-to-date services. How very difficult it must be for him to clearly think, plan his work and explain his contemporary ideas and policies in an office where he surrounds himself with furniture designed and planned for totally different use, hundreds of years ago. The use of occasional fine, old pieces—at times traditional accessories—in a predominately contemporary interior will always be handsome when done in good taste. Consequently, I think a sound, functional contemporary design approach is the one we will see more of in the future."

Mr. Risom foresees interesting solutions to the many new and changing problems in business methods and, therefore, in office design, machinery, and furniture needed by the executive. However, he does not believe that we will find the average executive changed so drastically that there is no longer a need for a pleasant, harmonious office in which to work, think, and in general perform the executive duties for which he is hired. No matter how many new electrical computers and closed-circuit TV sets are added to the office, there will always be the need for people to have offices in which to work, think, and meet people. The building, especially the modern one, consists of structural and architectural materials . . . steel, glass, concrete, marble, etc.

"Office furniture, in my opinion," says Mr. Risom, "should not be planned and designed as miniature versions of the building, but rather in design and materials which comfortably bridge the gap between the hard structure of the building and the man who is occupying the office. It is important that this person, who is there to be productive and creative, be given the best possible working environment. Here, in my opinion, wood comes through as the best material because its texture, color, depth, and warmth seem to satisfy the need for a comfortable working atmosphere. We will also find greater and greater use of color, objects of art, and other accessories important to the personality, comfort, and productivity of the occupant.

"Designers, manufacturers, and office-furniture dealers with design departments are beginning to play a greater and more important role in space planning, actual office design, and careful furniture specification. For years people bought office furniture the same way they bought wastepaper baskets. No real thought was even given to what the furniture was supposed to do for the man who would occupy the office, and only rarely was good design and quality to be found in the average dealer's showroom. Designers, manufacturers, and dealers have the very important job of upgrading the taste of the purchasers, to expose them to good products, good interiors, and carefully explain and sell furniture as well as they do typewriters, machines, etc. Good design and quality are available on any price level. You can have a well-designed and well-made chair for $50 as well as a poor chair for $50. Good design and quality products exist on every level and it is up to the professional to guide the consumer and advise him on how to wisely spend his money.

"Most people who are buying office furniture today have not previously done so, and until someone points out what is available, as well as the importance of good design and quality in furniture to the success of their business, it is difficult for them to understand the need for good professional service and top products. More and more companies are realizing that the trained designer is best equipped to solve the many new and changing problems in office planning and office equipment and that with the professional advice they will be better able to meet the needs of the future. It is for this very same reason that the dealer who plans to grow and prosper will need a competent design staff in order to adequately service his customer.

"The hope for a more sophisticated system that will take all the guesswork out of the enormously important field of office environment and furniture, can be best coped with by letter and more realistic planning by all concerned, independent designers as well as dealers. As more and more jobs are being ordered as complete installations rather than piecemeal purchases, the outlook for the future seems to be toward more professional performance from early space planning to final installation—a decent profit margin in order to offer the complete service which is necessary—and good display facilities in order to adequately show and sell the products necessary for a successful end result."

Executive Desks

There is no limit to the refinements and fittings which a custom-made executive desk can have. There are some fitted with bars, refrigerators, radios, intercommunication systems, even television.

The average executive, however, will be satisfied with the top-quality stock models of office furniture. These give him such refinements as built-in dictating equipment, personal file drawers, convenience trays, footrests, and similar features.

The typical executive office has a big desk and a companion table. A newcomer to the desk lines, however, gives evidence of doing away with the separate table to give added space and attractiveness to the office.

The executive conference desk has an oversize top which extends to the back and to either side in the manner of a counter. Staff members or visitors may draw up chairs to share the desk with the seated executive.

The conference desk gives the executive more desk space for himself and eliminates the need, in many instances, for the separate table. The use of the conference desk has made it possible for some firms to do away with a separate conference room, thus saving considerable floor space and expense.

Clerical Desks

The clerical desk is similar to the executive desk except for the de luxe refinements. It is used by those employees who do not require a typewriter at their work.

Today's office decor is quite like that of a well-furnished home. The executive desk, chair, and cabinet above were designed by Jens Risom, as was the reception room armchair at right.

Below, a filing cabinet by the Supreme Steel Equipment Corp. of Brooklyn is equipped with rods to accommodate hanging file folders.

Where floor space is at a premium, a single-pedestal clerical or flat-top desk can be used. It gives the same amount of drawer space as the secretarial desk.

The office desk has three principal types of drawers:

1. Storage drawers.

2. Center or knee-well drawer.

3. File drawers.

Storage drawers are commonly made so that vertical partitions may be added or adjusted to any position desired. This allows an unlimited number of combinations of compartment sizes and positions.

Storage drawer partitions can be moved to accommodate any width of card. The cards will fit crosswise in the drawer in easy reading and operating position.

Stationery racks are standard equipment in the secretarial and typist desk. They are fitted into a storage drawer to keep letterheads, carbon paper, and business forms in orderly arrangement. Executive and clerical desks, however, may also use the stationery rack to hold forms and other papers in order.

A coin and bill tray unit can be placed in one of the box drawers at positions which handle cash transactions.

The file drawer takes up the space of two storage drawers. A desk may have a file drawer in one or both pedestals and in either top or bottom position in the pedestal. In some desks, changes in drawer selection and location can be made after the desk is delivered.

Standard dictating equipment will fit into the file drawer of the desk. Some executive desks have a specially designed machine · drawer with space for the dictating equipment and built-in wiring and switch. This drawer keeps the desk top clear and helps prevent people from tripping over wires.

A special rack holding dictation machine cylinders and providing space for reference folders can be fitted into the standard file drawer.

Racks can be installed in the desk file drawer to hold suspended file folders. The racks will arrange the folders either lengthwise or crosswise in the drawer.

The standard arrangement for the file drawers is front-to-back filing. Side-to-side filing, however, can be provided by inserting a partition unit crosswise in the drawer, either in the legal-size or letter-size spacing. The inserts can provide for letter size in the front and legal size in the back, or vice versa.

Removable card index trays are available for use in any storage drawer. The standard storage drawer permits the cards to face the operator normally, but the removable trays are especially useful when the cards must be taken from the desk for reference or for use outside the office.

The center, or knee-well, drawer is used for a convenience tray of pencils, clips, and small articles. Back of the tray is space for the flat filing of large sheets of paper like plans and blueprints. Because the center drawer is awkward to use, it has been eliminated from some desks. On other desks it can sometimes be removed without detracting from the appearance of the desk. Without the center drawer, there is more knee space, a convenience for the taller person. When the center drawer is not used, the convenience tray is fitted into one of the storage drawers.

Sliding reference shelves are usually found at the top of the drawer pedestal. If the desk has two drawer pedestals, two sliding shelves can be had. Each sliding shelf increases the top area of a 60- by 30-inch desk by approximately 10 percent. The percentage is still greater on smaller desks.

In addition to providing extra writing surface for the desk occupant or visitor, the sliding shelf may be designed to serve other uses. Some can be reversed to make a tray for pencils and clips. It may be fitted with a glass under which can be positioned charts, telephone numbers, and other data frequently referred to. A visible reference file is also available which can be substituted for the sliding shelf in the same opening.

Secretarial Desks

The secretarial desk houses a typewriter in one of the pedestals when not in use. The desk is furnished with either a right- or left-hand typewriter pedestal, depending on how the desk is to be faced. The executive's secretary usually has a desk to match his, even though it may be in an adjoining room.

The common secretarial desk has two pedestals, one for the typewriter and one for stationery and other supplies. They are available, however, with only the typewriter pedestal.

The secretarial desk is the most popular desk for typists because the entire desk top can be used for other work when there is no typing to be done. There are some typing positions, however, especially in the larger offices, where the typewriter is used constantly and there is no need for a large top area on the desk. The fixed-bed type-writer desk, with a single or double pedestal, serves this purpose well.

With a fixed-bed typewriter desk, the machine remains on the desk immediately in front of the typist. When not in use, the type-writer is protected with a cloth or plastic cover. Typewriter men say this type of desk is best for a typewriter because it takes less abuse in moving about.

The fixed-bed desk is particularly suitable for heavy electric typewriters and wide-carriage machines. The portion of the desk immediately in front of the operator is at convenient typewriter height; the rest of the desk is full height. Adjustable bases are available separately to raise the typewriter to any height desired by the operator.

The familiar drop-head typing desk has been improved in design to allow more knee space when the desk is closed. It is losing out in popularity, however, to the secretarial desk and the fixed-bed typing desk.

Fanfold and Machine Desks

Continuous forms are being increasingly used by the business office. These forms are designed to furnish the required number of forms, complete with interleaved carbons. They eliminate the need for inserting and removing individual forms. Continuous forms are really a series of identical blank form packs attached together so that they form a long strip. For convenience in storing these long strips of paper and carbon paper, they are accordion-folded. For added protection, a fanfold desk can be had with a box attached to the back of the desk in which the unused portion of the continuous form is stored. The strip of forms moves easily from the box to the typewriter. Fanfold desks are particularly useful in order and traffic departments.

Many clerical operations, especially in the accounting department, require the use of adding and calculating machines or billing ma-chines of many descriptions. These machines are normally operated at the side of the desk so that the remainder of the desk can be used for the records that are being used in the work. A well, at the left or right of the desk as desired, allows the machine to be set lower than the standard desk height.

The calculating machine desk ordinarily has the machine well at the right side of the desk top. A similar desk with the well at the

Modular offices developed by The General Fireproofing Company include a desk, drop-leaf reference table, file and box drawers, book shelves, telephone, and dictating equipment. These components can be arranged in virtually any configuration.

left is commonly called a machine desk or an all-purpose machine desk.

The machine desk may come with a drawer pedestal or without the pedestal and having only end panels or legs. The well is slanted toward the operator to provide a more comfortable working position. She can use the machine from almost any seated position. A wiring opening is usually provided at the rear of the well so that the electric cord can be concealed.

Special Purpose Desks

Employees having contact with the public while seated at a desk, such as buyers, service department interviewers, receptionists, and the like, have need for the interview or contact desk. This is similar to the single-pedestal, flat-top desk except that the top has an extended overhang. Persons being interviewed can be comfortably seated at the overhang portion. The interview desk allows a reasonable degree of privacy and permits the conversation to be carried on in a tone that does not disturb the rest of the area. Doctors and other professionals like this type of desk for consulting with patients or clients.

A salesman's desk is almost a cross between a table and a desk and is used by any office worker or salesman who requires a writing surface but little storage area. It usually has one drawer almost the width of the desk, and no pedestal drawers. Desks may be obtained with paneled ends to match the rest of the office furniture.

823

Seating

The modern office requires several types of seating equipment. The chair at the desk is the most important because it exerts a great deal of influence on the quantity and quality of work produced by its occupant. Occasional chairs are required for visitors and for staff consultations. Davenports and settees are used in private offices and reception rooms. Special chairs are used by draftsmen, laboratory workers, and others who do not use standard desks.

Great strides have been made in recent years to provide seating comfort for the office worker. By means of the modern posture chair, each worker can be personally fitted for maximum comfort instead of having to contend with a chair designed for no one in particular.

A comfortably seated employee feels better, of course, but there is more than mere kindliness to management's motive. Many studies of worker fatigue have been made, and of the effects of fatigue on office production. Proper and comfortable seating helps to reduce that fatigue and improve the business operation through:

1. Increased production.
2. Fewer pauses for rest or diversion.
3. Higher quality of work.
4. Fewer errors.
5. Clearer mental decisions.
6. Reduced absenteeism.

A true "posture chair" is more than just a chair with an adjustment. The common swivel chair will turn at the base and can be adjusted for height. It may be perfectly comfortable, but it is not a posture chair.

The American Standards Association had a committee study the problem. Their decision was that a true posture chair had to have these three basic adjustments:

1. A seat adjustable in height.
2. A seat adjustable in depth.
3. A backrest adjustable vertically.

Two other adjustments may be offered: a backrest pitch adjustment and a spring tension adjustment.

Typists and others who work at fairly stationary positions prefer the solid backrest with the vertical adjustment. Executives and receptionists who move about prefer a backrest with spring tension. The tension can be adjusted to give full support to the back while in working position, yet allowing one to push back for relaxation with a slight additional pressure.

Types of Upholstery

The upholstery of the seat, arms, and backrest is provided in three broad classifications: leather, simulated leathers or plastics, and cloth. Each has an important place in the posture seating field and each has certain advantages over the other.

Although the most expensive of the three classes, top-grade genuine leather is preferred for long wear and prestige, especially in the executive chairs. When distributed over the life of the chair, the higher cost is relatively unimportant and may, in fact, prove a better investment. As with all leather products, one must be aware that leather has a number of grades and corresponding wearability. When using chairs made by reputable manufacturers, this is less of a problem, since they are careful to specify the leather used.

Plastics and plastic-coated fabrics are popular for those who want a long-wearing upholstery at moderate cost. Modern plastics are very tough and very resistant to abrasion. Susceptibility to punctures is modified by coating the plastic on a cloth backing, making what is called a "supported plastic." The cloth reduces the danger of the puncture spreading. Impregnated colors, and colors printed on the back of the plastic so that they show through the transparent covering, add beauty that lasts as long as the cover itself.

Fabrics introduce a homelike beauty to the office and offer a wider range of color selections. They are less conductive to heat than the leather and plastic and so are cooler feeling in summer and warmer in winter. The fabric will never shine a blue serge suit. Whether or not they wear better than plastics is debatable, but they are more difficult to clean. Some manufacturers apply removable covers which can be taken off easily for dry cleaning. These covers also make any necessary reupholstering easier and more economical.

Most manufacturers offer several types of cushioning and the cost of the chair depends to a great extent on the type used. The amount of labor and the cost of materials can quickly add dollars to the manufacturer's cost.

Foam rubber is generally accepted as the best cushioning material in use today, although it is quite expensive and can account for a considerable proportion of the chair cost if used in large quantities. The quantity and use of the foam is important, however, for it is not a magic name that automatically means the best. A saddle seat covered with one inch of foam is less desirable than a good coiled spring covered with hair.

The office equipment supplier will provide the selling points for his foam, but here are some of the qualities outlined by the Natural Rubber Bureau, Washington, D.C.:

1. Light. 85 to 95 percent air.

2. Clean. It "breathes," so no dust collects. Makes no dust itself. Ideal for allergic persons.

3. Resilient. Equalizes pressure against every point of contact. Springs back to original shape. No sag, bumps, or matting down.

4. Cool. Room temperature air going through all the time. Absorbs body heat and "exhales" it.

5. Odorless. No rubber or chemical smell.

6. Durable. Nothing to break down. Even cuts and tears can be mended with rubber cement.

7. Economical. Lasts longer. Less labor for production.

8. Quiet. No creaking. Absorbs sound.

9. Sanitary. Moth-, vermin-, mold-, and damp-proof.

10. Comfortable. More resilient. Compression in direct proportion to pressure.

Curled hair has a resiliency and springiness that makes it a good softening material. Coating the hair with latex rubber adds to its firmness and reduces the tendency to pack down.

Cotton felt is used for shaping and for distributing the weight within the cushion, but it is not used for softening alone.

Sisal, moss, excelsior, and cheaper materials found in household types of furniture are rarely found in office furniture because they cannot take the abuse. It does not pay to invest in this kind of upholstery.

Sponge rubber is rarely used in cushioning because it does not hold up as well as the other materials.

Base and Casters

The primary function of the chair base is to provide a stable foundation, one that does not tip easily. It must also give freedom of movement to the feet and legs. The bearing section that joins the chair to the base is one of the chair's most important features. Besides supporting the weight of the chair and occupant, the bearing must take sideward thrusts and rotation with ease and without excessive wear.

A commercial chair receives a great amount of use, and the casters receive every moment of it. A few dollars can be saved on a chair by selecting less expensive casters, but this should be discouraged. Most chairs can be furnished in two or more qualities of casters. Better bearings and better construction pay dividends.

Ball bearings are preferred in the axle and where the base rests on the caster. They give longer caster life and easier swiveling. The wheel diameter may be 1⅝ or 2 inches. The 2-inch wheels are preferred because they change position and "track" easier, are safer in rolling over objects on the floor, and are easier on the floor.

Caster treads are of two types. A rubber tread over a hard core is recommended on hard floors for more safety and working stability. They absorb vibration, do not roll as easily, and do not pit the floor. The hard tread is recommended for rugs or wherever free rolling is preferred.

WOOD FURNITURE vs. METAL FURNITURE

Wood and metal are naturally competitive in the office furniture industry. The fact that both continue to be used, often side by side, shows that each must have a place in the modern business office. Many office equipment dealers stock both wood and metal furniture.

As with other competitive products, advertising and sales tactics are not always of the best, and many careless statements are made on both sides. Metal and wood can each stand on its merits, and reputable manufacturers and salesmen do not make unfair comparisons.

The principal selling point for wood is its beauty—the same beauty that makes the business executive and secretary, alike, choose wood furniture for their homes.

Despite improved manufacturing processes, wood furniture has no "assembly line" look. No two desks are identical, since no two pieces of wood are exactly alike in pattern or design. The skill of the wood craftsmen in matching the grains of the woods brings out their beauty and personality.

No one will be able to tell you how durable wood is because, so far, no one knows. There are many pieces of wood furniture in existence today which are just as strong as when built hundreds of years ago. The Metropolitan Museum of Art has Jacobean furniture built in 1683. Other museums can produce thousands of antiques from all over the world to show that there is no limit on the length of time that wood will endure.

Should a wood desk become scratched or damaged, it can be easily repaired by the average reasonably competent workman, often right in the office. No long waits while the desk goes to the welder and spray booth.

The average metal desk weighs over 100 pounds more than a comparable wood desk. Because of the wood's lighter weight, wood furniture can be more quickly and economically moved when rearrangement is necessary, with less danger of damage.

No one will deny that wood will burn, whereas metal will not. If there were a lengthy, hot office fire, the wood desks might possibly be ignited, whereas metal desks would not. The *records* inside the desks, however, would be consumed in either case as if they were in a furnace. Any metal left would be twisted or warped beyond salvage. In fact, if the fire were not hot enough to ignite the desk, the insulation qualities of wood would do a better job of protecting the papers than would a metal desk which conducts heat rapidly. Only an *insulated*, fire-resistant metal desk would give better fire protection.

With the cooperation of the American Standards Association, the Administrative Management Society, and the Wood Office Furniture Institute, standards have been developed for wood furniture so that interchange of pieces and the matching of new pieces have been made easier. With close color control exercised by manufacturers, future matching of furniture is always possible. Even custom office interiors of wood paneling and built-ins can be matched with stock wood office furniture in color, finish, and style.

Modern metal desks are rugged, functionally designed, and durable. They have no splinters or rough edges to tear hosiery or clothing, or to injure the body. They will not warp in the presence of moisture, dryness, heat, or cold. They will not swell or shrink or absorb odors.

Replaceable parts are a distinct advantage of metal desks. Legs, tops, bases, suspensions, and even whole pedestals are easily replaced in the field if damaged. Drawers can also be rearranged to suit the need and convenience of the user, even after the desk has been in service for some time. Interchangeable units reduce the amount of inventory required by the office furniture dealer and yet make a wider selection possible.

Unsightly extension cords and equipment leads can be concealed in modern metal desks by the utilization of punch-outs in the bottom of the pedestals and in end panels and by the use of built-in clips for attaching connecting blocks. Manufacturers will furnish wiring diagrams if desired. Inside wiring retains the full beauty of the desk and reduces the hazard of tripping over exposed wires.

A sound-deadening material is frequently used to insulate the desk interiors. This makes the drawers quieter in operation, and also deadens the sound of bumps against the top or side panels.

DESK AND TABLE STANDARD DIMENSIONS
(American Standards Association)

	Wood	Metal
Double Pedestal	50 by 32 inches	50 by 30 inches
	52 by 32 inches	55 by 30 inches
	58 by 32 inches	60 by 30 inches
	60 by 34 inches	60 by 34 inches
Single Pedestal	42 by 32 inches	40 by 30 inches
	44 by 32 inches	45 by 30 inches
		45 by 34 inches
Tables	42 by 32 inches	45 by 30 inches
	44 by 32 inches	50 by 30 inches
	50 by 32 inches	55 by 30 inches
	52 by 32 inches	60 by 30 inches
	58 by 32 inches	60 by 34 inches
	60 by 34 inches	

Newer types of construction in steel desks allow for the interchangeability of the storage and file drawers so that the user can readjust the existing desk to fit any new requirement. The large file drawer normally takes up the space of two storage drawers, so that any two adjacent storage drawers can be taken out and a file drawer substituted. In most cases, a screwdriver and hammer are all the tools necessary to change the position of the file drawer. The storage drawers can be changed without tools.

Standard desk heights, recommended by the American Standards Association, are 29 inches or 30½ inches, or adjustable between these two heights. Most metal desks today are fitted with adjustable glides which allow the desks to be raised as much as 1½ inches to fit the proper seating requirements of the occupant. Adjustable glides also permit compensation for uneven floors, leveling the desk and eliminating rocking and vibration.

FILING EQUIPMENT

The top-grade file cabinets of today are more efficient in operation and hold more records than their counterparts of several years ago. New beauty in design, fittings, and color also improves the appearance of the modern office.

When you buy a file cabinet, you are primarily interested in getting a house for your records. But there are other considerations, too, or you would be just as satisfied with an equivalent number of packing boxes. In general, you want:

1. Space for records.
2. Ease of operation.
3. Durability.
4. Reasonable cost.

The better file cabinets will have improved methods for suspending the drawers, sturdier construction, and faster, quieter action. They will also have extra features like drop fronts and backs that increase the working space, dividers that keep contents in order, quick-acting compressors and follower-blocks that increase the pay load of the drawer.

A "file cabinet" is usually a standard correspondence file unless described otherwise. This is probably because correspondence files far outnumber all others in use. When discussing files, then, the logical place to start is with the correspondence file.

Correspondence Files

The various systems for filing correspondence have very little influence on the type of housing. The standard letter paper is 11 by 8½ inches and the office manager is interested in getting as many letters in as small a space as is practical, economical, and convenient. Aside from his interest in quality, he must consider the depth of the drawer from front to back and the number of drawers in the housing so as to balance floor area with utility. The actual drawer depths and the "available depths" after allowances for compressors, fronts, backs, and other fixtures, vary slightly from model to model and from manufacturer to manufacturer. The number of drawers to a cabinet, however, is a uniform selection available in all top-grade lines.

One-Drawer Cabinet. The single-drawer unit may be used alone or stacked on other cabinets. It is used frequently to increase the height of the standard four-drawer cabinets where floor space is not available and expansion is required. It is used for special or personal records on desks or tables, under windows, or for special space requirements. The single-drawer cabinet can be moved easily and so is useful in the small office, or where active records must be moved from place to place frequently. Traveling salesmen use this cabinet in the trunk of the car. As a word of advice, be sure that the back of the cabinet is anchored to prevent tipping when the full drawer is pulled open.

Two-Drawer Cabinet. The two-drawer cabinet is commonly called "desk high." It is popular for housing personal correspondence or active records which are better located alongside an employee's desk. It is often fitted with a composition top to match the desk and thus increase the desk's working area. Filing engineers point out that much wasted time and travel can be saved by a careful placement of pertinent, active records near the employees who use them most.

The desk-height unit will increase the working area of desks or tables and at the same time provide file space in the otherwise open area that would be wasted under a table. It is useful under windows, counters, tables, or wherever height is limited. A handy arrangement for active files is the use of a desk-height unit with a hinged or removable top which can be opened to expose the contents of the top drawer for faster reference. In this instance, the top drawer may be fixed so that it is actually a bin, while the bottom drawer functions in the normal way. Where it must be moved about frequently, the unit may be fitted with casters.

Three-Drawer Cabinet. The three-drawer cabinet is commonly called "counter high." It is used principally for constructing natural counters to separate the public from the office. It places those records close at hand which the employees use to serve the customer. For better appearance, the cabinet forming the counter may be fitted with composition top and special back trims or filler strips for the side facing the public. Special superstructures and grilles can also be attached to make collection counters. Similar counters may be used for working areas within the office or for making partitions between the various office departments without obstructing the view. A wide variety of drawers, cash drawers, safes, shelves, cupboards, and other units are often combined to utilize the entire counter area.

Four-Drawer Cabinet. This is the most popular office file cabinet size. The top drawer is at a height which makes it easily accessible for the average employee and the additional drawer provides a savings in valuable floor space over the counter-high units. A variety of drawer sizes can be obtained in the same cabinet. When placed in batteries, either in a single row or back to back, they serve very well as partitions for the departmental offices. They provide privacy without cutting off light and air circulation.

Five-Drawer Cabinet. The five-drawer cabinets are used when floor space is a problem, since they provide 25 percent more filing space than the conventional four-drawer cabinet in the same floor space area. This means that four five-drawer cabinets will give the same storage space as five four-drawer units. When used in a central file department, operating efficiency is generally increased because of the decreased distances required to operate the files. One extra drawer in height might lead one to wonder whether it would make the cabinet too high for the file clerk to operate efficiently. Actually, by trimming base heights and other space conservations, manufacturers produce a five-drawer unit that is only about half a drawer higher than the conventional four-drawer cabinet. Some models eliminate guide rods, others do not.

Most offices keep the records of the immediately previous period in the same cabinets with the active records because of the frequent reference. In the four-drawer cabinets, the two lower drawers are usually used for this storage. When five-drawer cabinets are used, the top drawer may also be used for inactive storage if the operators feel that it is too high for frequent operation.

Sectional Cabinets. An expanding upright cabinet is available for the small businessman who does not wish to start out with the standard sizes. The starter unit is made up of a top section and a base. Intermediate sections can then be added as needed between the top section and the base. No overall locking device can be used, of course, but individual drawer locks can be provided. The drawer inserts, described later, are usually not applicable to these sectional units. For an equivalent amount of filing capacity, the sectional upright is more expensive than the standard cabinets, so the businessman should be encouraged to purchase the solid cabinet in most cases.

Other Cabinet Selections

There are a number of other records sizes used in the modern office that require drawers of different sizes if the utmost in space economy and savings in operation are to be accomplished. Fortunately, business has standardized on forms sufficiently to allow the equipment manufacturers to offer these special-purpose cabinets as a standard line with resultant economy in production and final cost. Here are the more common special-purpose file cabinets:

Cap- or Legal-Size File. Legal forms are 13 by 8½ inches in the East and 14 by 8½ inches in the South and West. When stored vertically, they require a wider drawer than the correspondence file. Hence we find the legal- or cap-size files used especially in attorneys' offices, trust departments of banks, legal departments of banks and business offices, and government court and legal offices.

Document File. When the legal papers described above are folded, as in the case of insurance policies, deeds, leases, and the like, they are commonly filed upright, resting on the narrow dimension. The standard drawer depth and widths are used, but the drawer is divided into two or three compartments and labeled accordingly. The compartments are proportionately wider in the cap-size drawers.

Legal-Blank File. The legal-blank file holds a number of shallow drawers for the flat filing of legal blanks. Removable partitions within the drawer allow several stacks of blanks to be filed in one drawer without intermixing. Colored separators or other methods can be used to allow storing several forms in one stack. Lawyers, insurance firms, and stationers are common users of legal-blank files.

These deeper files are not limited to legal blanks. They have been used successfully for such materials as blueprints, circulars, contracts, electros and halftones, paper samples, photographs, proofs, sheet music, and advertising materials.

Storage File. File cabinets with drawers the same size as the standard letter, cap, or file drawers may be obtained for general or specific purposes. The drawer will be the same general dimension but will have flat bottom and side panels. The sides will also be higher to provide greater capacity than regular drawers used for storage.

The standard-size drawer is for "deep storage," the half-size drawer for "shallow storage." A "jumbo" file with oversize drawers is also available for photographs, X-ray films, artwork, and stencils. Art and photography come high. One spoiled job could easily pay for the cabinet.

Instead of a drawer, a door may be fitted to the standard drawer opening in the cabinet to form a storage compartment. Ordinary shelves or roller shelves may be included. A combination of storage compartments and regular drawers in one cabinet is especially popular for counter units.

A roller shelf is used for record books, drawings, charts, maps, and similar large or bulky materials. It is used especially by public departments, banks, and private businesses using heavy record books, catalogs, and the like. In many cases, roller units are combined with document file sections in vaults or record storage areas. Any record housed in heavy binders can be handled and stored easily on roller shelves.

Check File. Every modern business pays its bills by check. It is the safe way to transfer cash and provides an evidence and record of payment. The returned canceled checks are kept by the originator for audit and for evidence of payment. A check file with a slightly narrower width and with drawers shorter in height is ideal for large businesses and banks to use for storage and reference. The cabinet contains approximately nine drawers. Fillers can be placed in the drawers to fit them for shorter checks.

Banks require large numbers of check files for guiding and guarding the checks until they are turned over to the depositor. Savings and thrift departments also use check files for withdrawal forms which are permanently retained. Collection departments use them for their own forms and for payment checks. Business offices, especially payroll and accounting departments, are likely prospects.

Invoice File. Most invoices are narrower than the standard letter paper and when large quantities of invoices must be handled, it is more economical to conserve space with an invoice file. The file is narrower and the drawers are shorter so that five drawers are usually available in a standard-height cabinet. Although insert fillers and spacers may be obtained to convert the standard file drawer, an invoice file should be used whenever five or more drawers are needed.

Ledger File. Offices using card ledgers, either machine or hand posted, must have some housing for the filled and closed account cards or sheets. While they are active, they are commonly kept in tub equipment for faster reference and recording operations. The ledger record is usually longer than the other types and calls for a higher drawer than the standard. Consequently, the ledger file has drawers of standard width, but higher. Three drawers will usually be provided in a standard height cabinet. Other records of similar size, such as daily reports, auditors' reports, and schedules, will also use a ledger file.

Standard Card File. Although the regular letter- and cap-size cabinets can be altered to house card files, the larger offices which use quantities of card records prefer to use special cabinets designed especially for them. A greater number of records can be filed in an equivalent amount of cabinet space, and the cost of rent, equipment, and operating time is consequently less. Through space conservation during construction, these special cabinets will hold a larger number of drawers in the standard heights than will the converted letter cabinets.

The common card sizes in inches are 5 by 3, 6 by 4, 5 by 8, 8 by 8, and 9 by 6. The widths of cabinets vary to fit the card size. Ordinarily, two rows of cards are provided for in each drawer. In the case of the 5- by 3-inch card, however, three rows are possible in a cap-size drawer.

Card Record Desk. A special desk which combines a card cabinet with a working table surface is especially popular for use when one operator works on a selected portion of the card records for reference or posting. The cards are filed in trays which can be removed and placed on the adjacent desk during posting. The trays may run from front to back or they may be placed crosswise in the drawer and facing the operator for easier reference. The drawers are generally proportioned to take five 5- by 3-inch card trays, four 6- by 4-inch card trays, or three 8- by 5-inch card trays. Five- or six-drawer heights are most common.

Tabulating Card File. Cards used in tabulating equipment must be kept in perfect order and condition. Torn or bent edges will cause trouble with the machines. The drawers or card trays must also be removable for transporting the cards to the tabulating machines and back again. During the moving, the compressors must hold the cards securely to keep them from falling out and becoming damaged and disordered.

Impairment Card File. Insurance companies have a standard form called an impairment card. It is about 2¼ by 3 inches, and is filed on the short dimension. A drawer of standard width, though shallower, will contain four compartments for four rows of cards. Twelve drawers high is the usual cabinet capacity.

Magnetic Card Trays. Metal strips are imbedded in the record card during manufacture. A special card tray utilizes the repelling force of the magnet to separate one record card from the other when the pressure is released. The amount of separation is sufficient to make the top edge of the card visible in the same manner as other visible systems. Additional information can be obtained from the manufacturer.

Desk Files. Some types of records are housed best in a desk. Many of the modern desks are equipped with a letter-file drawer, but they may also contain cap-size files, card files, or any of the other combinations. When the pertinent records are kept near the person using them most frequently, much traveling time and delay can be saved. Even with the efficient central filing systems, provision is usually made for certain essential records to be kept by executives, and for active records to be kept near the employee using them most frequently.

Portable Files. A portable file may be used for personal records, records used primarily by one individual, followup or pending material, and for materials borrowed for a time from the regular files. The portable file is also used frequently for a sorter to place papers in sequence before filing. A bin resembling a standard file drawer is fitted with four legs to bring it up to. desk height. Casters are added for portability and a removable or hinged lid gives added protection. Locks may also be added. Hanging or regular folders and guides may be used in the same manner as in standard file drawers. Executive models frequently have a regular file drawer under the bin, making the portable file equivalent in storage to the two-drawer cabinet.

All-in-One File. A combination for the small office is the storage cabinet and file placed side by side in the same cabinet. The height is usually about counter high. Various combinations of letter and card drawers may be had for one side and the storage side may have shelves and drawers. The whole unit may be enclosed by doors or the door may close off only the storage portion.

Vault Truck File. Although the popular vault truck is one built from selected horizontal file sections, unusual conditions sometimes require custom-built trucks. Besides inclusion of the standard record drawers, provisions may be made for including removable ledger and card trays. Hinged covers provide protection for the records when not in use.

The vault truck saves many miles of walking on the part of office employees who would otherwise have to walk to and from the vault when working with the records. Walking might be a healthful activity, but it still costs the boss money without any production to show for it. There is added safety in case of fire. With a reasonable amount of warning, the truck can be wheeled into the vault before the office is evacuated, thus saving valuable records. Part of the office fire drill should include this maneuver.

Standardizing Office Equipment

Standardization of equipment is an important consideration in the purchase of office furniture. Standardization and uniformity of material, color, and design of the desks, chairs, tables, filing equipment, bookcases, and similar equipment provide easier interchangeability, possible lower cost on quantity purchases, and better appearance of the office.

Needless to say, extreme thought and care should be given to the selection of the line in which to standardize. A poor choice at the beginning will be magnified each time new equipment is added until the standard is modified or abandoned.

Complete replacement is naturally the best plan if the desk and chairs are old and obsolete. But if the budget will not stand the immediate cost, and if the executive heads will not make a special appropriation, the next best plan is the modernization of one or two units at a time. This is better than replacing isolated desks and chairs throughout the whole office in a hit-and-miss fashion.

Let's suppose, for example, that you located a total of 10 desks throughout the office which needed immediate replacement. If they were replaced where they stood by modern desks, the new desks would look strangely out of place and employee dissatisfaction and jealousy might result.

LEASING vs. PURCHASING EQUIPMENT

A trend that seems to be gaining momentum is the idea of leasing capital equipment rather than buying it. Business firms now lease rather than own their buildings; railroads lease rolling stock; and offices lease furniture and machines. Here are some reasons advanced for leasing:

1. It ties up less working capital. There is less cash outlay than in outright purchase. The same money invested in merchandise or in other projects can bring greater return.

2. Leasing is practical for cost-plus contracts which require strict allocation of expense.

3. It is helpful to companies whose future needs are uncertain. Equipment needed at the moment may not be permanently useful.

4. It provides a new way to write off expense for tax purposes. Rather than being required to use an accepted method of depreciation, the lessee can write off each payment as current operating expense.

5. Under leasing, there is no need to retain obsolescent equipment.

Leasing Plans

Leasing plans vary according to location and the methods of operation of individual dealers. Leasing rates depend on the age of the equipment and the length of the lease. Rate of obsolescence is also a factor. A machine, for example, may become obsolete sooner than a desk, so the dealer will want to get his cost back sooner.

Assuming that new equipment is leased, a typical monthly rental charge for short-term leases is 10 percent of the selling price with the first month's rent increased slightly to reflect delivery and installation charges. Typewriters and adding machines are usually rented at flat weekly or monthly rates.

The most common long-term leasing contract is for three years. While some contracts have flat monthly rates, the more common schedule is one with gradually declining rates.

An option to purchase is frequently a part of the contract. Such contracts usually allow a few months' rent to apply toward the purchase price should the lessee decide to buy.

Contracts can be written to permit title of the equipment to pass to the lessee after a given number of payments, or with the payment of a token amount. While often posed as a tax saving, this type of contract actually has doubtful tax advantage. The Internal Revenue Service treats these agreements, whether stated or implied, as conditional sales or installment sales and will not permit such payments to be charged to operating expense. Better check with your accountant or tax attorney first.

Traditional filing cabinets are giving ground to new units that take less space and hold more information. Above, a Remington Records Retrieval shelf.

An Expert Predicts Office Furniture Trends

One of the best-known names in the office-furniture field is that of The Globe-Wernicke Co., of Cincinnati, Ohio. Asked by the editors of this HANDBOOK to give our readers the benefit of his expert opinion on trends in office furniture, R. Herman Hammer, president of Globe-Wernicke, replied:

The growth of the office furniture industry in the past 10 years has been dynamic but during this period the concept of office furniture has changed drastically. There are several reasons for this.

First of all, the architect, designer, and interior decorator play an ever-increasingly important role in the selection of office furniture. Previously, the architect felt that his assignment was complete when the new building was completely erected and ready for occupancy; he was not involved in the selection of the furniture that was going to be placed in the offices that he had so carefully designed. That was, more or less, left up to the office manager or the office furniture supply house.

That is all changed now. Today the architect is not only concerned with, but in most cases actually dictates the type of furniture that he believes is suitable for the new building he has engineered. He wants to be sure that it further enhances the appearance of the building and that it is harmonious, colorful, and efficient.

The same is true of the interior decorator, who is stressing color coordination and design not only in private offices but in general offices as well. Henry Ford once said "I will give you any color car you want as long as it is black," and we office-furniture manufacturers used to say that we would give a customer any color he wanted as long as it was either green or gray. Today we furnish equipment in scores of colors and in most cases our equipment is multicolored in order to match the decor of the office itself. Color will continue to play an increasingly important part in the selection of office furniture.

New materials are being developed almost daily that can be used in office furniture to make them more attractive and more practical. Laminated plastics have replaced linoleum tops. Desks formerly made entirely of wood or of metal are now a combination of wood, metal, plastics, Fiberglas, etc. This trend will continue.

The use of conventional flat-top desks will diminish, as these are replaced with what will be termed "work stations." These will be either L-shaped or U-shaped for maximum efficiency. The executive who has his desk top cluttered with gadgets be believes he needs will find that more and more of these are built into his work station.

Examples of this are the Visible Reference Card File which is built directly into the arm slide of a desk; the telephone installed into the L-shaped or credenza unit; cupboard sections and sliding bookcase doors—all within his arm's length.

Using "Prefab" Combinations in Office Furniture

Homer B. Smith, Director of Merchandising and Training for the National Stationery and Office Equipment Association, said recently:

"Office executives, faced with the task of getting out more work, with rising space costs, and with the difficulty of attracting and keeping good workers, will increasingly replace desks with stock modular office furniture units available from their local office furniture dealers.

"Only a few years ago they had to design the units themselves and pay the high cost of custom building. Now the local dealer can bolt together any of hundreds of combinations of tops, pedestals, drawers, and cabinets to build a work station around each employee that is not only more efficient, but more comfortable and more beautiful as well.

"The new L-shaped and U-shaped units are replacing the space-wasting older desks, not only in the general office but also in the executive offices. Beautiful wood and colorful metal modular units go together as easily as Junior's Erector set to give every office worker his working tools within arm's reach."

The Burroughs E1100 Electronic Computing/Accounting machine speeds up production through instant electronic multiplication and storage of fixed factors in the memory. Unit automatically computes and prints a new balance for account and stores the amount to provide an overall total.

Chapter 49

OFFICE MACHINERY AND EQUIPMENT

L ABOR costs constitute the largest single expense item in operating an office. Good management dictates, therefore, that office workers be furnished the best tools which will get the work done most efficiently. A scarcity of qualified workers stimulated the greater use of office machines, and current high wages continue the demand and search for machines which will reduce labor costs in a greater amount than the investment in the machines.

Equipment is not an expense, it is an investment. It is a good investment if it can pay for itself in a reasonable time in reduced labor costs. It is a good investment if it produces needed information for more profitable operation of the business even at the expense of increased labor costs, providing that management considers the information worth more than the cost of producing it. If a piece of equipment cannot justify its cost in either of these ways, then it is not a good investment. These are the usual justifications for new or additional equipment:

1. To produce needed records available in no other way.

2. To produce records more conveniently, faster, in better condition than the current method.

3. To reduce labor and thus the cost of labor.

4. To bring specialization which increases speed, reduces cost.

5. To provide information important to the function and control of business not now available.

People starting new businesses or opening new offices frequently go overboard in buying expensive equipment. It is obviously better to start with the minimum amount of essential equipment and add new items as their need is justified and the money to buy them becomes available.

Standardization of Equipment

Standardization of make and kind of equipment may bring about some savings and conveniences, but it can also have enough limitations so that it should not be followed blindly. These are the main points that are usually advanced in favor of standardizing office equipment:

1. It reduces the need for training transferred employees.

2. It simplifies maintenance and repair work.

3. It permits quantity discounts in purchasing.

As long as management is willing to provide the best equipment for the job to be done regardless of standardization, then a reasonable amount of standardization can be beneficial. Standardization for its own sake, however, can be costly in efficiency.

Trade-in Policies

As modern office machines continually improve, the ones in use are more apt to become obsolete than become worn out. At the same time, a company cannot buy every new machine that comes out. Some plan is usually adopted whereby the company buys the best new machine for the job and keeps it until its efficiency has been reduced to the point where it can be traded in on a new machine without too much loss.

Normal accounting procedure frequently depreciates office assets over a period of 10 years. Some special-purpose machines, like book-keeping machines, may depreciate through obsolescence much sooner. But for income-tax purposes, most office equipment may be depreciated over a period of 10 years. For these reasons, it might be wise to establish a depreciation policy which will permit absorbing the cost of the machines and making them available for trade-in at that time. While machines may give satisfactory service after the depreciation period, the cost of repairs, trade-in values, and tax considerations should induce the office manager to study the use of each machine carefully.

Selecting Office Machines

The existence of a machine which will perform a task now done manually does not, in itself, justify its purchase. Manual operation of the task may still be more satisfactory. While machines usually offer advantages, there should be a careful determination of the need for a machine before buying it.

Here are some factors to consider when determining the need for an office machine:

1. *Volume of work.* Will the savings in clerical time, better service, or faster completion of the work justify the new machine?

2. *Accuracy requirements.* What is the degree of accuracy required? Will the machine eliminate checking and rechecking steps through its features?

3. *Speed.* A machine is often justified for work involving deadlines, rush jobs, and peak loads.

4. *Routine work.* Some tasks are so monotonous that it is difficult to procure and keep employees at the job. Even where no savings are obtained, a machine may be justified for morale and employee relations benefits.

5. *Reduced costs.* This is the area that is given the greatest consideration when purchase of a machine is contemplated. If the machine will reduce clerical costs sufficiently to pay for itself in three years, it is usually considered a good investment. The clerical labor it releases, of course, should be utilized in other work before it can be credited as a saving through the use of the machine.

It is sometimes difficult to distinguish between several machines which will do a particular job well, yet the choice must still be made. Here are some factors to consider:

1. *Ease of operation.* Faster operation, less fatigue, and fewer errors go with ease of operation. Here are some contributing factors: indexing the amounts, operating the motor bar or handle, operating control keys, visibility of printed result, recording the answer. Simplicity of operation is an important factor in training operators efficiently and with the least expense.

2. *Flexibility.* Unless there is enough work to keep a highly specialized machine busy, it is usually better to select one with sufficient flexibility to be used for different types of work. Often, without this flexibility, a machine would not be justified at all.

3. *Durability.* A machine is used by different people under varying conditions. Without durability, the machine becomes a poor investment.

4. *Portability.* A machine is frequently moved from user to user or from various spots in the same work area. Compactness and ease of handling save time and energy and increase the use of the machine. Modern machines have been reduced in size and weight without sacrificing quality.

5. *Adaptability.* If the machine can be used without disrupting an existing system, it is possibly a better choice than one which requires considerable rearrangement of the forms and records involved, extensive recopying of information, and adjustments in related procedures.

6. *Service.* Reliable and continuous performance demands quick repairs and proper maintenance. The machine which can be serviced promptly has the advantage.

7. *Operating cost.* This includes such things as supplies, space occupied, special equipment, forms, repairs, etc.

8. *Reputation of the supplier.* Few of us are experts in judging the mechanical qualities of a machine, so we must depend upon the integrity of the manufacturer and the dealer to furnish a good machine and to back up claims and guarantees.

9. *Styling.* Modern offices require machines which are pleasing and modern in design, compatible in color. In addition to the elements pleasing to the eye, however, there are other design functions which should appeal to the touch and hearing, too. These include convenient keyboard; simple motor bars; properly placed control keys; uniform action of all keys and levers; quiet operation; and neat, legible printing.

10. *Cost.* Cost, not necessarily purchase price, is a major factor in buying a machine. Frequently a machine higher in purchase price than another proves to be a better buy in the long run. If two machines are still comparable when checked against the factors of labor savings, maintenance costs, supplies and durability, and the rest, then the net purchase price may be the deciding factor. The net price considers trade-in allowances for present equipment and the expected residual values after depreciation is taken into account.

Control of Office Machines

Records of each machine should be maintained in a central spot, preferably in the possession of the person in charge of maintenance. These records will identify each machine in the offices, show their location, the work they do, and the amount and frequency of maintenance charges. A typical method of keeping the records is to have separate cards for each machine so that replacements can be made easily.

A complete inventory of all machines should be made to set up the records. The record card will show such information as the serial number of the machine, the model number, name of manufacturer, date of purchase, new or used when purchased, cost, and location. Machines should also be identified as to purpose (calculator, adder, etc.), and the records may be filed initially by purpose.

Space should be provided on the machine record card for the date and description of maintenance work and repair charges. The recorded dates of maintenance work will help to make sure the machines are inspected regularly.

12 QUESTIONS TO ASK BEFORE BUYING A SECONDHAND ADDING MACHINE

1. What kind of use has it had? In some places, an adding machine gets more use in two years than it would normally in 15.

2. Has the machine been dropped? If it has, parts may be sprung or cracked which will cause it to add wrong after a short time.

3. How old is it? Outward appearances tell little. The serial number helps, but it can be altered or disguised.

4. Has it been in a fire? Fire takes the temper out of metal. Such a machine could not be expected to hold up. Damaged cases can be refinished to look good.

5. Has the outside case been refinished or transferred from another machine to hide its age or damage?

6. Where has the machine been used? Damp areas? In dusty areas? Rust and grit do damage to parts.

7. Has the mechanism been strained? Forcing the machine can spring parts which cause trouble later.

8. Has the machine been regularly cleaned and oiled? Bad care shortens machine life.

9. Have worn and broken parts been replaced with factory parts? Substitute parts and homemade parts may work for a time, give out later.

10. Has the machine been stolen? A bill of sale doesn't necessarily mean a clear title. Legal entanglements and ill will, plus loss of the machine, could occur if the title isn't clear.

11. What is the new price of the machine? Sellers may jack up the new list price beyond what it is worth to make the machine look like a bargain. Even though the machine originally sold for the price mentioned, a new one might cost much less today.

12. What about a guarantee? Could the seller back up his guarantee? What is his reputation? Is there danger he could be out of business in a few weeks?

The advantages of centralized control of machines are:

1. Dates for orderly buying and selling of machines are established and observed.

2. Such control allows timing of trading machines to secure maximum service and allowances.

3. It permits machines to be used on jobs for which they are best suited.

4. It makes it possible to use the machines where they are actually needed throughout the office.

5. Adequate maintenance with controlled costs is assured.

How 600 Companies Care For and Maintain Office Equipment

Whether they represent large or small offices, executives contributing to this study are in complete accord that it is not only good business but common sense that policies be established and followed for the care and maintenance of office equipment. Systems vary, but not one of the 600 contributing executives said, "We have no policy whatsoever." Total number of employees working in the 600 surveyed offices is 430,168. Size of work forces ranges from three employees to 17,132. Types of business included in the study range from insurance companies, publishing concerns, banks, hospitals, and paperboard manufacturers to shoe manufacturers, utilities, metal products, and personal loan establishments. Thirty-eight states are represented in the survey.

Who Is Responsible?

The office manager is the executive charged with seeing that equipment is properly maintained and cared for in 50 percent of the companies. Here is the tabulation:

Office manager	50 percent
Ass't. office manager	3 percent
Office service manager	3 percent
Office department heads	6 percent
Other executives	38 percent

"Other department heads" include such executives as "respective department heads," "vice-president," "operations manager," "manager of purchasing," "operations officers." Nationwide Insurance Company, Columbus, Ohio, has a property maintenance supervisor who is responsible for sanitation and maintenance of grounds, buildings, and equipment. In the case of Weston Instruments, Newark, New Jersey, the manager of office services says, "Usually the department head where the equipment is located assumes the responsibility. In other instances an office service clerk keeps the equipment records."

Who Does the Work?

Outside services do the actual maintenance and repair work in 73 percent of the responding companies. However, some executives qualified their statements as follows:

"Outsiders are used for IBM and specialized equipment. Our own maintenance staff takes care of typewriters and simple machines. Isolated locations use local factory maintenance men to clear trouble—bills are checked by centralized maintenance group."

"Factory maintenance men take care of calculators, printing equipment, and Dictaphones. We use an independent service agency for typewriters, adding machines, etc."

"Both outside servicemen and our own maintenance staff care for office equipment. Typewriters, adding machines, and so forth, are maintained by our staff. Calculators, Dictaphones, IBM equipment handled by outsiders."

Advantages of Present Procedures

Reasons why most companies prefer to have equipment maintenance handled by factory representatives range from "makes life simpler for all of us" to "uniformity of recordkeeping." Typical comments follow:

"Uniformity of recordkeeping. Scheduling of work at office convenience. Clear line of responsibility."

"We are in the process of changing over most of our service from a contract to a call basis. This involves a little more clerical work on our part, but so far indicates a savings over maintenance contracts without appreciable loss of efficiency."

"They (outside service groups) do a better job of maintaining their own products. Periodic service and inspection is good preventive maintenance."

"I do not believe our procedure has any particular advantages unless it is simplicity. Except on our tabulating machines, we have very few service calls. It has been our experience that the charges for service on typewriters is less than 25 percent of what a service agreement would be."

"We have consolidated almost all of our maintenance work with one local firm, by contract, on a trial basis, rather than have work done by manufacturers. So far it is working well."

"Equipment seems to last longer and give less trouble when under regular maintenance contract."

Arguments for use of a company maintenance staff are found in the comments of some executives whose concerns use such staffs:

"Having our own serviceman for majority of equipment saves greatly, especially in time saved. If we had to call a serviceman for each typewriter or calculating machine, we would either have to carry a supply of loan machines or lose the time while the machine is out of condition. Now it is done on the spot. Also, the cost of maintenance would be greater than the salary paid to servicemen."

"With the large number of typewriters in service we feel we can do our own repair and inspection cheaper, and better, than by regular maintenance contract."

"Two bad experiences with manufacturer service led us to a policy of employing a man to do all of the work at our main office. He has been with us two years and we can show quite a saving over outside service and inspection. Of course, this man isn't doing equipment servicing full time, but he has proved very valuable."

Analyzing types of companies doing service within the organization, Dartnell editors found this type of office care usually is associated with larger concerns, the smaller offices relying on outside service. However, in the 73 percent using factory service, there are a number of large companies listed, too.

Encouraging Employees to Take Care of Office Equipment

Twenty percent of the office executives contributing to this survey represent firms with "no set policy" in encouraging employee care of office equipment. However, one executive qualifies his reply by adding, "This doesn't mean that we are careless about it. Abuses are handled individually; new employees are encouraged to treat machines well as part of their orientation."

Twenty percent of the offices require employees to use covers on their equipment and keep machines dusted. An executive of the Herbst Shoe Manufacturing Company, Milwaukee, Wisconsin, says employees get memos at periodic intervals on the matter of care of office equipment. The employee handbook also covers the matter.

Standard practice at Public Service Company of New Mexico, Albuquerque, is a policy whereby "employees are cautioned and instructed, when found in error." Training classes and individual instruction are used by Hardware Mutuals, Newark, New Jersey. The office manager of Franklin Electric Company, Inc., Bluffton, Indiana, tells Dartnell editors, "Necessary material for first-echelon maintenance is given each machine operator together with full instructions on its use. Service necessitated by poor employee practices is called to their attention."

Some of the late-model electric figuring machines available for the modern office. Above, an electric adding machine by Olivetti Underwood. Right, the Victor 3900 electronic calculator which saves staff and executives hours of paper-and-pencil figurework. Below, Royal electric adding machine has standard-size keyboard, a 10-column listing and an 11-column total.

Using Manuals or Written Instructions on Machine Care

Except for instruction books that come with new equipment, less than 80 percent of the offices use manuals or written instructions on care and maintenance of equipment. The Kimberly-Clark executive joining in this exchange of experience says, "We have no manuals other than those included with equipment like Dictaphones or typewriters. Our servicemen have service manuals. We tell our people to call them when anything seems out of operating condition. The simple cleaning of typewriters is done by the individual."

Experience With Maintenance Contracts

Here is the way respondents indicated success with service contracts:

Excellent	10 percent
Very good	6 percent
Good	43 percent
Fair	6 percent
Poor	12 percent

"Too expensive" was a complaint of six executives. Other comments follow:

"Favorable with more expensive pieces of equipment."

"Varied—most maintenance contracts have been of some value."

"Can be too costly if 'across the board.' "

"We feel we do not get full use of them, as our machines don't get heavy usage and service calls are infrequent."

Basic Types of Figuring Machines

Figuring devices range from simple charts, tables, and scales to the most involved electronic equipment. Many specialized departments do a large portion of their figuring work with tables and charts previously prepared. Plastic scales operating on the slide-rule principle are used for simple jobs like computing wages, discounts, prices, and the like.

As we get into figuring machines, we find simple ones like the small desk-type unit with a series of rotating dials operated by hand like dialing a telephone. Other units could almost be called pocket calculators.

True figuring machines, such as are used in the office today, can be divided into the following classifications:

1. Adding and calculating.
2. Listing and nonlisting.

3. Full keyboard and 10-key.

4. Key-driven and rotary-driven.

5. Hand-operated and electric.

1. *Adding and calculating machines.* Technically, a machine which performs the four fundamental arithmetic operations is a calculating machine. Since multiplication and division *can* be done on an adding machine, we must distinguish further. The calculator is made to do the multiplication, and particularly the division problems, much more quickly than the standard adding machine. Another distinction is that it is most often a nonlisting machine rather than listing.

2. *Listing and nonlisting.* A listing machine prints the numbers of the problem on a roll of tape or sheet of paper. A nonlisting machine records the numbers only in a register so that the answers must be copied. Checking on a nonlisting machine can be done only by reworking the problem.

3. *Full keyboard and 10-key.* The full-keyboard machine has from 6 to 14 columns of numbers from 1 to 9. The zero is printed automatically in any column in which no number key is depressed. On the 10-key machine, there is only one key for each digit, zero through 9, or a total of 10 keys plus controls. The digits of a number must be recorded in the proper order, including the zeros. The relative speed of these two types of machines with equally skilled operators is so similar that it is usually just a matter of personal preference.

4. *Key-driven and rotary-driven.* In a key-driven machine, a number is added into the machine as soon as its key is depressed. In a rotary machine, the complete number is first set up and then a motor bar or lever is depressed to record the number into the machine. The key-driven machine is always nonlisting and full keyboard. The rotary machine may be full or 10-key.

5. *Hand-operated and electric.* While the less expensive machines are the hand-operated type, electric models have been reduced in cost to the extent that approximately 80 percent of adding machine sales are now electric models.

Accounting Machines

Accounting machines are distinguished from standard adding and calculating machines through their capacities to do other jobs besides figuring. They can print descriptive information in billing, sort figures into separate registers for separate totals, and tabulate automatically to fit preprinted record forms. Their degree of complexity can vary greatly, increasing with the number of registers and with the type of descriptive keyboard offered.

Accounting machines take many forms, often classified additionally as billing machines, posting machines, bookkeeping machines, etc., although there is no clear distinction between them. While they can be designed for many different uses, they all perform the same operations: writing and calculating.

The combination of writing and calculating in any one machine is determined by its purpose. Some do only writing, like the hand-operated autographic registers. Others do both writing and computing, like the flat-bed billing machine. In principle, the operator must depress the proper keys to enter the information, but the movement of the machine for the proper entries on the forms is preset to function automatically.

NCR adding machines combine a number of features, including automatic step-over multiplication, automatic clear signal, selective answer-only printing, choice of single or multiple cipher bars, and paper spacing before and after printing the totals. The "answer-printer" avoids unnecessary printing of computation detail where only the total is desired.

Electric and Automatic Typewriters

Although the electric typewriter is almost as old as the manual typewriter, it is only in recent years that it has gained popularity for general office typing. At first preferred because of its more uniform and more forceful stroke in making carbon copies, the electric is now becoming popular for executive correspondence, typing for reproduction, and even general correspondence where good appearance is important.

While speed tests are now commonly won by typists using electric typewriters, the relative speed of the electric and manual in an office is not too important in the selection of one or the other machine.

Since the stroking and carriage return are performed mechanically, operators say there is less fatigue. The newer manual typewriters, however, have improved ease of manipulation.

Increased use of offset duplication has brought into being the carbon paper ribbon for the electric typewriter. This eliminates the pattern of the cloth ribbon and makes sharper characters.

Electric typewriters can be obtained with "proportional" spacing which simulates the spacing of regular printing. Attachments are also available which permit the typist to justify or align the right margin more easily. These features, plus the selection of a printing-style type and the carbon ribbon, make it possible to produce typing for offset work which closely resembles actual type-set printing.

Offsetting the advantages of the electric typewriter is its increased cost and the period of readjustment for the typist.

When form or part-form letters are practical and when the effect of actual typing is desired, the automatic typewriter may provide the answer. The automatic typewriter is a combination electric typewriter and an actuating mechanism which reproduces letters of identical text except where personal items like address and salutation are typed manually. One model utilizes a player-piano-type paper roll with punched holes to actuate the typing mechanism. Another type operates on punched tape. One operator can keep a bank of several machines operating simultaneously, going from one to the other to insert paper and type the personal items manually, then starting the automatic typewriter to finish the letter.

Punched Card Machines

Two basic types of machines use punched cards. One type uses punched holes and notches located around the card edges, and the other type uses cards punched throughout the card area.

Notched card machines (McBee Keysort) are used principally to speed up sorting. Holes around the edges are assigned meanings depending on their location. Identification is made by cutting out or notching the portion of the card between the hole and the edge. The machine selector picks out the cards with sorting needles. The cards notched at a particular classification position drop away from the needle while those with the hole still intact remain on the needle.

Punched card accounting machines are of two types, the Hollerith (International Business Machines) and the Powers (Remington Rand Div., Sperry Rand). They are similar in function, but different in motivating power. The former uses rectangular holes, the latter round holes.

The basic machines for a punched card system are:

1. A punching machine: to insert the information on the card by punching the holes according to a predetermined code. The machine can be operated manually or as a gang punch.

2. A sorting machine: to arrange the cards quickly according to any desired alphabetic or numerical sequence.

3. A tabulator: to prepare printed reports from the data on the punched and sorted cards.

Punched cards were first used only for statistical analysis, but now they can be used for almost any accounting function. Except for the original punching, all other processing can be entirely automatic once the cards are inserted in the machines. The volume of work rather than the size of a company is the criterion for deciding whether the cost of a card equipment installation is justified. The cost of the machines is high, so they must be in almost continual use.

Addressing and Listing Machines

There are two basic types of addressing and listing machines: embossed metal plates and fiber stencils. The stencils can be prepared on a typewriter but the metal plates require a special embossing machine. In general, the metal plate is preferred where the volume is large and the plates are used frequently.

Addressing machines are used to address letters, cards, tags, and labels. They also can be set to prepare lists accurately spaced, and are used in many accounting systems for imprinting repetitive data of any kind. Punched holes can be used to translate information like punched-card machines do.

A cutoff device can be used which permits only part of a plate to print. A selector can also be used which permits preselected plates to pass through the machine while others are stopped for printing. The advantage of the selector is that the sequence of the plates remains the same after the run.

10 WAYS TO USE EQUIPMENT EFFICIENTLY

1. *Schedule the Use of Equipment.* Equipment falls into two categories from the standpoint of use: Regular equipment needed on a day-to-day basis, which is integrated into the procedures used in handling paper work; standby equipment required for the peak production period, which is used on a temporary basis. By scheduling

such equipment as calculators and adding machines, greater economy of operation can be attained with less investment than if each department is equipped with full-load equipment, part of which is idle during the month.

2. *Provide Proper Maintenance.* Maintenance of mechanical equipment is the biggest problem of the medium- to small-sized office. Many large companies, with several hundred pieces of equipment, have their own maintenance departments. Smaller companies cannot afford to do this. Almost all equipment manufacturers provide maintenance service under contract terms. A maintenance contract on mechanical equipment provides for regular inspection and ordinary maintenance which will prolong the useful life of the equipment. It is suggested that this service be contracted for, and a record kept on each piece of equipment, showing maintenance expense and the service rendered under the contract.

3. *See That Equipment Is Covered at Night.* Dust and dirt are the principal enemies of office equipment, particularly machines having moving parts, such as typewriters, bookkeeping machines, calculators, and dictating equipment. All machines should be covered at night to protect the equipment from dust which may be raised during the cleaning of the offices.

4. *Train Employees in the Proper Use of Equipment.* Any machine used by an untrained person will suffer more wear than when operated by a trained employee. Training will include ordinary care of the machine, such as preventing eraser dust from falling into the key mechanism—ink erasers contain abrasives. When the eraser dust falls into the machine, it adds to the wear and tear of operation. Training will include the proper understanding and use of the machine for highest efficiency. Many equipment manufacturers operate training schools in order to provide skilled personnel.

5. *Survey Each System Before Purchasing Equipment.* The machine should fit the system and not the system fit the machine. This seems rather elementary, but often a machine is purchased and the system built around the machine. Most equipment manufacturers maintain research and methods departments that can render invaluable assistance in developing a system which will accomplish the desired objective by the use of certain mechanical equipment. Survey and analyze the problem. Study each step in the routine before purchasing any equipment.

6. *Centralize Office Functions of a Related Nature.* Office equipment, to do its best work, requires volume. Office equipment is essen-

tially a means of doing volume work without a proportional increase in manual labor. In order to produce sufficient volume, related functions are centralized. Central service departments which handle duplicating, transcribing, typing, and calculating are becoming common in industry. Centralization produces flexibility and economy of operation.

7. *Standardize on Kind, Size, and Type of Equipment.* To get the greatest use out of office machines, many people must be able to use them. Training becomes more difficult when different makes of the same type of machine are used. It may be necessary to standardize on certain makes, rather than buy several different types of calculators, typewriters, or duplicators. The equipment industry would be the first to agree that some standardization is essential to the efficient use of office machines.

8. *Develop a Trade-In Policy.* Few office managers have developed a policy to guide them on equipment replacement under normal circumstances. One policy, which is effective, states that when the cost of repairing a machine is equal to, or greater than, the book value (cost, less depreciation) there is a case for replacement and trade-in. This formula recognizes: (1) depreciated value, (2) operating charges. Assuming that there are sufficient budget funds for the purchase of a new machine, it is less costly from an operating standpoint to charge off the undepreciated value of equipment than to charge a greater sum (or even an equal sum) for maintenance and still have an old machine.

9. *Develop a "Pay Out" Policy.* Office managers have not gotten into the habit of thinking in terms of pay out—the period during which the initial investment is returned through savings. Companies often refrain from mechanization because of the size of the original investment. The size of the investment is of less importance than the pay-out period. Any investment in new equipment (initial or replacement) is justified if the savings from the machine will return the original investment in two to five years. Mechanization will be advanced if a definite policy is established.

10. *Take an Inventory of All Equipment Once Each Year.* The purpose of taking an equipment inventory is twofold: (a) It verifies that the equipment carried on the books is still in the company's possession (in large companies this can be important), and (b) it provides an opportunity to inspect the condition of the equipment and to appraise its care and operation. Idle equipment can be spotted during an equipment inventory.

Suggestions for Better Care of Equipment

The office services manager of the Nationwide Insurance Company suggests the following procedure for better equipment standards:

1. Use of service contracts.
2. Schedule for cleaning and oiling.
3. Periodic classes held by office machine representatives on proper cleaning and care of machines. We have one girl trained by the various office machine companies to orient new employees on proper care and maintenance.

The office manager of *The Journal* Company, Milwaukee, Wisconsin, says, "Our experience shows that when employees have pride in the condition and appearance of their office, this attitude carries over in the way they use and care for equipment needed in their jobs."

The manager of office services, Weston Instruments, Newark, New Jersey, explains a way the company saved $360 a year. He says, "Certain office machines on a service contract are serviced too often. Revise the contract so that service (and resulting cost) is reduced. As an example, a lubrication contract called for service every two months. It has now been changed to twice a year."

The office manager, Janitrol Divisions, Surface Combustion Corporation, Columbus, Ohio, feels, "A good independent service agency that can service machines of all types (particularly typewriters) has the advantage of better control over service and cuts down on the number of different service agencies. Also, it can handle more items on one call, thus reducing overall service cost. If machines are not on service calls, service records should be kept to insure periodic inspection and cleaning for all machines."

This Litton EBS 1210 electronic business system provides billing and invoicing facilities for the small business, or remote billing application for outlying branches of a large corporation.

Chapter 50

OFFICE DUPLICATING PROCESSES

A FEW years ago, a wonderful cartoon appeared in one of our national magazines. It showed a high-ranking Army officer dictating to his clerk. The caption read something like this:

" '. . . and because this excessive paper work is extremely inefficient and costly, it must be eliminated.' Now, Jenkins, get me 100 copies of that."

Every office manager in America could probably recite—with more rancor than humor—some similar experience. And usually, when the command "make a hundred copies!" is flung at the office manager, there is this added injunction: "And do it right away."

At that point, the office manager is confronted with the problem of finding the easiest, fastest, and least costly way of carrying out his orders. And this thrusts him into the field of office duplicating.

Time was when the office duplicating equipment of most offices consisted of a worn-out, dusty machine off in an obscure corner of the premises, which was occasionally operated by the office boy. But times have changed. And with them have changed the demands of business for copies of letters, forms, memos, reports, and brochures. This enormous diet of paper upon which modern business feeds has prompted the manufacturers of duplicating equipment to literally outdo themselves in developing new reproduction methods and machines. Today, the duplicating equipment field offers to the office manager a score or more different machines to obtain multiple copies of a page.

At the outset, it might be well to list and give a thumbnail description of the principal office duplicating methods.

Mimeographing

To produce office bulletins on mimeograph equipment, the operator types or draws directly on the stencil. This operation is the crucial step in obtaining quality copy results. For added effectiveness, however, it is possible to patch prepared cartoons and illustrations onto the stencil.

The mimeograph process is suited for short, medium, and long runs. It is fast and it is economical. Stencil duplicator prices cover a wide range. Hand-operated models sell for as little as $195; modern, electrically driven models may run up to $1,000. Speed, versatility, and copy quality results account for the price difference.

The electronic stencil process has been developed to help the mimeograph attain copy quality results previously reserved for the offset process. These stencils make it possible to reproduce linework, solids, and remarkable halftone facsimiles. From 5,000 to 10,000 copies can be reproduced from one electronic stencil.

Direct process duplicators, like that pictured here, are widely used for systems work. Keynote of this system is single writing which reproduces all records from one master form, effecting greater accuracy and impressive savings.

Photocopy

The photocopy process provides a quick way to obtain from one to any number of copies of an original document, such as reports, letters, invoices, etc. Some photocopiers will even copy pages in bound volumes, photographs, and blueprints. Generally, it takes only seconds and costs only a few cents to make a photocopy.

Some companies have found photocopy equipment especially handy for answering correspondence. Reply is made in the margin of the original letter; then a photocopy of the letter is made. The original letter is returned to the sender, and the copy is kept on file. This method of correspondence saves time and frees clerical personnel for more productive tasks but it does make a poor impression on many people who consider the return of their marked-up original as an affront.

Offset Printing

Compared to the cost of other office duplicating equipment, the initial cost of offset equipment is comparatively high, with most machines priced between $2,500 and $5,000. However, only the offset process can produce bulletins with print-like quality at a real saving of printing costs—including the reproduction of linework, solid areas, and halftones.

Offset equipment can also be used to produce letterheads, office forms, advertising literature, catalog pages, etc.

Any number of bulletins can be economically reproduced by this process at speeds up to 9,000 impressions an hour. Paper masters may economically be used for the production of a few hundred copies; metal plates are more economical when thousands of copies are needed.

Quantitative Decisions Needed

How shall an office executive choose the equipment required? There are a half dozen basic factors which must be considered and evaluated before a choice is made.

First, something must be known about the load factor, which involves not only the total amount of work to be done each day, but also the number and type of specific jobs to be done. Duplicating processes that are economically sound must provide for long-, medium-, or short-run reproduction or any combination of the three. (A short run is 20 copies or less; a medium run from 20 to 500 copies; and a long run above 500 copies.) The method that is best suited to reproducing 5,000 copies of a form is not the most economical for obtaining 10 copies of engineering drawings, for example. Long-run work should be done by either stencil duplicating or by offset; short-run work can best be done by whiteprint duplicating, or photocopy equipment. When it comes to medium-run work, usually letters, price lists, or bulletins—hectograph, stencil duplicating, and offset all offer good possibilities for economical reproduction.

So, the first economic determination in solving an office duplicating problem—that of load factor—cannot be easily resolved, nor is it completely determinative in itself. The unresolved question is this: Is it economically more sound to have the best duplicating methods tor the varied demands of the office and tolerate some idle machine time, or is it better to have less variety in the number of processes available and have fuller utilization of the equipment? There are other factors which will help resolve this question.

Quality Requirements

The second important consideration is the quality of the work to be done. This involves more than the caliber of work done by different operators, which will be subsequently dealt with as a separate factor; rather, the quality factor is the degree of complexity of the finished work and the level of its distribution.

If halftone reproductions must be made, an offset duplicator should be included among the office's reproduction equipment. While the stencil duplicating manufacturers have developed electronic stencil cutters and other devices that can approximate halftones on stencils, offset equipment, because of its more even ink distribution, is more capable of handling this sort of work.

For the short-run duplicating problem, where copies up to 34 by 22 inches are required, all other methods must be ruled out except the diazo process of whiteprint duplicating. This machine can also handle small-size work as well and can be readily adapted to order-invoice operations. Also, duplication on whiteprint of material on tracing paper or tracing cloth is a relatively simple matter. Although diazo process duplicators are available in desk-size machines, they can also be obtained in widths up to 54 inches.

When very short-run work is confined to standard letter or legal sizes, a photocopy machine, which is in some respects in competition with whiteprint equipment, may very well be adequate. Some photocopy machines are capable of enlargements and reductions, but none of those on the market can accommodate copy larger than 19 inches in width. If six or seven copies of letter-size material is to be reproduced, the desk-size photocopy machine is a very handy piece of equipment to have.

Generally speaking, a small offset machine is best to handle long-run work; a stencil duplicator and a spirit hectograph machine to reproduce medium-run work; and a diazo process whiteprint machine to do short-run work.

Other important considerations in the quality factor are the questions of who is going to get the finished work, and how it will be used. If the distribution level is within a single department and the material of only temporary use, the quality would obviously be of less consequence than a price list sent to customers for their use over a six-month period.

Office-size offset machines are capable of high-quality reproduction work, rivaling, to the untrained eye at least, the work of a commercial printer. By the use of photographic film negatives and paper negatives, presensitized or other plates can be prepared for high-quality, long-run reproductions. In addition, recent developments in the use of electrically sensitized metal transfer plates have made offset master preparation considerably easier and less costly, with very little loss in quality.

Operating the Equipment

Office duplicating equipment operators range from office boys fresh out of high school to experienced union pressmen who are expert craftsmen.

Because the various types of equipment place different demands upon operator skill, it is not possible to give a categorical answer to the duplicating personnel problem of any given office. Generally, however, it can be said that mimeograph, hectograph, photocopy, and whiteprint equipment have all been manufactured with an eye toward ease and simplicity of operation. For normal office requirements, employees at junior clerical levels can operate this equipment without difficulty. Some of the advanced mimeograph work such as preparation of photographic stencils by a photochemical process requires a more expert hand. Similarly, obtaining copies from an opaque master on whiteprint equipment calls for a more experienced operator.

The manufacturers of offset equipment have done a great deal to simplify the operation of their machines, but they still require a somewhat higher degree of operating skill than the other principal office duplicating processes. The blending of the ink and water in the proper amount requires that the operator be, in effect, a junior-grade pressman. When photographic and electrical dry processes are used, additional skills are required.

Installing the Equipment

Before installation can become a reality, a decision must be reached on where to place the equipment to fit conveniently and efficiently into an office layout. If photographic equipment is to be used, a closet-size darkroom must be provided. Floor space must be allowed as needed.

There are several minor considerations that must be provided for in the installation. One is to reduce the noise of the equipment, which might prove annoying if the machines are located too near typists or other clerical workers. A second is that, if the type of whiteprint machine that uses ammonia vapor as a developer is purchased, the removal of the ammonia fumes will have to be arranged for. The answer to both these problems is to enclose the equipment in a well-ventilated, noiseproof room.

Operating Costs

Before recommendations can be drawn up on the duplicating equipment to be installed, analysis of initial costs and operating costs must be undertaken.

A look at the range of price tags on the various duplicating machines on the market shows that the standard sizes of hectograph duplicators and photocopy equipment are about one-third less expensive than the standard size of stencil duplicators. Also, in the standard sizes, it is possible to spend from two to five times as much for whiteprint and offset machines as for standard stencil duplicators. (The wide range in price results from refinements and optional equipment available.) This same relationship, with hectograph and photocopy the least expensive, followed by stencil duplicators, then whiteprint and offset, applies also to the smaller and larger versions of the equipment. There is some overlap, though. The most expensive standard size stencil duplicator is approximately the same price as the least expensive small size offset machine; and the standard size photocopy and hectograph machines are about as expensive as the least expensive whiteprint equipment.

There are plenty of price differentials between different processes and between the machines of various manufacturers within the same process. Prices, however, are established in a free and highly competitive market, and the buyer can find processes and machines to fit any size of corporate pocketbook.

Fixed costs are established, such as the office floor space occupied by the machines, the straight-line depreciation of the machines, and the superintendence. To this must be added the rental cost of a valuable piece of equipment—an electrical dry process machine with a camera that will make it possible to prepare offset paper plates quickly and at low cost.

The office manager should next estimate the number of copies to be produced each month, the size of the initial base load, and the number of "extra" jobs.

Commercial duplicating concerns add, on the average, a flat percentage charge of 30 percent for overhead and profit to their time

Office copying machines continue to improve and provide flexibility for various needs. The A.B. Dick Model 610 above is useful in large offices where several copiers are required rather than one central station. Below, the Xerox 2400 III delivers sparkling copies of anything, including halftone photographs.

and material costs. When the volume is high enough that the fixed cost portion of such bills runs considerably more than the office manager's own forecasted fixed costs, it becomes economical to have an internal duplicating setup.

Variable costs include the operators' time, the cost of paper, ink, stencils, hectograph carbon, offset plates, photographic material, ammonia or developing fluid, and the other supplies necessary to reproduce the anticipated number of copies.

The possibility should not be ruled out that some work, too big or too complex for office duplicating equipment, will have to be sent out to letter shops. In fact, this is the kind of work that commercial duplicating firms are geared to do most effectively and economically. In simple work, however, where the volume is reasonably steady and the quantity 5,000 copies or less, the individual office can invariably do its own work cheaper than the letter shops and with no noticeable difference in the quality of reproduction.

Another Look at Costs

Looking at the cost problem from a different angle, there are two different types of costs in office duplicating work, preparatory costs and production costs. A common maxim in the field, expressed variously by different authorities, is that duplicating processes which have a low preparatory cost normally have a high per copy cost and processes which have a high preparatory cost have a low per copy cost. For example, the whiteprint machine requires virtually no preparatory cost. The master, once typed, is inserted in the machine as soon as the operator receives it, and the cost per copy (8½ by 11 inches), including operator's time and the materials, is extremely low. But the cost for the second copy and every copy thereafter is the same as that for the first copy. Here we see low preparation costs, but high production costs.

Contrariwise, the preparation of one 8½- by 11-inch offset plate, if done photographically, may run extremely high, and if only 10 copies are run, the cost becomes prohibitive. But, at 100 copies the total price begins to come into the realm of reason and for 1,000 copies the incremental cost per copy is in fractions of a cent per copy.

One of the most useful applications of cost per copy figures is in the determination of the economic break-even point on the number of copies to be run on a given machine. While the exact break-even point varies in each office because of the variables in operating costs, once the office manager has such figures prepared, he can chart the

Office printing plants now rival those of the commercial printer. The A.B. Dick 100-bin automatic sorter (above) is hooked up to the offset duplicator to enable the printing and assembling of copies in one continuous operation. At right, the IBM introduces to offset duplication the roll paper concept used by commercial printing plants to cut paper costs.

cost lines on a graph and readily pick off the break-even points at the various intersections.

Getting back to the main track of preparatory *versus* production costs, it must be understood that any realistic figures arrived at along these lines presume a 100 percent load factor on the machines. Under these conditions, the preparatory cost becomes a sort of service charge for getting ready to print, whereas the production cost— whether for 10 copies or 10,000—is the cost of operating the machine after the investment for the master has been made.

As a last word on reproduction costs, it would appear that in as dynamic a field as office duplicating, no sweeping analysis is possible nor can general conclusions be reached for a universal application. Inherent in these costs are so many *"x"* factors that each office manager must evaluate his own specific and individual cost elements before he can arrive at a well-reasoned and reliable estimate.

Every process mentioned has justified its existence by meeting the demands of some particular office duplicating problem. The choice of one method above another must be determined by each individual office, on the basis of value received from the equipment. This value may only be measured in terms of the legibility of the copies, the versatility, speed, and operating ease of the machines, and the ability of the company to meet the overall costs of purchasing and operating the equipment.

Other Methods of Office Duplicating

In addition to the methods already described, office duplicating or copying is done in the following manners:

Carbon paper: The use of carbon paper in duplicating needs no further description. Its sale has increased considerably in recent years due to its adaptation to other duplicating processes.

Automatic typewriter: Primarily used for correspondence, the automatic typewriter reproduces individually typewritten letters mechanically, with the name, address, date, and salutation being typed manually by the operator. The speed is more than twice that of the average typist and fill-ins may be inserted at certain points. For sales and collection letters and other repetitive correspondence where it is important that an original be mailed, the automatic typewriter saves a great deal of time. One operator can handle four or five machines.

NCR (no carbon required): Specially treated paper developed by The National Cash Register Company permits multiple copies without the use of carbon inserts. The back of the original paper is treated with a colorless chemical, the face of the copy paper coated with another chemical. The pressure of writing on the original forces the two treated surfaces into contact with each other, producing a chemical reaction that results in a blue-green impression. NCR can make seven typewritten or four handwritten copies. It is being used primarily as a substitute for carbon interleaved forms.

AUTOMATIC TYPING

Without doubt a letter which seems to have been typewritten just for the particular individual to whom it is sent carries with it a special "buying" inducement, whether the letter is selling a product, service, prestige, or whatever. The potential customer is flattered. If the letter sounds as if it were directed to one person, particularized instead of being merely general in tone, and if the proper type of sales appeal is used, the chances of this seemingly individualized letter (which actually is automatic) getting results are excellent.

While automatic letter-writing equipment can serve many purposes in an office, we are concerned here only with three applications for promoting sales or building good will:

1. The letter sent out "cold"—asking for an order, for money, or only for information.

2. A followup to this letter sent to a "cold" list; the followup to be an acknowledgment, a thank you, or perhaps another sales effort.

3. The purely good-will letter which uses a friendly tone to build still better relationships between the writer and his customers—a letter designed to do an institutional job.

A point to keep in mind when preparing a promotional letter that will be written on automatic equipment is to make it *sound* as if it had been personally dictated, just as it is made to look as if it had been individually typed. Of course the letter will be addressed to the prospect by name—his full name or initials—but experience has proved that it produces a much more powerful impact if still further personalized. The prospect's name should appear as a fill-in within the body of the letter. Or the name of the prospect's product or service—an individualization almost as dear to him as the sound of his own name—should be used. Perhaps the fill-in could more logically be the name of the prospect's city, or state, or even some precise date that makes the letter individual: "When I called at your (name of city) .... office on (here insert date) ....," In any case, at least one fill-in which includes the man's name, the sweetest sound to any individual's ears, should be used. By taking a little thought, a fill-in can be devised, sometimes even two in one sentence, that not only sounds completely natural but that makes the prospect feel only one letter was mailed, and it was written just for him.

One of the many advantages that grow out of using a typewritten letter for sales or promotional purposes is that the carbon copy provides splendid material for a followup. For years this idea has been used by many companies, particularly publishers, with excellent results. Its popularity is partly due to its low cost, simply the carbon and extra sheet of paper when it is typed with the original letter. While the plan should not be used too often on the same mailing list, records show that if the original sales letter is built around a good basic appeal the carbon copy may pull larger returns than the original.

The method of using carbon copies as followup letters involves very little work. They should carry the company's name, address, etc., and the full imprint that appears on the letterhead. All carbon copies of those letters to which replies were received on the original mailing should be destroyed. On the others, a brief paragraph can be added— a little block of typing, preferably in red—which says something like this: "Perhaps my letter of (date of original letter) .... failed to reach you. Won't you please let me know if you're interested in . . ." If there were carbons with the original letter, the same ones can be sent with the carbon copy. A reply card may also be included which is "personalized" by having the prospect's name, company, and address already typed on it, with space below for the individual to sign his name or initials. This sort of personalized card, experiments have proved, increases replies from any mailing.

In the same way, an answer to an inquiry, a thank you letter, or one acknowledging an order, makes a much more favorable impression if it seems to have been individually typed. After spending large sums of money to draw inquiries, many firms send out a cheap-looking form letter or mailing piece in reply. The resultant lack of response on the prospect's part makes much of the previous large expenditure a complete waste. Conversely, with automatic equipment and some skill applied to working up fill-ins, a reply letter or an acknowledgment can be personalized, adding still more sales appeal.

Completely Automatic Letter Writing

It is possible to add still further refinements to the automatic letter-writing job with the result that even the fill-in is accomplished automatically. The Friden Flexowriter Duplex can do this, using a prepunched paper tape which contains all the names and addresses of recipients and a tape which contains the date and body of the letter. The tape in the Flexowriter Reader causes the machine to type the date and line space to the position for inside address. At this point a code in the tape switches the operation automatically to a Motorized Tape Reader which holds the name and address tape. The tape actuates the Flexowriter to type in name, address, and salutation. At the same time, a by-product address tape is punched on the Flexowriter Tape Punch. When this information has been typed, a code switches back to the Flexowriter tape which then types the remainder of the letter. Coding in the tape automatically positions succeeding continuous form letterheads. Marginally punched, continuous form envelopes are addressed automatically on Flexowriter from by-product address tape.

Paper for Duplicating Equipment

When it comes to supplies for duplicating equipment, options are somewhat limited. Inks, fluids, and chemicals for the operating end of the machinery are pretty well fixed by the nature of the equipment, but in the matter of paper there are some alternatives. The photographic type of duplicating equipment, both photocopy and whiteprint, have their own special brands of sensitized paper, but offset, mimeograph, and hectograph reproduction machines can be fed several different kinds of paper.

Liquid hectograph machines use as their master copy a 24-pound specially treated paper. (Pound-weights are assigned to paper on the basis of the scale-weight of a ream—500 sheets—cut to 17 by 22 inches.) There are several weights of run-off paper for liquid hectograph machines, but the most common is a 20-pound paper that dries quickly and is especially made for this process.

In the mimeograph field, a 20-pound mimeo bond, suitable for two-sided work, is probably the most useful for most purposes. This is a highly absorbent paper but has a fairly hard finish. For offset machinery there is a somewhat wider range of papers with a minimum weight of 13-pound sulphite stock and a normal maximum of 24-pound ledger stock. Card stock can also be readily used on offset equipment.

The normal offset paper is a 20-pound sulphite paper of No. 4 grade. This paper has a hard finish but is not watermarked, as is grade No. 1. Standard sizes for duplicating with hectograph, mimeograph, and offset machines are 8½ by 11 inches and 8½ by 13 inches, although machines are flexible enough to receive paper cut to any size inside those dimensions. Similarly, for special jobs, colored papers of similar weights are available for both mimeograph and offset equipment.

How Hansen Glove Speeds Orders

A critical problem area for the fashion industry is the profitable matching of customers' requirements with inventory. Hansen Glove Corporation of Milwaukee, a foremost maker of women's fashion gloves, has been attacking this problem since 1965 through an IBM 1440 computer system.

Viewing the computer as a management tool, as opposed to a high-speed printer of conventional paper work, Hansen systems personnel, with the blessing of top management and with the expert guidance of IBM systems engineers and programmers, contrived a system that prints, tallies, computes, classifies, and analyzes incoming customer orders by style, color, and size. A parallel system of inventory records was programmed to run concurrently with the order analyses to provide detailed data of inventory in finished goods and goods in process.

A typical management-oriented coverage report is read out from the disc-stored order and inventory records. This coverage report summarizes for each style and color, by size, the total orders received to date as compared to quantities in goods finished and in process. In addition, this same report compares the quantities in finished goods with order requirements for each delivery period, and a print-out is made of the net position of inventory at each delivery period. Negative balances, of course, indicate inventory shortages, and trigger management action to expedite deliveries to stock of such items.

Though no mention has been made up to this point of the possible use of this computer-based information system in the area of sales forecasting, Hansen Glove is alert to this potentially priceless by-product. Realizing full well that it is an impossibility to reduce the whims and fancies of fashion-conscious women to a mathematical formula, nonetheless, they are convinced trends do exist in fashion glove preferences. Based on the premise that analyses of its own sales over a period of years might disclose such cyclical trends, Hansen has devised a 13-factor code of generic glove characteristics, and each glove style is classified according to this code. Compilation of sales data under these various factors will significantly help to reduce the error in future sales forecasting.

Other Uses

Though the management-control aspects of Hansen's 1440 system have been stressed up to this point, there are many "bread and butter" accomplishments achieved in the course of developing the control reports. For example, stock-available reports are produced that permit judgment as to whether orders for immediate shipment of goods can be met. On future orders—those previously placed by the customer for delivery in some future period—the IBM cards representing each line item of each order are processed through the computer which then, by comparison internally with the stock position of each item, produces a distinguishing punch in the cards for all items that can be shipped. Having determined that items are in stock for a particular order, the cards are processed under an invoicing program to produce a multicarbon stock selection, an invoice set which also includes shipping labels and packing slip. Concurrent with this procedure, shipped-sales data is compiled for salesmen by accounting and sales classifications and by style number for use in deriving the cost of goods sold.

The Punched Card

Though its existence has been inferred, this discussion has not mentioned the seemingly insignificant paper record upon which all the workings of this computer are based—the conventional punched card. These cards are punched at the time a customer's order is received for style, color, size scale, customer number, selling price, product classification, and other factors, and serve as the unit record behind all the order analysis and invoicing routine which make up the system. Similarly, with respect to the inventory control aspects of the system, punched cards are created to reflect the inventory status of all styles and colors by size.

In summary then, Hansen Glove is using a carefully systematized and programmed IBM 1440 computer to more effectively manage its rather complex fashion glove business, declares L. J. Stanton, assistant treasurer.

Moncrief Lenoir Reduces Invoicing Time

A three- to five-day speedup in invoicing and a substantial saving in overhead expense has been attained by a southwest sheet metal and steel products firm, as a result of a new billing system.

Moncrief Lenoir Manufacturing Company, with headquarters in Houston and branches in six other Texas cities, faced a serious delay in invoicing customers as soon as shipments were made, largely because of the wide open spaces of Texas.

After a customer in El Paso or Amarillo received his merchandise, it frequently was two days before the signed delivery ticket reached Moncrief Lenoir's home office, another day before the invoice could be produced, and two more days until the mailman had delivered the invoice to the customer's office.

This was a serious inconvenience to many customers, who based their own prices on suppliers' invoices. And since the geography of Texas couldn't be changed, Moncrief Lenoir set out to revise its own paper work routine.

The goal was delivery of an invoice within 24 hours of a shipment. This clearly indicated a transfer of invoicing operations from a central department in Houston to separate departments in each branch city. There was no other way to beat the delay in mail across Texas.

But this transfer became practical only when the company found a system which would create less overhead expense and fewer operational problems in seven locations than had been present in one. The central office at Houston had been renting tabulating billing equipment, at a monthly rental of $740. It would be poor business to multiply this expenditure by seven.

Duplicating Provides the Answer

The solution turned out to be a duplicating system which gives Moncrief Lenoir a single-writing system. The office salesman writes an order on a four-part delivery ticket, the top copy of which is a stain-free master.

The master accompanies the order to the customer's office. The customer signs it, and the Moncrief Lenoir driver returns it to the branch office the same day. It is checked, priced, and extended; and copies of the invoice are duplicated in a matter of minutes. In most instances, the invoice is in the mail the same day the shipment is made, and on the customer's desk, ready for processing, at the start of business the next morning.

And in finding a system which provided such speed, the company also gave itself and customers two other advantages.

First, the new delivery ticket contains a back-order column. If some items ordered are not in stock, the truck driver asks the customer if he wants to back order the merchandise and then makes the necessary notation.

A machine which automatically jogs, staples, and stacks sheets for an in-plant duplicating department will handle 54,000 sheets or 720 complete sets of 75 sheets each per hour. The unit will apply either one or two staples.

Courtesy Greenville Industries, Inc.

When the invoice is run, the amount to be back ordered is clearly indicated on both the customer's copy and Moncrief Lenoir's own record for its back-order file. This provision eliminates 30 to 50 exchanges of correspondence each day, concerning whether out-of-stock merchandise should or should not be back ordered.

A second advantage is that a complete description of merchandise appears on both the delivery ticket and the duplicated invoice. Most customers demand this description, but it was a problem when the company used a tabulating system to produce invoices. Even though Moncrief Lenoir used a two-card method, there was not room on the cards for an adequate description of merchandise.

The company's present investment in duplicating equipment is about $1,800 for seven hand-operated machines. On the other hand, the company has reduced its rental for tabulating equipment by $740 a month, and needs five fewer people in its Houston general office. The annual saving is known to be substantial, although the company will not quote an exact figure. The cost of master sets is slightly lower than the combined cost of the old delivery tickets and tabulated invoices previously used.

Chapter 51

INTRODUCTION TO WORK SIMPLIFICATION

T HERE are few companies," once said John L. McCaffrey, former chairman of International Harvester Company, to shareholders gathered in Chicago for an annual meeting, "whose income per dollar of sales has not gone down in recent years, which means that the cost of goods in relation to the price you can get for them is producing a squeeze." Then he added: "This problem has worried me, probably more than it has worried you, because we are in it from the time we get to the office in the morning until we leave at night."

Management men are frankly concerned over the possibility, unless ways can be found to arrest the upward drift of costs, of another period of "profitless prosperity," when in spite of high sales volume there will be barely enough earnings to cover dividends. So it is not surprising that they are considering carefully every possible way of cutting costs—not only in production and in distribution, but in the day-to-day administration of the business as well. Nor is it surprising that those directly concerned with paper work are talking a great deal about the pros and cons of "Operation Office Work Simplification"—which means, simply, finding better ways to do any job by eliminating all unnecessary parts and combining the necessary parts so as to get maximum efficiency with a minimum expenditure of time, material, and equipment.

Actually, work simplification is not new at all. It is the application of common sense management principles to the doing of a specific job. It is important in the quest for lower costs.

Objectives of Work Simplification

In a survey of 300 companies made by Dartnell, 99 percent of respondents agreed that the prime objectives of a work-simplification program are one or more of the following company goals:

To increase efficiency.

To reduce costs.

To eliminate duplication.

To speed up operations and eliminate waste.

These are the generally accepted reasons, but they hardly satisfy the executive who demands facts. Confronted with such replies, the president of an eastern railroad said it reminded him of sin: "Everybody is in favor of eliminating inefficiency and waste, but there's sure little sign of its losing favor."

Those members of top management who have taken the most interest and given the most support to their work-simplification programs see it as something more than might be indicated by listed specific objectives. To them it provides a method of improving relations with customers, clients, and prospects. It may also improve employee relations through the demonstration it provides of management interest in operating efficiently.

Some executives have learned to look upon the work-simplification programs in their companies as a method of developing present and future executives. Carrying out the projects involved gives all concerned a better knowledge of company operations and of mutual problems between departments. Through the interchange of information and the contacts between executives and employees in departments at all levels of operation, the work-simplification program improves communications, opening breaches in the barriers that often exist between various departments.

An executive of one of the world's largest insurance firms says that the specific objective of his organization's work-simplification program was "primarily to promote the idea that there is always a better way, and to let supervisors and clerks know that management wants them to suggest improvements."

S. J. Fecht, the president of S. J. Fecht & Associates, states the objectives in an equally down-to-earth manner: "To make better men of the supervisors. To reduce costs by teaching the supervisors how to determine and analyze . . . what is being done in their departments; where, when, and how it is being done; who is doing it; and how much it will cost."

A Toni Co. officer adds a final, highly convincing objective: "To indoctrinate that portion of lower and middle management which can reasonably be expected to advance to top-level positions in the philosophy of cooperative work simplification. When this indoctrination becomes a daily concern of every level of management, we will have attained a major objective."

Prevalence of Work-Simplification Programs

Although known by many different titles, office work-simplification programs in one form or another are in operation or being developed by about 50 percent of the major corporations surveyed.

THE SPECIFIC OBJECTIVES OF WORK SIMPLIFICATION

To strengthen supervisory controls and improve accuracy.

To better customer service.

To process all paper work faster.

To make better supervisors.

To reduce the cost of training supervisors.

To provide constant study and review of the effectiveness of management policies and organization structure.

To undertake specific management surveys, recommend improvements, and put them into effect.

To reduce or eliminate nonessential clerical operations.

To provide adequate management controls and information at minimum cost.

To develop a climate receptive to change.

To create dissatisfaction with present methods.

To train supervisors in analytical approach to problem-solving.

To mechanize large volume routine paper work activities.

To cut red tape.

To increase the productivity of office employees.

To reduce clerical time and effort while improving quality.

Among smaller and medium-sized companies, the percentage falls to less than 30 percent. But many firms in this group are engaged in efficiency programs which, in part, would fall under the general office work-simplification label. A very few companies use the realistic title, "Job enlargement." Not included in this generalization, however, is another important factor. Of the companies that report having no office work-simplification program, over half indicate that they are studying the subject to determine whether to initiate such a program or not.

Among the largest companies surveyed, general work-simplification programs appear to be carried out on an overall organization basis. Office work phases are likely to be handled in a piecemeal or partial fashion, except for very high-level functions where top management seeks and gets streamlined, companywide operation. The piecemeal approach to office simplification, according to the experts, is in large measure the result of top management's failure to see how the problem of office work simplification cuts across the organizational structure.

The result has its somewhat comical side. In one corporation, several offices have organized highly effective office procedures which result in significant savings in both time and labor. Since the functions of these offices are necessarily linked with those of divisions in which no simplification has been attempted, the gains made are, in a measure, lost by the inefficiency of the other divisions. Thus, while several bottlenecks have been cleared up, new ones are created by the increased efficiency of the reorganized departments. Further delays and needless overloading have resulted in departments where the new system has been slow in taking hold.

John Lubeck, executive vice-president of R. L. Majors, Incorporated, says that "while office work simplification can be approached on a specific department basis, it must be part of a general overall scheme to be extended to all departments or its long-range effectiveness will be lost."

Other questions asked in the course of Dartnell's survey follow, along with the answers given by participating companies:

What levels of management are actively involved in the operation of work-simplification programs? How? In almost all cases reporting significant results, all levels of management (including top management) were indicated as being actively involved. Specifically included were vice-presidents, treasurers, controllers, department managers, general managers, plant managers, sales managers, and "operating managers."

In answer to how such management was involved, following are some direct quotations: "To coordinate"; "daily decisions affecting procedures"; "analyzing, planning, discussion"; "consultation"; "initiation, approval, review"; for "establishment of policies and compliance with them"; "meetings to discuss problems and changes"; "recommend changes"; "top levels push lower levels into active participation in the program!"

Experienced executives are practically unanimous in their opinion that successful work-simplification projects depend on top-management support and on the daily active participation of middle and lower management. A long-time officer of the Bowery Savings Bank, in New York, has reported, as have many others, "Work simplification works best from the top down—from the top management down through the supervisors."

It should be added, however, that the confidential replies to this survey clearly indicate that the most difficult operations problem faced by the work-simplification staff is to get continuous support from the highest management level.

What is the title of the individual specifically responsible for implementing the office work-simplification program? Only 45 percent of the companies surveyed put their programs in the hands of executives designated as systems, procedures, or methods managers, or supervisors. Twenty-five percent are directed by executives whose primary duties are connected with finance: cost accountant, internal auditor, payroll and expense controller, manager of internal audit and methods, director of systems and budgets, controller, and treasurer. The remaining 30 percent of the companies surveyed have designated office manager, industrial engineer, assistant vice-president, president, director of personnel, or factory manager as the administrator in charge of their office work-simplification programs.

Management, according to this survey, has found that the most successful work-simplification programs are those directed by an official charged specifically with that task. To obtain the objectivity, as well as the time, necessary to supervise such a program, he must be free from the daily operations routine. Ralph Peck, research analyst for the American Surety Company in New York, cites the experience of his organization in this way: "We came to the conclusion—toward the end of the first year—that operating people, no matter how well instructed, or how well motivated in particular meetings, just don't find the time to continue a specific program once the workshops have been completed." Of course, much will depend on the size of the company, its specific problems, and personnel available.

What background or professional training did this administrator have in office work simplification? Most administrators had no specialized training for this kind of work, other than experience in business (from five to 25 years of office work) and their college work. About 50 percent had attended special clinics or seminars in addition to formal training in business administration, accounting, or industrial engineering.

It is at this point that one of the weakest factors in work-simplification programs appeared. While half of the administrators had attended clinics or seminars in work simplification, only about 10 percent of these had made any concentrated study of the subject or had been specifically trained in the methods and techniques involved. Too many had to "play it by ear"—carry on programs while they were frantically trying to get abreast of the theory and practice involved!

Management is also becoming aware of the work-simplification director's difficulty in securing a competent staff for operating his program and projects. Sixty-five percent of those selected to aid the executive have little, if any, specific training for the job. Only 10 percent have had even a two-day work-simplification seminar or clinic. Fortunately, those selected are usually men or women with from two to five years' experience in the company, and therefore understand the existing system. While some have degrees in business administration, accounting, or industrial management, they are generally in need of specific training in the theory and techniques of office simplification.

How many people make up the work-simplification staff? No significant figure could be determined. Staffs varied from just the administrator—as in the case of a rubber manufacturer and a nationally known electrical appliance firm, to 10 assistants reported by both a book publisher and a major petroleum company. The figure itself is meaningless, however, since it is the staff functions involved that provide the key to the size of staff.

"If the administrator's function is purely advisory, little staff is required," according to Charles Faulkner, computing-center manager at Spiegel's. "But if his job is to survey each department, to study and recommend specific projects or techniques, and to follow up to see that work simplification is a reality, he may need a staff of from two to 20. If the program is properly operated, each staff member should be able to save at least three to five times his annual salary by the efficiency he develops in office administration and procedures."

Did the training include a specific course for executives? For supervisors? Training for office work simplification is widely divergent, according to management reports. These are the determinable trends:

1. Some form of top-management indoctrination program is a must, if the program is to get off the ground.

2. Middle management and the supervisory level must be sold on the need and value of the program, have training in its specifics, be given an incentive to carry it out, and then provided with a management follow through so as to prevent lulls and backsliding. The training element is just one of the critical components.

3. General employee training in office work simplification appears to be impractical because of turnover, time involved, and current business pressure. The regular practice is to charge the supervisor with doing a local selling job and giving such in-service training as employees will find helpful in their specific jobs.

4. The technical job should be supervised and followed through by trained personnel. Most of these, to date, have been trained on the job, but an increasing number are taking outside formal training in order to learn the new methods, techniques, and equipment uses. Educational institutions are adding to established business courses to cover these subjects.

Only 20 percent reported some type of orientation course meant specifically for top management, but 90 percent of the total said that this was an absolute necessity to secure the support and understanding needed to initiate an active, practical program of office work simplification. Present programs for executives vary from one hour to two days and are designed to acquaint management with the philosophy, need, techniques, cost, and results to be expected. Emphasis in such courses or seminars is on management's responsibility to make the program work.

Eighty percent of the companies surveyed had specific training courses for supervisors. Some of these have already processed more than 500 supervisors. Both the subject material and the time devoted to these sessions vary widely. Most popular are seminar-type programs in which free discussion and broad participation by the supervisors are sought. Training courses are conducted on company time and last from a minimum of 12 one-hour sessions held over 12 weeks to 16 two-hour sessions.

Because of their basic operations responsibility, as well as relatively low turnover in comparison with other employees, the department head or supervisor is usually selected as the best bet for indoctrination in work-simplification methods. It is then expected that the supervisors will indoctrinate the employees under them.

One other type of training has reached important proportions. There is an increasing trend toward establishing specific training courses for work-simplification analysts, who then become the active assistants of the administrator. Such training is intense and detailed.

Getting Top Management's Support

Not all office management men have the ability or skill required to "sell" a work-simplification program to those who must okay the expenditure. For that reason many companies are getting along with inefficient, outdated methods.

To get the support of top management in an undertaking as vital as this, it is necessary to prepare understandable charts showing present and proposed methods. The distances traveled should be tabulated, the storage times, the number of operations involved, the total time consumed from start to finish. The figures must be accurate; they will provide the proof—the facts that will combat mere opinion.

The facts, then, should be prepared in understandable and even dramatic fashion. For example, to say that 13,527 miles of walking will be saved each year instead of saying that four feet of travel are saved on each operation lends dramatic flavor to the argument. Management might be told further: "You are paying $1.19 for each of the 4,509 hours spent in walking those 13,527 miles without getting one minute's production work done. You have an unseen person on your payroll whom you pay to do nothing but walk four round trips to Podunk each year."

Before a proposal is submitted for approval, it should be checked by someone other than the person who made the study to make sure there are no "blind spots" in it.

Preparing for Work Simplification

More than 65 percent of the companies covered by Dartnell's survey reported that their employees—rather than the office work-simplification staff members—came up with over half of the work-simplification ideas which are now part of their regular programs. This is, of course, the objective of every worthwhile office work-simplification program, for, as A. A. Hillner, secretary of Sligo, Inc., points out, "It is most important of all to have your own employees join in that research—in fact get them to feel that the 'discovery' of work-simplification steps and projects is theirs. They'll love it."

By using trained systems supervisors and the office executives directly concerned, some 80 percent of companies now engaging in office work simplification conduct regular weekly (30 percent), bimonthly (10 percent), or monthly (60 percent), employee meetings to discuss projects, review overall progress and individual reports. These meetings are conducted by the office manager (30 percent); systems and procedures or office work-simplification director (55 percent); company secretary, controller (or assistant), auditor or treasurer (15 percent).

The greatest results are obtained in those organizations having regularly scheduled meetings where members of top management take both an active interest and participate. Additionally, where work simplification is considered a regularly reportable office function, with each department and section expected to show actual efficiency or dollar-and-cents results, initiative, and pride of accomplishment may be measured and evaluated. A good example is found in the following employee report from the auditing section of Thomas J. Lipton, Inc.:

"A worksheet has been devised which makes it easier to isolate and identify differences between finished stock control records and the general ledger. Maintenance of the worksheet requires some additional clerical time, but considerable time can be saved at the end of the month in trying to reconcile differences. The keeping of this worksheet has considerably reduced the volume of differences. While a definite dollar value for the time saved cannot be estimated, it is significant to note that differences are now down to a very small fraction of 1 percent for the stock handled."

Management reports clearly indicate that the most successful work-simplification meetings are those which combine instruction, discussion, and actual case studies of problem areas in which the employees directly concerned are urged to speak up and offer their solutions. On the supervisory level, however, seminar or round-table meetings are the most productive when each participant is active in considering and solving all work-simplification problems, even though some problems do not directly concern his section.

Training Aids

According to officials of the Toni Company and of Carrier Corporation (whose opinions were echoed by some 85 percent of the experts reporting), the most effective aids used in connection with regularly scheduled office work-simplification meetings are:

1. Manuals
2. Flow charts
3. Motion pictures
4. Sound-slidefilms (and slides)
5. Flannel and block boards
6. Pegboards
7. Templates.

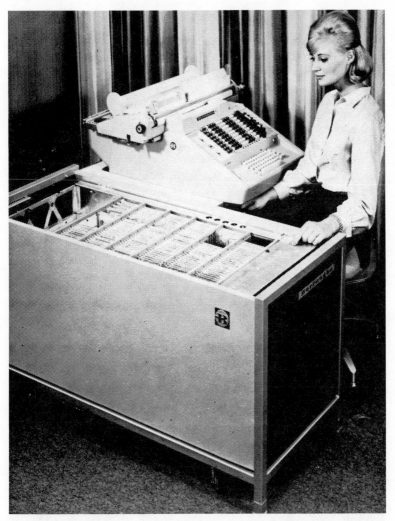

Payroll, billing, labor and cost distribution reports and other applications are possible on small units such as this Burroughs E2190 Electronic Direct Accounting Computer. One hundred words of electronic memory enables an operator to enter data quickly and perform only a limited number of functions on the virtually automatic desk-size computer.

Experts almost universally warn of the danger in letting either the employee or the supervisory sessions bog down in a morass of immaterial details. They suggest a program which:

1. Locates among the staff and general employees those best able, by temperament and interest, to get the most from office work-simplification training.

2. Keeps groups to workable size—12 to 15 persons.

3. Selects specific problem areas which can be handled on the employee-supervisory level, freeing professional systems people and management to make important, overall decisions relating to office work simplification.

4. After detailed training in analyzing the problem involved, undertakes the actual charting of workflow—simplifying, combining, and revising so as to produce the most effective system.

Initiative and enthusiasm are the result of making the employee, as well as the supervisor, feel he is part of the office work-simplification scheme. At the outset, it is necessary not only to educate and get the active support of management, but to convince employees that office work simplification is not designed to eliminate jobs, to increase or "speed up" work loads, or to place them on a machinery level productionwise.

Magnetic Ink Character Recognition units, such as this Burroughs electronic sorter/reader, can sort bank checks up to 1,560 a minute.

Some form of incentive is offered office employees in about 40 percent of the companies covered by Dartnell's survey. Cash payments for office work-simplification ideas put into action, production bonus plans, and incentive and wage-scale increases are as effective in offices as in plants, according to Chas. W. Faulkner of Spiegel, Inc., where a large volume of routine paper work has been highly simplified and systematized.

Cash incentive plans have been effectively used, although the amounts awarded vary widely. In most instances they are substantial enough to be attractive to the average office employee.

The Role of the Consultant

Since the end of World War II—and probably as a result of the tremendous problems resulting from the widespread industrial expansion as well as systems innovations during that struggle—there has been an astounding growth in the number of consultants in the office work-simplification field. Almost every state has from one to several dozen individuals and firms directly engaged in studying office operations, in redesigning office systems, and installing new methods.

What has been the most effective role of the consultants? There are two prime answers to the question: (1) Individual consultants have done excellent work in companies where management had a real desire to do something about office work simplification—"firing up" employee enthusiasm and interest through a short series (varying from two days to three weeks) of lectures, speeches, and seminars. These were promptly followed by company programs directed by trained company systems or methods men, or other management personnel. (2) Consulting firms have quietly entered the field, made detailed basic studies of office operations in a number of medium-sized and large firms, developed and presented specific programs of office work simplification, and then either turned them over to company supervisors or, on contract, put the approved program into operation.

How successful are such consulting programs? Experiences vary widely. The frequently used "pep-talk" consultants have temporary effect, but it appears their long-range effectiveness is limited by circumstances over which they have little control. Where management has quickly followed up with well-planned and supervised office work-simplification programs tailored to specific needs of the company, programs initiated by competent consultants have been quite successful.

Programs developed by the larger consulting firms, though initially costly, have been very successful. Largely management engineers or accounting specialists, a number of such companies have success-fully "saved" their clients several times the consulting fee within a single year. In most instances, however, these organizations survey, plan, initiate, train, staff, and supervise the work-simplification pro-gram until it is fully operative.

Choosing a Consultant

Actually, management should closely investigate before employing any consultant or consulting firm, a utility company president warns. "This is one field where experience counts. Check up before invest-ing in any service that is going to make changes in a system that is already working, even though it be a relatively inefficient one. It is better than one so messed up that you will have to start over!"

In addition, experience proves that, from its very outset, all such work-simplification programs should be under the active operational control of a company executive, a systems or methods manager, who will later have direct responsibility for continuing the program when the consultants or management engineers have completed their in-stallation.

What do consultants cost? Again figures supplied by companies that have had experience vary widely, and are dependent upon the precise job accomplished. Some fees may run as low as $100 a day; initial records systems surveys cost from $1,500 to $5,000; design-ing, training, installing new programs fluctuate from $5,000 for a small operation to $100,000 for continuing multiunit systems. A nationwide survey indicates that since almost every consulting job is "tailormade," fees are also adjusted to each case, often with more reference to a company's Dun & Bradstreet rating than to the job to be done.

Business Machines and Work Simplification

What part do improved business machines play in modern office work simplification? New high-speed office equipment—electro-mechanical as well as electronic—is having a profound impact on office work simplification, but there is a widespread tendency to put the cart before the horse. Office efficiency and effectiveness are de-pendent on well-designed, integrated systems into which equipment is fitted to eliminate unnecessary routine handling and to speed up mathematical, combining, sorting, or other data-processing or handling functions. The key, however, is not the type, variety, or speed of the equipment, but the effectiveness of the system.

As demonstrated by such companies as Westinghouse, Columbia Broadcasting System, Oneida Mills, John Plain, Spiegel, Thomas J. Lipton, and Acme Steel, when emphasis is placed on combining the most efficient system with the right kind of high-speed equipment, substantial savings in time, labor, and material are but a few results. There are also such tangible gains as greater management efficiency with less human wear and tear, and better customer and employee relationships.

Many companies, however, are getting a remarkably high degree of efficiency using traditional standard equipment combined with well-developed systems designed to get maximum use from such equipment. Others are just getting around to changing from manual or key-operated machines to the high-speed, versatile punched-card systems. Only a relatively small percentage of firms—even the largest ones—has made maximum use of punched-card technology. Research indicates that much remains to be done by these companies to attain effective machine loading as well as efficient methods of flow and control.

Less than 5 percent of some 300 major firms have taken any real steps in the direction of preparing for or securing electronic data-processing equipment. Of those that have, however, top management reports that, in planning the revised, simplified, and detailed systems necessary for the new equipment, large savings were realized before the equipment had been installed. Again the system, not the equipment, proves to be the basic element in good office management!

When Obsolescence Sets In

Obsolescent office equipment—as actually judged by the companies' own standards—was reported in over 80 percent of the organizations covered by Dartnell's survey. By far the greatest percentage of obsolescence, "as high as 100 percent," is in typewriters, keyboard equipment (adding, accounting, and bookkeeping machines), addressing devices, dictating machines, and duplicating equipment.

Almost 85 percent of those surveyed reported a need for new machines; 75 percent needed new office furniture and equipment; 65 percent had leased or purchased new equipment since beginning their office work-simplification programs; and 85 percent were planning additional purchases or leasing of new office equipment "in the immediate future."

Anticipated purchases or leasing by these companies vary in dollars and cents from $500 a month to a cash outlay of $125,000 a year. Companies reported new equipment budgets at $10,000, $30,-000, $50,000, $75,000, and $100,000; and rental costs for as many as 100 new units.

The list of new equipment to be purchased or leased by companies surveyed runs from adding machines, electric typewriters, new electronic computers, calculators, microfilm machines, a wide variety of facsimile printers and reproducers to large-scale communications systems employing Teletype printers, as well as network and telegraph systems. It would appear that the office machine industry is actually at the dawn of a new boom with a tremendous present market only some 30 to 35 percent "modernized" and with scores of new enterprises starting up monthly!

One reported trend of particular importance to management and the office machine industry is the result of the variety of the new equipment, its multiple and complex uses, and the planning and programing problem for its effective operation under speeded up and decentralized administration. More and more people are having a hand in the actual decision to purchase, lease, or install the new equipment. In spite of reports to the contrary, company purchasing agents are becoming less a factor in the selection of specific brand, size, and type of high-speed, multiuse office equipment than formerly. Because of these factors, the actual operations officers (vice-presidents, controllers, treasurers, auditors), supervisors, and methods and systems directors are the ones who have to be sold on the relative merits of new and competitive machinery.

While this makes selling more difficult, the "big ticket" equipment involved is causing management to critically study and analyze equipment purchases, even of small, relatively inexpensive units. In the long run, this augurs well for management. "If those who are actually going to use the equipment have a voice in its purchase, it increases their responsibility and makes them conscious of the need for using judgment in involving the company in increased costs," states the executive vice-president of one of the nation's largest insurance firms.

Chapter 52

MECHANICS OF WORK SIMPLIFICATION

IF a company has over 50 employees, it must be alert to systems as a management function. For whether or not there is a systems man, most of the supervisory and administrative employees are doing systems work every day they are on the job.

Function of a Systems Staff

A systems staff improves business management by applying creative thinking to problems of business communication. Its medium is usually paper work, the cheapest reliable means of communication. Its products are policies and procedures, systems studies recommending management action, forms designed to best utilize the printed medium, and flow charts to picture the sequence of steps in a procedure.

If the function goes unrecognized, the work may somehow get done; but probably in an unskilled, haphazard way. Effective systems work takes a high degree of management skill. It follows that the skill of a trained specialist is a real asset.

What if the systems job does get done haphazardly?

Profits are hurt. A good systems operation is a big moneymaker. The systems man who saves his company less than $25,000 a year is not doing his job, and often $100,000 a year is closer to his value. Not many business tasks are so directly productive.

When Minneapolis-Honeywell's former Aero Division began to realize this fact, top management decided that something should be done. The position of divisional systems administrator was established, with the administrator reporting to the director of administration.

Major task of the new post was to study the divisional systems picture that existed, study how systems groups operate in other companies, and propose an organizational plan of action. Management's criterion was that the administrator be a man of considerable systems background; well versed in the practical, operating problems of the systems field and of the company.

The proposal was developed, presented, and accepted by management. The research included not only Honeywell and its divisions, but several major systems departments in companies throughout the United States and Canada, plus weeks of study, discussion, and revision, to arrive at the most workable result.

What Is an Effective Systems Staff?

The carefully picked, trained, and skilled systems staff is a strong bridge that links daily company progress to the long-range, broad-scope plans and policies of management. By its awareness of working problems, it conveys management's intent with the full cooperation of the workers themselves. And by its creative approach, it often improves upon original plans.

In a real sense, the systems staff is responsible for the network of company communications, written and verbal—between groups and departments, between management and the employees—linking present operations of the organization to its future planning.

When systems men are not hand-picked, and training is a stumbling, find-out-for-yourself affair; when management casts a jaundiced eye on the whole systems operation, and little problems keep the systems man wrapped up in busy-work, the company gets only a minor assist from its systems staff.

To Whom Should the Systems Staff Report?

For the systems staff to reflect the corporate viewpoint, it must report to a person whose function and viewpoint are also corporate. This may not be the company president, but it should certainly be someone in the upper management circle. His allegiance should not be with a specialized segment of the company such as manufacturing or accounting, for such an alliance would entangle the systems effort in the web of departmental specialized interests.

To a detail man, a "line" manager, or one who directs a large clerical staff, the ways of the systems staff might seem illogical and confusing; for systems is a creative task in which the imaginative, sometimes blue-sky approach is common. Standard methods and scheduled results will hamstring its vitality.

The staff should report to a man of some creative imagination, one who appreciates that creative output does not follow a predictable time schedule. He should know how to pick a capable manager, give him the help and backing he needs to do the job well, and then leave the details of the operation to him except for the matters of management policy and direction, and long-range planning.

The man himself may be more important than his title. Generally, the functions of an administrative vice-president are best suited to head the systems effort, although the comptroller or other official may be effective if he can fully divorce his departmental bias from systems decisions.

Systems sees each problem from management's point of view; yet, to accomplish the most, it must be close to the whole gamut of company activities.

The staff, through its systems manager, keeps open the channels to company management. The means of keeping intimately in contact with daily operations at the factory and office level is more complex but just as vital to the systems staff's success. This is where the planning of organizational relationships and of physical location of the systems men can make a world of difference.

Organization

There are, generally, two types of systems men: The general practitioner, responsible for all the efforts of a certain department or area; and the specialist, who probes certain fields in depth, such as reproduction equipment, tabulating systems, the special requirements of electronic data processing, and so forth. Each reports directly to the systems manager and works closely with the other systems men.

Area Systems Men: By physically locating the general practitioners in their respective areas in the company, they acquire the personal "feel" for the area and its problems and are most available to the people who are experiencing these problems. Yet, by their direct job responsibility to the systems manager, by constant association with the other systems men, and by periodic staff meetings they can maintain the company concept over departmental narrowness. Their greatest strength is in the intimate understanding they have for the area they are a part of and for the personalities that make it up. They are continuously working with these people and their problems, and are depended upon to best present the area needs in interarea and management decisions.

Systems Specialists: Usually the systems specialists work for no particular area, but provide technical ability on certain types of problems. They work with and through the area systems men, often coordinating the problems of factory or office with the reproduction department, with tabulating or electronic data processing, or with cost and financial requirements—whatever their specialty requires. They are usually men with general systems backgrounds who have advanced by aptitude and experience into these positions.

Levels of Area Systems Men: Within the group of area systems men are juniors, acquiring the basic year or two of training and experience, and whose training and work direction come from the area systems man who also reviews and approves the results of their work before it is acted upon.

Systems man (center) works out a revised manufacturing system with production people at Minneapolis-Honeywell.

The area systems men represent a particular department or area. Large departments may have two or more working together, small areas may share one with other areas. These men have completed their systems training and have up to five years of working experience in systems.

The senior systems man may head the systems activity of a major department, or he may work from area to area or interdepartmentally on the tougher, broader problems. He may be the right-hand man of the systems manager on company planning or on systems problems of major reorganizational import. He usually has more than five years of heavy experience, and his salary is in the range of the specialist.

Other Functions: Forms-design skill is part of the training of every systems man; but except in the smaller companies, much of the actual design work is handled by forms designers, who report to the systems manager and handle work from several systems men. Forms control is also their bailiwick; they order forms, control reorders, and see that the proper systems man knows about the placement of orders for forms he may be concerned with, so that a form is not changed a week after a year's supply has been ordered.

Procedure writers are men with systems aptitude who can take the basic write up of a system and turn it into a brief, grammatically correct procedure which can be clearly understood by all levels of personnel. A good procedure writer is invaluable; often he is a man who is spotted for later advancement into the full scope of systems work.

These are the reasons why systems people should report to a systems head:

1. To avoid the dangers which internal bias can produce when the systems man is controlled by the manager of any operating department.

2. To permit hiring and full control of systems men by a manager skilled in systems.

3. To allow for movement of systems men among departments, for better coverage, for more thorough experience, and for promotional opportunity within the systems group. It is important that staff members do not become stale.

4. To provide a systems staff for group efforts on problems of major proportions.

5. To coordinate the writing and use of individual studies, procedures, and equipment information for the benefit of the entire company.

Requirements of a Good Systems Man

Behind any acquired trait, the systems man must have analytical ability, creative ability, and sales ability. He should have management potential, with the aptitude to advance well beyond the job for which he is hired.

His work will be superficial if he bridles at detail, but he is just as useless if he can lose himself by the hour in statistical contemplation. In short, he must keep always on track, not detouring around some bitter detail nor wandering off tangentially when a door is left open.

He must be hard-nosed on occasion; but unless tact and patience are strong features of his personality, he can never have the cooperation and respect of the people he works with. Human relations is the most important single tool of systems.

Common sense—the ability to keep his perspective, to sense the value and direction of his efforts—is his strong ally when the going is rough and the pressure heavy.

He is skeptical, trusting only cold facts, making unemotional decisions, being wary of the radical until he can justify it.

He must have a sense of humor. Frustrations are inherent in systems work, and without this safety valve the job will sour him. Too often, perhaps, every systems man finds himself backed into a corner; sometimes his only graceful way out is through humor.

He will be a drag on the staff if he lacks real enthusiasm for systems work, plus directed energy—plenty of initiative and a large capacity for hard work.

A college education is almost a necessity, but the particular field of concentration in which the degree is earned apparently makes no measurable difference. In his formal training he should have developed a good speaking vocabulary and a simple and clear manner of writing.

Ways to Combat Ineffectiveness

Even the best systems staff can lose its touch and become ineffective. Sometimes the weakening is hard to find; but unless it is located and corrected, the staff becomes impotent, its results superficial.

It may be the systems manager himself; he may lose sight of his goal, or fail to apply the strong guidance the staff needs. He may, through his intense concern for a major project such as electronic data processing or a departmental reshuffling, get out of touch with some of his men. Or he may be resting on his laurels.

Management backing may become weak. Nothing is so damaging to staff morale as to work out a tough problem, get agreement and support clear to the doorstep of management, then watch it wither and fade from inaction.

The systems men themselves may cause the slump. Perhaps they become absorbed in small problems, lose their drive, or fail in the human side of problems and so lose the faith of the people they work for. Or they may be too willing to compromise a problem to avoid dissension.

There are ways to counter these problems. Perhaps the most fundamental is that the reward of good income keep pace with growing abilities. Good men will not last without it.

The training program should be a continuous thing, with new ideas continuously injected, discussed, and applied. Broadening a man's experience by rotation to other areas or assignments keeps him on his toes and progressing.

But most of all, the staff must feel the constant stimulation of new and more challenging projects.

What Is a Good Systems Man Worth?

Systems has only recently begun to be recognized as a skilled profession. Some companies still hire or transfer a man to the systems job, give him a desk, and tell him to go to work. This requires the least out-of-pocket expense to the company; it is also most likely to discourage management on the whole subject of systems.

For such a systems man is a fire fighter equipped with only a watering pot; when there is a problem to solve, he keeps busy without doing much of anything. The results of his efforts have no comparison, either in scope or in accomplishments, with the work of the trained and experienced professional.

It costs more to hire a skilled systems man of management caliber, for good management men are hard to come by. When you find one, his fee is likely to fit into this national picture:

Trainee or junior—up to two years' experience............................to $ 8,000

Systems man—two to five years' experience.................$ 8,000 to $10,000

Senior systems man or systems specialist—with over
five years' experience...$10,000 to $18,000

Systems manager—over five years' experience...................$18,000 to $22,000

A good systems staff is dynamic; its impact on the well-being of the entire enterprise can be profound. The accepted, successful staff finds itself in the midst of the company's long-range planning, its systems manager a working member of the top management team. And—perhaps the best indicator—this systems operation is well regarded within the company by the employees themselves.

THE TOOLS OF WORK SIMPLIFICATION

If you want a quick idea of your production efficiency make a diagram of your office and trace the work flow with a pencil.

This advice to business executives is offered by Kenneth H. Ripnen, New York architect and planning consultant for the Wood Office Furniture Institute.

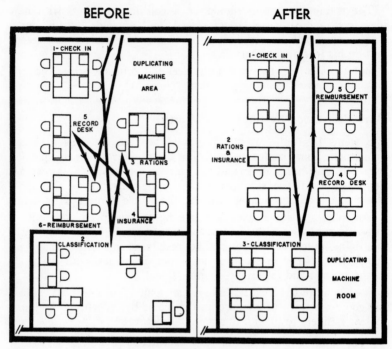

At left, the torturous path of a typical office process before a simplification program. At right, a highly efficient work flow results from a rearrangement of work steps and stations.

Following the simple geometric axiom—that a straight line is the shortest distance between two points—can save management time and money, Mr. Ripnen points out.

In straight-line work flow, paperwork moves from one desk to another with the least amount of handling, travel, and delay. A chart of an efficient office flow should look like a railroad map—no turning back, but a general forward movement.

Mr. Ripnen points out that the size of the office makes no difference. It takes just as long for a person to walk 10 feet too far in a small office as in a large one.

Other suggestions which tie into the work-flow pattern are that office records and machines be centralized so they will be available to many departments without needless effort; that the use of cubicles be held to a minimum; that related departments be located next to each other; and that employees be placed in front of or around their own supervisors.

According to Mr. Ripnen, the most effective use of available office space can be achieved by systematic planning which takes into account all factors, including type of work, floor plan, equipment, lighting, color, and wall and floor coverings.

Lately, some consultants are concerned with an aspect of work flow often ignored. This is the social aspect of work. Many people go out of their way in the course of executing a "mission" in order to talk to various people in the office. When the problem is serious, it usually can be solved by a different arrangement of working locations, or by improving discipline.

Usually there is one person to whom others gravitate for their "talk break." Placing this person closer to the supervisor usually reduces such visits.

Often, an additional office machine in a new location can make the difference between miles of extra walking and hours of time. A check on who uses what machines may possibly eliminate a lot of waste motion.

Motion Study

Supervisors will understand work simplification better when they know the basic elements of motion study. Often, hours of time can be saved by spending a few moments observing and experimenting with the motions of employees as they work at their jobs. Even in offices, time can be cut on such operations as folding, sorting, assembling, and distributing of papers.

The following rules of motion economy should be checked at the start of operations or in advance, if possible:

1. Are both hands of the employee moving at the same time?
2. Is the path followed by hands and arms smooth and continuous?
3. Is the work arranged so that motions are the simplest possible?
4. Where applicable, is it possible to use both hand and foot motions?
5. Are materials moved with a sliding motion or aided by gravity, rather than a lifting motion?
6. Are materials and tools placed within the work area—the space outlined when employee's elbows are on edge of desk and hands move in an arc?
7. Are materials and tools placed so that the best sequence of motions may be used?
8. Is it possible to have everything in position before the employee begins work, and the stock of materials maintained throughout the operation?
9. Are there any fixtures that could be used to increase the productive work done by the hands? Racks, hangers, etc.?
10. Is the employee comfortable, the work level right for good posture?

Motion study often fails in getting a warm reception from employees or unions. But it is not "speed-up"; it's efficiency. Some supervisors say they observe the employee at work and then try out a new technique unobserved by the employee. Then they attempt to have the employee think it is his own idea—that the new way is the best way. At the least, they talk things over with the employee and lead into the suggestion gradually.

Steps to Simplification

A well-organized description of the paperwork-simplification procedure has been recorded by Charles O. Libby, former head of the office-methods staff, Tennessee Valley Authority. The following paragraphs are Mr. Libby's advice:

If the routine or paperwork you wish to review is simple and involves few steps, a list of the steps in the operation, with the employees who perform them, may serve the purpose. List all details from actual observation and questioning of the employees. Some supervisors prefer to work from a list of breakdowns gathered in this manner rather than from a chart. The list would be similar to the "Description" on the process chart which follows. If the routines are complex, or paper work is large in volume, or there are many steps involved, you may want a detailed chart for review.

Here is what you will want to know:

1. *What* is being done and *why?*
2. *Who* is doing it and *why?*
3. *Where* is it being done and is the step performed in the right place?
4. *When* is it being done and are the steps in proper sequence?
5. *How* is it being done and can it be simplified?

You will want the facts in graphic form so you can study them together objectively. Is there a bottleneck? Are there steps which take a lot of time? Do activities result in needless running about? A good review for improvement will eliminate unnecessary steps, combine steps where appropriate, change the sequence for more direct operation, and simplify the remaining steps.

Several charts are used for this purpose and you may have preferences. Any chart or form which will display the facts graphically will serve the purpose.

Gather the Facts: When you have selected the paperwork to be charted, you will want to explain to each person interviewed what information you require and what you are going to do with it. There should be no mystery about it; all you want is to get the facts as they are now. Select a starting and an ending point of the operation for your review. Identify and describe fully each specific step in the operation, however minor. You should note time required for each step and the distance traveled.

The Process Chart: The process chart is useful in studying a series of steps in one continuous operation. It is not as complicated as it may appear at first glance, and many people like to use it once they become familiar with it. From it can be seen the flow as a whole; the storages and transportations can be selected for special study, or the individual steps examined for refinement.

Forms Flow Chart: The forms flow chart is useful in studying office forms; where each copy goes, who handles it, and what disposition is made of it. The chart affords an opportunity to study the distribution and to determine whether or not each step is necessary, whether one copy can take the place of two, or whether two copies can get some steps in the work done at the same time. The objective is to eliminate steps, copies, backtracking, and waiting time.

The charts should give the answers to what, why, who, where, when, and how. By studying the procedure as a whole and by questioning each step, four possible ways to simplify the work will be found:

1. *Eliminate all unnecessary work.* You should question every step and even the procedure itself. Can it or any part of it be eliminated? Particularly you will want to examine those steps in which work is delayed, such as transportation and storage. Study how to cut down waiting time and distance traveled. Can time be reduced by eliminating this step as a separate operation and placing the work in another step? Is there any backtracking of copies? Every step you cut out or cut down will speed up the work, will be a convenience to employees, and will be cumulative in effect. Can interruptions be avoided? Every bottleneck where papers pile up is a signal for special study. The use of a window envelope eliminates addressing. A form letter will eliminate individual memoranda. You may be able to use a stamp or a check mark instead of posting. Do you have to file every copy?

2. *Combine steps in the procedure.* Can you combine the steps or even the procedure itself with any duplicating activities? Sometimes work has been broken down too far and can be made easier by combining two steps. Can the use of another copy of the form for information purposes get work done concurrently with a step? Can rewriting be avoided by an extra copy? Can a step be performed

	LEGEND				PROCESS CHART of Order Routine (Before Revision)
(a) Mail Clk.	(e) Sales Anal.				
(b) Order Inter.	(f) Stock Clk.				
(c) Calc.	(g) Shipp. Clk.				
(d) Cash Clk.	( )				

O In Feet	△ Time in Min.	Operation / Transport	Storage	Inspect	Step No.	DESCRIPTION
		(a) ○	△	□	1	Mail Clerk receives order and remittance in mail
		○ (b)	△	□	2	Sends order and remittance to Order Interpreter
		○ ○	△ [b]	□	3	Checks to see if Cat. numbers and descriptions are correct
		○ (c)	△	□	4	Sends to Calculator
		○ ○	△ [c]	□	5	Checks extensions and amounts
		○ (d)	△	□	6	Sends to Cash Clerk
		○ ○	△ [d]	□	7	Checks amount of remittance and amount of order
		(d) ○	△	□	8	Posts remittance
		○ (e)	△	□	9	Sends to Sales Analysis Clerk
		(e) ○	△	□	10	Records items for statistical purposes
		○ (f)	△	□	11	Sends to Stock Clerk
		(f) ○	△	□	12	Looks up locations of items and marks on order
		(f) ○	△	□	13	Removes items from shelves and sends to Shipping Clerk
		(g) C	△	□	14	Prepares shipping label
		(g) ○	△	□	15	Prepares packing slip and notice of shipment
		(g) ○	△	□	16	Packs and ships order
		○ (g)	△	□	17	Releases notice of shipment to customer
		○ ○	△	□		
		○ ○	△	□		
		○ ○	△	□		
		○ ○	△	□		
		○ ○	△	□		
		○ ○	△	□		
		○ ○	△	□		

Order routine before simplification

LEGEND		PROCESS CHART
(a) Mail Clk. (d) Stock Clk.		of
(b) Calc. (e) Ship. Clk.		Order Routine
(c) Cash Clk. ◯		(As Revised)

O In Feet	△ Time in Min.	Operation	Transport	Storage	Inspect	Step No.	DESCRIPTION
		(a)	○	△	□	1	Mail Clerk receives order and remittance in mail
		○	●	△	□	2	Sends order and remittance to Calculator
		○	○	△	(b)	3	Inspects for proper remittance - checks extensions
		○	●	△	□	4	Sends to Cash Clerk
		(c)	○	△	□	5	Prepares set of forms including Stat. Anal., Pack. Slip, etc. and makes posting at same time
		○	●	△	□	6	Sends Stat. Analysis to Sales Dept.
		○	●	△	□	7	Sends Packing Slip, Notice of Shipt. and Shipping Label to Stock Clerk
		(d)	○	△	□	8	Looks up locations of items and marks on order
		(d)	○	△	□	9	Removes items from shelves and sends to Shipping Clerk
		(e)	○	△	□	10	Packs and ships order
		○	●	△	□	11	Releases Notice of Shipment to Customer
		○	○	△	□		
		○	○	△	□		
		○	○	△	□		
		○	○	△	□		
		○	○	△	□		
		○	○	△	□		
		○	○	△	□		
		○	○	△	□		
		○	○	△	□		
		○	○	△	□		
		○	○	△	□		
		○	○	△	□		

Order routine after simplification

during the waiting time of another operation? You may find that separate checking and inspection steps are not warranted. Or you may find that checking a larger quantity at one time will be more efficient. The work load of each step will affect the waiting time in steps which follow, and some of the work load may be better distributed. Possibly a visible record pocket can combine several forms and so combine steps. Sometimes a pegboard will permit a spread-sheet arrangement of separate reports. Can a monthly report take the place of a more frequent one? Will a punch-card system combine two or more card files?

3. *Change sequence of steps.* You will want to question the order in which the work advances to completion. The elimination or combination of steps may require a different sequence. Work should pass from desk to desk with a minimum of distance and time. Will a change of sequence cut down transportation or waiting time? Can storage points be moved advantageously? Are the items of the form in the proper sequence for rapid posting to another? Does the form have to go back to a desk again for additional information? The arrangement of furniture and use of communications may affect the steady flow of work. Are desks for related work grouped together? Can dictation take place at a regular time instead of interrupting operations? Can mail or forms be signed or forwarded regularly instead of developing peak periods?

4. *Simplify the remaining steps.* When you have eliminated unnecessary steps, combined steps where possible, and determined the most direct sequence, you can refine the operations further by study of details. You will be carrying on the same process of elimination, combination, and checking the sequence in a single step. Where there is a volume of work you may want to apply the principles of motion economy. Supplies and equipment should be in easy reach. Reference materials should be convenient to the worker. Should the form be redesigned for rapid handling? Are data furnished in usable form? Is the followup method cumbersome? Can a checklist increase the accuracy? Will classification of data by signals on a visible record simplify reference or reporting? Correspondence constitutes a large part of routine work. Have you streamlined it? Would mechanical devices save time or labor? You are working with details which are not trivia because through repetition they consume a large amount of time. That is why a new appliance will often pay for itself.

These statements can only be suggestive and the process chart will reveal other opportunities for simplification. When you have studied the steps sufficiently, try drawing them up in the new order. Be sure to check all proposed changes with those doing the work, for they may suggest further revision, and all will benefit by their participation.

SYMBOLS FOR PROCESS CHARTING

By use of four standard symbols the basic steps in any procedure can be graphically portrayed on a process chart. However, the essential thought in process charting is the identification of each step—not the symbols. Figures or letters may be used, or no separate indications. The steps can then be studied without other identification.

OPERATION

When something is being changed or created or added to.

TRANSPORTATION

When something is moved from one place to another.

STORAGE

When something remains in one place awaiting action, or is filed.

INSPECTION

When something is checked or verified.

HOW A COMPANY METHODS STAFF OPERATES

PLANNING, ORGANIZING, AND DIRECTING

Like all other segments of the company, Methods must plan, organize, and direct its work in the same way that the company as a whole performs its management obligations. Whether a methods office is composed of a single individual, who spends part or full time on methods work, or has numerous employees, its work is conducted systematically according to a planned approach, a sound allocation of activities, and close technical supervision.

Planning the work is primarily a matter of specifying in written form the functions assigned to the office and developing specific programs which will lead to a systematic attainment of the goals indicated in the functional statement. Organizing the work involves the assignment of the programs to the personnel of the office. Programs are divided into major subjects, and ordinarily the assignment of analyst personnel follows the natural subject division of the programs, with one or more analysts assigned to carry out each program. In a small organization several programs may be assigned to a single analyst or to a group of analysts. Directing the work involves the development of projects by means of which the programs will be carried out and supervising their execution. While the programs indicate the subject fields into which the functions have been divided, the projects are specific assignments in these fields.

PLANNING THROUGH PROGRAMS

Since the place of Methods in the company's scheme of things is to advise general management and to assist operating and supervisory management in the realm of administrative analysis, these responsibilities are prescribed in the Organization Plan and Manual as follows:

RESPONSIBILITIES OF THE METHODS STAFF

Develop programs involving organizational and procedural planning; develop projects for improving effectiveness or coordination in assigned fields.

Analyze current policies, procedures, practices, forms, and records; prepare charts and analyses reflecting work flows and performance, distribution of forms, maintenance of records and specific action taken on such forms and records; ascertain essentiality of existing activities and determine the necessary improvements to simplify or reduce clerical and administrative work and processing time.

Prepare manuals covering new or improved office methods; assist with the installation of such methods and arrange for training of employees in the required techniques.

Coordinate studies of office methods and equipment conducted in branch offices; keep informed of the progress made on each study and disseminate results to all interested Head Office departments and branch offices.

Develop job performance standards as a tool for office management and for comparative purposes when evaluating methods.

Maintain a current study of office furniture and equipment and develop new applications for existing, improved or new types of office equipment. Keep all offices informed of new or improved types of office equipment and possible application. Establish standards and recommend the use of office equipment which will result in improved efficiency or control.

Maintain continuous research in new management practices and disseminate information to improve administration operations.

These are the technical functions which Methods performs on behalf of management. Because Methods keeps itself technically informed in detail of administrative practices, it is in a position to compare and evaluate methods and to recommend improvements as the need becomes evident. The statement of functions, however, provides only advisory authority. Methods issues no orders. It analyzes, develops, and recommends. Solely upon the force of the facts gathered and the demonstrable worth of the recommendations made do methods analysts achieve the goals which management desires.

With the basic planning complete in the form of a statement of functions, the next consideration is to develop the programs to implement the general aims. The programs are grouped according to a logical arrangement by the major subjects which they embrace, and the responsibilities contained in the statement of functions are restated in somewhat more detail in the programs.

Each program is developed according to the type of work which will be assigned to the methods analysts. The technical skills which analysts are called upon to use in the course of their duties are as varied as the problems to which the skills are directed. Ideally, all analysts in a methods office should possess the knowledge and experience required to meet all technical situations which they would be likely to encounter. Even if this were normally true, the analytical work of the office would nevertheless have to be apportioned among the staff. The most convenient apportionment has generally been found to be in accordance with the specialties usually found separately in methods personnel. Each specialty also happens to be a natural division of the analytical elements common to methods problems. Close coordination of the specialties is requisite, however, if the programs are to be properly integrated.

How Methods has followed this natural division of specialties in developing its programs is evident from a consideration of each program.

OFFICE SYSTEMS PROGRAM

Conduct surveys of procedures and organizational relationships in Head Office and branch offices, in terms of the practicable extent of standardization, simplification, and production measurement. Coordinate with all other programs.

The office systems program, although the most comprehensive of all, places its emphasis upon administrative work flows and the organizational relationships established to process the work. In this program, measurable units of work are developed and related to the number of employees required to process a given volume of work. Of necessity this program is closely coordinated with the other programs. Analysts responsible for the office systems program possess the most general type of methods knowledge, although they must, from time to time, call for assistance from the specialists engaged in other programs.

EQUIPMENT STANDARDS PROGRAM

Conduct detailed studies and test makes and models of office machines and equipment for the purpose of making specific recommendations for practical application, proper utilization, and economical operation of equipment recommended. Establish basic requirements for the justification of purchase and for budgetary control purposes.

The equipment standards program is the most technical of all the programs. It deals with the best applications of office equipment, in accordance with the requirements of the procedures in which they are employed. Since procedural variations frequently govern whether or not a process will be performed manually or by machine, the equipment program is closely allied and coordinated with the office systems program. Likewise, the manner of housing filed records in cabinets becomes a joint consideration of analysts engaged in the records management program and the equipment program.

RECORDS MANAGEMENT PROGRAM

Develop filing systems and standards for the effective management of records. Develop recommendations concerning the retention of records in accordance with prescribed company policies. Coordinate with all other programs.

The records management program comprehends filing systems and the administration of records generally, including their arrangement, accessibility, and preservation. Clearly a specialty, records management as a program must be conducted in terms of the procedures of which the records are a part.

ADMINISTRATIVE EVALUATION PROGRAM

Follow up new methods installations and periodically review on a comparative basis the effectiveness of office systems, using data derived from the production measurement phase of the office systems program. Coordinate activities with all other programs.

The administrative evaluation program, although it may be considered as a final phase of the office systems program, is developed separately. This is primarily because its emphasis is upon the comparative measurement of work performed, following the standardization which results from the development of revised procedures. The program starts only after sufficient time has elapsed to permit an accurate evaluation of results and final adjustment of procedural and organizational details.

COORDINATION PROGRAM

Establish a systematic means of correlating forms and reports with related administrative procedures and coordinate the dissemination of information concerning policies and procedures.

COORDINATION OF FORMS: Within existing company requirements, develop and maintain a system for review and clearance of forms for purposes of analysis and standardization prior to use. Coordinate standardization with the office systems program.

COORDINATION OF RECURRING REPORTS AND STATEMENTS: Develop and maintain a system for review and clearance of recurring reports and statements initiated or requested, to avoid duplication and overlapping of data. Coordinate operation of the plan with the office systems program.

COORDINATION OF PUBLICATIONS: Develop and maintain a system for review and clearance for standardization of format and consistency of content of manuals, instructions, and other publications involving policies, procedures, organization, reports, statements, or forms.

Each of the three segments of the coordination program could of itself become a separate program if the volume of work were sufficient to warrant separate emphasis. Methods has grouped them together for the sake of simplicity. The coordination of forms, recurring reports, and publications is basic to administrative management. Without forms coordination, many duplicating forms, ill designed for ease of use, could be allowed to slow down procedures and retard prompt operating action. Without reports coordination, independent segments of the organization could impose reporting requirements upon other offices of an unduly burdensome or overlapping nature. Without publications coordination, conflicting instructions could be issued. Coordination provides a clearance which prevents administrative confusion and unnecessary expense.

RESEARCH AND TRAINING PROGRAM

Establish and maintain relationships with professional management societies and with other companies for the mutual exchange of information relative to management improvements in policies, organization, procedures, equipment, and methods-development techniques.

Develop, by laboratory methods, systems applications to company problems; test the applications; maintain bibliography and file of data representing the most effective proven solutions to typical methods problems.

Prepare training material on all phases of methods work for the systematic use of employees engaged in this field.

Conduct regularly scheduled seminars in methods problems and techniques.

Coordinate activities with all other methods programs.

The research and training program embraces the development and exchange of technical data relating to methods work between internal and outside sources. Data are available to train new analysts and for refresher material for the staff.

ORGANIZING THROUGH ASSIGNMENTS

To as great an extent as is practical, the personnel of a methods office should be interchangeable for purposes of assignment of work. So closely allied are the various programs that the entire staff must at all times be familiar with the nature and progress of all active and future projects of the office. For purposes of production of work, however, analysts should be confined for specified periods to a single program.

DIRECTING THROUGH PROJECTS

Projects constitute the nonroutine, nonrecurring studies which are made by methods analysts to further the goals of the programs. The result of a project ordinarily is the development of a new or the modification of an existing plan, policy, or procedure. Results normally are accomplished by means of a special report, revision of published instructions, issuance of a manual or other appropriate media. The purpose of a status of project report is to establish internal control over the work, by establishing a target date for the completion of each project, by measuring progress and by scheduling work.

TECHNIQUES OF ANALYSIS

PREPARATION FOR ANALYSIS

PLANNING THE PROJECT

Following the assignment of a project to the methods analyst, there are preliminary preparations which must be made prior to the commencement of the study. Regardless of the type of analytical survey involved, these preparations always are basically the same. Their object is to insure that the course of the project is determined beforehand and that the desired result is kept in sight during all phases of the study. There are four steps in planning the project:

STEP 1. DETERMINE WHO, WHAT, AND HOW LONG

WHO: Decide to whom the results of the project will be beneficial. Is the study directed toward management controls, or toward assisting operating personnel in performing assigned functions? Decide also whose assistance will be required. Consider asking assistance from specialists in the field under study. Opportunities should be taken to discuss the problems with those who are most familiar with it, as a prime source of ideas.

WHAT: Determine what the end result of the project will be, such as a report, a manual, or a letter of instructions.

HOW LONG: Determine how long it will take to complete the project. Although this may be difficult because of unforeseen circumstances, it is desirable to set a target date and to try conscientiously to meet that date, although it may later have to be revised.

STEP 2. OBTAIN BACKGROUND DATA

REVIEW pertinent reference material already available both within and outside the company. What has already been accomplished? What have the results been? Study reports, manuals, instruction letters, and other records pertaining to the subject to obtain a broad picture of the problem and to select authoritative reference material for later detailed study.

DISCUSS the problem generally with persons who have a working knowledge of how the work is performed. Obtain from them their experiences and problems. Ask for constructive suggestions for improvements.

STEP 3. SELECT LOCATION FOR CONDUCTING STUDY

SELECT the office in which the survey may be made most appropriately.

STEP 4. PREPARE TENTATIVE PLAN

DEVELOP the course of the project in outline form setting forth the objectives of the study and the method of attack. The plan should include in chronological sequence the steps which it is proposed to follow from the start to the end of the project.

ANALYSIS OF OFFICE SYSTEMS

GENERAL

Although the material in this section is confined to some of the techniques for analyzing organization, procedures, and office layout, and for the measurement of work production, many office systems projects will also involve other types of analyses, such as those which deal with office equipment, forms, and other records.

ORGANIZATION

The organization of a company may be considered in terms of function and structure. Function is used in its physiological sense of the normal and special action of any part of an organism. Functions are the means of accomplishing the objectives, or goals, for which a business is established. Structure is used to mean the arrangement of the parts which perform functions.

The structure of an organization may be of several types or combinations of types. The line of authority may flow directly downward from the president of the company through intermediate executives to the operating supervisors. In this type of organization, called "line," each executive has direct authority over subordinate units, which look to him for orders. Each executive, likewise, looks to his superior for instructions.

PLAN FOR METHODS SURVEY IN PRODUCTION AREA OFFICES

OBJECTIVE

The general purpose of the survey is to develop, in manual form, standard instructions for all activities under the jurisdiction of the Treasury managers in area offices. The subject matter will include policies, organizational and functional relationships, office procedures and records, and the preparation of reports.

METHOD

The surveys will be conducted in the areas by the Methods and Statistics Department in collaboration with selected area personnel. The surveys will be divided into eight phases; planning, fact-finding, analysis, development of test manuals, testing, publication, installation, and followup.

PHASE 1. PLANNING

This phase will take place in Head Office and will be divided into four steps as follows:

Step A. Select uniform methods techniques to be used for the collection of data.

Step B. Designate offices to be surveyed and notify local management of the survey plan. Request that one copy of each work paper, report, and form be collected.

Step C. Prepare checklist of procedures to be studied.

Step D. Establish target dates for ensuing phases as the result of preliminary sampling study in one office.

PHASE 2. FACT-FINDING

This phase will take place at the designated offices and will be divided into ten steps as follows:

Step A. Review overall plan with the Treasury manager, who will designate representative of area office as member of team. Hold meeting of section supervisors at which purpose of survey is outlined and method of approach discussed.

Step B. Review with area office representative on team the preliminary checklist of procedures to be studied; revise list and distribute copies to all supervisors.

Step C. Provide area office member of team with examples of techniques to be used in the fact-finding phase of the survey.

Step D. Classify documents collected by area office into the following categories.

  1. Work Papers
  2. Reports
  3. Flow of Work

PLAN FOR METHODS SURVEY IN PRODUCTION AREA OFFICES (Cont.)

Step E. Determine starting point of survey and assign team members to procedures to be studied.

Step F. Determine by observation and interview the existing procedure to disclose:

1. All documents and number of copies, such as transaction papers including vouchers, checks, run-tickets, working papers, and bookkeeping records, such as accounts receivable ledger and stock reports.

2. Flow of documents through organization.

3. Actions taken during each step of the procedure; all document entries will be identified as to source and document to which posted.

4. Utilization of business machines and equipment in the processing.

NOTE: The data obtained in Step F above should be recorded with the utmost care on the procedure analysis worksheet. By so doing, the preparation of process charts becomes a simplified operation.

Step G. Collect a specimen copy of each document involved.

Step H. Compile statistics indicating work load and scheduling of work load by type of employee.

Step I. Encourage personnel on the job to submit recommendations for procedural and other improvements.

Step J. Prepare flow charts from the procedure analysis worksheet. Review the flow chart with operating personnel and with supervisors concerned— obtain signature of supervisor to confirm the fact that the chart has been reviewed and is an accurate presentation of fact.

PHASE 3. ANALYSIS

In this phase, Steps A, B, C will take place in the branch offices and Step D in Head Office, as follows:

Step A. From work load and scheduling data, develop man-hour factors for measurable work units and analyze in terms of possible revised scheduling of work. Determine unit cost, where possible, in dollars and number of employees under existing procedures.

Step B. Develop charts of the reporting system as a whole, showing the sequence and relationship of the component financial and statistical statements used.

Step C. Analyze reports in terms of:

1. Use by recipients of copies distributed.

2. Unnecessary data on reports.

3. Duplicate postings.

4. Unnecessary posting steps.

5. Consolidation of reports.

6. Frequency and timing of reports.

PLAN FOR METHODS SURVEY IN PRODUCTION AREA OFFICES (Cont.)

Step D. Compare charts and work papers reflecting varying procedures in similar offices and analyze in terms of:

1. Straight line flow of work.

2. Unnecessary steps.

3. Unnecessary documents or copies of documents.

4. Forms design and utilization.

5. Equipment utilization.

6. Organizational relationship to functions performed.

7. Unit cost of producing or processing.

8. Improvement volunteered by branch office personnel.

NOTE: This phase will require assistance of equipment, forms, and files specialists.

PHASE 4. DEVELOPMENT OF TEST MANUALS

This phase will take place in Head Office and will be divided into two steps as follows:

Step A. Develop uniform procedure on basis of conclusions derived from the analysis phase and local concurrence.

Step B. Revise charts of procedures. Develop and prepare test manual.

PHASE 5. TESTING

This phase will take place in a designated pilot branch office and will be divided into three steps as follows:

Step A. Select a pilot office in which to test the tentative manual.

Step B. Secure necessary approvals for testing.

Step C. Install test procedures and revise as required on the basis of operating experience and general concurrences.

PHASE 6. PUBLICATION

This phase will take place in Head Office and will be divided into two steps as follows:

Step A. Revise test manuals to incorporate changes and suggestions.

Step B. Publish the final manuals.

PLAN FOR METHODS SURVEY IN PRODUCTION
AREA OFFICES (Cont.)

PHASE 7. INSTALLATION

This phase will be divided into three steps as follows:

Step A. Conduct training seminars for Chief Accountants for instructions in new procedure installation and distribute manuals.

Step B. Develop a timetable for installation of the various procedures in all offices and secure local management approvals thereto.

Step C. Provide technical assistance to branch offices during the period of installation.

PHASE 8. FOLLOWUP

This phase will be divided into two steps as follows:

Step A. Establish a systematic followup of new systems installed.

Step B. Develop a method of evaluation for:

　　1. New or revised procedures compared with former procedures on the basis of unit cost of measurable work units.

　　2. Comparison of performance of various offices on the basis of work load and unit cost of measurable work units.

Another type of organization introduces the so-called "staff" principle. The staff is used primarily in large companies, where the variety of functions is numerous and specialized. Staff executives have only advisory authority in their special fields and can issue no orders to subordinate units. Thus a minor executive may be advised by several higher executives in specialized activities, while reporting to another superior in the line of authority.

Differences in structural characteristics arise from the manner in which functions are grouped. The structure is called "departmental" if similar functions are performed by several organizational units and each unit is to a great extent self-sufficient in the accomplishment of its objectives. The structure is called "functional" if all similar functions are performed in one organizational unit, and this unit is dependent upon other units for the performance of related but not similar functions. The functional unit may serve other units.

Structural differences also exist in field organizations. Branch offices of a large company may be established in several ways. They may be set up on a geographical basis, to serve a given territory. They may be arranged according to the product manufactured, or they may be established on a functional basis, according to the function they perform.

PRINCIPLES OF ORGANIZATION

In applying organizational principles, the analyst should be aware that they are not universal truths. Practical factors, such as personnel limitations and expediencies occasioned by economy requirements, always enter into mature consideration of industrial organization. Among the essential considerations in an analysis of organization are the following principles. The first two principles deal with function, the second two with structure.

1. *Functions should be properly assigned.*

   Each function should be assigned to a unit of the organization so that all essential tasks will be performed.

   A function should not be assigned to more than one unit, to prevent confusion and duplication of effort.

   Each function should be clearly understood by employees to avoid conflicts and overlapping of activities.

2. *Responsibility and equivalent authority should be decentralized to the unit actually performing a function, without loss of overall control.*

   Responsibility for operating performance should be decentralized to prevent bottlenecks at a central point.

   Full authority to carry out assigned responsibilities should be provided to accelerate action at the operating point.

   Central controls should be established as a check on effectiveness of operations and propriety in the use of delegated authority.

3. *The organization should be standard and as simple as its size will allow.*

   A pattern should prevail at each level of the organization which is standard as to function and terminology. This will assure a general understanding of the location of major functions at all levels.

   The number of units should be as few as the variety of major functions will permit to obtain maximum work accomplishment.

4. *Supervisory and executive relationships should be clearly defined.*

   Each employee should know to whom he reports and who reports to him, to avoid confusion in assignments of work.

   No employee should be answerable to more than one supervisor, although functional guidance may be provided by several supervisors with purely advisory authority.

   The number of persons or units reporting to a supervisor should not exceed the number which can be supervised effectively. The number, called the "span of control," should be determined by the amount of supervision required for a particular type and volume of work.

ANALYSIS OF ORGANIZATION

   To disclose violations of these principles in an organization or in one or more parts of the organization, the analyst will use two means: an analysis worksheet, and a chart of the structure of the organization. The analysis worksheet is so devised that, upon completion, the degree of adherence to the functional principles will be readily observed and corrective recommendations will suggest themselves as they appear to be necessary. The organization chart, which will be analyzed in conjunction with the worksheet, will reveal lack of standardization, complexity, confusion in supervisory relationships, and too great a span of control.

The organization chart is prepared in a form which will reveal structural weaknesses when they exist. There are three basic types of organization charts: (1) structural, (2) functional, and (3) personnel. The functional chart includes the corresponding functions in the box representing each organizational element. The personnel chart omits the functions but includes the employees by title, name, or numbers in the chart boxes. From these charts the degree of conformity of the organization to structural principles may be determined readily.

For ease of operating use as well as for convenience of analysis, organization charts should be prepared according to the following elementary rules:

SIZE. All related charts should be prepared on sheets of paper of the same size.

IDENTIFICATION. Each chart should carry an identification section in the upper right-hand corner indicating the type of chart (structural, functional, personnel) and the name of the part of the organization represented. The name of the company should appear in the upper left-hand corner.

AUTHENTICATION. Each chart should carry its authentication and the date in the lower left-hand corner.

LEGENDS. A legend may be placed in the upper left-hand corner of the chart for identification of symbols or to specify other pertinent information.

PAGE NUMBERS. When more than one sheet is used, each sheet should be numbered in the lower right-hand corner.

CONSTRUCTION. Each chart should be drawn simply and should present a balanced structure insofar as practical.

TITLES. The title of each organization element should be indicative of the major function or functions performed.

PRESENTATION. Rectangular boxes should be used.

Boxes which contain the same types of responsibilities should be placed on the same horizontal level. If space is limited, boxes may be dropped to a lower level but should be connected by the same type of lines.

If it is not feasible to place all subdivisions of the same level on a horizontal line, one or more of the principal boxes may be dropped to a lower level.

Boxes on the highest level may be wider than those on subordinate levels.

Boxes representing elements of the same organization level should be the same size.

For purposes of symmetry, the depth of the longest box should determine the depth of other boxes on the same level.

TYPES OF BOXES. Geometrical shapes should be used.

A solid-line box indicates actual existence of the functions within the organization.

A broken-line box indicates proposed functions, or those not part of the organization but vitally concerned with its internal organization.

GROUPING OF BOXES. Groups of boxes which represent different functions should be so located as to indicate their relationship to other functions, as well as to the basic function. For constructing the organizational chart, the following criteria should be used in locating different functions.

"Consulting" or related boxes should be slightly lower than the functional box to which they are related. The line should emerge from the right or left of the top of the "consulting" box and enter the side of the related functional box.

"Service" functions should be shown immediately under and to either the left or right of the directing supervisor.

"Operating" functions should be shown in direct line under supervisory officials.

Only one line indicating the same type of functional relationship should emerge from or enter the same side of a box.

LINES OF RESPONSIBILITY. Solid lines————————————represent lines of administrative authority. They indicate direct supervision or a direct relationship in regard to assignment and work.

Dashed lines — — — — — — indicate special kinds of supervision and normally should be noted in the legend.

Dotted lines . . . . indicate contact or coordinate relationship with units outside the organization being charted.

TERMS. Functional statements should be in the present tense and should be brief, clear, and all-inclusive.

Chapter 53

CASE STUDIES IN WORK SIMPLIFICATION

WHEN employees of The Cleveland Electric Illuminating Co. reported for work one Monday morning, they literally had to cut red tape to sit down at their desks. Red streamers carrying the challenge, "Does your paper work red tape get in your way?" had been taped across every desk chair, from the top of the back to the front edge of the seat, to focus attention on a drive for paperwork simplification.

Cleveland Electric officials report that the increased paperwork simplification suggestions and the accompanying savings far exceeded the $1,100 spent on the campaign. Although suggestions from the office force had been coming in regularly under the company's work-simplification program, they usually ran far below those from the operating departments. As a result of the drive, however, 120 of 200 proposals turned in that month suggested paperwork simplification. The following month, still under the effects of the drive, 150 out of 232 suggestions offered were in the office work category.

During the campaign, questions such as the following were asked:

1. Are you keeping a record or file identical to one kept by someone else in your office?

2. Can you get the information you need by telephoning?

3. How often do you use each of the files or records you keep? In customer's accounting, a "record correction" form was kept for one year in the general files, although once the corrections were made, the form had no further value. Now, the last department using it to correct their records is instructed to destroy it.

Another example of unused files is a form which was filed in the telephone information division of customer's service. A check revealed that the copies were *never* referred to. They have now been eliminated.

4. How often do you need information that is not current?

5. Do you trust the records you keep, or do you have to check other sources anyway?

6. Are you keeping a complex record or file because the boss wanted information in a hurry a year ago? Has he asked for it since? Will he need that information again? Is he getting it from another source?

7. Are all copies *really* used? Numerous proposals were received to discontinue extra copies of reports. For example, three copies of an "install and disconnect" report were formerly prepared and sent to the treasury mailroom, to the Addressograph department, and the service record department. The latter two departments no longer need the report and thus it has been discontinued.

8. Is the information always valuable enough to justify the time and expense of keeping the file or record?

9. Does all your paperwork really help you do your job, or is some of it an end job in itself?

10. Why do you do each of your paperwork jobs? Ask yourself, ask your supervisor, ask your work-simplification committee— and, *get* an answer!

Eliminating Unnecessary Paper

"Work simplification can be practiced every day by throwing away unnecessary paper," commented Elmer L. Lindseth, Cleveland Electric's chairman. Consider the cost of maintaining a four-drawer file. The cost of originating the material to fill the file may run well over $10,000. When the value of the cabinet, floor space, filing labor, and all other costs are evaluated, the annual cost of maintaining a four-drawer file may be more than $325.

One of the "gimmicks" employees received to make them aware of paperwork simplification was a note pad with printed hints and paperwork shortcuts. For example, "If you find you are doing any unnecessary paperwork job that involves *only* yourself, *scrap it yourself.*" When the work involves the department operations, supervisors should be asked to explain why the work is necessary.

If the challenge reveals that it is unnecessary, then it is the supervisor's responsibility to scrap it. If the challenge goes into an area outside one's own department, the plan is to first approach the immediate supervisor, and then submit a work-simplification proposal in the usual manner.

Four other paperwork shortcuts which were adopted by Cleveland Electric were:

1. *Forms.* A duplicating form has been eliminated by typing figures directly from a ledger book onto a monthly summary sheet, rather than waiting for a form to be prepared listing the figures to be included on the summary sheet.

2. *Cards.* A 3- by 5-inch card file divided into three sections—current leaves of absence, returns from L. O. A., and previous year's leaves—is now used for employees on leave. The cards with employees' names and other pertinent information are filed alphabetically, retained for a two-year period, and then destroyed.

3. *Tear-Off Sections.* The statistical department now sends one photostatic copy of a requisition at the end of the month for material received daily during the month. The operator then sends it to the accounting department after checking. This procedure enables the accounting department to get the monthly total from this one requisition, rather than adding up one for each day as was previously done.

4. *Desks, Equipment.* An index card file was moved to make it more accessible to the clerk who uses it. He formerly had to leave his chair and walk 28 feet to use the file.

Getting Outside Help

Cleveland Electric selected work simplification to encourage and assist its own people to take a more active part in improving their job performance. The program looked good because it could be carried on by the employees, results could be accomplished quickly, morale could be raised, and it could provide a continuing effort toward cost reduction and job improvement.

To begin the program, one man from the company was sent to Lake Placid, New York, to study work simplification under Allan H. Mogensen. Later Mr. Mogensen came to Cleveland to train top executives, and then two more men were enrolled for study under Mr. Mogensen. The three men formed the nucleus of the program. One of them, R. W. Rix, now heads the department.

Mr. Rix and his staff recently made a survey to determine the source of these proposals. Most revealing was the fact that 358 union people, who had not as yet had work-simplification training, had turned in proposals as the result of being exposed to the principles through promotional campaigns and through their work with those who had been trained. Also, 210 office people without previous work-simplification training had turned in proposals. Among those who had been trained, some had turned in as many as 21 ideas for improvement. About 130 employees had turned in at least five or more suggestions apiece.

CLERICAL COST CONTROL AT CURTISS

Procedural changes made to eliminate duplicate or unnecessary work in offices will result in a greater productivity on the part of clerical employees, declares Carl Aspinall, accounting manager, Curtiss Candy Company, Chicago. Increased office productivity is the only way to reduce total office costs and provide other benefits such as better office discipline; better customer service; a better basis for evaluating methods, procedures, and policy changes; and a basis for changes in personnel policies and changing staff to meet changing volumes and conditions.

Clerical cost control can increase productivity in instances where mechanization is not feasible, and where work activities are definable. Typical activities include calculating, filing, posting, typing, and billing.

In the past 75 years, office productivity has been increased by the use of typewriters, adding machines, addressing machines, and, in recent years, by electronic computers. But has the office kept up with the factory and with science? The answer is an emphatic "no."

In a recent 10-year period, output of the factory employee doubled, but output per office employee remained essentially unchanged. Johns Hopkins University reports that engineering and technology doubles itself every 15 years, while in management science—the people who decide what use to make of our scientific capabilities—knowledge doubles only every 50 years!

We all know that salary rates have been rising rapidly in recent years. We also know that fringe benefits are an increasingly important part of payroll costs. The ratio of office employees to factory employees is rising rapidly. In 1900, for example, 10 office employees were required for each 100 factory employees. By 1960, 25 office employees were required for each 100 factory employees.

Obviously, increased office productivity is the only way to reduce total office costs. Improved office productivity and control can also effect the benefits mentioned previously.

Normally, we associate increased productivity with some form of mechanization, all the way from one-write systems to large-scale computers. The use of mechanization has grown rapidly in recent years. Certainly mechanization has played an important role in combating rising costs of clerical operations, but mechanization is not the only answer to rising office costs, and it does not insure efficient operation. For example, what about office employees who are left after mechanization? And what about the opportunity for increasing productivity in those instances where mechanization is not feasible?

Clerical Cost Control

These are the areas where the technique known at Curtiss as clerical cost control is being applied. Clerical cost control encompasses both measurement and system revision.

The technique can be used anywhere the work activities are definable. To be most effective, the majority of the work should be repetitive (not necessarily routine), and the individual elements of work should have clearly determined beginnings and completions. Typical activities include such office functions as calculating, filing, posting, typing, and billing. In addition, clerical cost control is used outside the office in such areas as material-handling, order-picking, bank telling, switchboard operating, janitorial duties, laboratory testing, and routine engineering.

The greatest benefits in a clerical cost-control program do not come necessarily from work measurement, but rather from procedural changes made to eliminate duplicate or unnecessary work and which permit a more balanced and controlled work load.

There also are improvements in organization made possible by clarifying functions, combining duties to increase flexibility, eliminating duplication of responsibility, simplifying complex organizations, improving office layout, reducing the number of levels of supervision, and establishing realistic ratios of supervision to personnel being supervised.

Increased flexibility, for example, comes from combining duties so that each person can do a larger portion of a given job. This means that imbalance in work load between detailed steps can be reduced or eliminated, often resulting in lower total time requirements to complete a given volume of work.

After making the systems and organization changes, the next step to improving productivity through a clerical cost-control program is to measure the individual activities. Work measurement has two components: (1) a measure of the volume of work, and (2) a measure of the time required. These two factors are expressed as the time to perform one unit of work. For example, typing an invoice may require 2 minutes.

The measure of volume for the work element must furnish a good basis for measurement and must reflect accurately the actual procedures and volumes incurred. For example, in an order-entry system, the work unit could be either the customer order or the number of line items on the order. The choice of the unit would depend on the average number of line items per invoice and the variation from that average.

Work-measurement techniques can be classified as either predetermined standards or actual performance standards. Actual performance standards can be either historical or current. We will discuss, in detail, each of the methods of work measurement:

Predetermined Standards

Predetermined time values are used to establish standards by analyzing the motions required to perform the job and applying time values to them from reference tables. Predetermined standards are relatively inexpensive to apply. They require no pace judgment, are consistent between analysts, and require a minimum of employee interpretation.

They require, however, extensive training to administer. Since minute analysis of the motions is necessary, their usefulness is limited to high-volume, repetitive tasks. In addition, their accuracy is open to question by supervisors. Furthermore, establishment of the standard provides no method for continued control.

The reference tables used for predetermined standard data can be very detailed. For example, to determine the time required to attach a paper clip to a piece of paper, you must know the distance of the hand from the clip at the beginning of the operation. If the reach is 7 to 12 inches and it is a normal attachment, it takes .0396 minutes to attach the clip. However, if the clerk also must press the clip to spread it, the time is .0498 minutes.

Historical Data Standards

Historical data standards are derived by analysis of past performance. This method of setting standards is relatively low in cost and is useful for nonroutine jobs. It creates a minimum of employee disturbance and is generally acceptable to supervisors.

However, built-in inefficiencies are perpetuated, and adequate data is frequently not available. The standards developed do not recognize pace or lost time and, therefore, they do not result in precise standards. In addition, it provides no method to continue control, and it is difficult to change standards to reflect procedure changes. Furthermore, the standards cannot be used to evaluate employee performance.

Work Sampling

Work sampling, sometimes called "ratio delay," uses random observations to determine the relative time spent on the various work elements. Work sampling is relatively inexpensive and is useful for both routine and nonroutine jobs. Standards can be established in a short time. Little employee interruption or reaction is experienced. The standards are easy to adjust for procedural changes.

However, work sampling cannot be applied to a large number of operations, because the number of observations required becomes very large. In addition, it is difficult to get supervisory acceptance of the standards developed. A further limitation is that statistical training is required to apply the work sampling.

Work-sampling standards are set by dividing the total available time into the separate duties, based on the ratio of the number of observations of each duty to the total number of observations. A pace-rating factor may or may not be introduced. The observed time multiplied by the pace-rating factor gives the corrected time. By dividing the total number of units processed into the corrected time, the unit time is developed.

Duty B, for example, was observed 300 times or 30 percent of the total observations. Thirty percent of the total minutes is 4,500. The analyst pace-rated the work being performed at 80 percent, so the corrected time is 3,600 minutes. If 1,800 units were processed, the time standard would be 2 minutes per unit.

For nonvolume jobs, only the total amount of time required can be determined.

Work sampling is best applied when there are only a few duties involved. Obviously, due to the total number of observations necessary, work sampling becomes very expensive if a large number of duties are involved.

Batching

Batching is used to set standards by giving employees work in small units and observing the time taken. Batching has good supervisor acceptance, eliminates fine detail, eliminates lost time from the data collected, averages easy and difficult units, is relatively inexpensive to apply, and provides a method of continuing control after the standards have been set.

It cannot be used, however, for nonroutine duties. It requires employee reporting and disrupts the regular routine of the office.

To illustrate the method of setting standards by batch control, let's use invoices as an example. If we were to take the simple average of the batch times, we would set a standard of 48 minutes per batch or 31 invoices per hour. However, batches five and eight required considerably more than the average time. A review of the contents of these two batches showed that they included certain items which required far more than the normal amount of time per invoice. By excluding these two batches from the total time, we set a standard of 42 minutes per batch or 35 invoices an hour. When operating the control system, invoices that require abnormal amounts of time are excluded from the batches and are processed as exceptions outside the routine flow of work.

Log Sheets

In the log-sheet method of work measurement, employees record their activities throughout the day. The sheets are summarized to set the time standards. The use of log sheets requires little training. They provide detail about how all the time in a department is spent, are applicable to nonroutine duties, and provide a means of continuing control.

However, they may contain errors either accidental or deliberate. Employee annoyance is created by interference with their routine, the collection of data is time-consuming, and employees can adjust actual time to "bury" personal and lost time.

When a daily log sheet is used in a work-measurement program, each operation is assigned a number, which is inserted on the sheet opposite the applicable time span. To indicate the start and stop times, the employee merely draws a line across the sheet at the appropriate times. The time required to summarize the data can be considerable. On some larger jobs, data is keypunched from the survey sheets and mechanically summarized.

Time Study

Time study is analysis and measurement of the work elements through the use of a stopwatch. Time study has been widely accepted in industry and results in precise standards. Standards are quickly set on simple, routine jobs.

However, the stopwatch creates a very unfavorable employee reaction in the office and is costly to apply. It requires extensive training and considerable pace judgment. Accuracy is open to question by supervisors. No method to continued control is provided.

Micromotion

Micromotion is used to set standards by analysis of motion pictures of the work performed. It provides a detailed analysis of the work; good employee reaction is generally experienced.

It is, however, quite slow and expensive and is limited to simple manual operations. Micromotion requires pace judgment.

Control Is Key Factor

As indicated above, each measurement technique has its advantages as well as its disadvantages. There are no hard and fast rules in selecting the techniques. Many times, combinations of the techniques are used. The point is that the control aspect of the system is where the emphasis should be placed, not on the mechanics of establishing the rate.

After the various work-measurement techniques have been applied to the activities, it is necessary to determine the performance rates for each of the work elements rated and to develop the fixed-time allowances for the nonrated jobs. The activity rates for rated activities may be stated as rate per hour or hours per unit. For example, pricing invoices may be stated as 10 per hour or .100 hours each.

The first step in establishing control is to take the backlog of work away from the employees and give it to the supervisor. This accomplishes two things: First, we now control the employees so that the work cannot be expanded to fill all the available time. Second, we now know what the backlog is. Knowing the backlog leads us into the next important control tool—leveling the work flow.

For example, there is a typical pattern for receipt of documents in the mail. Monday is typically a high-volume day, let's say 160 documents. Tuesday is generally a low-volume day, say 20 documents. Many times it is the practice of companies to process all of the work received each day on the same day. As can be seen, Monday requires considerably more work than Tuesday. By determining exactly how many hours are required on each day, it becomes obvious that some work should be carried over from day to day so that the same amount of work can be performed each day. If 180 documents are received on two days, 90 documents each day should be processed, rather than processing them as received. This means that immediately we can reduce our capacity from 160 documents per day to 90 documents per day, a reduction of nearly 45 percent.

As another example, take the variations in the number of invoices received by accounts payable each day through a one-month cycle. The number varies from 220 to 460 per day. With the rule of processing each day's invoices on the same day, the department would be staffed for a capacity of 460 invoices per day. Actually, an average of only 330 invoices arrives each day. If the capacity is reduced to handle 330 invoices per day, a backlog would be carried over each day. However, the backlog would never exceed or even approach one day's work, and in some cases no work would be left.

In terms of hours, the effect of leveling might look like this on a weekly work load control sheet: On Monday, 15 hours of work would be received; but because of the reduced capacity, only 8 hours would be completed, leaving 7 hours for the next day. On Tuesday, 2 hours would be received. As 8 hours could be processed, the backlog would be cut to 1 hour. Within the week, we would have processed the same total number of invoices with a controlled backlog with approximately 45 percent less time available.

Accurate Reporting System Needed

We have discussed the various work-measurement techniques used to develop activity rates and the application of the rates to the work load by batch controls and balancing. The final success of any work-measurement program, however, depends upon setting up an accurate system to report the results of the program to management so that they will know how well the organization is meeting the standards and the objectives which have been set forth. These reports should include current efficiency, the trend of the efficiency, a comparison of actual time to standard time by duty and possibly by individual, and the reasons for out-of-line performance. Reports should also show the relative amounts of variable and fixed work load within the various departments. In addition, it may be desirable to report the quality of work being performed if a review program is in effect.

A simple weekly activity report separates the variable work load from the fixed work load. The volumes and rates are shown for the variable duties. Auditing of vouchers is performed at 15 per hour, requiring 83 standard hours with 89 actual hours taken.

In the fixed work load, certain activities cannot have detailed standards developed. In this case, training is necessary only when new employees are in the department. When time is available, a quality-control program is conducted. This is an area where excess hours can be absorbed.

The net available hours are compared with the total standard hours. Several factors such as overtime, vacations, and illness can affect the available hours, so these are detailed.

Unaccounted-for Hours

The key indicator of employee utilization is unaccounted-for hours, the difference between net available hours and total standard hours. The trend of this indicator (unaccounted-for hours) determines when personnel changes are required. For example, when unaccounted-for hours consistently exceed 37 hours per week, one person might be taken from the department.

Certain factors can significantly affect the key indicator (unaccounted-for hours), and these also should be plotted. In some cases, vacation and illness, training and quality control, and overtime are the important factors. If, for example, vacation and illness are less than average, personnel reductions probably would not be made, unless it is expected that the average will change.

The training and quality-control functions give the supervisor an opportunity to absorb temporary slack. If these factors continually stay above the expected average, it is a sign of overstaffing.

Conversely, if overtime continually occurs when the key indicator (unaccounted-for hours) is below 37 hours per week, additional personnel may be required.

Daily Reporting

For a department with very little variable work load, actual time is maintained by daily reporting. Any significant variations from the standard for the month must be explained.

Such a department also may have frequent special duties which cannot be rated. Actual time for these items is reported in detail. Should the expected amount of special duties not develop, steps would be taken to reduce the staffing in the department to the required level to perform the work that is available. The same key indicators discussed previously also apply to a department like this one.

In large departments with several persons doing the same jobs, it may be desirable to report efficiency and quality by employee. Let us assume that management has established the following guidelines: A clerk's speed should be such that the average batch time is between plus or minus 10 percent of the standard, and the error level is less than 8 percent. Miss A is an ideal employee, whose speed and quality are within the guidelines. Fast but inaccurate, Miss B should slow down to improve her quality. Miss F is new in the department, so her speed and quality are both low. If she does not meet the standards within the 6-month probationary period, she will be dismissed.

By using the activity rates developed and the anticipated volume, it is possible to determine the total man-hour requirements for the department. The hourly rates multiplied by the expected volumes, together with the fixed duties, give the total direct man-hour requirements. With the additional allowances for vacations, sick leave, and personal time, the total weekly hours required for each quarter are determined. The total hours are then translated into the number of positions required, based on an 8-hour day.

At this point, management must decide on its objectives in terms of cost, of service, and the level of service to be provided by the department. This is a managerial decision and cannot be made solely by the results of work measurement. In reaching this decision, the total cost of providing the service must be considered, weighing the amount of overtime and idle time that would develop from any given level of service.

We chart the relation of work load, expressed as persons, to the various manning levels which might be selected. If a staff of nine persons is desired, considerable amounts of overtime must be worked, but little idle time is experienced. If the staff is set at 11 persons, very little overtime is necessary, but considerable idle time results.

Job Descriptions

Once management has determined the level of service to be provided and the staffing necessary to provide that service, job descriptions must be prepared for each position. These job descriptions should reflect an evenly distributed work load. In addition, these descriptions help to pinpoint responsibility for the various duties, something which is frequently vague both in the eyes of the supervisor and employees. Supervisors frequently do not know all of the minor jobs in the department, so the job descriptions clarify these.

For example, take a job description for a job which combines both variable and fixed duties. Preparing vouchers is performed at the rate of 20 per hour; with an expected volume of 2,520 vouchers per month, 126 hours will be required. The fixed duties balance the job to a full 158 hours per month (21 days x 8 hours less $\frac{1}{2}$ hour a day personal time).

Once staffing requirements have been determined, the savings must be realized—the excess employees must go off the payroll. The reduction is most likely the reason a clerical cost-control program was undertaken in the first place, and if the goal is not realized, the program has not succeeded. To prove the savings, it is necessary to show who has gone off the payroll or where the hiring of additional personnel has been prevented.

HOW SPIEGEL SIMPLIFIED FORMS

Most of the glamour of a mail-order operation is in its order-handling activities, with its complicated clerical functions carefully arranged in a straight-line production flow, for efficient handling of the rigidly scheduled picking, assembling, packing, and billing of the customers' orders.

Needless to say, this is the process most visitors see at Spiegel's. Their observations reveal that it is highly engineered, carefully integrated, and has been subjected to continued efforts of paperwork simplification.

Behind the scenes, however, there are hundreds of other processes, many of them far-reaching in their effects. And many of them also involve activity and expense that make paperwork simplification a "must." These processes may be localized in one activity or extend into several activities such as merchandising, advertising, returned goods handlings, warehousing, customer correspondence, accounting, traffic, package engineering, payroll, credits, collections, and dozens of others.

A factor that is common to many of the backstage operations, as well as being integral to the order flow, is the catalog number. The catalog number is the link with the customer, and it is a common-language medium of the activities throughout the plant. It is used to identify, classify, validate, evaluate, communicate, and remunerate.

Ordinarily, however, the catalog number cannot be used by itself, because it cannot be unique to each of the conditions, descriptions, and variations peculiar to the item that it represents. In some cases,

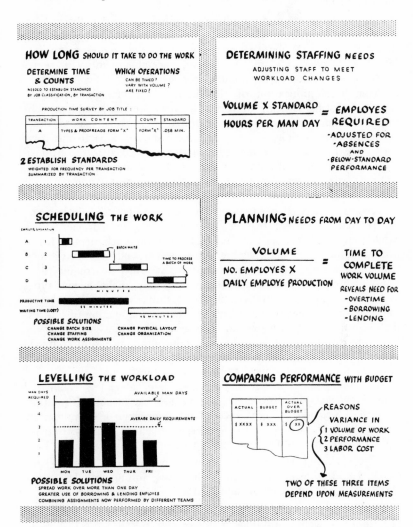

Because every step of the budgetary planning and control plan is a selling job, the visuals used are developed like those in a salesman's presentation portfolio.

it must be qualified by the colors and sizes that are offered in the number; in other cases, it will require prices, weights, number of labels, and so forth, in conjunction with it. Still another instance will require the sales estimate for each stockkeeping unit within the catalog number; and there are many other such requirements, representing similar needs.

It is, however, common to all forms. This means that the number itself could be written, printed, typed, or otherwise reproduced many times a season. When the quantity of catalog numbers exceeds 10,000 a season (six months), a very respectable quantity of reproductions on various forms is built up over a year's time.

Prior to simplification of this kind of paperwork through a repetitive listing system, all forms were created independently, by many different agencies, being generated from work papers, other forms, or combinations of both. In some instances, a particular form was created by one of several control agencies which were responsible for issuance, while others were created on a completely decentralized basis, some by buyers' secretaries, merchandise record clerks, stockmen, and other personnel.

Needless to say, this situation pyramided costs, bred delays, and contributed to format discrepancies and data inaccuracies. Each catalog number was written at least once for each of the forms produced, and other data pertinent to it was reproduced many times, depending upon the number of forms for which it was required.

Following a survey of the problem and study of the various types of business equipment that could offer a simple means of producing the necessary forms, it was concluded that a combination of address plates and offset printing would be most economical. Since all of the different forms do not have to be produced at once, and complete information is available sufficiently early to meet all deadlines, the same equipment can be used to produce all the forms.

Addressing plates are commonly considered a mailing room tool only. However, they represent a very flexible means of multiple printings, providing high speed and accuracy. Clever, simply operated accessories enable the addressing machine to perform tasks far removed from addressing mailing labels.

Offset printing is becoming more important to office systems every day. It offers economical short-run printing with less muss and fuss, easier preparation and correction, and cleaner copy.

Combining the two, it is possible to list many items rapidly and accurately as well as produce many copies. Because the task is to produce multiple copies of compiled data, this combination offers an admirable solution.

At this point, the most important objectives of paperwork simplification were:

1. Reduction of copies printed and distributed.
2. Reduction of data to minimum necessary for efficient operation.
3. Design of a format to provide legibility, proper allocation of space, and the most efficient use of the forms.

Spiegel produces multiple copies from master forms at rapid rate on press.

This can only be accomplished by asking the question "Why?" at each turn, by ascertaining the "How" of every use, and planning for the maximum integration of effort.

The "Master Line-Up"

A form called the "master line-up" contains complete information on all items offered for sale, so this form is used as a basis for all other forms. Accordingly, handwritten data is now entered on that form by the respective merchandise departments. They are then passed along to the other data sources, and finally subjected to a searching audit against catalog copy.

After audit, the forms are sent, on schedule, to a plate-embossing service bureau. A service bureau is used because the concentrated volume does not justify the purchase of equipment to do the job in the office, nor the building up of a trained staff for handling it in the short period available.

The address plate is embossed in a three-line format, with particular sectors of the plate allocated for each category of information. The plates are divided into two categories: Basic and follower. The basic plate represents the first stockkeeping unit of a catalog number and carries all data pertinent to the catalog number, as a whole, as well as all data relating to the particular stockkeeping unit itself, such as color, size, and percent of sales to the total for the catalog number.

The follower plate carries the information that is pertinent to the stockkeeping unit only. The ratio of follower plates to basic plates is about 5 to 1. Accordingly, because there is little information on follower plates, the embossing cost is much less.

The plates are proofed and inserted in frames by the embossing service, and they are further proofed and tabbed upon their return. Tabs are inserted to indicate the basic plates and those plates that are representative of catalog number and color.

The master line-up form is then run on a standard automatic addressing machine equipped with a three-column listing device. This device enables the machine to print the first line of the plate on the left-hand third of the form, the center line in the center third of the form, and the third line at the right. Using a grease-type ribbon, this addressing is stamped on an offset master that is preprinted with the master line-up format. Thus, multiple copies can be run off on a standard, automatic feed offset press, equipped with a chrome cylinder. Use of a quick-change clamp affords rapid master changes, enabling the printing of 35 copies from each of 50 to 65 masters an hour.

By tabbing the frames, advantage is taken of the selecting feature of the machine; and on the next form that is run, only those plates that are necessary to provide a complete listing of each catalog number and color are printed. Also, by cutting out spaces on the platen corresponding to information that is not required, only the necessary information is printed for each item to be listed.

Over 40,000 plates are required at the outset of the season's operation, with the quantity increasing to about 60,000 during the course of the season. No attempt is made to reuse any of the plates in subsequent seasons, although the major part of the information may be usable, *because the cost of segregation and alteration would exceed the cost of embossing a new plate.*

These techniques have resulted in very satisfactory savings over the old method. In addition, this system has:

1. Reduced floor space needed for operation.
2. Increased efficiency, by making forms more legible and more accurate.
3. Reduced paper waste, through centralized operation, under adequate supervision.

MANUAL METHODS AT HIGH STANDARD

Holding paperwork on small-parts orders within bounds and keeping shipments up to date call for the simplest possible systems consistent with good control. The High Standard Manufacturing Corporation of Hamden, Connecticut, achieved a new high in simplicity by eliminating a rather complex use of typewritten order-invoice forms and substituting a handwritten register invoice.

In making this change the typing time of two persons was saved, shipping time was cut from as much as 10 days to one day, and form cost was reduced.

High Standard has grown rapidly in recent years through combining craftsmanship with high-production levels in making pistol, gun, and rifle parts.

It used to be that a 12-part form was typed for pistol and parts orders. A customer's order was first edited by the sales department and sent to the credit department for approval. Then the form was typed; a shipping set portion was sent to the shipping department, the goods were shipped, and a billing copy was returned to the accounting department where the invoice set had been filed. This set was pulled from the file, extended, and the information summarized in a handwritten sales journal.

A lot of work was being done and *at the wrong time*. Many back-orders occurred, and this meant waste motion going over the same steps twice. Today the job is being done much more efficiently by one man in the parts-shipping department.

Simplified System

When an order is received, the shipper checks a credit reference file on his desk. If the order is approved by this simple check, he immediately lays out the parts from the bins—nearly 1,000 different items are stocked in this department. Then he handwrites a five-part invoice in a Standard Form Flow Register.

The first copy of this set is the original invoice, which also serves as a mailing-address medium, through a window envelope attached to the parts bag. Also provided are a duplicate invoice, packing list, accounts receivable and accounting copies.

As the written form is ejected these last two copies are refolded in continuous strip in a locked compartment of the register. They are removed once a day and sent to the accounting department. One of them is placed in a numerical file as a sales register, while the other is put into a pocket of the ledgerless receivable file, thus eliminating any further paperwork in the accounting phase of the order.

The new streamlined system safeguards the cost of handling a number of individual sales for relatively small amounts by giving all necessary paperwork on parts orders in a single writing by hand and deriving all required documents and records from it.

Chapter 54

ELECTRONIC DATA PROCESSING

T HE founders of American Data Processing, Inc. (formerly Gille Associates, Inc.) began their first data-processing information service in 1950. Their initial publication, *The Punched Card Annual*, was the first regularly published reference work on data-processing systems.

Today ADP publishes a *Data-Processing Systems Encyclopedia* with a monthly updating service, a *Computer Yearbook and Directory*, a monthly computer applications service, monthly letters on information retrieval and forms and systems, and many other publications.

This and similar activities in the field of electronic data processing suggest the impossibility of offering up-to-the-minute handbook material on such a complex, ever-changing subject like this, even under Dartnell's careful revision program. We will, however, attempt to give you an overall view of the importance of electronic data processing to modern office administration.

IS YOUR COMPANY READY FOR IT?

When a company says "no" to EDP today, it usually adds "not yet." Electronic data processing is advancing at such a pace that both users and nonusers feel they must constantly re-evaluate the equipment field. A Research Institute of America survey of 1,500 member companies disclosed a surprising extent of successful computer-usage among small firms.

The Institute does not advocate that EDP is now ready for every firm, nor that every company is ready for EDP. In fact, it may at the moment be uneconomical for your firm. But—on the basis of extensive investigation—we do maintain that no company should consider EDP a closed issue. Here are the facts and implications that can be drawn from the experiences of the companies who participated in the survey:

1. *Small business is becoming a big user.* A surprising 35 percent of the companies responding to our survey said they are currently using computers—either their own installation or an outside bureau. Of the firms using outside installations, about one-third had fewer than 100 employees, another third had from 100 to 200 employees, and the rest were scattered up to 1,000 or more.

2. *Users are convinced they are getting their money's worth.* Among almost 400 firms that reported direct savings, the average yearly savings mentioned were $80,000. Even 143 firms that checked "no savings" on this question were usually satisfied that their investment was paying for itself through indirect benefits.

3. *Most EDP users are planning to expand their usage.* After the usual startup on routine work like payrolls, the tendency is to move rapidly to nonroutine jobs. Three areas were noted most often: inventory control, operations scheduling, and purchasing.

4. *Wide-scale and integrated EDP holds the real payoff.* Among surveyed companies, those with three or more related jobs being done on their machines reported about twice the direct savings and tended to be more impressed with the indirect benefits.

5. *Most would-be users cannot economically justify EDP.* The 913 reporting firms that have not used EDP cite these reasons: company too small (588); high costs (411); EDP doesn't answer our problems (127). (Figures add up to over 913 since several reasons were sometimes given.) But note this fact: 40 percent of the non-users are still actively and seriously investigating computer applications.

The "Savings" Lure of EDP

Smaller companies have learned that they can reap the benefits of an EDP program by renting time on a machine outside the company or turning to a service bureau. But to gain the advantages, a company must be ready for the jump.

Direct savings are usually a result of substituting EDP for manual office jobs, like updating a customer's account or calculating payroll checks. Main savings here, if any, are the result of eliminating personnel on routine jobs. One small Midwestern insurance company reported that a computer installation allowed it to eliminate most of the clerks in its policy-writing section. This and other savings added up to a net annual savings of $143,000.

Indirect savings can also be measured accurately in dollars if a company has efficient cost-accounting. A West Coast electronics firm estimates that its ratio of successful bids on contracts has increased from 12 percent to 21 percent as a result of calculating them with a computer. It expects that savings in the preparation of elaborate bids will be between $50,000 and $100,000 a year. Many of the surveyed companies were able to point to other indirect savings of equal magnitude. Frequently mentioned were inventories, where computer control often resulted in reductions in stock of 20 to 40 percent with comparable savings on maintenance, insurance, and other carrying charges.

Management information benefits are usually impossible to pin down in dollars and cents, although a majority of surveyed companies considered this a very profitable area. A West Coast bathing suit manufacturer, for example, is able to keep extremely close coordination between incoming sales orders and production schedules. During a critical reorder period, he kept his EDP operation going around the clock, six days a week. As a result, he was able to handle a much higher percentage of reorders than ever before. Other benefits: Only half as many orders were shipped late, and fewer retail outlets complained that they ran out of stock on his popular lines.

A midwestern business-forms manufacturer is equally impressed by the fact that his service-center run inventory-control system "improves control by substituting computer decision-making for clerical judgment." As a result, he says, management receives a faster and more accurate picture of potential problems and is better able to make sure that high priority orders get proper attention. This has improved customer satisfaction and has meant fewer production bottlenecks and less overtime.

The key to EDP's management-information role is that it lets executives know, while they can still take effective action, how an order or any other business event will affect overall company operations. When this third level of EDP use is properly understood and installed in a company, it enables management to optimize its primary job, decision-making. The result is less hesitation, less seat-of-the-pants guessing, and a greater ability to concentrate on those business problems which will have the greatest effect on overall costs and profits.

The Cost of Getting Aboard

As might be expected, the Research Institute survey indicated a wide range of cost figures. Although the average expenditure in setting up a private installation was about $150,000, the range reported was between $20,000 and $300,000. When you consider the work that must go into preparing and installing the average computer installation, it is obvious that many of the companies were referring only to the cost of actual physical installation. Most firms, even small ones, must be prepared to invest at least the average $150,000 figure in a normal internal installation of EDP equipment.

Obviously, costs will vary sharply depending upon the level of a company's involvement, and any single figure is meaningless without a detailed description of the precise facts.

The reported range of operating costs was just as great, with an average of about $16,500 a month. In this case, however, it should be pointed out that the costs of large installations included in the survey had a very great effect on the average. A great many companies reported costs under the $5,000- to $8,000-a-month range.

In the case of companies using service bureaus, there was also a wide variance in expenses. The mean of $650 a month included everything from a company that spent $50 a month to obtain a relatively simple breakdown of its sales of auto parts to an electronics manufacturer who spent almost $4,000 a month on a complete EDP accounting system.

Naturally, not every company surveyed had a happy story to tell. In fact, 65 reported that they had tried EDP and abandoned it when it had not lived up to their expectations. Significantly, only 27 of these singled out cost as the primary reason for dropping their computer program. Most cited reasons like these:

... "Our internal organization was not able to cope with the discipline required for success."

... "We had to abandon EDP because of poor planning by management people."

... "We decided we did not want our work to go outside the company to a data-processing center."

But the interesting note was this: Even those companies that had less than satisfactory experience with EDP do not plan to ignore the rapid changes in the industry. In fact, companies with aggressive growth plans report that they intend to maintain a running study of rapid changes in the field as they occur. Basically they are looking for answers to two vital questions:

1. *Can my current routine data be handled better by a computer?*

2. *Can EDP improve management information and control?*

A study of operations could begin with rough estimates of at least the following basic clerical costs:

... Salaries and overhead chargeable to office operations.

... Cost of paperwork outside the office proper: warehouse record-keeping, production scheduling, periodic inventory inspection, etc.

... Purchase and rental costs of existing office machines and forms.

... Man-hours devoted to job estimating, report writing, and other routine clerical tasks by supervisors, materials specialists, office managers, etc.

Automation can handle routine responsibilities for a store manager while he spends more time with his department managers and customers. An assistant at the control panel keeps an eye on routine activities and calls the manager himself only when an exceptional situation arises. The alarm panel, data storage and retrieval, and teleprinter equipment were provided by Honeywell Inc. The closed-circuit television and internal communications equipment were provided by Motorola, Inc. Super Market Institute developed the store control center idea, and a special grant from Pepsi Cola Co. was used to finance the prototype design and construction.

It is likely that most companies will be unable to put a direct dollars-and-cents label on each of these costs, but even a rough estimate is enough to indicate the magnitude of data-processing expenses. At least, you will be able to pinpoint the largest cost areas—those that might easily be shifted to a service bureau—even if you cannot justify a more complete study.

Impact on the Existing "Establishment"

There are three essential questions top management must be willing to answer in the affirmative before making a commitment to install EDP:

1. *Am I willing to reorganize my company for EDP?* Many companies that already have a computer recognize—sometimes too late

in the game—that an EDP system cannot fit easily into their old organization. Tradition-bound information and report "needs" are clogging a computer's schedule, preventing the preparation of data that can really make a computer pay its way.

2. *Am I willing to spend money for EDP personnel?* Unfortunately, many top executives have assumed that their existing office personnel can easily be adapted to working with a computer. This kind of short-cutting may well prevent disruption initially, but it is bound to be very expensive over the long haul either in inefficient use of a company's own machine or in missed opportunities. At the least, a company must be prepared to send several of its employees through extended periods of formal training. In most cases, it will also be necessary to hire computer specialists or arrange for a consultant to assist in the planning and installation.

3. *Am I willing to invest heavily in planning for EDP?* It's a rare company that can adapt itself to even a few relatively routine EDP applications without a lot of hard planning work. Many firms, however, try to short-cut this step and wind up with unnecessary costs.

A Feasibility Study

Preliminary investigation will give you a yes/no answer on the company's potential use of EDP. But the major job of deciding how and with what equipment is still only partially done. For reliable answers, a feasibility study, should be undertaken to gather specific information:

...A detailed analysis of existing data systems.

...Plans for adapting your procedures to a computerized operation; revamping wherever necessary to fit the new information-handling abilities of the computer.

...Recommendations of specific computer equipment, based on capabilities and costs.

...A complete plan and timetable for changing over to EDP.

As the costs and procedures of EDP change, a periodic review of the questions raised in a feasibility study can help management see whether the company is actually getting anticipated benefits and whether opportunities are being overlooked.

In a very small company the top executive may be tempted to undertake the major responsibility for the feasibility study himself. In some companies, it might be handed over to the controller or office manager, or to a special employee with the proper EDP systems background. However, it is usually best to get the assistance

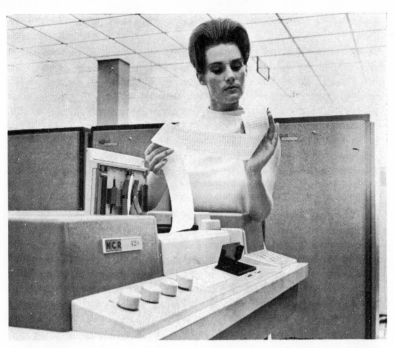

Although few offices have cash registers, optical accounting systems are bringing cash register tapes into many offices. Above, an optical scanning machine of The National Cash Register Company reads tapes from cash registers, accounting, or adding machines for input to a computer. Below, left, a Victor cash register features absentee management control with a locked-in detail tape. Below, right, an NCR register can "read" plastic credit cards. All details of charge account sales are registered and mingled with cash sales recorded. Combined data is then fed to computer control center for accounting and inventory information.

of an outside consultant. There will be important pros and cons to consider:

1. *Running the survey with home talent.* If you cannot afford to look outside for advice, it may be possible to turn one or more of your present employees into a computer specialist. In most sections of the country, there are courses available at colleges or other educational institutions. It may also be possible to have employees attend the schools of equipment makers even before you have committed yourself to a particular installation.

Caution: It is very unlikely that an employee you send to a school will emerge with anything more than the most rudimentary knowledge of selecting and implementing a computer system. He may, however, be able to get you started in EDP by running a few of your routine jobs at a nearby data-processing center or bank.

2. *The full-time EDP systems specialist.* There are many obvious advantages to hiring your own EDP specialist to do the initial feasibility study, either alone or with some assistance from outside consultants. However, there are also cautions you must be aware of. Most experienced EDP specialists have gotten their training in large corporations. When this orientation isn't carefully controlled, small firms can wind up with a proposed EDP system that they simply can't afford to install or run.

3. *Hire a consultant.* One of the easiest ways to short-circuit many problems of the computer installation is to hire a specialist. Consultant fees can be stiff, running as high as $50,000 in an average medium-sized manufacturing company. And here, of course, everything depends upon the individual you select.

Caution: Consultants who guarantee that a computer installation will pay for itself quickly on routine work should generally be avoided. Very few companies have achieved this result in less than a year or two after installation, and many never do balance costs and direct savings.

On the other hand, an experienced consultant can help you choose the best procedure and equipment for your company. Obvious reason is that a good consultant has been through the process many times in the past and is not likely to stumble into many of the traps that trip up executives unfamiliar with EDP. As one company president recently expressed it, "A consultant has hindsight beforehand and that's when it does the most good."

Recommendation: Even if an outside consultant is hired, it's often a good idea to make one of the company's own people the project manager, with the responsibility of coordinating all the work of the planning group. The danger is that the outside consultant may wind up doing too much of the work, with the result that nobody in the company really understands what's going on. When this happens, the consultant must be retained long after his main job is done, or else he leaves, and within a short time everything is chaotic.

Automation of the modern office requires an increasing number of electronic devices like the Steelcase computer console above, the Mc-Bee keysort data punch at right, and the new Wang Laboratories system below. The Wang unit enables as many as four low-cost console keyboard units to be operated simultaneously from a single electronics calculator.

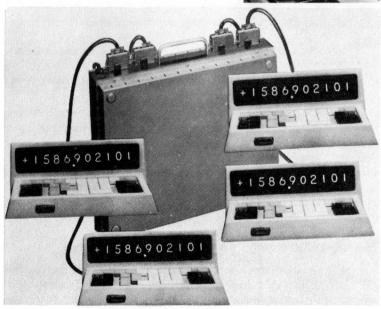

Evaluating Data Flow

First and possibly the most important job of the planning group in making the feasibility study is carrying out a detailed analysis of existing data systems. This will provide the basic framework for installing an efficient EDP operation or instituting work at a service bureau. But your survey of existing systems will be of equal value even if it should show that EDP is not needed. Many companies have never really fully evaluated their paperwork in terms of costs, efficiency, and the timeliness and usefulness of the data which is generated. When this job is done in the ordinary course of a feasibility study, it inevitably points up possible improvements and savings in the old manual system itself.

Evaluating an office system is a tedious job, the dimensions of which are easily underestimated by a nonspecialist. The following are just a few of the steps that must be taken to obtain the needed information:

...Evaluate information on every form used by the company—where it originates, where it goes, what it is used for.

...Estimate the cost of every item of equipment used in producing and distributing information.

...Find out exactly what every office worker does and estimate if his job has any peak periods, such as the end of the day, week, or month.

...Measure the value of every office operation and every report or study made.

...Spot all the existing bottlenecks in office procedures for the gathering of original data.

...Determine what information every manager gets and evaluate whether it's worthwhile or incomplete, etc.

A study of this type will easily take a three-man team between three and six months in the average small or medium-sized company. It may take even longer since an unpredictable number of value judgments must be made by top managers on the worth of specific information. In many cases, the people doing the work are not in agreement with their supervisors on the need for long-established reports and procedures. Here, too, top management will have to meditate.

New Data Goals

Companies who have weathered the storm agree that the toughest job starts at this point. After examining all of these factors, with a view to transferring existing operations to a computer, the feasibility study group must turn to the new jobs that EDP might accomplish. The following list includes those often mentioned by the surveyed companies:

1. *Inventory reduction.* What savings would a computer effect in terms of lower carrying costs, insurance, material handling, spoilage, etc.? Companies with several thousand items in stock and many small orders often report direct savings of 20 to 40 percent.

2. *Production control.* Estimates should be made of present costs of factors such as idle machine time and wasted manpower, especially if there are consistent overtime expenses over management estimates.

3. *Customer service.* A properly designed computer system can usually reduce stock outages and the resultant sales losses. And the overtime to meet rush orders can also be cut back drastically.

4. *Credit control.* Since customer accounts can be reviewed much more frequently with a computer system—daily if needed—unpaid

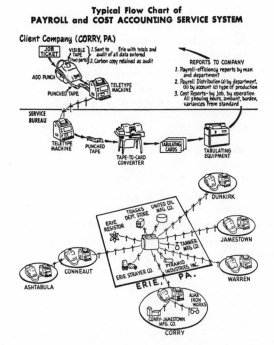

How a data-processing center services several small business organizations.

balances can be more easily held to policy limits and management can often spot problem areas before they become serious.

5. *Forecast and followup.* Not only can a computer improve company forecasting, but by processing information fast it can flag management when any segment of the business is not living up to expectations.

6. *Sales analysis.* A computer makes possible a continuous watch on salesmen's activities, product mix, and breakdowns of profit and loss items.

Caution: Many managers with a new data-processing system are entranced with the idea that they can get more detailed information than ever before. The result is that the EDP system makes their everyday job harder instead of easier because it overloads them with more information than they can easily absorb. In one case, a new sales manager of a small manufacturing company instituted an elaborate quota system for his men in the field. Trouble was he found himself spending most of the week analyzing the data on each man that the computer spewed out. The solution to this problem was to set a percentage figure below each salesman's goal and have the computer deliver only the weekly reports of the men who were below that goal.

Once the feasibility study team has completed its analysis of existing information systems and the potential data needs of a company, it must answer a long list of questions about how these needs can be met by EDP.

It's necessary, at this point, to start drawing up the specifications of the job that will help determine what equipment to use. These are just a few of the details that must be considered:

... Will input data arrive in the form of punch cards or other documents that are machine-readable and can be entered directly into the computer? Must information be sorted or processed again before being used?

... How can information jobs be combined and scheduled on the machine so input documents are used a minimum number of times?

... What are the requirements in terms of input and output speeds and computer memory if all the data needs of the company are to be met?

... What is the average daily volume of work that must be done?

... Are there any seasonal or other peaks and can these be rearranged to provide a more even flow of work into and out of the computer?

It's also necessary to think in terms of specific company problems when it comes to such things as files, for example. Whenever possible, an efficient EDP system eliminates files by maintaining records in the computer memory. This can mean a major cost saving in inventory record-keeping where many companies are now eliminating individual ledger cards on the many thousands of items in their

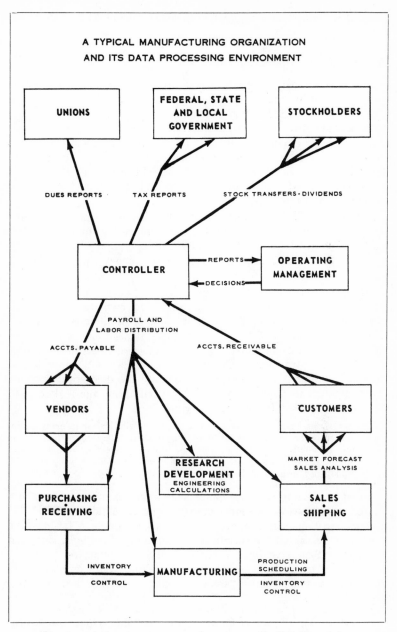

A TYPICAL MANUFACTURING ORGANIZATION
AND ITS DATA PROCESSING ENVIRONMENT

UNIONS

FEDERAL, STATE
AND LOCAL
GOVERNMENT

STOCKHOLDERS

DUES REPORTS

TAX REPORTS

STOCK TRANSFERS - DIVIDENDS

CONTROLLER

REPORTS

OPERATING
MANAGEMENT

DECISIONS

PAYROLL AND
LABOR DISTRIBUTION

ACCTS. PAYABLE

ACCTS. RECEIVABLE

VENDORS

CUSTOMERS

RESEARCH
DEVELOPMENT
ENGINEERING
CALCULATIONS

MARKET FORECAST
SALES ANALYSIS

PURCHASING
•
RECEIVING

SALES
•
SHIPPING

INVENTORY

CONTROL

MANUFACTURING

PRODUCTION
SCHEDULING

INVENTORY
CONTROL

The flow of data in a representative company is diagrammed here inventories and relying on computer memory alone as their primary record.

Solving the Equipment Riddle

When a company decides to set up a computer installation, it faces a confusing array of possible equipment. And no matter how carefully he has tried to cost out his new installation ahead of time, an office administrator can never really know which system is best.

Under these circumstances, it is no surprise that most companies do not buy, but lease their equipment. Even a company with the financial resources to buy computers outright usually prefers to pay the extra costs of leasing in order to be able to retain flexibility or change its decision later.

The fact is, 75 percent of companies with their own installations are using them less than the frequent contract minimum of 160 hours a month. In other words, speed of operation often has little to do with whether a company is getting its money's worth from its computer room.

For similar reasons, an executive deciding on a computer should be very skeptical about memory claims. Most computer systems on the market today are very flexible in the size of the memory which can be hooked up to them. In most cases if a special company requirement, such as an unusually large number of items in inventory, calls for an extra large memory capacity, this can be provided in accessory units. It is important to separate the theoretical costs of the equipment if it were used at full capacity from the real costs to you in terms related to the actual work done.

Caution: Costs alone are never the whole story. A vital factor in many equipment choices is the availability of similar equipment in case of a breakdown. A similar installation within a reasonable distance, where time can be bought or borrowed, allows you to get work done while your machine is being repaired. Such "emergency insurance" is worth considering.

Final bargaining with computer sales representatives can make a major difference in the efficiency of your transition to EDP. Of course, most managers approaching this decision in a businesslike way have submitted the specifications for competitive bids. But even companies that have firm prices will often negotiate on "extras," and offer a great deal more help in installing your computer than ordinarily available under "standard" contract. These are just four examples:

1. *Pretesting of your programs with "live" data from your operations is a necessity.* Most manufacturers provide computer time on

their own machines for this work—a common standard is 40 hours. If you bargain, however, you are likely to be able to increase this as much as double or triple the standard.

2. *Systems analysis and programming assistance is a vital part of every manufacturer's services for a new installation.* Whenever possible, nail down in writing exactly what you are entitled to. For example, you may be able to get a systems analyst assigned to your job on a full-time basis for three to six months. Also, if a company ordinarily supplies one programmer during the installation phase, you may be able to negotiate for two.

3. *Training of your personnel is included in most installation packages.* IBM, for example, usually runs a two- or three-day orientation program for your people, such as keypunch operators and clerks who will be making the transition from manual to a computer system. In addition, IBM gives an aptitude test to anyone you select to determine who will be the best bet for further training as a programmer or other specialist. It may be possible to arrange for even more extensive training programs, to better prepare your people.

4. *Programming assistance in the form of canned programs for routine jobs and computer languages like Cobol, Fortran, etc., is available to cut down your own programming costs.* Adapting many of these aids for use may be difficult unless you have your own specialist. It may be possible to get the company to agree to do the special modification for you.

Programming

An electronic computer has often been called a moron with a gift for doing arithmetic. It must be told exactly what to do with all the information it receives. Once its instructions or programs are written, it will follow them explicitly. It will not, however, look at a customer's balance and say, "This looks like trouble," unless it has been given specific instructions on how much of an outstanding balance that customer is allowed to carry.

Unfortunately, this job that many managements think ought to be routine can be the biggest problem area in a new computer installation. Often, companies that are willing to spend $80,000 to $100,000 a year on a computer installation are unwilling to hire the programming specialists who can make it really pay.

A programmer is really a computer's teacher, since he is responsible for the precise instructions that tell the machine how to do the specific job. And even though programming has become vastly more of a routine operation than it was just a few years ago, efficient programming can mean the difference between an EDP operation that runs smoothly soon after installation and one that is hampered for many months by errors and breakdowns.

Maximize the Return

In most companies, the initial efforts in EDP involve transferring jobs like payroll, billing, and accounts receivable to a computer. Main reason: these tasks are well understood by management. In the parlance of the computer expert, they are "well structured." That is, companies know exactly what information is needed, exactly how it must be manipulated, and exactly what output or results are required by the various management levels.

Starting to run even the most routine applications on a new installation is essentially a two-step process: Providing accurate input data and checking out the program.

Too many companies assume that their data-gathering and reporting techniques are adequate because they served the manual system efficiently. But, in a manual system, experienced people are able to sift out mistakes and take care of exceptions that would foul up even the best-programmed computer.

Two simple but vital jobs must be done before a new installation can even be properly tested:

> ...*Account coding.* This is the simple but crucial job of assigning an identification number to every piece of paper involved in your system.

> ...*Standardize data.* Provision must be made for a standardized method of preparing all input documents to your EDP system and all controls needed to insure that the information is accurate and in the proper form.

Next big question that must be decided is how much parallel operation of your system you must run before the computer takes over all responsibility. Most specialists agree that there are no rules that will work in every situation. Some companies report that it is impossible to run parallel operations at all. Some claim they do not have the personnel needed to run both of the systems since old personnel are the ones who were trained to take over the new system.

Whenever possible, however, a program should be run on an outside computer such as a service bureau, or rented time at a nearby company, until enough of the bugs are removed so that you can competently shut down your routine operations and run them on your new installation.

Caution: Many companies attempt to rush a number of applications like payroll and billing onto a computer only to discover later that they have to go back and redesign them before it's possible to introduce new applications. For example, it may be inexpensive and easy to program your incoming orders so that invoices are produced automatically. Later, however, when you are ready to ask the machine to generate market analyses you may find that the original program does not provide the kind of information that makes this possible.

Where the Payoff Is

Payroll is probably the simplest and most straightforward application in most companies. That's because the input information is well known and exact and the output documents, including checks, can be easily evaluated for errors in the computer program.

A small electronics military subcontractor recently won a contract which required him to double his payroll within a year from 800 to over 1,600 employees. He decided that the added expense of increasing his payroll office operations under the existing manual system would make it worthwhile to install a computer. While his savings on office payroll are obviously not enough to pay for his computer installation, they do provide a way to make his *total* EDP system economical.

Sales analysis is harder to evaluate in dollar savings than payroll and other applications, but most companies that use a computer on this job are sure that they are getting their money's worth. Comments like these are typical:

> ... "Now that we get sales reports at 9 o'clock on Monday morning, we drastically cut down the lag between what's happening in the field and changes in our merchandising strategy."

> ... "Our sales manager now has a running tally of how every product is doing in each territory. He doesn't have to wait for quarterly reports to adjust his advertising and other expenses to meet changing needs."

Accounts receivable can be a profitable area for computer applications in small and medium-sized companies. Not only is it possible to cut down the office staff and paperwork, but many companies find that they have fewer losses on late and unpaid accounts because they're able to spot problems faster. One metals warehouse was able to get out its monthly bills within three days instead of the usual two weeks. Over the first year of operation it estimates a savings of $40,000 in lower financing charges and unpaid accounts.

Inventory Control

Companies with successful EDP experience are often eager to expand it into other phases of company operations. Inventory management is the most frequently mentioned target for such expansion.

Most companies tend to think about computerizing this job as a problem of improving record-keeping. The fact is, however, that the real problem is forecasting. No mechanization of paperwork can make your inventory system really effective unless it can take future market changes into account.

Most smaller companies neglect this forecasting job. They either use a simple rule of thumb like the Alka-Seltzer slogan, "When tablets get down to four, that's the time to order more." Or else, even when they use a more sophisticated idea like "economic order quantities," they don't review the system often enough. Most common method is to set reorder points only once a year. In effect, this is a forecast that the demand for a product will be constant over the entire year.

A computerized inventory system, on the other hand, can make forecasting a continuous process—keep a day-by-day watch on inventory levels and automatically, according to a predetermined program, recalculate order point and reorder quantity. For a smaller company, it can be modified to a weekly basis.

Recommendation: Even if you don't have a computerized inventory system, it may be worthwhile to run a computerized inventory analysis periodically at a service bureau. The information you obtain from this process will help you manage your manual system better.

Extending EDP to Purchasing

Even the most sophisticated computer users in industry tend to neglect the purchasing department. What can a computer system do for the purchasing department of even a relatively small company? Biggest savings are realized by cutting down the time spent on routine orders. "It is not uncommon," says one specialist, "to find situations where 80 or even 90 percent of the buyer's workload is routine." But in many companies only 5 percent of the orders account for 70 to 80 percent of the money spent.

The primary purchasing EDP system is geared directly to handling routine purchase orders. The computer does such tasks as writing orders, maintaining files and records, selecting supplies on the basis of previously established rules, keeping track of each supplier's delivery record and quality standards.

In companies with a more sophisticated EDP approach, the computer literally handles the whole purchasing job on routine orders without a single human decision. One company, for example, has tied its purchasing operation directly to its computerized inventory control. When an inventory item falls to a predetermined level, a purchase order is automatically printed out of the machine and mailed to a preselected supplier. The computer program also provides for a notice to the purchasing department if the order is not delivered in a reasonable time.

More detailed analysis of suppliers is easy to obtain. In a few minutes, for example, the computer can produce an evaluation of the supplier's delivery record on how much money the company is spending with a particular subcontractor. Information like this, coupled with the elimination of routine work, can allow buyers to do a more careful job of negotiation contracts and cutting costs.

An unexpected byproduct of a computerized purchasing system is that it often gets top management more involved in the purchasing function. While purchasing may account for over 50 percent of the average manufacturing company's expenditures, management often has little to do with the department unless it consistently runs into problems. Only when late delivery holds up a production line or if raw materials fail to meet specifications does the president of the company start trying to find out why. A properly organized computer system will enable him to establish this control on a regular basis.

SOME APPLICATIONS OF ELECTRONIC DATA PROCESSING IN OFFICE MANAGEMENT

accounts payable	order entry-billing
accounts receivable	payroll distribution
bid evaluations	point-of-sale accounting
billing	production control
cost accounting	production scheduling
customer demand anticipation	profit analysis
distribution problems	sales analysis
dividend accounting	shop-order writing
freight movement	statistical analysis
inventory control	stock transfers
job-ticket analysis	tax data
labor distribution	transportation problems
management analysis problems	union reports
market forecasting	withholding calculations
material control	

APPENDIX

ADMINISTRATIVE

Purposes and Organization

The Administrative Management Society is the development of the efforts of a small group of office administrators who met in Chicopee Falls, Massachusetts, in June 1919.

AMS is a nonprofit organization, devoted to rendering special service to office executives who are interested in the many problems of methods, procedures, personnel, layout, and equipment which continually present themselves in the modern office.

The charter of the association makes use of such formal phrases as "To encourage the work of standardization . . . ," "To initiate and effect the application of scientific methods . . . ," and "General standards of office work" . . . all of which are fitting and proper. But, simply stated, AMS is devoted to furthering the welfare of its members by promoting the free exchange of ideas in the field of office management, thus assisting the members in their work for the companies which the members represent.

AMS serves the members by carrying discussions of topics of current interest in its publication, *AMS Professional Management Bulletin,* scheduling and arranging with the host chapter an Annual Conference on Administrative Management. The association undertakes to supply helpful suggestions to those making specific requests for assistance and encouraging the chapters to activity in research projects in their own localities. The findings of these research projects appear regularly in AMS publications for future reference.

While AMS is a business organization, it takes great pride in the fellowship and lasting friendships among its members which have come from the frequent contacts in Chapter Meetings and National Conferences.

MANAGEMENT SOCIETY

Code of Ethics

As a member of the Administrative
Management Society

I ACKNOWLEDGE

That I have an obligation to the science and art of management. I will uphold the standards of my profession, continually search for new truths and disseminate my findings. I will keep myself fully informed of developments in the field of management and cooperate with others in the use of our common knowledge.

That I have an obligation to my employer, whose trust I hold. I will endeavor, to the best of my ability, to guard his interests, and to advise him wisely and honestly.

That I have an obligation to do all in my power to assure the progress and contentment of my fellow workers. I will at all times deal with them fairly and openly, sharing of my acquired knowledge and experience freely.

That I have a dual obligation to society, arising through my personal and company relations in the social and economic life of our Nation; further,

That I have a continuing obligation to my country and to the chosen way of life of my fellow citizens.

I ACCEPT MEMBERSHIP IN THIS ASSOCIATION AS A PERSONAL RESPONSIBILITY TO ACTIVELY DISCHARGE THESE OBLIGATIONS AND I DEDICATE MYSELF TO THAT END.

ADMINISTRATIVE MANAGEMENT
SOCIETY CHAPTERS

Akron
Albany
Albuquerque
Athens
Atlanta
Bakersfield
Baltimore
Baton Rouge
Battle Creek-Kalamazoo
Beaumont
Birmingham
Boise
Boston
Brantford
Bridgeport
Buffalo
Butler County
Calgary
Cedar Rapids
Central Florida
Charleston
Charlotte
Chattanooga
Chester County
Chicago
Cincinnati
Cleveland
Colorado Springs
Columbia, Mo.
Columbia, S. C.
Columbus
Corpus Christie
Dallas
Dayton
Decatur
Delaware
Delmarva
Denver
Des Moines
Detroit
Dubuque
Duluth
East Tennessee
   (Kingsport, Johnson City,
   Bristol, Tenn.)
Edmonton

El Paso
Erie
Eugene
Evansville
Fargo-Moorhead
Finger Lakes
   (Newark, Seneca Falls,
   Geneva, N. Y.)
Fort Wayne
Fort Worth
Fresno
Galveston
Grand Rapids
Grand Valley
Greensboro
Greenville
Halifax-Dartmouth
Hamilton
Harrisburg
Hartford
High Point
Houston
Huntington
Indianapolis
Inland Empire
International
   (Port Huron, Mich.
   Sarnia, Ont.)
Jacksonville
Jamaica
Joplin
Kanawha Valley
Kansas City
Knoxville
Lakeland
Lancaster
Lansing
Lexington
Lincoln
Little Rock
London
Long Beach
Long Island
Los Angeles
Louisville
Lynchburg

ADMINISTRATIVE MANAGEMENT
SOCIETY CHAPTERS (Cont.)

Madison
Memphis
Miami
Michiana
Milwaukee
Minneapolis-St. Paul
Montgomery County
   (Norristown, Lansdale, Pa.)
Montreal
Muskegon
Nashville
Newark
New Haven-Waterbury
New Orleans
New York
Niagara
Norfolk
North Alabama
   (Huntsville)
Oakland-East Bay
Oklahoma City
Omaha
Ottawa
Paducah
Palm Beach
Peoria
Philadelphia
Phoenix
Pittsburgh
Portland, Me.
Portland, Ore.
Providence
Quad-Cities
   (Davenport, Iowa; Moline,
   E. Moline, Rock Island, Ill.)
Raleigh
Reading
Regina
Richmond
Roanoke
Rochester
Rockford
Sacramento
St. John's, Nfld.
St. Louis
Salt Lake City

San Antonio
San Diego
San Fernar.do Valley
San Francisco
San Gabriel Valley
San Jose
Scranton-Wilkes Barre
Seattle
Sequoia
Shreveport
Sierra-Nevada
Southeastern Mass.
Southern Minnesota
Southern New Jersey
Spartanburg
Spokane
Springfield, Ill.
Springfield, Mass.
Springfield, Mo.
Springfield, Ohio
Stamford
Stockton
Syracuse
Tacoma
Tampa
Thunder Bay
Toledo
Topeka
Toronto
Trenton
Triple Cities
   (Endicott, Binghamton,
   Johnson City, N. Y.)
Tucson
Tulsa
Vancouver
Victoria
Washington
Westchester
Wichita
Windsor
Winnipeg
Winston-Salem
Worcester
York
Youngstown

SELECTED SOURCES OF INFORMATION
FOR OFFICE MANAGERS

ASSOCIATIONS

AEROSPACE INDUSTRIES ASSOCIATION OF AMERICA, 1725 DeSales Street, N. W., Washington, D. C. 20036.

AIR TRANSPORT ASSOCIATION OF AMERICA, 1000 Connecticut Avenue, N. W., Washington, D. C. 20406.

AMERICAN AUTOMOBILE ASSOCIATION, 1712 G Street, N. W., Washington, D. C. 20406.

AMERICAN FARM BUREAU FEDERATION, 1000 Merchandise Mart, Chicago, Illinois 60654.

AMERICAN GAS ASSOCIATION, 605 Third Avenue, New York, New York 10016.

AMERICAN HOME ECONOMICS ASSOCIATION, 1600 20th Street, N. W., Washington, D. C. 20409.

AMERICAN HOTEL AND MOTEL ASSOCIATION, 221 W. 57th Street, New York, New York 10019.

AMERICAN INSTITUTE OF BAKING, 400 E. Ontario Street, Chicago, Illinois 60611.

AMERICAN INSTITUTE OF LAUNDERING, Doris and Chicago Avenues, Joliet, Illinois 60433.

AMERICAN IRON AND STEEL INSTITUTE, 150 E. 42nd Street, New York, New York 10017.

AMERICAN MEAT INSTITUTE, 59 E. Van Buren Street, Chicago, Illinois 60605.

AMERICAN MEDICAL ASSOCIATION, 535 N. Dearborn Street, Chicago, Illinois 60610.

AMERICAN NEWSPAPER PUBLISHERS ASSOCIATION, 750 Third Avenue, New York, New York 10017.

AMERICAN PAPER INSTITUTE, 122 E. 42nd Street, New York, New York 10017.

AMERICAN PETROLEUM INSTITUTE, 1271 Avenue of the Americas, New York, New York 10020.

AMERICAN PHARMACEUTICAL ASSOCIATION, 2215 Constitution Avenue, N. W., Washington, D. C. 20007.

AMERICAN SOCIETY OF ASSOCIATION EXECUTIVES, 2000 K Street, N. W., Washington, D. C. 20406.

SELECTED SOURCES OF INFORMATION
FOR OFFICE MANAGERS (Cont.)

AMERICAN STANDARDS ASSOCIATION, 10 E. 40th Street, New York, New York 10016.

AMERICAN TRUCKING ASSOCIATION, INC., 1616 P Street, N. W., Washington, D. C. 20006.

ASSOCIATED GENERAL CONTRACTORS OF AMERICA, 1957 E Street, N. W., Washington, D. C. 20406.

ASSOCIATION OF AMERICAN RAILROADS, Transportation Building, Washington, D. C. 20006.

AUTOMOBILE MANUFACTURERS ASSOCIATION, 320 New Center Building, Detroit, Michigan 48202.

COTTON COUNCIL INTERNATIONAL, 1918 North Parkway, Memphis, Tennessee 38112.

ELECTRONIC INDUSTRIES ASSOCIATION, 2001 I Street, N. W., Washington, D. C. 20006.

INSTITUTE OF LIFE INSURANCE, 277 Park Avenue, New York, New York 10017.

LUGGAGE AND LEATHER GOODS MANUFACTURERS OF AMERICA, 220 Fifth Avenue, New York, New York 10001.

MILK INDUSTRY FOUNDATION, 910 17th Street, N. W., Washington, D. C. 20006.

NATIONAL ASSOCIATION OF SECURITIES DEALERS, 888 17th Street, N. W., Washington, D.C. 20006.

NATIONAL ASSOCIATION OF TEXTILE & APPAREL WHOLESALERS, 110 W. 40th St., New York, New York 10018.

NATIONAL FOOD DISTRIBUTORS ASSOCIATION, 333 N. Michigan Avenue, Chicago, Illinois 60601.

NATIONAL FOREST PRODUCTS ASSOCIATION, 1619 Massachusetts Avenue, N. W., Washington, D. C. 20036.

NATIONAL INDUSTRIAL DISTRIBUTORS ASSOCIATION, 1900 Arch Street, Philadelphia, Pennsylvania 19103.

NATIONAL INDUSTRIAL TRAFFIC LEAGUE, 711 14th Street, N. W., Washington, D. C. 20005.

NATIONAL INSTITUTE OF REAL ESTATE BROKERS, 155 E. Superior Street, Chicago, Illinois 60606.

NATIONAL MACHINE TOOL BUILDERS ASSOCIATION, 2139 Wisconsin Avenue, N. W., Washington, D. C. 20007.

SELECTED SOURCES OF INFORMATION
FOR OFFICE MANAGERS (Cont.)

NATIONAL RETAIL FURNITURE ASSOCIATION, 1150 Merchandise Mart, Chicago, Illinois 60654.

NATIONAL RETAIL HARDWARE ASSOCIATION, 964 N. Pennsylvania Street, Indianapolis, Indiana 46204.

NATIONAL RETAIL MERCHANTS ASSOCIATION, 100 W. 31st Street, New York, New York 10001.

PACKAGING INSTITUTE, 342 Madison Avenue, New York, New York 10017.

RUBBER MANUFACTURERS ASSOCIATION, 444 Madison Avenue, New York, New York 10022.

SOCIETY FOR THE ADVANCEMENT OF MANAGEMENT, 16 W. 40th Street, New York, New York 10018.

SPECIAL LIBRARIES ASSOCIATION, 31 E. Tenth Street, New York, New York 10003.

SUPER MARKET INSTITUTE, INC., 200 E. Ontario Street, Chicago, Illinois 60611.

U.S. JUNIOR CHAMBER OF COMMERCE, Boulder Park, Box 7, Tulsa, Oklahoma 74102.

CREDITS AND COLLECTIONS

DUN & BRADSTREET, INC., Box 803, Church Street Station, New York, New York 10008.

INTERNATIONAL CONSUMER CREDIT ASSOCIATION, 375 Jackson Avenue, St. Louis, Missouri 63130.

NATIONAL ASSOCIATION OF CREDIT MANAGEMENT, 44 E. 23rd Street, New York, New York 10010.

NATIONAL CONSUMER FINANCE ASSOCIATION, 1000 16th Street, N. W., Washington, D. C. 20036.

INDUSTRIAL AND PERSONNEL RELATIONS

AMERICAN ARBITRATION ASSOCIATION, 140 W. 51st Street, New York, New York 10020.

AMERICAN MANAGEMENT ASSOCIATION, 135 W. 50th Street, New York, New York 10020.

SELECTED SOURCES OF INFORMATION
FOR OFFICE MANAGERS (Cont.)

AMERICAN SOCIETY OF TRAINING DIRECTORS, 2020 University Avenue, Madison, Wisconsin 53705.

AMERICAN VOCATIONAL ASSOCIATION, 1025 15th Street, N. W., Washington, D. C. 20005.

ASSOCIATION OF CONSULTING MANAGEMENT ENGINEERS, INC., 347 Madison Avenue, New York, New York 10017.

NATIONAL ASSOCIATION OF MANUFACTURERS, 277 Park Avenue, New York, New York 10017.

NATIONAL ASSOCIATION OF SUGGESTION SYSTEMS, 28 E. Jackson Boulevard, Suite 522, Chicago, Illinois 60604.

NATIONAL INDUSTRIAL CONFERENCE BOARD, 845 3rd Avenue, New York, New York 10022.

NATIONAL RECREATION ASSOCIATION, 8 W. 8th Street, New York, New York 10011.

NATIONAL SAFETY COUNCIL, 425 N. Michigan Avenue, Chicago, Illinois 60611.

OFFICE ADMINISTRATION SERVICE, The Dartnell Corporation, 4660 Ravenswood Avenue, Chicago, Illinois 60640.

PRODUCTION

McGRAW-HILL BOOK CO., 330 W. 42nd Street, New York, New York 10036.

NATIONAL MANAGEMENT ASSOCIATION, 333 W. First Street, Dayton, Ohio 45402.

PURCHASING

NATIONAL ASSOCIATION OF PURCHASING AGENTS, 11 Park Place, New York, New York 10007.

PURCHASING (Magazine), 205 E. 42nd Street, New York, New York 10017.

OFFICE MANAGEMENT

ADMINISTRATIVE MANAGEMENT SOCIETY, World Headquarters, 1927 Old York Road, Willow Grove, Pennsylvania 19090.

OFFICE ADMINISTRATION SERVICE, The Dartnell Corporation, 4660 Ravenswood Avenue, Chicago, Illinois 60640.

INDEX

INDEX

American Pharmaceutical Assn., 962
American Society of Association Executives, 964
American Society of Training Directors, 965
American Standards Assn., 963
American Trucking Assn., Inc., 963
American Vocational Assn., 965
Ammonia fumes, 862
Analyses of financial results, availability, 28
Analysis of office forms, 700-704
Analysis of office systems and projects, 910-914
Analysts, in work simplification, 897, 910
Analytical ability of employee, 52
Analytical approach for supervisors' use, 213
Analyzing office jobs, *see* Job Analysis and Evaluation
Anniversary bouquets, 265
Annual Conference on Administrative Management, 958
Annual salaries, table of, 184
Annuities payable at retirement, 360-362, 369-370
Anonymity promised in suggestion system, 340-341
Appeals to higher officers, 28
Application form, *see* Hiring Procedures
Application for credit union loan, 429
Appraising employee performance, *see* Merit Rating
Aptitude tests, 78
Architect, office building and layout, 763-766, 772-774, 839-840
Archives, *see* Records Management
Area per worker, 767, 771
Area systems personnel, 893
Art in the office, 787
Assembly line in mailing, 629
Assistant office manager, compensation of, 193
Associated General Contractors of America, 963
Association lists, 962-965
Association of American Railroads, 963
Association of Consulting Management Engineers, 965
Associations, employees' insurance benefit, 374
Assuming responsibility, 525
Athletic programs, *see* Recreational Activities
Attendance, record of employee, 523
Attendance, rewarding, 173, 406-407
Attitude survey, *see* Employee Opinion Surveys

Automatic gathering and sealing machines, 636-637
Automatic order recording system, 798
Automatic staplers, 630
Automatic telephones, 804
Automatic typewriter, 281, 583, 852, 868

AUTOMATION
  see also Electronic Data Processing
  automatic letter writing, 869-870
  bank units, MICR, 886
  computer, use of, 233-235
  designing the office for, 792
  filing, automatic, 645, 651
  inventory control applications, *see* Inventory Control
  payroll, *see* Payroll and Labor Distribution
  private wire systems, 814-815
  programming, 233-235, 951
  punched card or tape applications, 693, 853, 904
  savings realized through, 773
  typical setup, 772
  union opposition, 458
Automobile Club of Michigan, 491
Automobile Manufacturers Assn., 963
Auto-typist, 583
Auxiliary Lighting, 786
Awards, *see* Recognition and Rewards *or* Suggestion Systems

Bags for filing tape, 697
Ballbearings, in casters, 826-827
Bank automation, MICR units, 886
Bank employees, training, 233-240
Bank tellers, speeded by TV eye installation, 806

BARGAINING
  employee benefits, 348
  letters to employees during organization, 282
Barriers to communication, 271
Bars on skylight windows, 747
Basic salary structure, preparing, 165-168
Beginners' training, *see* Training Office Workers
Beneficiary of insured employee, 359, 370-371, 383
Benefits, *see* Employee Benefits
Bias, internal, effect on systems man, 895-896

BILLING
  compensation of supervisor, 193-194
  cycle billing machines, 660, 665
  invoice file, 834
  invoices, time required for, 754
  shortcuts in, 873-874
  use of microfilm, 665

INDEX

Binders, 697, 714, 743
"Birthday" bouquets after long service, 265
Block boards, 884
Blueprints, protection against loss, 688
Board rooms, design of, 772
Bond paper, 745
see also Incentives *or* Profit Sharing

BONUSES

Christmas, 192, 421-423
contingent, 176
days off for perfect attendance, 406, 488-499
deferring, 177
half-yearly, for long service, 266
irrevocable trust, payment from, 174
office managers, bonuses for, 192
repercussion when not forthcoming, 174
supervisors, 193
vacation bonuses, 345
Bookkeeping machines, 842-843
Booklet racks, 247
Booklets for secretaries, 243, 614
Booklets to take home, 246, 256
Bottlenecks, elimination of, 899, 904
Bouquet for "birthday," after long service, 265
Boxes on charts (size and grouping), 916
Branch offices, shipping supplies to, 735
Break-even point, on duplicating machine, 865
Breakfast, importance of, 507
Brevity in writing, 593
Broadcasting systems, to employees, 277
Buckpassing, 28

BUDGETS

cost of obsolescence, 889
direct labor expense, 750-752, 754
importance of office records, 23
projecting clerical work, 753-756, 757
purposes and requirements of, 748
variable expenses, 756

BUILDINGS AND LAYOUTS

air-conditioning problems, *see* Air Conditioning
architect function of, 763, 765, 772
automation, designing for, 772
city and rural sites, 759, 762
cleaning office buildings, standards for, 789-792
color, *see* Color in the Office
construction, 763, 765, 772
core-type, 758, 760
expansion, planning for, 761, 764
flooring construction, 772

home office building, 762-765
interior design, 770, 772
layout of office, 768-779
leasing office space, 760
lighting, *see* Lighting
mailroom layout, 624
maintenance, *see* Office Maintenance
modules, use of, 758
moving the office, 776-777
needs of large corporation, 758
orientation of private offices, 764
partitions, 765-766, 779
physical survey of site, 763
private offices, 765-766, 770
refrigerating system, 773
reviewing the layout, 770
rural setting, 762, 764
shortcomings of speculative buildings, 758
templates, use of, 769-771, 774-775, 884
windows, 758, 762, 764
working drawings and specifications 768
Bulb or lamp replacement, 767, 785

BULLETIN BOARDS

advantages and disadvantages, 294-295
board for union use only, 471
checklist, 291
departmental boards, 292-294
error control charts, 503-504
maintaining, 289-294
need of posters telling of suggestion awards, 330
readership, 279, 289
removal date of notices, 293, 295
requisites of the perfect bulletin board, 295
rules for using, 290-294
survey of, 279, 290

BULLETINS

announcing company rules and policies, 271-272
bulletins vs. magazines, 302-304
combating gossip, 303
daily office bulletins, 303-304
descriptions of job openings in company, 231
improving employees' health habits, 506
newsletters for employees, 281-284, 306
preparing for job analysis, 117
printing methods, 858-860
testing program for office jobs, 253
Burglary protection, 747
Burroughs equipment, use of, 84, 660, 840
Business letter, cost of, 584-589, 794
Business-Letter Deskbook, 280
Business machine standards, 84
Business machines, *see* Office Machinery

968

INDEX

INDEX

National Association for the Advancement of Colored People, 45
National Council of Negro Women, 46
National Urban League, Inc., 46
procedure, 47, 51-57
Southern Christian Leadership Conference, 47
union contracts, 53
Classification method of job evaluation, 129-130
Classification of records, 669, 679-680, 685-687

Classified ads for office workers, 69
Classifying jobs and salaries, 151-158
Cleaning, *see* Office Maintenance
Clerical desks, 818
Clerical job classifications, 151
Clerical salaries, 157, 161-162
Clerical standards for new employees, 84-85
Clerical work, budgeting of, 750-757
Clerical workers' training, 251-256
Clerks' duties, in work analysis program, 502

Closed-circuit TV, 805
Closed-shop requirement, 464-465
Clubs for company veterans, 268
Code of ethics, Administrative Management Society, 960
Coding personnel records, 93-94
Coffee breaks *see* Rest Periods and Coffee Breaks
Coffee carts, 400
Collective bargaining, *see* Labor Unions

COLOR IN THE OFFICE

art in the office, 787
avoiding extremes, 787
color scheme chosen by employees, 262
current trends, 839
effect on production, 787
form design and use, 723, 725-731
paintings, 787-788
reflection of light, 783, 785
templates, 767, 771, 774-775
use on moving day, 777
warm and stimulating vs. cool and relaxing, 786-787
Colored trays in mail-handling system, 803
Column spacing for office areas, 765
Combining steps or operations, 904
Comfort in seating, 824-825
Comma, rules for using, 596
Commands vs. suggestions, 31
Committee approach to records management, 643

COMMITTEES

controlling suggestion system, 339-340

employee, for safety work, 514-515
in charge of office manual, 564
job analysis, 120-122
moving day, 776
stationery, 734

COMMUNICATIONS

see also Counseling *or* Interviews
analysis of, 273, 275
bulletin boards, use of, *see* Bulletin Boards
company policy, explaining, 271-272
complex process, 274
Correspondence Manual, 815
developing customer-consciousness, 513
different interpretations of same item, 273
do's and don'ts of letter writing, 282
employee magazines, 301
facilitated by procedures manuals, 553
failure of, as cause of grievances, 453-454
failure of "open door" policy, 273
field trips for employees, 277
finding the "peg" for letters, 281
getting employees to listen, 281
gossip, combating, 303
grievances as to, 438
How to Take the Fog Out of Writing, 594
improved by opinion surveys, 316
improving letters, *see* Correspondence
information meetings, 275
in-plant television, 277
latitude for employer in writing to employees, 282
newsletters and bulletins, 281, 284, 300-309
office grievances, responsibility for, 452
overcoming barriers to, 271
personalizing letters to employees, 281
plastic recordings, 277, 288
policies, explaining to new employees, 101
public address systems, 271, 277
"Rumor Clinic," 278-279
should flow in three directions, 275-276
sixteen points on letters to employees, 283-284
three essentials, 275
250 Tested Credit and Collection Letters, 598
250 Tested Sales Letters, 598
union, letters about, 282-283
welcoming new employees, 106
writing vs. telephoning, 794-795
Communications supervisor, compensation of, 193

INDEX

INDEX

INDEX

INDEX

billing system, small business, 857
Burroughs E1100 Computing/Accounting machine, 840
Burroughs B251 Visible Record Computer, 691
catalog number, 930-931
centers for small businesses, 947
charge account and cash sale recording, 943
coding, 952
computers, 233-235, 691, 872
Conservascan, data and retrieval system, 645
credit card reading, 943
credit control, 947
developments in communication, 807-814
evaluation of data flow, 946
flow charts, 946-947
G. E. 225 Information Processing System, 691
IBM 1440 computer, 872
inventory reduction, 954
job descriptions, 929
Litton EBS 1210, system of billing and invoicing, 857
National Cash Register optical scanning machine, 943
number of companies using, 888, 937
Olivetti Underwood Victor 3900 calculator, 849
Oxford rotary sorter, 684
punched-card personnel records, 92-93
programming, 951
production control, 955
reorganization of company for EDP, 942
Royal 11-column total adding machine, 849
savings, 932
specialists, 944
storage and retrieval system, 645
training of personnel, 951
Electronic Industries Assn., 963
Electronic longhand, 810
Electronic routing of mail, 803
Electronic stencils, 859
Elevators, 518, 718
Elimination of unnecessary work or papers, 901, 919-920
Embossed address plate, 933
Emotional maturity, appraising, 69
Employee appraisal, see Merit Rating
Employee appraisal form, 158

EMPLOYEE BENEFITS

bargaining with the union, 348, 459
cancellation of some, during pregnancy, 390

coffee breaks, see Rest Periods and Coffee Breaks
dramatizing employee benefits, 350-351, 353
employer obligations, 374
explaining to new employees, 105, 579
fringe benefits, 345, 352
grievances as to, 438
high cost of, 345, 347-351
holidays, see Vacations and Holidays
insurance, 372-383
loans, see Credit Unions
recreational programs, see Recreational Activities
rest periods, see Rest Periods and Coffee Breaks
retirement plans, 351-352
"selling" the benefits, 349-352, 380
sick leave practices, see Employee Health
survey questionnaire available, 319-320
union view of, 351
vacations, see Vacations and Holidays
Employee counseling, see Counseling
Employee development, see Training Office Workers
Employee efficiency when noise reduced, 766

EMPLOYEE HANDBOOKS AND MANUALS

checklist for preparing, 298-299
company policy, explaining to employees, 271-272
customer-consciousness, developing, 513
induction manuals, 101-106, 578-581
job evaluation manual, 138
office manuals, see Office Manuals
procedures manual, 26, 553-559
secretarial manuals, see Secretarial Manuals
training aids, 208
what employees want to know, 296
work-simplification training, 883-886

EMPLOYEE HEALTH

accident sickness insurance, 388
effect of poor health on production, 506-507
explaining health facilities to new employees, 105, 578-581
factor in merit rating, 540
film on, for new workers, 105
health benefits offered employees, 345-351
insurance programs, see Insurance
leave of absence policy, 387
sick-leave practices, 385-389
sick leaves and pension plans, 385
sick pay formulas, 387

974

INDEX

INDEX

INDEX

Job satisfaction, 175, 196, 262-263, 525
Job testing, *see* Testing Programs
Job titles, descriptive, 150
Judgment, employee's, 542
Jumbo file, 833
Jury duty, 412

Keeping subordinates informed, 32, 33
Key employees, held by split-dollar insurance plan, 383
Key punch standards, 93
Knowledge of job, employee's, 540

Labeling machinery, 631
Labels, 632-633, 636, 667, 685, 697, 777
Labor distribution, *see* Payroll and Labor Distribution
Labor expense, budgeting, 750-752, 754-757

LABOR UNIONS

see also Unionization
accident and health protection, negotiating, 373
allocation of overtime, 472
attitude toward long-service awards, 268-269
attitude toward opinion surveys, 316
authority of management recognized, 469-470
benefits, bargaining as to, 349-351, 373, 460-461
benefits of membership, 459
benefits, view of, 345-352
bulletin board for union use only, 471
continuation of wages in illness, 471-472
cooperation in job analysis, 116, 122-123
craft vs. industrial, 462
discrimination, prohibitions against, 53
foremen's unions, 462
grievances, 437
intervening for discharged member, 222
layoffs, contemplated, voice in, 471, 474
leave of absence for pregnancy, 471
letters to employees, 282-285
managerial employees not to do members' work, 471
medical reports, copy to member's doctor, 471
membership required for employment, 465
monopolizing job skills, 553
no-strike record credited to house organ, 298
office manuals conform to agreements, 565
office workers on hourly rate, 162
represented at company information meetings, 276
rest periods and smoking provisions, 471

seniority in white-collar contracts, 462, 473
seniority retained despite promotion, 471
time spent in negotiations, etc., 471
transfer of job between departments, 471
typical office workers' agreement, 464-476
Lamson conveyors, use of, 803
Lawn maintenance, 792
Lawsuits, retention of records, 770
Layoffs, 471, 473-475
Layout of office, 768-776
Leadership ability of employee, 542
"Leakage" of office supplies, 738
Leases, retention of, 684
Leasing office equipment, 837-838, 889-890
Leasing office space, 760
Leather upholstery, 825
Leave of absence, 389-392, 545
Ledger file, 834
Legal aid for debt-ridden employees, 180
Legal aspects of microfilming, 656-658
Legal-blank file, 833
Legal holidays, 472-473
Legal records, 677, 683
Legal-size file, 706, 833

LEGISLATION

Act of 1966, 36
Civil Rights Act, 51
Equal Employment Opportunity Act, 38, 54, 59-64
Equal Pay Act, 1963, 43
Length of lease, 760

LENGTH OF SERVICE

see also Seniority
breaks in continuity of service, 473-474
insurance benefits used to reward, 380
morale-building effect of service awards, 264
pay based on, 169
rewards for, *see* Recognition and Rewards
sick-leave formulas based on, 387
Letter-writing contests, 589-590
Letter-writing techniques, improving, 249
Letterhead stationery, 745
Letterpress printing, 583
Letters, *see also* Correspondence

LETTERS TO EMPLOYEES

details to remember, 280, 283
do's and don't's of letter writing, 282
finding the "peg," 281
receipt of suggestion award entry, 335-336, 342
union organization, letters about, 282

INDEX

INDEX

Married couples, employment of both, 73-74

"Master lineup," 933-934

Maternity leaves of absence, 388-392

Mechanical facilities of office building, 765

Mechanics of work simplification, 891-892

Mechanization, *see* Automation

Median salaries of office managers, 190-191

Medical examinations, 91, 372, 376, 471

Medium-run duplicating, 860

Meetings, *see* Communications

Memoranda, office, *see* Bulletins

Merchandise awards for suggestions, 337

Mergers, union opposition to, 458-459

MERIT RATING

see also Salaries and Salary Administration

benefits of, 522, 534, 536-537

career progression program, 543

checklists, 520, 523-529

common mistakes in, 521

continuing process, 519

determination of all job duties, 531

evaluation of each employee, 531-533, 544

factors to be included, 523, 535, 540-544

formal vs. informal approach, 520

"general merit review" form, 528

grading method, 539

interval between ratings, 537

interviewer-rater discussions, 533

interviews, 522, 528, 535, 544-551

less than eight employees on same job, 528

more than eight employees on same job, 530

new employee 30-day rating, 539

over-all ratings, 532, 543

performance analysis form, 539

pointers, 529

prejudice favoring older employees, 534

promotability of employee, 527, 532, 535-544

salary administration plan, as part of, 150

selection and evaluation form, 69

small company's experience, 533

standards for sound merit rating, 520

use in training programs, 253

worker's chief strength and weakness, 543

Messenger services, 634

Metal furniture, 827-829

Metering mail, 630, 632, 635, 637

Methods, *see* Work Simplification

Methods, manager, 880, 888, 891-895, 897

Metropolitan Museum of Art, 827

MICROFILMING

admissibility as legal evidence, 657

advantages and disadvantages of, 598, 607, 659-663, 656-665, 690

automatic, new machine, 955

case studies, 657-663

checklist of, 657

color of paper, 706

costs and savings, 657-665

duty of stenographic pool, 607

economy of, 657

film aperture cards, 664

Reliant Microfilmer, 659

replacement of valuable records, 639

storage space savings, 657

Military reserve training, 406

Milk Industry Foundation, 963

Mimeographing, 617, 858-864

Minimum of overtime guaranteed, 473

MINORITY GROUPS

applicants, hiring of, 48

apprenticeship training, 48

civil rights groups, approaches, 47-49, 51-57

commitments, 51

discrimination, types of alleged, 58

equal employment opportunity records, 57

layoffs, 48

negotiations, failure of, 54

percentage of, 48

recruiting, 49

training programs, 48

union contracts, 53

Mistakes, *see* Quality Control

Modernization of office equipment, 838

Module, use of, 758

Monopolizing job skills, 553

Monotonous job operations, reducing, 492, 495

Monthly salaries, table of, 184

MORALE OF EMPLOYEES

see also Employee Relations

acceptability of timeclocks, 491-492

air conditioning, effect on, 778, 780

art in the office, 787

better lighting, 783-784

central typing pool, 603

chance of advancement, 230, 238, 255-256

comfortable seating, 824

company parties, 423

daily office bulletin helps maintain, 305

discovering work-simplification ideas, 883-887

effect of good supervision, 197

effect of noise reduction, 507

INDEX

INDEX

INDEX

INDEX

Opinion poll, packaged, 318-319
Opinion Research Corporation, 316
Opinions of employee not asked, 441
Order department supervisor, compensation of, 193

ORDER PROCESSING
case studies, 675-676, 935
process chart of, 902-903

ORGANIZATION
analysis of, 915
charts, 26-27, 31, 650, 916
checking points, 26-28
departmental vs. functional, 914
principles of, 914-915
systems staff, 893-896
Organization manual, 552-556
Organizational filing, 668
Organizational titles, 151
Organizing a suggestion award system, 338
Organizing ability, 526
Organizing employees, *see* Labor Unions

ORIENTING OFFICE EMPLOYEES
checking up on proper placement, 107
developing personal pride in job, 203
explaining personnel policies, 105
films, use of, 104
indoctrination schedules, 104-111, 252
induction checklist, 110, 201
induction manual checklist, 578-580
induction manuals, 101-104
interviewing new employees, 107-108
letters to employees, 106
probationary review, 204
sponsoring new employees, 109
supervisor's part in, 100-101, 104
thorough orienting important, 199
use of bulletin board, 271-279
what an employee wants to know, 296
Outgoing mail, *see* Mailroom Procedures
Outside consultants conducting surveys, 314-320
Outside consultants used as instructors, 256
Outside interests of workers, 246
Overcrowding, 25, 29
Overexpansion of business, 24

OVERTIME
allocating overtime evenly, 471
clerical load in maximum sales period, 795-797
factors for eliminating, 187, 480
guaranteed minimum, 473
moving day, 776
reasons for, 479-480

reduced when job monotony reduced, 494-495
replacement by hourly work on call-in basis, 484
work analysis form, 500

Packaging Institute, Inc., 964
Page service for mail department, 634
Paging systems, 794-796, 808-811
Paper clips, 736, 742
Paper for duplicating equipment, 870
Paper, standard sheet sizes, 713, 723
Paper tapes and cards, filing of, 692-694
Paper weights and grades, 724, 726-727, 732, 738, 745, 870
Paperwork simplification, 918-919, 932-934
Paragraphing, 567-568
Parking space, 764
Part-time help, 629
Parties, *see* Recreational Activities
Partitions, office, 766, 823
Passive verbs, 591
Patents, disposition of, 681
Patterned interview, 88
Patterned merit review procedure, 528
P-A-X systems, 804-805
Pay-as-you-go retirement plan, 368
Pay differentials, 162
Pay grievances, 441, 452
Pay-out period for office machinery, 856
Pay rates for stenographers, 162

PAYROLL AND LABOR DISTRIBUTION
change form, 160
electronic data processing, 233-235
frequency of payment, 163
payroll messages for employees, 165
records, 682
responsibility of office manager, 189
supervisor, compensation of, 193
weekly time requirement, 754
Payroll sheets vs. timecards, etc., 164
PBX, *see* Telephone
Pegboards, 884, 904
Pencils and pencil sharpeners, 735, 742
Pens for office use, 742
Pensions, *see* Retirement
Perfect attendance rewarded, 406, 489-490
Performance analysis, 537-551
Performance rating, *see* Merit Rating
Performance rewards, 269
Performance standards, *see* Office Standards
Permanent disability insurance, 376
Personal appearance and hygiene, 447, 540, 617
Personal mail, 625-626
Personal packages, removal from plant, 740-741

988

INDEX

INDEX

INDEX

disadvantages, 397-400, 402-403
incidence of, 397
length, 393-394, 397-402
monthly "coffee caucus," 396
morale improved, 395-397
policing coffee breaks, 399
profits from vending machines, 403
union contract provision, 471
vending machines in the office, 400-404
Restrictions in leases, 761-762
Retention of records, *see* Records Management

RETIREMENT

age of retirement, 357-360 363-368, 370
annuities payable at retirement, 360-364, 369-371
benefit formula, 353-354
benefits for beneficiary also, 360, 368-371
contributory plans, 358, 365-370
cost of pension plans, 355
deferred profit sharing, 353-354
do pension plans pay? 351-352
explaining the pension plan, 351-352
group pension plans, 356-357
half-pay retirement, 360
how to set up a pension plan, 358-360
investing pension funds, 360, 365-370
kinds of pension plans in use, 358
noncontributory plans, 358-363, 369-371
pay-as-you-go plan, 368
pension trusts, 359, 362-363
profit-sharing retirement, 364-365
refunding pension contributions, 361-362, 366-368
resignation or dismissal, 361-362
retirement income contract, 175
self-administered pension plans, 360-361
sick leaves and pension plans, 385-392
stock purchase plans, 367-368
tax status, 362-363
withdrawals from pension funds, 368-371
Return envelopes, addressed, 586
Reviewing salaries, 154
Reviewing the office layout, 770
Revising a manual, 571, 574-578, 616-617, 622
Revising forms, 715
Rewards, *see* Recognition and Rewards
Rivalry between company stores played up in house organ, 305
Roller shelves, 834
Royal McBee equipment, use of, 853
Rubber bands, storing, 685, 743
Rubber Manufacturers Assn., 964
Rubber stamps, use of, 743
Rug vacuuming, 790
Rules, *see* Regulations
Rulings, on forms, 730-731

"Rumor Clinic," 279

RUMORS

case study, 279
daily office bulletin used to dispel, 303-304
exposure through employee publication, 298-299
Rural setting for office building, 762

Safes or vaults, 688-690, 747, 778

SAFETY

accidents as cause of absence, 486
committees, 513-515
educating employees, 515-516
factor in merit awards, 173
films and film strips, 515
hazards in the office, 517-518
place in indoctrination program, 105
regulations, 516

SALARIES AND SALARY ADMINISTRATION

adjusting salaries to a wage increase, 157
administrator's duties, 147-148
assistant office manager, compensation of, 192-193
average weekly office earnings, 183
benefits of salary administration, 147
billing supervisor, compensation of, 193
cash payment vs. checks, 163
change in employee's status, 160
check-cashing service for employees, 164
checklist for salary administration, 201
Christmas bonuses, 421-423
classifying and describing jobs and salaries, 151-153
communications supervisor, compensation of, 193
comparing rates with other companies, 154
contingent bonuses, 176-177
deduction for frequent tardiness, 487-488
determining ranges, 149, 157
discrimination based on race, etc., 58
dismissal pay, 177-178
employee appraisal form, 158
extra compensation, *see* Bonuses *or* Incentives
failure to grant raise, 441
files supervisor, compensation of, 193
fixed salary vs. hourly rate, 162
frequency of payments, 163
general accounting supervisor, compensation of, 193
grievances as to, 438
how deductions are shown, 164

INDEX

INDEX

INDEX

breaking in new employees, 100-101, 104, 110, 621

budgetary activities, responsibility for, 757

checklist for supervision, 201

communications requirement survey, 794-795

compensating office supervisors, 192-193

conference leadership training, 216

control of coffee breaks or vending machines, 407

cost control, 749

dictators and transcribers, liaison between, 600

discipline, maintaining, 218-224

duties of supervisors, 199-201

excessive overtime reflects on, 481

giving supervisors objectives, 31, 877-884

handling of grievances, 440, 454-456

human relations test for supervisors, 206

inadequate supervision, 25-26

indoctrination and training, supervisors' responsibility for, 104, 252

influencing morale through supervision, 197

mail department supervisor, job description, 634-635

merit rating, responsibility for, 173, 519, 522-523, 528-544

motivating employees through supervision, 198

need to know cost of employee benefits, 350

not to do union member's work, 471

office manuals, help from, 553, 558

office manuals, responsibility for, 557, 576-577, 622

payment periods and methods, 163

performance analyzed yearly, 544

place in office layout, 778

procedure charts, 752

reducing telephone costs, 794-798, 804-805, 808-810

reports to or by, 26

reprimanding by, *see* Reprimands

responsibility for workers' errors, 505

selecting supervisors, 202, 205

States' credit union supervision, 431-432

suggestion system, 329-344

supervision of stenographic pool, 600, 609-610

supervisor handling both mail and files, 692

supervisor's part in job evaluation, 114, 126-127

supervisors, complaints about, 441-442, 448, 450-451, 486, 519

supervisors included in opinion surveys, 313-314, 320

supervisors of filing system, 653

survey questionnaire available as to, 320-321

training programs for supervisors, 28, 207-217, 334-335, 341, 529, 877-882

why workers quit, 196-197

women employees, managing, 205

work analysis program, 500

Supervisory training, *see* Supervisors and Supervision *or* Training Office Workers

SUPPLIES CONTROL

built-in check on oversupplying, 739

competitive bids asked, 735

paper savings, 713, 732

paper, selection of, 743-746

pilferage, controlling, 738-741

purchasing economies, 738-742

requisition handling, 735-736

stationery committee, 734

storage of supplies, 738, 740, 744

surveys, 733-738

waste, controlling, 732, 741, 877

SURVEYS

absenteeism, 486-487

acoustical treatment of office, 508

attitude, *see* Employee Opinion Surveys

better lighting, 781-783

bulletin boards, 279

communications requirements, 794-795

company policies, "selling" to employees, 273

compensation of office managers and supervisors, 192-195

cost of business letter, 584

credit unions, 436

employee counseling services, 285

employee publications, 297-299

forms, 699, 708-711

forms control, 710-711

fringe benefits, 345-352

health examinations, 91

hiring relatives, 71-74

holidays, 409-412

letters received by customers, 587-588

life and health insurance, 379-380

lunch periods, 478

methods survey, plan for, 952

noise in offices, 507

office air conditioning, 780

office gripes, 438-441

office manuals, 552

opening the mail, 624-626

reasons for job dissatisfaction, 197

recognizing length of service, 263-269

INDEX

INDEX

INDEX

INDEX

NOTES

NOTES

NOTES

NOTES

NOTES

NOTES

NOTES